*Europe in the
Nineteenth
Century*

BRISON D. GOOCH

University of Connecticut

Europe in the Nineteenth Century

A HISTORY

THE MACMILLAN COMPANY
COLLIER-MACMILLAN LIMITED / LONDON

Library of Congress catalog card number: 74–95300

THE MACMILLAN COMPANY
866 Third Avenue, New York, New York 10022
COLLIER-MACMILLAN CANADA, LTD., TORONTO, ONTARIO

PRINTED IN THE UNITED STATES OF AMERICA

To Dorothy, Linda,
and David

PREFACE

This book relates the course of nineteenth-century European political, diplomatic, cultural, and economic history, primarily from 1815 to 1890, with attention to the era preceding 1815 and a briefer consideration of the period following 1890. The narrative presumes some earlier familiarity with the personalities and events of the century. Although the presentation is generally chronological, it is not a recapitulation of bills and treaty provisions. Rather, it is a series of discussions of the contexts in which such documents occurred, with concern for the overriding issues and complexities of choice faced by those in positions of authority. Developing intellectual and ideological moods are an important part of history and have been given considerable space. Many textbook clichés are true and deserve to be repeated, but many of history's judgments are highly conditional. They require continual questioning, as well as reconsiderations regarding the motives and meaning behind men's actions. This volume of course is also subject to the questioning process as more and more new monographs appear.

To write a text is an exercise in humility, for such a task vividly demonstrates to an author his utter reliance on the work of others. The bibliographical section indicates only a few of the more obvious debts in this case. Over the years many fine teachers and colleagues have contributed remarks which found their way into this manuscript. Graduate students in European history at the University of Oklahoma are responsible for a number of insights in this volume and special mention should be made of Joseph Johnson and Assistant Professor James Chastain of Ohio University. Jack Ridley, assistant professor of history at the University of Missouri at Rolla, kindly read most of the manuscript and made a number of constructive suggestions.

B.D.G.

CONTENTS

III

The Changing Condition of Life

IV

The Romantic Movement

V

Liberal and Nationalistic Adjustments, 1820–1832

VI

Another Attempt at Stability and Order: The Limited Recognition of New Forces

VII

1848—Western and Central Europe in Turmoil

VIII

Peaceful Domestic Progress

IX

Nineteenth-Century Intellectual Vitality

X

Change Through Violence

XI

A New Politics of the Status Quo, 1870–1890

XII

Conclusion

ILLUSTRATIONS

MAPS

*Europe in the
Nineteenth
Century*

I

A Century and Its Birth

CHAPTER 1

Introduction

Europe in the nineteenth century was turbulent. An unprecedented tidal wave of progress and change swept over the continent. The static characteristics of much of earlier society in Europe became sharply altered after 1800. Social, political, and religious hierarchies had regulated life; and the emphasis through much of history had been on order and stability, the precious prerequisites for civilization. Basic alterations had usually required generations and centuries. Sons had lived largely as their fathers and grandfathers before them, with change at so slow a pace that the results were hardly apparent within a lifespan.

By the middle of the eighteenth century a different mood, a skepticism about knowledge and institutions tempered by a new optimism, appeared in intellectual circles. The scholars of the Enlightenment not only recognized that change was taking place and at an accelerating rate, but believed that an improvement in humans and in the human condition was in store. Rational attention to nature's definite and systematic laws would assure beneficial change for mankind. Instead of looking backward to a golden age, they were confident that another lay ahead. To assure and to hasten its coming, they diligently searched for nature's basic principles, collecting and publishing them in the *Grande Encyclopédie*.

In the nineteenth century many of the improvements predicted by the *philosophes* and rationalists came to pass. Instead of coming systematically, however, they occurred in rapid and overlapping profusion. Spontaneity and a disregard for order often appeared as hallmarks of the new age. Increased knowledge and its applications put traditional values under attack as society was caught up in new and evolving standards and ideologies. It was all regarded as "progress," however, and the new golden age abounded in conflicting impulses, loyalties, and frustrations.

The nineteenth century in Europe was the first in which the pace of change was so rapid that society was vastly altered within a lifetime. Technologically, the Biblical Noah was closer to Lord Nelson than Napoleon was to Erich von Ludendorff. Vast social and cultural alterations occurred in only a hundred years. After 1900 the pace quickened anew, with the complex problems and issues of our own day assuming staggering proportions.

The purpose of this book is to observe and discuss major aspects of nineteenth-century Europe, with the acceleration of change and its multiplicity of attendant problems commanding our primary attention. Because European leaders were self-conscious and acutely aware of their own roles in the midst of these dynamic forces, their conflicting efforts and judgments regarding how best "progress" was to occur also constitutes an important part of the narrative. A basic setting for our study is the noisy dialectic between the proponents of stability and order, on the one hand, and of change and progress, on the other.

It has become a truism that the nineteenth century began in 1789 with the calling of the Estates General in France. Few periods in history constitute such a break with the past as the French Revolution. Although under Napoleon there was a reassertion of many values and attitudes of the *ancien régime,* the revolutionary upheaval was so profound that a complete return to old practices was out of the question. The reforms of the Revolution encompassed an unleashing of human energy and a direct attack on a political hierarchy which had sufficed for centuries. The old system was bluntly challenged from the Atlantic to the Urals as, for the first time, whole classes reveled in political power and freedom. First Napoleon Bonaparte and later the monarchs of Europe managed to gain control and curb the Revolution. Its impact, however, was so great that for generations it stood as a rallying cry for the discontented. Supporters of conservative, divine-right monarchy saw the Revolution as a continuing, metaphysical threat to their position. Although military and political suppression eventually ended the French Revolution, this proved a temporary setback, and the history of the nineteenth century may be viewed as the story of the struggle and process by which the principles of the French Revolution gradually won acceptance in much of Europe.

The handmaidens of this political and social reform were liberalism and nationalism. Both received a marked impetus in the wake of the French Revolution. Nationalism became an especially dynamic and militant threat to established monarchies, where unifying principles had been based on loyalty to a dynasty. In a number of forms nationalism was centuries old even by the end of the eighteenth century—Luther had addressed many of his remarks to "we Germans" and in *Richard II,* Shakespeare put into the mouth of a dying John of Gaunt a moving, lyrical statement of nationalistic affection for "this sceptred isle." Nationalism had earlier joined militarism only sporadically, but after the Revolution, the union was more frequent, both finding another ally in the secular state. Nineteenth-century nationalism was a vibrant force, frequently serving the cause of political liberalism. As such, it became the object of intense opposition on the part of entrenched conservatives. There were some interesting exceptions, especially in the Russian nationalism promoted by Tsar Nicholas I; but, in general, nationalism was ranged squarely against the dynastic remnants of a feudal society.

Meanwhile, a remarkable increase in man's control over his environment was taking place. Society's productive capacity witnessed vast increases as the use of steam power became commonplace. Industrialization increased at a prodigious rate; and as more machines produced an amazing array of products, reformers began to cry for their more equitable distribution. Various schemes and plans were put forward, most being variants of socialism. The century was thus a period of intense, theoretical study of an evolving materialistic society, as well as the environment for a number of more practical socialist parties. Like nationalism, socialism found itself frequently allied with liberalism. It also lent itself to more radical, extremist movements, often characterized by a marked humanitarianism, as many selfless and dedicated men came to the fore.

While the proper distribution of goods was being debated, Europeans were extending their control overseas. Especially in the latter third of the century a vigorous wave of imperialism seized the imaginations of diplomats, entrepreneurs and clergymen alike. Combining with several aspects of nationalism, the new imperialism introduced European standards to many far reaches of the world. Although imperialism often meant vicious economic exploitation, the most serious related problem troubling some statesmen was that war might come in Europe as a result of rivalry over a remote and uncivilized area. Salving consciences, however, was the assurance that whatever else was going on, European Christian missionaries were engaged in a good and holy work among unenlightened savages.

During the nineteenth century a vigorous intellectual life prevailed in Europe. The Enlightenment had given way to the romantic movement, which pervaded virtually all creative activities. Often regarded as most prevalent in the early decades, it was also evident later in the century. Most readily identified with literature, music, and philosophy, it was a major influence in nationalism, socialism, and imperialism. It lent its perspectives and attitudes to the age, providing a historical, humanistic, or moral temper to all the feverish activity and struggle. Dignity, grandeur, and warmth were also given to projects that otherwise appeared to be only ruthless Machiavellian opportunism.

Men and movements acted in a bewildering interplay of personal hopes and ambitions. The French Revolution had signaled an unleashing of human talent and energy but how these were to be channeled and to what end was not clear. While the exhilaration and excitement of struggle and change were bringing out both man's better and baser instincts, they were accompanied by a vast accumulation of sheer wealth. Representatives of industrial complexes insisted on having a voice in state policy making, as wealth based on land had become progressively less powerful. Enormous physical change occurred in Europe, just between 1815 and 1870, and by 1900 much of the continent had become unrecognizable by the landmarks of 1789 or 1815. Let us now consider the course of this transformation, the high points in this century of turbulence and progress.

CHAPTER 2

The Ancien Régime and the Need for Reform

The Middle Ages established institutions of remarkable durability. Its class-structured society composed of social, political, and religious hierarchies encompassed most of Europe, its main features lasting for centuries. By 1750 this elaborate structure had undergone considerable erosion and further alterations were urgently required. In the eighteenth century the Roman Catholic Church was no longer the universal church for all Christians in Western Europe but remained a major property owner. In France, for example, it held between 6 and 19 per cent of all the land. Clerics comprised less than 1 per cent of the French population. Of these, less than 10 per cent, or between 10,000 and 11,000, were upper clergy and lived in sumptuous circumstances.

The landed nobility were the best-educated class and important patrons of the arts; but, although they owned about twice the amount of property as the Church and still provided military leadership, they no longer completely controlled secular affairs. The greatest aristocrats were, of course, the monarchs, but their circumstances were also changing. The Hapsburgs now lacked the power of Charles V, although they still controlled the Imperial crown of the Holy Roman Empire and were a considerable influence in European affairs. The Bourbons in France were another major dynasty and, after the reign of Louis XIV, they also sat on the throne of Spain. In Prussia the Hohenzollerns had been vigorously building a strong state in a relatively barren land. With the reign of Frederick the Great, Prussia became a ranking power, and to the east the Romanovs ruled Russia with an authoritarianism far more rigid than any other in Europe. Other dynasties of secondary powers frequently were energetic and from time to time produced an extraordinary leader, such as Gustavus Adolphus of the House of Vasa in Sweden. In England the Hanoverians ruled but this crown had lost much of its power in the seventeenth century.

While many old families were still at the apex of power, others of the nobility failed to maintain or enhance their position. In France the rustic nobility frequently were impoverished and bereft of the charm and bearing associated with an aristocracy. Poor and boorish, they constituted a barrier to progress and a blight on society. The more capable in this class responded to financial pressures by engaging in business, a distinctly nonaristocratic function but often a matter of sheer survival. The extent to which nobles in France were active in business has not been exactly determined but recent research makes clear that their numbers were considerable. At the same time that poverty was overtaking these aristocrats, their position as administrators for the crown was being eroded. After Cardinal Richelieu came to power, the middle class became more prominent in government and the intendants gradually came to rival local nobles in authority and prestige.

The growth of trade and royal administrative functions stimulated further development of the middle class. Talented commoners found law and government service open to them, and by 1750 the numbers of distinguished and able men drawn from nonnoble classes had markedly increased. Also they now possessed great wealth, often at the expense of the old nobility. The medieval structure inadequately provided for such a class, but through the practice in France of creating "Nobles of the Robe" a device evolved whereby they could be incorporated into the system.

Elsewhere in Europe there was also an increase in the middle class, although the rate of growth was not so marked. Better communications and increased trade enhanced the established business communities in Holland, the old Hansa cities, and the imperial free cities of Central Europe. Venice was also important, although the high point of Venetian trade and wealth was long since past. These commercial centers were becoming enlarged but this created little friction because their roots and privileges went back to the Middle Ages and their increased vitality posed no basic problem for the system.

The position of the peasants had changed little in Central and Eastern Europe. In Western Europe, however, many had become virtually free men. France, especially, had large numbers of peasant proprietors who had escaped from manorial and feudal obligations.

Across the English Channel was the society that had most altered its feudal structure. Here the business community spoke in national affairs with an assured voice reflecting its wealth and power. Medieval restrictions on the peasantry existed as bare vestigial remnants and the whole realm stood as a remarkable example of freedom, with a high living standard compared to the Continent. Parliament represented a major evolution from its medieval status, when, like many similar bodies in Europe, its function was expected to be advisory and a support for the monarch. Political-religious struggles prior to the eighteenth century had changed this relationship; and, in the execution of Charles I, the Continent's aristocracies were given a grim foretaste of the price of failure.

Orthodox Christianity was the dominant faith in large areas of Eastern Europe, including Russia. In Central and Western Europe the Reformation had badly crippled Catholicism. Despite a remarkable partial recovery during the Counter-Reformation, the unity of Western Christendom had been destroyed. The Lutheran movement was supreme in much of Germany and in Scandinavia; Calvinism was entrenched in portions of Switzerland, Hungary, the Netherlands, and Scotland; and the Anglican church was the official religion in England. The Roman Church was weakened even further by 1750. In France, for example, the Jansenist movement created dissension within the hierarchy and a sort of Gallican revival occurred also under Louis XIV. The hand of the state in religious affairs was prominent as the Church struggled to maintain its position in the face of heresy. At the same time a spirit of secularism and rationalism attracted many of the intellectuals and made serious inroads among the upper classes.

The political and diplomatic structure of Europe had also undergone important changes since 1500. Nationalism made its appearance with telling effect. When Spain proved unable to control the revolt of her Dutch provinces, her influence was markedly diminished in Western Europe. After the Wars of Religion in France, the revitalized monarchy saw its best interests served by alliances with Protestant states in Central Europe during the Thirty Years' War. This costly struggle resulted in a considerable weakening of Central Europe, in terms of specific losses in both lives and property during the conflicts and also in relative diplomatic strength with outside states after the war. The Netherlands and Switzerland were completely severed from the Empire, which also lost Pomerania and Alsace. A plethora of small and petty German states between France and Austria created a serious power vacuum that the declining Empire was unable to fill.

The Holy Roman Empire always had serious problems but by 1750 it was in marked decline. Emperors after Charles V never enjoyed his prominence in European affairs. Unable to count on much help from the Imperial Diet, their real power was derived from personal dynastic lands, now limited to the Austrian Hapsburg holdings entered around Vienna. The elective character of the emperor was still a problem and there were worrisome uncertainties about ensuring the succession of Maria Theresa in 1740.

Most serious for the Empire were the growing and changing ambitions of many of the statesmen in Central Europe during the century following the Peace of Westphalia. To begin with, conditions established in that treaty gave foreign leaders too much of a voice in imperial affairs. French interests were made clear in the Diet through Alsatian clergy and nobles, while the king of Sweden participated through his Pomeranian holdings. In addition to these nonimperial participants, a more ominous circumstance existed. Imperial resources were being expended in vast amounts on personal and dynastic ventures which were not in the interest of the Empire. The Hapsburgs spent freely on campaigns to seize lands from the Ottoman Empire. The electors of Brandenburg worked hard to enhance their holdings outside the Empire, becoming kings in Prussia in 1701. The electors of Hanover aspired to wear the crown of England. Their success in 1714 gave influence in imperial affairs to yet another power. In addition, two electors of Saxony (Augustus II, 1697; Augustus III, 1734) spent prodigious sums in successful efforts to be elected kings of Poland. One looks nearly in vain to see leaders of comparable stature within the Empire who were working to strengthen their holdings in a fashion consistent with the best interests of the Empire. An exception was the electoral dynasty of Bavaria, the old and prominent Wittelsbach family, now aspiring to regal status. Lacking both unity and effective institutions of government, with resources being drained for centrifugal ventures and outsiders taking part in her domestic discussions in the wake of the Thirty Years' War, the Empire was largely barren of real power. What strength she might muster on a given occasion depended on the degree of current Austrian involvement with the Turks. In the middle of the eighteenth century Austrian weakness was exploited by Frederick the Great, who occupied Silesia, adding it to Prussia. Twenty-three years of intermittent warfare encompassing a maze of diplomatic maneuvering failed to deliver Silesia back to Austria—she had lost one of her most productive provinces. Thus by 1750 the Empire was deathly weak and the medieval example of universal empire had proved no more durable than the idea of a universal church.

In modern intellectual history the century which saw the Thirty Years' War was also of crucial importance in the development of new scientific attitudes. The apex of the seventeenth-century scientific movement may be regarded as Isaac Newton's *Principia Mathematica,* published in 1687. From this work was derived a view of the world which came to be known as the Newtonian World-Machine. The entire universe acted according to basic laws which were everywhere the same and which allowed no favorites. Whether God had created these laws, as the deists would hold, was really beside the point. The important thing was that the laws existed. This key to physical events became the foundation for the Enlightenment, the dominant eighteenth-century intellectual movement.

The knowledge that unchanging laws governed man and his world led to a determined search for those laws. These could be discovered through the careful study of man's experience as recorded through his senses. The psychology of knowledge underlying this was that of John Locke whose works cast a long shadow indeed. Clearly, proper knowledge would allow not only a better understanding of the world but also a more rational ordering of one's life. Vast improvements in living standards were thus to be had, merely by finding and heeding the laws of the universe. In the process man would become morally better, for, as Socrates had observed, to know the good would be to do the good. A new golden age was within reach as a feverish study began of man's world and behavior. A "Newton of the social sciences" was awaited with high expectation

ticated, superficial lip service to the Enlightenment, Frederick soberly and wholeheartedly partook of its ideals and objectives.

In 1780 another ruler in Central Europe embarked on a singular mission of enlightened despotism. Joseph II, the son of Maria Theresa, was determined to reorganize his realm and its society in accord with the latest theories. He attempted far more in the way of fundamental change than Frederick and was, in fact, an ideologue dedicated to basic reform. Unfortunately he lacked his mother's sense of moderation and Frederick's pragmatic instincts. The result was that many of his changes were rescinded shortly after his death (1790) and those remaining were substantially moderated.

The intensity, rapidity, and apparent sincerity with which Joseph freed serfs, reformed laws, and tried to unify his realm have made him an attractive figure. There is, however, the view that much of what he inaugurated constituted merely an extension and intensification of his mother's policies. After the loss of Silesia, Austria had to become stronger and more efficient if it were to continue to play a major role in European affairs. Although there is much to this perspective, perhaps it fails to do justice to Joseph's emotional commitment to eliminate serfdom and to have equality before the law throughout his kingdom. Like Frederick he endorsed religious toleration, and his granting of civil rights to Jews far exceeded the requirements of proper despotic action. Unlike Frederick, instead of intensifying class divisions, he wanted to eliminate them completely and he hoped that his reforms might end the harsh misery that most peasants endured. The clergy and nobility to him were hated reminders of the Middle Ages, an unenlightened age of tyranny and oppression. Naturally, such views earned the wrath of these classes. His attempts to bring unity to Hapsburg lands led him to embark on a linguistic Germanization of his non-German populations, stirring up resentment everywhere and especially incensing the Hungarians.

Aside from being too tactless and hasty, his failure was also due to his virtual isolation. Very few sympathized with his ideas and he had no capable class to support him. The middle class was too small to be effective; thus he was essentially attempting an enormous task alone. When he sensed opposition from key people, he instituted a hated police system to keep him informed of violations. Hence an attempt to bring enlightened social progress was to be powered and enforced by autocracy and police vigilance.

Eastern Europe's prime example of enlightened despotism was Catherine the Great, a member of the minor German nobility, who came to rule Russia between 1762 and 1796. Like Frederick she achieved a considerable stature as a person of intellect and learning. She was, however, enormously vain. In her mind she set the *philosophes* on a pedestal and anxiously craved to win their praise and acceptance. The degree of her success is evident, for both Voltaire and Diderot were impressed with her insights; and her voluminous correspondence included thoughtful exchanges with Jean d'Alembert, Frederick II, and Joseph II. Her court glistened with a brilliance and protocol worthy of Versailles as her rule constituted a superficial resumption of the Westernization movement undertaken by Peter the Great. Catherine was especially well read and the authors she had studied included Plato, Montesquieu, and Rousseau. She read with particular care William Blackstone's *Commentaries on the Laws of England* while she was personally composing a work on the basic principles that should govern an enlightened state. Based heavily on Montesquieu, her document breathed the spirit of the Enlightenment and was to be a guide for a Legislative Commission which she expected to devise a comprehensive legal code. The commission failed in its basic assignment, although it did collect a great deal of legal and social information that aided Catherine in later efforts at more modest reform.

Catherine as a reformer was disappointing. There can be no question but what she consciously imitated the *philosophes* and, indeed, profoundly shared many of their basic beliefs. When it came to action, however, her reforms were secondary: local administrative reorganization, somewhat improved conditions for 14 million state-owned serfs, the founding of various schools, and a lowering of tariffs. Important as these reforms were—and they were carried out in a deliberate spirit of Enlightenment—they pale before other contemporary domestic changes. During her reign the living conditions of 20 million nonstate-owned serfs became far more wretched. Catherine's insecure and precarious political position had forced her into a kind of alliance with the landed aristocracy. She recoiled with horror at news of the French Revolution and in a bid for noble support, she allowed them complete control on their estates; thus each became a despot in his own right and few were enlightened. A system with opportunities for exploitation gave way to virtual slavery. This horrible development, with the Tsarina's sanction and combined with her known vanity, has inspired skepticism about Catherine's basic sincerity. Critics also have faulted her ruthless foreign policy, which dramatically increased Russian territory. A fair judgment is extremely difficult because aggrandizement at the expense of other powers was commonplace; and it would be hasty, indeed, to overlook the dangers a monarch of Russia would face if the aristocracy were in opposition, particularly when, as in Catherine's case, the monarch was not a native Russian.

There can be no question that enlightened despotism was consciously allied with the *philosophe* movement. What sort of an alliance this was, however, is an interesting question and invites a number of intriguing observations. The example of Louis XIV looms in the background. When despots enlarged their states through guile and warfare, they were surely close to the Grand Monarch. When they reorganized their governments with an eye to centralization and efficiency (order, rationalism, authoritarianism), they, likewise, had an example earlier than the Enlightenment. In fact, the point has been made that what eighteenth-century monarchs of Central and Eastern Europe were really doing was applying seventeenth-century concepts to backward areas, but using the terminology of their own day. Of course, there were some differences; the theme that "the monarch is first servant of the state" could apply to Louis XIV, who certainly labored for his state. The expression was recurring among the despots but its emphasis on duty and services was quite different from the monarch-oriented *"L'État, c'est moi."* One notes also an absence of deity among the despots; and although in theory the format was still that of divine-right monarchy, there was little talk and insistence on the idea by the late eighteenth century. Absolutism in the seventeenth and eighteenth century is an intriguing topic and obviously relevant. While pondering the extent to which Frederick, Joseph, Catherine, or others were sincere *philosophes* or *philosophe*-supporters, it is worth considering whether these monarchs were merely taking advantage of the intellectuals, finding that the new theories were convenient covers for old-fashioned autocracy. The values of Machiavelli were part of the scene for better or worse. Also, these despots are often viewed from a *philosophe*-like perspective and it has become clear that although these eighteenth-century intellectuals truly desired reform and believed their ideas to be practical, they were basically theoreticians and ideologues. Most possessed little administrative experience and none ever faced such a real crisis as Pugachev's rebellion of 1773. Some were uncritical admirers of reform and encouraged it without sensing that the deep-seated habits of centuries often gave an ignorant comfort to a wretched situation. Frederick seemed to know what could and could not be changed and, being a sober intellectual as well as king, he had a rare perspective on his world and its problems.

It was one thing to write essays for discussion at salons and quite another to alter the administrative and legal practices of a kingdom.

While French intellectuals were diligently promoting the values of the Enlightenment and watching the activities of reforming despots with particular interest, the need for such a monarch in France became obvious. Lethargic and haphazard administration had followed the forceful government of Louis XIV, and by mid-century the nation stood in need of both effective leadership and reform. This was clear to the *philosophes*, with Voltaire being especially critical. His incisive wit ridiculed the society's shortcomings. Corruption, fraud, and incompetence were central themes for his attacks. An evil-ridden priesthood posing as the moral leadership of the nation felt the thrust of his barbs, for nothing was immune from his pen. Merely to point out how things were, was enough to suggest that the society was not rationally organized. Such attacks lessened respect for established institutions, as it became commonplace for intellectuals to brand their government as nonrational and their church as immoral. Voltaire attacked the Church more strongly than the government because he regarded its roguish priests as the deliberate enemies of free thought and hence outright enemies of progress.

Unfortunately, there was much in France to criticize. The conflicting jealousies, hatreds, and frustrations, rapidly becoming more intense, are a common story in discussions of the origins of the French Revolution. The usual social divisions derived from a feudal past were themselves rent by further divisions and antagonisms. Many of these were generations old and could, perhaps, have continued but for an acute problem of financing the monarchy in the eighteenth century. Attempts to get more money intensified and acerbated existing domestic frictions, and resulted finally in outright revolution.

The economic problem was that the monarchy needed to acquire more funds to meet rising costs and the expenses incurred by the Seven Years' War. Because France was a wealthy nation, it became a matter of finding a device to extract the money from those who possessed it. Unfortunately, the tax structure made it possible for those with wealth to avoid or evade payment, letting the heaviest burden fall on the peasantry. It was an obvious situation calling for an enlightened despot, but a brief attempt to solve the problem within the Enlightenment tradition failed and France lost her prospects for orderly reform without bloodshed.

Enlightened reform in France had its opportunity between 1770 and 1776. In December of 1770, the Duke of Choiseul (1719–1785) left office as a result of failure to solve the problems of finance. The key issue resolved about the *parlements.* Strongholds of resistance to royal attempts to levy taxes against the wealthy, these bodies stood in defiance of the king's ministry. A point of crisis had been reached by 1770 and Choiseul had the choice of resolutely moving against the *parlements* or merely allowing financial affairs to worsen, undermining royal authority. As well as representing wealthy interests, the *parlements* enjoyed a considerable popular following; thus Choiseul refused to move against them. Because of this, he was dismissed and power was given to a former president of the *parlement* of Paris, René Nicolas de Maupeou (1714–1792), and to the Abbé Joseph-Marie Terray (1715–1778).

Maupeou at once struck out against the *parlements,* a course he had been suggesting for some time. He simply closed down the *parlements,* forcibly retiring and exiling the magistrates. He then established new *parlements* which he could control and altered their authority. It was a bold move calling forth a torrent of abuse, but Maupeou remained firm as he looked ahead to a recasting of legal procedures, a codification of the law, equal justice, and a recovery of royal prestige. Meanwhile, Terray created further criticism by starting fiscal reform by resorting to bankruptcy and repudiating the government's obligations for previous debts. More to his credit were his improvements in assessment procedures for the income tax (*vingtième*) and the poll tax (*capitation*), which at once produced additional revenues. Maupeou and Terray had crushed the obstacle to reform and successfully faced the basic problem of raising money. Unfortunately the mainstay of their authority disappeared when Louis XV died in 1774. At his death, royal authority was being reasserted, and although the outcry of the wounded vested interests was considerable, others, including Voltaire, recognized and defended the new course.

Louis XVI (1754–1793) came to the throne in the midst of a wave of popular optimism and good feeling which he managed to dissipate. The hornet's nest of entrenched privilege stirred up by Maupeou looked for aid from the new king. Maupeou and Terray were shortly dismissed and the old *parlements* re-established in a move almost completely reversing the constructive efforts of the previous ministry. The pressures for reform, however, were also strong and Louis XVI and his advisor, the Count of Maurepas (1701–1781), wanted at least to appear dedicated to change and progress. In this spirit they appointed as controller-general one of the intendants, Baron Anne Robert Jacques Turgot (1727–1781), a respected writer on economic subjects with a reputation as an effective administrator. Turgot proved, in his less than two years in office, to be interested in substance rather than appearance and far more dedicated to practical reform than Maurepas had suspected. He should have seen, however, from Turgot's record as an intendant that he had very little respect for mere tradition or for entrenched privilege.

Turgot was a physiocrat, one of the *philosophes* especially interested in the economic theories of Quesnay, who held that wealth came from the land, thus all landowners should pay taxes and there should be free trade in all products of the land. A specific follower of the physiocrat Vincent de Gournay, Turgot's wide range of social acquaintances included Montesquieu, D'Alembert, Helvetius, Galiani, and Voltaire. A believer in Newtonian physics and an author of many essays on economic topics and of articles in the *Encyclopédie,* his credentials as an intellectual were impressive.

His practical administrative qualifications were even more significant. From 1761 to 1774 Turgot had been the intendant at Limoges. Of all the intendancies it was the most backward and poverty-ridden and typified most of the ills in French society. Turgot's appointment was the occasion for his friends' sorrow because Limoges was the graveyard of reputations. A succession of poor harvests were to complicate his other problems at Limoges, and in 1769 outright famine stalked the land.

Turgot at once began a systematic attack on this provincial sample of the *ancien régime.* Reforms were introduced in rapid succession and the area's productivity began to increase. The *taille* and its administration was completely overhauled as well as the working of the *corvée.* He implemented at Limoges the program of free trade in grain which came to France in 1763–1764 and occasioned a great deal of local hostility. While he was working to counteract the harsh impact of poor harvests through relief measures, he was also supervising an important program of public works. The results of his labors were remarkable but what Maurepas should have noted was that Turgot was embroiled much of the time in litigation with the *parlement* of Bordeaux. Many of his actions were of questionable technical legality and he often by-passed the courts. While the magistrates pondered, he pushed his reforms hoping for quick vindication. Clearly he did not hold previous custom or the *parlements* in great awe.

Turgot entered the office of controller-general in 1774 with very clear ideas. He explained to Louis XVI that he expected no additional loans, no new taxes, and no bankruptcy. Sensible standards of thrift and reform would ease the fiscal situation and spread the burden of taxation fairly. He counted on royal support for specific portions of his program and expected to work with or around the restored *parlements*. Both of these expectations proved too optimistic and he left office in May, 1776.

Though he was controller-general less than two years, what he attempted and accomplished was noteworthy. He brought free trade to both the grain trade and the wine industry. The administration of both the *taille* and *corvée* were drastically altered. He attacked guild privileges and introduced a host of lesser reforms, ranging from the elimination of sinecures to apprehension of persons defrauding the government. Eventually the chorus of vested interests became too strong for Louis XVI and he dismissed his offending minister. Turgot had acted with speed but little tact, perhaps because at Limoges he had gained no experience in dealing with the likes of an intriguing court nobility. The *parlements,* combined with the aristocracy at Versailles, including Queen Marie Antoinette, had brought him down. In the end he proved no more successful than Maupeou.

Nevertheless, under Turgot there was a dramatic improvement in royal finances. In the year he took office, government income was 276.7 million livres, expenses were 325.3 million livres—a *deficit* of 48.6 million livres. In 1775 there was a *surplus* of 5 million livres. Five months after Turgot's dismissal the deficit had returned, 37 million livres, along with 60 million of future revenue committed. Obviously Turgot had temporarily reversed the trend and proved that the financial plight of the monarchy was not unsolvable. Terray's earlier efforts were also partially responsible but the conclusion is clear. Interestingly, Turgot opposed involvement in the American Revolution on grounds that it would cost too much. It ultimately cost France 2 billion livres and hastened the desperate financial plight which resulted in the events of 1789. One can only speculate on what might or might not have transpired had Maupeou and Terray or Turgot been given a decade of power.

France thus failed to take advantage of the wisdom of her own *philosophes.* This group, properly supported, could have solved the most serious financial problems of the state and would also have given the population a unified and thorough law code ensuring equal justice. French reform efforts in the decade before 1787 were superficial and even fraudulent and the stage was passed where improvement could be either moderate or rational. The Revolution was in sight.

CHAPTER 3

The French Revolution

In 1789 the festering grievances and problems of many generations finally burst out into the open. The land of Saint Louis, Henry IV, and Louis XIV underwent a complete revolt against royal absolutism and entrenched privilege. The world of classicism and of elegant Cartesian dualism, of balance and order, gave way to the phrases and values of Rousseau pronounced with an intense emotional fervor.

The French Revolution was to alter profoundly the course of both French and European history. It represented as basic and cataclysmic a break with the past as the human record provides and its multifaceted nature has made it an intriguing and worthwhile object of study. Fortunately, extensive contemporary documentation survived so that research in depth is possible in economic, cultural, social, political, administrative, diplomatic, and military fields alike. For more than a century careful scholars have produced a variety of perspectives on the upheaval but today it still poses important interpretive questions where considerable disagreement exists. Historians are continuing their study and the flow of articles and books to join those thousands already on the shelves will surely be maintained into the foreseeable future. Our task is not to join this group in detailing the Revolution but rather to note some of its more interesting aspects.

As we have seen, the need for economic, social, and judicial reform was apparent in much of eighteenth-century Europe; and a mechanism for that reform, the appearance of enlightened despots, proved only partially able to solve the problem. Beyond this general truth about the period prior to the Revolution, disagreements abound. There are many explanations of the economic origins of the Revolution, learned opinion ranging all the way between emphases on French poverty and on French wealth. Descriptions branding a system that allowed government destitution in the midst of national wealth have been especially popular. Urban hardships and peasant poverty before 1789 have been important ingredients in narratives of the revolutionary situation, but are balanced by accounts emphasizing that with all her admitted need and administrative incompetence, France and her citizens were wealthy and well-off compared with much of Europe.

The role of ideas has also proved intriguing. Besides helping to establish a climate of opinion calling for and expecting reform, in what other ways was the Enlightenment related to the Revolution? Were the ideas and slogans of the Enlightenment which were implemented during the Revolution a result of their long-range impact or of the pragmatic necessities of the moment? How much more was there to the ideology of revolution than simply the failure to reform?

Marxism has, of course, a theory of history and of revolution which owes much to Karl Marx's study of the French Revolution. Ideology and economic considerations blend in an interesting interpretation where the growing ranks of the bourgeoisie, the class struggle, and the patterns of history bring reason and order to the bloody conflagration. Wealth, want, and struggle are all neatly accounted for—so well, in fact, that the burden of proof has fallen on those who would offer other basic explanations.

Another perspective suggests that the French Revolution is better understood when seen in the context of other revolts and revolutions going on in Europe and America between 1763 and 1801. A sort of "World Revolution of the West" or a democratic Atlantic revolution of vast proportions was underway and many of its characteristics were evident in the upheaval in France. It was an age and area in ferment and to see it whole is merely to see it as it was.

The French Revolution has achieved the status of a classic, thanks largely to its rich documentation. The period of resistance to established authority, the revolutionary regime itself, and then its stiffening against various forms of counterrevolution can all be clearly traced and used as a yardstick to evaluate and study other revolts. As various explanations have come to emphasize ideologies and large movements, the problem arises of how to trace adequately the roles of particular people caught in the upheaval. In this case it is especially intriguing because, although moods and movements may be clearly seen, so also can we document the human condition, the men who were buffeted by the tides of change as well as those who understood and led, challenged, or diverted these epic influences. Basic problems in explaining all human history are thus to be confronted in a study of the French Revolution.

When the Estates General convened on May 5, 1789, a first stage of the Revolution was well underway. The calling of this assembly represented a triumph for the nobility in a struggle for more political power. By dominating the clergy as well as their own order, they expected to control the whole assembly. The King would be forced to institute reforms along lines they prescribed, in effect, coming to share political power with them. They would return as a class to a position they enjoyed in France before Richelieu. Not only did this prospect seem clear in the King's call for the *cahiers de doléances* and the convening of the Estates, but it appeared a certainty when Louis XVI declared that the Estates would meet by order. Although they had finally pushed the King to the point where he was preparing to share his authority, they failed to foresee his similar retreat before bourgeoise pressures. When, on June 27, Louis finally acceded to the demands for votes by head in a combined assembly, the aristocracy had lost its best opportunity and another interest group took its place.

The successive struggles for ascendency during the Revolution are fascinating. There were competing cliques within competing classes and competing persons within the cliques. Although there were a host of interesting combinations, successes and failures, ebbs and flows in the struggle for power, until the later days of the Convention the center of authority generally moved from right to left. Each group found allies to its left in its initial struggle but then lost leadership to these elements. Also, as the Revolution went further left (broadened and deepened), there was a drawing together of some of those who had allowed power to slip from their grasp. Thus an aristocratic revolt, with help from enlightened business and legal interests, lost control to the middle class. When the bourgeoisie felt endangered, it found allies among the lower classes, the workers or "masses," who in turn controlled the Revolution for a time. The clear pattern of this "drift to the left" appears so obvious that it could be questioned whether any of the actors in this drama were free to steer its course in any other direction. Basic to the success of the earliest stages of the Revolution was the amiable, lethargic, and hardly competent Louis XVI. In a decade and a half he managed to dissipate much of the popularity and goodwill evident upon his ascending the throne. A marked deterioration in economic conditions had followed his failure to reform. His compelling sin was not that he was despotic but that he was not enlightened. After Turgot he drifted from one expediency-oriented minister to another, little interested in the details of governing and generally annoyed and irritated at the increasing grievances being placed before him. When pressures built up against a minister, he merely turned to one of the critics, entrusting him with the office until the next round of protest. His backing down before demands for a single house was a characteristic response to crisis. An unfortunate sample of royalty, Louis XVI exemplified a glaring weakness in the hereditary principle of succession.

A striking feature of the early Revolution is the dearth of leadership ability on the right. Not only was the King's grasp of the situation inadequate but none about him appeared capable. Louis XVI had a gift for inaccurately sensing a situation and several times missed chances to moderate the early course of the Revolution. After personally irritating many of the bourgeois members of the Third Estate, he failed to realize their determination to play an effective role in legislative decisions. Tactless threats of force only stiffened and energized the opposition.

Within the Third Estate a number of capable men appeared, the most prominent at first being the Count of Mirabeau (1749–1791). This renegade noble with a sordid reputation was able to mobilize the opposition to entrenched privilege, conveying a sense of unity and importance to the Third Estate. Conversion of the Estates General into a National (Constituent) Assembly may be largely credited to his initiative and ability.

During the month of July, 1789, the discussions at Versailles were forced to consider a number of serious breaches of royal authority. Social revolution now accompanied political revolution; and, at first, militant members of the Assembly delighted in the Crown's demonstrated weakness. An urban mob successfully attacked the Bastille with approval of the Parisian bourgeoisie, while in the countryside riots and disorder spread like a plague. Mere rumors ("The brigands are coming") were enough to motivate whole communities to turn systematically on all symbols of authority and privilege, killing tax officials, nobles, and estate managers and destroying manorial records. Many private grievances were avenged as the normal restraints of law and order disappeared. This violence in the countryside, the so-called *Grande Peur,* caused an immediate end to tax collection so that the financial problem was now completely out of hand. Simultaneously, there were urban demonstrations in the other major cities. On the heels of a series of earlier bread riots, the results of the violence and the direction it took bore little relation to its initial causes.

Although bands of farmers with pitchforks and firebrands are more difficult to document than politicians angling for power in a formal assembly, the causes and psychology of both urban and rural mob violence are now receiving the careful study of historians. The monarchy was caught between the Assembly and an echoing crescendo of urban and rural upheaval. That affairs could come to such a state was a sad commentary on the King. At this point, he needed help from the Assembly but it proved hesitant to rescue royal authority. Where rests the responsibility for this attitude?

On the evening of August 4, members of the Assembly finally voted measure after measure which in theory dismantled the feudal regime. In fact it had been long altered in its essential respects and several of the measures of August 4 were mere validation of long-standing conditions. Nominal aristocrats lacking privileges moved the abolition of the rights of their wealthier peers as internal jealousies and revenge played their part. Some changes, however, related directly to the rural violence, and although the Assembly claimed moral credit for these reforms, had it acted earlier, its position would have been far more creditable. Despite the forced character of some reforms and the emptiness of others, the Assembly did seem seized by a spirit of concern for the public welfare and perhaps their collective action could even be regarded as a manifestation of the general will. While privileges were being surrendered, the dominant bourgeois group was not so revolutionary but what it recognized that these were forms of property requiring indemnification, posing a subsequent additional financial problem for the Assembly. The show of goodwill evinced by the nobility during the proceedings strengthened the determination that they should receive justice, and so the need for money was intensified.

If there were any doubts about the enlightened middle-class character of the Assembly, they were dispelled by the values evident in the Declaration of the Rights of Man, passed August 21, 1789, a preface to the constitution still to be drawn up. These "rights" were rooted in the seventeenth- and eighteenth-century concept of natural law and breathed the spirit of the Enlightenment: "Men are born and remain free and equal in rights"; property is "a sacred and inviolable right"; "the source of all sovereignty resides essentially in the nation"; "law is the expression of the general will"; and "every society in which the guarantee of rights is not assured or the separation of powers not determined has no constitution." When finally added to the constitution (of 1791) the initial Declaration was altered to emphasize the opposition to inherited distinctions and privilege. It is interesting to observe that portions of the Declaration were ignored in the constitution itself. Serving a propaganda function, the Declaration attracted followers to the cause of the Revolution and may also be regarded as a strictly utilitarian document of the moment. In this light its emphasis on freedom and equality are not a result of philosophic conviction but of a need to eliminate privilege with its sinecures in government. The King's earlier support of the aristocracy had given the bourgeoisie a sense of abandonment —even betrayal after the monarchy had governed *with* them for well over a century—and now they needed an assurance that careers would be open to talent rather than lineage. As a group they never doubted that such a standard would assure them power nor did they have in mind a provision by which the lower classes would assume control. Thus the Declaration had its roots in the practical past frustrations and ambitions of the middle class, especially those members with legal and administrative experience. Although the earlier American experience in framing a similar statement of rights was common knowledge and widely discussed, the French also possessed adequate historical, political, and ideological background to formulate their own statement. The insistence that sovereignty resided in the whole nation attacked royal absolutism and at the same time led to a system whereby an assembly representing the nation could itself be absolutist. The middle class may have been consciously following its own interests, but by and large it did so with the presumption that its perspectives were those best for the nation.

After the peasants had been completely freed of manorial obligations, they became essentially a conservative force and rioting in the countryside became less frequent. Urban unrest flared in early October as a horde of women and the Marquis de Lafayette (1757–1834) with the National Guard brought Louis XVI to Paris. After this, however, violence ended for nearly two years. It had started in the spring and accompanied the various political decisions made during the summer. With both the Assembly and the monarch in Paris, the King finally approved Assembly actions taken since August 4. Louis XVI was virtually a prisoner and many deputies began to wonder whether the Revolution had gone too far. A number departed for their homes and others emigrated, leaving the Assembly weaker on the right and much more susceptible to the liberal influence of the Parisian government and the various clubs, and to threats of urban insurrection.

Louis XVI had failed to make effective use of the army during 1789. Some royal forces sympathized with the Revolution, but not all by any means. There were also mercenary troops but the King managed to derive no positive advantage from these, incurring only public distrust and ill will by their mere presence. This, however, must be regarded as only one of his minor errors.

Although the King and his family had been moved into Paris and the rural turbulence had subsided, the National Assembly still had not resolved the financial problem. In its desperate need for funds the Assembly finally turned on the Church. Blending its solution to financial problems with the general mood for clerical reform, it nationalized Church lands and made the clergy state employees. As a source of tremendous landed wealth, it was probably inevitable that the Revolution would attack the Church if other measures to raise money failed. With the aristocratic right weakened and the King's role diminished, there was inadequate strength within the Assembly to protect the Church, and when one of its own prelates, Maurice de Talleyrand (1754–1838), the Bishop of Autun, introduced and argued for the initial spoliation, its fate at the hands of the Assembly was clear. Although the issuance of *assignats* based on Church lands and the Civil Constitution of the Clergy may be seen as two programs, in reality a number of specific measures were involved which represented a massive attack on the Church.

Of all the Assembly's reforms, this was perhaps the most profound. Louis XVI finally became alert and deeply concerned about the course of the Revolution. Its other measures paled in his eyes compared with these acts of spoliation which he regarded as evil and

Godless. A specious mechanism had been devised for the transfer of Church property to members of the middle class and to long-suppressed Jansenists. At the same time all who acquired these lands and all who dealt in the *assignats* now had a stake in the progress of the Revolution. Thus, within a very short time, an extensive backing for the Assembly had been created and it could finish establishing its constitutional system with the expectation that it would succeed. Self-interest and human greed would make counterrevolution almost impossible. Politically the Assembly's judgment was shrewd and a success. Economically the *assignats* were a failure and the fiscal problem was to continue. The sale of Church lands never kept up with the printing of more *assignats* and an orgy of speculation, depression, and inflation complicated economic affairs. As the income from the confiscated lands failed to meet expectations and the cost of supporting the clerical establishment had been added to the state budget, deficits became larger than ever.

In addition to taking over Church property and making employees of the clerics, the Assembly also reorganized the Church in France, forcing the clergy to take an oath of support to the new system. Although the general attack on the Church could have been expected and perhaps defended, the Assembly made a serious mistake in the extent to which it involved itself in strictly religious affairs. Heretofore its opponents had been the aristocracy and the court. Now many devout believers of all strata—especially those in Alsace, the west, and the north—joined the ranks against the Revolution, the so-called nonjuring clergy (which the Assembly, in effect, created) being natural leaders in moral opposition to the government.

An opportunity for counterrevolution was at hand but required of the King a measure of inspired leadership. Unfortunately this would have been completely out of character for Louis XVI. He halfheartedly listened to advice from Mirabeau, who was steering a suspicious course between the monarch and the Assembly. Questionable as Mirabeau's motives may have been, after his death on April 2, 1791, Louis XVI never received adequate counsel and continued to be incapable of making correct judgments. Local insurrections were widespread and many more were threatened but Louis XVI failed to put himself at their head. Instead, after correspondence with *émigrés*, he decided on a military demonstration just over the northeast border. He left Paris, heading for the chateau of Moldave, where his brother, the Count of Artois (1757–1836), awaited him, but was intercepted at Varennes and forced to return. Thoroughly discredited, his actions were now regarded by many as nothing less than treason.

The King's flight doomed to failure the attempt to create a constitutional monarchy. Although Louis accepted the constitution and wholly new faces appeared in the membership of the Legislative Assembly, too much suspicion of the King's ill will existed. A grim combination of circumstances then combined to guarantee the country's involvement in war. Most factions saw their own advantage being served if war were to come, leaving the voices against it too few and too weak. Both the King and his critics united in the belief that the war would somehow solve the domestic problem—to their separate ends and satisfactions.

The story of the coming of the war is almost a classic illustration of how domestic political groups may attempt to seize advantage from a progressively deteriorating foreign policy. It also demonstrates clearly the relationship between underlying and immediate causes for a conflict. Intriguing questions also abound. Did a struggle against royal absolutism in France really have to become a conflict against other monarchs? Was freedom in France incompatible with its absence in other areas of Europe? Seeing war mainly as a ramification of the attack on privilege, secular and ecclesiastical, could it have been avoided but for the dynastic connection between the Bourbon and Hapsburg houses? It is worth noting that the Revolutionary leaders at this juncture saw themselves and the system as under attack from outside elements which were suspected of collusion with the King. Although the reformers were not yet talking aggressively about freeing enslaved mankind, the continued existence of the Revolution itself carried such an implication. Does it have any meaning to ask such a simple question as who or what caused the war?

Speculation on these and other questions remains. Men and parties moved to war as though pushed by unseen forces. Louis XVI hoped for rescue from abroad and expected that if by some miracle French arms should be successful, the credit would rebound to himself. This proved an amazingly simplistic perspective. Within the Revolutionary clubs, fierce debates raged over how the crisis should be used to solidify or extend the Revolution. Robespierre was virtually alone in foreseeing the danger of a military dictator. From the point of view of other European monarchs, the dangers in attacking a nation shorn of most of its aristocratic leadership seemed minimal and there could have been no way to anticipate the militant brand of nationalism that was to emerge in France. Few, if any, who balanced the issues of peace or war in the spring of 1792 could properly sense the vast issues at stake. Compounding the situation was the position of the Church. Papal opposition to the Revolution gave a moral sanction to the enemies of France, and the "juring" clergy within the nation also lent an emotional support to the war effort. With God's agents on both sides, what wonder that mere mortals made terrible errors!

By summer of 1792 enormous changes had taken place since the convening of the Estates General in May of 1789 at Versailles. The King had been personally discredited and legislative action involved the interaction of a number of cohesive groups. The war introduced a new militancy. Political opposition now meant treason, for loyalty to the constitution and the Revolution assumed the highest value. In this light the King's continued contact with *émigrés* and other monarchs was especially dangerous. He had a right to be bitter regarding the Duke of Brunswick's proclamation, which brought him down. This document was far more sweeping than Louis had anticipated and, well intentioned though it may have been, its language was close to betrayal. Louis XVI had not asked for condemnation of the Revolution or the Assembly but merely of its most radical faction. Such a declaration would possibly have isolated this group and enhanced the Assembly's more moderate and conservative elements. The misunderstanding involved here was fatal for Louis XVI.

The role of extralegal elements (mob violence and pressure at balloting) in the transition from constitutional monarchy to a republic was ironic but probably inevitable. In the orgy of murder and mass violence of the September Days, the urban proletariat ran wild as agitators spurred them on. Responsibility for the insurrection is difficult to document but Danton and Marat are highly suspect. Private justice occurred on a wide scale as an apprehension of conquest by invaders seized the population. The battle of Valmy (September 20) was a strange and insignificant military encounter in itself but it assured a brief period of security for the organization of the new government. With the Convention in session, the trial of the King was given high priority. Heightened emotions made it difficult for one to defend the monarch without appearing to be an enemy of the Revolution and of France. The young firebrand Saint-Just even maintained that Louis should be treated like a captured prisoner of war. Much has been made of the irregularity of the charges and the voting, and the absence of a plebiscite. Also the closeness of the vote has led to special criticism of particular persons who cast their ballots for death. However, much of this is really beside the point. From the fall of the monarchy on August 10, irregularity was common and Louis XVI had become an unnecessary embarrassment. The execution of Louis XVI (January 21, 1793) was essential to assure the permanence of this last stage of the Revolution, but it also brought more countries into war against France. Conservative opinion went underground or abroad and the monarchs of Europe saw clearly the sinister side of the Revolution. The Convention girded for all-out war.

Under the National Convention the Revolution took its most extreme form. In the name of liberty, equality, and fraternity, an authoritarianism of appalling rigor assumed control and prior reforms paled before measures now introduced. Rousseau had made the point that under certain conditions a small group might find that it truly embodied the "General Will." The Committee of Public Safety took this position, for Maximilien Robespierre (1758–1794) saw himself and the Committee as conscious examples of what Rousseau had described. Buttressed by a confidence that their ideas embodied those of the whole nation, they acted decisively. Loyalty to "the people" was the supreme virtue, especially because the nation was under attack. A particularly militant nationalism took on many religious attributes, while the truncated Church, which had survived the earlier stages of the Revolution, now succumbed. The new nationalism, stressing loyalty to the Revolution, had its own emotional demands and satisfactions, achieved through slogans, songs, martyrs, and credos. Clearly the middle class had lost control of the Revolution and orators catered to the shouts and approval of the workers and the Parisian mob. Ironically, some very capable and educated leaders emerged; thus although the motive power for the Revolution at this stage was often at a level of the urban rabble, its leadership was particularly distinguished. Talent had found its way to the counsels of power, a belated symbol of the indirect success of earlier phases of the Revolution.

In military affairs the passion for reform was thorough, for the nation was in deadly peril. The old officer class had been decimated and a system of merit established. The idea of careers open to talent was most effectively implemented and the *levée en masse* provided for many new recruits. The deputies *en mission* were a military version of the Terror. Bonaparte was only one of many who were able to rise swiftly when the Revolution weeded out the upper ranks and rewarded obvious ability. The idea that the entire nation was involved in a war was new and gave to their struggle a sense of unity and desperation lacking among their opponents, whose peasant armies approaching France were led by uninspired aristocrats. French enthusiasm for the liberties granted by the Revolution led them to see their struggle as now directed against all entrenched privilege. Having freed Frenchmen, the Revolution was now a mission to free the masses of Europe. This sense of crusading zeal constituted a serious threat to Europe's old order. This was especially clear when the armies of the Republic began to enjoy marked success in the field and France could annex Savoy and territories to the Rhine. Annexation brought not only the current French version of liberty but also the *assignats* to the conquered areas. In 1793 there were temporary French retreats on these frontiers, but by early 1794 the new revolutionary armies were again successfully repeling the enemy.

Within France executions assumed a mass character—domestic "enemies" were being discovered in great numbers. Insurrections also added to the tension as the various clubs competed for power. The Jacobin Club eventually provided the leadership for the Convention and demonstrated the force which a highly disciplined and authoritarian group can exert within a larger unit. An interesting struggle was developing between Robespierre and Georges Jacques Danton (1759–1794) and their rivalry has provided the grounds for a continuing debate among historians. Which of these men represented the best of the Revolutionary values: Danton (defended by F. A. Aulard) who enjoyed power from April to June in 1793, or Robespierre (the hero of A. Mathiez, student of Aulard) the more radical leader who engineered Danton's execution (April 5, 1794) and was himself a victim of the guillotine on 10 Thermidor (July 28, 1794)? In any case, the dictatorial government had carried out its domestic repression in the name of the Revolution; but after Robespierre's death it lost much of its initial fervor and spontaneity. A Calvinistic grimness pervaded the scene as the Terror gradually began to create its own opposition—not from treasonous elements or remnants of conservatism but from its own leaders, who came to realize their own insecurity. The Terror subsided after the fall of Robespierre as the Thermidorian reaction set in, giving France a constitutional government in 1795.

With the Directory the middle class returned to power. It continued most of the reforms of the Convention but the Terror was gone. Historians are divided on the true nature of the Directory but fear and brutal repression gave way to appearances of opportunism and corruption. The provision that two thirds of both new chambers had to be *Conventionnels* invited suspicion, and tampered elections confirmed public skepticism. Indeed, the brilliance and efficiency of Bonaparte's 1796 campaign in Italy contrasted markedly with the sleazy and devious immorality of the system installed in Paris. When the grim sterility of the Terror receded, concern for the purity of the Revolution gave way to an interest in creature comforts. With the lessening of revolutionary zeal on the part of the government, opportunity opened for plots against the regime—the Directory faced a major threat in 1796 from the left (the Babeuf plot, the Conspiracy of Equals) and in 1797 from the right (a royalist plot involving General Pichegru). Jacobin plots abounded, and perhaps the remarkable thing is not that the Directory fell to Bonaparte and his associates in late 1799 but that it lasted that long.

With Bonaparte's coming to power, a military leader had at last emerged, as both Robespierre and Edmund Burke had predicted. Some historians regard the next fifteen years as an integral part of the Revolution, but many regard it as sufficiently different to say that the Revolution had run its course in the 1789–1799 decade. Although the Robespierre-Danton (Aulard-Mathiez) controversy has been referred to, a number of additional perspectives regarding the Revolution may be noted.

A basically conservative interpretation sees the Enlightenment and the *philosophes* as subverting legal order and undermining a legitimate system capable of reform. Once the events of 1789 occurred, destruction of the system was inevitable along with the final emergence of a strong man. Robespierre was this man, the epitome of the Revolution, a fanatic and a result of Rousseau's ideas. Interesting as this view is, it overlooks the force of the basic economic and social problems that beset France.

A more liberal view argues that the Revolution was necessary and its high point came under Danton. The Girondins are seen as an educated, nonnoble élite and Robespierre emerges as a villain. This view also ignores deep-seated economic problems and class conflict.

A radical interpretation emphasizes the conflicts of classes in France. The upper bourgeoisie started the Revolution, attempted to use the *sans culottes,* but lost control. The establishment of a republic became necessary when the King showed that he could not be trusted. Robespierre is the hero of this explanation, which sees the Directory as the return of the upper bourgeoisie to power.

To these views should be added the specifically Marxist interpretation, which emphasizes class problems and economic considerations. The basic problem was that dynamic capitalism was developing within a frozen feudal society. The story of the Revolution is the story of various strata of the bourgeoisie trying to break up the feudal arrangements. Robespierre's impact and failure is explained by his economic policies, for *"the people" really never led* the Revolution.

All these analyses have many versions and shadings. Indeed, the facts of what happened are far clearer than the reasons why. A reform movement had clearly gotten out of hand, leading to terror and a military autocrat. As a result, Europe saw its first attempt by a major modern state to rule without either a monarch or an aristocracy. The entrenched rulers, or at least many of them, may perhaps be pardoned for joining coalition after coalition to erase such a precedent.

CHAPTER 4

Napoleon

The beginning of the nineteenth century saw the meteoric rise of Napoleon Bonaparte (1769–1821). It was fitting that an age of such extraordinary vitality and ingenuity should begin under the influence of a figure of epic proportions, a man who declared that his task was nothing less than civilizing the Revolution, making its benefits acceptable and palatable to the rest of Europe. He was both the Revolution's product and solution, and one aspect of his legacy was that his career, like the Revolution itself, loomed ominously over the decades following his death. Closely resembling the later enlightened despots, he was a nineteenth-century replica of the eighteenth-century absolutism of Louis XIV.

By the close of 1815 Napoleon and his regime in Europe were defeated, and, appropriately, even this defeat had a heroic quality. His greatest triumphs, failures, and personal shortcomings have been carefully studied and described, but the reasons for his early successes—so rapid, numerous, and variegated—are hardly clear. It begs the question merely to say that the man was extraordinary and the age was ripe.

An enormous amount of propaganda has made the truth about Napoleon as elusive to historians as it was for his own contemporaries. He was a popular hero, adored by his followers and hated by opponents. Objectivity in the study of the Emperor was to come slowly in the decades after 1870. Because few writers were neutral, grossly uncritical praise rests on the book shelves beside various levels of character assassination. Much of Napoleon's own writing has added to the difficulty of finding the truth. A particularly astute propagandist, he wrote as often to conceal as to reveal. His Caesarism made a mockery of his post-Waterloo claims that, as a dedicated child of the Revolution, he was truly working for the welfare of the people of France. Yet it must not be forgotten that he did bring order to a situation which the Revolution had created and failed to stabilize. Although many of his claims may be discounted, where to draw the line is not clear. There can be no disputing that he was ambitious and egotistical, that his mind operated rationally and was capable of shrewd insights. Unquestionably his self-centeredness led him to irrational decisions; but when he faced calmly a problem not directly involving his ambition, then its solution was usually approached systematically. This quality made him a superb administrator and practical reformer. Despite his having read widely in the authors of the eighteenth century, his rationalism came from his basic nature rather than from the Age of Reason, however tempting such a thought may be. In addition to having a passion for orderly and logical patterns in human affairs, he possessed the rare facility of being able to see in a body of data possibilities that escaped less flexible minds. On many occasions he noted opportunities in a military situation which his generals and marshals failed to see. His supreme frustration occurred in Moscow in 1812 when after hours of map study, he could see only the same few disastrous choices that others saw.

His appointment to command the Army of Italy on March 2, 1796, typified the difficulties historians have in evaluating much of Bonaparte's career. From the wisdom of hindsight he was clearly an inspired selection, but given the situation at the time, why was he chosen? Josephine's "intimate" friendship with Barras, a director, has often been cited as a major factor, and considering the general caliber of the Directory, this is not an unreasonable explanation and has been especially tempting to Bonaparte's critics. Certainly influence and contacts counted for as much under the Directory as they ever had under the monarchy, where even Turgot had owed his appointment of controller-general to a friend in Maurepas' confidence rather than to his own good record at Limoges. Intriguing as such a view is, and Josephine's closeness to Barras surely did not hurt Bonaparte's prospects, another explanation is apparent. Napoleon had already been with the army in Italy and had formulated plans for offensive action which had been partially tried with success. Further, he was the only general officer with both confidence and ideas for victory in this sector where morale was low and failure threatening. It is a distinct possibility that he was appointed for professional reasons which were soon justified. We may choose either explanation, or both—but choose we must, because certainty is lacking.

How important a figure was Napoleon in early 1796? Known as an officer with Jacobin associates (especially Robespierre), he had been instrumental in the raising of the British siege of Toulon in December of 1793. Perhaps the *perpetuels* remembered him as playing a part in turning aside a mob in their defense during the dying days of the Convention. Just what his role was in the revolt of 13 Vendémaire (October 5, 1795), however, is something of a mystery. In later years he frequently referred to the incident, but with each telling the account took on new coloration. He was neither the first in command nor responsible for the crucial moving of heavy guns into position. A variety of his stories have been accepted at face value by generations of historians, but *the documents do not bear out any* of his versions. That the command in Italy resulted from gratitude for this action is a very tenuous explanation at best.

The Italian campaign of 1796 was a classic in military history, but only partly for the reasons and actions which Napoleon chose to dramatize. From him we get a view of rapierlike thrusts. of inspired victories in actions where the French were vastly outnumbered. Again his versions of how he energized a lethargic, poorly equipped force and led it swiftly into green valleys and great riches have been taken largely at face value. He wrote with a modicum of truth, but no amount of propaganda or later theatrical references, could, for example, make a significant military action out of Lodi (May 10, 1796). It is more instructive to look at the situation that led him to claim Lodi as a triumph. He had by then succeeded in his command beyond the Directory's most optimistic hopes. He had forced Sardinia out of the alliance and the Austrians were racing for the protective walls of Mantua. This was a great accomplishment in itself but had been done with no major pitched battle, no engagement which focused and compelled attention; thus he dramatized the minor engagement at Lodi. He really succeeded because of careful planning and brilliant maneuvering of troops, operating against officers committed to the cordon system rather than a war of movement and control of strategic areas. Had there been no siege of Mantua (July, 1796–February, 1797), his campaign to this point would have been important enough for study in military schools. His destruction of successive armies trying to relieve Mantua likewise shows careful planning and an awareness of how to take special advantage of geographical features. Bonaparte's decisions here were prudent, based on sound principles and an incisive judgment of the intellectual prowess of his opposing commanders. Little was left to chance. While he was moving against Mantua, he was also negotiating with Italian states to the south, deftly dovetailing diplomatic and political demands to the military situation. After Mantua's fall, Napoleon advanced into Austria, making a series of tactical errors. The armistice of Leoben and Treaty of Campo Formio he characteristically claimed as personal triumphs but they masked his mistakes and were really Austrian diplomatic successes.

Almost every episode in Napoleon's career is intrinsically fascinating, and the Egyptian campaign (July, 1798–August, 1799) is no exception. This was a struggle larger than life, with an extraordinary man accomplishing amazing feats only to be defeated by circumstances he could not control. Tactical brilliance and ingenuity proved inadequate in the face of profound strategic disadvantages, but for Napoleon to have awakened Egypt from a sort of lethargic medievalism was no mean accomplishment, by-product though it was to his main objectives. The symbol of his failure is that today the Rosetta Stone is in the British Museum. Characteristically he returned unscathed to France to the accompaniment of his own propaganda, which presented his unsuccessful mission as a great victory. By the time better information was available in France, he had virtually complete control of the government.

In 1799, Paris witnessed the progressive weakening of the Directory, its position threatened anew from both royalist right and republican Jacobin left. The opprobrium of corruption and military reverses in Europe had settled upon the government and the main political question seemed to be *what sort of coup* would be best. There was little loyalty to the Directory.

Untainted by recent scandals, a new director appeared, the Abbé Siéyès (1748–1836). Author of the influential pamphlet *What Is the Third Estate?*, he had subsequently voted for the death of Louis XVI, had been a member of the Committee of Public Safety and a *perpetuel,* and had recently returned from a year at the embassy in Berlin. It was presumed that as a director he would restore integrity to the government. Having survived ten years of crisis himself, he was believed to be the man who could save the Republic. His immediate task was to secure himself against threat of an uprising led by Bernadotte. After pressuring this general out of the war ministry and winning time for more permanent planning, he decided on an alliance with Napoleon. He needed the support of a general, and most of the other prominent soldiers proved unsuitable. That Napoleon should land at Fréjus on October 9 while Siéyès was pondering the selection was fateful. The public displays of affection for this taciturn thirty-year-old officer during the week-long trip to Paris were obviously suggestive. Siéyès had already worked with Lucien Bonaparte and now decided—although with some foreboding—to work with Napoleon. The coup of 18 Brumaire (November 9) went off smoothly, but Siéyès' doubts were to prove well founded.

Siéyès' role at this juncture is of some interest. A decade earlier he had worked eloquently for a strong representative assembly. But his ideas had changed and now he favored a strong executive and participated in the establishment of a consulate with chambers possessing little power. The danger of a Jacobin coup was gone with Masséna's victories in Switzerland during the summer. The best opportunity for a soldier with Jacobin connections to overthrow the government had passed by the time Napoleon landed at Fréjus. Ironically, although Bonaparte was approached by others also, he fit neatly into Siéyès plan, and despite his past Jacobin associations, the coup was justified by an alleged Jacobin plot, of all things.

Napoleon has, of course, been accused of participating in an illegal seizure of power and of showing a callous disregard for the constitution. As he pointed out, however, the constitution had been violated by many groups and, with the Directory enjoying little respect, many responsible people wanted a change. The coup of 18 Brumaire was a popular act accomplished without bloodshed. It may be cogently argued that the emergence of Bonaparte was in accord with the general will and was a victory of integrity over a system of corruption and graft.

For Napoleon another victory was necessary to bring him full power. Allowed three months in which to prepare a new constitution, the provisional consuls (Bonaparte, Siéyès, Roger Ducos) completed the task in half the time. This period was a psychological test of will between Bonaparte and Siéyès. The durable old constitutionalist, who had been prepared to flee for his life on 18 Brumaire, approached the task with a feeling of responsibility for his legislative followers who had helped give the coup its façade of legality. Napoleon sensed this and at once let Siéyès appear as a special pleader for discredited politicians while he posed as both the military support for the new regime and as the man without and above party, speaking for the entire nation and its welfare. Siéyès proved no match for Napoleon, who allowed him vast patronage but little political power. As a result, Siéyès was blamed for creating new *perpetuels* and Bonaparte emerged as First Consul, aided by two other consuls, Cambacérès (1753–1824) and Lebrun (1739–1824). Not only was Siéyès nudged from nominal power but his future was also undercut. In the plebescite on the constitution, Bonaparte's name alone was specifically on the document, so he interpreted its massive approval as a sign of national personal support. The popular general finishing an unsuccessful campaign and possessing little organized political support had taken over a plot planned by others, emerging in January, 1800, as the most powerful man in France. As implied by the understatement years later of his nephew, Prince Louis Napoleon, this man was much more than merely "a lucky general."

The new government was a striking application of military procedures to civil administration. The Senate along with the Tribunate and Legislative Body with their Siéyès-appointed holdovers (65 and 230, respectively) were powerless but allowed as gestures to Revolutionary tradition. Not completely docile, they were expected mainly to authorize programs. Thus a Council of State was founded to advise and to plan measures which the First Consul desired. These then were forwarded to the two houses for passage. The Council was a collection of about forty men of distinction and Bonaparte ruled through this agency. The heads of the ministries never met together as a cabinet. A series of special boards, within ministries but controlled by the Council, assured Bonaparte that the ministries themselves would never become solid bases of power for a political opponent to use against him. Throughout the nation, prefects implemented the policies enunciated in Paris. Local democratic councils had never been effective and were now brushed aside. The prefect wore a splendid costume but was an outsider to the area he administered. His assistants, subprefects, were local men. Thus an administrative centralization emphasizing efficiency rather than justice was achieved, with Bonaparte at its head.

Centralization was not a new idea but now it was more thoroughly implemented. A more careful check was kept on the prefect than had ever been the case with intendants and, generally speaking, care was taken to select capable administrators. This bureaucratic reordering of French administration was to prove one of Napoleon's most enduring achievements.

Napoleon's appointees were a remarkable group. He had come to power on the specious excuse of moving against Jacobins but he kept as minister of police Joseph Fouché (1759–1820), an old Jacobin who had helped bring down Robespierre. Cambacérès was a regicide but a moderate lawyer with great prestige. Lebrun, a respected literary figure suspected of still harboring royalist sentiments, had been a secretary to Maupeou. Many *ancien régime* officials and Jacobins found new positions as Bonaparte made good on his statement that all with ability were welcome, provided they were loyal. He even made it easier for *émigrés* to return to France as careers were made open to talent to an extent heretofore unknown in France.

The Legion of Honor was to be the capstone of this recognition of talent. Although "careers open to talent" had a democratic ring and was a product of the Revolution, Napoleon's objective was to identify an elite to serve the state with loyalty and distinction. At first unpopular and opposed by the republicans, the Legion of Honor acquired enormous prestige. Because there appeared to be a place for capable men of whatever party, widely disparate groups became hopeful for a better future and the immediate result was an upsurge of confidence in the government and in Bonaparte.

While completing the formation of his administrative bureaucracy, Napoleon began working on several basic problems unsolved by the Directory. His success in dealing with these problems, after providing the nation with a rational structure of government, made the Consulate one of the most constructive periods in French history.

The working of an effective bureaucracy made other reforms easier. For example, control of assessments and tax collection was now exercised in Paris (under Gaudin, an official from *ancien régime* days) and much more money was collected. The Bank of France was founded. With additional revenue, the debt reversed its upward spiral, which created even more confidence in the government. The Bank was given the sole right to issue notes, ending the decade of the *assignats*. A balanced budget (1801–1802) completed the financial miracle. Bonaparte, like Turgot, had proved that effective administration could solve the economic problems of France. Finances, however, were not the most fundamental problem, for incessant warfare made the achievement of 1801–1802 impossible to maintain.

In the domain of law and order, Napoleon immediately faced two separate problems. Western France seethed with royalist revolt and insurrectionary threats which had begun during the latter days of the Directory. Bonaparte refused rebel attempts at negotiation, quartered an army in their midst, and suspended constitutional rights for the area until their forces were crushed. Republican plots were also frustrated and domestic order was quickly assured.

The Second Coalition was still intact when Bonaparte became First Consul. Switzerland had been secured by Masséna, and Napoleon decided to attack the Austrians once more in Italy. His Second Italian Campaign lacked the brilliance of his first but similarly ended with a barrage of personal propaganda and a settlement which handed control of Italy over to France. He had boldly led his army through the Alps "like Hannibal" and the issue was settled at the battle of Marengo (June 14, 1800). One of his least impressive victories, he nearly lost the encounter. Meanwhile General Moreau had moved across the Rhine and defeated the Austrians in striking fashion at the battle of Hohenlinden (December 3, 1800). The Austrians quickly came to terms while Napoleon returned to Paris, arranging his arrival to coincide with Bastille Day. He returned to an acclaim dwarfing his earlier receptions, and those anxiously hoping he would be defeated or killed in battle realized that popular support for a movement against him would now be extremely difficult to organize.

While campaigning in Italy against Austria, Napoleon began negotiations with the Papacy regarding a new religious settlement within France. Pius VII (1742–1823) proved no match. This placid and monkish figure, formerly Cardinal Chiaramonti, had just been elected and had never been a strong opponent of the Revolution. With Austria's defeat he felt abandoned in Italy and was anxious to see Catholicism legally and completely restored in France. Discussions were involved and lengthy as both the First Consul and the Pope tried to get the best possible arrangement. Bonaparte kept referring to Henry VIII's successful nationalization of the Church while in the background the Bourbon pretender (Count of Provence, Louis XVIII, 1755–1824) was intriguing against any sort of new settlement. Pius VII, however, was prepared to accept the most reasonable agreement he could get. The Concordat re-established Catholicism in France and, for all practical purposes, healed the breach which dated from the Civil Constitution of the Clergy. The Church was restored in such a subservient position in relation to the state that the criticism of the settlement in the Council of State was surprising. Although there had been a tradition in France of state control and interference in religion, probably very few persons had any idea of the control Napoleon expected to exercise. Despite the shackling of the Church in France, from a papal view the faith was openly restored in Europe's strongest Catholic country and Rome was no longer drifting without a powerful defender. As for Bonaparte, he had solved the religious problem along with the vexing issue of Church lands, and in a compliant clergy he had a powerful propaganda agency throughout the nation. It was a major success that seemed to give a moral sanction to Napoleon and the aspects of the Revolution he maintained. It was also a powerful blow against the royalists and an important building block in the new royalism emerging about Napoleon.

Meanwhile another monumental task was being pursued, codification of the law. Napoleon again was responsible for this work, which finally resulted in a series of codes, including the Code Napoleon. The project had been authorized and started under the Convention but was only lethargically pursued. Napoleon energized the staff and participated in some of its discussions. Lacking legal knowledge himself, he nevertheless was able to get substantial results from his experts, who produced the finished codes. Some of Bonaparte's ideas were incorporated in the new legal structure—suspicion of bankers, a diminished status for women, ascendancy for fathers within the family—but, by and large, the codes preserved many of the basic ideals of the Revolution, especially the principle of equality before the law. The codes were a major triumph of lasting importance.

In the field of education he adapted the system left by the Revolution, making it more comprehensive and patriotic. The *lycées* were founded and their functioning carefully regulated. The University referred to the whole educational system, directed from Paris. The object of education was considered to be obedience and secular control, although loyalty to Catholicism was emphasized. The Church did have schools but they were controlled by the state, and the tradition of a system of secular education was established.

Thus Bonaparte engaged in a series of basic reforms which were at once successful and which tended to belie their inherent difficulties. Capping his entire program was the Peace of Amiens signed in March, 1802. A new government (Addington) in London responded to war weariness and a desire for continental markets which hostilities had closed. It negotiated a peace which Bonaparte also desired so he could consolidate his domestic and continental position. For the first time since 1792, France was not at war. Napoleon had incorporated the best features of the Revolution while solving the problems of religion and war which it had created. The Count of Provence concluded that now France was ready for a Bourbon return. Napoleon, however, was determined to rule himself.

In establishing the Empire Napoleon argued that the French people wanted monarchy but not the Bourbons. Taking the imperial title after he had established so many dramatic reforms gave Napoleon an enormous personal following. He had proved himself a brilliant reformer as well as a successful general. Considering the men of capacity who failed to survive the Revolution or failed to solve its problems, Napoleon clearly was extraordinary. The Consulate was as brilliant and constructive a period of leadership as any nation can boast.

As consul, Bonaparte had brought peace, but this was of short duration and for this he was as much to blame as "perfidious Albion." During the Empire the problem of war was continuous and ever more costly as its scope grew larger. Sheer militarism took the place of struggling to secure revolutionary ideals, resulting in the patterns of power on the continent being altered completely. The Consulate had brought profound changes to France in only four years. A decade was now to change the face of Europe.

Within France the imperial structure was ostensibly to be an extension of the idea of "careers open to talent." Titles and distinction awaited those who proved themselves worthy, with the exception of Bonaparte's brothers. Lucien, Joseph, and Louis were men of some ability but to give a crown to Jerome on any basis of merit was utterly incomprehensible. As the Empire wore on, a surprising number of former nobles joined those Napoleon had created. In the administration and even in the ranks of generals he proved able to accommodate many of the old aristocracy. Those who would support him rather than a Bourbon claimant were able to gain his acceptance. His marriage to Marie Louise was another indication of this attempt to win acceptance for his regime from the old nobility. Had it not been for his militarism he might have succeeded.

It was unlikely that the Peace of Amiens might have lasted, but there can be no question that Napoleon used the cessation of hostilities as an open license to continue French expansion on the continent. French foreign policy after 1804 was clearly imperialistic, but was accompanied by barrages of propaganda about bringing the principles of freedom to the rest of Europe. His victories on the battlefield were striking enough in themselves but their publicity gave them an epic character. If Napoleon filled the role of an enlightened despot in France, he now assumed the function of being one for all of Europe; his objectives dwarfed the attempts of such monarchs as Charles V, Louis XIV, and Frederick II. Almost casually, he rid Europe of the Holy Roman Empire. Freed of this anachronism, Austria, Prussia, and the other German states could have a clearer view of their own identity and best interests. Of course, Napoleon did not stop at this point but transformed Central Europe into a client status. The Germany and Italy which Austria had earlier dominated now were controlled by France. The French appearance in these areas is often regarded as bald aggression, but it needs to be observed that the areas of French control witnessed more enlightened progress in the brief period of French ascendancy than they had for ages under the Hapsburgs. Eliminating most of the petty German states while introducing various revolutionary ideals did the inhabitants a great service. As usual, Napoleon's reforms were rigorously rational and calculated to increase efficiency and loyalty, but the by-product was a true administrative and political renaissance in Western Germany. Although principles of the Revolution were moderated considerably (liberty was conspicuously missing) in this form, they were carried wherever French armies were triumphant, and when the tide of victory at last turned against Napoleon, many of these ideas had been so successfully implanted that a complete return to the customs and practices of the earlier age was out of the question.

After 1805 Napoleon went far beyond assuring French security and he was not nearly as careful in weighing military involvements. French nationalism become imperialism had carried aspects of the Revolution to most of Europe, but in the process it had awakened and energized the nationalistic spirit in other peoples. Although Napoleon gave lip service to nationalism, he seemed unable to realize that a people might prefer inefficiency and even exploitation from their own kind over enlightened reform and efficiency at the hand of a foreigner. Spain was, of course, the supreme example of this attitude and, in the long run, it was the Spanish problem that led to his downfall. The Russian fiasco in 1812 was a military failure of heroic proportions which gave the signal for revolt in Germany but it was never as expensive in men and equipment as Spain. From 1808 on, Spain not only sapped the Empire's resources but was also

EUROPE IN 1810

French Empire
Grand Empire
Allied with Napoleon
States Independent or
Hostile to Napoleon
* Battles or Historical
Events

NORTH SEA

DENMARK

KDM.

Edinburg

Belfast
UNITED KDM. OF

New Castle

Dublin

GREAT BRITAIN AND IRELAND

Bristol
London

Plymouth

Amsterdam

Antwerp
Brussels
Cologne
Waterloo,
1815
Frankfurt

ENGLISH CHANNEL

FRENCH

WEST

Brest

Seine R.
Paris
Metz

Rhine R.

BADEN
WÜRT.

Marne R.

EMPIRE

Nantes
Orleans

Loire R.

Zurich

SWITZ.

ATLANTIC OCEAN

Lyons

LOMBARDY

Milan

SAVOY

Marengo, 180
Genoa

BAY OF BISCAY

Bordeaux

Garonne R.

Rhone R.

PIEDMONT

Coruna

Bayonne
Toulouse

Nice

Marseilles

CORSIC.

Burgos

Oporto

Ebro R.

KDM. OF

Salmanca

Saragossa

SARDINI

Cagliar

KDM. OF

Barcelona

Madrid

PORTUGAL

Tagus R.

KDM. OF SPAIN

Toledo

Valencia

Lisbon

BALEARIC ISLES

Bailen

Guadalquivir R.

MEDITERRANEAN

Seville
Granada

Cadiz

Trafalgar, 1805 *
Gibraltar (BR.)

Tangier

46

Napoleonic Europe (1810).

47

a graveyard for the reputations of her generals. Napoleon never personally lost an engagement in Spain but he was forever diverted by problems elsewhere in Europe.

Napoleon's conduct of the campaign in France (January–March 1814) after losing the battle of Leipzig (October 16–19, 1813) eloquently refutes, the view that he had become sluggish and lacked his earlier mental agility. Although alert to opportunity, he had allowed the forces at his disposition to be too flagrantly used for too long. A telling criticism of his conduct as a general was his disregard for casualties when the outcome would enhance his personal position. But he understood that one result of the eighteenth-century's despots had been an administrative centralization giving capitals great strategic importance. Thus his campaigns were characterized by direct assaults on capitals, which, once taken, gave firm control of the country's administration, making fewer battles necessary.

The return from Elba became one of the most important parts of the Napoleonic Legend, and it was an amazing accomplishment. The failure at the battle of Waterloo (June 18, 1815) was appropriately of epic proportions. Few historians have taken the Hundred Days (March 20–June 29) very seriously, perhaps because historians are often mere chroniclers of winners and losers and here Napoleon lost. They point out that his path to Paris avoided former strongholds of royalism and that the middle class, earlier hurt by the Continental System, was not enthusiastic over his return. His *Acte Additionnel* was insincere and the Waterloo campaign was useless because the rest of Europe would never have acquiesced in his return. The way the coalition against him combined, despite his publication of proof of Austro-English plotting against Prussia and Russia, indicates the solidarity against him.

Although such a presentation has much to commend it, nonetheless it lacks a sufficient appreciation for the strategic possibilities at the time of Waterloo and also ignores the added resources Napoleon would have had if he could have lasted another three months. Waterloo is justly remembered because a great deal did hinge on its outcome. It does matter who wins battles, and Blücher's arrival in time to assure victory for the Duke of Wellington (1769–1852) doomed much of Europe to decades of illiberal, conservative reaction.

Napoleon's impact proved to be so pervasive that in his wake European monarchs generally found a changed world. It was true that the values of the French Revolution had been introduced into much of Europe but these ideas had been modified by Napoleon. He had even demonstrated how these could be adapted to a monarchical system. The nineteenth century's challenge was how to do better, particularly since its statesmen had combined to overthrow Napoleon.

Within France his administrative system and the codes survived dynasties, as did his arrangement with the Church. The reforms of the Consulate had over ten years in which to take root and were so practical that they were maintained long after Napoleon had passed from the scene. He had proved the wealth and power of an efficiently administered France, and, by example, posed a considerable challenge to those who would succeed him. He lasted long enough to make utterly impossible a complete restoration of the pre-1789 system—in this sense he had not only civilized but saved the Revolution.

Outside France, the areas most susceptible to French influence included northern Italy and central and south Germany. Here the middle class saw its advantage in the reduced power of their nobility and appreciated the idea of written constitutions sanctifying both property and equality. The impact of modified revolutionary ideas was especially strong in the Rhineland and in Bavaria, where the codes exercised a profound influence. In these areas of special Catholic strength, French influence, building on an already striking eighteenth-century cultural impact, was pronounced. Successive humbling of Austria had allowed a non-Austrian, German nationalism to take root, as nationalism generally received an enormous impetus. Few problems were more serious for nineteenth-century statesmen, most of whom had to deal with nationalism without wanting to accept it. Poland, Greece, Belgium, Italy, and Germany were the most prominent areas creating problems for reactionary leaders in Europe. Nationalism also swept Latin America as many aspects of French influence were apparent, particularly the idea of a military figure controlling all aspects of the society. There can be no doubt of nationalism's vitality later in the nineteenth century, but there is some question about its role in Napoleon's fall. He helped circulate the idea that he conquered when opposing mere kings but fell before great peoples. No nationalistic uprising in France supported him in 1814 and no such movement forced him from power. Only the Spanish people really turned against him. The divisions which opposed him at Waterloo were not markedly different in this regard from those he had been facing for over a decade. Mass desertions from his own ranks in 1813–1814 were a more important factor in his defeat than any new nationalism in the armies he faced.

Another major Napoleonic contribution to the nineteenth century was the romantic attitude toward war stimulated by his dramatic military successes. This, combined with nationalism, led to numerous heroic attempts at freedom on the part of many subject peoples.

Formal judgments on Napoleon must necessarily be cautious but some questions and observations are especially appropriate. How many who have condemned his despotism and autocracy ever lived through anything like the Terror? Of those who have penned vigorous criticisms of the man, how many were themselves noteworthy in terms of leadership or intellectual prowess? Has Napoleon ever been judged by minds nearly the equal of his own? Democracy on a wide scale in a major European country was an untried principle with dangerous possibilities in the 1790s. Consider society's obligation to the man who ensured a common system of weights and measures in most of Europe while disbanding guilds and confiscating monastic lands in Central Europe. He emancipated the middle class in much of Europe from feudal restrictions, and in Germany he made possible enormous strides forward in the decades of the nineteenth century. For this many Germans paid money and some Germans died but many Frenchmen both paid and died. Consuming ambition was clearly a weakness but perhaps understandable in a man who saw about him vast incompetence. A brilliant man, a vain and ambitious man, and probably a lonely man, his exile at St. Helena gave his career a fitting classic ending. His admirers would insist that during his life he had met nobody his equal and, like Socrates, perished in the midst of men markedly his inferior. Critics would suggest that Caesar and Charlemagne were more appropriate comparisons but all would agree that, for good or ill, enlightened despot, absolutist, or egocentric militarist, this man's career had an epic quality which touched the lives of millions.

II

The Conditions
of Peace

CHAPTER 5

The Congress of Vienna

The conditions of peace for a century beginning in 1815 were enunciated at the Congress of Vienna. Although basic problems in the structure appeared within a decade and massive readjustments occurred regularly thereafter, this formula for general peace in Europe was still recognizable by 1900. The peacemakers in 1814–1815 labored in a context of compelling, immediate difficulties and it was remarkable that a settlement providing long-range stability should result. Political conservatism then dominated in the victors' councils and a brief consideration of the European power structure in the centuries before 1789 will demonstrate how very conservative their decisions were.

Under Charles V the Hapsburgs dominated Central and Western Europe and France felt menaced from the north, east, and south.

After Hapsburg holdings were divided, France began a struggle for supremacy in Western Europe which, despite later losses and coalitions against her, she won between 1618 and 1714. In Central Europe the Austrian Hapsburgs still were dominant, although a weakened Empire after 1648 and a strengthened Prussia by 1763 considerably reduced the dynasty's over-all ascendency. Before 1750 Russia and the Ottoman Empire were not crucial to European considerations of power and peace.

Aside from the social implications of the French Revolution, the Napoleonic experience amounted to a domination of Western and Central Europe, with only its fringes (England, Russia, Ottoman Empire) retaining freedom. Napoleon's Confederation of the Rhine was a French version of the domination of Germany which the Hapsburgs had enjoyed for centuries through control of the Holy Roman Empire. After Napoleon's fall, the major change was that Russia now threatened to replace France as the menace to Central Europe.

In its broad lines the settlement was a return to the general situation prior to 1789. France remained a major power in the West, though now suspect as in the last decades of Louis XIV. In Germany, Prussia and Austria were restored to positions of uneasy rivalry with the domination of much of Germany by Austria provided for by a shallow reconstruction of the Empire, the Germanic Confederation. Mid-eighteenth century warfare had attracted Russia to the orbit of Central European politics, a situation even more pronounced after 1815. Historians can see that Vienna had loosely but essentially restored the status quo *ante bellum,* but to the statesmen involved, the welter of conflicting ambitions and problems facing them obscured any such simple-sounding formula for peace.

The Treaty of Chaumont (March, 1814) may be regarded as the first stage in a series of diplomatic discussions and documents culminating in the Vienna settlement, itself a package of many parts. The Treaty of Chaumont was negotiated as Napoleon's phenomenal retreat from Leipzig was entering its last days. As a wartime agreement, it reflected the exigencies of the moment with an intensity lacking in later treaties and may be regarded as a brilliant success for Britain's foreign secretary, Lord Castlereagh (1769–1822). From her enemies' viewpoint, France had produced the Revolution and was responsible for over two decades of warfare. Although menaced least by the Revolution's social impact, England had been the most consistent opponent of France, granting numerous subsidies to any on the Continent who could be persuaded to take up arms against Napoleon. English war aims looked toward a return of French power to her historic boundaries. Other governments opposing Napoleon did so for their own reasons but, although their actions served England's objective, there was no coordinated agreement, no real Grand Alliance embracing all of Napoleon's enemies. There was a continual prospect that Napoleon might be able to make a separate peace, especially after he had abandoned areas east of the Rhine, and in retreat his army again appeared revitalized.

Chaumont provided for a unified alliance (really the first since 1792) with no separate peace. It also presumed that a peace would soon be made with Napoleon, with both him and France needing surveillance for at least twenty years. In terms of separate war aims, Austria's Prince Klemens von Metternich (1773–1859) acquiesced in the idea of an enlarged Netherlands, receiving English support for a Central Europe (including Italy) modeled on Austrian designs. Prussia and Russia were not especially hostile to the terms of the agreement but both presumed more extensive later diplomacy. It is surprising that Metternich allowed so much of the initiative here to rest with Castlereagh but England's subsidies were still needed as well as her later support in discussions on Central Europe. Metternich was further handicapped by his concern for Napoleon's personal position. While accepting the English emphasis on long-range surveillance of France, he feared that should Napoleon be unseated, the full force and fury of the Revolution might again break out. Thus he was an influence for moderation and tried to convince Napoleon to accept reasonable terms while they were yet possible. There was the ironic prospect that the Hapsburgs might save Bonaparte, not because he had married into their house, but because he was mistakenly thought to be essential for European social order. Although Napoleon refused these overtures, this consideration weakened Metternich in his dealing with the English at Chaumont.

Russia's Tsar Alexander (1775–1825) entered Paris on March 31, the day following its capture, to discover that virtually by default his was the choice that would decide the future government of France. Although he had considered the problem, he had made no decision and he turned to Talleyrand for advice. This wily diplomat lectured the Tsar on the principle of legitimacy, encouraging a Bourbon return. He argued so persuasively that Alexander and the King of Prussia, Frederick William III (1770–1840), issued a declaration (April 1) that no negotiations would be held with Napoleon or any of his family. In the wake of this, the normally placid Senate declared Napoleon deposed. Influence was crucial as the Tsar vacillated between alternatives. Napoleon learned of the Senate action two days later while pondering his next attack. After considerable debate, he abdicated (April 4) in favor of his son, the King of Rome. This action reopened the question of dealing with one of Napoleon's family and Alexander wavered, impressed by the thought that Napoleon's son would be a focal point commanding the army's loyalty, thus assuring law and order and a government the nation would accept. Talleyrand again played a key role in convincing the Tsar to adhere to his earlier decision. Napoleon was left with the Treaty of Fontainebleau, a personal settlement for himself and his family, offered on a take-it-or-leave-it basis. On April 13, he accepted the treaty, and he departed for Elba on April 20.

Talleyrand could clearly have argued in favor of some sort of Napoleonic regency which Alexander would have accepted. Instead, he suggested that a regency under the King of Rome would result in Napoleon's return within a year. As it developed, Napoleon returned anyway, and it seems preposterous in retrospect that Alexander and Talleyrand, both of whom knew Napoleon, could have believed such a man would rest content on the isle of Elba. Metternich and Castlereagh arrived in Paris too late for these discussions but both regarded Elba as particularly inappropriate.

With Napoleon gone and the Bourbons re-established, it was fitting that treaties of peace between Austria, Russia, Prussia, Great Britain (and also Spain, Portugal, and Sweden), and France would be signed (May 30, 1814) by Talleyrand. Because Napoleon was regarded as the basic enemy, this First Peace of Paris was remarkably generous. France retained her November, 1792, boundaries, which allowed her retention of Avignon and portions of Savoy and the Palatinate. There was no spirit of harshness with France, no reparations, and no systematic looting. There was rather a feeling that larger issues elsewhere in Europe needed to be settled, and therefore a major provision in the treaties was Article 32, calling for a congress to be held shortly at Vienna to consider the whole range of European territorial problems. A number of interesting secret articles proved to be partially binding at Vienna. One of these established Austria's boundaries in Italy, and another repeated the stipulation at Chaumont that the German states should be independent but formed in a larger confederation, obviously a provision aimed against Prussia. France recognized the transfer of Belgian provinces to Holland and, in an intriguing blank check, also said she would approve any territorial changes decided on by her conquerors. No arrangements were made regarding the Polish and Saxon questions, which were deferred to the later meeting. The problem of France was now settled (temporarily, it proved) but other issues involving the major powers needed to be resolved. The diplomats gathering in Vienna were forced to adopt a genuinely European perspective to balance their narrower allegiances as they worked to find arrangements that would assure peace for the whole Continent. Few earlier statesmen ever had such a broad outlook as these who earnestly tried to find Europe's common good by placating personal or regional greed without resorting to acts of revenge. Could this group have been the embodiment of the Continent's general will?

In mid-September of 1814, diplomats and nobility of all ranks began drifting into Vienna, the most majestic arrivals being those of Tsar Alexander and Prussia's Frederick William III, on September 25. An amazing horde, comprising both the important and the nearly insignificant, became guests to be lavishly fed and entertained by the nearly bankrupt government of Austria. No formal agenda had been drawn up as the Congress had initially been construed simply as an occasion for public announcement of decisions by the four larger powers regarding the postwar settlement. The major diplomats realized after the treaty negotiated in Paris that there were vast unresolved issues, but the general public, presuming the Four Powers had already reached basic agreement, speculated publicly and wildly on what the Congress might decide. Lasting peace was on everyone's lips but the formula for it was elusive. Freedom of the seas was not a concept admired by English statesmen and both disarmament and the end of traffic in African slaves failed to enlist unanimous support. There was in Vienna an air of casualness and carefree gaiety appropriate to the lack of planning, and the many high hopes for the Congress were inundated by sumptuous diversions. As a formal gathering the Congress of Vienna never held an official meeting.

Despite the lighthearted atmosphere, many major decisions were made. The basic mechanism of the Congress consisted of regular morning meetings in Metternich's apartment. Here spokesmen for Austria, Russia, Prussia, and Great Britain discussed and decided the most pressing issues. The continual round of social functions enabled many decisions to be made over an extended period and gave opportunity for private consultations with spokesmen for secondary states, who were present on a sort of stand-by consultative basis. This practice accustomed the participants to the idea of the Great Powers making basic decisions for not only themselves but also the second-rank states. This viewpoint extended through the nineteenth century, the Great Powers being those most important in the alliance against Napoleon, in addition to France which was later admitted to the charmed group during the Vienna Congress.

Beyond question, the most important figures were Metternich, Tsar Alexander, Castlereagh (later Wellington), and Talleyrand. Prussia's position and claims were crucial but her spokesmen were less effective. It is worth noting that most of these leaders in recon-

Prince Metternich. (Courtesy of Historical Pictures Service, Chicago.)

structing Europe were then barely middle-aged. Britain's spokesmen were both forty-five (Napoleon's age also in 1814), Metternich was forty-one, the Russian Tsar was only thirty-seven, and Prussia's Wilhelm von Humbolt was forty-seven. By contrast Talleyrand was sixty and Prussia's half-deaf Hardenberg was sixty-four.

Naturally *émigrés* and reactionaries abounded but also present were many "Napoleonic" statesmen who had been able to cooperate with the French. In one sense even Metternich, Talleyrand, and Alexander fit this category, although each preferred that this aspect of his past be forgotten. More to our point were those many German rulers who had enjoyed Napoleon's favor, especially the kings of Württemberg and Bavaria. The King of Saxony had not betrayed Napoleon early enough to win the good graces of the Congress, and was not even allowed in Vienna. Among unexpected dignitaries was Napoleon's stepson and former viceroy in Italy, Eugene Beauharnais, who hoped that his marriage to a Bavarian princess might lead to some German holding.

Although the Congress is often viewed as a great watershed which established a pattern that endured for a century, it began its discussions with distinct handicaps. Rather than beginning with a tabula rasa, the diplomats inherited a number of previous agreements within whose provisions they now attempted to devise a stable peace. Most obvious among these were the treaties of Chaumont and Paris. France had been re-established as a power in good standing after the latter treaty and, although welcome at Vienna, she was treaty-bound not to object to decisions by the four major victors. This proved an embarrassing condition when expediency required Talleyrand's admission to the innermost decision-making group. The principle of legitimacy had been effectively introduced and its author was in Vienna. The idea of later congresses and of French surveillance stemmed from Chaumont, as well as the promise of English subsidies if France proved again to be a menace. Napoleon's return from Elba activated this aspect of the earlier agreement and canceled as well the Treaty of Fontainebleau. Austria, for example, despoiled the holdings of Marie Louise as even the father-daughter relationship proved flimsy. In the Second Peace of Paris (November 20, 1815), France was treated somewhat more harshly, her status at best being probationary. Her monarch, Louis XVIII, had demonstrated that he was insecurely on his throne and Napoleon had proved that his mere presence in France was disruptive.

More of the ground rules stemming from the earlier agreements were the Austrian boundary in Italy, the idea of an enlarged Netherlands including the Belgian provinces, some sort of Germanic confederation, and independence for Switzerland.

More serious complications were to arise from a series of 1813 treaties: Kalish (February 28, 1813) between Prussia and Russia; Reichenbach (June 27, 1813) between Prussia, Russia, and Austria; and Teplitz (September 9, 1813) between the same three powers. Kalish had formalized a Prussian agreement to renounce in Russia's favor most of her claims to Polish territory in return for similar amounts of land in Germany. Reichenbach and Teplitz simply agreed to a tripartite division of the Grand Duchy of Warsaw between the three powers, with nothing said of appropriate Prussian compensation. Early discussions had revealed a complete impasse and this problem had been tactfully put aside at the First Peace of Paris. At Vienna, however, it had to be faced and its settlement required considerable patience.

The Polish problem revealed the differing political orientations regarding a balance of power in Europe and Central Europe. Essentially, for Russia to acquire more of Poland upset the other powers' view of a proper balance in Europe and it was difficult to reach agreement on how to make an appropriate counteradjustment after it finally became clear that Russia was not to be denied in Poland.

The English view of the situation was fairly simple. She wanted it guaranteed that the Low Countries would be independent and that no country would dominate Europe as France had under Napoleon. Because Russian encroachment in Poland threatened to be just such an ascendancy, appropriate readjustments were necessary to counteract any increase in Russian influence in the rest of Europe. An enlarged Prussia would be a protection against both France and Russia, but any such Prussian increase in Central Europe must not endanger Hanover.

Prussia was content to relinquish her claims in Poland but expected to be compensated elsewhere. Blocking her in much of northern Germany was Hanover with its English tie and the general provision ensuring a Germany of independent states. Prussia's answer to the problem was that she should acquire Saxony, whose king, after all, deserved punishment and had little sympathy in Vienna. Russia also supported this solution.

Austria regarded this proposal as completely unacceptable, partly for the very reasons that made the plan attractive to Prussia. The addition of the bulk of Saxon lands to Prussia would make her a much stronger and more cohesive North German power, a more dangerous rival to Austrian influence in German affairs. For Prussia to give up recalcitrant Poles for capable Germans who would readily be assimilated was out of the question, because, as Metternich saw it, it would threaten the independence of many other smaller German states and upset the balance in Central Europe. Essentially, Metternich was more concerned with Central Europe than with Europe as a whole once the over-all menace disappeared. Such an enlarged Prussia would constitute a threat to Hanover; so a natural

English-Austrian coalition against Prussia and Russia began to develop. When the principle of legitimacy was brought up in support of the Saxon king, the Prussians responded that this unfortunate monarch could be given former Prussian lands along the Rhine. Austria viewed this solution as a device to make the Saxon monarch a Prussian satellite, whereas the English felt that Prussia's flag was essential along the Rhine as a symbol of support for the Netherlands should France again become aggressive.

By the end of the year the impasse was clear, as various proposals had all been rejected for one reason or another, and France (represented by Talleyrand) was now invited to participate in the discussions, raising "The Four" to "The Five." Most historians have rather uncritically accepted Talleyrand's account of how this was achieved. He gave himself the chief credit, and his record of personal diplomatic triumphs is so extensive that, on the surface, it seems feasible to attribute it to his cunning and skill. No amount of guile on his part, however, would have gained him admittance to the inner group had a solution to the Polish-Saxon issue been possible without him. Talleyrand was called in because France was believed essential to a solution. Thus, his presence represented a failure on the part of the other four powers. Castlereagh is as responsible as anyone for "The Four" becoming "The Five," for he thought of France as added support for England and Austria in a showdown. When the impasse was reached, he was thinking in terms not of "The Four" or "The Five" but of "The Three." He initiated a secret defensive alliance (January 3, 1815) between these three powers (and also Bavaria, Hanover, Hesse, and Württemberg) and against Prussia should she continue to insist on Saxony. Thus the architect of the alliance against France now personally broke up his own coalition in favor of a new system of powers which included France. Meanwhile Russia was showing herself more willing to cooperate. As a result, Prussia had less support for her militancy regarding Saxony. Ironically, France had emerged from her suspect position before Prussia received what she regarded as a just reward for being on the winning side. Napoleon's return largely nullified this striking comeback for France which was a tribute to her basic importance in the over-all power structure of Europe.

One simple solution was the suggested restoration to Prussia of the portions of Poland she had acquired from the eighteenth-century partitions. This, however, would have required a struggle against Russia. Prussia was willing to turn on Russia if Austria would acquiesce on Saxony but Metternich still refused. When the

Russians learned of the sort of probing going on behind their back and realized that they could not count on Prussia, Russia became more amenable to cooperation, especially after hearing rumors of the secret Franco-Austrian-English alliance. Her "moral" position now proved open to a number of possibilities and diplomacy could proceed more fruitfully.

The Russian position as enunciated by Alexander was that the partitions of Poland (1772, 1793, 1795) had been acts of frightful immorality and, as Russia's tsar, he had an obligation to give back to the Poles their sense of statehood. He would eliminate the divisions and give them a constitution whose working he would supervise to ensure justice. The sanctimonious nature of Alexander's position made discussions difficult but he had to be taken seriously because the Russian army was in Poland. It was, of course, galling to both Austria and Prussia to have it openly stated that the partitions had been evil when obviously they still felt no qualms. Alexander hardly belonged in such a group of crafty cynics as Metternich, Castlereagh, and Talleyrand.

The well-known solution finally agreed on pleased and relieved everyone. Russia stayed in "Congress Poland," a somewhat diminished version of what she initially had claimed, and Prussia and Austria retained portions of their earlier holdings derived from the partitions. Prussia received part of Saxony but made significant additions on the middle and lower Rhine. Thus she had been strengthened enough to be an effective buttress to the new Netherlands and a bulwark against French influence in the Rhineland, without being a menace to Hanover. Her continued division did not make her too much of a threat to Austria and the King of Saxony had been punished. At the same time negotiations had showed that the Tsar lacked the strength to avoid moderating his position. Thus, England's vision of an enlarged Prussia in a Europe not dominated by any one power was achieved. Despite its gains in land, Prussia emerged still territorially divided and indefensible and continued to worry about the Russians in Poland and French interest in the Rhine.

The difficulty of solving the Polish-Saxon problem has diverted attention from two other vexing issues which the Congress readily settled. Neither Genoa nor Switzerland could be disposed of by a facile application of the principle of legitimacy. Although the solution resembled a pattern of creating buffer states on the borders of France, this was not a practical guiding principle consciously applied by the statesmen who wrestled with these two situations.

Genoa had been a republic and under Napoleon was known as the Ligurian Republic. Restoration of a republican government in northern Italy, either in Genoa or Venice, was out of the question to Austria, which worried more about republicanism than about French imperialism. The decision to add Genoese territory to the Kingdom of Sardinia, thus creating a sizable buffer state on this French approach to Italy, offended none of the four victorious powers (France and Spain disapproved) and came to be seen as a sort of equivalent action to the transfer of Belgian provinces to the Netherlands. By this means, two second-rank states, supported by the major powers, had been created on French boundaries. Between these two newly enlarged states lay Switzerland, then torn by internal dissension as both Bern and Zurich moved into the breach created by the fall of Napoleon. The Congress achieved a settlement that included an interesting contradiction. Geneva was transferred from Sardinia (and also Neuchatel from Prussia) to Switzerland to give it more strength as yet another buffer, but the relatively loose confederation which emerged was distinctly weaker than before. The competing Swiss rivals compromised and the result was a constitutional arrangement much like that of Napoleon in 1803, although the country was now larger but less unified. In the course of the negotiations, France and Austria had argued for the more reactionary solutions and Russia had supported the liberals. The basic problem had been to create an acceptable situation for the various cantons, and the result was another buffer state on the border of France. Its neutrality was guaranteed and "The Four" were bound to its defense should French imperialism reappear.

As implied in the case of Genoa, restorations guided by the principle of legitimacy were carried out on a selective basis, with each case considered on its "merits." When the most reasonable course suggested the return of the dynasty in power prior to 1789, then legitimacy was a triumphant principle. Although deposed or dispossessed nobility and royalty were assured a hearing, there was no guarantee whatever that the decision of the Congress would automatically be in their favor. Metternich proved as skeptical and critical as any regarding incompetence and medievalism supported only by claims of "legitimacy." He was not implacably against rational reform or constitutions. He was properly dubious about the wisdom of restoring the Bourbons in Spain and accepted most of Napoleon's sweeping amalgamations of petty states in Central Germany. Legitimacy did not save these nobles but was a talking point in the dispute over Saxony.

The European Settlement of 1814–1815.

Because Metternich proved to be an especially able negotiator, Austria was one of the great victors at the Congress. The dimensions of her success were remarkable in relation to the role of Austrian arms in the overthrow of Napoleon. She acquired territory from Bavaria, and in the Presidency of the new German Confederation she returned to a prominence in German affairs somewhat comparable to what she had enjoyed during the Holy Roman Empire. The Confederation still had its outside interference (Denmark and Holland, besides Prussia and Austria) but Austria had exchanged the Belgian provinces for a massive accretion of power in Italy. Her new Lombard-Venetian kingdom became a portion of the Austrian Empire, which also now included the Valtelline, a strategic invasion route toward Vienna from Italy. Austria was a much stronger power than she had been in 1789.

No significant objections were raised against the newly defined status of Austria, although Metternich had a voice in nearly every other basic decision taken by the Congress. Few historians have blamed Austria for the loss of Venetian independence, although Napoleon's initial overthrow of that republic has been described in terms suggesting the blackest infamy. Once her independence was lost, it appears to have been accepted, and Austrian continuation of what Napoleon had started did not result in any special condemnation. Austrian unpopularity in northern Italy dates from a later day, when Italian nationalism developed more vitality.

The over-all settlement in Italy largely followed Austrian interests. In Naples Joachim Murat (1767?–1815) nearly reigned despite Napoleon's final fall. Although this Napoleonic subordinate had fought for the Emperor as recently as Leipzig, the Austrians had negotiated a treaty with him in January of 1814 to persuade him to abandon Napoleon. For this he was assured his crown. The three other major powers recognized this treaty and, much as they disliked the idea, there was agreement that Murat should be left in power. Had Napoleon not returned from Elba or had Murat not supported him during the Hundred Days, he could, like Bernadotte in Sweden, have emerged with his crown, surviving the downfall of the man who had raised him up. Murat, however, believed the Congress would not really allow him to survive. Events flowing from his decision to return to Napoleon's cause led him to his death before a firing squad.

England made no territorial gains in Europe but on its fringes she acquired Malta, Heligoland, and control of the Ionian Islands. Overseas she retained the Dutch colonies of Ceylon and the Cape Colony.

Dutch compensation for these was supposed to be the Belgian provinces, giving the Netherlands more status in Europe. By the First Treaty of Paris, England had formally acquired the French colonies of Tobago, Ste. Lucia, and Mauritius. These former French holdings were so small that England appeared magnanimous in retaining them instead of other vast French and Dutch holdings which she voluntarily returned.

Most of the basic decisions to emerge from the Congress had been decided by February of 1815, although many details were yet unresolved. Word that Napoleon had returned from Elba was received in Vienna March 4, 1815, and an air of suspense hung over all the decisions until after Waterloo. Napoleon had not dissolved the Congress but he did delay its completion. Murat's actions relieved the Powers of their embarrassment in southern Italy and led to a Bourbon restoration in Naples. The Hundred Days appeared to prove the wisdom of buffer areas around France, because the French people had demonstrated that Louis XVIII's throne was not very secure.

The Congress achieved a great deal despite obvious shortcomings and its air of shallow formality. Norway was transferred to Sweden and Finland to Russia and all the major Continental powers who won were strengthened. The Germanic Confederation was a stronger instrument than the old Holy Roman Empire had been, although this was due more to Napoleon's policies in Germany than to any allied planning. Despite this new strength, however, it was still too weak by itself to assure containment of either France or Russia. Ironically, France was also more powerful than she had been in 1789 and far stronger than any of her neighbors. The wars had forced a better organization of men and materials in all the states of Europe. After the Second Treaty of Paris French borders were modestly altered. Much has been made of the post-Waterloo occupation and indemnity, but essentially France was treated with moderation. All of these arrangements in Vienna largely ignored nationalism and there was little concern for overseas colonies, despite the obvious problem regarding Spanish colonies in the New World.

Within Europe the careful attempt to create a balance of power, with all its shortcomings, was the most comprehensive in the modern period to date. It must continually be kept in mind that the force of the Congress was restricted to the victorious powers emerging from the struggles against Napoleon and that whatever changes were made had to be compatible with the foreign-policy objectives of the Four Powers. Warfare since 1792, accompanied by advanced ideas of reform, had created a chaotic situation by the time Napoleon was defeated. The Congress had to create in Europe a different basis for order than the French hegemony, knowing that it was impossible to return to 1789. Considering its limitations and the perspectives of the major participants, the Congress was remarkably successful.

Aside from the basic territorial adjustment concluded at Vienna, two other agreements of particular importance emerged: the Quadruple Alliance of November 20, 1815, and the Holy Alliance of September 26, 1815. The Congress had provided for a redrawing of boundaries and a validation of the various governments in Europe in its efforts to settle problems created by over two decades of war and revolution. The Quadruple Alliance and the Holy Alliance enunciated formulas for future policy, and they were devised especially for the preservation of the decisions at Vienna.

The Quadruple Alliance had its origin in the Treaty of Chaumont and must be regarded as the work of Castlereagh. The object was to continue the coalition that had defeated Napoleon twice—to protect Europe from a renewal of French aggression. Should such a contingency again occur each nation's obligation to cooperate in crushing this threat to European order was stipulated. Also included was the statement that the Great Powers would meet periodically to discuss problems of peace and prosperity. In this "Concert of Europe" the major powers would "stand together in support of the established principles of social order." The particular "established principles" were those that guided the Congress of Vienna. This Congress had been an example of the earlier sentiment at Chaumont and the current provision was to be the basis for what came to be called the *Congress System*. Because the victors in the war opposed the values of the French Revolution, it was probably inevitable that when they met to discuss problems, it always became an occasion to plot the suppression of liberal principles. This development came to be associated closely with Metternich's policies, rather than England's, and how this occurred is the story of the Congresses, which must be discussed later. It is interesting that the spokesman of such a liberal power as England framed the stipulations that led to formal sanction for the policing of reaction. England, however, proved unable to tolerate the implications of the Alliance and abandoned it before half of the agreed twenty years. Despite the alteration of the role it was intended to fill, historians have agreed that this Quadruple Alliance was a practical and explicit provision to guide future policy, hopefully in the enforcement of the peaceful settlement Vienna believed it had devised.

The Holy Alliance was quite another type of international agreement. Often seen as an utterly impractical and nearly useless document, it deserves consideration as part of a romantic, pietistic movement then attracting wide attention. (See Part IV.) As a scheme for world peace it belongs to a long series, which in the modern period would include Henry IV's Grand Design and the Kellogg-Briand Pact. In its immediate diplomatic context, it was regarded with incredulity and scant respect by both Castlereagh and Metternich. Alexander, however, like Wilson over a century later, appeared as the spokesman for a nation whose power could not be denied, and attention had to be given to his suggestions. The Christian message of brotherhood struck the hardened and Machiavellian statesmen of the struggle against Napoleon as both banal and naive. Suggested by a spokesman from a second-rank power, it would surely have been ignored.

Alexander I. (Courtesy of Historical Pictures Service, Chicago.)

Alexander was a man of integrity whose mind and personality prompted erratic behavior in the long run but intense consistency for shorter periods. From his father, Paul, he had acquired a feeling for military excellence despite the antipathy he felt for this parent. Alexander had approved the deposition of his father but was shaken when it led to his murder. It offended a nature sensitive to literature and the many aspects of the Enlightenment to which he had been exposed by his grandmother Catherine. Alexander had then moved to acquire a reputation as a great liberal. This would not have been difficult after Paul's reign but Alexander even seemed to admire the French Revolution. His character at times was so chameleonic that it was difficult to tell what the man really stood for. Sincerity seemed always apparent in his statements and he made a striking impression on those dealing with him. Napoleon, Castlereagh, and Metternich, however, were models of straightforwardness compared with the Russian Tsar, whose actions represented more a confused personality than a talent for duplicity.

In 1815 he was nearing the climax of an intensely emotional religious experience. He claimed that the burning of Moscow in 1812 gave him a realization of how puny men's efforts were, and since that episode he had become a devout reader of the Bible. As various problems arose, more and more he turned to religion for solace and guidance. In this mood he saw Russia's success in repelling Napoleon as God's use of his country as an agent in the French Emperor's punishment. This autocrat was now fervently determined to carry out the Lord's work. Reinforcing this view were Alexander's contacts with a number of mystics, the most prominent being the Baroness Juliana von Krüdener (1761–1824). He learned from her letters to ladies in the Tsarina's court that she regarded him as "God's Elect" who would "slay the dragon," bringing peace on Earth. The Russian people and their leader had been "chosen" to accomplish this mighty and holy task. This naturally buoyed his ego and he became eager to meet her. A chance meeting at Heilbronn in 1815 seemed heaven-inspired and she joined him in regular worship sessions in his garden in Paris. It was primarily while under her influence that Alexander drew up the Holy Alliance and he took the document so seriously that he was offended at the inference that it had political implications.

His proposal was simplicity itself. Monarchs would take care of their subjects as if they were children in a large family. They would regard themselves as brothers and a spirit of Christianity would pervade human relations, resulting in peace. It was to be an alliance between sovereigns, a watering down suggested by Castlereagh, from an original version which included peoples. The emphasis on Christianity served to emphasize the variety of Western Christendom represented in the coalition against France. Naturally the Papacy objected to what it regarded as preachments from a schismatic. To ensure lasting peace in Europe the document would also have needed the adherence of the Sultan, but he was not included.

Although in itself the Holy Alliance lacked force, its idea of co-operating sovereigns became generally confused with the Quadruple Alliance provision for periodic meetings. As these gatherings proved to be especially dominated by Austria, Prussia, and Russia, the key signatories of the Holy Alliance, it became common parlance to think of their actions as those of the Holy Alliance. As a matter of fact, Metternich came to use the Holy Alliance as an excuse for violations of the sovereignty of other states when the particular action could not be justified in any other fashion. Thus the Holy Alliance came to be regarded as a religious sanction for reaction and repression and in this regard it is of particular importance. The document may have been shallow and impractical but its deliberate misinterpretation was significant. Further, it gave its name to the commonality of Russian-Austrian-Prussian foreign policy evident decades later, so that to refer to the Holy Alliance powers or the neo-Holy Alliance was a meaningful reference in the early 1850s.

CHAPTER 6

The Metternich System

The period from 1815 to 1848 has been called, with a modicum of accuracy, the Age of Metternich. At Vienna this statesman had played a major role in reconstructing Europe; then for over three decades, he tried diligently to ensure the permanence of the settlement. He believed his struggle was in behalf of positive and enlightened values in opposition to smouldering, revolutionary attack which he saw as essentially evil and, above all, destructive. When liberal and nationalistic attitudes proved triumphant in later decades, Metternich appeared to many nineteenth-century historians as merely an obstacle to progress. Since 1900 the Austrian chancellor's efforts have received less criticism and much more appreciation.

As Metternich assessed Austria's position in Europe, he saw several natural enemies and few friends. To meet this circumstance, he devised a policy which, for over thirty years, prevented her rivals from open and effective opposition. From his early years in the Rhineland and living in Brussels he had acquired a lifelong hostility toward the French Revolution and revolutions in general. Within Germany, Austria's rival was clearly Prussia, and it was with mixed feelings that Metternich approved those gains in the Rhine area which made Prussia more than ever a *German* state. Russia was another rival, in the Balkans as well as in Poland. The Tsar's army was poised in Poland, and he thought of himself as a protector for the sovereignty of several of the smaller German states to which he was dynastically connected. His sympathy for many aspects of liberalism was a special worry. French ambitions in the Rhine area were to be constantly feared and the English antipathy for genuine repressive tactics was another source of insecurity. It was Metternich's triumph that in arranging for two of Austria's natural opponents (Prussia and Russia) to join her in a common policy against revolution and for the status quo, he created a bloc large enough to assure control of much of Europe. Metternich's actions during the congresses reveal how he used the fear of revolution to counteract the natural hostilities of his neighbors on the Continent, thus achieving for his day Austrian security and general European peace. He was able to provide enough flexibility so that part of the time France also cooperated, and although England disapproved, she did not openly combat his "system." Though there was much worried talk about revolution and various tactics for dealing with liberalism, the result was Austrian security and predominance in Central Europe. Considering the mediocre record of Austrian armies, the maintenance of peace was essential for stability within her polyglot empire.

In 1818 at Aix-la-Chapelle the Great Powers assembled to consider the ending of the French occupation, a goal toward which the Duke of Richelieu had been working for some time. A number of other parties had also decided to make formal requests of the Great Powers. Their petitions usually related to the earlier Vienna settlements, such as that of the former Elector of Hesse who pointed out that because his title had no meaning, he desired to be regarded as royalty, just as the former electors of Bavaria, Saxony, and Hanover had become kings. On the grounds that another king in Europe would merely weaken the title, he was refused. Another interesting plea was that of Letitia Bonaparte, Napoleon's mother, who asked that he be allowed to leave St. Helena. This request was also refused. These and a number of other petitions were all evidence that the major powers were, in effect, recognized as having *de facto* authority in Europe. The unity of the Great Powers in hammering out solutions to the major problems facing them at Vienna was continued here at Charlemagne's old capital. This, however, was to be the last of their meetings where agreement prevailed. Subsequently the authority of congressional decisions declined.

The question of removing foreign troops from French soil was readily settled; a treaty of October 9, 1818, pledged that allied troops would all be recalled before November 30. The Powers were concerned about the impact of their soldiers on French morale and Richelieu especially felt that their presence dramatized the weakness of Louis XVIII. It seemed wise to remove them before agitators might seize on their presence as an issue. Metternich was also concerned about the effect on the soldiers of too long a stay in France. Prussia suggested a compromise which would have placed troops poised in Belgium, ready to march at short notice; but the English opposed this adamantly and neither Metternich nor Alexander felt like insisting, despite their belief that the idea had merit.

Alexander arrived at Aix-la-Chapelle with several secondary suggestions for international collaboration, all of which the English strongly opposed on the grounds that little beyond the Quadruple Alliance was really needed. The Tsar wanted a broad religious sanction, such as the Holy Alliance, to provide firmer moral support for the political and diplomatic settlement but, then, the English noted that *all* treaties were in theory equally solemn and binding. In discussions of the Barbary Pirates and the slave trade, Alexander suggested the formation of international naval units, which England opposed. The Tsar's enthusiasm for more than token internationalism, his suggestions for reform, and his urging the adoption of constitutions provoked English opposition and Austrian apprehension. All these consistent and pointed refusals by England to support Russian initiatives served to ease Metternich's role.

With the occupation to end and satisfactory arrangements made regarding the indemnity, the question arose about readmitting France to Great Power discussions. England still viewed her basic treaty commitments stemming from Chaumont as mainly aimed at France. She argued that to admit France made little sense; at Vienna France was needed for support of the Anglo-Austrian position regarding the Polish-Saxon question. This issue had been solved, and France during the Hundred Days had forfeited the friendship of the Four Powers. Furthermore, the removal of troops carried no specific implication of readmission. Although this was the basic English attitude, another consideration proved more compelling. If not allowed to participate, then France would be a natural supporter for any plot against the system devised at Vienna, a pragmatic view which led the English to acquiesce on the question. Although in one sense the alliance had thus become a Quintuple Alliance, France really adhered to a somewhat general agreement, and the original Four Powers secretly reaffirmed their Quadruple Alliance, still aimed at France in Castlereagh's view.

This first Great Power meeting after Vienna appeared strikingly successful. It was surely the high-water mark of this phase of the Congress System, for although three more congresses met in rapid succession, these lacked final unanimity on their basic questions. The apparent success of Aix-la-Chapelle obscured the fact that no truly crucial question had then been confronted. That agreement really was illusory was demonstrated during the next few years. By a quirk of chance no major, divisive issue arose between 1815 and 1818, so that an appearance was created that decision by Great Power collaboration could effectively ensure peace. A few congressional decisions, however, did not constitute congressional government and the Powers later proved they could not agree even on the purpose for meeting. Nonetheless, an idea had been established which later generations would fondly recall and even imitate. For many of Metternich's contemporaries, the illusion disappeared shortly after the conference at Aix-la-Chapelle adjourned, for before the next meeting several disquieting episodes occurred.

In 1818 Metternich was widely known as a diplomat who supported conservatism, but he had not yet earned his reputation for domestic repression. This came when he then moved to counteract what he regarded as ominous symptoms of impending social disorder. In much of Germany the Napoleonic period had weakened the traditional nobility. After the War of Liberation, ideas of political liberty and independence had been planted, though often they took the form of protest against French interference. University professors, journalists, and student groups, whose numbers now included many veterans, attracted considerable attention by an orgy of criticism in anticonservative, liberal publications and speeches. This worried Metternich, who attributed to them an excessive vitality and sense of purpose and failed to recognize that the Burschenschaft movement had large ingredients of simple frivolity and horseplay. Jena was the most prominent center of this student enthusiasm, which existed also in other universities as demonstrated by a student festival at Wartburg in October, 1817, which highlighted the unrest. It should be recalled that the German universities provided their government with substantial numbers of bureaucrats, and after the Napoleonic reorganization they were even more important as a source of educated officials. Thus in Metternich's view the ideals of the next generations' leadership were being endangered and so the whole affair could not be dismissed as a harmless display of youth, especially when their antics attracted attention outside Germany. There was a haunting danger that ideas of a real German state encompassing "Germany" could also be a part of the program of these critics of autocracy. After all, why had they fought the War of Liberation? Because such a state could hardly be Austrian, Metternich worried lest Prussian leaders awaken to their opportunity. He was increasingly disturbed but the unrest had not quite come to a point of crisis when the Powers met at Aix-la-Chapelle. In the next two years, however, much of his time was devoted to silencing the voices of liberal protest then emerging from an environment of intense intellectual ferment.

Metternich's opportunity came on March 23, 1819. On that day at Mannheim August von Kotzebue was murdered by a Jena student named Karl Sand. Kotzebue had formerly espoused liberal views and had been an agent of Tsar Alexander. Before his assassination, however, he was writing attacks on student unrest in the German universities and Sand regarded him as a spokesman for reaction. His violent death brought applause from liberal, professorial circles and to Germany's princes dramatized the incipient danger of allowing irresponsible voices to go unchecked. In July, Metternich met with Frederick William III and convinced the Prussian monarch that university freedoms must be restricted. Building on this agreement, he then gained assent from the ministers of the member states of the Confederation to the regulations known as the Carlsbad Decrees. The Diet formally accepted these a year later and thus assumed the authority to supervise several aspects of the domestic affairs in the member states. When the princes failed to oppose this infringement on their sovereignty, the censorship of journals and university lectures alike came under the legal control of the Confederation. On the heels of this success Metternich called for a further adjustment, the right for the Confederation to use arms to assure order and the maintenance of conservative government within any member state. Thus the Confederation assumed more of a federal nature as the kings and princes approved of outside interference if their own regimes became threatened or even if they themselves decided to liberalize. Metternich had accomplished this basic change by May of 1820. Essentially there was now an agreement between monarchs aimed at their own peoples, an interesting perversion of the Holy Alliance within Germany. Austria's power now extended through much of the bureaucratic apparatus of the Confederation and a program of systematic repression of liberal sentiments in Germany was implemented. Paradoxically, although autocracy had received aid in Central Europe, the mechanism of that support involved a weakening of the authority of specific monarchs in the area. There would clearly be stability and order in Germany while Metternich was in power, but if Austrian leadership ever faltered, a great void would invitingly open.

While Metternich was consolidating his position in Germany, special problems in Spain and Italy prompted another formal meeting of the Congress. In addition to the earlier murder of Kotzebue, the assassination of the Duke de Berri (February 13, 1820) in Paris and the unsuccessful Cato Street Conspiracy (February 23, 1820) in London which envisioned nothing less than the murder of the entire English cabinet were two other specific symptoms of hostility to conservatism. Revolutionary successes in Italy and Spain, however, involved basic liberal changes of existing government. To counter this, the Austrian chancellor invited the Great Powers to agree to a European version of the same sort of arrangement he had just completed for Germany. The Powers should feel free to intervene in any state where stable and conservative governments were *threatened* or overthrown.

Although the Duke de Berri's murder was a direct attempt to end the Bourbon dynasty in France, Louis XVIII joined England in only sending observers to the meeting, rather than properly accredited agents who could engage in full-scale diplomatic talks. This meant that only Austria, Prussia, and Russia were prepared to make basic decisions, and that, more than ever, Metternich's views would carry the day. After the recent arrangements with Prussia's king over the German problem, there remained only Alexander's views for Metternich to face, though he was annoyed by the abstaining action of France and England which, of course, weakened the total impact of any decisions the truncated Congress might make. Nonetheless, Metternich went ahead, drawing up for the five states a "Troppau Protocol" which would authorize the Powers to interfere when internal affairs of any ruler constituted a direct or indirect threat to the conservative order of Europe. Prussia and finally Russia agreed to the document, which gave the appearance of making the Holy Alliance a force for the repression of liberalism. There was no specific statement to this effect, but with England and France deliberately refusing to sanction the Protocol, its provisions could not be justified in terms of the Quadruple Alliance or the treaty including France. The main leaders acceding to the Holy Alliance, that treaty between monarchs rather than states or peoples, now also had signed this Protocol aimed at peoples within other states. This had the effect of giving an international sanction to the earlier Carlsbad Decrees. By this time Alexander was having a number of doubts about liberalism. He worried about plots in his army, about Polish insincerity, and about the murders of Kotzebue and de Berri; and he strongly disapproved of constitutions being thrust on a nation's leaders by means of force from below. Constitutions were documents needing careful and wise study, to be granted in a spirit of moderation from above rather than from mob passion below. Because Spain and Italy both violated this aspect of propriety, he agreed on the principle of interference. He had initially come to the conference emphatically opposed to intervention and had opposed the Protocol. Now his only scruple was that, to Metternich's annoyance, he kept saying, as he had at Aix-la-Chapelle, that such actions should be international if possible. Metternich reacted by generally agreeing but suggesting that, in some cases, it would be more practical if a single power intervened. Italy was the cause of his immediate apprehension and he wanted a mandate for Austria to act alone. For him the Spanish situation appeared more remote at the moment and, furthermore, was sure to involve the English. Thus he emphasized the situation at Naples and received the Tsar's support.

The English disapproved of a blanket grant for Great Power interference in case of hypothetical future crises and specifically refused sanction of the Protocol. However, they suggested that so far as the situation in Italy was concerned, Austria should simply act on a unilateral basis to restore authoritarian government in Naples without consulting the Great Powers. The English were suggesting that Austria act in Italy in the same fashion that she was authorized to by the German states in Germany. Thus Castlereagh was willing to accept armed Austrian interference in various states in Italy but resented the "Protocol," which looked like a formal decision of the "concert"—*his* concert. The French memory of allied troops was still fresh and their opposition to the blanket authority of the Protocol was natural, although they approved of Metternich's specific tactic regarding the situation in Naples.

This brief account does not do justice to the tortuous course by which Metternich negotiated his "Protocol," achieving from all the

Great Powers agreement either for the document or its immediate implications. In July of 1820 Ferdinand I of Naples had acquiesced in the face of a *Carbonari*-inspired uprising and granted a constitution, following an example set earlier in the year by the King of Spain. The document was, by Austrian standards, revolutionary, and Metternich was determined that it be rescinded. His plan envisaged an invitation for Ferdinand to report in person to the Congress on the situation. If he did not come, it would be assumed that he was captive. If he did appear, it was presumed he would request aid in restoring a despotic regime. France approved of this device and Austria made preparations to intervene. Armed with his Protocol and varying degrees of approval from the Great Powers, Metternich then arranged a recess until Ferdinand could be contacted; the Congress agreed to reassemble at Laibach in early January, 1821.

At Laibach the major dignitaries recently at Troppau reconvened to make a final decision regarding Italy. At this meeting Ferdinand appeared and, predictably, appealed to the Powers for Austrian assistance, after condemning the concessions he claimed were forced on him. This was a characteristically perfidious performance. Before leaving Naples, he had solemnly announced that he wanted to appear at Laibach to convince the Powers of the virtues of the constitutional system he had sworn on a Bible to uphold. There was little for substantive discussion and the action for the Congress to take was obvious in light of its earlier acceptance of the Troppau Protocol. Metternich was free to intervene in Italy and could argue that he had the moral sanction of the Powers, though it was apparent that the spirit and substance of real cooperation between all the Great Powers had become almost nonexistent. No position was taken on Spain, which, combined with the international implications of unrest and insurrection in Greece, was to bring the complete disintegration of the Quadruple Alliance.

In Italy the Austrian army efficiently crushed the *Carbonari* forces which had rushed to war to defend their constitution, and despotic authoritarianism was again restored in Naples. A month later, in April, Austria also intervened in Sardinia, crushing an insurrection which supported a government based on the Spanish constitution of 1812. Absolutism thus prevailed in the entire peninsula, including a particularly wretched papal administration, and Metternich now felt secure in Italy.

In support of these actions Alexander had provided 100,000 men available as a reserve force. These troops were poised just over the Austrian border and worried officials in Vienna, who did not understand the subtlety of Metternich's diplomacy. Meanwhile an uprising in the Danubian principalities in February, 1821, invited outside interference on the same basis as the Italian revolts. Neither England nor Austria wanted Russia to intervene. Austria's army was still needed in Italy, but Metternich succeeded in convincing Alexander that, although Russia properly favored Slav independence from the Turk, this revolt was a calculated effort to destroy Austro-Russian solidarity. When the Tsar then withheld support to the Greek leaders of the insurrection, they were crushed by the Turks. By mere persuasion Metternich had prevented Russia from forcefully extending her influence in the Balkans after he had just received Russian support for the consolidation of Austrian control in Italy. Diplomacy had immobilized Austria's natural enemy, Russia. The liberal Alexander had become conservative and 100,000 Russian arms were virtually at the service of Austria. In terms of the winds of change in the nineteenth century and the values let loose by the French Revolution, Austria was an impossible combination of peoples, but Metternich's diplomacy helped it survive well beyond its time.

On May 5, 1821, Napoleon died on St. Helena and the haunting apprehension that he might return again disappeared from the chancelleries of Europe. An era closed with his death, which coincided with the disintegration of the alliance which had defeated him. Though there would be future meetings of the Great Powers during the century, very few evidences appeared of a true concert and the later solution of problems reflected coalitions against one or another of the countries. Metternich's last major congress, Verona, signaled the end of the Quadruple Alliance.

A year and a half after Laibach the Powers again met to discuss current problems. The agenda had been debated during a Vienna meeting in September, 1822. The obvious areas calling for collective discussions and possible action were Spain, Turkey, and Italy, but only Spain was selected for major consideration by the formal Congress. When the representatives of the Great Powers convened in Verona on October 20, the discussion was further limited to Spain as regarded by French policy. The government of Louis XVIII was anxious to intervene in Spain, thereby demonstrating its loyalty to conservative principles. Success in restoring Ferdinand's full authority would lend particular status to Bourbon military leaders who would gain, as mentioned earlier, from a superficial comparison with Napoleon's Spanish difficulties.

Alexander had long felt that this revolt should be crushed and was prepared to march large Russian contingents to a base area in Sardinia, from whence, he suggested, they could strike against Spain or, if need be, against any republican resurgence in France. Though Metternich agreed to the desirability of restoring absolutism in Spain, he was most uneasy about the thought of so many Russian troops in the West, especially in northern Italy. The deteriorating situation in Greece suggested that Russian troops might be needed elsewhere, but Metternich did not want Russia too active in the Balkans either.

England's position was absolutely adamant. She totally disagreed on the need for intervention and would not approve any sort of action. George Canning (1770–1827) had succeeded Castlereagh, but no basic policy change had occurred. As with Metternich, expediency ruled, but a cloak of principle was handy. England had acquiesced in the repression of liberal revolt in Italy but now took the position that nonintervention should be the rule. This position implied, interestingly, no Russian aid for Greek nationalists and no French aid for Spanish absolutists. It also meant no European interference with developments in former Spanish colonies. England was thus at a complete variance with the other Powers over the question of restoring absolutism in Madrid and made no efforts whatever to hide this disagreement.

At Verona Metternich had hoped that common Austrian and English apprehensions regarding the extension of Russian influence within Turkey might be the basis for restoring Anglo-Austrian cooperation. French initiatives regarding Spain, however, dashed this hope and destroyed the prospect of Anglo-French diplomatic cooperation which had been possible after Troppau. England was now alone, "insular," as Metternich put it, so far as Europe was concerned. Consequently, England became more receptive to cooperation with the United States, and after the French easily restored absolutism in Madrid, the Monroe Doctrine emerged as a result of this collaboration. There were few victories for English foreign policy that year, so Canning tried to present the American declaration as a success of his own, despite the fact that in its final form the document was aimed almost as much against England as the Holy Alliance powers.

The Quadruple Alliance had truly come to its end. The Holy Alliance had become formally reactionary at Troppau, and when the nation that authored the Quadruple Alliance argued that revolts in Spain, Spanish America, and Italy really were not items of common interest to the major powers of Europe, clearly both documents had been largely redefined and a new period in diplomacy was at hand. For the future the Holy Alliance amounted to the status quo, antiliberal, antinational policies of Russia, Prussia, and Austria. Without France and England it could not pretend to be an effective European system. The Quadruple Alliance was simply dead. Congressional governing of Europe had amounted to spasmodic reaction to crises and ended with a lack of unanimity among the Great Powers after Aix-la-Chapelle. No major power altered its basic foreign policy because of the congresses, except perhaps Russia. Alexander's disillusionment with a vague liberalism represented a change but, more important, his manipulation by Metternich meant that Russian power and prospects in Europe were never fully utilized. Metternich exploited the fear of revolution to keep both Prussia and Russia from vigorous policies inimical to Austria, and English apprehension of French policies regarding Spain prevented formation of a really effective Anglo-French alliance. Peace and Austrian security were maintained but both were highly fragile. The Congress of Vienna had ignored the basic force of nationalism and its ramifications created problems for the rest of the century. The Eastern Question was also overlooked at Vienna, and, imbued with nationalism, it too became a major problem lasting for decades. Another element disregarded was the progress of industrial development. This, combined with nationalism, created awesome problems which progressively made the settlement of 1815 appear sterile and archaic.

CHAPTER 7

Domestic Compliance with the Spirit of the Vienna System: Legitimate and Authoritarian Rule in Practice

The air at Vienna had reeked with the spirit of the entrenched conservatism. Nevertheless, the assembled statesmen who carefully composed antirevolutionary documents consciously saw themselves as products of the Enlightenment. Though the era had long since passed, in the form and format of refined enlightenment they enunciated anew the bases for despotic government. Considering also the exhaustion of Europe after Napoleon's defeat, it was no wonder that in a number of instances, events failed to fit neatly into the pattern designed in Vienna.

Russia, after 1815, was a prime example of the gulf between words and action. According to Alexander's early public statements, the nation could have expected substantial reform, granted from above in the spirit of enlightened despotism. He had talked in a liberal vein for nearly twenty years, but changed the tenor of his remarks during his last five. Because the Tsar appeared shaken by events near 1820, it has been widely assumed that the once liberal monarch turned conservative and even reactionary. Among possible questions of this view is the matter of his earlier liberalism. How sincere had he really been? It is not enough to compare and debate his earlier and later pronouncements. They must also be considered in light of Russian domestic conditions and policy during his reign. In terms of living standards and the impact of the imperial government at the local level, the reign shows few signs of liberalism; it had remained a grimly consistent autocracy. An almost inescapable conclusion is that Alexander's mind was filled with a ramshackle assortment of ideas. Motivated by a chameleonlike personality particularly susceptible to suggestion, given to whims of fancy with a vague and vain ambition, he gave voice to ideas as they came to him. It is a mistake to assume a rational and orderly connection between many of his public utterances and Russian imperial policy. He did toy with some liberal ideas, but in Russia proper, effective measures for reform were not a marked feature of his reign.

The most practical evidence of enlightened direction could be seen in three fringe areas, Finland, the Baltic provinces, and Poland. Finland had been taken by conquest and remained Russian after 1815. Nominally the Russians allowed the Finns to retain their basic autonomy, with the Tsar merely becoming their Grand Duke. After the defeat of Napoleon, however, a number of violations of their basic statutes were introduced, and by the time of Alexander's death the familiar features of Russian absolutism were apparent. Censorship had been introduced, the legal checks on legislation and use of funds were disregarded, and compliance with the Finnish preference that all officials be native Lutherans became archaic as Orthodox Russians were given appointments in the Finnish bureaucracy.

South of Finland, in the Baltic provinces, Alexander did carry through a measure of reform. By 1819 he had gradually freed the serfs of Estonia, Kurland, and Livonia. The emancipation had to be accomplished in a fashion acceptable to the area's Germanic nobility. This was achieved by freeing the serfs without giving them land. They then became paid workers for the most part, with the more ambitious among them eventually obtaining land and becoming free farmers.

Within Russia itself nothing came of plans to modify serfdom. Alexander showed interest in a number of schemes but none were ever implemented even though serf wretchedness was indescribable.

During the desperate struggle with Napoleon, serf emancipation was described as coming after peace was secured. Rather than freedom, however, Alexander personally devised a new system of military colonies. These were a further degradation which, in reducing whole communities to military regimentation, made American slavery appear mild. The idea was to allow peasant conscripts (twenty-five-year terms) to live with their families while providing for their own subsistence. The result was practical slavery. Because so much time was given over to drill that the more mundane aspects of farming were neglected, crops were poor and resulted in even more hardship. By Alexander's death a third of the Russian army was organized in this fashion and the Tsar was looking ahead to this arrangement for the whole army. The vastness of the system can be imagined by recalling that Russia's army after 1815 was not reduced. Her peacetime army was deliberately kept as large as that of Prussia and Austria combined.

Despite this system the burden of military expenditures was enormous and the budgetary situation resembled prerevolutionary France; there were consistent deficits with some attempts to hide the situation through fraudulent bookkeeping. This came naturally to a bureaucracy honeycombed with corruption and vice and sadly in need of reform. Bribery was a way of life and the common people were systematically robbed and cheated by petty officials. *Ancien régime* France was a model of integrity and enlightened administration compared with the corrupt ruthlessness of ordinary government in Russia in the last decade of Alexander's reign.

The educated were largely nobles and they were, from Alexander's view, increasingly suspect. As officers many spent years in Germany, Poland, or France and, like some peasant conscripts, imbibed ideas which made them critical of conditions back in Russia. Several secret societies were founded during Alexander's reign but there was never much agreement on how conditions could be changed or what sort of progress was most desirable. Possibilities ranged from moderate reform to murder of the entire royal family. The Tsar was aware of these organizations and they were driven underground, where they continued despite severe handicaps.

In the universities many civil servants were trained but here too the hand of autocracy and censorship appeared. Divine-right monarchy was to be extolled and truth in all subjects had to be in accord with Biblical wisdom. There was no room for revolutionary or liberal doctrines: Machiavelli and Hobbes were regarded as especially despicable. Obedience was the great civic virtue.

Alexander was perhaps his most enlightened regarding the Poles. He may have been sincere about wanting to restore their nationhood, and he spoke of their situation after 1815 as though they were now better off. Under his reign Russia controlled more of Poland than she had earlier as a result of the partitions; but he saw this not as an increase of Russian control, but as a restoration of Poland, a returning of good for evil, a Christian act of extending his hand to help the less fortunate. It seems not to have occurred to him that he was acting somewhat like Napoleon had in bringing enlightened institutions to Spain and that, like the Spaniards, the Poles simply were too proud to accept such condescension from an outside autocrat. Although he pondered ways to increase the size of Poland, he was also receptive to a plan to terminate Poland as a kingdom, making it one of the major Russian provinces. As usual, several possibilities vied for attention in his mind and the result was a gradual drift toward more autocracy in Poland. Historians have taken special note of Alexander's supposed change from liberalism to conservative reaction, but many people in any society go a similar route. In Alexander's case, an added ominous factor continuously present was that he owed his position to the murder of his father. This act was a standing example of what a plot can accomplish and was not to be overlooked in an age where ideas attacking the social order were to be seen or suspected on every hand.

Although Alexander's autocracy was accompanied by numerous pious statements of a liberal nature, no such inconsistency marked the conduct of domestic affairs in Austria. The official government policy was not only crystal clear but applied to a much enlarged Austria. Despite the mediocre showing of its arms, it emerged from the struggle against Napoleon with 10 million more inhabitants living on 2,300 square miles. By comparison the Russian gain had been 3 million people living on 2,100 square miles and Prussia acquired 5.36 million people residing in 2,217 square miles. The Lombard-Venetian kingdom annexed by Austria probably felt the yoke of rule by Vienna as lightly as any part of the Empire. Here Vienna's authoritarianism was its least onerous and there was relative prosperity. Despite this, however, Austrian censorship, spies, and police measures created resentments to such an extent that the occupation appeared no better than that of the French which had at least paid lip service to Italian nationalism and given them reformed codes.

North of Italy, Austria was a polyglot empire with a German core and German leadership. Ironically, she was intent on increasing her ascendency over non-Germans, leaving a large share of the problem of defense of the Confederation to the Prussians while maintaining direct influence in the German states through the Carlsbad Decrees. Though Prussia was in a defensive posture against both France and Russia, her gains at the expense of smaller German princes hurt her position within the Confederation, thus making Austria's influence the more pronounced and assuring the retardation of liberalism in the Germanies.

If it were important to Austria that liberal influences be combatted in the Confederation, it was crucial that they be crushed within her own borders. Fortunately for the dynasty, this was a relatively simple task. The French had never completely occupied or administered Austria, and the initial impact of revolutionary ideas was therefore negligible. The maintenance of conservatism became a matter of simple surveillance, so that no new ideas appeared. Censorship and police supervision were important to the government, and appropriately, the police were the most efficient branch of the bureaucracy. A pall of medievalism and reaction pervaded the Empire as both the Emperor Francis and Metternich deliberately tried to shut out the tides of change. The effectiveness with which Metternich isolated Austria and retarded liberal growth within the Confederation was to make Central Europe almost defenseless when finally Prussia awakened from her own torpor. With Austrian trade and commerce restricted by high tariffs, her middle class remained small and the traditional medieval social pattern existed, a massive peasantry supporting a predominantly unenlightened nobility. Both the Church and the universities were simply expected to preach obedience; no new ideas were desired from any source. Even Austria's rulers came to realize that their state was becoming an anachronism in the nineteenth century. In the subject territories there were assemblies or estates which existed according to dispensations and grants centuries old. Their meetings were irregular and always docile. Aside from the police, the Empire's administration was lethargic and generally incompetent. There was no real cabinet in the modern sense but rather heads of ministries who went their own way, although all were imbued with the Emperor's general sense of conservatism. Metternich had a few ideas for increased efficiency but these were casually brushed aside. Although Metternich helped set the tenor of government and had vast influence, he was primarily a diplomat and not an administrator. He had very little control over finances, for example, and enjoyed no authority over the heads of ministries.

The greatest menace to the Empire was the spirit of nationalism.

Austria was the most prominent example of a state where nationalism really meant disintegration. An efficient bureaucracy promoting loyalty might have counteracted some of the dangers, but this was lacking. A vast Hungarian nobility chaffed at German control from Vienna; Italians similarly resented German domination; Poles in Galicia mourned for their former position as part of an independent state; Bohemians resented limitations on their autonomy; and many smaller ethnic groups also resented control by "outsiders." To all, the government in Vienna turned the same face. A deadly "stand-pattism" was assuring a major disaster, should the day come when the leadership faltered. Although the government successfully kept outside influence to a bare minimum, the various sections of Empire developed their own nationalistic identification, largely through their awareness of cultural unity and growth. A change of reign in 1835 resulted in no basic change, for the new Emperor Ferdinand 1793–1875) was not only conservative, but ignorant as well.

Once Metternich had removed Austria from being *mainly* concerned with German affairs, her success or failure depended on whether or not the nineteenth century was to be an age of nationalism. Napoleon had helped Austria to be a non-German state when he disbanded the Holy Roman Empire, and later Bismarck would also emphasize the trend. Metternich saw no need for a nationalistic core for Austria. He proved to be a cultivated eighteenth-century aristocrat who temporarily stemmed the tide of both progress and nationalism. His negative insistence on order for its own sake proved ultimately inadequate to the forces released by the French Revolution.

In Italy the Papacy made a partially successful effort to steer an independent course. Austrian influence was strong during the last years of the pontificate of Pius VII, but neutrality in diplomatic affairs was an expressed Papal ideal and Rome rebuffed pressure to support the Holy Alliance. Napoleon had brought an order to Papal finances which lasted for a decade. His rule also disrupted the papal contact with many of its major churches and resulted in a need for redefinition of the Church's position in much of Europe. The period after Napoleon's fall thus witnessed a complex negotiation of concordats. After the death of both Cardinal Consalvi (January 24, 1824) and Pius VII (August 21, 1823), Austrian influence gave way briefly to that of France, although in 1831 Gregory XVI (1765–1846) required aid from Austrian troops and the myth of an independent policy was exposed. Leo XII (1823–28) was a papal version of Austrian reaction. The decades between 1815–45 were filled with religious ferment, and the Papacy, alternately caught between the weight of tradition and the glitter of new ideas, functioned as both spiritual leader and secular government and was buffeted by enormous social, political, and intellectual forces. That the popes following Pius VII were unable to give imaginative and successful leadership is hardly surprising.

The Prussian monarchy after 1815 was both weak and reactionary. Frederick William III showed no personal qualities of strength and his reign in the quarter century preceding his death in 1840 is marked by few evidences of regal distinction. He lacked three years of ruling as long as Frederick the Great, and though there were opportunities to mold the course of events, he assumed a passive role. Pious and unimaginative, he made little effort to compete in an arena containing Napoleon, Metternich, and Alexander. He was humiliated by Napoleon's easy successes over Prussian arms and his cavalier rearranging of German territories. To have been left on the bank of the Nieman while two non-German emperors discussed the fate of his kingdom along with other issues was insultingly appropriate. A viewer of Prussian disintegration, he was a little more responsible for Prussian resurgence and German regeneration. In the wave of popular excitement and enthusiasm accompanying the War of Liberation, he was given a rare chance to create a new and vital Prussia. His failure to assume this role is only one of a series of tragic factors affecting the course of modern German history. He also neglected to capitalize on the prominence of Prussian arms in the battle of Leipzig and in the French retreat. They were also crucial in the success at Waterloo. No consequent increment in Prussia's diplomatic role occurred, however, because Frederick William was easily dominated alternately by Alexander and Metternich.

Within Germany the French domination had temporarily enhanced Prussian prestige, even as she was shorn of her most Germanic territories. While members of the Confederation of the Rhine involuntarily submitted to French influences, they looked to Prussia to bring about their deliverance. German nationalism received a great stimulus and Prussia itself was caught up in this. Constructive social reforms of the French National Assembly were credited with providing the sinews for French victories and Baron vom Stein argued that the elimination of serfdom in Prussia would have the same effect. To defeat the French they must become, in some measure, like the French. The reform was successful in this regard and when Napoleon's control in Central Europe was broken, a wave of enthusiasm greeted Prussian and Russian troops as deliverers from the French.

Prussia at this time possessed an opportunity to head a potent German liberal movement, powered for the moment by a surge of nationalistic goodwill. Enlightened institutions had been planted in West Germany and though there was relief at seeing the French go, there was no intention whatever of going back to *ancien régime* standards. The new Prussia could have been a genuine leader of a vast area if she had been more progressive after 1815. As it was, once the danger of renewed French rule subsided, Prussia gave up its reforming posture and its more traditional values came to the fore. This was a great blow to many German liberals, who were now left without support.

Despite promises made during the War of Liberation, the court of Frederick William III regarded the principles of the French Revolution as anathema, and after the Napoleonic threat was over had no intention of extending them. In rather unimaginative fashion it regarded the immediate task as the introduction of Prussian bureaucratic practices into its new territories, especially integrating the lands acquired along the Rhine. To Prussia's advantage none of these lands had ever really known independence. They had always been part of some other unit and so in no sense did Prussian rule come to areas formerly free. In Polish and Saxon territories a measure of autonomy was allowed. Along the Rhine the disparate territories were effectively brought together by Prussia's bureaucracy while French measures pertaining to the entire area and enhancing its unity (such as tax measures and the codes) were maintained. In all the new areas, there was virtually no real feeling of *Prussian* nationalism. The acquired lands were integrated within the system but felt much like Lombardy under Austria or Finland under Russia.

The rigor of Prussian administration was unpopular along the Rhine, especially as it became more conservative and suppressed a number of journals. A further complication was religion. Of the new Prussian citizens, many were Roman Catholics who found Lutheranism particularly distasteful. The Prussians were sensible enough not to wage a religious crusade against them, but despite attempts to avoid friction, the problem of mixed marriages brought the Prussian state and Catholicism to an impasse. The crucial issue was the control of children's education in mixed marriages. Many Prussian officials moving into the Rhine married local Catholic girls and insisted that a father controlled the education of his children, a view Rome found offensive. Prussian efforts to deal with specific bishops were no more successful than negotiations with Rome and an open rupture came after the government forcibly removed the Archbishop of Cologne and jailed the Archbishop of Posen. The Pope in Rome and the hierarchy in Germany emphatically opposed the coercive measures taken by Berlin as unrest prevailed along the Rhine. Feeding this smouldering disaffection for Prussia were Roman Catholics in Bavaria, to the southeast, and in Belgium and France, to the west. The whole dispute was also enmeshed in an unsuccessful attempt to limit papal control within the German Church. Rome proved to have a much different view of what properly constituted Germany than did Berlin, and from the perspective of some in the Rhineland both were outsiders. Particularism in Germany remained an especially important continuing problem.

The question of a national representative body for Prussia was debated and generally delayed. Some zealots had been so moved by enthusiasm over the liberation that they had expected such a body to be established shortly after 1815. They became disillusioned, after 1820 especially, when it became clear that the government was opposed to such a measure. Their hopes had been legitimate while Frederick William was dominated by Alexander rather than Metternich, but as Alexander's sentiments changed after 1818, the outlook for a constitutional and representative regime was bleak. The liberals wanted a national assembly, a Reichstag, which would be composed of delegates chosen from provincial assemblies, the Landtage. It was agreed that such a representative structure should be developed on constitutional and historical bases already in existence. Open to debate was the question of whether peasants should be represented in the various assemblies. The old medieval estates were appropriate but extremely susceptible to particularistic influences. Considerable debate centered on the need for any but regional assemblies. The old nobility saw revolutionary ideas in many of these suggestions, especially those coming from along the Rhine, where the French had resided the longest. The issues were not unlike those in Paris in 1789. The government delayed the whole question until well into the 1840s and sought instead to bring a kind of unity to its disparate territories through rigorous administration. The king and his appointees ruled their state with little collaboration from its citizens.

In 1815 the flow of economic goods in Prussia was handicapped by an unenlightened mass of tariff walls. The result was so to handicap trade that smuggling was the most flourishing industry. While extremely high tariffs hindered the various segments of Prussia from trading with one another, finished goods poured in from outside, especially from England. The Confederation exercised little control of economic life for the same reason that it was of limited effectiveness in political affairs; large segments of her territory were integrated into the affairs of outside states. With budgetary deficits and no help expected from the Confederation, Prussia was left to her own resources in finding corrective measures to improve her economy. The forthright solution to this problem was of enormous consequences for latter Prussian success; its story is incompatible with the conservative line stemming from Vienna and will be discussed later. Equally counter to the spirit of reaction were several educational moves. More opportunities for *gymnasium* instruction and an emphasis on compulsory education were particularly important. A new university was founded at Bonn and that at Halle was strengthened. Education thus became more accessible but its doctrines were carefully watched to make sure that revolutionary ideas were absent and that devotion to the state was emphasized.

If Vienna represented a spirit of responsible conservatism, the regime restored in Spain was nothing but blind reaction. Napoleon had allowed Ferdinand VII (1784–1833) to return in 1814 and the allies never questioned his right to the crown. Back in Madrid he engaged in a studied program of repression against all who previously had supported any sort of reform. He canceled the Constitution of 1812 and disbanded the Cortes, the legislative body which had written the constitution. This was a reasonable reaction yet Ferdinand went much further in harassing particular political leaders than was necessary.

The Constitution of 1812 was an interesting but hardly original document. Ideas from the United States were mingled with material taken bodily from the French Constitution of 1791. It established a limited hereditary monarchy with the king as the primary administrator. The Cortes was the main legislative organ and a fine separation of powers indicated a respect for English experience. The Rights of Man were proclaimed and feudalism was wiped out, along with the Inquisition. The document embodied the best of the early French Revolutionary experience and had been formulated by a dedicated and learned group of Spaniards who believed that this constitution represented a normal extension and growth of modest reforms instituted during the 18th century. It was *not* a system devised for them in Paris and given to them at the sufferance of Napoleon. The men who framed it were ardent supporters of the Bourbon monarchy in Spain, had plotted against Napoleon, had worked to keep public devotion to the dynasty alive, and deserved more understanding than Ferdinand granted. The new system involved too many concessions from the royal family, the Church, and the nobility for them to accept it when the circumstances of Napoleon's defeat made it possible for them to refuse. The Constitution later became an object of blind loyalty to many Spanish intellectuals, a rallying point not only for them but also for agitators in Italy as well. Many reasonable and educated men regarded this constitution and the French Charter of 1814 as standing for responsibility and enlightened government. Neither document, of course, was close to the French Revolutionary system as it existed at its peak under Robespierre.

Ferdinand, however, was not a "reasonable" man and his repressive autocracy stimulated intense opposition, particularly among army officers. Four unsuccessful uprisings between 1814 and 1817 were led by officers attempting to restore the Constitution. Though these men had fought the French bitterly, they had imbibed many of the invaders' ideas and were insisting on an enlightened government. The Freemasonry movement provided a further sense of solidarity which in this context made the order appear dedicated to revolution: the whole situation was complicated by the upheavals in Spanish America. Finally, in 1820 (January–March) Colonel Rafael del Riego (1775–1823) carried through a military revolt which restored the Constitution of 1812 and the Cortes. On March 9 Ferdinand blandly accepted the change, promising constitutional leadership. The Great Powers of Europe leisurely debated a plea for help from Ferdinand. In October of 1822 the Congress of Verona, over English objections, authorized the intervention of France to restore Ferdinand to his former position. A French army readily put down the revolt. A constitutional system had lasted for three years and the memory of this experience was to last. With the restoration of Ferdinand to complete power, a wave of repression appeared which dwarfed the government's harsh measures of eight years before. Metternich regarded Spanish diplomats as utterly reactionary and looked down on them despite the enormous importance of Spain in Napoleon's downfall. After Riego's short success, however, Metternich supported forceful domestic measures to root out revolutionary ideas. The hanging of Riego was a signal for unbridled terrorism; autocracy of the worst sort now ran virtually unchecked in Spain for over five years.

In France after 1815 repression was somewhat muted as Louis XVIII refused to give full rein to the passions moving many of the returned *émigrés*. Historians have generally sympathized with Louis, mainly because he was not thoroughly given over to revenge and avoided espousing the reactionary ultraroyalism of his brother, the Count of Artois. The period of 1815–28 in France has not inspired very much intensive and comprehensive study; consequently, our knowledge of it rests on stereotypes of contemporary views. Current research appears to be only moderately altering or refining our understanding of Louis XVIII's reign, despite the need for considerably more information about French social and economic history in the decade after 1815.

The Charter of 1814 "granted" by Louis XVIII was a wise and moderate document in light of the passions of the day. Like the Spanish Constitution of 1812 and the National Assembly's Constitution of 1791, it established constitutional monarchy and accepted many of the basic advances of the French Revolution. The Charter became the rallying cry for liberals outside of portions of Europe where the Spanish constitution was the symbol of political freedom and progress. To Louis' credit he accepted the document as reasonable and conscientiously lived within its provisions for a decade.

If agitators for reform were watching France, so also were many conservatives who sympathized with the returning *émigrés* and regarded Artois as their main spokesman. These aristocrats returning from exile were no longer cultivated examples of the enlightenment who found *philosophe* ideas exciting. They were narrowly proclerical and their view of monarchy reeked with images of Louis XIV or Philip Augustus. A number were also young and knew France and the republic as the land which had, in Machiavellian terms, robbed them of their patrimony. A reaction of sorts was probably inevitable and in 1815–1816 the so-called White Terror was a beginning of Ultraroyalist revenge which threatened to assume the proportions of repression current in Spain. In France, however, there was always more of a show of legality—Marshal Ney did receive a trial by his peers and the Chamber of Deputies was dominated by reactionary opinion. Republican and revolutionary writers have made much of this French repression, but it surely lacked the vigor of either the policies of Ferdinand VII or those of the Jacobin ascendancy. Because France had been the cause of so much trouble for Europe, Metternich was concerned about the stability of the new regime. Its initial unpopularity had been proved by the ease which which Napoleon assumed power on his return from Elba, and the Austrian chancellor had visions of the Ultra repression leading to an uprising against Louis. There was also the possibility of another Napoleonic return. Thus he counseled a measure of moderation and the French monarch dismissed the Chamber and called for new elections. The Ultras, who had been essentially opposed to the Charter, were now (1816) replaced as a majority in the Chamber by a group supporting the system. These were upper-middle-class moderates who believed in both the Charter and the monarchy. These "Constitutionals" gave France four years of reasonable, responsible government, though divisive issues made serious inroads and the voices of moderation were gradually weakened in the face of attacks by right-wing Ultras and left-wing critics of the dynasty and the Charter. The Duke de Richelieu's government gave way to a ministry headed by Duke Decazes (1780–1860), who possessed a remarkably clear view of the dangers and needs of French politics. These two leaders were largely responsible for implementing much of the moderation associated with Louis XVIII, but the government's position was simply too weak to survive the Ultra pressure, which was continued and strong. The election of a regicide (Abbé de Grégoire) coupled with the assassination of the Duke de Berri gave added strength to the Ultra cries that the franchise was too broad and the voices of moderation were in error.

From 1820 to 1824, when Louis XVIII died, the Ultras were in a position of political ascendancy, buoyed by the confidence that their leader would shortly ascend the throne. A conservative interpretation of the Charter was the guide of the Count of Villèle (1773–1854) who tried to implement the Ultra program. Debates over a press law and the veto power of the king (vaguely left open in the Charter) had characterized the early days of Louis' reign, but now as the Ultras grew progressively stronger, the Charter itself was on increasingly unstable foundations. The peers were a clearly Ultra body, despite including some Napoleonic nobility. A measure of the reactionary character of the Ultra program can be seen from Villèle's need to manipulate an already Ultra body. As reaction was becoming more pronounced, the monarchy thought it saw a major opportunity in the events in Spain. Allied troops no longer occupied France and the nation had ostensibly been readmitted to good standing in the councils of European Great Powers, although the renewal of the Quadruple Alliance indicates that there were some reservations on this score. For the French army under Bourbon leadership (Duke of Angoulême) to succeed in Spain would not only enhance the position of the crown among the conservative powers in Europe but a superficial comparison with Napoleon's failure in Spain would be of importance within France as indication that international military prestige could come from Bourbon as well as from republican or Napoleonic leadership. That Napoleon's involvement in Spain was not comparable to the events of 1823 was disregarded as the restoration of Ferdinand comprised little more for the French army than an exercise in logistics and field maneuver. While Metternich viewed Franco-English relations with suspicion, he approved the Ultra successes within France so long as insurrection did not result. He was also delighted that the French intervention in Spain made diplomatic cooperation between France and England more difficult.

Thus after 1820 France moved domestically in much the same direction as Alexander's Russia. Reaction was strong by 1824 and the nation was about to embark on a more conservative reign. Charles X was a French version of Russia's Nicholas I (1796–1855), but in France potent forces existed requiring greater finesse and wisdom on the part of a monarch dedicated to conservative and reactionary principles. France had a substantial middle class which believed in many eighteenth-century principles and had memories of efficient government under Napoleon. In France much of the Revolution had been accepted by the time the old monarchy returned. In Russia the Revolution was never experienced, let alone accepted. Charles X had many problems but his most serious shortcoming was that he seemed not to recognize that he ruled in a nation which had accepted more of the Revolution than it had retained of the old monarchy.

At the Vienna settlement the Netherlands received the Belgian provinces, thus making the kingdom ruled by William I (1770–1843) larger and presumably a stronger bulwark against any later French efforts to expand. The union made economic sense, for Holland was essentially commercial whereas the Belgian provinces were both agrarian and industrial. The Belgians had never experienced real independence and in this respect their transfer was much like the Prussian gains along the Rhine. Catholicism and French influences were very strong, even in Flemish areas. The Belgians possessed a popular nobility which cooperated with its large and growing middle class. Accustomed to non-Belgian rulers, a wise and tactful regime could probably have governed these provinces with a minimum of discord. Unfortunately, William was neither wise nor tactful. He saw himself as an eighteenth-century enlightened despot who granted privileges. In this spirit in 1815 he gave his kingdom a "Fundamental Law," a document influenced by the French Charter. In its details there were many features which Belgians found objectionable (equality of creeds, even division of deputies in the lower house despite the Belgians comprising three fifths of the population), and after Belgian notables were invited to consider the Law and rejected it (527 against, out of 796, with 100 abstentions), William decreed its acceptance. This naturally infuriated the Belgians but William believed he was following a proper course. He started new schools in the Belgian provinces, aided Belgian industry by building new canals and roads as well as by enlarging port facilities in Antwerp and Ostend. Hoping that through education the southern provinces would gradually assume a sense of Dutch nationality, he overlooked Belgian pride and sense of justice. They saw legal equality of creeds as a clear religious intrusion and resented his failure to give more official appointments to Belgians. Similarly, it appeared to Belgians that their wealth and ingenuity were being taxed to make up for the debts incurred by the northern provinces. Bitter friction had developed well before 1821 and it was remarkable that more serious difficulty did not occur sooner. In his conservatism William was not nearly as narrow as many in his day but his rule appeared harsher and more unjust to Belgians than he ever intended it. His policies were to survive the 1820s but only barely.

Across the Channel in England, conservatism was similarly installed. Political reform was long overdue and had been delayed by patriotism's priority on victory in the long struggle against Napoleon. The progress of industry had accelerated during wartime so that the need for change was now acute. Though the English Tories were far more enlightened than their conservative Continental brethren, they did not embark on thoroughgoing reform once peace was at hand. Like most of the Continent, England experienced poor harvests after 1815 and a major depression heightened discontent, which took the form of demands for a reform of the electoral system. Tory leaders refused to consider such fundamental change but did introduce a few ineffective measures calculated to lessen the widespread economic distress. When the aggrieved took to rioting and barn burning, the Tory response was unmistakable. Regarding such acts as essentially revolutionary and the result of the sinister influence of Robespierre, they adopted an authoritarian stance (Coercion Acts, 1817) which in turn made the discontented even more militant. The two protagonists met head on in the Peterloo Massacre, giving the cause of reform its martyrs. With little apology the Tories then enacted the "Six Acts" which markedly limited free speech and freedom of press and assembly. As a clearly reactionary measure, it would have been devastating to the prestige of the government had a plot not been discovered to murder the entire cabinet. Thus reaction earned a grudging measure of approval and somewhat delayed the insistent demands for reform. After 1822 the Tories began a series of important reform measures, although they failed to move quickly enough on the question of modernizing the representative system. France was becoming progressively less enlightened during the 1820s, but the reverse was happening in England. Like most of the status quo powers in 1815, England was conservative for the first few years but in the 1820s took a different course, paralleling its divergence from the Continental powers in foreign policy.

III

The Changing
Condition of Life

CHAPTER 8

Population Growth and Industrialization

The conditions of peace drawn up at Vienna in 1815 were derived from what appeared to be the necessities and dangers of the moment. The peacemakers viewed Europe largely as a collection of dynastic states and it was merely a matter of adapting past formulas to devise a way of assuring everyone's security without leaving any combination of important powers with basic grievances. Concern for actual peoples extended only to whether their rulers were "legitimate" and conservative. Napoleon's Continental System had called attention to the importance of economic factors in national life, but despite this the statesmen at Vienna paid little attention to current economic problems or developments. They presumed a stable society where economic life followed traditional patterns. That a vast economic upheaval—indeed, an industrial revolution—had already begun was

101

hardly noted by the diplomats then trying to arrange a durable peace. This oversight led to significant breaches in the settlement and to untold headache and worry for Metternich, who seems never to have understood the basic economic transformation then underway. As the century progressed, enormous economic and social change occurred. A remarkable thing about the Vienna settlement was not that important modifications were later made, but that it was still recognizable in 1900.

European society had been overwhelmingly oriented to an agrarian base prior to 1800. Both the cities and the aristocracy depended on the slender margins which the countryside produced beyond its own need. Rural productivity was geared to rural needs with a goal of uniform self-sufficiency. Surpluses and peasant comforts were rare, whereas malnutrition and starvation were continuing dangers. When bad harvests brought famine, tax collectors became an especially hated group. Peasants had little sense of nonlocal political involvement and were ideologically inert on national issues. A vast and hardworking peasantry, organized in village units and supporting a local aristocracy and clergy, formed the basic centuries-old rural pattern of life, which did not abruptly change with the nineteenth century. Vast social alterations did occur in the generations after 1789, but it needs constantly to be recalled that a basic stability and tradition-bound pattern existing in 1800 extended for decades into the century, in some areas even continuing beyond 1900. Instinctively, the nobles guarded their local prerogatives and were anxious that the monarch lack power to enforce nationwide obedience and conformity. The aristocracy and monarchy were both strong defenders of the entrenched Church, and all three were driven together by the growing middle class and the French Revolution. Thus by the early nineteenth century the cleavage between the middle class and the traditionally powerful groups was wider and more explicit than it had been before the Revolution.

Though European society had a tradition-bound, hierarchical structure, there were innumerable varieties and exceptions. A striking difference divided the Continent into two distinctive areas. Eastern Europe, the area roughly east of the Elbe, contained few cities, and those which did exist were largely bureaucratic. The middle class was very small and politically insignificant. The nobles owned enormous estates and enjoyed extensive power while the lot of their serfs was especially wretched. The forces of tradition were more firmly entrenched and patterns of living had experienced much less modification than in most of Western Europe, where southern

Italy and southern Spain were exceptions. Even after the French Revolution and Napoleon, the prospects of basic social change in Eastern Europe were remote and the obvious conclusion an observer of these areas would derive was that, outside of Prussia, the traditional patterns had hardly been disturbed.

Western, Central, and Northwestern Europe had witnessed major alterations. A number of sizable cities had developed and, compared with Eastern Europe, a thriving trade existed. The middle class enjoyed considerable wealth and aspired to political power, and the aristocracy was more defensive in face of real threats to its privileges. Land was held in much smaller units and those aristocrats still living on estates were much less powerful than their Eastern European counterparts. Many of the old medieval, serf obligations had disappeared and ownership was more diffuse. Peasants and the middle class both shared in the management of property. The peasant's life was hard but he was not bought and sold, or flogged and exploited in the fashion of Eastern Europe. In the West the aristocracy and middle class were better educated and literacy was common among artisans, so that ideas could be understood and communicated much more readily than in Eastern Europe. The impact of revolutionary ideas was by far the most pronounced in the West, and in this context, Metternich's manipulation of the peace settlement in the few years after 1815 represents an attempt to apply to the coalition against Napoleon, the values of the social system of the Eastern landed aristocracy. That England, differing even more from Eastern Europe than France, had financed and largely powered the coalition, was beside the point in terms of efforts to achieve long-range stability. England's diplomacy aimed merely at containing France, whereas Metternich, a noble originally from the Rhineland, was trying to preserve a way of life.

With the wisdom of hindsight we can see that the social and political order Metternich was defending could not withstand the forces promoting change in the nineteenth century. In his defense, however, a stodgy, social stability with very little basic change had characterized European life for centuries and there was no recent parallel that would suggest the massive alterations about to occur. Napoleon was seen as merely another aggressive French leader, like Louis XIV, who for a time dominated and menaced other powers; but with his fall, there was no reason to expect that European society would not fall back into its old routines.

In 1815 Europe was crossing the threshold into a new era and Napoleon's defeat merely disguised the extent to which the forces

promoting change were already at work. The sheer increase in population is a striking feature of the nineteenth century and contrasts
sharply with the rather static preceding periods. In the century before 1750 the Continent's population had increased by only 3 per
cent. After 1750 the growth was rapid, though geographically spotty,
because some areas started their growth as much as a century after
others. By 1900 the population growth encompassed the whole Continent. The 188 million people living in Europe in 1800 had become
over 400 million a century later. While more than doubling in numbers, the Europeans also sent *another* 10 per cent overseas, scattering
European methods, values, and vitality over the globe.

Studies of this demographic upheaval suggest that it was characterized by two distinct phases—first a period of phenomenal increase,
and then a distinct decline in the rate of increase, though the growth
continued. Clearly evident in France, which first went through the
pattern, it also occurred in other areas of Europe.

The first phase of growth followed a number of eighteenth-century developments which altered the monotonous rhythm of high
death rates accompanying high birth rates. Infant mortality was
dramatically cut; and, through hygienic advances, life expectancy
soared; in France it increased from twenty-eight years to nearly fifty
between 1800 and 1900. A better diet similarly added six inches to
the average French male's height, which in 1800 was only five feet.
Better standards of sanitation combined with more vigilance to
hamper the spread of disease. The familiar pattern of plagues from
the Eastern Mediterranean spreading through the Balkans and into
Central and then Western Europe was broken by the Hapsburg
bureaucracy, which had instituted more stringent border surveillance. In addition to improved controls against disease, the amount
of arable land was significantly increased. Through swamp drainage
and more intense colonizing of barren regions, more people could
be supported, and with the widespread adoption of the potato, a
better diet further stimulated population growth. The new land encouraged peasants to marry earlier and to have more children as a
spirit of expansion and opportunity appeared at the very base of the
social spectrum.

In the second phase (a slowing down of the rate of increase) the
most crucial group was the middle class. More family units were
reproducing but the emphasis on many children gave way to control
over the number of births in the interest of assuring a reasonable
inheritance and family continuity in property holdings. France
reached this position by about 1820. She had grown by a third (20

million to 29 million) since 1750, but with the reduction in rate, nearly a century was required to add another third (to 39 million). While French growth was slowing down, other areas began to double and even triple their numbers, so that France experienced a relative decline. This tendency to slow down as the middle class and other urban elements became prominent came to the rest of Europe as the century progressed. These shifting population pressures created specific political and social problems which crucially affected the course of nineteenth-century history. The energetic turbulence of youth became a significant ingredient of political life as more young people were competing in a world in which the middle class had just created social cleavages and opportunity. An entrenched system of privileged orders came increasingly under attack. Traditional institutional values were challenged and movements of "de-Christianization" were common. The family as a social unit remained secure, though it was to be questioned by theorists and its circumstances were greatly altered in terms of marriage ages, number of children, and interest in child welfare. A work force of enormous proportions had been created as growing urban centers teemed with new vitality. Egalitarianism and demands for property rights were shouted in an ever-rising chorus as, in the decades after 1800, so many new people wanted basic changes that political leaders were forced to consider more than simple modest reforms.

Increases in population among the peasant class both accompanied and promoted land reform and new methods of agricultural production. Though the French Revolution was concerned with property rights, so many variations and alterations in property holding had occurred over the centuries that many European statesmen overlooked this basic feature of the French upheaval. Because the Revolution was a recent and highly emotional experience, propagandists and reformers seized on it as a convenient reference that most people would recognize.

The story of peasant freedom in Europe—his emergence with personal liberty and ownership of his own land—encompassed centuries and still was not complete in 1900. By 1800 the peasant had made significant progress in some areas, and in the next century the ideal was widely achieved. Peasant emancipation had been taking place sporadically since late Middle Ages. Feudalism was a cumbersome structure consisting of a vast mosaic of individual legal relationships. This was everywhere being altered at differing rates to accommodate local, economic, or political changes, so that by 1789 there was a substantial variation in the degree to which further freedom and land-owning potential was needed. In some localities emancipation was so far advanced that formal national or regional legislation—the sort usually noted by historians—made no practical impact. Such was the case, for example, in widely scattered portions of France, in Hanover, and in some sections of Württemberg, where peasant freedom and landownership came formally between the sixteenth and eighteenth centuries. A considerable amount of serf emancipation came in the wake of the German Peasant Uprising in the sixteenth century. Zwingli had abolished serfdom at Zurich in 1525 and substantial freedom had earlier been achieved by peasants in Austrian Swabia, Alsace, and Breisgau. Tenant farming in the Netherlands and lower Rhine also involved considerable emancipation. In parts of Württemberg, in Baden, and in Bavaria, emancipation meant merely the abrogation of long archaic legal stipulations which had remained on the books. In much of Germany, when the French swept in bringing "freedom and liberty," they did not create a chaotic social readjustment but did bring about a formal uniformity which increased bureaucratic efficiency.

One by-product of nineteenth-century emancipation was the creation of a seasonal, migratory agricultural work force, particularly, but not exclusively, in Eastern Europe. At the same time there was extensive emigration from the countryside to the city, and rural populations were still more than doubling. New methods and new lands held out opportunity, but east of the Elbe the rapid rise in population by 1840 had quickly changed the situation to one of increased poverty. Industrialization of the Ruhr, the growth of Berlin, and emigration to America took up some of the surplus; but it was only after 1870 that industrialization absorbed a sufficient number to ease the situation. By then the rate of increase had also begun to decline and the situation became less menacing. Thus in the nineteenth century the increase in population was often accompanied by significant urban and industrial growth. In Eastern Europe, however (excluding Bohemia and Moravia and also the Baltic provinces of Russia, where the land was sparsely settled), there was no parallel industrial development and no migration to industrial areas. The result was an overcrowding of the countryside and the creation of major social problems. Emancipation in much of Eastern Europe in the nineteenth century meant a partitioning of the land beyond the requirements of sound agricultural practice and led to strong support among reasonable men for schemes of collectivization.

The population increase, continuing steadily after 1750, was essential to European industrialization. The widescale development of

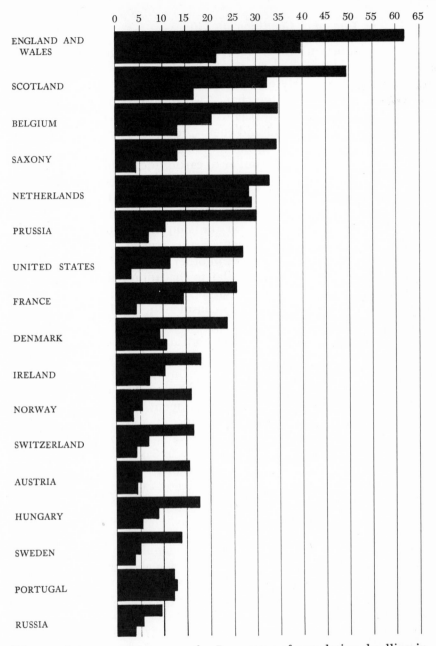

Nineteenth-century urban growth. Percentage of population dwelling in cities of 10,000 or more in 1800, 1850, and 1890, or the nearest census years. (Top bar represents percentage in 1890, bottom represents percentage in 1800.) (From A. F. Weber, *The Growth of Cities in the Nineteenth Century*, 1899.)

107

factory production which occurred in nineteenth-century Europe followed swiftly on the heels of the English experience in the latter eighteenth century. Here a number of factors had fortuitously combined to make possible the change which historians now call an industrial revolution. It has been commonplace to regard this process as developing in England and then spreading, during the course of the nineteenth century, from the English Channel eastward and southward. Such a view is similar to earlier ideas which described the Renaissance somewhat erroneously as an Italian cultural flowering which spread northward. There is no question that an industrial system developed first in England (from 1780s on) and that it influenced later developments on the Continent, but it should constantly be kept in mind that many factors crucial to industrialization in England were equally present in other areas and that swift change in the direction of a course similar to that followed by England was taking place independent of, but behind, the English experience. We must restrain the impulse to consider the English experience as a unique forerunner which brought industrialization to Europe.

By 1750 the added population had already made its impact on English production. The medieval, guild-oriented system of production had long since distintegrated, freeing labor from guild restrictions and regulations. Reforms in land tenure had made the peasant more mobile, and agricultural improvements, especially cultivation of the potato, had created an abundance of food allowing cities to expand rapidly. Before food surpluses, a cottage or home-based industry (putting-out) had developed (also in Saxony and elsewhere on the Continent) and was the most advanced system of production consistent with the need for a huge labor force in the fields. The population pressure not only provided more personnel but more demand for finished products. The manufacture of textiles (cotton especially) was of particular significance in new developments as industries tested themselves and their ingenuity to adjust to the increased requirement of society. In the demand for more clothing, textile leaders progressively became more efficient and were receptive to new ideas and suggestions. A series of inventions or technological improvements at once found practical application. Striking advances stemmed from the flying shuttle (John Day), the spinning jenny (James Hargreaves), and the water frame (Richard Arkwright). A new technique for weaving was introduced by the power loom (Edmund Cartwright), and the cotton gin (Eli Whitney) assured a larger supply of raw American cotton. The principle behind the steam engine dated from antiquity but the practical steam engine for the needs of the late eighteenth century was a result of work by Thomas Newcomen and James Watt. The use of steam as a motive force resulted in soaring production as a worker's yield was enormously increased. With the application of steam engines and more sophisticated machinery, the manufacturer discovered that he was producing an unprecedented volume of goods with *proportionally* fewer employees. With large markets, an overabundant labor supply, and an adequate source of raw materials, the continued prospects for enormous wealth and economic power were fulfilled. The social ramifications of this advent of industrial production were also to create friction and unrest for much of the century.

When water or steam became the basic source of power, the modern factory was born. Production could no longer be scattered through the homes of the community, for it was now essential that the workers be near the energy source, that is, the water wheel or the engine. Managers were enabled to organize the work more effectively, taking advantage of the basic idea of the division of labor. Larger machines proved more productive than smaller ones; consequently, the movement toward large factory units was swift. While production soared, costs also increased. The entrepreneur now had to provide for a large building as well as expensive machinery. These items were so costly that he felt impelled to introduce all possible economies while engaging in a vigorous search for ever new markets. The Napoleonic Wars had an enormous impact on English industry. European markets were legally restricted through the Continental System, though this proved only partially effective. The demands of the war itself to supply England's forces and those of her allies were a particular stimulus to production. Of special importance was the English role as a supplier of finished goods to the Spanish colonies in Central and South America. This market was so lucrative that England was loath to surrender it after Napoleon had fallen and the Continent was again open. To compete in all these markets, however, required that tariffs be at least moderate, and so England became the great spokesman for lowered tariffs. Confident of her ability to produce cheaper and better products through her head start in industrializing, she embarked on a program of free trade and tried to encourage others to follow.

In the new productive system, sources of coal and iron were of crucial importance. England had deposits of both in relative abundance besides an excellent system of water transportation so that they could be readily brought together. Coal and iron located in reasonable proximity came to be recognized as basic to industrial development. Where they existed but could not be brought together through cheap water transportation, the process of industrialization was delayed until the railroad appeared. Both Russia and Germany are examples of this latter circumstance, and it is interesting that the development of rail transport was essential to early industrial development in some areas but barely incidental in others. In addition to bringing raw materials together, the railroad was often instrumental in providing access to larger markets, thereby stimulating growth. It was also a consumer itself, requiring rails, locomotives and rail cars in increasing numbers.

The steam engine came to be recognized as central to industrial development. With the recognition that coal and coke were more effective as power sources than charcoal, coal mining became a basic industry, and with steam engines, deeper shafts could be sunk to exploit deeper seams. At the same time, the use of coal and steam power in the smelting and refining process made it possible to expand iron production, so that the increase in both of these basic products powered early industrial growth.

Another essential element in the industrial revolution was the availability of capital. The new business ventures and techniques were often highly experimental and, by the standards of the day, extremely costly. In general, the money as well as the leadership came from the growing middle class. Once the nature of industrial development became fairly clear, a number of governments sponsored investment banks, making capital available to begin specific industrial projects. Occasionally, one man would have enough money to finance a manufacturing venture; but more often a number of prominent businessmen pooled resources and formed a corporation, which then was able to attract the aid of banks and government. Once a number of areas were industrialized, opportunistic business leaders sought out less "advanced" areas as markets and as places for investment, if they should appear on the threshold of industrial development. As well as capital, the middle class provided talent and intellectual leadership in Europe's expanding economies. Success in a competitive setting spurred on this class, which had always resented its relative lack of social acceptability among the aristocracy. It eagerly showed its ingenuity as those above it revealed insecurity. Indeed, wealth could no longer be reliably measured in land. The industrial middle class was dynamic and, providing ability in abundance, its ranks were continuously being replenished from below. This was a middle class quite distinct from those which the traditional patterns of commerce had produced. These men of business, leaders of industry, were not bankers or money lenders, nor were they traders who extracted a livelihood from the exchange of goods and money or their transportation. Their virtue was that they "made" things; they took raw products and "created" items of considerable utility, and in doing so, they added notably to the standard of living. This vibrant and growing element of the population enshrined competition and believed itself the real source of ability. It had, however, appeared in the midst of peoples where the remnants of a medieval, class-structured society, though grossly moribund, had managed to defeat Napoleon and worked to subvert ideas like the Rights of Man. It is little wonder that traditional aristocrats were disturbed by these people whom they did not understand. To aristocrats on the Continent the middle class was more often thought of (with apprehension) in terms of the difficulties of Louis XVI or of the government of the Directory. Later, journalists, bureaucrats, and professional men came also to mind, but the industrialist was not quite the same.

As mentioned earlier, the combination of factors which assured the early industrial development of England was also present in other areas, though to a lesser degree. Although there were several attempts simply to duplicate what England had done, the over-all trend toward industrialism was more pronounced than the borrowing from English experience. Belgium was especially advanced, with northern France close behind. Silesia had long been known as an industrial area; Bohemia and Saxony were also major centers of production which became more prominent late in the nineteenth century. Among new industrial complexes, the Ruhr became especially important. By the 1870s most of Europe's major cities had taken on an industrial function, and cities as disparate as Toulouse and Budapest were familiar both with the problems of the factory worker and the factory owner. This development was to continue in the twentieth century and would ultimately result in an almost total reshaping of society as its ramifications in many fields, such as communications and sanitation, made Europe—and much of the planet—a different place in which to live.

As industrial development occurred at differing paces, the more advanced areas tended to take advantage of those which had not yet developed their productive capacity. This is a major aspect of nineteenth-century imperialism and will be discussed later. Within Europe itself the same sort of relationship existed. Urban industrial areas viewed the agrarian countryside as retarded and as a source of cheap labor as well as a place to dump goods. Less opportunistic, however, were the natural markets and outlets which the vagaries of economic laws seemed to create. French economic interests involved her in two potentially huge markets, Germany and Italy. Until the 1860s when the German productive plant became significant, the French, along with the English, supplied a large portion of the German and Italian market. French finance played a major role in railroad construction in Germany, Italy, and elsewhere in Europe, and the relationship between such French economic activities in Central Europe and French foreign policy between 1840 and 1880 still merits more study by historians.

England's early industrialization owed a great deal to chance and circumstance. Her crucial inventions were less sophisticated than French products at the time and were the work of skilled artisans experimenting in their workshops. They reflect no great technical or scientific expertise, and English education, particularly technical education, lagged behind that of both France and Germany. England had nothing like Prussia's *Bergakademie* or the French *École Polytechnique;* nonetheless, her craftsmen wrought a technological revolution.

A striking illustration of English economic progress was the cotton industry. Both its raw materials and markets were mainly overseas, and slave labor and the backwardness of other areas were crucial to prosperity. In the interest of her own sales, England acted to reduce the industrial development of India. Her view, properly imperial, took in the whole of Europe as a potential and real market which she hoped to serve, aside from being active in other continents and satisfying her own home needs. For most of the nineteenth century no other European nation even remotely aspired to this goal which England assumed as a matter of course.

CHAPTER 9

Patterns of Trade and English Population Relocation

While Napoleon brooded on St. Helena, the patterns of European economic life, as we have seen, underwent a major adjustment. In the West an enlarged and growing middle class moved quickly to take advantage of its restored contact with English businessmen. The enthusiasm engendered by learning new techniques rapidly gave way to an insistence on government protection for their own production, resulting in tariff barriers to restrict the freer flow of goods. By now English industrial development was so significant that London had superseded Amsterdam as the banking center where the great banking houses were located or had major offices. High finance had attracted many Jewish families, the most prominent being the Rothschilds, who, like the funds they controlled, moved readily across borders wherever the vagaries of economic laws and opportunity seemed to beckon. On the Continent, new roads contributed significantly to the flow of goods, especially within national borders. Before the Revolution, highway construction in much of Europe had progressed at a very slow pace and in some areas the network left by the Romans still constituted the major arteries. With Napoleon vast projects of highway construction and improved port facilities were begun and well advanced before his defeat. These programs were continued and expanded as the century progressed. When railway construction became extensive in the decades after 1830, supplementing the highway network, the demand for transport required that both types of construction be continued, and later there occurred a resurgence of canal building. Thus with industrialization the communications network became more sophisticated, and the growth of both was apparent first in Western Europe and then in the East.

English businessmen found the opportunities in South and Central America particularly alluring. The English had such a significant commerce and their investments were so extensive in the Southern Hemisphere that a lessening of economic ties was out of the question. To them a restoration of Spanish authority was conceivable only if it failed to carry any rights to alter the economic pattern which had developed. This position of English commercial interests was very clear and its diplomatic implications will be noted later.

The New World had its own evolving patterns of trade and commerce which impinged on Europe's economy. The United States became a major industrial power during the century and ceased to exist in any sort of colonial status. In the Caribbean, France, England, and the United States were all political and economic rivals. The elimination of slavery had been an object in diplomacy since 1800, with Denmark providing much of the initiative. A major factor which temporarily affected England's competitive position adversely was her decision to abolish slavery. For example, the effect of emancipation in 1834 was to make Jamaican products, like sugar, more expensive on the open market than the products of slave-holding Cuba or Puerto Rico. This sort of obvious disadvantage, in fact, explains why Denmark lagged behind other major powers in freeing slaves in her Caribbean islands, an ironic point considering the diplomatic initiative provided by her monarchs.

Another aspect of England's overseas trade was her commerce with the Far East. Formerly conducted through chartered companies, like the East India Company, this trade gradually dwindled and by 1833 was turned over wholly to private traders, who enjoyed increases in the latter half of the century, following a resurgence of Dutch trade. The Netherlands East Indian empire had shown an interesting economic vitality after 1815, but by 1830 the net effect for Holland was an imbalance in receipts which the government unwisely attempted to correct by an unfair tax structure expected to raise most of the money from her southern (Belgian) provinces.

A new supplier of wheat appeared on the European scene after 1815. Russia began exporting wheat through the Dardanelles and, as the century progressed, was joined by Moldavia and Wallachia. By 1850 a formidable, competitive situation developed in the Black Sea basin over the wheat trade. Also the Ottoman Empire appeared as a vast and unexploited market, attracting both Russia and England and bringing a new interest and urgency to the Eastern Question. The patterns of economic competition created new problems for statesmen as the capacity to produce quantities of finished goods tempted advanced states to adopt virtually a colonial attitude toward their nonindustrialized neighbors.

An interesting illustration of this development occurred in the French trade with Central Europe. France exported to non-Austrian areas of the Confederation finished goods of a semiluxury nature— silks, woolens, wine, leather—while receiving raw materials such as cattle, coal, and wool, and she profited substantially in the exchange. With Sardinia she also had a high volume of trade with a favorable balance, and her trade with the Hanseatic port of Hamburg was substantial. Central Europe from Hamburg to Florence was an enormous market, tempting to outsiders, and the French competed here successfully. Her trade with Sardinia was so important that she could not help but share Sardinian hopes that Venetia and Lombardy might be freed from Austria to join Sardinia, thus resulting in a near tripling of French economic opportunity in nothern Italy. Austria deliberately concentrated on trying to satisfy her own needs and was an outsider so far as the basic German markets were concerned. In the decades after 1850, when Central Europe became more industrial, the pattern of trade with non-Germans became far more complex and was conducted on a basis of equality. France found her trade with the German states especially hampered after mid-century by German tariff policy. Political unity and strength accompanied economic independence, and the relationship between these elements is both important and intriguing.

The most basic economic development in Central Europe after 1815 was the formation and growth of the *Zollverein*, a massive customs union which had its origin in 1819. The previous year a policy of internal free trade had been adopted by Prussia. Deficits, poor harvests, and floods had brought depression conditions to Germany in the wake of 1815. While Prussia's government was reverting to some of the ideals of the *ancien régime* and becoming less liberal in its outlook on political questions, it heeded the advice of its economists, like Friedrich List (1789–1846), who were promoting the ideas of Adam Smith on the virtues of free trade. List was insisting that a customs union was essential to business growth and a united Germany. Internal restrictions had simply made Prussia a greater market for outsiders, and so in May of 1818 internal free trade on a broad basis came to Prussia. This provided an enormous stimulus to commerce within Prussia and was a body blow to smuggling. The success of the venture was so obvious that Prussia engaged in a steady effort to extend the system to other states of the Confederation, excluding Austria. Her success in this has been seen as a triumph in the long struggle of Prussia against Austria for ascendency in Germany and a crucial step in the unification of Germany.

This is, of course, an oversimplified view typifying many histories which assess a period mainly in terms of the author's knowledge of later developments. In such accounts the multiplicity of choice often becomes lost as the investigator follows threads or chains of events which he seeks to follow to a known conclusion. In Germany a growing middle class which had accepted the idea of a Prussian-oriented free trade area without Austria would not be expected as a class to oppose political unity with Prussia. True as this is, it is a partial view which does not explain why other political and economic patterns did not emerge. Why this particular combination?

Austria's economic policy was unenlightened, to say the least. High tariffs were expected to keep foreign goods out to satisfy her own producers and internal barriers prevented the efficient flow of products with the Empire. Doubly inefficient, Austrian economic development largely stagnated while she deliberately cut herself off from the economic life of the rest of the Confederation. There was no economic parallel to Metternich's aggressive efforts of political and domestic control in Central Europe. Metternich's view of European economic life was distinctly pre-1789 and reflected no justice to his years spent along the Rhine and in Brussels. Austria therefore was no economic competitor of Prussia and thought more in terms of protecting Viennese producers of luxury items from French and English competition.

So far as fiscal policy was concerned, Central Germany was virtually abandoned to Prussia by Austria. Some attempts were made to oppose the extension of Prussian influence but ultimately all failed. A scheme to unify Baden, Hesse-Darmstadt, Hesse-Cassel, Württemberg, Bavaria, and the Thuringian states in a rival customs union failed. This movement, led for a time by Baden and then by the Duke of Anhalt-Kothen, completely disintegrated by 1827 and in 1828 many of its smaller members had made commercial agreements with Prussia. Austria underrated the long-run danger to its position in Central Europe and gave inadequate support to attempts which the smaller German states made to remain outside the Prussian orbit. Their public denunciations of Prussian economic policy brought no strong Austrian help and eventually they all succumbed. An important and surprising asset for Prussia was her lack of geographic unity. As a result of her scattered domains, Prussia surrounded many of the small states and placed others at a serious disadvantage. Her territories in the West athwart the Rhine gave her additional leverage, which, in the absence of any effective Austrian policy, led to Prussian success. Through her economic policy she was continuing the process of amalgamation of small German states begun by Napoleon. In 1828, Württemberg and Bavaria were the core of a southern customs union which put the central German states in a difficult position. Some, the most important being Hesse-Darmstadt, came to terms with Prussia, but the remnant of old Saxony now erected a customs union of central and northern states which included Hanover, Brunswick, and the cities of Hamburg, Frankfurt, and Bremen. This effort also failed, and when Prussia came to terms with the southern (Bavaria-Württemberg) union in 1829, it was only a matter of time until non-Austrian Germany was following Prussian fiscal leadership. Prussia's aggressiveness and forward thinking in economic policies contrasts markedly with her otherwise conservative and unimaginative political leadership. The revolts of 1830 delayed somewhat the final economic unification, but in 1834 the last major German state, Saxony, adhered to the *Zollverein*, and by 1844 it was virtually complete. Within Germany the result of the customs union was similar to other attempts at free trade, an impressive increase in domestic trade and an all-important incentive to local entrepreneurial instincts. All segments within the union prospered from the association and all had a sense of autonomy, because each had its own special arrangement with Prussia. Thus some ego-serving aspects of particularism survived while increased commercial efficiency and greater prosperity made the arrangement appear especially worthwhile. A by-product of this development was the gradual appearance of a pro-Prussian bloc in the Diet whenever questions with commercial ramifications came up. Prussia's success in the economic sphere was so complete that Austria could count, at best, on seven votes out of the Diet's seventeen; but despite this obvious Prussian ascendency and despite the increased wealth occurring as a result of the *Zollverein*, Austria never seriously fought its development and never accepted opportunities to join. In the growth of German trade Austria was being left behind. By 1840 the Germany of 1815 had changed substantially. Another quarter century was to render much of it unrecognizable.

While Prussia was pursuing her aggressive and enlightened commercial diplomacy during the 1820s, the industrial revolution in England had produced social maladjustments which fueled demands for political reform. As earlier and elsewhere, the most energetic and vocal pleas for reform came from elements of the middle class who based their arguments largely on the idea that the system of representation in the House of Commons was antiquated. "Pocket" and "rotten" boroughs were elequently criticized and the worst examples given wide currency: Old Sarum's spokesman represented a green mound of land; Dunwich was now under the North Sea; Gatton had five voters, Malmesbury thirteen, and Orford twenty. No new boroughs had been added since the seventeenth century, and industrial development had intensified relocation of the expanding population. No adjustment in Parliament had recognized that Manchester, Leeds, and Birmingham were large cities contributing enormously to the nation's economic life. It was obvious that equality of representation did not exist despite the insistence in the Civil War that "every he that is a he in England" deserved a voice. Simple pleas for reform based on the idea of population reconcentration were rational arguments which, like *philosophe* logic in eighteenth-century France, could be used with equal validity by more than one class. In England of the 1820s, the cries for political reform did not come from the masses laboring at near subsistence levels in the new cities. Instead, it came from their employers, though the language of their protest proved hardly exclusive.

England's commercial classes had long had a voice in national policy-making and until the 1760s it could be argued that the interests of the middle class were adequately represented. The new industrial system, however, produced another variety of businessmen. These were not younger sons of the landed aristocracy but were often from an artisan background. A breed of "self-made men," they came to view affairs from the perspectives of their own particular industries. Like the commercial middle class, they were interested in harbor development, banking facilities, and tariff policy, but they differed in that they had no voice in government. When these industrial leaders began amassing wealth, it was clear that some device had to be found to give them the political voice they desired. Their wealth was not only highly regarded in itself but the trade of these new businessmen dovetailed with many of the interests of the old commercial aristocracy, thus winning their cause a number of influential allies.

As various formulas for reapportioning the House of Commons were being considered, little thought at first was given to the plight of the laboring population. If the cities of Manchester or Birmingham were important enough to merit more of a voice in Parliament, it was assumed that their spokesmen would be from the new managerial elite, a mere adjustment of the rotten borough system rather than its elimination. While the leaders of industry were trying to gain a place in the Commons, factory working and living conditions grew perceptibly worse. A smoke-laden atmosphere permeated the shack cities which had grown up surrounding the mills and a vicious exploitation of labor kept the workers in utter poverty. A particularly abhorrent feature of the new system was the extensive use of women and children. Women had always been part of the labor force but had rarely worked under such exploitative circumstances. Children were of special value in the costly mines, because they could crawl through smaller openings than adults and thus make possible a more effective tapping of the veins. Every new improvement in machinery progressively enhanced the position of the employers while the workers merely had to accept a greater level of malnutrition. Sporadic worker riots and destruction of machinery in themselves failed to deter the exploitative process. The system was not slavery, but the abundance of labor and the prospects of ever-increasing profits, as well as threat of a depression (as in 1825–26), made life for laborers extremely difficult.

CHAPTER 10

New Identities in the Demands for Social and Political Change

The industrial revolution spawned two important and interesting offspring, the liberal and the socialist. Both of these nineteenth-century creations were ideological positions and both gave to the language of an earlier era a new meaning.

The nineteenth-century English liberal became a stereotype, faithfully reproduced on the Continent wherever the industrial process flourished. Building, in both cases, on the Enlightenment, there were interesting differences in the evolution of liberal ideas. In England's case, the liberal saw his position in the context of concessions made by the monarchy in the seventeenth century and his own appearance as a new part of the middle class (really the bourgeoisie, ironically the middle class is too diverse and conglomerate to be regarded truly a class) meant that he had some natural allies within the existing struc-

120

ture. As he amassed economic strength, he could not be ignored; specifically, his cause would be taken up by the Whigs. Politically a child of John Locke, the liberal believed strongly that a major function of government was the protection of property and property rights and, naturally, that property owners had a special right to a voice in public affairs. In England the tradition of Parliamentary life was long established; it was simply a matter of finding a way in which this new element could be included in the existing political structure which by 1820 had long recognized the claims of property.

The economic ideas of the liberals were derived from the eighteenth-century writing of Adam Smith (1723–1790), which varied from the earlier mercantilistic doctrines current when English commercial groups were acquiring strength in Parliament. The emphasis was now on complete *laissez faire* and few government controls. Put rather simply, the businessman should have complete freedom in running his business, unchecked by artificial, moral, or government restrictions. The natural laws of economics were to determine the flow of goods and the fluctuations of market prices for both goods and labor. Government was, of course, to protect the property rights of the winners in the competitive free-for-all resulting in an increase in national productivity and wealth. Self-assertive and opportunistic, the English liberal never really doubted that he would be able to achieve his goals without challenging the concept of nationalism and was thus able to blend his objectives with the demands of patriotism. This was especially convenient where he was able to acquire outlets in the economic life of other nations without seriously embroiling his government. Occasionally, however (as in Latin America), his interests and those of the commercial aristocracy were so strong that government conduct of foreign policy was directly involved.

Continental liberals came close to the same position, though by a somewhat different route. Lacking a long tradition of parliamentary experience, popular assemblies and constitutional government were thought of in terms of the French Revolution, more specifically of the Jacobins. Such an association created special handicaps to these liberals struggling to win a voice in government affairs. A complication on the Continent was that in several areas of southern Europe the elements seeking liberal reform were the sort of commercial aristocracy which, in England, had long had the voice in government which the new industrialists were seeking to share. There was on the Continent less of a bifurcation between the new industrialist and the older commercial leaders, and the cry for liberal reform was much the same. As in England, the business community's striking success in amassing wealth forced the entrenched aristocracies ultimately to deal with it; its participation in government affairs corresponded closely to the progress of industrial development. The insistence on written statements of royal prerogatives sounded like the Revolution, although the intentions were more the slogans of the Enlightenment. Similarly, liberal economics were taken from Adam Smith and emphasized especially the idea of free trade within the state. They were much more oriented, for most of the century, to local and European patterns of trade than to global trade. Some were exceptions, especially the Dutch, but essentially the English faced little competition from other Europeans in non-European trade opportunities for the first two thirds of the century.

The liberals were relatively conservative so far as ideological innovation was concerned. They all leaned heavily on the past and came up with little that was new in terms of theory. Their borrowing was so pronounced that, in particular causes, it was easy for them to ally with other social elements. Their emphasis on freedom from the arbitrary authority of titled aristocrats and on constitutionalism meant that Jacobinlike agitators could join them in an emergency. Their interests seemed to be consistent with nationalism for much of the century, so that their economic power was available for struggles of unification and national independence. This aspect of their nature led them later in the century to promote economic and political imperialism in a narrower and more controlled fashion than England had previously tried. When religions were seen as hand in glove with nonliberal, authoritarian regimes, they branded the clerics as natural enemies and presented them as Voltaire had seen them, apostles of reaction and darkness in an age of progress and light. The liberal couched his basic ideas in terms of the general natural rights of man, thus making his position difficult for entrenched aristocrats to refute. This language, however, could not justify refusing further concessions when lower social groups became more restive. As in the French Revolution, an argument based on natural rights of all men could not last as a justification for what was essentially a middle group desiring concessions.

The other ideological by-product of industrialization, the socialist, was a very different sort of person, although he too had some roots in an earlier agrarian age. Socialism was imbued with a sense of humanitarianism as well as a broad perspective on society. Where the liberal wanted freedom for the producer, the socialist wanted fair treatment for those participating in the system. The concept of private property which the liberal held to be almost sacred, the socialist regarded as a cause of the most unspeakable injustice. A sense of Christian charity had been lost as well as the idea of human equality, and the problem seemed to be that machines were controlled without a sense of social responsibility. Although some critics approved of rioting against improved machinery which employed fewer workers and thus created more unemployment and although others promoted schemes involving essentially agrarian communities, most socialists believed the solution lay in assuring an equitable distribution of the profits. Early socialists, like Saint-Simon, and Fourier, put a premium on the logic of their arguments, believing that the governing groups would willingly alter the structure of industrial development with social and economic justice in mind. Thus they hoped for altruistic contributions to charity by industrial leaders; failing that, they wanted government regulation of industry and sponsorship of cooperatives. Because it was unnatural to expect a manager to pay higher wages than he had to, socialists finally concluded that the workers must become proprietors through communal ownership of the means of production. To the socialist, Adam Smith's virtually unfettered capitalism was resulting in a form of economic serfdom which made a mockery of England's official efforts to end slavery. Human beings were not receiving human justice.

Attacks on property were hardly new; much of socialism's vocabulary can be found in eighteenth-century France. Monasteries offered a concrete example of cooperative, collective production in the earlier agrarian society. When private property was criticized, it was usually as an oppressive hangover from feudalism. The language of protest launched against property owners and entrenched privilege was explicit. Jean Meslier, a priest who starved himself to death (in 1729 or 1733, the date of his death is uncertain), wrote that "all nobles should be hanged and strangled with the entrails of the priests" and urged "common ownership of property in every parish that you may all enjoy the earth and the fruits of your labor." Brissot in 1781 noted that in a state of nature all goods were common property and that the real thief was the rich man who by guile had sequestered more than his share. Under a system of private property all sorts of inequities occurred and Brissot penned the words which Proudhon made famous, "Property is theft!" These early attacks on property were all in the context of an agrarian society; after the 1820s the same language was employed to describe inequities resulting from machine production.

Adam Smith's *Wealth of Nations* had appeared in 1776 and exuded the rationalistic spirit of the Enlightenment. Freely motivated individuals naturally seeking personal gain were, through the working of the law of supply and demand, guided by an "invisible hand" in such a fashion that the outcome was a beneficial contribution to the general welfare. Written before mechanization had changed the face of England, this doctrine required very little alteration to serve the needs of the new entrepreneurs. Smith and his followers in the next generation are often loosely referred to as the "classical economists." The basic idea of freedom from government restraint, which they assume to be interference with the operation of natural economic laws such as supply and demand, runs through all their work.

The two names most closely associated with amplifying Smith are Thomas Malthus (1766–1834) and David Ricardo (1772–1823), writers who were mainly concerned with explaining the misery which accompanied growing industrialization, an unfortunate fact which all could see. In a somber deductive study entitled *Essay on the Principle of Population,* first published, appropriately, in 1789, Malthus suggested that the poverty was merely the price, in effect, of the system. The working of economic laws in human affairs was an aspect of natural population fluctuation which resulted in continually recurring competitive situations. Industrial misery was, then, a result of overpopulation among the lower classes who had not the will to practice self-restraint. Struggle and danger were everywhere, and in many forms. Population increases were putting too much strain on the food supply; therefore, natural checks on population growth had appeared—war, disease, and famine. Governments should not interfere, because if left unhindered, natural laws would arrive at a stabilization of population which would be appropriate to food supply. Malthus paid little attention to the idea of significant new sources of food or of dietary adjustments which would alter his calculations. He wanted to see the proper natural stabilization occur as soon as possible and his recommendation in the meantime was that lives of a high moral character would likely be less a prey to the ravages of poverty. The implication was of a grim sort of Calvinism. Success was justified, competition and struggle were justified, and poverty was justified. The conscience of the new businessman was eased, because it was right that he amass wealth and natural that others suffer malnutrition. Reason had explained why things were as they were and also why one should not hope for government intervention. A patronizing charity was about the best the poverty-stricken could hope for, but this was all the poor had ever had anyway.

Malthus' work carried enormous implications for English economic development, but his main perspective was on the broader topic of population growth. David Ricardo was an economist who wrote a number of searching studies. A remarkably successsful speculator, he lacked training in writing and exposition, and many of his works are so lacking in clarity that misunderstanding was virtually invited. An expert on money and taxation, he is most commonly regarded as first describing the "Iron Law of Wages." Here, because of the massive and continuous oversupply of labor, wages inexhorably sank to minimum, subsistence levels and the worker could expect no improvement in his lot through the normal progress of economic life. The struggle for survival was going on between various elements of society, and it was all natural. All in all, the range of Ricardo's economic wisdom was broad and many of his ideas were incorporated in Peel's economic reforms.

Additional work emphasizing *laissez faire* was carried on by a number of economists known as the Manchester School. These authors produced a host of studies which make tedious reading but which detail the workings of many aspects of England's growing industrialism. Free trade became a key objective of these economists who are best represented by Richard Cobden (1804–1865) and John Bright (1811–1889), optimistic reformers who were notably humanitarian.

While the apostles of *laissez faire* were analyzing English progress and poverty, Jeremy Bentham (1748–1832) was presenting another perspective on his age and its problems. Bentham was an interesting product of the Enlightenment who viewed problems from the perspective of personal liberty and happiness. In his statement of utilitarianism both of these basic concepts could be limited in the interests of specific groups. With a peculiarly English faith in the efficacy of representative institutions, he applied these perspectives to current social problems. Parliament should be composed of men of reason and learning who would be able to pass enlightened legislation assuring "the greatest happiness for the greatest number." He called for legislative reforms of all sort, beginning with Parliament itself. All questions were to be decided on the basis of pleasure, or utility, and he was sure that careful study would reveal a fund of specific data on which scientific decisions could be made. He had little praise and much criticism for natural law but strong enthusiasm for utility and legislation. Obviously an enlightened legislature, concerned with the general welfare, would not have allowed the human degradation surrounding the factories to continue unchecked. Special efforts were needed to ensure the happiness of workers, for Bentham saw society as a series of cooperating and relatively happy groups. While casting the legislator in the role of a wise adjudicator and shepherd who would labor to relieve distress, Bentham still had no specific doctrine for economic reform. He asked of a regulation not its origins nor philosophical bases, but merely that it work. Did it help more than it hampered? His ideas were an interesting amalgam of the French Enlightenment (esp., Helvétius) and faith in empirical data.

A group which accepted many but not all of the ideas of both the "classical economists" and the Benthamites were the "philosophical radicals," an intellectual elite whose most prominent figure was John Stuart Mill (1806–1873). His father, James Mill, shared the enthusiasm for Bentham which motivated most proponents for reform and did much to popularize and spread his ideas. With John Stuart Mill, however, Bentham's outlook seemed partially deficient and artificial, and he looked also to Coleridge for ideas. Although it was well and good to insist on popular voting and Parliamentary freedom, this did not assure the more important consideration, a legislative body of educated men. Further, John Stuart Mill was more oriented toward the plight of the industrial poor, finally coming to the position that justice really was not to be found through doctrines based on private property. Instead, the focus should be on the equitable distribution of the profits of industry. The radicals also disagreed with Malthus on the implications of population growth and were advanced enough in their thinking to argue that birth control would reverse the downward trend of wages. Individual freedom thus came, in English radical thinking, to be seen in terms of economic justice rather than simply as a political matter.

While the structure of English political life and practice was flexible enough that the new middle class could reasonably aspire to a voice in national affairs, on the Continent there was neither the tradition of political flexibility nor such an advanced middle class. Here the basic liberal goals were defined in the French Charter of 1814 and the Spanish Constitution of 1812. The Spanish Constitution had been declared null and void by Ferdinand VII when he returned to Madrid from France in 1814, but it existed as a memory of stated liberal objectives—a weakened monarchy possessing little more than a suspensive veto, a legislature indirectly elected by manhood suffrage which could not be dissolved by the king, the whole system resting ostensibly on the sovereignty of a people who constitutionally enjoyed freedom and equality. The French Charter was the only major liberal document in effect after 1815 and it represented a fusing of revolutionary tradition with the old Bourbon monarchy. This Charter "granted" by Louis XVIII was remarkably enlightened, considering the attitudes of revenge and ultrareaction held by the returning *émigrés,* including the King's brother. Frenchmen waged an active political life over the ambiguous provision for freedom of the press (a free press but laws restraining editorial excesses could be passed) and also debated the chambers' lack of power to introduce bills (a royal prerogative). The whole question of whether the crown possessed a veto was not mentioned in the Charter. Despite these limitations dividing Frenchmen, the Charter was still the most liberal basic document in use on the Continent.

In Central Europe liberal hopes rested very precariously on Article XIII of the Federal Act establishing the German Confederation. This article rather explicitly stated, "A constitution based on provincial estates will be established in all states of the Confederation." This was a simple declaratory statement which carried no compulsory provision and no time table. Members of the middle class in western Germany were especially heartened by what seemed to be an encouragement to adapt whatever local institutions had survived into representative bodies; but, other than the initial Article XIII, the Confederation itself did nothing to encourage the growth of constitutional practices within its borders. The lead was taken by a number of south German princes, especially in territories where French influence had been especially pronounced. First was the Grand Duke of Saxe-Weimar. In 1816 this ruler who had supported Goethe, among others, granted a constitution allowing complete freedom of the press and a popularly elected legislative body which could control taxes and demand redress of grievances. Even Russia's Alexander approved this document, and by 1820 the kings of Bavaria and Württemberg as well as the grand dukes of Baden and Hesse-Darmstadt also granted constitutions based on the French Charter of 1814. Considering the limited growth of liberalism in Central Europe, these were encouraging signs. Not quite so heartening was the situation in Prussia. Here Frederick William III had promised a national representative assembly in 1815 but wavered between the positions of various advisers. Some urged him to forget his promise, others declared he should copy the French Charter, and still others said he should approve a constitution based on provincial estates. Finally, between 1823 and 1829 provincial diets were set up with clear divisions between nobles, peasants, and burghers. There was vague talk of a later assembly at Berlin but the liberals became discouraged. In the West especially, where entrenched privilege had largely disappeared and trade was more brisk, there was special irritation at the crown thinking of the population in terms simply of nobles, peasants, and burghers. To compare the Prussian monarchy after 1815 with the French monarchy before 1789 is at least moderately appropriate. It should be noted that these modest gestures toward liberalism were made while Metternich was combatting the same ideas in Central Europe. Liberalism at least had made some small legal footholds within the Confederation, although one needs to remember that it was not yet the manufacturing elite whose voice and interests were finding their way into these basic documents of power.

IV

The Romantic Movement

CHAPTER 11

Romanticism Defined and Apparent in Politics and Diplomacy

As the Enlightenment reached its peak in the eighteenth century, a differing statement of man's nature and his world was being articulated by Jean-Jacques Rousseau (1712–1778). This theorist's natural man, essentially good with emotions which drove him to creative and nonrational actions, differed markedly from the man in nature which the ages before had loved to posit. Natural man had been imagined as rather helpless, responding mechanically to his primitive environment. An especially negative portrayal was that crude being whose life Hobbes had described as "solitary, poor, nasty, brutish, and short." In the world of the Enlightenment things had their proper place and the whole was exact and rational. As the carefully structured and classical world of enlightened despotism gave way to a chaotic social upheaval, surging outward from France,

131

so the new values called romantic became ascendant in much of Western and Central Europe. Romanticism dominated cultural life in Europe during much of the first half of the nineteenth century, and in some areas it lingered much longer. It affected nearly every social and cultural movement in the decades after 1815, giving to the nineteenth century much of its special claim to uniqueness. Although Rousseau was an important early figure in the movement, equally crucial was the impact of the Germanic storm and stress (*sturm und drang*) movement, a group of writers centered around Weimar between 1765 and 1785 who emphasized the emotional bases of human life and action. Both Schiller (1759–1805) and Goethe (1749–1832) were associated with this particular apogee in Weimar's cultural history, and the writings of both men were to be important in the particular direction taken by German national feeling. Thus while romantic action was seen on a wide scale during the French Revolution, the well-springs for similar values and action had been independently established in Central Europe.

Romanticism put great stress on one's uniqueness and struggle with the environment. An antirationalism rejected finitude and boundaries to human endeavor and emphasized one's purity of soul or strength of character. To identify in some mystic fashion with a spirit found in nature was also given the highest priority. To show emotion in public became common. (Especially appropriate were fainting spells for ladies of tender sensibilities.) The universe was seen as a bundle of passions with which humans strove for a sense of identity and emotional fulfillment. The heroic grandeur of the soul who succeeded in this quest set him even more apart from his fellows, and a sense of highly moral but lonely triumph became associated with rare accomplishment. Each person was a source of emotion and truth for himself, and the new movement deliberately opposed a view of the world which saw things as carefully structured and orderly. Ancient truths or lessons of history were often to be cast aside for judgments based on emotional reaction to current experience. Not only did people, like nature, have souls and spirits, but there was presumed to be such a thing as a spirit of the age which could be felt by one properly attuned to his environment. It was a period when institutions and authority were based on history and precedent, but leaders also sought desperately to prove their relevance in the vast array that was life. Many people found proper emotional company in various large collectives. The peace they sought was provided by a sense of identification with a nation, a church, or some group providing a meaningful destiny and an emotional fulfillment. Humanitarianism, socialism, nationalism, and Christianity all came to be colored and partially powered by this romantic movement.

In France during the Revolution there were numerous examples of romantic influence. Robespierre parroted Rousseau with remarkable success, but our attention is perhaps more appropriately directed to Marat or to other Jacobins during most of the National Convention. By this time a faith in "the people" had become far more than a rationalistic abstraction. They had become imbued with such merit and spiritual dignity that to succeed in debate, little more was necessary than to invoke their name. Liberty, equality, and fraternity became sacred and associated with "the people" in whose names the grossest forms of torture and murder were committed as revolution against the dynasty became one also against the conventions of legal and civilized practice. It was as though mankind was starting all over again and needed to reject the leadership and social values from the past. That France was at war with the rest of Europe merely emphasized the grandeur of the struggle and invested it with a special moral quality. One fought for "the people" and also for one's country, and the effort was not only worthwhile but glorious. In addition there were those who found their identity in The Revolution in the abstract. In these people, nationalism quickly became imperialism as the moral urge to carry the fruits of the Revolution to others was not to be denied. On a narrower plane, loyalty to one's club became a satisfying practical fashion in which to help "the people."

In the Continentwide upheaval between 1789 and 1815, changing sovereignties encouraged and introduced new attitudes. In many cases, however, new objects of loyalty did not emerge strong enough to replace those of the eighteenth century. Although there was an emotional character to the struggle against France, especially in Germany, this failed to create a fierce and defiant sense of independence. The briefness of the open war against Napoleon in Germany probably prevented the Liberation from being invested with very much emotional, heroic character. Romantic stories of the epic struggles of the Spanish and Russian peoples against Napoleon have been flamboyant, but a fundamentally altered sense of nationalism did not survive 1815.

Romantic action consisted of people moved by their own inner being to attempt identification with some outside element, an impulse which led, within the standards of the day, to both liberal and conservative conduct. Among the old ideals and symbols to which some romantics could adhere were those traditional institutions representing historic Europe—monarchy, church, and empire. The Empire, which had lasted over 1,000 years, was gone and nothing comparable was in its place. Monarchy, however, had survived and many noble dynasties were exacting loyalty and tribute from subjects who had exercised little choice in the matter. Although the aristocrats were objects of awe to many of their populace, they hardly provided the people with a vicarious existence. Within the noble ranks, however, a number found their sense of fulfillment in belonging to the group and labored to provide effective leadership. The Church had played a similar role for centuries, ministering to inner hungers and channeling actions to usually constructive ends. The Revolution had been seen as anti-Christian and its ultimate defeat thus appeared as a victory for Roman Catholicism. The Church attracted many romantic supporters, but a number were repelled by its detailed regulations.

New symbols mentioned earlier were liberty, equality, and fraternity. Romantics struggling for these ends were often opposed by others who were as sincerely imbued with respect for tradition and civilization. A believer in the Burkean defense of institutions could only have watched the fall of Louis XVI with alarm. The romantic reliance on emotional rather than intellectual guidance resulted in a glorification of struggle and of piety. Personal freedom was central to the search for meaning, and so movements that would attract romantic supporters had to appear particularly flexible. Many humanitarian groups working for "the people" simply provided an outlet for a host of dedicated altruists who would otherwise have been most frustrated.

A prominent example of conservative romantic thinking was the Holy Alliance. This agreement, eventually sanctioned by Europe's leading monarchs, showed a lack of faith in rationalistic or constitutional bases of power and indicated that, despite the experiences since 1789, there was still abundant faith in the idea of divine-right monarchy. The historical development of Europe was to be seen in the unfolding of God's will, and that Autocrat favored kings. There were too many different kinds of Christians to get further agreement, but this proved unnecessary. Each dynasty's legitimacy was decided to the satisfaction of the Great Powers, and where competing claims made judgment difficult, the delegates presumed God's grace was guiding them. In this union of politics and religion the Holy Alliance pledged the monarchs (Austria, Prussia, Russia, France) to cooperate with one another in bringing justice, peace, and Christian charity to their realms. Although Metternich used the agreement as an excuse for conservative repression within the boundaries of his neighbors, its origin stemmed clearly from the wave of romantic pietism which swept over Central and Eastern Europe after the turn of the century. That Alexander soberly believed in the document merely guaranteed that other statesmen were forced to consider it, and somewhat to his surprise Metternich found its practical role.

Another demonstration of romanticism taking the form of a conservative union of throne and altar was the reign of Charles X in France. This younger brother of Louis XVI had been far more militant in his opposition to the Revolution than his older brother, Louis XVIII. He had watched, as the next in line, while the Charter was issued and Louis made compromises with both the Revolution and its Napoleonic aftermath. As the Count of Artois, he took charge of the Ultra leadership and largely controlled policy after 1820. The champion of the old landed aristocracy, the Count had never personally accepted the legitimacy of the concessions to revolution made in the Charter. On February 13, 1820, his son, the Duke de Berri, was assassinated but the Duchess de Berri happened to be pregnant and gave her deceased husband a son, who was known for much of the century as the Count of Chambord (1820–1883), unsuccessful Bourbon pretender to the French throne. The public outcry against the murderous attempt to end the dynasty brought it support and the Ultras to power.

The period of the Restoration in France, the reigns of Louis XVIII and Charles X, has attracted relatively few scholars. The era has been overlooked as the Revolution and Napoleon have maintained an almost pathological hold on the imagination of historians. Our view of these monarchs and their ministers—Decazes, Richelieu, Villèle, and Polignac—is today little altered from that presented by liberal opinion in the 1830s. This lack of detached study typifies a situation also true of other portions of the century. The disruptive movements of revolution, liberalism, socialism, and nationalism (imperialism) have been so attractive to intellectuals that the study of conservative, right-wing positions in most of nineteenth-century Europe has been neglected. Historians have generally repeated the contemporary, middle-class, liberal interpretations of the conservatives rather than themselves pursuing depth studies. Hence the widely accepted perspective of the right wing as composed of mossback aristocrats with an entrenched interest in opposing "progress" persists. The most glaring example of this was Russia's Nicholas I, who has yet to receive justice from historians. Metternich began to fare better only in the 1920s. In this context Charles X has emerged as an unrealistic and narrow-minded representative of the worst features of the *ancien régime*. The despotism of the Enlightenment had been imbued with a sense of service and the best of the eighteenth-century rulers had been working monarchs, but there appeared little of this emphasis in Charles X. Instead he seemed dominated by the idea that the crown and the old aristocracy should be restored to their prerogatives enjoyed before 1789. From the liberal point of view, he seemed utterly unrealistic, and among the most disturbing features of his reign was the prominence given to the Roman Catholic clergy. His emphasis on the Church role in royal functions made the throne and altar appear extremely close. The restored Church under Napoleon had been carefully regulated but now it seemed to share the councils of power as the signs of an eerie medievalism were openly displayed. Obsequious ceremonies reminiscent of the *levées* of Louis XIV at Versailles were restored, and for the crowning of the sixty-seven-year-old King at Rhiems, special oil was used which was purported by some miracle to have survived since Clovis. A religious revival was prevalent in much of Europe and so some emphasis on the Church might have been acceptable, but Charles went entirely too far. For all that France had been through, he was too blunt and thoroughgoing in his alliance with the Church. He sponsored a law against sacrilege which was particularly offensive, and the death penalty for theft of sacred objects from a church as well as for profaning communion was simply tactless and too severe. There was no widespread need for such legislation. When the Jesuits illegally returned and began appearing in positions of prestige, even a number of the Ultraroyalists at last became critical of Charles.

While the King was steadily bringing the crown and clergy closer together, he was similarly alienating the middle class. At the same time he was aiding the development of a political myth, the Napoleonic Legend. In his determination to restore the crown to all its prerevolutionary prerogatives, he misinterpreted the extent to which Napoleon's rule had enjoyed public support. In dismissing over 150 Napoleonic generals, he underrated their public esteem and the pride with which many Frenchmen looked back on various phases of the Empire. The Legend had more of a basis than Charles' antiquated notion of true kingship. It rested on a body of factual data, Bonaparte's career, which received its first formulation at the hands of the fallen Emperor himself. His followers in the next generation had only to place his idealized version of the Empire beside the shallow pretentions and failures of the Restoration monarchs.

As noted earlier, Napoleon was careful that the episodes in his career were reported to his best advantage. While at St. Helena he reminisced and further embellished the truth with a view both to his reputation and the future possibilities of his son. Many events had passed with fleeting documentation, but in the leisure of his confinement in the South Atlantic, he produced detailed recollections and commentaries. In Europe some chancelleries and policies took on a highly conditional air as Napoleon's confinement was continually in mind. After his first departure to Elba a few scandalous sheets purporting to be confidential exposés of the Emperor found eager readers. When he proved how shallow the roots of Bourbon support were by casually brushing aside Louis XVIII's government merely by returning from Elba, the sensationalists went at once under cover. After his second abdication, there was no similar outpouring of anti-Napoleonic pamphlets by alleged former confidantes of the Emperor. He might return again; only his death would be an adequate guarantee that he could be publicly reviled with impunity. When he died on May 5 in 1821, the critics again hastened into print. Many rose in his defense and the air was filled with many intemperate versions of the imperial period. In France the Bourbons invited comparison between themselves and Napoleon in their Spanish campaign in 1823. Soldiers, however, knew the difference and so did the public at large. Napoleon fared so well in the comparison that episodes from the Empire were featured in plays which an increasingly sophisticated middle class patronized. Sporadic bursts of goodwill for the Empire flared in the late 1820s as Charles X became progressively less popular. It is impossible to say how pervasive this sentiment was, but there is no question that for many, Napoleon stood larger than life, an exciting and thrilling example of French superiority. That the record contained misrepresentations was beside the point; Bonaparte appeared as a brilliant leader for France. In an age of idealistic fervor the Emperor was seen as a heroic type, never truly understood by the peoples he sought to serve. His peers were presented as Caesar and Charlemagne, his figure assumed fully cosmic proportions. The true impact of the Legend will never be known but the election of Louis Napoleon to the presidency of France in 1848 is the compelling historic fact. The "how" and "why" of this is particularly debatable, but the fact remains that a man whose name was Napoleon struck a responsive chord at the polls. It was appropriate to an age of romanticism that the Emperor's figure cast such a shadow.

CHAPTER 12

Romanticism in Literature, Political Theory, Historical Writing, and Music

By 1800 literary vitality and maturity were widely evident in most of Europe and only barely related to any local political cohesion or independence. German and English literary activity were equally pronounced; advanced study may also be profitably pursued in the literature of such politically exploited lands as Italy and Poland. The pervasive nature of Romanticism found its way indiscriminately across political boundaries as well as into many aspects of life. The Enlightenment had been a brief but encompassing synthesis, a world view, comforting in its rationalistic assurances and imitative classicism. That it justified much of the prerevolutionary social organization helped to make believers in that structure more emphatically enlightened, so that as romanticism spread, the attitudes of the earlier period persisted, even as the romantic movement produced its own type of defenders of autocracy and reaction.

In Germany the ideas of Johann Gottfried von Herder (1744–1803) were particularly influential and breathed the spirit of the Enlightenment. Herder saw all mankind as having been divided into various groups through the influence of geography, with separate customs and language then developing naturally. As a consequence each group had its own special character, which was to be highly prized. There were no superior peoples and education would make clear to all the uniqueness or "national soul" of the various cultures. Herder wrote with great affection for humanity and for national independence. He opposed imperialism on the ground that for one nation to control another was unnatural and impinged on a people's basic character. The application of his perspectives to the European scene in the early nineteenth century is highly suggestive, although there are some practical problems. Just how different must groups be to remain politically separate, considering, for example, Italy, Switzerland, and Germany? Herder's cultural nationalism breathes the spirit of the Enlightenment but has aspects which readily found acceptance and survived in a romantic age.

Metternich could not be regarded as a literary figure but he expressed himself explicitly in eighteenth-century terms. Man was a creature of nature and natural law. Like man himself, his institutions and his society obeyed natural law and followed a cyclical pattern through infancy, youth, maturity, and old age. Evil results when the stabilizing moral precepts of religion and custom are disregarded. (To Metternich in 1820 the world was full of evil.) The specific causes of evil he ascribed to printing, gunpowder, discovery of the New World, and the Reformation. These were responsible for the problems of his day. These historic events had accelerated human knowledge faster than the growth of wisdom and produced a liberation of passion and error not appropriately counterbalanced by wisdom. He saw it appropriate that the Italians were in revolt; they were a people with great knowledge and intense passion. A casting aside of tradition coupled with an emphasis on equality had given to society an emotional basis, a sort of moral gangrene affecting the middle class, which selected constitutionalism as its rallying cry. Governments, he insisted, must strongly maintain stability and order and support religion while stamping out secret societies in the interest of the whole of civilized society. Many an old aristocrat shared such pre-1789 ideas and was little moved by any urge to accept new and romantic arguments for reactionary policies.

The transition from the Enlightenment to the romantic period is clearly seen in English literature, especially in poetry. The eighteenth century's classicism, with its balanced treatment of themes taken from Greece and Rome, had resulted in sterile, mechanical verse which reflected artificiality and neither instructed nor amused. The insights and dignity of Alexander Pope characterized a much earlier phase, when the main alternative was the democratic and vernacular-oriented Robert Burns. These were both worthy antecedents but the new breed of poets deliberately set themselves apart. In revolt against prior themes, in proper romantic fashion they wrote of how they found nature and themselves in it. The so-called Lake School was comprised of many prominent poets whose impact was profound. In William Wordsworth (1770–1850) the world of nature became worthy of the poet's central attention. The nature which he portrayed was not that of polished society nor of the Newtonian world order; it was rather the world of heaving oceans and floating clouds, of mountains, trees, and intricately beautiful flowers mirrored in still and glasslike ponds, and Wordsworth's descriptive language communicated both its awesome and fragile qualities. With Samuel Taylor Coleridge (1772–1834) the emphasis was on the personal imaginative power of the poet himself. By rigorous self-examination and brilliant recasting of the conventional use of language patterns, he probed for basic emotional truth. An intellectually facile person, he enhanced his inventive powers by use of such aids as opium and communicated his reactions in verse. Coleridge and Wordsworth were close associates, but the general characteristic of the Lake School was that its members wrote almost to the exclusion of other people or their problems. They were not motivated by political ideology or social objectives even though most held identifiable positions regarding the French Revolution and various issues in English politics. In Robert Southey's (1774–1843) work, so little interest in the reader is apparent that we have a rare example of romantic poetry which was turgid, abstract, and dull. Few writers have felt more emphatically free to write as one will than Percy Bysshe Shelley (1792–1822), whose themes dealt with freedom and equality. His friend, John Keats (1795–1821), was also a giant among those romantic poets whose power of language imagery and sensitivity to beauty were combined in a series of exquisite poems. Lord Byron (1788–1824) was justly well known in his day, but the circumstances of his life and death drew a disproportionate attention to his work, which was no more noteworthy than that of several others. The brilliance of English poetry in the decades before 1840 is extraordinary and her poets wrote with an awareness of their own uniqueness.

While a golden age for English poetry, it was also a period of vitality for the novel. Indeed, both Viscount René de Chateaubriand (1768–1848) and Madame de Staël (1766–1817) believed the novel had become the dominant literary form during this period. Madame de Staël was an incisive analyst of the cultural and political scene and carefully explained how the new writers were free of the strictures binding eighteenth-century authors. This was as apparent on the Continent as in England, but there were few ways in which the various novelists might be linked together in a group. Many, however, may be associated in their imaginative sense of the past, especially as developed in the historical novel. This device has been credited to Sir Walter Scott (1771–1832), who had a great sense of the past and viewed it with special reverence. He gave full rein to his attraction for the Middle Ages in *Ivanhoe* and the *Talisman.* In Italy, Alessandro Manzoni (1785–1873) wrote *The Betrothed (I Promessi Sposi)*, a brilliant historical novel which convincingly evoked the conditions of life in seventeenth-century Lombardy. A frankly romantic French writer who also illustrates the acceptance of the historical novel was the renowned Victor Hugo (1802–1885). His *Notre-Dame de Paris* was set in fifteenth-century Paris and was, in his language, a work of "imagination, caprice, and fantasy."

In France romanticism shared the general characteristic found elsewhere but was more avowedly political. Appropriate to a reign where church and altar were in close accord were the works of Bonald, Maistre, and Chateaubriand. The sheer emotional content of the Christian faith was emphatically pronounced in René de Chateaubriand's *Le Génie du Christianisme*. Here one finds no reasoned defense or exposition of dogma, but its "spirit"; God's being is here viewed as apparent in human events. Chateaubriand had an amazing career. He grew up in a fog-bound, eerie castle in Brittany before he embarked on a life which mingled exile and contact with the greatest men of his day (Washington, Napoleon, Louis XVIII, Alexander, Pius VII, Gregory XVI, Fox, Burke, Pitt, Capodistrias, Nelson, Bolívar, Mirabeau, and others). In his *Mémoires* he tells how he had camped in "Iroquois shelters and Arab tents, in the wigwams of the Hurons, amid the remains of Athens, Jerusalem, Memphis, Carthage, Grenada . . . after enduring poverty, hunger, thirst and exile, I have sat, as minister and ambassador, in a gold-laced coat . . . at the feasts of princes and princesses, only to relapse into indigence and to receive a taste of prison." He was a lonely wanderer who found true solace only in the mysteries of his Church. He was not a defender of divine-right monarchy, but believed in traditional monarchy combined with constitutional liberties, in effect, the Charter of 1814 with minor alterations. His writing emphasized the importance of historical development. God played his part in events, thus making the present closely bound up with the past. There was no denying the Revolution but its lessons must be incorporated into the continuing institutional structure. Not really an original thinker, Chateaubriand's particular formulation was uniquely relevant for France after 1814. Clearly a romantic and a practical man of the world, at the same time he was both Ultraroyalist and liberal. To a generation disturbed by revolution and regicide, he provided a comforting reassurance of Christianity's divine mystery.

Count Joseph de Maistre (1753–1821) was another aristocratic exile who found great value in the union of throne and altar. An absolutist, he would go back to the principles of the prerevolutionary period, when divine-right monarchy was properly functioning beside the hierarchical system of the Catholic Church. This was, to say the least, an idealized view of how things had been in eighteenth-century France, but a broad enough reference to include the reign of Louis XIV would make it at least understandable. The carefully structured society, in both its secular and religious aspects, would produce order, and for Maistre, the *émigré* from revolution and Napoleon, this was his main interest. A cooperating throne and altar such as Charles X seemed to be moving toward was what Maistre wanted. There could be no ascendency of one over the other; this would lead to either tyranny or anarchy. Though he died in 1821, his was very much the spirit of the reign of Charles X. Revolution to him meant regicide, the distintegration of order, and the outlawing of the Church. Such complete evil could only be the work of Satan.

The Viscount Louis de Bonald (1754–1840) was also a confirmed absolutist, though his writing was somewhat less original and more polemical. To Bonald, mankind required the control which a strong monarch and a strict church could provide. Otherwise man would be a depraved being and resort to such barbarisms as revolution. Like Edmund Burke, Bonald was much impressed with history and historic institutions. Both believed the Church and monarchy had real roots, but the Revolution appeared essentially rootless. Whereas Burke emphasized the near sacred character of institutions (those sole ties between the living, the dead, and the yet unborn), Bonald was particularly interested in language. He regarded speech as a gift from God, a divinely given basis for social cohesion and order. Language became the distinguishing mark of nationality, and as a good Frenchman, he concluded that the French had the most perfect language. French history included the blending of Roman, Gallic, and German blood; and of all the peoples of Europe, they were the most enlightened—except for the Jacobins in their midst. Christendom represented to Bonald a holy alliance; through the Church and autocratic states, peace and advances in civilization would be possible in Europe. Consequently, to Maistre and Bonald, 1815 seemed a high point in the triumph of God's will, wherein particular people could submerge their identities and find their true being in the romantic and historic entities of Christendom and monarchy.

Another French writer moved by romantic impulses was an abbot, Félicité Robert de Lamennais (1782–1854), who, like Bonald, Maistre, and Chateaubriand, strongly believed in the importance of Catholicism. He began as a defender of absolute monarchy, where the duty of a king is to promote religion, but as the 1820s wore on, he became less convinced of the propriety of the Church being so close to the crown and he turned aside an opportunity to wear a cardinal's hat. By 1830 he had modified his ideas considerably as was evident in his journal *L'Avenir,* where he presented his perspectives on various contemporary issues. He moved close to constitutional republicanism in his apprehensions that a corrupt monarchy might contaminate the Church. An eloquent Ultramontane spokesman, his democratic ideas were utterly condemned in 1832 by Gregory XVI in the encyclical *Mirari vos.* In Lamennais the Church produced a defender who was wholly romantic but who was capable of moving from a strongly autocratic position to one of republicanism, as the tides of change and experience made him continually ponder the proper relations of church and state, all the while defending an Ultramontane position.

This France of the Restoration which had its reactionary defenders also had its critics who viewed the system as a great tragedy borne by the French people. Among these was Marie Henri Beyle (1783–1842) who wrote under the name of Stendhal. In *The Charterhouse of Parma* and *The Red and the Black* he showed himself completely at odds with the official values of his age. He combined many elements in his indictments of the regime succeeding Napoleon. Stendhal presents the Emperor as bringing opportunity for all classes of mankind. He made it possible for men of ability to rise above any low station to which they may have been born. Careers *were* open to talent, and corporals *did* become marshals. Napoleon made possible a reshuffling of people and positions based on ability. One of Stendhal's problems, however, is that although he called for the equality and freedom of opportunity which would allow an individual to rise, he still retained an admiration for the neatly structured society of the Enlightenment. He admired velvet and elegance but overlooked the point that neither Napoleon nor Danton were very elegant. The society of the 1820s is scathingly criticized through its limitations on opportunity. Further, Stendhal's characters are corrupt and contemptible people, caught up in petty projects. The institutions and practices of the *ancien régime* resurrected after 1815 had resulted in artificiality. The salon, a device which had provided challenges for the minds of Voltaire and Turgot, had become turgid and utterly lacking in vitality or freshness. The stultifying pressures of the 1820s are so comprehensive that Stendhal saw no real hope in the future; there was no burning ideology to cling to. The problem was to discover how a sensitive person might survive with his integrity and amount to more than a mere flunkey in an age of mediocrity and reaction. Living before socialism's great appeal, Standhal's gaze went back to Napoleon, the man who had created so much opportunity. True justice had briefly been possible in human affairs; but, alas, the Emperor had fallen.

The impact of such writing for the Napoleonic Legend is obvious, but its importance goes deeper. Stendhal did not look ahead to a Bonapartist restoration and he really lacked faith in "the people," despite his agonized call for equality of opportunity. In *The Red and the Black* Stendhal presented society as broken into classes essentially at war with one another. Their friction was a playing out of political issues in an age when real, open, political competition was illegal. Thus society was stabilized through economic pressures and the normal political instincts appeared as personal ambition, hatred, and banditry. All of these motivated the central character in the novel, Julien Sorel, who acted like a strange blend of Lord Byron and Karl Marx. Stendhal wrote a political novel about an age when politics was really impossible. His voice was an agonized cry from a part of society which recognized opportunity under Napoleon but did not know what to do after the Empire's fall. Heroism and spontaneity are lost in the Restoration, where society cramped the human spirit. The case for merit versus rank was Stendhal's basic complaint and became a crucial problem for the whole century. Stendhal's picture of France after Napoleon was harshly drawn, yet there is much truth in his portrayals. His heroic figure who conquered through *will* and achieves *success* is quite different from the man of attainment, born to position and privilege. Stendhal wrote with little hope and a feeling of betrayal at the hands of history.

The nineteenth century was the age in which historical writing became a specialized discipline rather than a memoir, a chronicle, or an apologia. This development came to fruition, however, later in the century and occurred in large measure in spite of romanticism. Much of the history written between 1820 and 1845 bears unmistakable marks of the romantic movement. In the absence of fixed standards, historical writers followed their own whims and the age saw a flowering of highly imaginative presentations.

The credentials for history as a creative literary art were impressively established by Augustin Thierry (1795–1856), Jules Michelet (1798–1874), and Thomas Carlyle (1795–1881). Thierry was repelled by the formalism and dullness with which the Middle Ages had been presented and he determined to write colorful narratives which would attribute to people and events centuries past the intensity and passion of current affairs. His critical sense thus was responsible for his definition of what historical writing needed but was not so apparent in his dealing with source material. His basic contribution was his artistic ability to imagine the past and to record it vividly. In identifying with the ambitions and frustrations of his subjects, he made them seem more understandable, but unfortunately such involvement was a handicap in that he took sides mainly on an emotional basis. His best-known work, *The Conquest of England by the Normans,* demonstrates this shortcoming, but there is no better example of history as creative and artistic literature.

Jules Michelet shared some of the abilities and objectives of Thierry but was moved by far stronger passions. His history was often a blending of fact and myth, with an emphasis on colorful reproduction calculated to impress through its poetic impact and basic message. His most important works were a massive *History of France* to the death of Louis XI and a *History of the French Revolution.* No writer ever described "the people" caught up in the Revolution with more intensity and narrative power. He produced striking rhetorical flourishes to describe crucial events, overwhelming the reader with tales of heroism, suffering, and sacrifice. Exhibiting virtually no critical quality, the value of Michelet's writing is that on occasion his portraits ring true. His "people" during the Revolution do give us a sense of the meaning of social revolution. His descriptive prose in narrating group action provides a more accurate picture than if he had followed the more common practice and restricted his focus to the words and actions of specific leaders. In his setting of scenes within near cosmic perspectives, serious errors of fact crept in. His history is literary and emotional, peopled with both villains and heroes etched in bold relief. In his affection for France and "the people," he fashioned patriotic eulogies that were widely read and brought many to a love of both history and France. His unrestrained and romantic history thus served an admirable function in the practical unfolding of nineteenth-century French intellectual history.

Whereas Michelet's vision was focused on large masses of people, Thomas Carlyle was virtually incapable of seeing anything but particular persons. In true romantic fashion his eye was on the extraordinary person, the man of heroic stature, and his history constituted a number of biographies presented in rhetorical language. He never lost sight of how a situation appeared to those caught up in it and so his writing carried a sense of immediacy which many generations have found appealing. Carlyle was at his best in creating striking word portraits, but when dealing with social history, he made serious errors of analysis. Not only was he much interested in heroes, but he idolized them to such a degree that he often attributed to them qualities they may have lacked. Further, he tended to see mankind as composed of extremes, the leaders and the led. His history was peopled with heroes and villains. Men and leaders were not seen in the context of developments extending over generations. This was true of his history of the French Revolution, of his study of Cromwell, and of all his other major works. His ideas about great men were clearly stated in his *Heroes and Hero Worship* and are most interesting considering that in Frederick the Great and Napoleon Europe had just experienced two bona fide heroic types. To read Carlyle on Napoleon and then to reflect on Stendhal's presentation of the Emperor's importance is especially engaging. As in Michelet, the over-all merit of Carlyle makes his errors of fact and interpretation almost appear beside the point. After these two writers, no serious historian could fail to take into account either the perspective of group involvement and striving or the importance of biographical presentation. Both are important contributions of romanticism to the developing craft of historical study and will be later joined to rigorous standards of analysis and criticism.

In music the impact of romanticism was most pronounced. The late eighteenth century, known in music history as the classical period, had been an age of brilliance in harmonic composition. In the wake of Johann Sebastian Bach (1685–1750), the dominant figures were his six sons and Christoph von Gluck (1714–1787), Franz

Joseph Haydn (1732–1809), Wolfgang Amadeus Mozart (1756–1791) and the young Beethoven (1770–1827). The orchestra had developed to its modern form, and "sonata form" as a method of shaping symphonies, concertos, and sonatas had also been established. Acceptance of the piano as the chief keyboard instrument was of enormous importance for the opening of a new age. The piano was able to produce extensive variations in sound between loud and soft and was far more flexible in this regard than the harpsichord or clavichord. Its pedals also enhanced a player's ability to control sound. The piano developed in England became a particular favorite of romantic composers because it generally produced a more powerful tone than the alternative, the Viennese piano. Recognition of the artistic possibilities of the song as an art form had also just occurred, as well as the beginnings of true musicology. These were major developments in music history and legacies for the nineteenth century.

Romantic composers seized on the possibilities for greater flexibility that the piano especially had opened up. They became less interested in working within rigorously defined structural laws and more concerned with the creation of impressions through sound, of scene painting through composition. This gave to sound a new significance, making it all-important rather than merely a complement to structure and form. This development permeated the entire course of music history in the nineteenth century.

Ludwig van Beethoven was an extraordinary Viennese composer. The greatest composer of his age, and perhaps of any age, he represented a transition from classicism to romanticism. His early compositions (1792–1802) show the strong influence of Haydn and Mozart with their emphasis on grace, balance, and order. In his second period (1802–1815) he broke away from many accepted standards so that his music might better express his personal feelings. The classical emphasis on perfection of order and balance was all well and good, but he decided it should not limit the expression of personal emotions. As Beethoven's skill matured, his hearing began to fail; but, nonetheless, he produced a host of sonatas, symphonies, and quartettes which showed striking originality and individuality. In his last period (1815–1827) his output was somewhat less prolific but included some of his finest compositions. Then completely deaf, he composed works of extreme personal intensity which helped to establish the idea that music might properly express emotions rather than manipulate sound mechanically to produce ordered patterns.

Contemporaneous in Vienna but overshadowed by Beethoven was Franz Schubert (1797–1828), whose symphonies and quartettes stamped him as clearly romantic. Essentially a lyricist, he made important contributions to the song as a musical art form; his compositions tended to be lengthy but with absolutely regular measures, a holdover from the classical era. A shy and meticulous worker, he received little recognition in his lifetime.

Ludwig van Beethoven. (Courtesy of Historical Pictures Service, Chicago.)

Romanticism was especially pronounced in opera, where mythological characters were now unacceptable on stage and were replaced by legendary persons from chivalry or fantasy. The orchestra and the overture became integral parts of the production. Experimentation with instruments became common also, with a use of the picturesque and fantastic. In Italian opera the old emphasis on virtuosity and florid arias still survived but was subordinated to the plot line rather than dominating the entire work. Karl von Weber (1786–1826) really brought romanticism to opera and helped transfer the leadership in operatic production from Italy and France to Germany. He freed opera from restrictions of a fixed musical structure, thereby making considerable experimentation possible. Along with Louis Spohr (1784–1859) he helped to make melodramatic themes common. In Italian opera Gioacchino Rossini (1792–1868), Gaetano Donizetti (1797–1848), and Vincenzo Bellini (1801–1835) especially welcomed the new romantic freedoms. In French opera the first half of the nineteenth century was a golden age. The *opéra comique* used dialogue and put a premium on fanciful character, whereas French grand opera usually featured works on historical, tragic, or patriotic themes and were completely sung. Leading composers in this latter medium were Gasparo Spontini (1774–1851), M. L. Carlo Cherubini (1760–1842), Étienne Méhul (1763–1817), and Giacomo Meyerbeer (1791–1864). The extensive operatic experimentation following Weber contributed a sense of vitality and musical freedom which helped set the stage for the meteoric careers of Giuseppe Verdi (1813–1901) and Richard Wagner (1813–1883).

Romanticism in music extended through the rest of the century and is clearly apparent in the various nationalistic schools developing after 1865. By midcentury sheer romanticism dominated musical compositions and may be best seen in the works of Hector Berlioz (1803–1869), Felix Mendelssohn (1809–1847), Robert Schumann (1810–1856), and Frederick Chopin (1810–1849). Independence of style and personal warmth marked most serious music, with Germany becoming decidedly the most prominent of the nations through work at Leipzig, Vienna, Weimar, and Berlin. Piano playing as a specialty became widely popular in both intimate and elegant salon music and in the orchestral concert, and the symphonic poem began to replace the formal symphony. Full recognition of the song and the ballad as art forms of high rank now corresponded with a revival of choral music in both England and Germany.

The careers of Mendelssohn and Schumann both illustrated and helped secure the prominence of Germany in the realm of music. These two, along with Chopin, represent the height of romanticism in music. Mendelssohn came from a family of wealth and was quickly recognized as a musician of rare talent. All of his music had qualities of warmth and emotional freedom. He composed almost spontaneously and produced works in all forms except opera. He was also noted as a conductor and pianist, and in 1842, he established the

Leipzig Conservatory. A particularly prolific composer, concertos, trios, duets, overtures, songs, two oratorias, and five symphonies flowed rapidly from his pen. His was a romanticism emphasizing warmth and intensity rather than freedom in technique, which, compared with Schumann, was a bit conservative.

Robert Schumann came to music from the study of law and was especially attracted to the piano. His career had its frustrations. An injured finger ended an unusual promise as a pianist; as a director of opera both at Dresden and Dusseldorf he was unsuccessful; he similarly failed as a conductor. He did manage to found a music journal in 1837 but his forte was in composition. He wrote songs, symphonies, chamber music, and a vast repertoire for piano. A man of intense nervous energy, his music showed a disregard for traditional patterns or popular taste. His music had a freshness and a sort of nobility which connoted both independence and authority. His songs frequently had piano parts strikingly interwoven and were really ensembles. There were many other prominent German composers, theorists, and performers, including the so-called Leipzig Circle, but none were as well known as Schumann.

Although nationalistic schools developed later, passionate patriotism in music is no better represented than in the compositions of Chopin. Like many other Polish refugees in the 1830s, he found refuge in France and his talent made him welcome in Parisian society. Much less versatile than most other major figures in the history of music, he wrote essentially for only one medium, the piano. A fine pianist himself, he popularized piano playing and devised innovative pedal techniques which expanded the instrument's potential beyond what his predecessors had believed possible. He composed a few Polish songs and no orchestral works, but a veritable flood of sonatas, waltzes, polonaises, mazurkas, and nocturnes for the piano. These are all sentimental, moving pieces, showing great freedom in conception. Chopin's music is both personal and extremely patriotic and his style is so distinctive that virtually all his pieces are readily identifiable.

In orchestration the most important figure before Wagner was probably Hector Berlioz, whose romanticism was unmistakable but tinged with realism. Berlioz strongly believed that music could often present an idea which was impossible otherwise and that pieces which truly lasted did so mainly because of the music rather than the prose which might accompany it. Nonetheless he was a firm admirer of good literature and saw to it that in his own work he borrowed from the best, Goethe and Shakespeare. A rebel against prior symphonic restrictions, he experimented with grandiose orchestras. The vast scale of his productions won him acclaim as the greatest of all orchestrators, the sheer solidity and power of his music standing as his most prominent achievement.

Of the areas permeated by romanticism, music perhaps best illustrates its liberating sense of freedom and individuality. An unleashing of human energy and initiative had freed the imagination from the order and strictures of the Enlightenment view of the world and in all areas man's personal relationship to his environment was being freshly re-examined. Were objects in nature attracted or repelled by one another and was man merely another object? And what really was change and how did it come about? In the face of such uncertainties some men found solace in the institutions and wisdom of the ages; others found their identity in their drastic modification. Some found man at one with nature in a sort of mystical correspondence; others saw life as a heroic struggle in defiance. Taken altogether, an era of incomparable intellectual vitality had begun.

CHAPTER 13

Romanticism in Philosophy and Religion

Among the disciplines influenced by romanticism, none underwent a more basic or challenging reorientation than philosophy. As a segment in the history of philosophy, this period is characterized by a resurgence of philosophic idealism culminating in a sequence of thinkers whose work did for modern idealism what Plato's had in antiquity.

By the middle of the eighteenth century, philosophy had come under the domination of empiricism, with the ideas of Hobbes and Locke commanding great attention. In France Cartesian thought was similarly respected and contributed to the empirical and rationalistic base of the Enlightenment. Idealism as a philosophy was simply out of fashion; virtually its only creative proponent then was Bishop Berkeley (1685–1753), whose particular version found few

152

followers. Berkeley sought to relate human knowledge and experience, raising questions about how we know what we know and how we communicate with others. He explained experience and common experience through positing God acting in a volitional capacity. Berkeley came to a position of near denial of reality to the world of experience, which we know only through ideas placed in our mind by God. An honest God, however, plants accurate ideas; thus, the objective world is real. Though Berkeley's version of idealism was not widely accepted, philosophers appreciated his probing of the epistemological problem.

David Hume (1711–1776) was a penetrating thinker (as well as the author of a respected history of England) and may be regarded as producing the rationalistic critique of rationalism. The basic problem was still that of epistemology, and he began with the sensationalist psychology of Locke. Berkeley had accepted the idea that the self (which has experiences) had continuity. Hume took the position that there was no self which could be identified as anything other than agglomerations of sense data. This was Lockean with a vengeance. He then went on to examine how portions of our experiences appeared to be related and suggested that an idea such as causation arose from our own force of habit rather than as an object of real knowledge. Necessary connection between events simply cannot be proved. People act on the basis of hunches, expectations, and guesswork, but not on wisdom or knowledge. Indeed, we are unable to get real knowledge of the world, because for us mortals there is only data about which we make fuzzy assumptions. There is no other truth.

Such ideas as these of David Hume obviously destroyed the pretensions that concepts of natural law had scientific validity; he had lanced the heart of the whole Enlightenment. The rationalistic religion of deism was as weak as Berkeley's whole system, because God's existence could not be proved. Ironically, Hume seemed to destroy the grounds for certainty in rationalism by rationalistic reasoning. He was equally against nonrationalistic, religious, or authoritarian explanations; and an ironic major result of his writing was a stimulus to religious evangelicalism, more belief in absolute values, and the development of an elaborate metaphysical structure. Immanuel Kant (1724–1804) authored the first stage in the evolution of a new idealism and he first presented his ideas in terms of issues raised by Hume.

As a professor at the University of Konigsberg in East Prussia, Immanuel Kant had been living a life of spartan austerity and regularity while teaching what he believed was true information in the natural sciences. Unlike many contemporaries, he at once saw Hume's implied challenge. Although scholars have since questioned just how much Kant really knew of Hume, he declared that Hume had awakened him from his "dogmatic slumbers" and he set for

Immanuel Kant. (Courtesy of Historical Pictures Service, Chicago.)

himself the task of formulating a response. The result was Kant's most important work, *The Critique of Pure Reason,* as well as a number of derivative studies in which he employed an involved, specialized vocabulary in a closely reasoned attempt to reconstruct (or to explain) the world of certainty which Hume had cast in doubt.

In a careful consideration of perception and perceptual experience, Kant concluded that there was more to experience than a mere stringing together of sense data. There were at least four extra elements and he identified these as the concepts of space, time, substance and causation. These were not simply a matter of habit, but rather were *a priori,* existing *aside from the data* as devices or principles by which our mind orders or interprets the data. *A priori* concepts, he decided, existed *at the beginning* of experience as we comprehend it. A mind, or self, or ego, is also a reality outside of experience; it must be to grasp the data or experience and order it in accord with the previously mentioned *a priori* principles. Thus laws in nature, the regularities, are products of our mind, so far as we know.

Having found at least five elements outside the customary world of sense data, Kant then postulated the existence of another whole world beyond the world of phenomena which we experience. Because the five he had isolated were all of the character of mind or idea, he suggested that this extra world was of a nonexperiential character, which he called "noumenal" or transcendental. In this noumenal (reality beyond experience) world there are "things-in-themselves," which are the true realities. It is these which impose the sense data upon us for our minds to grasp and organize.

This bare sketch hardly does justice to Kant's incisive logic, but perhaps enough has been given to make intelligible a number of important inferences which he was able to draw. First of all, Kant has agreed with much of Hume's position, especially with the idea that we cannot *know* reality itself because it is beyond our comprehension. To Hume's statement that he could find no self, but only more sense data, Kant is also in agreement, although he refines the position considerably. It is to be noted that time, space, substance, and causation are attributes only of *our* mind and *may or may not* also apply to the rest of the noumenal world. The noumenal mind exists to contain the law which it forces on the data it perceives. This aspect of the noumenal world is definite and may provide clues to other aspects of *that other true* world. An example of another characteristic of the noumenal world may *perhaps* be found in man's moral life, since ethical demands cannot be derived from study of experience by itself. Going further, Kant made it *reasonable to have faith* in a God or a religious system. At the same time he noted that so far as understanding experience was concerned, our minds only perceive it in terms of time, space, substance, and causation; therefore, for us experience will always appear with these characteristics or be explainable in these terms. In short, Kant had erected a limited grounds for certainty in science. Experience and its order may be studied with confidence though we should be aware that what is studied is a very limited facet of truth. Within these limitations, however, we should study and probe as carefully as we can. Kant had rescued science from Hume while making religion respectable for intellectuals.

A proper study of Immanuel Kant would require an intensive examination of his work in all its convolutions and nuances. There were innumerable major problems in the history of philosophy for which he suggested at least partial solutions. For example, there was the ethical problem of personal freedom in a world which appeared to be strongly deterministic. Within his structure, Kant attempted to resolve this issue. Determinism, or events occurring in a causally related sequence, obtained in the world of phenomena. The "ought," or ethical demand, is grasped intuitively, not from any experience but as an aspect of the noumenal world. In the true world of "things-in-themselves," there is freedom (and goodness and justice and beauty, and so on), whereas causation and determinism are only in our ordering of experience. When Kant attributed both causation and freedom to the noumenal category, he had transferred the basic ethical problem to the nonmaterial world. Indeed it has suggested to critics that his whole noumenal world was merely a convenient place for anything not otherwise understood. Kant's analyses were by no means universally accepted, but he had opened the door to a restatement of idealism and offered a stiff challenge for those who would reject it. As it developed, several major idealists now appeared and the study of metaphysics blossomed. Kant also was concerned about the practical world and, as well as "saving" science and making religious faith "reasonable," he worked out a scheme for universal peace based on regional federalisms.

The first important modification of Kant's ideas occurred at the hands of an avowed follower, Gottlieb Johann Fichte (1762–1814), who produced a thoroughgoing idealism. In his own person Fichte is an admirable example of the working of intellectual history. He wrestled with the most abstract and technical problems of philosophy and made major contributions at that level. He was able, as well, to put his ideas into practical form and then to influence others to act in accord with his conclusions. As the first rector of the University of Berlin when it was founded in 1810, he promoted a fervent German nationalism which called for union under Prussia, leading to "freedom," that is, the expulsion of Napoleon. Thought thus became action, so that, aside from his position as a philosopher,

Fichte had imposing credentials as a German patriot, educator, and writer.

Fichte's philosophy may be found in the *Wissenschaftslehre* (science of knowledge), a bold, imaginative study which encompassed transitions of thought which Kant would probably have disputed. Less intellectually satisfying than Kant and more open to criticism, his intent was to demonstrate the existence of a basic principle which would explain everything. This he took to be the real goal of philosophy and he believed that consciousness was the principle he sought. Dropping Kant's differentiation between the world of experience and the transcendent, noumenal world, Fichte suggested that it was all transcendent and unified, a vast transcendent consciousness, a sort of ultimate mind or thinker. The only alternative explanation he saw was materialism, which he rejected as unable to explain consciousness and not doing justice to man's ethical nature. In Fichte's view the existence of matter was no problem. The material world he presented as merely a bit of consciousness which had become self-conscious. Experience was merely the great transcendental subject (ego) experiencing a partial self-awareness. Because this self-awareness was generated by the subject itself, subject and object are identified. The whole world of objects (nonego) became illusory, composed of diverse, complex thought patterns all derived from the active nature of consciousness. The differentiation of subject and object were necessary for thought but Fichte maintained that, in fact, the subject had created the object; or, to put it into more abstract language, the ego had postulated the nonego. Progressive and involved differentiation might then occur but it would all come from the transcendental ego. As to why this occurred, Fichte weakly explained that activity was part of the ego's nature. Creation for creation's sake, activity or play for its own sake was his answer. Thus the universe was simply activity or enjoyment in the mind of the transcendental ego (or absolute). Evil became merely an obstacle to be overcome to make the activity more rewarding and real. Like sand traps on a golf course, evil was really good from the ego's standpoint. This hardly did justice to the problem of evil, but Fichte could insist that it indicated the essential goodness of the ego and that immortal man lived in a moral universe, which was no mean achievement. Obviously the ego could be thought of as God, a creative and moral power, but Fichte was clear that this God was not to be thought of as a personal being. The possibilities for religious interpretation were so tempting and led to such unorthodox (pantheistic, atheistic) positions that Fichte aroused the hostility of the theologians at Jena, where he taught before moving to Berlin.

Because to Fichte each person was a creative self-expression of the absolute, each had an important place and function in the universe which was properly realized when an individual found his proper vocation. Society's outstanding people clearly were among those who had found their proper niche. This aspect of philosophy made a major impact in a romantic culture which avidly seized on the importance of "men of destiny" and such a personal identification with nature. It fed fuel to the demands of artists, writers, and scientists for more personal freedom, and Fichte was emphatic that the major task of the state was the protection of freedom.

Following Kant and Fichte a wave of idealism spread through the philosophy faculties in German universities. A number of intermediary figures worked with various aspects of the position, but perhaps Friedrich W. J. von Schelling (1775–1854) may be regarded as the most significant of this group. An associate of both Fichte and Hegel at Jena, he went through a number of phases, never formulating a settled and complete position. He worked on the dialectical process by which various categories were developed by the absolute, especially being concerned with the differences in its sense qualities. He amplified the relevance of it all for the romantic movement, especially noting the importance of the artist. Through art and morality he perceived that laws clearly existed which could not be arbitrarily violated. For all his insights, Schelling remained a suggestive and brilliant transitional figure.

Idealism in philosophy achieved its high point with Georg Wilhelm Friedrich Hegel (1770–1831), a professor at Jena who, like Fichte, went on to Berlin. The main elements in Hegel's philosophy may be found in his *Phenomenology of Mind,* in *The Logic,* and in the *Philosophy of History.* As a professor he expounded his ideas to hordes of students in courses which, for most, were memorable experiences. Hegel was an energetic and driving person with passionately held ideas. Along with Schelling, he had been a republican at Jena and his radicalism led him to a special lifetime concern for freedom. Like Kant, his writing was especially difficult but crucially important. Hegel's was to be the supreme modern statement of idealism, spawning many followers as well as some vigorous intellectual countertrends.

In what at first appeared as a vigorous clearing away of useless ideas, he rejected outright Kant's noumenal world with its "things-in-themselves." *Experience* to him *was the sole reality* and no grounds whatever existed to postulate another whole world of nonexperience, a procedure which ridiculously tried to explain a problem by doubling it. Hegel denied a distinction between experienc*ing* and the experienc*ed*, maintaining that some experience holds together and makes what appears to be a self, whereas other elements

Georg Wilhelm Friedrich Hegel. (Courtesy of Historical Pictures Service, Chicago.)

hold together as objects or as not-self. Interestingly, he somewhat agreed at this point with Hume, who could not find the "I." Hegel found it but it was only sense data as Hume had said it was. In the totality of experience which he called the absolute he found no inner qualitative distinctions but rather a vast organic arrangement, a state of flux with changing forms and points of cohesion. As a cohesive clustering within this absolute, each person by analyzing himself might discover an insight into basic reality and the nature of the absolute. By analyzing the mind, Hegel then found a host of categories existing in dialectical relationships with one another. To Hegel, mind itself was merely a principle of order from a particular point of view within experience. The absolute itself was timeless and eternally conscious. From its viewpoint all men are eternally present, though our existence is finite. The absolute alone possesses a timeless quality as past and future are indistinguishable. Theologians were attracted to this idea of an absolute being a timeless eternal but were disturbed by the idea that real foreknowledge on the part of the absolute meant an absence of true freedom, thus determinism and a negation of moral choice. Evil to Hegel was a matter of appearance from our finite point of view. He believed the whole universe was good.

To understand all experience he then examined its organization, which for him was mind. For Hegel mind did not impose order on experience, as Kant suggested, but rather *was the order in experience* and he identified a number of levels or degrees of order (or mind). The first level he called the *subjective* stage (theoretical mind), where subject is differentiated from object. At this point a self is not aware of other selves. With the recognition of other selves and of order that is supraindividual, an *objective* stage (practical mind) has been reached. Here selves grow as parts of social groups and we might study the principles of intrasubjective order or the rise of law and morality. The self-conscious individual here has become rational. At the third stage (free mind) of complete cooperation and freedom, the self is in complete accord with its environment and has limited its wants. Persons will the moral law and find freedom in morality. Thus far, Hegel has described how beings see the universe and not necessarily how it is. In the achievement of free mind, an idyllic condition of happiness and peace would exist, for in effect objective mind would have encompassed all persons. There yet remained an additional stage called absolute mind or the absolute idea, an awareness of the total formal order of all that exists, a condition reached by thought and only on very rare occasions. Hegel believed he had had such a view of the absolute. At this level subject and object differentiation disappeared, thought and will being in complete union. There is no higher order of thought, the whole universe is seen as real, good, and rational.

In absolute mind (no subject-object distinction) he found three stages. In art the mind has created its own object thus making subject-object differentiation disappear. In religion the idea that the objective world results from a mind like our own tends to lessen the subject-object friction. He regarded this as a myth but it still made the subject more in harmony with the object. In the third stage of philosophy the whole structure of the objective world is seen as an expansion of the structure of the philosopher's mind; thus the absolute has become truly aware of itself.

In his explanation of the various stages of order, or mind, he presented a situation where from the earliest (subject-object differentiation) stage there existed friction and a sense of opposition. As the area of order, or mind, expanded, friction declined and freedom expanded. Most people live at levels somewhere between the first and second stage; and so, the world for them is full of competition, a struggle with both other men and the environment. In their limited understanding, virtues will be made of struggle and strife, whereas the premium should really be on cooperation. A nation is a large area of organization and cooperation, a higher order of mind, and hence freedom, than a region and so is more deserving of our loyalty. This message had an obvious potential for the development of German nationalism under Prussian hegemony.

In *The Logic,* especially, Hegel analyzed the absolute idea in terms of categories of thought. This sober and abstract work has attracted considerable controversy. He saw the formal construction of the absolute as being composed of interlocking ideas, each implying others. By starting with any basic idea, Hegel believed that by a dialectical process all the other categories might be deduced. In a somewhat Thomistic fashion he erected a complex but complete intellectual structure. By illustration Hegel suggested beginning with the most abstract (simplest) idea, *being* (thesis). Merely by definition and recognition it is separated from *nonbeing,* (antithesis). Because these are opposite, there is friction or struggle which produces a synthesis containing qualities of both the initial protagonists but existing on a higher level. In this case, *becoming* is the synthesis and is itself a new thesis generating another antithesis, more friction, and another synthesis. By a tortuous and complex route Hegel leads his readers to an idea called *infinite of measure,* which is another way of saying *concrete being,* and we have had a tour of all the categories.

Hegel's debt to Fichte is clear; the formal structure for a segment of Marxism is obviously outlined. *The Logic* was popular for over two decades, and many people enthusiastically accepted the heady idea that the world was full of blind opposing forces. People and things in conflict became understandable, especially when the dimensions of the struggle were large. World historical individuals were essential to break up smaller units of order to create larger units of order and freedom. Great men with inflated egos were necessary for the working out of the absolute idea. The evil instincts of particular persons thus fit into a total picture and were really good. The example of Napoleon destroying the Holy Roman Empire to make possible more enlightened government in Central Europe appeared as an obvious contemporary vindication of Hegel's argument, and a later generation would excuse Bismarck's international immorality on the same grounds.

Hegel applied his insights to the course of human history in his

Philosophy of History. As in much of his other writing, things occur usually in three stages or steps and the entire narrative is absorbing. He naturally saw history as a dialectical process and he was especially interested in freedom's progress. This he saw as having three stages. First, in Oriental history *one* person was free, the despot. Later at the time of Greece and Rome, *some* were free, the citizen class which possessed slaves. Finally, in what Hegel calls Christian Germany, *all* were free, man as man was free. In terms of citizenship, freedom arose from obedience to the law because law was always an expression of the general will, even if it were the decree of a tyrant. Our duty, as well as our best interest, is to obey the law.

Although Hegel had an enormous following, he stimulated both sarcasm and criticism over the next century. Many complained that his ideas contributed to a resurgence of Germanic Prussian nationalism; but on sober philosophic grounds, his entire structure had three basic flaws, which of course made possible more particular criticisms of details in his system. Writers have insisted that there was more to becoming than being and nonbeing and that Hegel was simply wrong in this basic triangular relationship. If sustained, this simple criticism would jettison *The Logic.* Another drawback was that Hegel's subject-object distinction omitted the mental act and the role of expectation. The mind is a thing apart from experience; the knower is not the same as the known. This objection may also apply to pragmatism, positivism, the new realism, and Hume. Hegel would not have accepted these points as effective criticisms. A final objection (though more an observation) is one made of all idealists; they argue from the egocentric predicament. They start by saying human knowledge is limited to what we apprehend from experience and so all else is denied while they analyze their reactions to the experience, hunting for fundamental truth. This procedure is inevitably an exercise in introspection but is nearly irrefutable logically.

In Hegel's wake were many idealists who were less rigorous than he but similarly moved by a grandiose view of the universe. Many nonidealists condescendingly brushed aside the import of the whole school, charging them with overactive imaginations and inadequate attention to the world of solid data. Hegelian studies have tended to flourish in Central Europe and never received comparable attention in Anglo-Saxon areas.

While public attention was largely on Hegel, another seminal thinker was espousing a different variation of idealism. Arthur Schopenhauer (1788–1860) was a younger contemporary of Hegel who was bold enough to schedule his lectures at Berlin at the same hour as Hegel's. Such youthful arrogance was rewarded by few students and loss of his position, making an essentially skeptical and pessimistic outlook on the world turn even more sour. A man of especially strong sex drives, he hated women and maintained his venomous attitudes to the end of his life. In his last twenty years he

Arthur Schopenhauer. (Courtesy of Historical Pictures Service, Chicago.)

finally achieved the recognition he felt he deserved and then presided at a salon of some distinction.

His most important work was *The World as Will and Idea,* which in classic idealistic fashion argued from the egocentric predicament and presented matter as an aspect of mind or spirit. Otherwise, it was distinctly and deliberately non-Hegelian. Schopenhauer represented another line of development from Kant, whose things-in-themselves were reasserted as basic in *The World as Will and Idea*. Much impressed by passion, energy, and drive, Schopenhauer posited that this was the nature of the reality beyond experience. Things-in-themselves were of the nature of *will*. This will created in us a world of ideas (or forms) which may be divided into two types: those of particular objects and a more general and basic category. The latter has a nearly universal character (like Plato's Ideas) and is seen in such things as natural law and species. A kind of blind energy which is necessarily active continually creates and re-creates the forms which humans perceive. Seeing only these, our rational instincts drive us to formulate explanations based on these representations. The probabilities for error were vast but Schopenhauer was convinced that his view was sound. He saw himself as building directly on the work of Kant but also reasserting the importance of Berkeley.

In our knowledge of the world, he insisted that it all rests on our own individual will. The world exists as a matter of our consciousness. *The world is our will and our idea.* We *will* the ideas, and what we call knowledge is merely a matter of generalizations about these ideas. Reason creates speech and although scientific study is possible, it does not probe ultimate reality. Much of Schopenhauer was frankly speculative, but he noted that this was a proper function of philosophy, especially because he was disputing Hegel's attempt through rigorous logical thought to produce knowledge of reality.

His consideration of aesthetics clearly indicated his perspectives and their potential. Defining aesthetic activity as the contemplation of the basic forms or near permanent ideas, the function of art was to present these forms which the artist has discovered in the multiplicity of changing particular objects or lesser ideas. The forms are intuitively grasped. To recognize the forms, the viewer must set aside personal, practical desires and become abstract. Knowledge (science) is moved by practical objectives in particular problems and hence misses the forms. When we intuitively grasp the form, we have subordinated thought to will and our distinction of subject and object have disappeared. Eternal ideas are thus discovered in nature or art and genius is the highest capacity for such contemplation. In this union of subject and object, our will becomes blended with others and we have escaped from our human condition of frustrated desire, want, and unsatisfaction. Thus we feel a sense of purification or regeneration after a truly aesthetic experience. The great tragedy of the universe was the creation of persons, which is to be seen as a division of will. Art is an escape from this world, where men groan.

Schopenhauer's pessimistic philosophy was lacking in specific political advice but helped to spread interest in Indian philosophy. He found the doctrine of reincarnation consistent with his concept of will and thus incorporated in his thinking another intellectual tradition. It was appropriate to romanticism that his system was admittedly speculative and owed a great deal to a pessimistic attitude. In the will he made a basic contribution to thought which proved strikingly suggestive in the context of the mid-nineteenth century.

In religion the impact of romanticism was both profound and pervasive. Multitudes were touched by pietism, an emotional rededication to Christian principles presented in moving but simple language. For aristocratic intellectuals faith based on the heart was available in sophisticated language.

During the eighteenth century the pietistic movement had been progressively gathering strength as a reaction to a number of current attitudes. In Germany it was a rebellion against an unemotional and rigid dogmatism which had developed in the Lutheran church. It similarly opposed the emphasis on science and the whole set of rationalistic attitudes comprising the Enlightenment, including deism, which pietists regarded as a concoction of the human mind utterly unworthy of God. Human reason to them was presumptuous and clearly irreligious in its constructions. Thus they looked with condescension on the scientific and artistic achievements of the Enlightenment and saw in public life merely an unfortunate exposure to rampant evil.

To the pietists true religion was a matter of individual conscience, an inner experience which touched the heart. A mystical emotionalism seemed to them a far sounder guide than reason, whose errors were often demonstrable and whose successes were handmaidens to the human failing of pride. Usually fundamentalists, their morality was puritanical.

The origins of the movement antedated the Enlightenment, a Calvinistic pietism seeping into central and south Germany (especially Württemberg) from Dutch universities in the seventeenth century. Pietists acquired positions in German theological schools, particularly at Halle, and thus trained large numbers of Lutheran pastors and powered a sort of mystical religious renaissance within the church. The emphasis on personal feeling and conviction made practical organization difficult, and no massive, purely pietistic organization emerged, although many small groups existed erratically for short periods. The Moravian Brethren became thoroughly pietistic and were perhaps the most successful.

By 1800 pietism remained a major influence and was producing numerous prophets. These appeared at all social levels; through prayer and contemplation they claimed a clairvoyance which was widely credited. The crescendo of events between 1789 and 1815 fed their imaginations, and the idea that the millennium was at hand echoed and re-echoed. The Baroness von Krüdener had such visions and was widely known for her prophecies. Converted in 1805 by one of the Moravians, she brought her simplistic religion of the heart directly to the Tsar and other dignitaries assembled at Paris in 1815. The leaders in the struggle against Napoleon were especially susceptible to pietistic equations of Napoleon with anti-Christ and themselves as agents of God in His struggle with evil. A re-emphasis on personal morality was apparent in all churches in the early nineteenth century. Outdoor services in "natural" settings became popular, especially with the lower classes. The trees and the soil seemed to suggest purity and in such a setting provided for a greater awareness of one's identity as a creature of nature and a child of God.

Heavily pietistic was the Methodist movement, which stemmed directly from the 1738 conversion, by a Moravian, of John Wesley. Methodism was an emotional reaction to several English circumstances in the eighteenth century and succeeded to a welter of religious ideas current in seventeenth-century England. Justification by faith and personal salvation received renewed emphasis, and religious oratory took on the aura of a fine art. Masses of people hearing impassioned sermons were converted in droves. An enormous pamphlet literature appeared, along with a splurge of hymn writing, as the leaders in the movement were immersed in immediate practical tasks. No towering philosophic figure emerged from Methodism, where the emphasis was on eloquent preaching. As a protest movement within Anglicanism, Methodism was mainly a religion for Englishmen. Thus, it was very weak on the Continent, but in England and North America it became a potent force. One of the intriguing imponderables is the relationship between the growth of Methodism and the Reform movement in England. Methodist preachers were eloquent on the idea of political loyalty and the maintenance of law and order. The force of Methodism tended to diminish the resentments against the rotten borough system during the long struggles against the French and quite possibly was responsible for a delay of practical reform.

During the nineteenth century the Protestant movement was continuously undergoing divisions and subdivisions as new sects appeared. These were mostly in the pietistic tradition and served as a needed stimulus to the older and more tradition-oriented churches.

Evangelicalism became a feature of most Christian faiths as a consequence of the pietistic movement. By and large, the new sects were composed of the lower classes, where the subtleties of Enlightenment learning had barely penetrated. In the upper classes, where rationalism's deism and skepticism had taken hold, pietistic romanticism was present but was not as obviously successful. A strong sense of piety had motivated Kant, who provided a rational argument for turning to faith. Similarly, Chateaubriand made religion respectable for many sophisticated intellectuals. A deliberately romantic presentation of religion, however, was most impressively stated by Friedrich Schleiermacher (1768–1834), a philosopher-theologian who taught at Berlin.

Friedrich Schleiermacher. (Courtesy of Historical Pictures Service, Chicago.)

Schleiermacher's ideas are best presented in the early chapters of *The Christian Faith,* a ponderous work published in 1821 which philosophically stated the basic position he had worked out over two decades earlier. Writing as a theologian, Schleiermacher was a distinct break with the past. Reflecting various degrees of loyalty to the logical model devised by Aquinas, theology for five centuries had been heavily rationalistic; its various positions all had proofs, even for God's existence. Schleiermacher, however, insisted that a rational metaphysics simply was not possible, a position close to that of Kant, who would have equated it to certainty regarding the noumenal world. Religion was not based on certain knowledge but rather on a sense of piety. Religious life was a response to a religious feeling and not something to be proved or disproved. Kant had shown that it was reasonable for men to believe; Schleiermacher proceeded to examine the nature and consequences of belief, pointing out that verification regarding the object of belief was virtually beside the point. He went on to the first basically empirical approach to religion, seeing it as a psychological and sociological phenomenon. The insight that religious beliefs arose from kinds of experience rather than reasoning led to extensive comparative study of world religion and religious practice. Theologians since Schleiermacher have largely abandoned attempts to prove God's existence and have put a heavy emphasis on exploring the nature of religious experience.

Schleiermacher insisted that piety, a type of feeling rather than a matter of knowledge or action, was essential to all religion. He maintained that knowledge of religion did not guarantee religious experience, nor could it come through deeds. The specific feeling was intensely subjective and stimulated knowing and doing. The function of the church was to promote and encourage this special feeling, this sense of piety. Piety consisted of a sense of absolute dependence. Between persons and the objective finite world a relationship of mutual dependence exists. However, religion comprises a sense of finitude before the infinite, which we call God. God is therefore to be understood as the origin of the feeling of piety, and this is all humans can know of God. It follows that the most pious are the most religious. Recognition of the sense of absolute dependence requires the highest level of consciousness, in which the soul is in tune with the infinite. Persons thus oriented are capable of extraordinary feats of thought and action, especially when united as a common body or church. Unfortunately, religious action can be misplaced. A corruption of religion (idolatry) occurs when a figure becomes the object of piety. Because all feelings interpenetrate one another, religious action can be turned in many directions. In the course of religious history, three types of monotheism gradually emerged— Christianity, Mohammedanism, and Judaism. Monotheism is the highest type of religion because, Schleiermacher observed, it is most appropriate to a sense of *absolute* dependence. A feeling of *absolute* dependence is simply not possible where there is more than one God. He concluded that no religious doctrine may be said to be true or truer than others in any factual sense, because they are all neither true nor false. Doctrines merely serve as an aid for inculcating a sense of piety and for directing religious feeling into socially useful channels. Doctrine or theology is simply man's interpretation of his reaction before a sense of infinity. Therefore, no religion practices doctrinal truth and none can declare that the doctrines of others are false. Roman Catholicism, Calvinism, or Lutheranism are mere myths, although, of course, the myths may be true. His basic point was that truth or knowledge has nothing to do with the feeling of piety. The time-worn proofs of God's existence had not resulted directly in piety, and obviously rationalism in religion was beside the point. Man believed because of a feeling and he thus accepted something which evidence had not forced upon him. He believed in spite of data and reason.

Schleiermacher suggested that the Lutheran faith best promoted the sense of piety, and much of his writing explores this topic in detail. The Lutheran church and many other Protestant sects were influenced by his observations on piety. In the face of a basic statement that factual truth was unattainable, it could not be expected that dogma or any so-called truth would be very staunchly defended. Relativism could more readily be accepted as well as easy accommodation with changing political regimes. Besides making religion fashionable and acceptable on an emotional basis, Schleiermacher's ideas also helped to create religious groups who could later acquiesce to a society like that of the Third Reich.

V

Liberal and Nationalistic Adjustments, 1820–1832

CHAPTER 14

International Unrest and the End of the Concert

The coalition which had emerged from the struggle against Napoleon failed to survive the 1820s. This decade saw the basic divergence of Austrian and English policies exposed over issues largely ignored by the congresses. The formulas derived at Vienna and Troppau were inadequate for the crises posed by the Eastern Question and by the revolt of Spanish colonies in the New World. Further, in Italy, there was, despite autocratic vigilance, a disquieting spread of underground conspiracy aimed at instituting government on a constitutional basis. Metternich's abilities were sorely tested as he achieved a qualified success in Italy but proved unable to control events where England was directly involved.

The 1821 suppression of constitutional supporters in Naples and Sardinia demonstrated Austrian ascendancy in Italian affairs. The

173

speed and ease with which absolutist elements were restored discouraged open attempts at revolt in the peninsula for a decade.
While Austria had proved she could maintain control in the face
of uncoordinated uprisings, it was not as though Metternich had it
all his own way. He had wanted a tighter control of the whole peninsula through treaties with each state, providing for a large measure
of Austrian supervision. Naples and Tuscany agreed but the Papacy
and Sardinia stoutly declined the obvious client status. Partially
rebuffed, Metternich then suggested an Italian Confederation which,
through Lombardy-Venetia, Austria would easily control. This idea
similarly failed as the Viennese statesman was unable to erect a more
formal and comprehensive political structure in Italy. His efforts,
however, had the paradoxical effect of sharpening the sense of dependence on Austria among Italian leaders while promoting the
idea of the peninsula as a unit.

As in Germany, police spies and paid informers appeared everywhere; and through a series of postal agreements, the foreign correspondence of the Italian states was routed through Vienna where
it was systematically opened, often copied, and then resealed and
sent on. In this fashion Metternich remained well informed on Italy
and realized that although open insurrection was not in progress,
widespread nationalistic and liberal discontent was only barely con-
cealed. The *prospect* of revolt was thus continuous as, from the
1820s on, a vibrant romantic movement in Italian literature was
actively promoting ideas of national independence.

Politically, Napoleon was largely responsible for broadening
Italian perspectives to encompass the peninsula rather than one of
its subdivisions. Prince Eugene had been his Viceroy for *Italy*. After
1815, secret societies composed of members of the aristocracy and
bourgeoisie worked throughout the peninsula for constitutional government, the specific documentary model being Spain's Constitution
of 1812. These societies were not yet unified on a national basis, but
after the debacles of 1821, they increasingly thought in terms of a
united Italy under some Italian prince. As in Germany, Napoleon's
impact had been to lessen political barriers while providing more
bases for common perspectives through widespread adoption of the
codes and elements of French Revolutionary ideology.

A less immediate but equally serious problem for Metternich was
the issue of revolution in Spain and Spanish America. If legitimacy
and absolutism were bona fide guiding principles, then Spain's problems could have been as readily settled as the 1821 revolts in Italy.
However, the issues involving Spain were complicated by England's

special interest. Metternich realized this difference and tried to delay facing the problem, hoping circumstances would improve. The revolt against Ferdinand VII (January, 1820) had antedated and inspired a revolution in Portugal (August, 1820) resulting in a short-lived constitution (until June, 1823) modeled on the Spanish Constitution and that produced by the Neapolitan uprising (July, 1820). At Verona in October of 1822, the problem could not be further delayed and Metternich realized that the ideal of the Great Powers reaching agreement in periodic congresses was no longer possible. The English had understood Austria's interest in putting down revolts in Italy but were adamantly against intervention as a principle and especially opposed the forceful restoration of absolutism in Spain by outsiders. Castlereagh's death brought to England's foreign office the more militantly liberal George Canning. Thus at Verona, Wellington had been instructed not to commit England to any sort of coordinated action, leaving Metternich with little room for maneuver. The French were volunteering to restore Ferdinand to his former prerogatives and Alexander supported their proposal. Metternich, like Prussia, was left with little option but to acquiesce; he could neither soften the issue for the English nor get their support for the decision. When Wellington informed the Congress point-blank on October 30 that England would have nothing to do with intervention in Spain, the Quadruple Alliance was dead and the guise of unanimity and Great Power approval for Metternich's conservative program was no longer possible. With the disintegration of the wartime alliance, both liberalism and nationalism gained in potential; indeed, a Tory English government, hated at home by liberals, now appeared to be supporting liberal revolutionary movements on the Continent. France, against whom the Alliance had been directed, was the agent of reaction in restoring Ferdinand; but after 1829 she became a Continental version of England, a haven and exporter of ideas disturbing for conservatives.

After Verona, England pursued a strictly independent policy, watching apprehensively while French troops easily restored autocracy in Spain. She was much more active, however, in the problem created by unrest and revolution in Spain's American territories.

The breakup of Spanish holdings in America is an interesting and complex story. Despite a myriad of petty internal frictions and difficulties, Spain had successfully governed her vast American holdings for over two centuries. Theoretically, they were not colonies, but rather, extensions of Spain itself, ruled by the king in the manner that Charles V had ruled over much of Europe outside his Iberian lands. The revolt from Spain seriously began when, in 1808, Napoleon casually brushed aside the Bourbon dynasty and established his brother Joseph as the king, a particularly unpopular act in much of Spanish America. To this situation were added agitators and volunteers who poured overseas from Europe, supported and abetted by friends in England. Some of these troublemakers (from the view of Spain) were American born, had been educated in Europe, and were imbued with those French Revolutionary ideas found in the Spanish Constitution of 1812. Especially noteworthy were Francisco de Miranda (1750–1816), José de San Martin (1778–1850), and Simón Bolívar (1783–1830). England openly admitted her stake in the situation, which was almost entirely economic. Her trade with Spanish America had grown enormously during the Napoleonic Wars and increased by over twenty times in one four-year period. The Continental System had driven her to expand into this area of trade as she assumed much of the mercantilistic posture of a mother country for the colonies now cut off from the Continent. With the coming of peace English merchants had no intention of relinquishing this profitable tie. Thus, ardent revolutionaries wanting to sever connections with the restored Bourbon monarchy in Spain found favor in England. Perhaps some arrangement could have been devised whereby the trade could continue with England while political allegiance was to Spain, but it would have required a man in Madrid with more wisdom than Ferdinand VII.

This wretched Bourbon had, in 1814, been returned to power by the success of Wellington's arms in the peninsula. A dedicated autocrat who at once annulled the Constitution of 1812, he was amazingly popular among the reactionary clergy and generally unenlightened peasantry. By this time the initial phase of the independence movement overseas was ended with royalism nominally secure, but a spirit of opposition and rebellion against the mother country had been firmly implanted. While liberal and revolutionary ideas were being brought in from Europe, the successive governments in Madrid expected obedience and submission from the overseas territories. This was even true of the Cortes after 1812, when it denied adequate colonial representation on grounds of expediency. When Ferdinand installed authoritarian rule in Madrid and pointedly spoke of restoring the proper economic relationship and control of Spanish America, the colonies embarked on a more vigorous drive for political freedom. Insurrection spread rapidly, but by 1819 the King had gathered an army at Cadiz for transport overseas. On January 1, 1820, a mutiny broke out and touched off what proved to be the Spanish Revolution of 1820, which culminated in Ferdinand's decision in March to restore the Constitution of 1812. This episode was a result of many factors, including poor provisioning for the troops and dedicated plotting by Freemasons in Cadiz. Initially, the revolt in Cadiz appeared short-lived, but as it was faltering, uprisings in the north gave the insurrection new life. From Ferdinand's view, the entire country seemed to be rising against him. His incompetent administration had helped cause the revolt and, in a state of paralysis and near terror, also allowed it to succeed. The monarchy now was in no position to restore its overseas authority and the independence movement entered its last phase. Restoration of the 1812 Constitution reduced much of the bitterness in the colonial struggle, where diplomacy now became more prominent. At the same time English investments markedly increased as London worked for formal recognition of the new states. There was also a significant United States economic involvement, which accounted for yet another voice in the chorus of diplomatic discussions. The leisurely pace of negotiations was terminated abruptly by the Congress of Verona's decision to approve French intervention in Spain, which allowed Ferdinand again to discard the liberal constitution. The ease with which this was accomplished in the summer of 1823, coupled with Ferdinand's call for another congress to decide on the restoration of Spanish America, spurred both English and American diplomats. The United States had wanted republican governments founded in the new states, whereas England supported the idea of constitutional monarchies. From the viewpoint of Metternich and other conservative leaders, it was a simple matter of legitimacy. Alexander had, from Aix-la-Chapelle on, been proposing intervention overseas to restore Spanish control and even sent a fleet (unseaworthy) to Cadiz in 1818 for Ferdinand's use. After the crushing of liberals in Spain, France suggested in October of 1823, a meeting of the powers to discuss Latin America. This idea failed because the Holy Alliance powers refused to deal with an agent of the United States, which to them symbolized republicanism. Shortly thereafter, in December of 1823, President Monroe made his statement on nonintervention, for which Canning boastfully tried to take the credit. Although the implied English–United States agreement to repel any European attempts to restore Spain's sovereignty gave pause to the Holy Alliance powers and may be seen as a response to the Troppau Protocol, there were interesting elements of disagreement. The United States had refused an English version which would have stated that *no* outsiders, *including the United States,* were to pursue ambitions looking to any change in sovereignty in Latin America. Further, Monroe's statement was directed as explicitly against England as against the conservative powers of Europe. In the wake of Monroe's statement, Canning moved swiftly to assure English formal recognition of the new states before important trade advantages might be lost to the United States. This required an overlooking of scant Latin American support for constitutional monarchy but did save considerable trade and influence for England. The English navy was the major compelling factor preventing the Continental powers from helping Ferdinand; but the success of English interests in the New World was modified by the independent policy of the United States, a new power which had only recently won its second armed struggle with England.

While Spain and Spanish America thus occasioned a sense of anxiety and crisis among diplomats, another trying dilemma, the Greek revolt, tested their collective skill and patience. The historian may discuss each subject separately, but foreign ministers found several issues at a time crying for attention. Few diplomatic studies give adequate attention to the complexity surrounding the task of formulating and implementing policy for a major state. In tracing a statesman's course, the historian writing decades and perhaps centuries later often sees and presents an oversimplified view of causes and events, and nineteenth-century diplomacy abounds in instances of such easy misrepresentation.

Of the crises testing the statesmen of Europe after 1800, none were more exasperating than those known collectively as the Eastern Question. The major European powers looked upon the Ottoman Empire as being in a state of rapid decline, to the point of disintegration. Since 1700 the Turks had gradually been giving way before Austrian and Russian encroachments as their government seethed with corruption and incompetence. The Turks evoked little sympathy but great concern over impending political alterations should the Ottoman Empire collapse. Prussia had no direct interest but Austria and Russia saw any Turkish decline as resulting in a direct accretion of territory for themselves. France had ties with the Ottoman Empire and Near Eastern trade which dated from many centuries. England entered the picture mainly after 1800. The question concerning alterations in Ottoman sovereignty centered on areas of the Empire west of the Bosphorus, with control of the Bosphorus and the Dardanelles a crucial consideration. In its nineteenth-century form, the Eastern Question may be regarded as being solved after World War I, when the Turks were left with scant holdings west of

Constantinople and their former holdings comprised a number of sovereign, second-rank states. In 1815, the statesmen at Vienna had deliberately made no formal arrangements regarding the Ottoman Empire. Having just acquired Bessarabia (Treaty of Bucharest, 1812) Russia wanted no study of the Ottoman situation, and the Powers were anxious to avoid any unnecessary disputes. They had quite enough to worry about with problems in Poland and the rest of Europe; in the absence of a crisis calling for immediate decision, the implications of Ottoman decadence and political decline were willingly overlooked.

To evade the issue may have been the proper course at Vienna, but obviously this did nothing to abate the problem and the specific issue of the Greek revolt soon appeared. There had been previous uprisings within the Ottoman Empire, but this time the over-all situation contained new ingredients and was markedly different. For one thing, outside interference was much more certain. The effect of Napoleon's campaign in Egypt and the subsequent (1806–1809) English involvement in war against the Turks was to give England, and Europe generally, more of an awareness of the Near East. The Ottoman Empire was recognized as including a major part of Europe.

The French Revolutionary stimulus to nationalism made inroads among the Balkan populations, although this can be easily overrated. Equally important, many Western statesmen who viewed the Balkans in terms of nationalism concluded that Turkish rule was unjust. It was also easy to overlook the confusing differences and cultural divisions within the ranks of the subject Balkan peoples. That Islamic Turks were ruling over fellow Christians seemed especially unjust; it was easier to forget the gulf between Greek Orthodox Christianity and the religious varieties elsewhere in Europe. At the same time the romantic movement had made such an impact that, for the educated, it was virtually unthinkable that the descendants of the ancient (pre-Roman) Greeks would submit to domination from non-Greeks. Turkish oppression and misrule may have been harsh, but it was widespread and had been present in some sections of Europe since the fourteenth century. Many Western Europeans now became concerned, which contrasted sharply with their general indifference over similar Serb revolts which had begun in 1804 and were proving successful by 1817.

While the members of the Congress of Vienna were tactfully trying to avoid Ottoman involvement, the specific factors leading to the Greek revolt were already present. In 1814 at Odessa, the *Hetairia Philike* was founded, merely the latest of many secret Carbonarilike societies formed to plot against the Turk. Many Greeks were a well-to-do minority within the Empire and controlled an enormous amount of trade and filled many positions in the bureaucracy. The Russians had encouraged the Greeks to oppose their Turkish over-lords, and Count John Capodistrias (1776–1831), one of the Tsar's closest advisers, was supporting the plans for revolt. The first major Greek challenge to the Sultan's authority came with the revolt in Moldavia in March of 1821, which was led by Prince Alexander Ypsilanti (1792–1828), a Russian general of Greek extraction. Success of the movement focused on the expectation of Russian support. The intriguers, however, had underrated Metternich's ability to influence Alexander against intervention. Further, the native population in Moldavia proved no more endeared to the Greeks than to the Turks and the revolt was brutally crushed. Meanwhile, another *Hetairia*-inspired revolt flared in the Morea on April 2, 1821. Greek leaders had now turned to the more specific and fruitful objective of independence for Greece rather than for essentially non-Greek segments of the Empire, such as Moldavia. In a modern classic of aroused nationalism, Greek businessmen, clergymen, intellectuals, and peasants rose together against the Turk. Neither Turk nor Greek showed any mercy as thousands upon thousands were slaughtered in systematic butchery. The upheaval was complicated further by fratricidal cleavages within Greek ranks as, like the Serbs, they struggled with one another while fighting the oppressor. Finally, Western diplomats became openly concerned about the problem. Again Metternich tried to keep the problem localized and promoted a policy of concerted action among the Powers, but this time his efforts were nearly in vain.

The year 1823 may be regarded as especially crucial in the Greek revolt; for during the same year that Latin America was such a concern for George Canning, England formally recognized the Greeks as belligerents. This significant upgrading of the insurgent's diplomatic status was one of the major changes in English policy clearly apparent after Castlereagh's replacement by Canning. Metternich had consistently argued that the Sultan was a legitimate monarch and that revolts in the Ottoman Empire were frequent and even normal. He desperately wanted to keep Alexander from intervening in support of the Greeks. To have the Russians in Poland was quite enough, and he regarded further extensions of Russian influence at the expense of the Turks also to be at the expense of Austria. Though Metternich tried to minimize it, a rivalry between Russia and Austria in the Balkans had, in fact, already begun. He thought in terms of limiting Russia in this sphere rather than working for compensatory Austrian gains in the Balkans. With all the cosmopolitanism necessary in a diplomat of a polyglot empire, Metternich seems to have acted with poise when dealing with problems in Europe to the south, west, and north of Vienna but with a sense of insecurity, aversion, and fear when looking east and southeast. The centuries-long, Hapsburg role as a bulwark against the Turk helps to explain his position, particularly his well-known remark that "Asia begins on the *Landstrasse.*"

Meanwhile, Alexander grew progressively uneasy as he recognized a clear opportunity to extend Russian influence. He now regretted the Troppau Protocol and he regretted that he had followed Metternich's advice so closely. He wanted a conference which would give him a mandate to intervene in behalf of fellow Christians. Canning bluntly refused to attend such a meeting, seeing a chance to divide Metternich and Alexander over the Greek issue. Earlier, Castlereagh had been willing to follow Metternich's views regarding unrest in the Ottoman Empire; now Canning sensed a growing public concern. Because the Turks had been unable to provide protection for commerce (ironically, the troublemakers were *Greek* pirates), formal recognition of the Greek insurgents appeared to make sense. There was the further satisfaction for Canning that, in adopting a partially Russian stance which made possible Anglo-Russian cooperation on the question, Metternich would be virtually isolated with legitimacy as a theory discredited in the face of nationalism. Brash over the progress of events in Latin America, he eagerly moved to this new triumph, carrying with him not only his colleagues in the ministry but public opinion and the French as well. His success was complete as Alexander became utterly exasperated at Metternich and finally declared that he simply could no longer work with the Austrian statesman. The Quadruple Alliance was dead, the Troppau Protocol was dead, and the Holy Alliance was dead. Metternich, rebuffed in both the New World and in the Balkans, was left in the wreckage of his system with only the unimaginative Frederick William III. However, Canning's final victory proved shortsighted as the defeat of Metternich on the Greek question signalled an increase of Russian stature in the Balkans, a circumstance hardly to England's advantage.

As the revolt grew more serious the Sultan called on the Pasha of Egypt, Mehemet Ali (1769–1849), for support. This strong subordinate sent his son, Ibrahim (1789–1848), to the Morea in February, 1825, to begin a systematic reconquest. Moving efficiently to his task, Ibrahim left behind a trail of blood which further inflamed tempers in England and France. At the Treaty of London, July 6, 1827, France joined England and Russia in support of the Greeks, and three and a half months later (October 20) a joint allied fleet sank the Turko-Egyptian fleet at Navarino Bay. Russia now declared open war and "volunteers" flooded east from France and England. A special French volunteer force arrived to aid in expelling the Egyptians from the Morea. Navarino had been a major setback to Ibrahim's conquest, which had been progressing efficiently. While the French were arriving, and fighting off Greek pirates in the process, the English were negotiating with Mohammed Ali for Ibrahim's withdrawal. The Turks were forced to make peace with the Russians, and the resulting treaty of Adrianople (September 14, 1829) opened the way for the later London Protocol (February 3, 1830), which established an independent Greece. Europe's revolutionary upheavals of 1830 caused some delay in negotiations, but finally, in January of 1833, the Greeks received their new king, Otto, the second son of the King of Bavaria. The new nation's independence was guaranteed not by the concert of Europe but specifically by England, France, and Russia. Since the final solution was negotiated in the wake of the revolutionary contagion of 1830, a major softening occurred in Russia's ambitions regarding the Ottoman Empire. Before 1830 it appeared that Russia would make enormous gains, but she acquired mainly supervisory rights in the principalities of Moldavia and Wallachia, gains much less than other powers had feared. The French minister of Charles X, the Prince de Polignac (1780–1847), had produced a scheme which involved a major revision of the Congress of Vienna's territorial decisions. Brushed aside as impractical, nonetheless it came from a major statesman. In terms of the Eastern Question it frankly proposed the partition of the Ottoman Empire, the same idea which the English later professed to find alarming when it came from a Russian tsar. Polignac suggested that both Russia and Austria acquire land at the Turk's expense, besides allowing for a fairly large Greek state. His candidate for the new Greek throne was the Netherlands' King William, whose former realm would be divided, with the Belgian provinces going to France and the northern provinces going to Prussia. The Dutch overseas empire would be given to England and Prussia would absorb the rest of Saxony; the Saxon king would be compensated with Prussian lands along the Rhine. All the major powers would gain new territory and only the Ottoman Turks would be victimized. Several of his proposals became realities as the century wore on, although at the time it appeared to many statesmen as only a shabby device to gain the Rhine frontier for France while discrediting the territorial arrangements made at Vienna. The idea of eliminating the Netherlands as a state was especially objectionable to diplomats who now believed the Continent needed strong secondary states on the frontiers of France to ensure security from French aggression.

CHAPTER 15

Revolt and Revolution: Russia, France, Belgium, Poland, and Italy, 1825–1832

"War in Greece means revolution in Europe." This perceptive observation by Metternich suggests why the Austrian diplomat shrank from open involvement in the growing crisis and tried to persuade other states not to intervene. Because plots and uprisings in Central, Western, and Southern Europe were being controlled only by dint of vigilance and outright force, he believed that support for the Greeks would incite other European nationalists and liberals to revolt. Further, the stabilizing influence of the army would be lessened as units were transferred to help Greece. To Metternich the danger was obvious, for despite censorship, liberal ideas were circulating broadly. The years 1830 and 1831 were to see the widescale upheavals he predicted, but earlier, in 1825, the potential danger came to the surface in Russia.

184

Alexander had not been the only liberal Russian. While this monarch was progressively adopting a more reactionary stance, relying heavily on the cruel General Alexis Arakcheiev, ideas for liberal reform were swiftly spreading, especially among the younger nobility and, as in Italy and Spain, among army officers. Informers notified the Tsar of various secret societies dedicated to liberalism, but he wistfully abstained from taking action, observing that he himself had earlier encouraged such ideas. After the struggle against Napoleon many officers compared Russian institutions unfavorably with those they had observed in Central and Western Europe. Formal liberal groups had appeared as early as 1814, and in 1816 the Society for Public Salvation was founded. Initially, Alexander approved of the Society but gradually a rift occurred. After 1818, the Society, now exasperated with the Tsar, took the name of the Union for Public Good. Disagreement over both tactics and specific reforms desired led to schisms formalized in the founding of a Northern Society, a Southern Society, and the United Slavs. Basically, the Northern Society of St. Petersburg, led by Condratij Ryleieff (1795–1826), wanted constitutional monarchy in Russia; the Southern Society, led by Paul Pestel (1793–1826), favored republicanism. These societies were both nationalistic; but by 1825, the United Slavs favored republicanism and international cooperation with other Slav secret societies, thus promoting Slavophile ideas and Panslavism. The participants were educated and earnest young nobles firmly believing in reform. They were intellectuals who had read widely such political theorists as Montesquieu, Rousseau, and Bentham, but unfortunately they had little contact with the rest of Russian society. As officers they did not share their ideas with ordinary soldiers, and the peasantry or urban dweller had no comprehension of schemes for political reform. Further, they lacked experience in plotting, as demonstrated when after correctly sensing their opportunity, they utterly failed.

The members of the Northern Society decided that their opportunity was at hand in December, 1825. Alexander had gone to Taganrog in September and died there on December 1. His death was unexpected, for despite his need for rest, he was only forty-eight years old. His abrupt and premature death, coupled with his earlier frequent statements about abdicating, helped give rise to a variety of rumors and speculation, almost as much among historians as among contemporaries. Intriguing as they may be, the stories of suicide, poisoning, or escape to a monastery must be regarded as erroneous. The best documentation indicates that Alexander died at Taganrog on December 1, 1825. He was succeeded by his twenty-nine-year-old brother Nicholas, who was finally convinced of his accession on December 24. For three weeks Russia lacked an acknowledged monarch and this circumstance encouraged the Northern Society to act.

Confusion arose because of another brother, Constantine (1779–1831), then forty-six years of age and the Viceroy in Poland. Three years earlier he had renounced his claims to the succession, but Nicholas was unaware of this. Constantine offered to step aside because he truly did not want the burden of administering the cumbersome empire. In this he was sincere, but another compelling factor was that, like Alexander, he had no children, whereas the young Nicholas had a son (the future Alexander II), born April 29, 1818. Nicholas had married a Prussian princess and so, if he were to follow Alexander, the dynasty's interests would be served and would carry a promise of closer relations with Prussia, a prospect which Alexander came to value more as he became impatient with Metternich. For these reasons the Tsar had urged Constantine to put his decision in writing. At the sudden death of Alexander, both Nicholas and Constantine proclaimed each other's accession and it took some time before it was clear to Nicholas that he was truly Russia's next monarch.

December 26 was selected as the day on which troops would swear allegiance to Nicholas. On the evening before, the Northern Society decided that conditions were ripe for an insurrection. By having troops refuse allegiance to Nicholas, they expected a national assembly to be called at once to debate the succession problem. Once convened, it would also institute reforms limiting the periods of army service and begin work on serf emancipation. Meanwhile, a dictatorial government under Prince (Colonel) Trubetskoi would rule.

The troops refused the oath to Nicholas and there were shouts of "Long live Constantine!" "Long live the Constitution!" and "Constantine and Constitution!" Then nothing else happened; there was an absolute absence of leadership. The soldiers did not know what they were calling for or why, and no large additions were made to their numbers by city residents or other regiments. After entreaties with them to change their minds, Nicholas called in other troops and the "revolt" was pitilessly crushed and its leaders were imprisoned. The Southern Society attempted an insurrection two weeks later which failed just as dismally. The "Decembrist" leaders were tried and in July, 1826, five of the most important, including Pestel and Ryleieff, were hanged and over 100 others were sent to Siberia. Russia's revolutionary tradition had its first martyrs.

As a revolt or an uprising, the affair had been amateurish and without a serious chance of success. Its impact, however, was enormous. Nicholas never forgot that his accession had been opposed not by his older brother, but by rebellious officers. He equated defiant and disobedient troops with revolution and was shaken that such a thing could occur in Russia. He began to rely on Germans as administrators rather than Russian nobles. As a dedicated conservative, his opposition to liberalism proved harsher by far than Metternich's. The Decembrist Revolt is often regarded as the beginning of a modern revolutionary movement in Russia. Also it was the first upheaval (if it merits such a word) in Russia with an ideological basis, a political program; thus it differed from earlier dynastic or personal conspiracies and from such uprisings as Pugachev's rebellion. It was the first use of palace troops for an ideological revolt, and it was the first time a palace revolution using troops failed in Russia. An amusing story of the revolt maintains that the troops in their ignorance thought Constitution was merely Constantine's wife. Varients of this tale crop up in several other European revolts in the next thirty years, and it is difficult to tell the extent to which it is apocryphal.

Shortly after Nicholas was securely in power, he embarked on a more militant policy regarding Greece and soon was also at war with Persia. This ended in 1828, but by then Russian arms were fighting the Turks. Nicholas was hardly a devout believer in Greek nationalism, but the opportunities for extending Russian power and prestige in the Balkans were too tempting. With the English and French also aiding the Greeks, Metternich anxiously wondered where stability and order would next be challenged. When revolution broke out in Paris, the omens could hardly have been more threatening.

Charles X has received very little sympathy from historians. He was so completely at home in the system of entrenched conservatism (reaction) defended by Metternich that liberal historians have given him short shrift. Until recent studies by Vincent W. Beach he has, in fact, been largely ignored by serious scholars. That Charles' policies and instincts were markedly conservative is clear but that he deserved dismissal because of them is less apparent. Even as he went into exile, he was insisting that his regime was well regarded in the country at large and that his difficulties really were limited to a few overly ambitious men. His error was not so much in this analysis but in underrating how much these few capable and ambitious men could do. During cabinet meetings he busied himself making unusually shaped paper cutouts but carefully followed the discussions on both the major questions and the minutiae of government. Utterly unwilling to compromise with positions he found disagreeable, the crown had not made him more cautious or moderated his views. Indeed he became intractable, declaring that rather than be like an English monarch he would prefer to saw wood. This man's strong sense of duty and personal integrity brings an element of tragedy into the story of his fall.

After coming to the throne in September of 1824, Charles consistently supported programs of an *ancien régime* character. His open alliance with the clergy reflected little awareness of widely held bitterness toward the Church. He further failed to understand the importance of many new leaders in Parisian society. As well as comprising remnants of the old aristocracy and Napoleon's nobility, an upper class of considerable wealth and sophistication had emerged. The world of business had proved to be an area where, to a remarkable degree, careers were open to talent and where those who succeeded aped many superficial aspects of the *ancien régime* aristocracy. They dressed in velvet, kept mistresses, and gloried in prestige and public attention. While resembling some of the pre-1789 aristocrats, they were not for a moment prepared to accept any sort of theocratic or medieval despotism, a point which Charles X seems never to have understood.

The resistance to reaction was demonstrated in the fate of a government attempt to reinstate primogeniture, a measure openly contrary to revolutionary egalitarianism. Explicitly stating that the principle of equal inheritance was contrary to monarchical government, the bill provided that the eldest son should receive more property than other children when there was no will. This would apply only to those few families paying 300 francs in direct taxes annually; it thus affected barely 1 per cent of the households in France. Nevertheless, the measure caused an uproar. After heated discussion, the Chamber of Deputies gave its approval but the Peers rejected it. The Chamber of Peers similarly killed a stringent press bill and, earlier, weakened the bill on sacrilege. These actions touched off celebrations in Paris and in major provincial centers and the regime steadily lost public confidence. The extent of opposition to Charles was clear from the loss of support by many Ultras. The Peers, after all, had rebuffed him, not the more popularly selected deputies. The Indemnification Act passed in 1825 had been a particularly ill-considered venture. It indemnified the old *émigré* nobility for lands lost during the Revolution through manipulation of bond interest rates. The *émigrés* were disgruntled that they did not get more and the bankers and bond holders were infuriated over what appeared to be a form of robbery. A further unsavory aspect, especially from the peasants' viewpoint, was that it looked as though persons who had fought with enemies of France were being rewarded.

Resentment against Charles X was not limited to the upper middle class, and among the politically alert an interesting society was formed, the *Aide-toi, le ciel t'aidera* (Help yourself and heaven will help you). Composed of disillusioned Ultras, frustrated businessmen, and even some republicans, it took particular interest in policing elections and working for a wider franchise. They also insisted that if the business classes were going to be taxed, the King should work closely with its elected representatives in governing the nation. An upper-class articulate opposition had developed while workers and dedicated republicans began debating revolution. In this context political events moved inexorably to the July Revolution.

Essentially, Charles had never accepted the idea of government according to the Charter. He believed in divine-right royalty in the manner of Louis XIV and made little effort to conceal this view. He created seventy-six new peers in 1827 in a bald effort to assure control of the Chamber of Peers and was clearly on a collision course with the dominant mood of French society. In the 1827 elections for a new Chamber of Deputies, opponents of the regime were markedly successful, despite press and electoral harassment. The Count de Villèle's ministry was forced out of office in January 1828. Villèle had served since 1821, and though he had proved himself an able administrator, he had grown progressively unpopular. Public opinion partially blamed him for the Ultra programs of the King and for not being more aggressive in aiding the Greeks. He was followed by the Viscount de Martignac, a moderate whose ministry endured for nineteen months. Charles was uncomfortable with Martignac's government and plotted his demise for seven months. He created a new ministry (August 8, 1829) under the reactionary Prince de Polignac, thereby serving notice that efforts to get along with opponents of his program were ended. The mere announcement of the new ministers created a public scandal, not only in Paris but in the other capitals of Europe, although Metternich observed that it was a bold but necessary move to the right. Polignac was known to share Charles' political views and to believe that the Bible was the only real charter and that God intervened in human affairs. His appointment was shocking to wide segments of the public, but equally disturbing were the names of the Count de la Bourdonnaye, a moving spirit in the White Terror and now minister of the interior, and the Count of Bourmont, a general who had deserted Napoleon before Waterloo and was now minister of war. A torrent of liberal protest met the new ministry; its opponents in the Chamber of Deputies became as intractable as the King himself and condemned "Milord" Polignac and "Judas" Bourmont.

The *Journal des Débats,* a moderately royalist organ, could see nothing in the new government but "national humiliation, misfortune, and danger." The only holdover was the minister of finance, the Count of Chabrol. La Bourdonnaye proved to be quarrelsome and unable to cooperate either with liberal deputies or his political allies. He readily alienated Polignac and when he resigned in November, a series of other ministerial adjustments occurred.

Controversy about the cabinet raged into the winter and new voices of criticism appeared, a prominent one being *Le National,* a newspaper founded in January of 1830 by Adolphe Thiers (1797–1877). Funded by the banker Jacques Lafitte and supported by Talleyrand, Thiers and Armand Carrel penned open criticisms of the regime, and pointedly observed that in the English Revolution of 1688 a constructive change had occurred merely by replacing the monarch with one of his relatives. What France needed, they suggested, was a "French 1688," where there would be "a change of persons but not of things." The implication that Charles could be replaced by a relative (the Duke of Orléans, 1773–1850) who would respect the Charter was obvious to the public.

A harsh winter following poor crops also saw a marked increase in destitution. Unemployment spread while thousands died of respiratory ailments. The aristocracy pursued a round of balls and gaiety, for current thinking encouraged the idea that entertainments created employment and were a duty of the higher classes. The literate public assumed that the government was formulating a program to meet the hardships and anxiously awaited the convening of the Chambers on March 2, 1830. Charles opened the sessions with a speech which for the most part was mild and noted a profit in the budget. It ended, however, with a threatening paragraph which asserted royal prerogatives in the face of "perfidious insinuations which malevolence seeks to propagate." The Peers responded with moderate criticism but the Deputies, on March 16, replied bluntly, approving by a vote of 221 to 181 an extremely critical response to the

Crown. The "221" were publicized as heroes but had acted precipitantly before learning any details of the government's program which a number of them might have been able to support. Charles retorted by calling for new elections which were held in July. The newly elected opposition deputies now numbered 270, another rebuff for the government (90,000 voters had selected the 5,000 electors who selected the deputies).

The impasse was clear. Talleyrand wrote that with the "decisive moment" approaching, he could "see neither compass nor pilot and nothing to prevent a shipwreck." The stage was set for a violation of the foundations of the system by either the King or his critics and Charles decided to act. A last-minute attempt at compromise by General Sebastiani was brushed aside by Polignac as the King was determined to carry through what amounted to a legal *coup d'état*. Interestingly enough, both Metternich and Nicholas of Russia opposed the course he was about to follow. The Austrian statesman predicted that any attempt to abolish freedom of the press or to tamper with existing electoral laws in France would cause the dynasty to fall. Nicholas equally felt that any violation of the Charter would lead to a "catastrophe."

The famous Ordinances of July 25, 1830, accomplished all that these observers had feared. There is no question whatever that Charles and the ministry signed these documents with full knowledge of the issues. Charles called them "momentous decisions" which involved "life or death." That he recognized this aspect of the situation makes his action even more difficult to explain, because proper precautions were obviously lacking to deal with any upheaval that the ordinances might touch off. Considering the history of the city of Paris between 1789 and 1799 and the fact that Charles was a brother of Louis XVI, it seems absolutely incredible that the prospect of an uprising was not more seriously weighed. Charles had concluded that decision was required and he took the fateful step with a boldness belying his seventy-three years. To presume that he could alter election laws, shackle the press, and cancel scheduled meetings of the newly elected chamber, all without opposition and a resort to force was amazing. Yet he left Paris in the hands of his prefect of police, who expected no difficulties, after placing local troops under the command of Marshal Marmont, another officer who had aided in Napoleon's fall. The garrison was below normal strength because of the campaign in Algeria; Algiers had fallen on July 5 giving Charles one of his few successes. Though the King may not have realized it, feeling against him and his ministry was so intense that this achievement brought virtually no political gain. At any rate, after he signed the Ordinances, he left Paris to go hunting and was out of town when they were published the next morning, Monday, July 26. Insurrection broke out and by Thursday night, royal troops had been beaten and driven from the city. Four days later Charles abdicated and headed for England while arrangements in Paris were being made to install the Duke of Orléans as Louis Philippe, King of the French, which was accomplished on August 9, 1830. France had had its 1688.

The problems of understanding Charles' lack of foresight and the inadequate preparations for violence are equaled by attempts to analyze the insurrection. It has become a truism that lower-class republican elements fought the revolution but had its gains taken over or assumed by the bourgeoisie. That the middle class was not at the barricades is clear. Who did man the barricades then, and why? Recent research has shed considerable light on the personnel of the crowds and now this query can be at least partially answered.

The harsh economic circumstances of 1830 must be seen in light of conditions since 1828. Bad as they were, there had been an improvement from the low point in 1829. Thus, economic distress must be seen as part of the background establishing a general tone of discontent, easy to blame on the government, but it cannot be regarded as the direct cause of the specific uprising in July, 1830. Similarly, anticlericalism may be seen as part of the context of the revolt but not the direct cause.

An immediate consequence of the Ordinances was a closing of print shops. Crowds on the 26th contained a large number of printers, and on the 27th, as the situation worsened, many printers and journalists were in evidence. They appear to have acted as catalysts, helping to stir up other city dwellers who then attacked the symbols of royalty. Printers were not particularly prominent in the crowds after the 27th, though other tradesmen were. The uprising was never manned by the lowest social classes, a circumstance which raises serious interpretive questions. Two events seem to have combined to encourage open insurrection. Knowledge that the unpopular Marmont was in command caused many to sympathize with the printers and agree with an objection to the Ordinances defiantly published and circulated by liberal journalists. Marmont was a symbol of national disgrace and his appointment focused popular hostility against the dynasty, not merely against the ministry. On Wednesday, the 28th, the tricolor appeared on a tower of Notre Dame and the bell of the cathedral boomed defiantly. It is difficult to assess the impact of this appeal to patriotism, but the uprising against the troops of the crown then became widespread and was completely out of control.

Leadership for the insurgents has been variously attributed, but it is now thought that mature veterans from the Revolutionary and Napoleonic period gave direction to the mob activity. Some former National Guardsmen (disbanded since 1827) appeared in uniform, but their numbers were small and few really fought on the barricades. Students from the *École polytechnique* were minor participants, with only sixty-one fighting on the last day. Republican agitators or Carbonari leaders were also negligible elements. Thus the forceful phase of the revolution was a genuinely patriotic uprising consciously against an unpopular dynasty and in behalf of those views symbolized by the tricolor. In its actions, the populace was thinking more of 1789 than of 1688.

In liberal newspaper circles, the Ordinances were regarded as absolutely outrageous. Thiers drew up a bold statement, signed by forty-three journalists, announcing that obedience to the regime was no longer a duty and that the required authorizations to publish would be defied as long as possible. Accordingly, *Le Temps, Le National, Le Globe,* and *Le Journal du Commerce* appeared on the 27th and carried Thiers' protest. Ironically, the debatable issues raised by the Ordinances were mainly political and little related to the mass of Parisian city dwellers composing the crowds who had few political rights under the Charter and virtually no direct reason to be concerned about either its defense or violation. Indeed, journalists noted a considerable apathy which first appeared as the popular reaction to the Ordinances. They were elated as the situation deepened, which would lead, they hoped, to recall of the Ordinances and the fall of the ministry. At the same time a number of like-minded deputies were anxiously meeting. The climactic day of the revolution was Thursday, which saw the royalist troops routed and the agreement by thirty deputies, meeting at Lafitte's house, on Lafayette as formal commander of the victorious insurgents. They also appointed a temporary municipal government for Paris that began to function the next day. Also on Friday placards appeared which Thiers and his associates had produced promoting the Duke of Orléans as one dedicated to the Revolution who would defend the Charter. Later that day a group of deputies declared him the Duke Lieutenant General of the Kingdom.

The politicians and journalists had thus set the stage for a transition of power to the Duke of Orléans. However, a number of republicans claimed that they had really won the revolution and they proposed Lafayette as president. At this juncture Lafayette decided in favor of a constitutional monarchy for France rather than a republic and consequently cooperated in the move to bring the Duke to the throne. On Saturday morning, the 31st, the crucial event occurred. The Duke went to the republican headquarters in the

Louis Philippe and his sons. (Courtesy of Historical Pictures Service, Chicago.)

Hotel de Ville and there on a balcony before an applauding crowd, he and Lafayette embraced. This approval of the mob was taken as sanction by the people for the accession of the Duke. It was now too late for Charles, who had been at St. Cloud most of the time and through a spyglass had seen the tricolor atop Notre Dame. Before abdicating he offered to withdraw the Ordinances and to replace the ministry but these decisions came too late. When he abdicated, he named his grandson, the Duke of Bordeaux (the future so-called Henry V), as his successor, and left the protection of his rights to the Duke of Orléans, a wistful and unrealistic gesture. With both Charles and his grandson in exile, Louis Philippe's position was that the throne had been vacated.

Interestingly enough, although some deputies were active in the move to bring the Duke of Orléans to the throne, few of the 428 had been active in the revolt. The fall of the regime came as a surprise to many but was virtually required to head off the more radical demands for a republic. In effect, the upper classes sacrificed Charles X in order to retain and extend their own privileges. The situation required a forthright assurance of loyalty to the Charter from the new monarch along with alterations of the document so as to preclude the offensive features of Bourbon rule in the future. The changes had to appear to have a marked republican character and many members of the Chamber of Deputies, which Charles had decided would not meet, met formally to revise the Charter. They also declared the throne vacant and invited Orléans' accession, provided he approve the alterations. He took the oath to the revised Charter on August 9, and thence began his reign. The deputies who accomplished all this numbered 219, a majority by only five; the Chamber of Peers had been unable to produce even a similar slender majority.

Changes in the Charter were intended to assure liberal influence in government. Naturally press censorship was forbidden and Catholicism was explicitly denied as a formal state religion. As King *of the French* the monarch was to hold his throne from the people and such medievalism as a coronation with holy oil at Rheims was not expected to be a part of the new reign. Both houses could now initiate legislation and the franchise was extended. The National Guard was solidly restored and the tricolor was affirmed as the nation's flag.

Thus autocracy was routed and a new regime came to power in France. It was the work of a minority with the nation at large accepting the change. There had been no massive popular upheaval and the population had not been particularly hostile to the dynasty. Most of France was politically inert, and in 1830, as so often in its history, the majority of the nation merely accepted the alterations made in Paris.

As the crisis had deepened Talleyrand played a key role, using his influence with members of the diplomatic corps to keep them from publicly supporting Charles X. Internationally, the fall of Charles was encouraging to liberals but disturbing to Metternich. The Tsar was similarly concerned and in diplomatic parlance coldly recognized Louis Philippe as a "friend" and not a "brother." A change of monarchs by mob action, especially in Paris, was particularly offensive to Metternich, but a series of other disturbances prevented him from any forthright action. Besides, the whole affair was over very quickly and Metternich could argue that, after all, Louis Philippe *was* royalty and Charles had not been very wise. Thus he accepted what amounted to a *fait accompli* and hoped that the French example would not be widely followed. This hope proved illusory.

Louis Philippe was barely established on the throne when riots and revolt broke out in Brussels. Ill will, pent up since the Fundamental Law had been imposed, gradually reached a fever pitch; on August 25, 1830, it burst forth and rapidly assumed the proportions of a major revolution.

The omens of trouble had been clear for some time but William failed to take them seriously. A landmark on the way to revolution was the 1828 formation of the Union of Belgian Catholics and Liberals, a temporary tactical fusion of the two major political groups in the southern provinces. Essentially conservative, the Catholic Party joined the Liberals in presenting their petitions of grievances. Both parties were interested in reform and wanted especially freedom of the press, ministerial responsibility, jury trials, and revision of both the tax structure and the requirements regarding the use of the Dutch language. Revolution was not even contemplated. William bluntly rejected these proposals, creating further unrest among the Belgians. Civic leaders took the King's rebuff personally and their indignation was communicated broadly among the population. These provinces had not known independence for centuries, but they were accustomed to deferential treatment and possessed a fierce sense of pride dating from their first documented appearance in history, when Caesar described them as the "bravest of these" tribes in Gaul.

By 1830, William's unresponsive attitude to grievances coupled with his meddling in Church affairs had welded the southern provinces into a kind of national unit. This represented an enormous change because the population was rent by a number of divisive characteristics. Over the centuries an intense municipal and provincial loyalty had developed and feeling toward foreign overlords was often more benevolent than that toward the other provinces. A cultural cleavage ran through the area and still creates problems today. To the north and west were Flemings, strongly religious with a fundamentalist Catholicism reflecting the early missionary activity of the Irish Church, with a literature and culture clearly Germanic but strongly independent. In the south and east were the Walloons, culturally oriented toward France and the builders of a rapidly growing industrial plant. That William's policies brought these two together in cooperation against him speaks volumes. Growing economic hardship after 1824 aggravated the existing grounds for discontent. Another factor in the deepening crisis was the appearance of a number of capable young journalists whose ideological comments revealed a large dose of French Revolutionary sentiment as well as a distaste for William and things Dutch. Adding to the incendiary situation were a host of exiles from all over Central and Western Europe. Only London was more of a haven for leaders of unsuccessful revolts than Brussels. The overthrow of Charles X was an obviously suggestive example, especially to young liberal journalists, but its importance in the specific sequence of events leading to the uprising has often been overrated. French radicals were intriguing in Brussels and Belgian critics of William were in contact with Louis Philippe, but these were not basic to the situation in late August, 1830. William had only himself to blame.

In August an industrial exhibition was held in Brussels and was visited by William. Its conclusion was to be observed on August 23 with fireworks. The 24th was also a scheduled occasion for celebration because it was William's fifty-ninth birthday. A few plotters, hoping for an upheaval, put out inflammatory leaflets proclaiming: "August 23, fireworks; August 24, the King's birthday; August 25, revolution." Local officials were aware of existing unrest but garrisons were not enlarged. The only special precaution was the cancelation of the fireworks and celebrations because of bad weather, a spurious excuse which irritated many people who saw nothing at all wrong with the weather. On August 25, the opera *La Muette de Portici* opened in Brussels. Its theme of revolt in Naples aroused the audience, which poured into the streets shouting anti-Dutch slogans. Assuming mob proportions, it roamed freely, looting and sacking the homes of Dutch officials. The 26th was also given over to mob action while local leaders hurriedly discussed means of ending the disturbances. Hastily, an assembly of notables, formed from nobles, businessmen, and local officials, met and drew up a polite address to the King, asking for a considerate hearing for their grievances. At this point William's kingdom was intact and would have remained so if he had been willing to grant a reasonable amount of administrative autonomy to the Belgian provinces. This was the most that the notables wanted, but by failing to agree at once, the King left them in a position where popular sentiment and militant pressure forced them to more radical demands as the only way in which they could maintain control. William's reaction was to send one of his sons, the Prince of Orange, to conduct discussions (September 1–3) with the notables while he collected troops, ultimately to be led against the insurgents by his other son, Prince Frederick. The Prince of Orange (the future William II) was politely welcomed and was reasonable in his discussions, showing sympathy for the idea of administrative separation. Alexander de Gendebien, speaking for the notables, suggested the Prince as a viceroy for the southern provinces. The Prince responded that he could only convey sentiments to his father but declared that he would urge acceptance of the notables' requests.

Throughout the Belgian provinces, news of the uprising in Brussels triggered a series of other revolts, a quite different reaction from that in France when word had spread of the revolt against Charles X. Except for Ghent and Antwerp, all the major cities were in open insurrection; Liège and Louvain were particularly violent. From these subsidiary revolts, local leaders and many of their followers came to Brussels, which contributed a more forceful element to the revolution. Foremost among new faces in the leadership was Charles Rogier (1800–1885), an energetic young leader who came to Brussels with his "Legion from Liège," a band of some 400 young zealots. In Brussels there was a situation of near anarchy when Prince Frederick, after his father refused to yield, moved toward the city on September 21 with an army of 12,000. With the approaching army, many notables lost heart and left Brussels, among them Gendebien and Sylvain van de Weyer. Barricades were put up but the city was unprepared for serious military defense. To the surprise of the leaders of the insurrection, Rogier's "Legion," augmented by other provincial volunteers who had entered Brussels and many urban rebels, fought furiously against elements of the Dutch force. After a few days of further encounters, Frederick and the Dutch troops left the city on September 26. Leaders of the revolt now organized a provisional government with an executive committee composed of Charles Rogier, Gendebien, and Van de Weyer (who had returned after the 23rd), Count Felix de Mérode, a member of a local family of great distinction, and Louis de Potter, a rabid and energetic young journalist who had long been agitating against William's policies. The revolution became committed to outright independence, and on October 4 the new government called for a national congress, which was elected and duly convened on November 10, 1830. Meanwhile the Prince of Orange sensed the trend of events and proclaimed the

Belgians independent, hoping to rule in Brussels in his father's name. For a time many statesmen saw such an arrangement as an obvious solution to the problem. William, however, would have none of this and called on England, Russia, Prussia, and Austria for aid in putting down the revolution. Considerable support would have been necessary because all the Belgian cities and towns applauded the success against the Dutch troops in Brussels and cooperated with the new provisional government, providing troops and assurances of monetary support. To await help while developing more careful plans for dealing with the Belgians, on October 21, William requested an armistice and a conference of the powers in London. His representatives and those of the powers signatory to the old Quadruple Alliance met and imposed an armistice. By this course, William added immeasurably to his problem, because this had the effect of granting belligerent status to the Belgians, technically making it much easier for outsiders to aid them. The first phase of the revolution was over.

The National Congress which sat from November 10, 1830 to July 21, 1831 established the bases for Belgian political life. Elected by a restricted suffrage, the Congress was composed of prestigious members of the upper class. It reiterated Belgian independence from Holland and established a constitutional hereditary monarchy, forever excluding the House of Orange-Nassau. The Congress then drafted a constitution and selected a king before it disbanded to allow political life according to the newly established rules. An unusually productive Congress, its work was completed during an increasing involvement of the Powers in Belgian affairs. No narrative does justice to the complexity and interrelationship of events which now occurred and tested the mettle of Europe's statesmen. Upheavals in Poland and Italy, ministerial crises in England, all in the wake of the fall of Charles X and the Belgian revolt, were virtually contemporaneous events that enhanced the dangers of miscalculation and that can be seen as the background in which the Belgians worked out the details of their separation from Holland.

By February 25, 1831, the new Constitution was prepared. A thoroughly liberal document, its debt to the French Revolution was obvious. It was a more explicit liberal statement than the revised charter which Louis Philippe had accepted. It gave considerable authority to local communes but was no simple outgrowth of medieval charters. The monarch was to be King of the Belgians. Ministers were responsible to the Chambers, which voted annually on the budget and the size of the army. Personal liberty and freedoms of the press, worship, and association were explicitly affirmed. After some debate over various royal prospects (including the Duke of Leuchtenberg, son of Eugène Beauharnais, a possibility utterly unacceptable to France) the Congress selected the Duke of Nemours, the second son of Louis Philippe. Such a choice was opposed by the English, especially because it lent credence to the idea that the whole revolution was French inspired and a shabby device for French expansion. Louis Philippe tactfully declined for his son; finally, in June of 1831, Prince Leopold (1790–1865) of Saxe-Coburg was selected. In retrospect, this proved a brilliant choice, although at the time it was attended by scant enthusiasm. He had recently declined the throne of Greece after his wife's untimely death denied him the prospect of being consort to an English Queen. His family contacts among the German nobility were extensive and he also was an uncle to both Victoria and Albert. He soon married Louise, a daughter of Louis Philippe; so, as nominal head of the new state, he had influence and prestige in the major capitals of Western Europe, an enormous diplomatic asset for the newly formed nation. He accepted the crown in the midst of trying conditions and worked hard to get diplomatic acceptance for his new country. In later years Leopold claimed he had really founded the country. Catholic and Liberal politicians, however, insisted rather that they had established the country before selecting Leopold. This disagreement rankled with him, and he never forgot that he was the second choice of the Congress.

When William invited the Powers to consider his situation, he had expected assistance. His view of the problem was clear and uncomplicated. Subject peoples had risen up against a legitimate sovereign, as in Naples and Spain, and he deserved assistance in restoring his authority. This was in accord with the Vienna settlement, where it had been emphasized that it was important for the peace of Europe that William's kingdom extend to the French frontier. That the formal structure of Vienna had earlier been eroded seemed not to alter the situation for the Dutch monarch.

As with all the diplomatic crises since 1815, Metternich closely followed these events. After the fall of Charles X, he and Count Nesselrode, Russia's foreign minister, had met at Carlsbad to discuss the situation. For the moment (August 6) they decided that nothing should be done so long as France merely experienced a domestic change of dynasty without assuming an aggressive foreign policy. Louis Philippe openly gave assurances of peaceful intentions, but the outbreak of violence in Brussels cast these in serious doubt. Prospects of unified Great Power intervention supporting William were curtailed when uprisings occurred in both Italy and Poland and all the Powers wanted the Belgian crisis somehow to pass without war. Metternich saw the entire situation as laden with variables he could not control and aimed at a solution which would keep France contained, avoid war, and retain Austrian domination in Italy. Belgian independence per se seems not to have worried him very much as long as France was not enlarged.

In both France and England the business classes provided liberal support for the Belgians. The two powers aimed at a diplomatic solution which would see the Belgians independent and secure. When William refused to approve Leopold as King of the Belgians and violated the armistice by sending an army into Belgium, the French at once provided a counterforce commanded by Marshal Gérard (1773–1852). At the same time, Anglo-French naval units blockaded Dutch cities and the Dutch were forced to withdraw. A French army in Belgium alarmed Metternich, but the need to protect Leopold was clear. Meanwhile another prospect was that Prussian troops might intervene. French statesmen pointedly declared themselves in favor of a doctrine of nonintervention and suggested that France would greet Prussian troops with force. The upheaval in Poland disturbed Prussia's leaders and Frederick William was prepared to turn his back on William, sacrificing him for the higher good of European peace. He declared that in this regard he "silenced his heart so as to hear only the dictates of public reason." England had not wanted French troops in Belgium but was helpless to disapprove when William resorted to arms. Despite the problems in Italy and Poland, both Metternich and Nicholas were concerned by the bold French action. As before, the acts of force were short-lived, so the period of greatest danger passed quickly. France acted as an independent power in this crisis and was really free from any sort of former probationary status. Nicholas was the monarch who most closely agreed with William, and he refused all ideas of compromise. Though the meetings in London eventually produced a solution, the Tsar declared that he would not accept the idea of an independent Belgium until William did. As a matter of fact, he held out over a decade longer than William.

The negotiators had many disputed points of detail to adjudicate. Obviously the new state could not be expected to fill the former Netherlands role of an effective buffer against France. Much quibbling ensued over the dismantling of specific fortresses, but the decision to admit Belgium as a forever neutral state whose independence would be guaranteed by the Powers solved this problem. There were interminable discussions about how the debt of the former kingdom was to be divided and boundary issues were especially vexing. The final settlement gave the Belgians less of Luxembourg than they desired and they also lost Maastricht and the duchy of Limburg. The Dutch monarch remained Grand Duke of Luxembourg, which belonged to the German Confederation. The talks dragged on for years while Leopold was presiding over a government which was fully operational, with its own army and diplomatic service. After final decisions were reached in 1838, the appropriate documents were signed on April 19, 1839. Forced to bow before the pressures of the Great Powers, William abdicated and his son, William II, witnessed the conclusion of the negotiations.

The revolutions in France and Belgium sent out shock waves over the rest of Europe, where a growing middle class reacted with enthusiasm and an often misguided optimism. In the Germanies especially, newspapers avidly reported events in Paris and Brussels as, despite censorship, the agitation led to outbreaks against the forces of the status quo. A number of additional constitutions were granted in the smaller German states (Hanover, Hesse-Cassel, Saxony, Brunswick), but generally the unrest was uncoordinated and lacked effective leadership.

Further east, in Poland, the impact of the revolt in the west was more pronounced. A revolutionary situation had gradually been developing for several years. As in Russia before the Decembrist episode, a number of secret societies had been formed, most of them of an anti-Russian, pro-Polish character. Irritation centered on Polish ambitions for lands to the east that she held prior to the eighteenth-century partitions and on the desire of Nicholas to use Polish troops in his struggle with Turkey in behalf of the Greeks. Constantine acted as a defender of their interests concerning the use of the Polish army, which only increased Nicholas' suspicion. In 1829, the Tsar was formally crowned in Warsaw as King of Poland, but in the 1830 Diet, ill will toward Russian rule was obvious. Revolt broke out in the wake of the Belgian uprising when word spread in Warsaw that Nicholas intended to march with Polish and Russian troops to put down the revolutionaries in both Brussels and Paris. A poorly led conspiracy composed of army officers and students broke out on November 29, 1830. An attempt to murder Constantine failed, but the Viceroy departed and took with him substantial military forces. The result was an enthusiastic show of support from urban workers and an immediate establishment by the elite of a provisional government which sent out pleas for help and girded itself for more serious military action.

Chance and poor judgment appeared on every hand in this revolt. To strike against Constantine was to move against their best friend in the councils of Russian power. Had the Viceroy stayed in Warsaw, the rebels could not have established themselves in a formal fashion. The aristocracy moved rapidly to take a hand in the new government, lest the workers assume a more radical role; as in France support of the lower urban classes was essential but they were finessed out of the councils of decision. The key leaders now were Prince Czartoryski (1770–1861), General Chlopicki (1771–1854), and General Skrznecki (1786–1860). Once in control they tried to negotiate with Nicholas, who refused to compromise with insurrection. He was especially intractable after January 25, 1831, when the Diet declared his deposition. They were thus driven to assume more openly the status of national revolutionary leaders, a position they could only partially fulfill because of a lack of peasant support. The revolt lasted until autumn of 1831, with Warsaw falling to the Russians September 8. Cholera and the need for troops along the Turkish frontier had allowed the revolt to continue as long as it had, but without outside help, it stood little chance of success. The Poles put undue hope on the idea of assistance from other powers, especially France. They believed that Russian attempts to crush them violated the Vienna settlement and therefore that Prussia, England, and Austria should support them. An ironic touch is that although prospects of outside intervention were illusory, they missed opportunities for striking military successes themselves. Their generals were defense-minded and especially concerned with surviving the period with the honor of Polish arms intact. The Tsar's unwillingness to negotiate after formally being deposed meant that the leaders of the revolt either had to fight with their current forces or had to institute broad land reforms to gain extra support from the population. French revolutionary ideals had already been partially introduced by Napoleon, but now the aristocracy shrank from further reform.

With the entry of Russian troops into Warsaw, a reign of terror began as Nicholas took a vicious revenge. The separate status of Poland provided for at Vienna was discarded and martial law applied to the occupied area. Most leaders of the revolt fled to Western Europe to be welcomed by the middle and upper classes; those who failed to escape were summarily executed. Far more of Nicholas' enemies were killed than was the case after the Decembrist Revolt, but then, the Polish upheaval was more widespread and a more serious challenge.

Though the Poles were crushed, the consequences of their attempt were far-reaching. The revolt had forestalled the Tsar's threat to send an army toward Brussels and Paris. Nicholas was revealed as a complete despot, and militarism within Russia became more pronounced. Polish intellectuals and officers in Western Europe were particularly embarrassing for diplomats who, while sympathizing with them personally, could hardly countenance their intensive and consistent anti-Russian intrigues. The revolt in Poland had added another dimension to the unrest already apparent in 1830 and doomed any hopes William had of aid from Prussia. It also made Metternich more willing to accept an accommodation with France and England that would recognize Belgium. The revolt assured the presence of more Russian troops in Eastern Europe, and Metternich was left free to deal with non-Prussian Central Europe. Unrest within the Confederation, though potentially dangerous, proved no real difficulty. His most serious challenge was in Italy, where the revolutionary news of Brussels and Paris also struck a responsive chord.

In 1830, Italy, like Poland, was on the verge of revolt. The Carbonari movement responsible for earlier violence had long been planning a massive uprising. This time there was extensive cooperation between the various secret organizations and coordination with international societies meeting in Paris and London. A leading member in the conspiracy was Enrico Misley (1801–1863) of Modena, who spent several years trying to arrange agreement among the various groups. The objective now was freeing most of Italy, not just one state. The conspirators hoped that Metternich would be too engrossed in watching Russia's activities against Turkey to embark on a new and vigorous program of repression against outbreaks in Italy. It was important that the revolt, when it appeared, encompass a substantial area and that it be led by a bona fide prince. Also the threat of outside assistance would help as a deterrent to Austrian action. For his prince, Misley selected Duke Francis IV of Modena. Misley obtained agreement on Francis among the conspirators only with great difficulty. Francis was ambitious and was suspected of being unreliable. That Misley had discussed the scheme with Capodistrias worried Francis, but he yearned for the greater prestige that he thought would come to him as king of a constitutional kingdom embracing Central Italy. By winning over Francis the conspirators felt that the total armed resources of at least one state (Modena) would be at their disposition as a dependable nucleus. Several of the mistakes of the earlier Italian uprisings would thus be avoided. In France, encouragement for the plotters came from several who wanted Louis Philippe to come to power. Unfortunately, the whole scheme appeared to disintegrate when, in September of 1829, Russian hostilities with Turkey ended. Austria now was less apprehensive about Russia and Francis feared that Metternich might learn from the Russians about his part in the intrigue.

Misley hastily tried to erect a new program which included revolts in Spain, Italy, and France. Before preparations for concerted upheavals were complete, Charles X had fallen, the Belgians were in revolt, and the French had made their statement about a doctrine of nonintervention. In Italy high prices because of food shortages had increased the prospects for mob support once an insurrection started and the situation seemed ripe for a massive Italian version of the Belgian revolt. The conspirators, however, were to be frustrated by Metternich's skill and the caution of Louis Philippe. With the Russians occupied in Poland, Metternich was free to take action in Central and Southern Europe, and he made this clear to France. As a consequence, a new and more cautious French government redefined the doctrine of nonintervention in such a way that, for Italy, it applied only to Piedmont. A sort of trading thus occurred, with Metternich countenancing Belgian independence and France recognizing Austrian prerogatives in Italy. Francis belatedly tried to crush the conspiracy before it could get started, but in February of 1831, revolts broke out. The Austrian army rapidly put them down and the hope of independence through secret societies was ended. The prospect of liberation had never been seen in terms of the entire peninsula, although the effort in 1831 was on a distinctly broader scale than that of previous uprisings. For Italy hope of aid from France was far more realistic than the expectations of many Poles. Metternich viewed the situation as merely another need for applying the Troppau Protocol, which he justified on much the same grounds as Russian suppression of revolt in Poland.

From the viewpoint of the conservative powers, the extremely dangerous years of 1830–1831 had passed with the general structure of Europe intact but for Belgian independence. France had backed down on her statement of nonintervention and, aside from Belgium, England had played a negligible role. The Greek struggle was over and Turkey was clearly weakened. Autocracy had been shaken but not seriously challenged. Germany still was in a client position, and in Italy, reaction was dominant. Italians were still not thinking in terms of a free Italy; indeed Metternich appeared to be the most prominent statesman with a view of the entire peninsula. The Italians were slowly groping toward a national image of themselves. In this respect they were way behind the Poles who remembered a historic Poland. In Italy there was nothing like this after Rome, and Italians thus had the double task of freeing themselves from the Austrians and of creating an Italian nationalism. They achieved this in the next generation.

VI

*Another Attempt at
Stability and Order:
The Limited Recognition
of New Forces*

CHAPTER 16

The English Example of Responsible Reform

Although the revolutions spawned in 1830 had been largely contained, they signalled the coming of a new era. A number of interesting domestic alterations in Europe had occurred largely because in many areas the conditions for life had altered markedly since 1815. Stability and order remained the objectives of European diplomacy but were now seen as a continuing problem. Some statesmen, like Nicholas and Metternich, found solutions by a reactionary resort to old methods, granting barely a minimum of recognition to new forces. In Western Europe, social and political structures were altered to accommodate a rapidly changing society. In England, deliberate efforts to adapt to new conditions successfully avoided the extremes of violence and repression which appeared to the east.

The Reform Bill of 1832 was a landmark in English political history. Its domestic implications constituted more of a real revolution than the fall of Charles X in France and the measure became the source of justified pride for decades of English historians. Parliamentary monarchy proved flexible enough to spare the nation from open revolution, after coming to its very edge. Her early solution of problems largely engendered by industrialization is worth particular study because the rest of Europe was later to experience similar situations although forced to deal with them in different contexts and without the parliamentary tradition that England possessed.

So much has been made of the Reform Bill that the earlier reform legislation of the 1820's has often been overlooked. The Tories stood staunchly opposed to any basic change of the rotten borough system and incurred after 1815 a public image of being antiliberal and antidemocratic; they stood ready to use force if necessary to maintain control. The Seditious Meetings Bill, suspension of the Habeas Corpus Act, the Peterloo Massacre, and the Six Acts reinforced this image; but such a view hardly does justice to important reforms which the Tories instituted prior to 1830. A significant new wing in the Tory party, headed by Sir Robert Peel (1788–1850), was receptive to liberal ideas and worked to make the party more responsive to changing conditions. The nominal Tory leader between 1812 and 1827 was Lord Liverpool (1770–1828), who sought to moderate differences between his various ministers. The year 1822 saw a sharp alteration in the leadership. George Canning succeeded Castlereagh as both foreign secretary and as leader of the House of Commons; Peel became home secretary; and William Huskisson (1770–1830) became president of the Board of Trade. The monarch was George IV, who ruled from January 29, 1820 to June 26, 1830; he was a selfish, untrustworthy reactionary. His reign appropriately began with a scandal when his wife (since 1795) Caroline sought full recognition as his queen. Her death on August 7, 1821, solved this particular problem, but the monarch's image never improved.

With Canning's support, Peel and Huskisson launched England on a reform program destined to continue for decades. Canning was endowed with a driving energy and, in marked contrast to Castlereagh, knew finance well enough to be amenable to Huskisson's ideas for fiscal reform. Careful concern for commercial policy reflected the government's awareness that two thirds of England's population no longer worked on the land. The new Tory reformers were recognizing that agriculture was no longer supreme and that middle-class values had to be recognized and protected. Naturally, this created rifts within the Tory ranks, and as more progressive reforms appeared, the opposition to government action was as vehement within Tory ranks as it was from the Whigs, with whom Peel openly cooperated on occasion. Canning supported the wide range of remedial legislation prepared by his associates but was completely adamant toward the growing demands for parliamentary reform. His death in 1828 occurred before this issue became crucial, but his blind spot in this regard is worth remembering.

Domestic, legal, and social legislation were of special interest to Peel. After consultations with Jeremy Bentham, he completely recast the nation's criminal code, reducing the number of crimes carrying the death sentence by 200. In many respects England had been the most advanced European state, but even the Russian Tsar, in 1814, had commented on their harsh system of punishment. He attributed the excessive punishments, paradoxically, to the greater basic freedom enjoyed by Englishmen—a government powerless to prevent crime in the first place must of necessity punish offenders harshly. The laws were so Draconian that jury convictions were difficult to attain, despite compelling evidence. Peel's initial reforms were continued until, by 1838, murder and treason remained the basic crimes meriting a punishment of death. Peel's establishment of a professional police force for London (the "Bobbies") was merely the most striking of a whole series of beneficial measures instituted by the new Tory leadership.

Huskisson's achievement was to put the economy on a more rational basis. Modifications in the Navigation Laws led eventually to their repeal in 1849. Instead of the mercantilistic monopoly of colonial trade, Huskisson argued for greater emphasis on the welfare of the colonies. The result was a loosening of restrictions on colonial trade and a pronounced increase in loyalty to the mother country. At the same time he thoroughly revised English tariffs and domestic taxation. Essentially a believer in free trade and no protection, his policies were a stimulus to industry, with shipbuilding and commerce showing an especially rapid growth. An orgy of speculation (deplored by Canning, Liverpool, and Huskisson) accompanying the prosperity in 1824 led to an acute crisis and depression starting late in the next year. A poor harvest in 1826 increased the widespread privation and prompted the government to set aside temporarily the restrictions embodied in the Corn Law of 1815. The landed interests thus acquiesced in the face of crisis. When relief followed, the Law appeared detrimental to the community at large. The ministry consequently began an unsuccessful move to revise the Corn

Law. This had the effect of making the Laws an open target for complaint, and they continued to be the object of withering attack through 1846. After Canning's death in August of 1827, the Tory leadership fell eventually to the Duke of Wellington, who presided over a government which enjoyed little sympathy from the followers of Canning. It is ironic that while consciously attempting to move back to a more obvious Tory position, Wellington was forced to support a reform which old Tories viewed as anathema, Catholic Emancipation. As Wellington began his movement to the right, he lost support from many of the Canning group who joined forces with the Whigs.

The apex of Tory reform came in 1829. In the year before, the Test and Corporation Acts had been modified in favor of granting equal political rights to non-Anglican Protestants. The obvious next step would bring political equality to the Roman Catholics. The effort to admit Catholics to the nation's political life through the vote and seats in Parliament had had a desultory and spasmodic history, with many frustrations and few successes. A high point had been the opening of all military ranks to Roman Catholics in 1817. Political rights for Catholics were appropriately tied to the Irish problem, England's perennial nightmare. Sensing the spirit of reform in the 1820s, Irish leaders made a concerted effort for political gains through attacking those restrictions clearly based on religion. In a blunt challenge to the system, Daniel O'Connell (1775–1847) ran for a seat in Parliament in county Clare. His was a shocking candidacy, because it was known that he could not be seated if he won. An O'Connell victory demonstrated a solidarity which infuriated many Tories, but Wellington decided that concessions to the Catholics were essential if a civil war was to be avoided. Historically, the English had often countenanced repression in Ireland when it seemed expedient, but now a chorus of voices counseling moderation and justice was raised in Parliament itself. Robert Peel and other Tories had opposed Catholic Emancipation because they anticipated that the rotten borough system would allow some wealthy Catholics to acquire a number of seats in Commons. These would be a direct threat to Tory control, but after O'Connell's election, this Tory opposition retreated before what was sensed as a greater threat. It was cogently argued that problems of Irish unrest were more practically faced through discussion with some Catholic spokesmen, whose mere presence in Parliament had a soothing effort on the population in Ireland, rather than encouraging a seething hotbed of rebellion and no effective communication with Irish leaders. It was, of course, an illusion that simple admission to Parliament would solve the problem. Indeed, Wellington's action only convinced many Irish that militancy gained practical results. Although the immediate crisis was past, a tactless attempt to keep O'Connell personally out of Parliament meant that the ministry's concession failed to bring the popular acclaim in Ireland that it merited. At the same time, Wellington's role brought him intense criticism from the more reactionary Tories, the group he normally found most congenial. As with the various Canningite reforms, the Whigs supported Emancipation as though it were their own issue. The admission of Catholics brought no advantage to the Tories, whose ranks now were badly fragmented. It may be argued that reform once started was incompatible with Toryism. The very nature of reform attitudes made it inevitable that eventually the foundations of the party itself would be eroded, still another of history's examples of conservatism being a continuously disintegrating position. It was a period of shifting loyalties, for the old party labels and clichés were hardly adequate to a political situation requiring imagination and flexibility. New elections after the death of George IV on June 26, 1830, brought all of this to a head.

Until the Tories began to heed the demands for reform, their political ascendancy was nearly unassailable. For decades they had kept the Whigs from office. Motions for parliamentary reform had been introduced at various intervals since 1745. Such reform, however, meant attacking institutions which Blackstone regarded as the height of human wisdom in government. Taking their arguments from Bentham, the Philosophic Radicals had launched scathing attacks on the system. These had been so bitter that as late as 1817, the Whigs found them reprehensible. During the 1820s, however, the Whigs sensed a political opportunity and became a party dedicated to widescale reform; late in 1830, they accepted the challenge of reforming Parliament itself. Tory reforms represented a gradual movement toward Whig views, a circumstance which encouraged a redoubling of Whig efforts. Lord John Russell (1792–1878) had introduced a bill for parliamentary reform in 1819, and this became the Whig political program. With the change of sovereigns in 1830, the Whigs noted a rising mood in support of reform and prepared to campaign explicitly on this issue. As generally understood, their electoral success brought Earl Grey (1764–1845) to office and guaranteed a struggle against last-ditch conservative elements. Emerging from this combat were the Reform Bill of 1832, a wave of new reform legislation, and a reorganization of the party structures. Between

1830 and 1832, English political life embarked on a new course, which ultimately resulted in parliamentary democracy.

The involved situation from which the Reform Bill emerged defies adequate description and its complexity is often underrated. Most accounts are oversimplified stereotypes, uncritically passed from one text to another. Although much of what occurred is still not clear, it is obvious that many aged generalizations regarding the two years after George IV's death must stand as patently false.

Amidst the uncertainty, the historian's penchant for attention to chronology serves him well and at least reduces the area of speculation. One such instance relates to the impact of the July Revolution on English politics in 1830. That the fall of Charles X coincided with new parliamentary elections was most suggestive. A popular interpretation has been that the upheaval in France provided incentives to radicalism and mob violence which affected the English elections. The time required for news of events in Paris to arrive in London assured ignorance of the July Revolution on the part of most of the English electorate. There was interest in England in the worsening situation in France, but this counted for little when the candidates for the Commons took to the stump. Though some called for reform, the evil of slavery was a more popular topic. The promptness of the general elections after the death of the King led to suggestions that Wellington was attempting a sort of legal *coup d'état,* like that of Polignac. Several proponents of reform in England had friends among the middle class in France, and many Tories were close to some Bourbon Ultras. Indeed, Polignac had assumed the premiership directly after coming from London, where he served as the French ambassador. Interesting as these relationships are, they beg the question so far as the English elections in 1830 are concerned. Whig gains really did not amount to a Whig triumph and Wellington remained the prime minister. Given the state of party fragmentation, Wellington could be said to have lacked a majority before as well as after the election. When Parliament reassembled after the elections, there was little feeling that the Duke should not continue as chief minister. By this time, however (early November), the events in France had made their impact on the thinking of English politicians and the revolution in Belgium was well under way. There was a widely held sympathy for reform which Wellington was expected to acknowledge, just as he had previously adopted the cause of Catholic Emancipation: he fell on November 16, because he stubbornly refused to provide leadership for this new "spirit" in the House of Commons. The previous election had little to do with it.

The new monarch, William IV, was popular and thought to favor reform, but almost anyone following George IV would have been so regarded. When the speech from the throne did not promise reform, Wellington was directly questioned about it and replied that the "full and entire confidence of the country" supported the existing system which he characterized, as Blackstone would have, as the best "the wit of man" could devise.

This open expression of a refusal to reform attracted a storm of indignation. Few moderate voices were heard and Wellington fell back before the combined wrath of proponents for major reform and the criticism of former Canningites who had hoped for mild gestures of reform. He also found himself abandoned by Tory die-hards who had not forgiven him for Catholic Emancipation. Amidst the tumult and the clamor, William called for Earl Grey, who had for twenty years declared himself ready to introduce measures for the reform of Parliament. Grey selected as ministers a distinguished group dominated by peers and containing four future prime ministers, an interesting demonstration of both Tory weakness and the fluctuating nature of the parties. Indeed, the urgency felt for reform blurred party lines as political leaders of all persuasions felt that the future course of orderly political life for England depended on a wise solution of the problem.

Complicating any analysis of the passage of the Reform Bill is the issue of how close England really was to revolution. Many, including Lord Grey, came to believe that "the Bill" was the only alternative; Grey challenged both the House of Lords and the King. The issue of open revolution depended largely on the middle and lower classes, especially the latter, whose role is imperfectly understood. After the newly elected Whiggish Commons passed the Bill (the Second Reform Bill, the first had died in committee in March, 1831) on September 21, 1831, the Lords rejected it on October 8, touching off a rash of violence. Rumors circulated of prepared plans for insurrection if Wellington ever succeeded in forming a new ministry. Historians are still divided on whether England's closeness to revolution in 1831 was real or rhetorical. In the campaigning for the general elections earlier in May of 1831, many rash statements had been made by politicians with dire warnings of what might happen. Were they genuinely perceptive or merely irresponsible? Reformers made so much of "the Bill" that when its progress was checked, they had, in fact, invited violence.

Part of the difficulty in assessing the danger lies in the question of how much the various political spokesmen truly represented widely held views. The Tory position was clear, but what of the exponents of lower-class views? The ideas of Bentham and the Philosophic Radicals were eloquently stated, but how widely were they held? Adult manhood suffrage was an obvious working-class objective, but how did the ambitions of the workers fit into the issues surrounding "the Bill"? Spokesmen for the lower classes, like Cobbett, had held all along that Parliament needed considerable reform, but they saw this as only part of their total program, in which manhood suffrage was more important. Laboring ranks were split into many segments and both objectives and tactics lacked unanimity. There had been agrarian violence in 1830, but there were urban disorders in 1831. When the Whigs openly adopted the cause of reform, most labor spokesmen expected their bill to be mild, making it possible to attack both Whigs and Tories with the same language. The actual provisions of the bill, however, put them in the position of having either to adopt a Torylike attitude in opposing the bill or to support what clearly amounted to a grant of political power to their employers. The Whigs were proposing, in effect, to take power from the landed aristocracy and give it to commercial and manufacturing leaders. In this situation most lower-class spokesmen decided that the bill should be supported as a major step toward further reforms which would ultimately benefit the workers. They saw their enemy at this time as the Tory monopoly in power, not the Whig party.

The extent to which this general pattern of motives is true may be questioned and cannot be answered by study of the speeches of men like Cobbett. Spokesmen for labor were a varied group and each spoke for such a narrow constituency that few inferences may be drawn from their statements beyond what they actually said. It is clear, however, that through the oratory of radicals and the impact of a radical press much of the working population became aroused by the idea that their economic welfare was related to political reform. This occurred largely between 1816 and 1819, when lower-class unrest became a continuing factor for political leaders to consider. The workers were aroused over "the Bill" and knowledge of this had a sobering effect not only on Whigs but on many Tories. This is, however, a far cry from saying that England was on the verge of revolution. Had a revolutionary situation truly developed? In 1831 many examples were at hand. The revolution in Paris was talked of as a model, even while many Frenchmen were congratulating themselves for having carried through a "French 1688." Francis Place was advocating a run on the bank if Wellington returned to power ("To stop the Duke, go for the Gold"), and a run did actually begin. But was this a practical solution to the situation? How loyal was the army? Would the ordinary soldiers really "fire high" if used against workers? There are many unresolved questions regarding the role of the workers and how close England was to physical revolution, but one clear result of the entire crisis was the massive extension of a sense of solidarity among the workers. In terms of the labor movement, this was an enormous asset and must be regarded as a major by-product of the struggle for the Reform Bill.

In struggling against reform, the Tories were motivated by an obvious narrow interest in retaining power. There was more, however, to their position. They insisted at the time, and the record since has vindicated their apprehensions, that what was being contemplated was, in effect, the end of a system which had served England well. As Burke would have argued, England's basic institutions were being attacked. The House of Lords, the church, and eventually the monarchy itself could become mere symbols or be swept away altogether. These historic institutions had provided leadership and saved the nation from the passions of mob violence. The third Reform Bill (finally passed by the Lords June 4, 1832 after royal pressure), coming after Catholic Emancipation, offered Tories a clear sign that aristocratic leadership was being sacrificed for a course which could only lead to democracy. Many historians have found the glory of the Reform Bill to be precisely this. The new consciousness created among the workers assured more concerted violence if the government were to show weakness, and the decades after 1832 were, indeed, rent with frequent industrial disturbances. There appeared to be more violence after the Reform than before; now, from a Tory view, the gates stood open to accommodate insurrection. The House of Lords had backed down when challenged, encouraging the idea that they would not, and could not, defy public opinion once it spoke with a clear voice. Although this overstated the meaning of the crisis, in any future dispute the Lords clearly would enter the struggle perceptibly weaker because of the results of the Reform Bill.

A vast increment of power now resided in the House of Commons and ministerial responsibility to the Commons had become a clear reality. The specific provisions of the bill redistributed 143 seats, thereby giving representation to new urban centers in the north and west. The vote was given to townsmen who held property with an annual rental value of ten pounds and to rural owners of property with a similar value. Thus the vote was tied to a property qualification, and in general, the requirements for renters were more stringent than those for owners. As a result of the reform, the electorate increased from 478,000 to 814,000. The consequence of this was profound, not so much because the voting lists had been nearly doubled but because the door to subsequent electoral reform had been opened. The pattern by which future reform could be accomplished was clear, for as Lord John Russell noted, the Reform Bill was a beginning rather than an end. The Commons had been significantly altered, and in the struggle both the Lords and the Crown had suffered from having yielded to pressure.

An interesting by-product of the contest for passage of the Reform Bill was the emergence of a new party structure. New labels appeared; the Tories became Conservatives and now adopted a posture of willingness to accept change "gradually, dispassionately, and deliberately." Led by Peel, the group suffered from internal divisions and retained many old country squires who were solidly opposed to the reforms of the previous decade. The Whigs now called themselves Liberals, a party committed to reform and progress. Made up of former Whigs, radicals, and some Canningites and boasting Lords Melbourne (1779–1848), John Russell, and Palmerston (1784–1865), this party dominated Parliament between 1832 and 1841, a nine-year golden age in reform legislation.

The new reformed Parliament which met in 1833 differed little from its predecessors in terms of classes represented, but its tone greatly changed. The leading politicians were returned but now the lower house was strongly anti-Tory and many of its members were enthusiastic for further reform. The crisis over passage of the Reform Bill had resulted in other measures being delayed or by-passed and now the Commons prepared to consider this old business in the spirit of reform, which they believed was dictated by the outcome of the Reform Bill struggle. Parliament had come a long way, indeed, in the short time since Canning had succeeded Castlereagh.

Another crisis in the perennial Irish problem was waiting for the new Parliament when it convened. Though the Tories had viewed Catholic Emancipation as the height of radicalism, in fact, it failed to go to the root of Ireland's basic problems. It had provided Irish agitators, such as O'Connell, with a more influential forum from which to attack the vested interests dominating the Irish. The entrenched church in Ireland, the Established Episcopal Church, claiming fewer than 900,000 members in a population of about 8 million, had gradually goaded the people into near open revolt by requiring support of a tithe system. The so-called Tithe War of 1831 resulted in widespread violence as agents attempting to collect the tithes were tortured and murdered and persons paying their tithes were unmercifully harassed. The government authorized the military to help enforce collection, which increased the hatred and bitterness of the poverty-ridden population. O'Connell's oratory waxed with righteous indignation while murder, property destruction, and sedition spread on the Emerald Isle. Parliament's response was a characteristic halfway measure which failed to eradicate the problem but eased the situation for a time. A Coercion Bill, passed in April of 1833, gave the lord lieutenant more despotic authority, especially in the suppression of public meetings and in the application of martial law. This show of force was tempered by the August passage of the Irish Church Temporalities Bill, which substantially reduced the size of the Episcopate to be supported. Two of the four archbishoprics and eight of the eighteen bishoprics were to be abolished as they became vacant. This was a major concession but the idea of using the money saved for secular projects in Ireland was defeated. This latter point resulted in more sarcastic oratory from O'Connell and Parliament enjoyed no sense of gratitude in Ireland for the real concessions it had allowed. O'Connell's partial defeat was blamed on opposition in the Lords, a patronizing excuse that understated the point that although the future trend may have been established, the upper house could not yet be readily disregarded.

In the background of political debates for years had been a sustained attack on the evils of slavery. This accorded with the spirit of reform set in motion by Canning and had been growing in eloquence since 1832, finding a continuously weakened opposition as trade with the West Indies was declining and humanitarians generally took up the cause. Complete defiance by Jamaican plantation owners only added support for the movement in England. In 1832, the question came up in the Commons as a private bill without the formal support of the cabinet. When it gained 136 votes the government decided to give the issue more priority. After the bitterness engendered over the Irish church, Lord Stanley was transferred from the office of Irish secretary to that of colonial secretary, in the hope that a new face might somewhat mollify Irish tempers. For Stanley, however, it was to move from the thick of one crusade to another as he immediately introduced a bill to abolish slavery. Jamaica was the most crucial area, possessing the highest percentage of slave labor.

As its markets had declined and the colony faced stiffer competition from other Caribbean islands producing the same products, the slave owners became more demanding and cruel. Emancipation in their minds was equated with an attack on property and a violation of the idea of *laissez faire*. It also meant that if they were required to pay wages for field labor, they would have no chance whatever to compete with other West Indian islands where slavery continued. The government in London, in effect, was destroying their livelihood in the name of a misguided humanitarianism. In 1833 these arguments carried little weight in London, where a £20 million payment was authorized for the slave owners as part of a scheme to phase out the system over a seven-year period. Complaints that this was less than the value of the "property" being lost failed to prevent passage of the bill. The projected seven years became four as, by the end of 1838, slavery was formally ended in the British Empire. There was widespread anxiety that freedom would mean Negro insurrections against their former owners, but there proved to be relatively little violence. For many the patterns of life changed little.

Another serious intrusion on the world of *laissez faire* also occurred in this session of Parliament, the Factory Act. Considering the nature of Parliament, this was an amazing piece of legislation and was one destined to have enormous repercussions. Basically addressed to the textile industry, the bill placed limitations on the use of child labor and set up a system of inspectors to gather information so the law could be enforced. It also required that children under thirteen spend two hours a day in school. Such a measure violated the precepts of both the manufacturers and the tradition-ridden Tories. The bill was later extended to include a broader spectrum of industry, the first major instance being the Mining Act of 1842. Evidence collected by the inspectors was published by Parliament and stands as eloquent testimony to the conditions of life in an early stage of capitalism. Unfortunately, the inspection system never worked. The abuses were recorded but continued, so that the reform resulted in a gesture and a mass of material for scholars to study.

Another reform of importance was the Poor Law Amendment Act (1834), which directly attacked the problem of the increasing pauperism which accompanied the nation's industrialization. Some intellectuals attacked this intensely humanitarian issue with appeals to Malthus, arguing that it was natural that more and more people would live in progressively poorer circumstances; it was all a matter of science and to help the poor through direct aid was really to flout the working of natural law.

Thus a plethora of reforms came swiftly in England, especially following the parliamentary Reform Bill. The Municipal Corporations Act in 1835 similarly brought reform to local city governments, where, consequently, effective control was passing to the well-to-do middle class. Rapid reform was to cause fiscal problems for the Liberals, but England's approach to a changing world was that of calm good sense, nudged occasionally by a riot or murder. For all the stubbornness of entrenched privilege, social and political reform carrying enormous implications for the future were allowed in full knowledge that there could be no turning back. Other nations proved to be less flexible.

CHAPTER 17

Liberal Stability—
The Reign
of Louis Philippe

Few regimes are as stereotyped as that of the July Monarchy in France, the reign of Louis Philippe from 1830 to 1848. Contemporaries described the monarch as a bourgeoise citizen-king who worked for peace and prosperity, sacrificing national honor and countenancing corruption in the process and finally creating an environment where Lamartine (1790–1869) could aptly remark that "France is bored." Most later accounts of the period may be summarized in the same manner, for only a handful of historians have carefully researched aspects of the reign and most of their writing merely amplifies the traditional interpretation. Such a bland overview, unfortunately, does little justice to Louis Philippe and to the complexity of the issues he faced.

The Orléanist succession to Charles X has properly been regarded as a triumph for upper-middle-class liberalism at the expense of a tradition-oriented and titled aristocracy. The men wielding economic power in France under Charles X had now moved into high political office. The revolution had resulted more in recognizing their ascendancy than in ushering in basic changes. Unlike the situation in England, liberal assumption of political power did not mean opening the door to forward-looking, liberal legislation. In fact, liberal rule under Louis Philippe aimed as much at achieving a posture of stability and little change as had ever been the case during Charles X. To a remarkable degree the membership in the Chamber of Deputies was unchanged and Casimir Périer was explicit in condemning the enthusiasm of those who expected that the July Revolution really meant change. In the Chamber of Peers modifications made in December of 1831 gave the King considerable power in naming new members and brought about a major change in its membership. Wealthy office holders and supporters of the regime appeared in force, whereas the old aristocracy disappeared, or, as many accounts say, retired to their chateaus. In an ego-serving change, the titles of power were now worn by men who had long been prominent and critical of a regime which had denied them opportunities for high office. An obeisant but shallow gesture to the cause of republicanism increased the franchise so that it was far larger than during the previous reign but still remained pitifully small, barely 3 per cent of all adult males. This miniscule *pays légal* was the continuous object of solicitation and favors by successive Orléanist governments. Hardly an election during the July Monarchy was free of official pressure, and in the 1840s electoral corruption was scandalous.

From the confusion attending the fall of Charles X, Louis Philippe had emerged with the royal title on August 9, 1830. Six years, however, were required before he was solidly established. In this period fraught with many pitfalls he proved himself an astute and determined leader. Up to 1834, the greatest danger lay in foreign affairs. Republican militants were jubilant over the upheavals elsewhere in Europe following the French Revolution of 1830, and editorially they encouraged other insurrections. They called out for French aid to other peoples struggling against autocracy; it is no wonder that many insurrectionists counted on French help. The republicans had been outwitted when the upper middle class secured the kingship for Louis Philippe. Now, in foreign policy, their aims were similarly blunted by the new king himself. Seeing the danger of a war against the conservative powers, he backed down on support for republican and nationalistic revolts except in Belgium. Here he was establishing an *entente cordiale* with England, which other powers could not prevent because of upheavals in Poland and Italy. Non-intervention proved a convenient principle. Domestically it was presented as assuring French security from attack. At the same time, it provided an excuse for not aiding Italian nationalists while insisting on supporting the Belgians against Dutch intervention! By 1834, the danger of foreign involvements had abated considerably and the franchise restrictions, coupled with royal selections for the upper house, had brought the upper middle class into the major offices. The republicans had been checked at almost every point, mainly by Louis Philippe, who had rewarded with political office those who had brought him to power. Consequently, by 1834, the King was politically independent, beholden to no one.

Besides the danger in foreign policy issues, until 1836 the new monarch faced more direct, physical challenges. He was a frequent target of assassins but somehow escaped each time. On April 30, 1832, in the name of her son and the cause of legitimacy, the Duchess de Berri raised the standard of revolt against Louis Philippe. She had little chance of ultimate success but did manage to stir up the population in the Vendée. The death of Périer (May 16) delayed action against her bold attempt, which finally was defeated in November after a regular military campaign. The unrest continued although the Duchess was captured and kept in genteel confinement in the fortress at Blaye, near Bordeaux. Pregnant at the time of her capture, she gave birth to a child in the prison and was then expelled from France when it was learned that she had secretly married a member of the minor Italian nobility, thus seriously diminishing her credentials as a legitimist Bourbon leader.

Less formal but more dangerous were a number of urban uprisings prior to 1836. Both Paris and Lyon had major revolts in 1831 and 1834, and Paris was the scene of insurrection in June of 1832. These were vigorously put down by the army, with Louis Philippe providing personal leadership, in marked contrast to Charles X's earlier continued absence while revolt spread. The reconstituted National Guard proved effective in Paris but untrustworthy in Lyon, where, in 1831, it aided the insurgents. Republican influences were clear in the Parisian disorders; in Lyon, economic considerations were more pronounced. Lyon's uprisings were labor or working-class revolts; the Parisian disturbances were more avowedly political. A factor contributing largely to urban unrest was the cholera epidemic of 1831–1832. This covered much of Europe and was especially lethal in larger cities like Paris, where over 20,000 died.

Besides direct military action the government tried to hamper the activities of radical groups through legislation. The assassination attempt by Giuseppe Fieschi on July 28, 1835, especially offended the public, which acquiesced in the passing of restrictive censorship laws in September of 1835. Now the government had stronger legal weapons to combat radical leaders and the upper middle class turned to measures of official control which they had regarded as unenlightened and oppressive under the Restoration.

By 1836 a revival of prosperity, after the extended slump between 1827 and 1832, lessened grievances among the workers and Louis Philippe's position was secure. The prospects of open revolt were diminished and the regime settled down to a program of domestic peace, prosperity, and the status quo. In foreign affairs Louis Philippe followed a bold course in allying with England in support of liberalism in both Spain and Portugal, but he retreated before the combined pressure of England and the other major powers in the War Scare of 1840. This rupture with England was followed by a further alienation over the question of the Spanish Marriages. These issues (discussed in Chapter 19) created potent ammunition for the critics of the regime. Countering these episodes was the systematic extension of French control in Algeria which brought satisfaction to the military but apprehensions in London. In addition to growing complaints about his foreign policy. Louis Philippe had the extra burden of a serious economic depression beginning in 1845. To skeptics, the surrender of national honor had not assured prosperity. Meanwhile, a new revolutionary situation had gradually developed; but despite the warnings of his friends, the King refused to believe it existed.

Louis Philippe's regime was one of control by the upper middle class, a collection of elites, all dedicated to the protection of property through constitutional guarantees. In the early days, bankers played an especially important role but they gradually gave way to other elite groups. Wealth was extremely important but the system was flexible enough that people of low birth or no vast inheritances could gain admission to high office. Intellectuals were welcome and because many scholars possessed scant means, devices were found to put them on the public payroll. Thiers typified how a person of modest birth could be accepted in society after acquiring wealth through marriage. The very well-to-do who served Louis Philippe were a combination of old families and the newly rich who had made their fortunes under the protectionist policies of Napoleon. Middle-class elements below these upper elites lacked the franchise but supported the regime nonetheless. They served in the National Guard and were proud of this privilege which set them above ordinary workers. Collectively, they concurred with the professions of support for property and stability put out by the government and saw themselves eventually gaining admission to the electorate. It was to this group that Thiers' schemes of broadening the franchise were obviously aimed, and he was the man that such a development would bring to power.

Adolphe Thiers was extremely ambitious and possessed little sense of compromise. His political career, which spanned over forty years, proved to be one of the most important in nineteenth-century French history. During the July Monarchy he led the Left Center Party of Movement (so called because it stood for modest reforms) against the Right Center Party of Resistance, led by Guizot, who opposed further change in the nation's political structure. After Périer's death, Louis Philippe tried to avoid having strong ministers. Thiers was so outspoken that he was especially by-passed, though on two occasions (for seven months in 1836 and for seven months in 1840) he came to power briefly. While the monarchy settled into a pattern of complacency and stability with no radical changes planned, a great hue and cry arose among the politicians, which gave the impression of an active political life. However, they were all liberals and the issues between the two parties were minimal (except on the franchise question) so that much of the struggling was merely to satisfy personal vanities by acquiring office.

Aside from the King himself, the most influential political figure of the reign was François Guizot (1789–1874). His ideas against change suited Louis Philippe completely and he was especially on the rise after Thiers' fall in October of 1840. Both Guizot and Thiers were respected historians and typified the July Monarchy's ability to effect interesting unions of scholarship and political service.

Guizot was a prime example of what historians have labeled liberal nationalism. Many liberals, influenced by romanticism and interest in local folk history, saw Europe composed of nationalities, each of which should comprise an independent state. To accomplish this clearly required some basic political alterations; some "unifications" and "dissolutions" were necessary in order that currently "enslaved" peoples might be "free" masters of their own country. Their liberties would be stipulated in constitutional documents which would assure the basic freedoms of association (speech, press, worship) as well as economic freedom. Free trade would end war and bring continent-wide peace. The middle class never doubted for a moment that it should manage the government. Although it gave lip-service to representative government, it had no faith in democracy. The middle class produced few real zealots, but there were many followers dedicated to both liberalism and nationalism. Guizot had concluded that the system established by the revised Charter was the best and most liberal that was possible in France. This was a government of constitutional guarantees with the middle class in control; its foreign policy stressed peace and stood domestically for industrial, intellectual, and religious freedom. It was a middle ground between aristocratic reaction and Jacobin democracy.

Ironically, while Louis Philippe's regime provided for religious freedom, under the Calvinist Guizot the Catholic Church played a subordinate role. The government explicitly limited freedoms of the press and association while maintaining economic protectionism. It also shrank from fully supporting national struggles in Poland and Italy—all contradictions disturbing to sensitive intellectuals.

Guizot's nationalism was fervent and utterly uncompromising regarding France and the French. He believed that French history was really the story of civilization itself, that "there is not a single idea, not a single great principle of civilization which, in order to become universally spread, has not first passed through France." Anglo-Saxons may especially marvel at such a statement by a historian who had carefully studied seventeenth-century England. Guizot was a zealous patriot presiding over a system where liberal ideas were being controlled and modified. His greatest contribution to French history lay in the field of education. In 1833, he authored a bill which broadened the scope of public education. It required a public primary school in every commune and set up new normal schools to train more teachers. Though many problems developed and a number of adaptations were made in subsequent legislation, France was now pointed in the direction of public education available to all. This was to create special problems in relation to the Church, issues which were finally settled only after 1900.

It has been widely assumed that the July Monarchy was a period of frenetic business activity and industrial progress, an impression which is only partially true. The government favored business and the King made a public show of bourgeoise habits; nonetheless, industrial and commercial growth came at a restrained pace in France. The 1830s and early 1840s were years of great change and vitality in Belgium, but France lagged behind her industrious neighbor. French coal production had increased but imports from both Belgium and England were still needed to power her growing manufacturing plant. While French pig-iron production was being doubled, English output was increasing nearly fivefold. French businessmen reflected centuries-old patterns of thinking and invested cautiously. Thus industrialization came to France more slowly and in a more deliberate fashion than it did in England and Belgium, and later Germany. This is clearly seen in railroad development. The government produced a plan for railway building in 1842 and the construction of lines radiating from Paris began shortly thereafter. This initiative characteristically lagged behind the Belgians and even the Prussians. Nevertheless, the government played an active role in encouraging industry and the *laissez-faire* liberals took this for granted, accepting concessions, franchises, and protection while expecting no interference whatever in dealings between the businessman and the workers. Thus important changes steadily occurred, especially in Paris, and a spirit of economic prosperity prevailed until the mid-1840s.

While industry was slowly changing the patterns of French urban life, the romantic impulses of the age were lending a special coloration to segments of Catholicism, socialism, and Bonapartism. In France by the 1830s the classical appeals to Empire, the thought of one's identity with nature, and the earlier symbolic majesty of a union of church and altar were tarnished and empty. In their place came a new concern for "the people," that laboring, amorphous mass which the First Republic had nearly deified.

During the Bourbon Restoration the Church in France was strongly Gallican and the Papacy meekly acquiescent. Louis Philippe broke with the pattern of his cousins and gave only nominal obeisance to Catholicism. Like many of the business leaders of his day, he was openly agnostic and was surrounded with men who shared his views. Guizot was a Protestant, but Thiers' view of religion was close to disgust. The King was determined to avoid the close association with the Church which had marked the rule of Charles X. While the Church in France was losing its favored position, it experienced a reform movement within its ranks. The seminal figure in this disturbance was Lamennais, the abbot from Brittany. The burden of his message amounted to a practical recognition of the basic principles of the French Revolution. He had concluded that a number of alterations were in order, beginning with the Gallican posture of the French Church. He supported a return to ultramontanism, with a corresponding diminution of clerical autonomy in France. It was for him a pietistic and religious truth that the Papacy was the divine agency of God's will and must tower above any local or nationalistic tendencies within the hierarchy. Rome should support popular efforts for political freedom where possible, and at the moment Poland was a case in point. Further, he believed the Church should show a greater sense of a social mission in an age where machine production was herding workers closer together in ever more degrading living circumstances. It should work for democracy and focus more on the problems of the common people, because the workers desperately needed the spiritual aid which only the Church could give, and the liberals needed the Church as a practical matter to assure orderly industrial growth. Indeed, the Church was crucial to social stability in a time of accelerating change.

Lamennais was not alone in his insistence that the Church needed to change some of its emphases. A. F. Ozanam (1813–1853), founder of the Society of Saint Vincent de Paul, was only the most successful of dozens of young priests who dedicated themselves fully to working on society's festering social problems, impressive evidence of a kind of pietistic renaissance underway within the lower ranks of the French clergy. Ultimately their values and objectives were to be successful, but for the moment they received little encouragement from their hierarchy and Lamennais was openly opposed.

The public call for a new Catholic liberalism or a program for Christian democracy appeared in the daily columns of *L'Avenir,* a short-lived paper which Lamennais, Jean Baptiste Lacordaire (1802–1861), and Charles de Montalembert (1810–1870) founded in 1830. The hierarchy in France emphatically rejected Lamennais' ideas, which were attracting a following mainly among young priests. In the face of hostility from his superiors, Lamennais appealed to the Papacy for support, further creating a situation tinged with irony because the basic ideas which he was preaching came to be accepted by the French hierarchy and by the Papacy itself later in the century. In 1832, however, Pope Gregory XVI saw much of Lamennais' doctrines as similar to those which had just opposed the Papacy in its secular lands. Lamennais had reasoned that an exaltation of papal power would set it above secular governments, thus freeing Rome from dependence on foreign bayonets. To the Pope the lesson of the moment seemed to demonstrate quite the reverse, and in August of 1832, he issued the encyclical *Mirari vos* condemning the ideas of Lamennais. At that time it was expecting too much for Rome to sanction revolt in Poland and to take the lead in promoting social democracy in Europe.

L'Avenir ceased publication but Lamennais, who had argued for papal superiority, found himself unable to accept the verdict against him. He moved further to the left and was excommunicated. Leaving the Church, he continued to write and became a heroic and martyred statesman in the cause of democracy. He provided an emotional and psychological stimulus for a movement he no longer led. The Papacy could condemn both him and his ideas but the lower strata of French society and the Church had been stirred, and many young priests began to preach a new social mission.

Other humanitarian ideologies gained wide favor during the July Monarchy as the miseries of the poor became a topic for theoretical study and sophisticated conversation. Collectively known as "utopian socialists" were a number of social critics whose ideas won large audiences in the 1830s and 1840s. Somewhat like Lamennais, their essays breathed a sense of piety and concern for the laboring poor and were addressed primarily to the literate nonpoor who possessed the means to institute practical change. It is interesting that most of the early theorizers of socialism were French rather than English. The land where industrial development was most advanced did, however, produce Robert Owen (1771–1858), a manufacturer who offended other industrialists with precise cooperative schemes and political procedures for investigating working conditions. In France a number of comprehensive programs for social reorganization appeared.

The earliest modern writer explicitly espousing socialism was Count Claude Henri de Saint-Simon (1760–1825), a descendant of the gossipy memoir writer. He had lived through the French Revolution and pondered its ideals. He also had engaged in business, as a manufacturer of playing cards and as a land speculator, and vast sums passed through his hands before he died in poverty in 1825. From his experience and observations, he concluded that society's ills were not to be corrected by any such simple device as a new constitution. Methods of production were in a state of flux, not static; and social organization needed to shift from feudal and religious foundations to more practical industrial and scientific bases. His was a mild sort of socialism, an interesting combination of business and religious idealism which inspired decades of other French social critics. In *Industry* and *The New Christianity* he explained how men were to be employed according to their abilities and rewarded according to their production. The workers' interests were to be protected by the leaders in industry, science, and the arts. He had described, in effect, a new feudalism whose nobility was made up of artists, scientists, and business leaders. In his restructured society he designated three categories of people: the priests (or artists), the savants (scientists), and the workers. The priests provide inspiration to the others and promote the general concepts which constitute the bonds of society. The scientists are concerned with applied knowledge and are themselves divisible into three categories: a research group, a teaching staff, and philosophers who prevent intellectual anarchy by coordinating the teaching and research efforts. The philosophers synthesize knowledge and direct efforts to find new knowledge. The last group, the workers, are to be organized into communities where production is regulated according to the results of careful statistical study of human needs. Saint-Simon's system would end anarchy in production, lessen misery, and result finally in justice, happiness, and progress. The whole system was oriented toward the poor: "All social institutions should have as their aim the physical and moral improvement of the most numerous and poorest class," another version of Bentham's "greatest good of the greatest number."

Saint-Simon's object was to help the poor but his appeal was to the business community, where he won many followers. These often forgot the apostolic side of his message and were quite content to accept merely the idea that they, as experts (scientists), should control the state and involve it in business. During the July Monarchy Saint-Simonianism was especially popular and its ranks included some of the most important business leaders, who often met in the offices of Jewish bankers to plan the "New Christianity," with its need for more railroads and canals. Their ardor was something more than opportunism and Saint-Simon's ideas spurred them to probe the possibilities of credit manipulation for social gain. They made their profits, but from their scheming came great events, especially a vast extension of the rail network and the digging of the Suez Canal. There developed a veritable cult of Saint-Simon. A number of disciples took up his doctrines and sought to reach a wide public by preaching and publishing masses of pamphlets. Père Enfantin was among the best known of Saint-Simon's followers and suggested programs attracting considerable discussion. A world wide league of nations would abolish competition; wealth might then be distributed according to works and the principle of heredity be abolished. With the international organization of industry, war would disappear. In the new scheme of things human exploitation would end and each person would feel a sense of responsibility. Work would be honorable and shared by all.

There were many variations of these ideas but generally they all were presented in a context of infectious humanitarian zeal. In the development of socialism this early version was merely one of several labeled as "utopian," in contrast to later varieties tinged with Marxism and termed "scientific." A major difference concerned the manner in which change might come. The utopians all hoped for reform through an altruistic attention to the problem by those already in power and close to the top of the economic hierarchy. The appeal to their sense of charity was unmistakable. The "scientific" school (which we will consider later) held that it was ridiculous and unreasonable, even unnatural, to expect people who were exploiting others, to change their practices voluntarily.

The utopians were essentially optimists in their view of man and human nature. Charles Fourier (1772–1837) shares with Saint-Simon the responsibility for the widespread introduction of early "Utopian" ideas of socialism. Unlike Saint-Simon he had little respect for those "captains of industry" so central to Saint-Simonian theory, and he positively loathed the competition, greed, and deceit associated with triumphs in the business world. Fourier based his proposals on a far more philosophical basis than most utopians. He worked out a cosmological explanation for behavior in which universal attraction was the basic law of nature. There were five classes of phenomena, which he identified as inorganic matter, life, mind, magnetism, and society. Their corresponding forms of attraction were material, organic, intellectual, animal, and social. He was convinced that, intrinsically, attraction was good and that consequently every passion or desire of man was good. Evil in the world comes not from passion but from artificial circumstances often attending the passion. In a natural society the law of attraction results in its expansion and love rather than restriction, secretiveness, or appeals based on a concept of duty. There are particular personal passions and group passions or drives. The reformer's role is to devise a plan where every passion is able to find a proper outlet and contribute its force to the common health and good of all.

Fourier suggested that society should be arranged in a series of harmonious cooperative communities called phalanstres. Each would comprise about 1,600 people who would live in a large, hotel-like structure and work an area of land about three miles square. Eventually, the whole of mankind should be so organized. Every citizen would work and the unpleasanter jobs would carry greater rewards. Because Fourier believed that all work was honorable, it was to be made as pleasant as possible: music would be played on the way to work and wine and pastries would be served regularly. For the necessary but dirty and unattractive tasks, Fourier suggested child labor.

Children basically love dirt, so they would be used to kill vermin, work in slaughterhouses, and work in the mines. Communal living would meet man's need for companionship and would also provide the human requirement for sex without the institution of marriage. As with Saint-Simon, this aspect of Fourier's planning was understood widely to be an espousal of free love and tended to bring the whole movement into disrepute.

Fourier had many followers, the most prominent of which was perhaps Victor Considerant (1808–1893). Of several model communities attempted, all failed; but, meanwhile, many thoughtful people were attracted to the idea of reducing suffering through some sort of planning. Fourier clubs sprang up, especially in France, Belgium, and Russia. While various attempts were failing, Fourier himself announced that he would be ready at noon daily to discuss the details of establishing "the new society" with any prosperous benefactor who wished to provide the capital. He waited for twelve years, but his altruistic appeal to men of wealth yielded no visitor.

While the ideas of Saint-Simon and Fourier were spreading in the 1830s and 1840s, a new wave of critics appeared who shared a common viewpoint in criticizing the new industrial exploitation of labor. Sismondi explicitly labeled profits as exploitation and observed that the machine rarely benefited the man who tended it. Like others, he believed that government should intervene in behalf of the worker. Another "utopian," Louis Blanc (1811–1882), proposed that the government should establish "social workshops." A system of producer cooperatives supported with government funds would flourish in a context of cheap communal life. Prices would be regulated and competition, which he saw as the source of evil, would be drastically modified. His ideas in *The Organization of Labor* caught the fancy of a wide audience, but he overlooked the point that the government, especially that of Louis Philippe, could not really be expected to support schemes which opposed the enrichment of its own members.

Social critics during the July Monarchy included several proponents of a republican tradition which dated back to the 1789 Revolution. More radical than the utopian socialists, because they often advocated violence they aimed their message directly at the new urban proletariat. Of special importance were Philippe Buonarroti (1761–1834) and Louis Blanqui (1805–1881). Buonarroti was widely known as a former collaborator of Babeuf, whereas Blanqui was a perennial revolutionary agitator who alternated jail sentences with plotting. Both favored a system of democracy that was heavily tinged with socialism. Meanwhile other indictments of the society came from Pierre Joseph Proudhon (1809–1865), whose most influential work, *What Is Property?*, was startling in the bluntness of its conclusion. Property, he declared, was theft, pure and simple. This was a disturbing idea in an age when opportunities for acquisition existed on a large scale and many of the regime's most respected citizens were noted for their land holdings. Thus while property as an institution was under attack, agitators were inciting the workers and the upper classes were being advised to reorganize society. Jules Michelet was writing his flamboyantly rhetorical *History of France,* a sheer glorification of "the people" rather than their aristocracy, clergy, or dynasty. As the reign continued, direct attempts on the monarch's life were less of a danger, but the lower ranks of society became more conscious of their exploitation and more aware that radical change was possible.

Another voice calling for change was that of Louis Napoleon Bonaparte (1808–1873), a nephew of the Emperor. An active leader in two unsuccessful coups, he contributed to the Napoleonic Legend through an extensive outpouring of formal writing and correspondence. Adapting Bonapartism to the current situation of France, he authored two particularly interesting works, *Napoleonic Ideas* (1839) and *The Extinction of Pauperism* (1844). In the former he presented a thorough criticism of French leadership since 1815. His propagandistic portrayal of Napoleon Bonaparte's ideals would have been both surprising and pleasing to the Emperor. Liberty, freedom, and peace were the prime virtues that this genius had supposedly advocated while being frustrated and succeeded by men of little minds and modest abilities. Napoleon had attempted too great a task too soon. His heroic effort, however, had shown the correctness of his instincts and France needed a return to Bonapartist leadership, the only sort of government properly consonant with changing social conditions under Louis Philippe, according to the judgment of the young pretender. What such a restoration could mean for France was spelled out in his work on pauperism, written during his imprisonment at Ham. This theoretical study showed a marked Saint-Simonian influence and a familiarity with other utopian socialistic schemes. He had numerous ideas for domestic social reorganization besides such suggestions as the construction of an isthmian canal across Nicaragua. His appeal was thus directed both to the lower classes and to the business community.

With all this ferment of ideas, the July Monarchy managed to drift along, countenancing mild corruption while aiding business, and avoided undue danger from domestic unrest until 1848. When prosperity ceased and economic hardship appeared on a broad scale, the regime was in danger. The system may have been appropriate for well over fifteen years, but in 1848 the limited recognition of new forces implicit in the July Monarchy proved insufficient.

CHAPTER 18

Ultraconservative Stability: Determined Hostility Toward New Forces

The liberal ideas current in Western Europe found little favor with Nicholas of Russia. He was so steadfastly opposed to anything suggestive of French Revolutionary principles or procedures that his personality and reign became thoroughly stereotyped, making objective appraisals especially difficult. In the three decades after Alexander, orthodoxy, autocracy, and nationality were explicitly named by S. S. Uvarov—Nicholas' minister of public education from 1833 to 1849—as the basic principles for the reign. They appeared as such obvious keys to understanding Russia's new regime that historians only gradually recognized the limitations such a slogan imposed on understanding Nicholas or his policies. A more accurate and sympathetic version of the Tsar has slowly emerged, modifying greatly the former image of him as a narrow-minded, conformity-demanding autocrat.

236

The Tsar was, of course, central to the making of Russian policy. A proud and strikingly attractive man (Victoria said he was the most handsome in Europe), he was unyielding when once he had taken a given position. The Decembrist Revolt inaugurating his

Nicholas I. (Courtesy of Historical Pictures Service, Chicago.)

rule provided an element of gnawing uncertainty about the loyalty of both his army and the aristocracy. To him constitutionalism represented a cluster of dangerous ideas which posed a constant threat to the course of European civilization. This viewpoint promoted a feeling of continuous insecurity, which he countered by being militantly alert to all sorts of dangers, some real, some imaginary. To note that his emphasis on orthodoxy, autocracy, and nationalism reflected these apprehensions is sound but fails to do justice to many of his initiatives and flexibility in both domestic and foreign affairs.

While Western Europe was experiencing a rapidly growing middle class with impressive changes in living conditions and communications, a somberness fell over Russia and much of Eastern Europe. After crushing the Decembrists in 1825 and the Poles in 1833, Nicholas felt a special responsibility to keep his vast holdings secure from revolt and revolution. In conversation he frequently referred to Pugachev's rebellion and to the general danger of revolution, an insidious disease which he blamed on Western Europe. He never felt truly secure and after widespread revolution broke out in Europe in 1848, he became increasingly ill at ease, to the point where nervous irritation undermined his health and contributed to his early death at the age of fifty-eight.

Nicholas found solace from his insecurity in the petty side of militarism and in the rituals of the Orthodox Church. He mastered the details and intricacies of parade ground maneuvers and enjoyed an emotional satisfaction from watching intricate drills and manuals of arms. His almost compulsive absorption in military precision and regimentation would not have been reprehensible if, meanwhile, he had better provided for the broader and more important military requirements of his realm. The peasants hated the army which, before 1834, conscripted them for terms as long as twenty-five years. The earlier military colonies were continued and various forms of quartering the soldiery on the population prevailed. Both cavalry and infantry were woefully inadequate for service against an up-to-date foe. For this lack of efficiency—but impressiveness on a parade ground—the price was high and even in peace constituted the nation's largest item of expense. The army under Nicholas proved to be capable of putting down domestic uprisings and was good enough for lackluster campaigns against the Poles, the Persians, the Turks, and the Hungarians. Nicholas was fortunate that a more formidable test like the Crimean War came at the close of his reign, because he was psychologically unable to face up to the sheer ineptitude of the military structure on which he had doted so intensely.

The Tsar's religious sense was also an important feature in his make-up. As with the military, he was absorbed in the minutiae of the experience, the punctual and systematic performance of ritual.

Absolutely dedicated, his faith was uncluttered by doctrinal or theological questions. He believed as his peasants believed, simply, pietistically, and fully; and he expected others to believe. His concept of duty required an absolute obedience from his followers as well as his own obeisance before God. Divine-right monarchy was an article of faith which for Nicholas was beyond question. A fatalistic acceptance of one's place and one's obligations flowed from all of this, along with a willingness to presume that others in authority also shared a high sense of honor, duty, and integrity. Such trust and openness were to lead Nicholas into serious miscalculations, especially in foreign policy.

Basically, the most fundamental issue for Russia under Nicholas was that posed for Europe by the French Revolution. Were liberal political ideals, born of the Enlightenment and given direction and force during the Revolution, to be allowed in Russia? The same question had plagued Alexander, who finally took a stand against liberal ideas. Nicholas was consistently against their intrusion from the very beginning. Although his reign gave scant opportunity for liberalism in politics, the issues were fostered in a growing literary movement. Despite a heavy-handed censorship, two major schools of thought debated Russia's situation. Those who most avidly criticized Russia as being behind the standards of Western Europe were loosely called Westerners. Prominent in this group were Vissarion Belinsky (1811–1848) and Nicholas Chernyshevsky (1828?–1889). Because politics, philosophy, and religion were so sterile, their functions, Chernyshevsky maintained, had to be taken over by literature. Those functions were to promote the triumphs of Enlightenment thought so that the people of Russia would acquire proper laws securing rights based on justice and common sense. Belinsky was most explicit in advancing these ideas and worked them into his analyses of other men's writing. Russian society was ripe for vast social change and these writers gave voice to undercurrents of unrest which should have received urgent attention. The Westerners were opposed by a group called the Slavophiles. These authors took the position that Russian civilization had its own special qualities and was not inferior to that of Western Europe. They equated the ideas emphasized by the Westerners with a weakening of religious ties, a worship of mammon, a deterioration of government strength, and personal isolation. Without being opposed to reform, the Slavophiles emphasized the special historic factors in Eastern European development and were ardently nationalistic. In their view Russia was the major example and defender of a unique and superior cultural development.

This intellectual debate was to continue after Nicholas, with the Westerners providing nourishment for a socialistic tradition. The Tsar, of course, opposed such "alien" ideas, and early in his reign (1826) he established the Third Section, a bureaucratic organ with special police functions and responsible directly to the crown. Despite police spies, censorship, and harrassment, the Westerners communicated their ideas among a slowly growing, literate public. The attempts to tighten up and become more autocratic gave the Third Section such an offensive reputation during the latter portion of the reign that it is common to characterize its activities by its harshness during the years after 1848.

The fundamental social problem in Russia was serfdom, which gave the views of the Westerners a special relevance and sharpness. The overwhelming urgency for peasant reform was strongly felt by Nicholas himself but he was unable to find a practical method for carrying it out. This was the basic domestic contradiction of his reign, and Nicholas here deserves more credit than he has received, though hardly enough to assuage his personal responsibility in not accomplishing more.

Nicholas consistently spoke of the need for reform and during his reign appointed ten special committees to study the problems of peasant emancipation, the first selected as early as 1826. He believed a considerable amount of serf unrest was directly traceable to harsh mistreatment by the nobles. While condemning this in the strongest language, at the same time he wanted a program for reform which would not diminish the privileges of the aristocracy. By and large, little resulted from the work of the various committees; a few decrees spasmodically appeared which lightened the burdens for some serfs and gained freedom for a few. Public discussion of the problem was muted as the committees worked in secret. Nicholas believed this procedure was essential and that open consideration of the issue would merely encourage waves of peasant unrest. Frustrated that he lacked a formula for solving the problem, he remained rigidly authoritarian in dealing with unrest while plaintively desiring some method leading to a "gradual transition." Those about him slowly became acclimated to the idea that reform was absolutely essential. Thus, although Nicholas failed to institute emancipation, he created a climate of opinion at the top which made it possible in the next reign. Nicholas' enthusiasm for reform was blunted after 1848, though he still recognized its need. An indication of his muted interest as the years passed may be seen from Third Section reports which, until 1848, continuously called for the reform of peasant conditions and presented the strength and vitality of Russia as welded to emancipation. The continuation of serfdom merely assured agrarian unrest which would put further difficult demands on the Third Section.

Although Nicholas agreed with this general perspective, he was dominated more by what he saw as the arrogance implied in revolution and insubordination to divinely ordained authority. His actions bespoke a harsh cruelty which was both strangely consistent and inconsistent with his beliefs and personality. On one occasion he praised God that there was no longer a death penalty in Russia and swore he would not allow it. In the same breath he recommended as a punishment the running of a 1,000-man gauntlet twelve times, an ordeal the victims failed to survive. This was his manner of revising a court sentence of death, a judgment, incidentally, meted out to two Jews for the crime of trying to cross the frontier to avoid the plague. Another instance of dubious moderation in criminal punishment under Nicholas was the substitution of the lash for the rod. The key to this reform was the compelling fact that those punished by the rod were rendered incapable for military service. Thus pious expressions of humanitarianism mixed with evidence of savage vindictiveness in this Tsar of all the Russias. A tragic and melancholy sense of frustration and isolation surrounded him in his later years as he grimly persisted in a domestic program which he intuitively knew was wrong but felt compelled to continue.

The worried but uncompromising autocrat at home was an equally determined enemy of revolution and upheavals against constituted authority in Central and Western Europe. His militance in this regard overshadowed Metternich, whose additional concern included the Russian zeal displayed outside her own boundaries. Nicholas consistently opposed constitutional liberalism and grudgingly acquiesced in the 1830 modifications in France and Belgium because of the trouble in Poland, closer to home.

Metternich was markedly less in control of events after 1830, though Nicholas' involvement with Poland masked this. The Austrian statesman welcomed the Tsar's staunch support for conservatism but was apprehensive about Russian initiatives. Alexander had slowly come to a break with Metternich but Nicholas pursued an independent course from the start. The Greek struggle for independence demonstrated how the latter pursued policies based solely on Russia's interests as he saw them. Almost ignoring Metternich, Nicholas could condemn the Belgian revolution, crush the Polish revolt, and yet be pious in support of Greeks engaged in a nationalistic uprising.

The year 1833 was particularly successful for Russian diplomacy. The Tsar was in the position of being the sole protector of the Sultan against his ambitious subordinate, Mehemet Ali, and was able to negotiate the Treaty of Unkiar Skelessi in July, which made Russia in effect the guarantor of Ottoman independence, a considerable reversal considering his role in assisting the Greek uprising. In September of 1833, he negotiated the Treaty of Münchengrätz with Austria. Here Austria joined Russia in guaranteeing the Ottoman Empire and explicitly agreed to oppose any further action Mehemet Ali might take against the Sultan. Prussia also agreed to these terms. What Nicholas had accomplished was to erect a Metternichlike arrangement regarding the Ottoman Empire. The diplomatic initiative was Russian rather than Austrian, and Nicholas now had the conservative powers as guarantors of an Ottoman Empire he had just weakened. For England and France to be able to pose as defenders of the Ottoman Empire in a war against Nicholas represents a diplomatic turn-about of major proportions. This disaster, which will be discussed elsewhere, was a product of many factors, but prominent among these was Nicholas' personal conduct of foreign policy, his assurance that in private meetings many of diplomacy's problems could be solved. He read too many of his own values into other men's remarks, insisting on occasion that between men of honor treaties are unnecessary. His word was good and he expected that of other aristocrats to be equally reliable. His miscalculations based on such thinking were monumental and help explain the supreme, final failure of his reign, the Crimean War.

Between 1833 and 1847 neither Prussia nor Austria were receptive to political liberalism. Austria was the most impervious to outside ideas and its cumbersome bureaucracy managed to maintain an atmosphere akin to stagnation. No significant changes had occurred in decades and no domestic crises loomed on the horizon. Indeed, from Metternich's vantage point, danger seemed confined to the periphery of Austria—in Italy and in the Balkans—and did not constitute a major domestic threat.

In Prussia there was also little in the way of significant change, aside from the impressive success registered by the Zollverein. This, of course, represented a complete compliance with recently recognized economic forces and succeeded through Prussian leadership rather than coercion. In 1840 Frederick William III was succeeded by Frederick William IV (1795–1861), whose first seven years are hardly distinguishable from those which preceded. The new monarch was especially interested in religion and felt that Protestants needed some sort of functionary to minister to their needs in the Holy Land. To this end he negotiated with England the establishment of the "Jerusalem Bishopric." By this scheme the monarchs of England and Prussia would alternate in naming a bishop to reside in Jerusalem. The nominee would be consecrated by the Archbishop of Canterbury, receive diplomatic support as needed, and do his best to win converts among the resident Jewish population. The first bishop, Michael Solomon Alexander, nominated by the British crown, was born a Jew in Prussia but had gone to England and converted to Anglicanism; he was a scholar of languages and taught Arabic and Hebrew at Kings College for twenty years. He lived only to see the bishopric established. His successor, appointed by Frederick William, was Samuel Gobat, a Swiss-Reform cleric fluent in Arabic as well as German and English. For over three decades Gobat vigorously proselytized in Jerusalem, enjoying considerable success but many frustrations. There were a series of bishops before the whole practice was abandoned later in the century. A lasting result was an unusual intrusion of German language and culture into the eastern Mediterranean. Mainly a curiosity, the episode speaks volumes when seen as a measure of the new Prussian King's interests. He was eagerly promoting this scheme while the chancellories of Europe were worried about the prospects for a general war in 1840.

In neither Austria nor Prussia was the autocracy so obvious or repressive as in Russia. A more sophisticated cultural life and a higher living standard for the masses made the system less harsh; but nonetheless, reform was needed and awaited a propitious moment. In 1848, as we shall see, that moment appeared to have arrived.

CHAPTER 19

International
Irritants and Harbingers
of Trouble

The uprisings associated with 1830 had largely subsided by the end of 1833, though diplomats were still discussing the details of Belgian independence. The next round of widespread upheaval would not occur until 1848, but in the interim a number of interesting and irritating Mediterranean developments posed difficult problems for the Great Powers. In each case armed conflict between major states was avoided but important legacies were bequeathed to the future.

As mentioned earlier, Louis Philippe had inherited a French foothold in Algeria. This invasion had been the largest amphibious expedition to date, but the whole affair was still sufficiently tenuous that it could have been readily abandoned. The new regime in Paris debated alternatives and delayed for over three years in deciding what to do about Algeria. This early hesitation stemmed, in part, from more pressing problems of consolidating the regime at home. In addition, the campaign in Algeria had initially failed to strike much of a responsive chord in France and there appeared little popular support for the venture. Another negative factor was a clear English hostility to such an extensive expansion of French control of the Mediterranean coast. That a near mythical Algerian connection with the Ottoman Empire was being destroyed was hardly considered; but French ascendancy here, combined with their strong influence in Egypt, was a source of great concern for England. The other major countries, however, preferred that France expand her energies in this direction instead of pursuing the Rhine frontier.

The various alternatives had their proponents in the French Chambers and extensive debate raged over what should be done. A plan of limited colonization in areas along the coast was briefly tried but came to ruin because of native forces led by Abd-el-Kadir (1807?–1883), an Arab chieftain who tried to drive the foreign invaders into the sea. His efforts were so intensive by mid-1835 that the French were forced to decide between a major war or virtual withdrawal. Opting for the former, the systematic conquest of the Arabs then began, with an objective of controlling the interior as well as the coastline. Progress was expensive and uneven as the enemy proved remarkably resourceful, considering the vast difference between the general cultural level of the protagonists. England continued to look askance at the whole operation while other developments required more of her attention.

The impact of the Algerian experience was especially important in the history of the French officer corps. There were a number of key engagements, the most crucial being the Battle of Isly on August 14, 1844, but the conquest soon settled into garrison commands with a series of regular raids made against the poorly armed natives. This pattern provided opportunities for rapid promotions while the chances of death were minimal. Action against the Arab enemy included suffocating them by the hundreds by setting fires at the entrance of caves where they had taken refuge. Such "conquest" opened the way for colonization. Critics claimed that the French acquired in Algeria a supply of officers who had risen from drummer to general without ever having been fired upon. While rising swiftly through the grades, they were also in contact with the Napoleonic Legend. Bonaparte's epic career was discussed continually and the Algerian officers came to equate their limited exploits with a Napoleonic campaign or engagement. The result was a breed of officer which was supremely confident but had had its native potential blunted. Perhaps even worse, the "African generals" formed a clique within the army and came to dominate major commands and policy-making, especially during the Second Empire.

Among these officers were a number who achieved a measure of popular acclaim as heroes. Most prominent was Marshal Bugeaud (1784–1849), appropriately titled the Duke d'Isly for having won this major triumph in the conquest. As a French military leader, Bugeaud was the successor to Napoleon and within the army was a kind of father figure. Officers who served with Bugeaud never forgot it. In the Crimean War, when these men had become major commanders themselves, it was to Bugeaud that their thoughts turned in difficult situations. "What would Bugeaud (or Père-Bugeaud) do now?" was the question they pondered while their allied counterparts were asking, "What would the Duke (of Wellington) do now?" That Bugeaud was their model rather than Napoleon was an interesting commentary on the force of the Legend. Bugeaud they had known personally, whereas Napoleon was an abstract historic figure by comparison. Thus their limited experiences in Algeria far outweighed their study and knowledge of campaigns of the Empire.

Less distinguished than Bugeaud was a whole echelon of "Heroes," the most prominent being Generals Cavaignac, Changarnier, and Lamoricière, men shortly to have frustrating political experiences. There were many other officers, not yet as well known to the public, who were destined for prominence later when they provided military leadership for France during the Second Empire. Many possessed great initiative, intelligence, and ambition. It was tragic for France that this generation of military leaders was so stunted by the Algerian experience that it proved unequal to the military demands of 1870. Ironically, it was widely assumed among European diplomats that Algeria was providing the basis for the renewal of French imperialism.

Less suggestive of the future but more dangerous for the Powers were the two Iberian succession struggles in the 1830s. In both Spain and Portugal, bitter civil war raged between the more liberal and constitutionally oriented supporters of a regency for a young girl and the traditional aristocratic forces favoring the claims of an uncle. In Portugal the situation was complicated initially by the issue of Portuguese and Brazilian separation. The Brazilian phase of the question was in the background by 1828 and the Portugese struggle was clearly between supporters of the ten-year-old Maria II (1819–1853) and those of Dom Miguel (1802–1866). The popular young prince accepted a crown offered him by the Cortes in 1825 and, as

Miguel I, moved systematically to root out liberalism. He might have enjoyed success and a long tenure but for the events of 1830 which brought to power the Whigs in England and Louis Philippe in France. These constitutional nations earlier had looked askance at Portuguese proceedings; but now, concerned for depradations against their nationals and openly hostile to the principles of absolutist "Miguelism," they prepared to provide help for Maria II. Her father Pedro (1798–1834) had abdicated (April 7, 1831) as Brazilian emperor and appeared with her in England and France, preparing to enter Portugal and to wrest the crown from his brother.

In Spain the basic issues between conservative absolutism and liberal constitutional forces were much the same, though the situation was less drawn out. Liberalism in both Spain and Portugal was associated more with trade and commerce than with manufacturing, but it shared the emphasis on constitutional guarantees for private property found in France and England. Issues came to a head in Spain at the death of Ferdinand VII on September 29, 1833. Debates on the Salic Law had ended with an affirmation by the Cortes that Maria Isabel (d. 1904), a child born on October 10, 1830, was the heir to the throne. Ferdinand's younger brother, Don Carlos (1788–1855), was furious and became the center of a conservative movement to wrest the throne from his niece. His main protagonist was the Queen Regent, Isabel's mother, Christina (1806–1878), who was also a sister to Carlos' wife. The traditional elements of strength in Spain, the landed aristocracy and the clergy, supported Carlos, who quickly commanded the loyalty of much of northern Spain and prepared to move against the rest of the nation. Christina was forced to rely on liberals and progressives. To keep their support she instituted reforms; but as her situation became more desperate, she turned to England and France for help.

Bitter civil war thus raged in both Iberian nations, and in both, sorely pressed liberals appealed to France and England for aid. At the same time the conservative forces, the Miguelists and Carlists, sought aid and encouragement from the traditionally conservative powers, Austria, Prussia, and Russia. Metternich closely followed developments, giving advice, some credit, but no troops. A welter of diplomatic activity came to a climax on April 15, 1834, when France, England, Portugal, and Spain signed a Quadruple Alliance providing for French and English assistance in securing the young queens their inheritances. Talleyrand, the French ambassador in London, had learned of the negotiations between England, Spain, and Portugal. When he confronted Palmerston, the English minister sheepishly admitted the talks and declared he had fully intended to invite French participation. This was to be the last international agreement carrying Talleyrand's name. His nation became formally a party to securing liberalism in the peninsula, but despite this commitment the burden of the task fell to the English.

Aided by volunteers and English naval cooperation, the Miguelists were soon defeated and Maria was secure on the Portuguese throne. In Spain, however, more direct outside aid was required. Carlism found in Tomas Zumalacarregui (1788–1835) an exceptional military commander. Christina's forces suffered defeat after defeat and her fiscal resources to continue the struggle all but disappeared. After acid debates in Parliament, a lackluster English "Legion" was authorized. It was to give one of the poorest accounts of itself of any force England ever sent overseas. Little direct financial aid came from London, and Paris was even less encouraging. Private bankers were reluctant to provide funds unless such loans were guaranteed by the English and French governments. Because such a commitment in London could have endangered the ministry, some other way of getting funds was needed. A series of hastily conceived expedients failed to improve a deteriorating situation, and in the midst of this mounting urgency appeared a plan to mortgage or sell Cuba, "the brightest jewel in the Spanish crown." In early 1837 efforts were made to raise money through this course, although the prospects at one point appeared so bleak that conversations turned to the idea of the child-queen becoming Isabella II of Cuba should she be driven from Spain. Britain had guaranteed the naval protection of the island and in view of such assurances, along with "aid" of the English "Legion," propositions regarding Cuba were probably made to the government in London. Rumors to change the status of Cuba were common among the United States consular personnel who also seized on these reports. When asked directly by the American ambassador, Andrew Stevenson, Palmerston failed to deny that some sort of proposition had been made. England refused her opportunity to curb the "slave sugar" which was hurting Jamaican "free sugar" in the marketplace, possibly because she might get the island anyway if she merely waited. In any event Christina's agents, finding no deal in London, turned furtively to Paris. Here Talleyrand helped arrange a tentative secret agreement whereby France would buy Cuba, Puerto Rico, and the Philippines. Louis Philippe's penchant for driving a good bargain, however, caused the whole plan to fall through when he demanded a reduction in price from 40 million reals to 37 million.

Still lacking funds, Christina's government then apparently made inquiries of Belgium's King Leopold. Evidence is lacking on the details of the approach to Leopold and also on whether still other states were contacted; but in April of 1837, Leopold believed that he saw an opportunity for Belgium to acquire Cuba as a colony. Unfortunately he lacked funds. Rather than see such an opportunity pass, he inquired of Palmerston if a loan might be possible. Palmerston must have been amused but gave no indication of prior English involvement. He soberly replied that Cuba was really a poor security for such large sums and that, while England had no funds for direct aid, if Belgium could find a smaller and more "suitable" prospective colony, English diplomatic aid could be relied upon. That Leopold was interested in a colony, even before the treaties assuring Belgian independence had been completed, was especially interesting.

Meanwhile Christina still lacked adequate funds, but the death of Zumalacarregui was having its effect. The Carlists had begun to lose ground, a trend which became clear late in 1837. As this occurred, Spanish credit improved, making more money available. An interesting index of the changed situation appeared in 1838–1839. Seizing Palmerston's hint of support for a smaller acquisition, the Belgians asked in Madrid of conditions regarding a transfer of the Isle of Pines, off the southwest Cuban coast. With the acute crisis over, the Spanish now were virtually uninterested. All the initiative regarding this scheme came from Brussels and met with casual indifference in Madrid. By 1839 and 1840 other colonial opportunities beckoned to Leopold and so the negotiations over the Isle of Pines ended. Belgian overseas ambitions were now well known to diplomats and a whole series of colonial schemes followed one another in rapid succession. All were to fail under Leopold I. As for Spain, Carlism was formally beaten by August of 1839. Peace nominally was restored but Carlism was to continue as a threat, to burst forth on later occasions. An important feature of the whole episode was how the Quadruple Alliance dramatized the liberalism of the nations in Western Europe at the very time order and conservatism were being assured in Eastern Europe through Münchengrätz. Europe was split into two vast camps with very little in the way of unifying tendencies at work.

As stability was restored in the Iberian peninsula, another chapter of the Eastern Question unfolded, typically disturbing the shaky status quo. The crisis, ultimately the War Scare of 1840, grew logically out of the earlier agreements made between the Sultan and Mehemet Ali. Resenting the situation which allowed his Egyptian vassal to have Syria, Mahmoud II (1808–1839) had carried through some minor reforms, including a modernization, with Prussian help, of the army. Impressed by his success in this, in April, 1839, he launched an offensive against Ibrahim's forces in Syria. The Sultan's troops were no match for Ibrahim and again the Powers were faced with the prospect, as in 1833, that unless the Sultan received aid, Mehemet Ali could readily march on Constantinople. The crisis developed largely because of a changed French role since 1833. France was now more concerned, as a result of her involvement in Algeria, with Mediterranean problems and was determined to support Mehemet Ali, her ally. The new vigor of French policy dramatized to the English that unless the Egyptians were stopped, France might end up controlling the entire southern coast and the whole eastern end of the Mediterranean. Consequently, Palmerston worked not only for the blocking of Mehemet Ali but for the return of Syria to the Sultan. This position placed England beside Russia in opposition to French policy. Preliminary negotiations masked somewhat the clash of interests; but in February, 1840, Thiers assumed the premiership in Paris. At once French policy took on a more truculent tone as he tried to put direct pressure on the Sultan. In response the Powers negotiated the Treaty of London (July 15, 1840), which assumed the proportions of an ultimatum to Mehemet Ali. He rejected its terms (hereditary rule in Egypt and Southern Syria for life only). The stage was set for war. Thiers was furious over the allied agreements negotiated without consultation with France and he was prepared to go to war. At this juncture Louis Philippe relieved Thiers of office while English military units forced Ibrahim out of Syria. Mehemet Ali settled for personal undisputed rule over Egypt as the crisis subsided. Further negotiation resulted in a Straits Convention (July, 1841) which closed the Dardanelles and the Bosphorus to warships in peace time. France joined the other powers in agreeing to this and on the surface a sort of European concert existed, at least on this issue. Domestically, Louis Philippe was tagged as selling out on a question of national honor. The Return of the Ashes occurred in 1840, and Thiers, working on a history of the Consulate and Empire, eloquently asked if Napoleon would have yielded before such pressure. This example of "timidity" in foreign affairs proved to be a charge the July Monarchy was unable to overcome. In the East, England had gained the most and, like Russia earlier, had saved the Turk. Russia's fleet was confined by treaty to the Black Sea and French influence had been restricted. Ironically, the apprehensions against Mehemet Ali were largely based on the near certainty that he would have made the Ottoman Empire more efficient and self-assertive.

The threat of major war had passed but two more incidents clearly indicated continued Russian and English interest in the area. In September, 1843, a revolution in Greece prompted King Otto to issue a liberal constitution on March 30, 1844. This constitution resulted in little immediate change; administrative neglect and incompetence merely gave way to corruption. In the negotiations following the resort to force, the Russian, British, and French governments all had spokesmen for their views among the Greek politicians. Nicholas grew especially concerned when it became clear that his sympathizers in Athens were unaware of or misinterpreted his position. Essentially concerned with the protection and growth of the Orthodox faith, he finally agreed with England in support of the constitution. Despite his anticonstitutional principles, the Tsar reasoned that in a moment of weakness Otto had promised a constitution, and that promise far outweighed any consideration of circumstances because a monarch had a basic obligation to keep his word. The French diplomatic role in the episode was negligible but English and Russian influences were pronounced and came to work for nearly identical ends in practice.

England and Russia had followed similar policies regarding both Greece and the Ottoman Empire. Their common interests were pointed up in 1844 during a visit to London by Nicholas. Between May 31 and June 9, the Tsar cordially and frankly discussed the Ottoman Empire with a number of English leaders, including Lord Aberdeen (1784–1860) and the Duke of Wellington. He carried from these talks the impression that he had effected a gentleman's agreement with the English that each would consult the other before taking direct action during any future crisis regarding the stability of the Ottoman Empire. However, because the talks were just that —"talks"—the English statesmen believed they had not obligated themselves. Nesselrode drew up a memorandum which summarized the talks, and the Russian ambassador in London, Brunnow, showed it to the successive prime ministers and their foreign secretaries. Tragically, in 1853 Aberdeen was prime minister and Nicholas believed that the talks of 1844 were still the basis for English policy. Though the conversations proved inaccurate as a measure of conditions in 1853, for 1844 they reflect a remarkable agreement between Russian and English attitudes toward the Ottoman Empire.

Few other diplomatic issues in the nineteenth century saw these two nations following similar courses. Even as England had intervened to protect the Sultan against Mehemet Ali, following the Russian example earlier, economic patterns were undermining the prospects of any genuine lasting Anglo-Russian cooperation in the Near East. The Ottoman Empire became an economic battleground where England and Russia were more and more in opposition. This was observed at the time by Karl Marx but for decades scholars failed to pay much attention to this insight. The economic ramifications of the Eastern Question were not indicated in the diplomatic correspondence which most historians studied and they remained unconfirmed until Vernon J. Puryear explained the implications of data available in Board of Trade records. The developing economic rivalry left very little room for diplomats to err, and in 1854 the two countries went to war.

A considerable amount of the blame for the danger in 1840 could be laid to Thiers; thus, after his removal from office, France could in good conscience rejoin the European concert by signing the Straits Convention. Both Paris and London tried to promote a sense of reconciliation, with Louis Philippe visiting London in 1844 and Victoria coming to the Chateau of Eu in 1843 and 1845. Personalities of the two nations' respective ministers made a considerable difference in policies, the difference between Thiers and Guizot in France being matched by Palmerston and Aberdeen in England. The royal visits proved to be superficial and unsuccessful and the two powers bitterly fell out over the issue known as the Spanish Marriages.

After the struggle against the Carlists, Spanish policy took a more reactionary turn. Constitutions issued in 1834 and in 1837 which reflected the values of 1812 were substantially amended and revised, until finally by 1845, the nation's basic governing document was rigorously reactionary. Under General Narváez' ministry a virtual dictatorship assured order and efficiency. Isabel had been declared of age on November 8, 1843, and the new constitution explicitly authorized her to select a husband without gaining permission of the Cortes. This made public a question which was being privately and furtively discussed, and diplomatic pouches now bulged with correspondence on the topic.

At the time of her majority, Isabel was thirteen years of age and headed for a life of flagrant immorality. On her sixteenth birthday, October 10, 1846, she and her younger sister, Maria Luisa Fernanda, were married in a double ceremony ending a series of complex diplomatic intrigues which created hostility between London and Paris. In addition, the issue had been a divisive influence in

Spanish politics, with Christina, now the ex-Regent, playing a shifting and dubious role on both fronts. Among the many candidates for the hand of Isabel were two sons of Louis Philippe, the Duke of Aumale and the Duke of Montpensier; a cousin of Victoria and Albert, Prince Leopold of Saxe-Coburg; the Carlist Pretender, the Count of Montemolín; an abnormal brother of Christina, the Count of Trapani and Christina's nephew, the Duke of Seville. During the talks at Eu, the English and French at one point agreed to the union of Montpensier with Maria Luisa Fernanda, but only after Isabel had married and produced an heir. This would prevent Montpensier from becoming a royal consort if Isabel happened to die unexpectedly. In return the English would withdraw their support of Leopold. From the viewpoint of London, the double marriage was an open violation of the Eu agreements. Montpensier married Maria at the very same time Isabel married a man not previously prominent in the discussions, the younger brother of the Duke of Seville, Don Francisco de Asís. This was a particularly objectionable choice because he was generally disreputable and regarded as physically unable to father children, thus enhancing the likelihood that Montpensier would become the practical ruler of Spain. Palmerston was furious over this threatened extension of French influence. There was nothing he could do directly, but Anglo-French relations chilled perceptibly. In Spain, Isabel followed a flighty course of immorality and paid scant attention to her husband, openly taking lovers. The angling for increased French prestige never paid off. Isabel had children and Montpensier never ruled.

By the end of January, 1848, two other episodes had made Anglo-French relations even more strained. The Duke of Wellington made a survey of English coastal defenses and reported that the entire southern coast was open to invasion. Intended as a confidential report, it found its way into the newspapers. Public feeling against the French began to rise, and in Paris there was resentment at the inference that the French planned an invasion. This all followed a drawn-out diplomacy regarding the Sonderbund in Switzerland. There a fleeting civil war had been won by liberal opponents of the Catholic Sonderbund. The powers had watched closely as Palmerston worked successfully to prevent outside intervention. Metternich and other Continental statesmen were irritated at the aggressiveness of English policy; plans went forward for a Continental alliance against England. France, Austria, Prussia, and Russia all agreed that specific measures should be devised to counter English intrigue on the Continent; March 15, 1848, was selected as the date on which arrangements to this effect would be settled. England was now the outsider, as France had been in 1840. This new situation, however, ended abruptly in February of 1848, when Louis Philippe fled to England, hardly giving a second thought about the propriety of such a refuge.

VII

1848 — Western and Central Europe in Turmoil

CHAPTER 20

France in 1848

In 1848 the pressures for change again broke through Europe's veneer of stability and order. A series of revolutionary upheavals burst forth and spread, feeding one another while toppling several of the established governments in Western and Central Europe. A euphoric optimism seized many intellectuals who sensed a moment of crucial historic change and believed themselves called to exert leadership. These well-meaning men of ideas, known to history as "forty-eighters," generally proved inadequate to the challenges which opened before them. The old system was not entirely bereft of leadership capacity and its emphatic restoration of order lent an air of tragedy to the ideologues' efforts to mold history.

The enduring and debatable cliché among historians of 1848 has been G. M. Trevelyan's observation that "1848 was the turning point at which modern history failed to turn." Opportunities for the success of liberal and nationalistic objectives were briefly at hand. The variety of factors present in the various upheavals makes evaluation and generalization particularly difficult. Few insurrectionary leaders knew how to proceed and they have been sorely criticized for enabling reactionary forces to survive a few more decades. Europe's traditional leadership faltered, and although the forces for change and progress lacked the sense of how to use their opportunity, it was no mean achievement on the part of the old order that it could emerge, shaken but still largely in control. Prussia and Austria were clear examples of this, and the French experience followed almost classic patterns of revolution and struggles for power. Extensive historical study has centered on 1848, but the year deserves still more investigation.

In 1847, despite some irritating problems, Louis Philippe's regime appeared stable. For seventeen years the nation had enjoyed an active political life which, in spite of suffrage limitations, saw the Chamber of Deputies functioning as a parliamentary body with many of the attributes of a constitutional representative system. Its very stability, however, was part of the July Monarchy's problem. The lower middle class was inadequately represented in the councils of power at the same time that the traditional aristocracy was becoming stronger. Even a majority of the lingering Napoleonic nobility was supporting the government, which by the mid-1840s was becoming progressively unresponsive to the interests and needs of the lower classes. Such a circumstance, of course, meant that basic change would require action against the regime itself. After 1845, economic depression dealt harshly with these classes, which made more responsible government action imperative. At the same time, several scandals gave Guizot's government a general reputation for corruption, a reputation which recent research has indicated was not merited.

Despite the obvious social problems, the monarchy seemed well entrenched, especially when compared with the more volatile decade of the 1830s. Both Louis Blanc and Lamartine were among those expecting no basic change until after Louis Philippe's death. The King was particularly confident and unresponsive to the needs for reform. When his son-in-law, Leopold of Belgium, warned him of signs of danger, the French monarch merely shrugged off his observations with the remark that he was so safely in the saddle that "neither banquets of cold veal nor (Louis) Bonaparte" could unseat him. This proved an erroneous analysis which underrated the potential of only two of the voices clamoring for change.

In Paris, 1848 began on a somber note following the death of Adelaide, the Kings' sister. In her passing Louis Philippe lost a particularly beloved confidante. He soon suffered a stroke and while he lay for several days in a semiconscious state, Guizot and a handful of other conservatives anxiously debated the details of an abdication. When he began to recover, such talk ceased and the government turned its attention to the banquet problem, which they utterly failed to understand. Like their monarch, they underrated the cries for electoral reform and were unaware of either the extent of society's developing grievances or the fashion in which the feeling for reform had taken on cohesive form and articulate leadership.

The banquet campaign beginning in July, 1847, was an adaptation of an English political practice. Dominated largely by republican critics of the regime, it attracted so many dissatisfied persons that banquets rapidly became commonplace. Oratory at these affairs directly attacked Guizot and demands for substantial electoral reform were applauded by audiences who had paid to hear the regime criticized. Louis Philippe, like Charles X before him, attributed the public discontent to disgruntled office seekers. It should have sobered him to note that, as in 1830, Thiers was encouraging the opposition. Louis Philippe refused to make concessions and in addressing the Chambers on December 27, 1847, he defended his version of constitutional monarchy, branding those who had supported the banquets as "blind or hostile passions," a tactless reference which merely served to inflame the sentiments against him. Plans for a massive banquet in Paris, a grand finale of the whole campaign, were hastened while cleavages began to appear in the opposition now that a sharp and deliberate confrontation with the government was clearly shaping up. In the planning for this final and crucial banquet, the leaders of the various local banquets now became aware of the breadth of passions they had aroused and realized that other elements in society were ready to support their demands.

By mid-February of 1848, Paris was a hotbed of intrigue, rumor, and unrest. Many of the instigators of the great banquet now assumed a distinctly moderate role. While Armand Marrast, editor of the republican *National,* called for an open challenge to the government's authority, Odilon Barrot, a central and conservative figure in the planning, now envisioned little more than a quiet but unlawful gathering which could become an issue for a legal decision.

Apprehensive over the interest being shown by the Parisian workers, the planners of the banquet decided to charge a higher admission fee and to hold it on a Tuesday (February 22) rather than on a Sunday in the expectation that few laborers could be present. The government became less apprehensive when it forbade the banquet and when, after hasty discussion, Barrot, Lamartine, and others canceled the banquet. Louis Philippe believed the situation had been resolved. Had Paris been like most cities in Europe at the time, he would have been correct.

The French capital, however, was alone in having not only a fairly large proletariat but also a number of intellectual agitators who for some time had been agitating among the workers. A host of secret societies had been formed with Proudhon, Barbès, Blanqui, Ledru-Rollin, and Louis Blanc ominously present and contributing to the cauldron of unrest. By February of 1848, republican demands for a broader franchise to include more of the lower middle classes had been presented by agitators as practical aid for the workers. In reality the basic position of men like Thiers and Barrot was far removed from that of Blanqui and Blanc but there were widespread lower-class expectations that the theories about restructuring society were coming to pass and depended on the holding of the banquet. In 1847 a major rise in basic food prices occurred as famine was widespread. By midwinter a third of the city's laboring force was on charity. When the police forbade the banquet, it seemed for a moment that the regime had saved its moderate critics from the consequences of having been too rash. Instead, however, it was committing suicide.

News that the banquet was canceled spread among workers like wildfire and on the 22nd they appeared in the streets in force. The holding of the banquet had come to be a symbol of their relief and its cancellation, coupled with dampness and rain, made them sullen and dangerous. As crowds roamed to and fro, Louis Philippe hoped for support from the National Guard. This, however, was an illusion, because the expanded franchise which the banquets had called for would have brought solid power to many in the Guard. On the 23rd Guardsmen shouted against Guizot and in favor of reform, and it became clear that they could not be relied on as a force to protect the regime. The King decided to replace Guizot, who was more of a symbol of the unenlightened system than even the monarch, and tried to induce Count Molé to form a ministry. Molé recognized the futility of such a course, for he both sympathized with Guizot and sensed that a greater shift to the left was needed. Thiers was then called to form a government, a concession which would have earned the King high praise from his critics had it occurred earlier. Late as it was, there was a sense of the crisis subsiding, because friends of reform, the National Guard and leaders like Barrot and Thiers, were satisfied. Unfortunately, the crowds were still in the streets. On the evening of the 23rd, an outbreak of violence and bloodshed signalled that real revolution was under way. In what became a grim precedent for the later violence associated with 1848, a shot was fired during a brush between troops and the crowds. Immediate confusion was followed by an organized volley which killed fifty-two of the crowd. Once open conflict had started, barricades went up over much of the city and authorities were presented with a major insurrection. The monarch's conciliatory gesture came too late. Offering power to Thiers failed to stop the revolution. The National Guard had proved unreliable, and the King faced the last resort of using the army to stay in power. Marshal Bugeaud, the foremost hero of the Algerian conquest, was in command, prepared to restore order in Paris as he had in 1834, but unwilling to take orders from a civilian minister. When the alternative came to a brutal crushing of the people of Paris by the army or losing his throne, Louis Philippe shrank from the horrors implicit in such a use of force. Almost matter-of-factly, on the 24th, he penned a simple abdication, indicating his grandson (the ten-year-old Count of Paris) as his successor, and took the traditional exile's route to England.

The abdication of Louis Philippe left most of the earlier voices calling for reform in as much of a quandary as the followers of Guizot. Thiers was no leader of the workers. For the King to leave at a time when insurrection was rife made the monarchy itself virtually indefensible. A dispute between middle and upper classes had allowed lower-class passions to be aroused, and when leadership faltered, a power vacuum opened which was filled by mob violence. As in 1830, the crowd provided the motive power in the crisis which toppled the monarch. Also like 1830, it was to lose out in the subsequent power struggle, but this time that conflict was to be more open, more protracted, and eventually result in a fearful toll of human life.

In the few hours which history had allowed Thiers for restoring order, he had urged the King to dissolve the Chambers and call for new elections. Because Louis Philippe had refused this, the legislative arm of government was in session when the King abdicated. It was natural that the supporters of monarchy thus turned to the Chamber of Deputies for sanction of a regency, but they were handicapped by the crowds which simultaneously entered the Chamber and desecrated the Tuileries. Law and order had reached its low point. Talk of a republic led the Chamber to turn its back on the question of a regency and to give roaring approval to a tentative list of members for a provisional government. It was a tumultuous session, reminiscent of scenes from the First Republic.

Meanwhile the leaders of the workers were also debating who should be in a new provisional government and drew up a list which only partially coincided with that proposed in the Chamber of Deputies. At a compromise meeting at the Hôtel de Ville the lists were merged to the roar of the crowd. The new government thus had the same popular sanction that the July Monarchy initially possessed, but now the product of the change was much more complex. The members selected by the Chamber with mob approval were generally republicans and bourgeoisie, whereas those selected in the name of the workers were essentially socialists who had been chosen by radical newspaper editors. Ironically, both groups were indiscriminantly cheered by the workers, who now presumed their problems would be solved. An early decree (February 25) obligated the government to provide work for all. The republicans would have preferred to leave the socialists out of the government but lacked the nerve to defy the cheering crowds. Among the new government's pressing problems was its basic composition. Its members were egocentric ideologues who hated and spied on one another. Many republicans were upper bourgeoisie who were undogmatic defenders of property and could believe in certain forms of socialistic practice while the socialists posing as working class leaders were bona fide intellectuals. The Orléanist regime had been brushed aside but the new government refused to move to a genuinely radical program. True Jacobin revolutionaries like Blanqui were disgusted at the moderation exhibited by the new leaders. Despised by both ends of the political spectrum, the government's task was made doubly difficult by its own internal dissension.

The Provisional Government faced two major problems at the outset. Something had to be done at once about alleviating worker distress, and it had to be accomplished while the rest of Europe was just learning with dread of Louis Philippe's abdication to the accompaniment of a Paris in barricades. In this situation three men came to the fore, Alphonse Lamartine, Louis Blanc, and Ledru-Rollin (1807–1874). Their interests and abilities symbolized both the intellectual idealism and the practical problems of 1848.

Lamartine was a nineteenth-century romantic liberal who supported republicanism in the face of the rigidity and inflexibility demonstrated by constitutional monarchy as it had developed in the later years of the July Monarchy. Enjoying a wide reputation as a poet, he provided an emotional leadership to the new government. The revolution which was not liberal enough for Blanqui was radicalism incarnate for the conservative states in Europe. While the new regime was debating specific domestic reforms, Lamartine's first major responsibility as foreign minister was to mollify and reassure the Continent's leading statesmen. For them, 1830, with its forceful change of government, had been galling, but at least a dynasty had emerged; and Louis Philippe, after all, was descended from the Bourbon family. Now more violence had toppled that monarch and in his place was a republic as in 1792.

To avert foreign intervention, Lamartine sent French ambassadors a circular notice (March 2) which explained how the new republic's diplomatic position should be presented to other governments. It was a carefully constructed message which tried to be conciliatory and reassuring while emphasizing the essential independence of the new regime. About a third of his message discussed how the situation differed from 1792. He noted that in merely coming into existence in 1848 the Republic had occasioned no aggression against any other established government in Europe and that the Republic was dedicated to peace. At the same time it would accept war if forced upon it. In a more disturbing but still conciliatory vein, he declared that so far as the French Republic was concerned "the treaties of 1815 exist no longer in law." The territorial agreements of 1815, however, were practical facts and common sense called for respecting them. Alternating from subtle defiance to compliance, he declared that the French would feel free to render military aid if "certain oppressed nationalities" were interfered with when on the verge of achieving significant democratic or nationalistic gains. He hinted that trouble could arise in Switzerland and Italy and then went on to declare that the French would never be responsible for plotting unrest among neighboring populations.

Lamartine's circular had its desired effect. Disturbed as they were, most European statesmen did not want to become involved in a war with France. Although they were irritated by the cavalier repudiation of the treaties of 1815, they were encouraged by the moderate tone of the entire communication and relieved that French republicanism per se might not be synonymous with war. In addition, there was a feeling of sympathy for Lamartine. He was, after all, a man of breeding and distinction. His word was itself a guarantee of peace and he represented a possible restraining influence within France. Meanwhile, the diplomats debated the protocol of recognition. France was not a new country; it had merely altered its governmental form. Discussions of a compromise tendering of de facto recognition led to the obvious conclusion that the Provisional Government was not de facto at all. The Belgians felt the brunt of the problem and gave quick recognition. To deny it would be tantamount to an invitation to war and she could only be that defiant if Prussian troops were massed on her frontier to give her instant support. The fact that Leopold was Louis Philippe's son-in-law made the Belgian leaders feel especially apprehensive. Lamartine's message brilliantly accomplished its objectives but what has not been so clear is the extent to which it reflected his personal ideas concerning French policy. How sincere was he, and was the document construed with any other intent than to buy time? These questions have a special relevance when seen in the context of French propaganda and intrigues. Part of the problem may have been that although Lamartine was spokesman for France to other governments, he possessed little control over others in the government. Thus, a zealot like Ledru-Rollin could plan to export revolution in utter disregard of Lamartine's formal pledges to other powers. Unfortunately, some documents seem to compromise Lamartine himself.

A feature of the history of 1848 which needs more attention is the development and activities of a number of so-called Legions. Formed in Paris, these were given missions of bringing republican institutions to several areas in Europe, especially Poland, Belgium, and Italy. Composed of unemployed foreign nationals (workers) or exiles resident in Paris in 1848, they were organized, propagandized, and given weapons. Late in March, two groups of the "Belgian Legion" approached the northern frontier but were turned back by Belgian troops. In addition to such units, a horde of republican agitators, financed from Paris, tried to stir up insurrection in Belgium, Luxemburg, and the Rhine area and enjoyed a few sporadic successes. The main point is that the Provisional Government did indeed work at exporting revolution and republicanism. Ledru-Rollin, as minister of the interior, was responsible for much of this, but Lamartine was also involved. The foreign minister favored the founding of other republican governments, whereas Ledru-Rollin felt that areas could best become republican by becoming part of France. Thus the more radical intriguers were basically imperialistic, whereas Lamartine was content simply to see agitators go forth to do what they could to further republican ideals without favoring a deliberate extension of French frontiers.

Foreign affairs consumed only part of Lamartine's energies in the early weeks of the Provisional Government. Virtually from its inception, the republican members waged a deliberate campaign against the socialists they had reluctantly accepted during the ceremony at the Hôtel de Ville. Karl Marx (1818–1883) analyzed the progress of events in France in 1848 as a clear unfolding of the class struggle. Paris in 1848 and during the earlier Great Revolution is as clear a demonstration of this position as the human record provides. Republican attempts to discredit the socialists and the chain of events leading through the June Days surely constituted a classic acting out of Marxian postulates.

The republicans who came to power in February were hardly prepared for responsibility. As banqueteers they had hoped for a broadening of the franchise and the fall of Guizot. Amazed at the flight of Louis Philippe, they found themselves the handy beneficiaries of his abdication. They assumed the posts of government with no obvious program other than to secure their position in the infant republic and to combat the socialists whose leaders they had uneasily accepted. Many of them were not as ideologically committed to the Republic as they were to the ideal of property. Consequently they encountered little difficulty in attracting business support, and many who had favored Louis Philippe's regime now ranged alongside the republicans in a struggle to oppose the spread of socialism.

In its early hours the Republic had made a solemn commitment to the workers to guarantee labor and the tactical implementation of this pledge sharpened the republican-socialist dichotomy. The need for a program was urgent, for crowds still roamed the streets. Unemployment was further aggravated when at the first indication of violence many of the upper classes left the city, thus abruptly ending work in a number of luxury trades and services. The workers themselves called for a ministry of progress to be headed by Louis Blanc. This ideologue was known to have a plan, enunciated in *The Organization of Labor*, which if put into practice would result in equitable and constructive employment. The workers believed that if Blanc were in authority, then their problems would be solved. In this euphoric expectation lay both the republicans' problem and its solution. They had to placate the workers by using Blanc; they had to reduce unemployment; and they somehow had to reduce the role of the socialists in the government. All this they had to do while hoping that foreign nations would not interfere. The spontaneity of the situation at the fall of Louis Philippe meant that the republicans faced this dilemma without planning; yet, as events developed, their every move regarding the socialists worked as well as if their strategy had been decided after intensive study.

The government launched a two-pronged attack on the problem of employment. As the workers' champion and an authority on labor, Blanc was put in charge of a commission (meeting at the Luxembourg Palace, hence the "Luxembourg Commission") which would make comprehensive studies and recommendations. He worked long hours, presiding over meetings of both workers and employers who debated the entire range of employment problems. A few practical changes emerged from these meetings, especially relating to length of the working day and to wages; but by and large a considerable amount of time and thought yielded negligible results. A number of the Commission's suggestions would have begun a movement toward a form of state socialism in France but most of their recommendations received no support from the republican majority in the government. At the same time, however, the idea had been firmly planted that Blanc was in charge of the government's program for labor.

While Blanc's work was being sidetracked, public attention was attracted to an impractical program of national workshops. These workshops were instituted under the ministry of public works which was headed by Alexandre Marie (1795–1870), a critic of Blanc's. The national workshops bore virtually no relationship whatever to the social workshops envisaged in *The Organization of Labor,* yet they were presented as fair samples of socialism. To make the perversion even more complete, the direct administration of the national workshops was entrusted to Emile Thomas, a young and brilliant engineer who desperately tried to make the workshops succeed. There was thus a sense of dedicated direction in the leadership which further suggested that the failure lay with the system rather than in faulty supervision. The workshops were devices to provide employment and income to those needing it, but they were established so quickly that there was inadequate planning. Despite this, Thomas was a fountainhead of ideas on how the unemployed could be used in such programs as railway and canal construction, but most of these were never approved in the ministry. His proposals, if implemented, would have employed many more people and kept them decentralized. As it was, the unemployed, including vagabonds, flooded into Paris in such numbers that they could not all be gainfully employed. Indeed, labor for only 10,000 could be found, out of an available force which by mid-June numbered over 150,000. A scheme of rotating employment and reduced payments to those not working failed to solve the problem; the whole program was easily presented as a system which merely encouraged laziness and the waste of public funds. It is tempting to speculate what Blanc and Thomas, working together and supported by a government, could have done. Fate, however, had not brought them together in such a happy circumstance, and the efforts of both failed.

An interesting social cleavage was apparent between the two working groups. Those represented at the Luxembourg Commission came from the trades and clubs of Paris. They were more highly skilled and possessed a sense of solidarity. Further, through the discussions in the Luxembourg they were becoming schooled in the heady hopes of socialism. Those in the workshops were less skilled and generally less responsible. Large numbers of these latter "workers" were encouraged to join the National Guard, a device by Marie and Lamartine to prepare a laboring counterforce should Blanc weld his workers into a revolutionary force.

The intrigue against Blanc and the socialists was hardly subtle. The elections for a National Constituent Assembly, though delayed through socialist efforts from March 17 to April 23, resulted in republican successes, largely because of the poor publicity gained by the national workshops. When the new Assembly convened on May 4, the Provisional Government ceased to function. The new executive committee was republican and formed after a debate in which Lamartine successfully opposed efforts to get rid of Ledru-Rollin. The republicans had discredited the socialists, beaten them at the polls, and then excluded them from the new government. For Louis Blanc and his followers the range of choice became drastically limited. His proposal that a ministry of labor be formed was rejected. With this there seemed little prospect for working through legitimate channels; the alternative of redress through mob action was clear.

On May 15, socialist-inspired mobs invaded the Assembly. They had demonstrated on March 17 and on April 16 and had merely succeeded in creating more apprehension in moderate republican ranks. Lacking the spontaneity of February, the May riot should have been more carefully planned. Some radical leaders, including Barbès and Blanqui, were insisting that circumstances were not yet propitious for such a use of force; Louis Blanc was himself a restraining influence. After surging into the Assembly, the mob then turned toward the Hôtel de Ville. The National Guard moved efficiently against them, clearing the workers from the Assembly and dispersing many on their way to the Hôtel de Ville. The whole insurrection collapsed. Had the Guard been as efficient or dedicated in February, Louis Philippe would never have fallen.

In the wake of the upheaval many of its leaders were in prison and the plight of the socialists seemed even more hopeless. Sentiment in the clubs against the government was pronounced while the executive committee debated how to deal with both the workers and the workshops. The government saw the uprising as a direct socialist assault on the representatives of property and the deputies believed that they and their system had only barely survived the challenge. Sensing that some of the laborers in the workshops were moving closer to those in the clubs, they decided that the workshops must be closed, a measure which had been contemplated before May 15. Believing the country at large would support them, they reasoned that they must act before even greater numbers congregated in Paris. Thus a direct confrontation was decided upon and the government girded itself for the task.

Late in May, Thomas was forcibly removed from Paris and many of the workers were reassigned to the army, to private industry, and to projects outside Paris. Decrees also ordered the closing of the clubs and worker unrest increased markedly. At this juncture a joining of ranks between the workers in the clubs and those in the workshops occurred which made the government's problem more acute. Many club leaders began planning for another banquet to be held in mid-June, but internal dissensions frustrated these hopes. When a decree on June 21 formally closed the workshops, the signal for insurrection had been given.

Immediately, barricades began to spring up and the government debated whether to attack them at once or to wait until the full extent of the insurrection was clear before attacking in force. While discussing the issue, the Assembly relieved the executive committee of its authority and transferred it to General Cavaignac (1802–1857). The situation was now far beyond what the Guard could be expected to handle. While military units were being collected near Paris, a call went out in the provinces for volunteers to aid in quelling the rebellion. A considerable response to this plea demonstrated the sentiment in favor of property and a widespread public disgust with the workshops. General Cavaignac, son of a *Conventionnel*, had been a successful zouave leader in the campaigns in Algeria. A dedicated republican, he now moved systematically to crush the insurrection.

In the "June Days" (June 23–26) he subdued the workers at a fearful price in blood. As the barricades repulsed wave upon wave of assault, the human toll mounted. The combat was ferocious. The struggle spontaneously ignored previous club organizations and drew in broad spectrums of the lower classes. Summary execution was the lot of many prisoners on both sides. The dead numbered approximately 1,500 and Cavaignac's dictatorship was reconfirmed by an Assembly shocked at the savage violence shown by the lower classes.

The June Days in Paris. (Courtesy of Historical Pictures Service, Chicago.)

The uprising was not nearly as comprehensive as a Marxist analysis would suggest, but the earmarks of a class conflict were uncomfortably present. Assembly members who were devout republicans were appalled at the bloodshed. In 1793 the Republic had been opposed by elements above the republicans in the social scale. This time the republicans were the defenders of property and had used the ultimate public weapon, military force, to coerce the lower, essentially nonpropertied classes. In retrospect they believed that they had been forced to this bloody extreme which had offended their consciences and sensibilities. Soberly they looked askance at the moral implications of what they had done and willingly entrusted Cavaignac to assure the framing of a constitution. Had he been a less dedicated republican, he could readily have installed a regime based on personal power and the army. If the episode had profoundly disturbed the republicans, this reaction was pale when seen beside the impact on the workers. A sense of worker solidarity and hatred toward property owners and managers had been created which still endures. Many families never forgot that property owners had sanctioned the use of the army against the workers. A somewhat similar situation in 1871 meant that in two generations such an event happened twice, and these two episodes go far to explain the particular truculence and friction which has characterized labor relations in France.

The emergence of Cavaignac was a relief to many people. Lamartine's ascendancy was over, though he appeared not to realize it. The republicans were shaken after the June Days and willingly allowed the general to set major policy. He appeared a welcome shield behind which a constitution could be prepared for the Republic. Cavaignac himself had much the same view of his role, but expected eventually to be elected president of the new system. To other rulers Cavaignac also represented an end to mob violence and a return to order as French foreign policy now promised to be more conservative and less imperialistic. Belgian officials were especially relieved, because Cavaignac was an old friend. His boyhood schooling had been in Belgium, where his father had found a haven during an exile shared with the father of General Chazal, Belgian war minister in 1848. There was clearly less danger of a French invasion of Belgium, and relations between the two nations perceptibly warmed. In late summer and fall, however, the forum for trouble lay in Italy and the pressures were strong on Cavaignac to intervene. He resolutely refused, maintaining that a strong garrison was needed in Paris, a priority that could hardly be questioned. Under Cavaignac there was also a marked decline in the *provocateurs* from France who sought to raise rebellions in Central Europe, although by then the forces of rebellion were already loose.

The retention of Cavaignac in power after the June Days was aptly symbolic of the marked reaction against the more advanced revolutionary forces of February. Leaders in the clubs had feared just such a reaction but were unable to exercise restraint in the emotional surge following the decree closing the workshops. In the resumed constitutional discussions, the trend to the right was clear. There now was little talk of a constitutional obligation to provide employment and the final document made no reference to the right to work. In this Assembly dominated by moderate republicans, the most absorbing discussions centered on the relationship between the popular body and the president. Learned discourses citing precedents and problems ranging from antiquity finally resulted in the creation of a strong executive with a unicameral legislature, two arms of government essentially coequal but with no mechanism established to resolve a deadlock. The legislators were to be elected for three-year terms. As a body they could not be dissolved, nor could new elections be called by the president. Correspondingly, they could not remove him from office. Thus the idea of separation of powers was rigorously followed. Realizing the danger but agreeing with Lamartine that "something had to be left to Providence," they finished the document on November 4 and scheduled elections for December 10. The president was to be elected to a four-year term by universal manhood suffrage. He was thus to speak with more authority than any person or clique in the Assembly, but this advantage was somewhat balanced by the stipulation that he would be ineligible for direct re-election.

In retrospect, the most important political development during Cavaignac's ascendancy was the appearance of a resurgent Bonapartism headed by Prince Louis Napoleon Bonaparte, nephew of the Emperor Napoleon. The only Bonaparte prince living in 1848 who had been acclaimed a prince at his birth in 1809, he had spent most of his life living in Switzerland, Italy, and England. For years he had been assiduously propagandizing himself and the Napoleonic Legend, insisting that what France and Europe needed was a Bonapartist restoration. In 1836 at Strasbourg and in 1840 at Boulogne he had attempted coups which were ludicrous failures but which served to keep his name before the public and secured his claim within the family as the main pretender. It was essential for a Bonaparte with political ambitions to be a military authority and so, in order to buttress his credentials as a military expert, he wrote an artillery manual for the Swiss army. A reputation for adventure came also from Carbonaro associations and revolutionary activities in Italy in 1831. While in prison at Ham (1840–1846) he wrote economic and political studies and corresponded voluminously with a wide range of social critics and ideologues. Meanwhile, Louis Philippe contributed to the Napoleonic Legend by arranging for the Return of the Ashes, completing the Arch of Triumph, and erecting numerous monuments to the glories of the Empire. The embittered Thiers was acidly criticizing what he regarded as a failure of leadership, especially after 1839, when the July Monarchy suffered in comparison with the reign of Napoleon. A considerable public sentiment for Bonapartism was suggested in the April (1848) elections, when seats in the Assembly were won by three of Louis' cousins: Prince Pierre, the son of Lucien; Prince Napoleon, son of Jerome; and Lucien Murat, the son of Caroline.

At the fall of Louis Philippe, Louis had sounded out Lamartine about his political prospects and was dissuaded for the moment. His devoted promoter, the Duke de Persigny (1808–1872), however, began an astute publicity campaign for him and his name was entered in the by-elections of June 4. He was elected by four departments, a gratifying result, but in the Assembly there were strong objections to the right of this escaped prisoner, who had been convicted of intriguing against France, to sit now as one of its members. Remaining in England, Louis bent gracefully before the storm and resigned the seat he had legally won. His restraint won praise as he awaited another opportunity. He was thus in England during the June Days, his record untainted by any of the issues surrounding the clubs, the workshops, or the insurrection. In September, he was again elected and crossed the Channel to take his seat. The more conservative Assembly now received him in a spirit of curiosity mixed with relief. His first speech accepting his seat amazed many deputies because it was delivered with the accent of a Swiss-German. Further, most had never seen him and he neither sounded nor looked like a dangerous person. His speech, which was sluggish, did not seem to reveal a clever mind. The common reaction was that he had been overrated because of his name and that it had been a mistake to worry about him. His supporters increased the publicity on his behalf and he became a candidate for the presidency, an amazingly bold step for one so recently returned from exile. As election day neared, help appeared from many places. Thiers supported him, predicting that with the fame of his name perhaps the election could be won, and if this occurred, the prince would need help in governing, because he clearly (to Thiers) lacked the potential to rule. Thus Thiers hoped to come back to office on the coat tails of Louis Napoleon. Many critics of policies dating from February similarly voted for Louis. The combined support for him was a complete surprise, for he swept the election with over 5.5 million votes. Cavaignac was chagrined only to receive about 1.5 million votes, virtually a betrayal for the man who had saved the Republic and steadfastly refused to abandon republican institutions. Ledru-Rollin and Lamartine received little support as the voters turned to a name which connoted prestige and authority. Implicit in their voting was an expectation for change and a repudiation of much that had happened since February. Louis therefore took the oath on December 20, 1848, as President of the Second Republic, with a mandate which could be interpreted as striking at the very foundations of the system. With his election, the revolutionary year came to an end; the end of the Republic, perhaps in sight, was not to come for three years.

CHAPTER 21

Revolt in Central Europe

The year 1848 saw a series of revolts stretching from Berlin to Naples. These uprisings were both liberal and nationalistic and, combined with events in France, made 1848 a banner year in the revolutionary tradition. In general, they followed the French experience of initial successes for liberal goals, succeeded by a conservative subversion or controlling of these objectives. The various insurrections took many forms and still offer the historian fruitful areas for investigation.

News that the barricades were up in Paris and that Louis Philippe had fled had an electric effect in Central Europe. It gave hope and encouragement to malcontents while causing consternation and apprehension for those in power. The years 1792 and 1830 came at once to mind; the mood of crisis appeared at every hand. Thus, indirectly, France was a factor in causing the outbreaks to come when they did. The French were directly responsible, however, for the unrest in much of Central Europe. As mentioned earlier, during the Provisional Government paid *provocateurs* and revolutionary firebrands poured out from Paris, creating discontent and local insurrection. They were special problems for the areas bordering France to the north and east. Through the efforts of Ledru-Rollin and to a lesser degree Lamartine, the revolution was being exported in a fashion which caused many statesmen to wonder whether it was possible for a republican government to exist peacefully in a monarchical family of nations. In the Grand Duchy of Luxembourg agitators called for union with the Belgian province of Luxembourg, which would then form a new republic under French protection. In Belgium speakers urged the overthrow of Leopold and the institution of republican government, and in the Moselle valley a mob controlled Trier and insurrection was widespread. Similar unrest swept through the Rhineland, where middle- and lower-class grievances were real and impulses to follow French actions were easily played upon by agitators. The year 1848 was busy for Karl Marx, who vigorously urged revolution in the whole area from Switzerland to the lower Rhine. The particular brand of republicanism born in the February Revolution was thus a direct menace to the parties in power on the borders of France; but before statesmen of the status quo could decide on what to do, they had either been overwhelmed and thrown from power or were fighting for their lives against revolution. Despite some notable casualties, their widespread survival showed a considerable amount of good luck as well as residues of real ability.

Most studies of 1848 in Central Europe concentrate on events in major cities, especially Berlin and Vienna, an emphasis justified in terms of the importance of change in these capitals. Fortunately, sources of information about urban uprisings are much more extensive and less fragmentary than those for rural disturbances. The documentation of unrest in the countryside in 1848 has largely been left for scholars working in local history. Such work has not yet been adequately made a part of the general narrative and our knowledge suffers accordingly. Bureaucratic and administrative studies would prove most interesting and monographs on strictly economic topics during 1848 would similarly be welcome. Through much of the Rhine basin, bands of discontented peasants were burning and looting, and in the cities proletarian unrest constituted a major threat to the middle and upper classes. These aspects of 1848 remain insufficiently explored; but, fortunately, the scholarship to date does seem to explain the most crucial upheavals in Berlin and Vienna. The temper and enthusiasms of those agitating for change are difficult to portray because so many factors were simultaneously at work and narrative accounts usually fail to capture this. This is especially true for the historian who generalizes and tries to identify basic trends and characteristics. News that Louis Philippe had fallen precipitated unrest in many widely separated areas; secondary reverberations occurred after word spread that Metternich had also fallen. Berlin was in insurrection; Hungary was in arms; and Italy was in revolt. The emotional intensity created by these circulating stories and heady rumors rarely is a part of scholarly accounts of any of the separate revolutions, but it was a major ingredient in many an insurrection.

Of all the unrest in Germany, perhaps the least ambitious objectives were apparent in Berlin. Chance played a key role during the March Days. On the 18th a couple of shots, fired possibly by accident, turned a well-mannered crowd of curious spectators into a frenzied mob of barricade builders. This was virtually a replay of events almost a month before in Paris. Fraught with dangers enhanced by the mediocre leadership of Frederick William IV, the insurrection lacked an emphasis on worker solidarity. As a consequence, extreme egalitarianism was not one of its driving forces. Indeed, the monarchy had merely to retreat along lines already staked out by liberals before 1848. Triggered by events in Paris, the upheaval in Berlin centered on issues more resembling the French revolution of 1830 than that of 1848. The bourgeoisie wanted a larger voice in public affairs and hoped to get this in a representative *Landtag* which would legislate for all Prussia, meet regularly, and have some control over finances. In 1847, they had been frustrated in this hope, but in the unrest of 1848, there was talk of a constitution and an end to censorship, and liberals felt that their expectations might yet be fulfilled. News of widespread rioting and the fall of Metternich emboldened liberals in Berlin, but at the same time they were apprehensive about the fervor with which workers threw up barricades and fought the regime. Thus they tempered their objectives when they saw the King being humbled by the lower classes. The monarchy had gained a resourceful ally in its subsequent turn to a more reactionary course.

Frederick William had earlier lost the respect of many liberals for his consistent refusal to make significant concessions. Because his regime made little use of their talents, they were hostile to the basic institutions which perpetuated the system, especially the army, which was controlled by the nobility, like much of the bureaucracy. Showered with prestige, the military was particularly resented by the middle class because of its domestic police function. When the King ordered the army out of Berlin in an effort to abate the revolution, the middle class found itself in an interesting dilemma. The opportunity for a constitution was clearly at hand, yet a defenseless monarch meant the danger of a real democratic movement.

Throughout the whole episode Frederick William was a curious figure. He found it an almost impossible idea that the people opposing his regime were really his subjects. He believed he was adored and that much of the difficulty stemmed from foreign agitators. Conservative statesmen found it incomprehensible that he had muzzled his own military, because the army probably could have restored order. The King's actions, however, need to be seen from another perspective, his deep and convoluted sense of Christianity and divine-right monarchy. That God had allowed the insurrection made it obvious to him that the proper course was not to use the army against it but to make the concession which the situation demanded. His curbing of the army, however, allowed the challenge to his authority to become more dangerous than it might have been, but his subsequent show of grief for the victims and his agreement to constitutional change allowed him to survive with his crown.

While acquiescing to the desire for liberal reform, Frederick William also made statements implying his support for a new Germany. He talked more of Germany than of Prussia and nationalists took his remarks to imply the end of the Metternich system and a modification of Austrian influence in Central Europe. With the fall of the Viennese statesman, events seemed to be moving pell mell toward Prussian leadership in the definition and founding of a new Germany; and in the perilous days of March, Prussia's King gave no hint that he had any serious reservations in playing such a role.

In the smaller German states liberal reform came quickly with a modicum of unrest, and the bourgeoisie saw in Austria's internal problems the need for new leadership in the Confederation. They showed remarkable initiative in the speed with which they organized the Frankfurt Assembly and prepared the way for Prussia to assume a dominant position. Meeting in Heidelberg on March 5, a band of liberals called for a larger meeting on the 31st. This would include local legislators from the various German states along with a number of others dedicated to reform. This *Vorparlament* purged itself of republican elements and called for elections by universal manhood suffrage. Those elected would meet in May to frame a constitution for Germany. The elections were speedily held, and on May 18, the Frankfurt Assembly duly convened in St. Paul's church. Elected president of the Assembly was Heinrich von Gagern (1799–1880), an emotional patriot who had decades before been a Burschenschaft activist and an acquaintance of Karl Sand.

For the forces of change to have come so far was a tribute to many things. Again, events in France served as a great catalyst, but change was also welcomed because of widespread disdain for the Confederation set up in 1815. This now had few defenders outside Austria, who saw it only as a device for exercising control beyond her own borders. A measure of the contagious enthusiasm for something different was clear in the approval given by the moribund Federal Diet to the calls for elections and to the presumed mandate of the Assembly to meet in Frankfurt. There was, in fact, no legal or constitutional authority whatever for the convening of such an assembly until the Diet meekly acquiesced in the face of the liberal initiatives. As in Prussia, had conservative leadership been initially vigorous, the liberal movement could readily have been coerced. Considering, however, that the Diet was influenced by the knowledge of royal hesitation in Berlin, by liberal reforms in the smaller states, and by the basic disintegrating movements within Austria, it may be pardoned for yielding in the face of liberal boldness.

The Frankfurt Assembly has been regarded as a tragic highwater mark in German history. It was liberalism's finest hour and its failure to survive has been presented as the last great alternative to the aggressive militarism which later dominated German politics and society. The point has often been made that the Assembly was a collection of erudite pedants, able in debate, skilled in writing a constitution, but deficient in the ways of practical politics. Such observations and criticisms tend to overrate the liberals' real opportunity. They never had, for example, control over the bureaucratic apparatus of a single state. They lacked the power to tax and they had no army. They flourished only during the power vacuum caused by problems in Berlin and Vienna; but once the conservatives saw their authority restored in these two cities, the prospects were remote that the Frankfurt Assembly could become an effective government for "Germany." That such an assembly ever was called and functioned at all was a miracle in itself. Indeed its members clearly recognized that they needed administrative and executive leadership; despite installing Austria's Archduke John as a temporary executive, they hoped that Prussia's king would rise to the opportunity. In this they banked too heavily on Frederick William's remarks about "Germany." It turned out that he had in mind, at most, something like a restored Holy Roman Empire containing a prominent place for Prussia. He was not energetic enough to contemplate the expulsion of Austria from "Germany" nor liberal enough to accept a crown "from the gutter," so the opportunity proved illusory when restored royal power in Berlin allowed the King again to support conservative institutions and to follow Austrian initiatives willingly. Thus Frederick William refused the crown offered him by the Assembly while accepting the reinstitution of the old Confederation and its Federal Diet. It had been unrealistic for liberals to expect that Frederick William IV would promote reform in Germany at large any more than he had in Prussia itself.

After Paris, perhaps the most critical and emphatic challenge to established authority occurred in Vienna. On the night of March 13, Prince Metternich resigned and fled. This symbol of an age had been easily swept aside and surprised zealots now expected that extensive reform was near at hand. In Austria there was a thorough mixing of national and liberal objectives which compounded the government's problems but also suggested some of its solutions, once the rulers adjusted to the double shock of Metternich's flight and the news of widespread riots all over Germany, including Berlin. Conservative leaders showed remarkable ability in subverting one of 1848's most explosive revolutionary situations. If Berlin resembled the French revolution of 1830, Vienna was closer to the situation of 1789, with peasant unrest more of a recognized problem than worker agitation. As in the Great French Revolution, once peasant grievances received some attention, they ceased to be vigorous supporters of further reform. An interesting new element was the appearance of students as a recognizable faction in the ranks of the protesters.

The problems besetting the Austrian Empire in 1848 were more definitely nationalistic than those troubling other states in that year of turmoil. To this time nationalism had been a major cause of trouble elsewhere in Europe, and Austria had assumed the posture of a concerned observer, from time to time aiding the forces of reaction. In Italy she had been drawn into a more active role but essentially she did not see nationalism as a profound domestic issue of her own. She recognized nationalism in the French, Prussians, Spanish, and English, and to a lesser extent in the Italians, Germans, and Poles. The Greek struggle for independence had suggested the problem that could be created within a political structure embracing many peoples, and in 1848 the full impact of such a situation came home to Austria. A developing Slav consciousness began to stir while specific Hungarian, Croat, Czech, and Italian revolts demonstrated the handicaps that the Austrian Empire faced in a growing age of nationalism. A series of upheavals in distant parts of the Empire, each demanding immediate and careful attention, came at a time when the city of Vienna itself was in the throes of a revolt. Compounding the danger, the dynasty was then represented by Ferdinand I (1793–1875), one of its weakest members. When Metternich resigned, the portents for disaster were everywhere.

As in Prussia and elsewhere in Central Europe, the spark which ignited the fires of revolution in Austria was the news of the fall of Louis Philippe. This had a simultaneous impact on liberals in Vienna, especially students at the University, and on Hungarian nationalist leaders who happened to be sitting as members of the Diet's lower house, then meeting at Pressburg. Vigorous statements by the Hungarian Louis Kossuth (1802–1894) served to enervate the crowd in Vienna which had gathered in response to the earlier news from Paris. At this point it would have required firm and determined leadership to restore order.

The Magyars had continually been a special problem for Austria. The gulf between peasant and noble was far less pronounced than in many areas of Europe and a unifying cultural and linguistic renaissance was under way. A moving force in this and in measures devised to assure economic improvement was Count Szechenyi (1792–1860), who believed in indirect progress toward national status. There was a long tradition of Magyar identity and constitutional history to build on, and by 1847 the stirrings for independence were pronounced. Szechenyi was to be overshadowed by Kossuth, who favored a more direct attack on the regime in Vienna and was able to express himself in more eloquent language. Further, Kossuth spoke with the martyr's credentials of three years in prison, and his public appeals for freedom of the press, freedom of speech, jury trial, and more autonomy created an openly revolutionary situation. At the news from Paris, Kossuth delivered one of the many great speeches of his career. He openly attacked the government of Vienna as a curse to the Hungarians. He insisted that Magyar loyalty to the Emperor was only possible if more autonomy were given Hungary and he argued that throughout the Empire similar constitutional procedures should be instituted. Vienna should copy a program defined by the Magyars in the East rather than the slogans from Paris in the West. The fervor of his remarks convinced the Diet and it voted to address these liberal and nationalistic demands to the Emperor.

News of Kossuth's speech and the Diet's address to the Emperor served as a second incendiary spark in Vienna. Students were already agitating when Kossuth's remarks concerning more constitutional government for the Empire became known. They now became further excited, sought out workers to join their cause and demanded arms and immediate reform. A weak and vacillating ministry did not know what to do and acquiesced in the demand for arms. Hoping to conciliate the crowd, it turned on Metternich, who resigned after a brief exchange in which he declared his reluctance to step down because he had promised Francis he would never abandon his weak son. There was little determination to coerce the mob; but, unlike the king of Prussia, the Crown never ordered the army from the scene.

When the students received arms to form a national guard, as they had been insisting, their demands for a constitution and major liberalization of the Empire naturally carried more force and the government readily acquiesced. Hungary's demands were similarly accepted and the Magyar lower house voted a series of bills collectively known as the March Laws. These served as a written constitution, embodying liberal demands and virtual independence, with Hungary remaining part of the Austrian Empire only through the figure of its king, who also ruled as emperor in Vienna.

The imperial government gave every appearance of being utterly at the mercy of events. Prince Windischgrätz (1787–1862) was virtually alone in favoring a blunt military solution to the deteriorating situation. Italy, Bohemia, and Croatia joined the ranks of insurrectionary centers and the ministry seemed paralyzed. On April 25, it offered the citizens of Vienna a constitution which was remarkably enlightened, considering its sponsorship. The students, however, rejected this concession and again poured into the streets. In response the Emperor called for a special assembly to draw up a constitution and left for Innsbruck with his family. The Assembly began its meetings in July, and after a number of interruptions and a change of meeting place to Kremsier it completed a constitution on March 1, 1849. Its work, unfortunately, had taken too long; as they had with the Frankfurt Assembly, events altered the conditions which had necessitated the document in the first place. This "Kremsier Constitution" was an anachronism on the day it appeared and three days later Prince Schwarzenberg (1800–1852) gave the Empire his own, more authoritarian constitution. By March of 1849 the Empire had more responsible leadership and a major counterrevolutionary movement was well under way. With multiple centers of major insurrection, the problem for Austrian leaders was far more complex than that faced by either Louis Philippe or Frederick William IV. Varying degrees of national and local autonomy were confused with standard liberal objectives and in the first months after February,

Revolution in Vienna. (Courtesy of Historical Pictures Service, Chicago.)

it seemed as though revolution was to be triumphant on a wide scale. For Austria's conservatives, the road back to power and control began in June, 1848, in Bohemia. The restoration of imperial authority proved possible because the rebellious nationalities were unable to cooperate and officialdom finally recovered its nerve. It should also be added that rarely in Austrian history had its generals performed so ably. In addition, outside help was needed, and as we shall see, was readily provided by Russia.

While the government in Vienna was at its most indecisive, the Bohemians in Prague agitated for a formal constituent assembly. An incipient Czech nationalism had been developing for some time and the appearance of barricades and mobs was as natural for them as the course taken by the Hungarians. Another factor complicating the situation in Bohemia was the presence of a numerous and sophisticated German minority which hoped for a reconstruction of Central Europe which would make them part of the new federation, whose National Assembly was then meeting in Frankfurt. The Czechs, however, wanted autonomy within Austria and looked askance at the idea of any Bohemian territory being considered responsive to a government at Frankfurt. On June 17, Windischgrätz used the army to crush Czech resistence to imperial authority, abruptly ending the heady spirit of revolution in Bohemia. The army's loyalty, coupled with efficient leadership, was to be the key to the restoration of Vienna's authority, not only in Bohemia but in other dissident areas as well.

Another conflict between subject nationalities was developing in Croatia. The Croats and Serbs had also been gradually infused with the spirit of nationalism and those within Hungary reacted sharply to the rigidity of Magyar rule. The loosened bond between Vienna and Budapest had not meant a more lenient treatment of non-Magyars. Indeed there was an insistence on control from Budapest. In this context a Croatian revolt developed, aimed against the Hungarians. It is interesting that at first Vienna openly condemned this action and relieved its leader, Jellachich (1801–1859), from his command in the imperial army. Jellachich, however, insisted that he was not only fighting for Croatian rights but for the unity of the Empire. By late summer both Bohemia and Italy were back under Viennese control and the ministry turned its full attention to Hungary. Jellachich now (October 3) was given formal command of troops to operate against Budapest. The earlier concessions made to the Magyars were obviously to be rescinded by force, but Hungarian valor and military prowess forced a longer and more drawn-out campaign than had been expected. Not only was Jellachich forced to retreat, he was hotly pursued. This turn in the war led to a fresh outbreak of violence in Vienna. Windischgrätz now marched from Bohemia and joined Jellachich. They turned back the Hungarians and bombarded Vienna, crushing the insurrection. Major military regrouping and also political adjustments were now possible and in the councils of power in Vienna an aggressive new personality had appeared. Prince Felix Schwarzenberg formed a new ministry that was characterized by ability and a sense of purpose. He was a brother-in-law of Windischgrätz and a firm believer that aid for Marshal Radetzsky (1766–1858) in Italy was crucial. The period of weakness and vacillation in the face of challenge was over. A conservative policy of force was agreed upon, a major point being that the dynasty needed a fresher and more vital representative at its head. Schwarzenberg insisted that Ferdinand abdicate and that his equally unimpressive brother, Francis, be by-passed so that the crown could go to the eighteen-year-old son of Francis, Francis Joseph (1830–1916). This occurred on December 2, 1848, and despite a few early liberal phrases, the way was cleared for a return to authoritarian control.

While these events took place north of the Alps, revolution was also creating problems for Austria in Italy. Here Austrian control of Lombardy and Venetia was part of the larger issue of Italian independence and unification. Thoughts on the latter were hazy but the idea of a "free" Italy had been widely circulating since 1831. Mazzini's vigorous propaganda was having its effect, but by the late 1840s it seemed clear that any "freedom" would have to come under the leadership of a native dynasty, the choice coming down to the Bourbon house in Naples or the house of Savoy in Turin. By 1848, as Ferdinand II proved a supporter of conservative principles, Charles Albert (1798–1849) in Turin seemed the better prospect.

Italy was one area where word of revolution in France was not required for unrest and insurrection. The year 1847 had been a troublesome one for conservatives. Pius IX (elected June 15, 1846) gave early indications of liberalism and of intention to reform the Papal States. The Sicilians anticipated the February Revolution in Paris by over a month and Ferdinand issued a constitution (February 10) which resembled the French revised Charter of 1830. This action touched off a burst of liberal enthusiasm elsewhere in the peninsula, and by March 15, constitutions also were granted by the Grand Duke of Tuscany, Charles Albert of Piedmont, and Pius IX. The big question was whether Austria would really allow these liberal changes to last. When news arrived that revolution had broken out in Vienna, Milan rose in revolt. The end of Austrian control of Italy seemed finally in view.

The fall of Metternich was the signal for rejoicing and revolution in Milan. The populace threw up barricades and hurled themselves against the Austrian garrison. In the so-called Five Days (March 18–22) the struggle went on, with the garrison being slowly worn down. Its commander, Radetzsky, had his troops (13,000) in the fortifications which ringed the city and prevented contact between the insurgents and the outside world. He lacked the numbers, however, to hold this position against prolonged attack, and on the 23rd he led his forces away from the city. At this sign of weakness, Charles Albert declared war on Austria and led his army toward Radetzsky. Meanwhile, Venice successfully revolted and a provisional government declared that it acted in the name of the Venetian Republic. Enthusiastic volunteers swarmed north to assist Charles Albert and Austria's role in Italy appeared to be at an end. Vienna's reaction to Radetzsky's plight was merely to imply that nothing could be done to help him. He was instructed to negotiate as well as he could and to offer independence for Lombardy, a course which the marshall refused. Schwarzenberg had been in Naples but now was with Austrian forces in Lombardy. While Radetzsky maneuvered in the famed Quadrilateral, Schwarzenberg convinced the government in Vienna to send 25,000 reinforcements for the campaign in Italy. On July 24, the marshall was able to defeat the Piedmontese soundly at the battle of Custozza. Charles Albert was forced to request an armistice and then to return to Piedmont. The Italian phase of the 1848 revolutionary movements was not yet over but after Custozza it had largely run its course and Austrian power had been sufficient to weather the storm. The enthusiasm of inexperienced troops led by a king responding mainly to public pressure had proved no match for the professional Austrian army led by Radetzsky, an unusually able commander. When Schwarzenberg became chief minister he remarked that the Empire had been saved by three talented commanders who had ignored imperial orders: Jellachich had attacked Hungary earlier in defiance of Vienna; Radetzsky had refused to yield in Italy as instructed; and Windischgrätz had turned cannon on the city of Vienna despite the Emperor's accession to the demands of the mob.

Italian unrest continued in 1849 but the problem was not nearly as pressing for Austria. Charles Albert again attacked Radetzsky but was thoroughly crushed at the battle of Novara on March 23. This was the end of this phase of Piedmontese efforts to expel Austria from Italy, and Charles Albert gave up his throne to his son, Victor Emmanuel II (1820–1878).

The year 1849 saw liberalism generally in defeat, with conservative forces back in power in Sicily and in Florence. In Rome the Pope was unable to prevent a swing toward radicalism and he became more conservative. A short-lived Roman Republic was founded but overthrown by a French action which will be discussed later. After restoring order in Lombardy, Austria turned on Venice to crush the independence movement there. It was a mopping-up year in Italy and the high hopes of liberals and patriots proved misplaced, even when Austria was beset by other problems.

In Vienna, Schwarzenberg viewed the beginning of 1849 with confidence. He believed his main problem was to subvert the Assembly, which was working on a constitution. This was easily accomplished when those who had forced the election of the Assembly in the first place had been coerced. The conservative reaction was succeeding everywhere from Naples to Berlin, except in Hungary, which was still independent. Under Windischgrätz, major campaigns now began against the Hungarians, but General Görgei proved remarkably resourceful and forced the Austrian troops to evacuate Hungary. It was clear that if the Hungarians could maintain their position, the Italians and Bohemians could be encouraged to further revolt. Adding to the insult for Austria, the Hungarian Diet on April 13 declared Hungary a republic. At this crucial juncture, Tsar Nicholas came to the aid of the government in Vienna and Hungary faced invasion from the North as well as the West. The outcome could not be long in doubt; by mid-August Hungary had been crushed. A blood bath of revenge occurred, but many prominent leaders, Kossuth among them, escaped to the Ottoman Empire.

In Central Europe liberalism's finest hour had passed. Peasant emancipation had occurred in Austria but seeds of bitterness, frustration, and discontent seemed to be the main results of all the rebellions. Prussia and Piedmont emerged with constitutions, but the former was by royal sufferance and the latter was hardly a source of liberal hope after the twin disasters of Custozza and Novara. Though Austria had survived, it was clear to thoughtful observers that her multinational character constituted a weakness in an age of increasing nationalism. Further, her ultimate dependence on Russia was obvious despite the brilliance of her own generals. She had survived a challenge to her being, the like of which even Metternich had never had to face, but there were ominous signs for her future.

CHAPTER 22

The Second French Republic and the Demise of the Hopes of 1848

As many cynics suspected, the man who swore to uphold the constitution of the Second French Republic entered office with explicit intentions to violate that document. Louis Napoleon had openly declared that he was going either to "the cemetery or the Tuileries." On the day he took the oath of office, he confided to a friend that he was "not at the summit yet" but only at "a halt by the way, a terrace where we stay a moment to rest as we gaze at the horizon . . . of men and things."

The constitution provided for a presidential term of four years, with the distinct provision that the incumbent could not run for re-election. To Louis this meant that he was to be allowed nearly four years in which either to alter the limitation on re-election or to overthrow the system by force. Should the latter be necessary he

287

needed the firm support of the army. Consequently, he authorized a systematic search within the army to find officers who would support his person rather than the Republic. An approach was made to Marshall Bugeaud, but this hero of the Algerian campaigns died of cholera on June 10, 1849. Behind Bugeaud, on a second echelon of prestige in the army, were Generals Cavaignac, Changarnier, and Lamoricière, but none of these would support Bonapartism. A number of others—Generals Castellane, Randon, Magnan, Vaillant—indicated they would cooperate with a nonrepublican regime but made clear that some other officer would have to hold the top command if the situation called for a *coup d'état*. The search for prominent men then turned to those actively serving in Algeria. Here several were found whose ambitions dwarfed their sense of loyalty to the Republic. The most important adherent to the President's cause was General de Saint-Arnaud (1789–1854), who was publicly acclaimed for a brief campaign against the Kabyles in May of 1851, quickly promoted, and then brought to Paris as minister of war. He was to play a crucial role in overthrowing the Republic. The ease with which the transition occurred testified to the care Louis Napoleon took to identify and reassign major officers who would support a new regime. These generals proved to be the main leaders of the French army during the Second Empire, and some, though too few, were men of great ability. In addition to loyalty to the Bonapartist cause, most of these generals shared a common experience in Algeria. They revered Bugeaud and romantically described their exploits against poorly armed natives as the equivalent of major campaigns. As a group they were relatively young and promotions had come rapidly, making them supremely self-confident. For his purposes the President had screened the military admirably, though until late in his term of office he hoped for a legal and non-authoritarian route to full power.

The new President was hardly in office when he faced a problem regarding the Roman Republic. With the reassertion of conservative and Austrian strength in the peninsula, the fate of this republic was jeopardized. In Paris there was strong sentiment for intervention. In fact, while Cavaignac had been in power he had resisted pressure to send an army into Italy in support of the Piedmontese. The situation now was markedly different and Louis Napoleon found himself caught between his personal leanings as a former Carbonaro in support of Italian independence and the opportunity to win clerical support at home by aiding the Pope. His decision favored the latter course and incurred the hostility of many republicans who deplored the idea that the arms of a French republic would be used to put down a republic in Rome. The best defense Louis put forth was that the Roman Republic was already doomed because three other forces—from Spain, Naples, and Austria—were marching against Rome. By sending a French army at once, the Papacy would be protected from Austrian pressure.

The decision to crush the Roman Republic was the beginning of a long-standing irritation. Instead of Rome being captured easily, the French army, led by General Oudinot, was repulsed on April 30 and retreated to await reinforcements. After a month Oudinot returned to the walls of the city with an army now numbering 30,000. The city's defenders, commanded by Giuseppe Mazzini (1805–1872) and Giuseppe Garibaldi (1807–1882), waged a heroic defense. Another month passed before Oudinot entered the city and restored papal control. A French garrison remained in Rome most of the time until 1870, becoming an irritating and embarrassing diplomatic issue during the 1860s. News of the initial repulse of the army was greeted with consternation among some members of the Assembly, who added their criticisms to those of the members who opposed the crushing of a republican government. This hostile indictment disappeared, however, when new elections returned a more conservative body. It had a right-wing, though not a Bonapartist, orientation and was more amenable to the Roman policy.

There can be little question that Louis Napoleon's aid to the Papacy was deliberately anti-Austrian and a bid for support from the Church in France. Domestically, he also supported passage of the Falloux Law (March, 1850) which enhanced the Church's role in education. In terms of prestige and prominence, French Catholicism made a remarkable comeback under Louis Napoleon. Louis Philippe had given few favors to the Church, but after the bloodshed of 1848, many people were more willing to support an institution which seemed to represent stability and continuity. The restoration of clerical (conservative) prominence paralleled the May 13th elections of 1849. By supporting the Pope and clerical interests in France, Louis Napoleon achieved a measure of support which he previously lacked, but this was to become a very expensive and demanding alliance.

At the same time that he was angling for Catholic support, he had to face an attack from the left. After the elections Ledru-Rollin, who had attracted 2 million votes in five districts, demanded the impeachment of the President on the Roman Question and called for a widescale socialist revolution. Riots occurred in many cities, with Paris and Lyons the scene of the most serious upheavals. In the capitol Changarnier easily put down the insurrection. The local commander in Lyons was General Magnan, who turned artillery on the mob and restored order after inflicting 200 deaths. The newly elected conservative Assembly applauded such firm action against the lower classes and the Church also supported this show of force. Public sentiment seemed to reveal a substantial swing to the right (even Lamartine and Garnier-Pagès had failed to win election to the new Assembly), and now the President's problem was to maintain his identity and disassociate himself from the Assembly. While the forms of a republic lingered on, the system clearly lacked effective support from either the President or the Assembly. The enthusiasms of 1848 had been subverted and it remained merely to see what right-wing alternative would take its place.

The elections of 1849 lessened Louis Napoleon's chances to remain in power by legal means. Since his election to the presidency, his supporters, especially the Duke de Persigny, had worked feverishly to find Bonapartist candidates to run for seats in the Assembly. Only a few of these were successful, despite the swing to the right. Consequently, the President's long-range personal goals were to be pursued outside of, and eventually in defiance of, the Assembly.

In his choice of ministers the President was in an awkward position. Some of the most prominent politicians refused to serve. He first asked republicans but these admirers of Cavaignac, and Cavaignac himself, declined. Lamartine was willing to head a ministry but was unable to find men who would serve with him. Ironically, at this point there was no Bonapartist party as such. One had to be created, but this took time. Louis turned to Thiers, who also refused to serve but suggested men who would. The result was a government headed by Odilon Barrot, who assembled a group of liberal royalists, more Orléanist than Legitimist. This ministry shared the earlier opinions of many who believed that the President was just a lucky plotter with little ability and they began to pay him scant attention. Louis at once created a scene to force them to treat his views with deference. His cooperation with these ministers not truly of his own choosing lasted less than a year. Out of the Roman expedition grew debates in the Assembly in which the President's policies were attacked and his cabinet failed to defend him. At this point, on October 31, 1849, he dismissed them and, turning his back completely on Thiers, appointed a ministry of relatively unknown men, the leader being General d'Hautpoul. This was the beginning of personal government, for these men with no prominent political past but a great future, scrupulously began to rid the bureaucracy of presidential critics. The ministries became agencies of Napoleonic propaganda; references to Empire were encouraged and military reviews were held at the slightest provocation. Aged veterans of the Empire were singled out for special honor and in a blatant act of nepotism, Jerome, the old ex-king of Westphalia, was made a marshall and Governor of the Invalides.

Both the President and the Assembly were pursuing conservative policies so far as republicanism was concerned and the chief executive carefully sought to find additional ways in which he could set himself apart from the Assembly. The conservative and royalist complexion of the Assembly needs to be especially noted because when the system was overthrown, Louis Napoleon was charged with destroying republican institutions. Many historians have echoed this view, but in reality the Assembly was dominated by men plotting some sort of Orléanist or Legitimist restoration. Continued republican government simply was not one of the alternatives during 1851.

New conflicts between the President and the Assembly occurred as though deliberately planned. Louis substantially exceeded his allowances for official expenditures and had to request more funds, which allowed caustic speeches by critics in the Assembly. A whole series of ministerial adjustments brought a succession of new faces and fresh barbs on each occasion. The background had been established for an open act against the Assembly and all that remained was a compelling issue and the tactical decision. These occurred in mid-1851.

The movement to the right had been steady and unrelieved. It was so pronounced that in espousing a step backward, the President sensed an opportunity. In May, the Assembly passed a bill limiting the suffrage. It required three consecutive years residence in one district and was aimed especially at urban workers. The object of the measure was to limit radical political strength; but Louis and his supporters realized that merely by supporting universal suffrage, he could win extensive middle- and lower-class support in any confrontation with the Assembly. While the squabbles over his expenses continued, he formally requested that the constitution be altered to allow his re-election. In the debates on this question the specter of Caesarism was roundly condemned and when the votes were counted, the President's proposal had a majority, but far less than the three fourths needed. There now seemed no legal way to remain in office and Louis moved toward a *coup d'état*. This was appropriate to his record of underhanded plotting, but characteristically, he vacillated down to the last moment and much of the coup's success must be credited to his fellow conspirators.

Specific plans for the coup were formulated during mid-September, 1851. De Saint-Arnaud as war minister saw to it that officers loyal to the Prince were in key commands; his judgment was validated when the crisis came. Nonmilitary preparations were in the hands of Louis' half-brother, the illegitimate Duke de Morny (1811–1865). Born of a liaison between Hortense and an illegitimate son of Talleyrand, Flahaut, he had proved himself an able businessman and had served in the Chamber of Deputies during the July Monarchy. Designated to be Minister of the Interior at the time of the coup, he supervised the issuance of proclamations and was a leading figure in decisions about personal arrests. The plan had been to strike while the Assembly was in recess; but Saint-Arnaud argued that while scattered throughout the countryside, the deputies were potential rallying points for opponents to Bonapartism. His logic convinced the others and December 2, anniversary alike of the founding of the First Empire in 1804 and of the battle of Austerlitz in 1805, was selected as the day. The Assembly had just been asked to restore universal suffrage. When it refused, the general public was reminded of the Assembly's distrust of the lower classes. The proclamation of the coup emphasized that Louis Napoleon was moving to restore universal suffrage and that the stubborn and intractable Assembly had made this illegal step necessary in the interests of liberty.

The coup went off smoothly. Key Assembly members—including Cavaignac, Changarnier, and Thiers—were arrested; the general public accepted the change quietly. There was even some humor in the idea that the President had put one over on the Assembly. A few deputies met in rump session but were arrested. A republican uprising crushed by the army with a moderate loss of life was the basis years later for propaganda charges against the Emperor. A number of arrests and deportations gave the change of power an authoritarian aspect which Louis Napoleon had authorized but regretted. A plebescite was hastily arranged by Morny and over 7 million voters approved the idea of the President preparing a new constitution. This document was quickly introduced in January and outlined the essential structure of the Empire. It provided for a presidential system and only a few changes were required when the formal transition to Empire was made in December of 1852.

The other powers of Europe had been watching Louis Napoleon with great interest. With so much unrest in 1848 and with Italy and Hungary uncontrolled until mid-1849, the conservative monarchs applauded the appearance of Louis Napoleon. Although somewhat apprehensive about his origins, to his credit was the idea that he could be relied on to maintain order; and this, above all, they wanted in France. They were especially reassured by his control of the riots in Paris and Lyons in 1849. The Tsar showed the most concern about Louis as a Bonaparte. Nicholas took the treaties of 1815 seriously and simply could not accept the idea of a Bonaparte dynasty being restored in France. This issue became an acute topic for diplomatic correspondence in the year between the coup and the proclamation of empire. This was a year of Napoleonic propaganda in France and open references to an empire. Louis' response to the point that treaties explicitly banned the Bonaparte dynasty in France was to observe that he held power not by dynastic succession, but from the ballots of a free people. To Nicholas this was just as bad and he tried to arouse other monarchs to the danger which he believed was present. Widespread speculation among many statesmen centered on what numeral Louis would use. Nicholas saw this sort of quibbling as largely beside the point but was unable to convince any other power to join him in opposing the proclamation of the Empire. He would willingly march, he said, in Europe's interest, but he did not think he should march alone. The founding of the Empire was unprotested and Europe gained a new emperor, Napoleon III. The Second Republic as even a name was gone. In France no essential remnants were left of 1848, other than the Emperor who remained a "48er" at heart.

The year 1848 passed into history as a tragic time of heroic revolt. The year of liberal and national sacrifices ended as a lesson in premature action and uncoordinated efforts. From the outset there were probably serious limits to how much cooperation was possible on the part of the rebellious groups. Political questions relating to liberalism were basic in Paris, Berlin, and Vienna; but in Paris, overriding social issues were also crucial. National independence or autonomy was at the heart of the Hungarian, Bohemian, and Italian problems. When Louis Philippe fell and mobs, quickly gathering in other European cities, shook the confidence of the rulers, then the various local discontents surfaced and created more disorder, with each movement serving as a catalyst to others. Thus the various revolts were connected while often being over quite different issues. In Bohemia and Hungary there were no real proletariats and no sense of worker solidarity. This was barely present in Vienna, which was mainly a bureaucratic city. The Hungarian revolt was the work of its nobility who were leading a national movement. Italy also followed this pattern; it was clear at the end that both Italy and Hungary were being controlled only by force.

In Hungary there was little sense of toleration for non-Hungarians and socialistic statements and ideology were almost meaningless. In Paris, on the other hand, socialistic objectives had to be taken very seriously. The image of a republican, property-owning government authorizing the army to shoot down propertyless workers lasted in France for generations. Nationalism was obviously a powerful force which might cause more trouble in Italy and Hungary. While it also lingered as a problem-laden memory regarding Germany, the idea of a government for "Germany" had been planted at Frankfurt. In general, the armies and bureacracies remained loyal to the nominal rulers who were able to use them effectively when they recovered their own nerve. Despite the overall failure of the revolts, a great deal of practical change did occur. Serfdom ended in all of the Austrian Empire, for example, and a wave of liberal reform had passed through the Rhineland. Prussia emerged with a constitution which allowed for a representative body to meet and deliberate policy. The old order had survived the storm but it had been badly shaken and its continuance was highly speculative considering the forces for change then at work in Europe. The fact that Austria had, in the end, needed Russian help, dramatized how very insecure her position was. Stability and international peace were sorely needed if reactionary conservatism was to remain for long. With the emergence of Louis Napoleon, however, peace was to give way regularly to war.

VIII

Peaceful Domestic Progress

CHAPTER 23

Three Decades of Victorian Progress

In 1837 Britain received a new monarch, eighteen-year-old Victoria, niece of William IV. She was to reign until 1901 and give her name to an age. A sensible person, she was often touchy on issues involving royal prerogatives and would not suffer being taken for granted. In 1840 she took as her Prince Consort, Albert (1819–1861) of Saxe-Coburg-Gotha, which completed a circle of advisers who were essentially German (including the Coburg King Leopold of Belgium and Baron Christian Friedrich von Stockmar). Albert proved an able adviser as well as an endearing husband. Following his death in 1861 Victoria, overwhelmed with sorrow, for years took little interest in public life, only gradually recovering from her bereavement.

Her reign was a highpoint of progress, intellectual vitality, and unparalleled prosperity. Industrial exhibitions and fairs became common, with the first being held in 1851 in Hyde Park, thanks to Albert's ingenuity. Britain was the world's economic leader and her statesmen were never more prominent. In her long life Victoria worked with Peel and Palmerston, Disraeli (1804–1881), and Gladstone (1809–1898); and to dramatize just how issues changed in her lifetime, she was two years old when Napoleon died and before her death she could look back over the entirety of Bismarck's public career.

Lord Palmerston. (Courtesy of Historical Pictures Service, Chicago.)

Lord Palmerston provided the clearest indirect challenge to her prerogatives early in her reign. Like Gladstone decades later, he tended to regard her views as those of an uninformed woman. She willingly accepted her position as a constitutional sovereign but insisted on being informed and consulted. She gave orders that important instructions to officials abroad were to be cleared through the palace, but Palmerston often disregarded her and sent out dispatches on his own authority. He was a proud statesman with experience in diplomacy stemming from the Napoleonic period and he presumed the Queen incapable of bringing much wisdom to the conduct of foreign policy. Further, he regarded the German Albert as having too much influence in strictly British affairs. The hostility which developed between Palmerston and Victoria kept him out of the prime ministry for years, an unfortunate circumstance, for he represented an active and strident foreign policy which the nation was prepared to support. In the Don Pacifico case (1850) he gave probably his greatest speech in Parliament. Don Pacifico was a Jew born in Gibraltar, hence a British subject. In an involved dispute over his claims against the Greek government, Palmerston called in the fleet and defended Don Pacifico on the basis largely of his British citizenship rather than on the basis of more relevant facts. Palmerston's oration on June 29th was a bold call of nationalism, particularly appropriate because England was supporting liberal revolution and nationalism during the chaotic years of mid-century. Palmerston preceded Disraeli in the energetic pursuit of enlarging Britain's place in the world. Her naval power over the globe went unchallenged in this era of imperial success and profit. Palmerston's touchy relations with the Queen obscured the extent of his popular following in the early 1850s. By this time the Liberal and Conservative parties had become fairly stabilized as the mediums for political rivalry; but after Peel and Wellington passed away, no great leader of comparable stature emerged. John Russell, Aberdeen, Derby, and Palmerston all played roles of prominence, but the Crown's opposition to Palmerston created a situation where policies were unpredictable. Palmerston had the strongest following, but it took the outbreak of the Crimean War to make this clear. Gladstone and Disraeli were prominent "comers" whose classic rivalry occurred after Palmerston's death in 1865.

Domestically, the 1840s were difficult; crops were poor and there was some famine. In the 1850s, however, production soared and the nation embraced the doctrine of free trade, which brought even greater prosperity as the century progressed. The reform movement continued apace. Political leaders generally adopted a stance of yielding before pressures could build up as they had preceding the Reform Bill of 1832. Among the laboring classes a sense of solidarity was rapidly spreading and revealed in the Chartist movement, an outgrowth of the Working Men's Association founded in 1836. This association was a labor movement which expected relief through further parliamentary reform. There was little support for socialism, but there was a firm conviction that workers must have spokesmen in Parliament if their lot was to improve. They approved of the earlier reforms, but too often these had been inadequately implemented. Chartism was a sporadic movement and fed on local discontents and shortages. In the *Northern Star* Fergus O'Connor tried to give some national cohesiveness to the movement but the over-all impact was negligible. It was a source of concern to authorities and served as a distinct phase in working-class history. Its leaders were more petitioners than revolutionaries; consequently, the movement took the form of devising a monster petition. This was presented to Parliament three times—in 1838, 1842, and 1848—but each time Parliament refused to act. Eventually, the specific program requested was largely accepted; but in 1848 the ruling classes were not prepared for universal manhood suffrage, annual elections for Commons, the secret ballot, equal electoral districts, payment for members of Parliament, and the abolition of property qualifications for a seat in Parliament. Only a few uncoordinated riots occurred during the attempts to win support for these demands. The Chartist petition carried no real threat, despite the fact that probably half the males in the country had signed. In 1848 Chartist leaders claimed 5 million signatures, but they had half that number. The discovery of many scurrilous signatures helped to discredit the whole movement. A crucial problem of Chartism was that whereas the leadership was visionary, the movement attracted practical extremists who discredited them. In 1848 Wellington anticipated difficulties by having 170,000 special constables sworn in (one was Louis Napoleon) and discreetly kept troops out of sight but prepared if the demonstration in London got out of hand. Chartist requests never had a chance in Parliament, where they received little sympathy. The workers accepted the rejection docilely and turned their attentions to the developing labor unions, which, being craft oriented, promised more direct attack on local problems. Instead of expecting help from the government, they now looked to their union leaders to bring them relief from the managers. Labor unions were informally allowed and even encouraged. Regarded as alternatives to socialism, a means of preventing outright attacks on property and order (as seen in 1848 in France), they were not expressly legalized until 1871. The 1850s saw a vast growth in the union movement and the support of many influential people. Most impressive was the disavowal by union leaders of violent and disruptive tactics. Rather, an emphasis was placed on arbitration, conciliation, and compromise. In the upper classes, unions acquired a reputation for reasonableness, which stood in comforting contrast to the strident violence being preached by Karl Marx and agitators on the Continent.

Victoria ascended the throne in the midst of a period of reforming zeal and keen competition between parties. The Liberals (Whigs) were vigorously implementing the promises implicit in the Great Reform Bill, but they were encountering serious fiscal problems. The impressive spurt of domestic legislation under liberal leadership ended on May 7, 1839, with the fall of the second ministry of Lord Melbourne. Besides the sheer costs of reform, his strength was further weakened by a simmering rebellion in Canada and a crisis in Jamaica. Living conditions of former slaves in that island colony had worsened since emancipation, partly because the plantation owners, unable to compete in markets where slave economies were also represented, put more restrictive measures on the Negroes. The constitution in Jamaica was suspended in an effort to control the situation; although this helped to restore better relations, the extremity of setting aside the constitution brought down a torrent of criticism on the prime minister. In addition, the perennial Irish problem lost him important support. Melbourne was naturally opposed by Conservatives when he extended to Ireland the Poor Law provisions for workhouses (in place of the dole), but the Irish members in Commons also opposed him because they felt that there simply were too many poor to suppose that their problem could be met through the labor (such as crushing piles of stone) provided in the workhouses. When his efforts to liberalize voting rights in Irish cities and to regulate tithes were equally unsuccessful in attracting support, he resigned. A dispute between Sir Robert Peel and Victoria over her ladies-in-waiting allowed Melbourne to return for a third ministry, which lasted two years. Essentially, however, his period of effective leadership had ended.

This era of reform was completed by Peel in his second ministry, which, with one brief interruption, lasted from September of 1841 until June 29, 1846. In the crucial fifteen years after 1831, the legislation was passed which set the stage for the industrial and commercial course followed by Britain for much of the remainder of the century. Rapid industrialization was speeded by the railroad, which contributed to the wide distribution of goods in ever-expanding consumer markets. Though workers continued to suffer, their lot

Sir Robert Peel. (Courtesy of Historical Pictures Service, Chicago.)

improved as part of the over-all prosperity which came in the 1850s.

Sir Robert Peel (1788–1850) stands as a prime example of a dedicated, patriotic, and pragmatic politician. A conservative by instinct and party, he was nondoctrinaire and provided vigorous leadership for distinctly nonconservative measures when he realized that their adoption was essential to the national welfare. Rather than coming into office with a coherent and preconceived program, he methodically dealt with problems as they arose. Because he was not oriented to a strong ideological base, he was able to formulate programs which were antithetical so far as theory was concerned. Thus through the Factory Act (1844) government supervision sharply regulated industrial activity while a whole series of tariff reductions made him appear almost an apostle of *laissez faire*.

Laissez faire had become virtually dogma to a number of Whigs and radicals by 1840. The Manchester economists, especially Richard Cobden and John Bright, so consistently wrote and lectured for the cause of free trade that it would be relatively easy to forget that the great spokesman for the doctrine was Adam Smith and that even he regarded its implementation as highly utopian. It was a visionary goal rather than a dogmatic requirement for this author of the *Wealth of Nations* who, by his indictment of mercantilism, was in close agreement with many other intellectuals of his day, including David Hume, François Quesnay and the Marquis d'Argenson, who originated the term *laissez faire*. Smith's ideas were widely accepted and a number of prominent English writers promoted the belief that economic prosperity was more likely to come from a lessening of government controls. Historically the most important adherent to free trade was David Ricardo. In his writing and speaking he emphasized the virtues of reducing the restrictions on trade. More than Cobden and Bright, it was Ricardo who firmly planted these ideas in the mind of Peel, though the Manchester economists must be given due credit for helping to create a climate of opinion where the concept of free trade would be welcomed.

The general impulse toward free trade was explicitly formulated in a demand to repeal the Corn Law. This was blamed for increasing the misery which the working classes were experiencing partly as a result of poor harvests. The Corn Law had been on the books for years as part of a whole package of restrictions hampering the free flow of goods. This particular law dated from 1815, with modifications in 1828. The purpose was to protect the agrarian landed interests by keeping foreign grain out until prices were substantially improved. This assured the consumption of the home yields; but, in times of hardship, it also assured very high prices. Meanwhile, restrictive tariffs on raw materials led to inflated costs, which meant diminished employment at a time when the demand for work was increasing rapidly as people flowed in from the countryside. The situation had many threatening possibilities; one, of course, was a proletarian uprising. It was to the credit of Cobden and Bright that the workers abandoned extremist elements in the Chartist movement and seized on free trade and especially repeal of the Corn Law as the manner in which their plight could be eased. In this context the Anti-Corn Law League (1839) developed from initiatives taken in Manchester in 1838 and was supported by manufacturers and workers alike. Cheap food was seen as essential by both major segments of the industrial community. The struggle was not so much liberal against conservative as it was the new industrial population against the landed squirearchy. In Manchester funds were raised for brochures and speakers, so that a major propaganda campaign was well advanced by the time Peel came into office in 1841.

The new prime minister was a long-standing protectionist and was not yet convinced of the necessity for repeal of the Corn Law, although he was thoroughly conversant with the reasoning of the League members. The landed Conservatives were forthrightly opposed to the efforts emanating from Manchester. A particularly telling argument against the Corn Law was that if food costs were low, then people would have more to spend for the products of industry, which in turn would provide greater employment. Peel's first problem concerned the deficits he inherited, and he met these by a series of enlightened economic measures. In 1828 the tariff on corn imports had been fixed to a sliding scale which Peel now liberalized to encourage foreign producers. He also lowered a number of duties on raw materials and foods and at the same time put new emphasis on the income tax as a source of revenue. He reduced the tariff on over half of 1,200 different taxable items and all duties were abolished in the wool trade. For a protectionist Peel had come a long way toward free trade, and he was much impressed when the results of all this legislation appeared to indicate that free trade did indeed lead to economic prosperity. Meanwhile, he had aroused antagonism in his own party, where die-hard Conservatives at last found a champion in Benjamin Disraeli, who led an attack against Peel. The drum-fire of publicity against the Corn Law continued as Peel's measures won him only modest support from Liberals, who did not feel he was doing enough. In 1845 he did away with all export duties and further lowered import tariffs, but the Corn Law remained as the main focus of agitation. In both parties humanitarian arguments against the Corn Law were telling and their repeal could not be delayed much longer.

By October, 1845, Peel had accepted the idea that the Corn Law had to be repealed. His prior budgets were testimonials to what free trade could accomplish, but he had hesitated to go all the way with the principle because he believed in the idea of self-sufficiency in time of war and a modest tariff would assure that corn production would not die out. Now, however, an overwhelming practical problem arose which compelled urgent attention. As so often happened for British statesmen, the trouble was associated with Ireland.

The 1845 potato crop failed as the result of a blight which was particularly intense in Ireland. The Irish population depended almost exclusively on the potato for food, and famine on a wide scale was imminent. Intense pressure was on the government; the Liberal (Whig) leader, Lord John Russell, published a key policy statement on November 22. Known as the "Edinburgh Letter," it abandoned protectionism and came out emphatically for free trade. Peel's area of choice now was narrowed to either declaring for complete free trade and undertaking repeal of the Corn Law or stepping aside and letting Russell do it. After several meetings he was unable to convince the rest of his ministers, and so he resigned on December 5. Russell proved unable to form a government and within three weeks, Peel returned to office and pledged further tariff reductions and the repeal of the Corn Law. At this point he lost all support from the Conservative landed gentry, who saw him as betraying the party. Disraeli became the leader of this faction and turned his sarcasm against Peel. The prime minister managed to get the Corn Law repealed (June 25, 1846), but the price had been the wreckage of his party. Peel resigned and the Conservative party was essentially out of power for two decades. The Liberals came to office under Lord John Russell and took credit for most of the reforming legislation of the 1830s. They also pointed to their championship of free trade and repeal of the Corn Law; but the record is clear that it was Peel who put Great Britain on the road to free trade, by his work in the 1820s as well as in his epochal Second Ministry. Free trade had been the work of Tories. The repeal of the Corn Law was a cardinal objective of the growing industrial community. The repeal showed that the Reform Bill had indeed made it possible for new voices to be heard; business leaders, with an assist from the Irish, now saw their views embodied into law.

Meanwhile the Irish situation worsened dramatically. Famine was widespread as the potato crop in 1846 was smaller than the year before. Other crops were also poor, but they were not as crucial to the diet. Repeal of the Corn Law meant little in these circumstances and both public and private charity, though extensive, were inadequate for the problem. The most cruel period occurred during the winter of 1846–1847; recovery came very slowly. There were still harsh conditions in 1849. Thousands died and more thousands emigrated to England and to the United States. In the five years after 1845 Ireland's population dropped by slightly over 20 per cent. There was some agrarian unrest and an unsuccessful peasant uprising in Tipperary (July, 1848); but, essentially, recovery came by natural causes as the government did little to correct basic land problems.

Free trade remained a point in the Liberal arsenal of political propaganda, and compared with earlier days and with other nations, Britain's trade was indeed "free." Actually, however, it was a system of low and moderate tariffs which all but a handful of economists approved. One of the most influential British documents embodying free-trade ideas was the Cobden-Chevlier Treaty signed with France on January 23, 1860. Hailed as a high-water mark in economic history, it was to have politically unfortunate ramifications for Napoleon III. Both of the negotiators, Richard Cobden for Britain and Michel Chevalier (1806–1879) for France, were devout believers in the principle of free trade and personally convinced their respective governments to accept the treaty. The intent of the negotiations was to open the French markets to the products of British industry and to allow French silk and wines to enter Britain more cheaply. The treaty, with later modifications, accomplished these objectives. British goods paid a reduced duty; French silks were imported duty-free; and wines from France paid only a moderate duty. British exports to France at once increased and remained high for five years, and the sale of French wines and silks in Britain increased steadily. The treaty was an unqualified economic success, although the British were disappointed that the Civil War in the United States restricted their supply of cotton and prevented them from properly exploiting an opportunity to sell finished cotton goods in France.

In the two decades after 1845, the dominating figure in British politics was clearly Lord Palmerston. Foreign policy problems occurred in such rapid succession that political attention centered especially on diplomacy. The Eastern Question remained alive after remarks during a visit to London by Tsar Nicholas in 1844. In Western Europe attention was drawn to the crisis over the Spanish Marriages. In the turbulent year of 1848, Britain sympathized with Continental liberal and nationalistic movements and then provided a haven for defeated agitators as prominent and diverse as Marx and Guizot, Kossuth and Metternich. Palmerston supported Louis Napoleon and endorsed his overthrow of the Second Republic. In a new phase of the Eastern Question leading to the Crimean War, Britain followed a confusing and ill-defined course which ultimately placed her as an incompetent comrade-in-arms with Bonapartist France and the non-Christian Ottoman Empire. At this struggle's nadir Palmerston was finally called by Victoria to become prime minister, a distinction long overdue. After the Crimean War Napoleon III led his army into Italy. Britain, suspicious of his motives but applauding Austrian defeat, merely looked on, with her energies diverted partially by a revolt in India. Before Palmerston's death there was the embarrassing early cooperation with France in the Mexican payments issue and the two nations both took a pro-Southern stance during the United States Civil War. Thus, although nominally the Liberals dominated policy in this period, there was virtually no significant reform legislation after the repeal of the Corn Law. At the same time there was so much economic expansion and general prosperity that little pressure existed for further reform. Efforts to generate enthusiasm for extending the franchise in the late 1850s and early 1860s attracted only modest support.

Between 1865 and 1867 a mild depression stimulated renewed interest in reform. Agitation of the Chartist variety was virtually nil, but the Reform League began to incite workers to clamor for electoral reform. Russell now was the prime minister and believed that the time was ripe for another major reform bill. His 1866 bill split liberal ranks. The radical wing, led by John Bright, favored extending the franchise to the extent of universal manhood suffrage; the conservative wing, led by Robert Lowe, did not want to see the vote given to the laboring classes. This latter group combined with Conservatives to assure the bill's defeat in the House of Lords. The measure had represented only moderate extension of the vote and the country at large seemed unexcited about the issue while it was being considered.

When Russell fell on the question, a victim of the right wing of his party, it seemed that the issue of reform had been considered and settled. However, a storm of worker protest broke loose. At mass meetings incendiary speakers were contemptuously critical of the decision of Parliament. Trade unions actively focused the protest. Russell's successor was the Conservative Lord Derby (1799–1869), who was heading his third ministry as a minority leader. Disraeli served as Derby's leader in the Commons and these Conservative leaders decided that reform was an issue which had to be brought up again and that, by supporting it themselves, they would gain future political allies from the ranks of the newly enfranchised. Their problem resembled that which Russell had just faced, loss of their right wing. A staunch group of Conservatives warned the leadership that they completely disagreed with the prospect of opening the door to democracy and mob rule. Disraeli found himself in Peel's position in

1845, when he had had to face Disraeli as the leader of right-wing, die-hard dissidents. He was now the dominant personality in the party, and in the face of this threat, he temporized, presenting first to the cabinet and then to Commons a series of lukewarm propositions for reform. As the debates raged in Parliament, amendment after amendment was added until finally a Reform Bill emerged which was far more radical than such politicians as Bright and his followers had envisioned. So many important features were added that it is more appropriate to regard the bill as the work of Parliament rather than of the Cabinet. The Bill passed; but Disraeli lost the right wing of his party while gaining no liberal support, for his whole performance had smacked of opportunism. Disraeli was to lose the 1868 elections, which opened up a new age in British history.

The Second Reform Bill ended an era by adding to the electorate the ordinary householder and worker. Britain was far from democracy but she had just doubled the electorate and this particular doubling meant that half of the new voters were poorer than virtually all of those voting before 1867. The lower classes now held the balance of power. A consequence of this was that Britain's political parties began to develop grass roots support for the first time and became responsive more to the electorate than to cliques in Parliament. In forty years the British aristocracy had accepted as colleagues in the political process the new industrialists; in turn, both of these admitted the workers to a voice in affairs. All this had been done without revolution and now the potential existed for a new type of political life. Responsible legislation was the British answer to forestall violence and to alleviate developing social problems. British leadership and institutions had thus proved flexible enough to adjust peacefully to the unique requirements of economic and industrial progress at a time when many other nations were solving their problems by military force.

CHAPTER 24

Two Decades of Napoleonic Progress

As in Great Britain at mid-century, France during the Second Empire underwent profound economic and social change. The government of Napoleon III played a paternalistic role, claiming for itself a large share of the credit for the striking advances that "Progress" was delivering.

The structure of the imperial system was set forth in the Constitution of 1852, which provided for an appointive upper house (Senate) and a popular Legislative Body whose 260 members served terms of six years. Louis Napoleon appointed the president and vice president of this lower body. He also was able to exert enormous influence in the local elections, where it was a considerable advantage to be the "official" candidate of the government. Most candidates were successful businessmen and essentially apolitical. They were an élite

Napoleon III. (Courtesy of Historical Pictures Service, Chicago.)

of service, *parvenu* like the Emperor. Napoleon extended the hand of friendship to many local men of prominence who happened not to be Bonapartists. By allowing local elites to run as government candidates, he gained the support of a good many former Orléanists. In return for this electoral endorsement, he required an oath of obedience to himself and the Constitution. Despite his own example as an oath-violator, he believed that most men did take oaths seriously. A few refused but large numbers cooperated when to be part of the government obviously would bring them increased local prestige and prominence in Paris. In this system initiatives came from Napoleon who was an essentially authoritarian ruler until November of 1860. After the turmoil of 1848, this firm regime provided a climate of stability which encouraged economic growth. The harsh depression years of the 1840s were almost forgotten as prosperity developed on such a broad scale that for a time it was difficult for opponents of the regime to attract much of a following.

The formal agencies of government were devised simply to carry out imperial programs and politics in the normal sense nearly disappeared. The Legislative Body was regarded as an administrative rather than a legislative organ; it was expected to pass bills but not to initiate policy. Montalembert was the only prestigious member who survived from earlier regimes. In the early days of the Empire many natural critics had been exiled and the press was rigorously controlled. In the absence of debates and public political criticism, interest in politics declined. Elections were "managed" and regarded as merely devices to select someone for a role of prestige rather than actually to name a representative of the people.

Exiles gathered in groups outside France but were powerless to do more than give solace to one another. Louis Napoleon confiscated Orléanist estates on January 22, 1852, but no other government would do anything about it except to listen with sympathy to Orléanist complaints. The republican exiles were much poorer than the royalists and had no friends in power in other nations. They had problems of financing themselves and were often harassed by police. Many republicans accepted pardon merely to be able to live in peace at home and became apolitical. Republicanism had very few supporters at the high point of Napoleon's reign at the end of the Crimean War. In the provinces the government was represented by the prefects who "managed" elections and supervised the issuance of patronage and government contracts. There was also the political police, which mainly reported local complaints and relayed local opinion to Paris, where it was taken into account in policy making. This feature was no worse than that employed under earlier regimes and was far from the sort of totalitarian state which some later scholars have suggested.

There was a continuous opposition to Napoleon III but before 1857 it had little opportunity to express itself. By this time Bonapartists were entrenched in office and an intricate network of commercial relationships effectively tied businessmen to the regime. The Empire was successful in providing stability and order, cherished conditions after 1848, but in its early years its citizens lacked liberty. Napoleon had declared that once he restored order in France, he would "crown the edifice with liberty." This crowning of the edifice took place in stages in the decade after 1859. This period of the so-called Liberal Empire saw the modification of the governmental structure in such a fashion that at the end of the Empire, a parliamentary system much like that of the British had been devised. There is no debate over what changes occurred but, an acute disagreement exists over why Napoleon made the modifications which liberalized the regime. His promise of the liberty which he granted was not enough to negate the observations that he seemed to make concessions at a time when criticisms of his regime were especially acute. Had he begun to liberalize before many of his foreign policies failed, he would have appeared more sincere. As it was, it looked as though he made concessions grudgingly and his critics could then claim that they had *forced* him to liberalize.

The first legal opposition of any consequence appeared in the elections of 1857, when 750,000 votes were cast for opponents of the regime. These votes were cast mostly in Paris, Marsailles, Bordeaux, and Lyons and resulted in five republicans being seated in the Legislative Body. These became a nucleus for a significant republican opposition as the 1860s wore on, but for a time they were barely recognized and played an insignificant role in proceedings.

By 1860 a Catholic opposition had also developed. This was a particularly interesting development in light of the favors showered on the clergy by the Emperor. After the example of the pro-clerical Charles X, Louis Philippe had kept the Church at arm's length; consequently, it watched him go into exile with no regrets. Alarmed at the violence of 1848, the Church had supported Louis Napoleon against Cavaignac because republican stability carried an inference of public *nonclerical* education. The local clergy wielded great influence among the peasantry and when the overwhelming returns came in from the provinces, Louis recognized the debt he owed to the Church. He at once began repayment by aiding the Pope in 1849 and by the Falloux Law of 1850. In turn, the Church supported the coup and mutual favors continued until 1859. The Emperor's campaign in Italy left the Papacy dangerously exposed to rampant nationalism. Many Catholics turned against him for this, although he continued to favor the Church within France. The loss of clerical support because of Italy came at about the time of the Cobden-Chevalier treaty, making that document appear as a shrewd effort to attract the loyalty of the liberal segment of the population to balance the support he had lost. Thus he failed to receive adequate popular recognition for his forward-looking ideas of free trade.

The Emperor's benevolence resulted in substantially increased clerical salaries and many new clerical offices, including 1,600 new parishes with virtually no government interference in the selection of personnel. Besides being richer the Church was also freer and received special exemptions from government restrictions on public assembly and on publications. Most journalists were harassed by the government, but the Catholic press flourished, its most prominent publication being *L'Univers* edited by Louis Veuillot. Many local journals were allowed (twenty-five by 1862) and most supported conservative issues while liberal Catholics like Montalembert grew bitter over their own lack of support. The Second Empire was an era of conservative Catholicism in France. The Church was dominated by ultramontaine sentiments and strongly supported authoritarianism. In contrast, its Gallican liberal wing, which had supported genuine parliamentary government, was now a victim of the reaction against the republicanism of 1848. Napoleon III's support of the Church is especially interesting when one recalls that Napoleon I had created the University explicitly to control and restrict clerical influence in education. The Falloux Law was an attack on the University. It guaranteed "freedom in teaching," a specious phrase which meant that clerical instructors who were "free" of the ideas of Voltaire and his sort could now teach the truth. Early in the presidency a clerical *Union électorale* was formed which brought together an otherwise disparate group who all believed in the need for a strong church. These men supported the Empire until 1860, when they became a source of criticism on non-Church issues, joining in temporary alliances with republicans, Orléanists, protectionists, and nationalists.

In 1859 the Emperor granted an amnesty allowing political exiles to return to France. The republicans interpreted this as a sign of weakness and increased their propaganda. By allowing agitators to return, Napoleon had increased the number of strident critics, and when the government closed down their papers, lawyers like Léon Gambetta (1838–1882) used the courtroom to attack the Empire and its institutions.

Additional critics appeared in the wake of the Italian war, which left ardent French nationalists irritated that the nation had not gained more. In enlarging Piedmont while irritating her by making peace prematurely, Napoleon had made a hostile second-rate power out of a fourth-rate power on an exposed French frontier. In addition, the Cobden-Chevalier Treaty had aroused a broad segment of protectionist French businessmen.

At this point Napoleon decided to liberalize the regime. The decrees accomplishing this (November 24, 1860) had every appearance of being granted to placate critics. He had waited too long to receive much credit for altruistic good will, but it should be noted that he could have tightened up the regime instead of making it freer. Among his advisors, Morny especially argued in favor of liberal reform. His reasoning, however, was hardly liberal. His view was that if the developing oppositions were allowed an open and public official forum, the result would be a continual babble of voices in open disagreement. The Emperor then would be the man above parties, the objective mediator who could take credit for policy successes while "the parties" would be blamed for failures. It is not clear to what extent Napoleon was swayed by logic of this sort, but his past suggested that his mind was certainly not closed to such Machiavellian considerations.

The decrees of 1860 began the dismantling of the authoritarian regime. The Legislative Body now could present an annual address to the Emperor. Its sessions were opened to the public and more of its proceedings were to be published. Limited as this beginning was, it was the start of a parliamentary regime and was as practical as the system in France during the July Monarchy. The Press Laws were soon relaxed and many republicans worried that the Emperor was slowly putting into effect their program. The liberalization created widespread speculation over whether the Emperor would be able to win liberal support by his action and also over the wisdom of his concessions. In 1863 the elections proved interesting. An opposition vote of 2 million elected thirty-five candidates to the Legislative Body, seventeen of them republicans. Official candidates attracted over 5.3 million votes, a reflection that the imperial system still had its adherents. Nonetheless, the size of the opposition vote was impressive. The new freedoms were being used to attack the regime and as a succession of diplomatic ventures failed, the Empire became ever more susceptible to criticism.

Among the opposition after 1863 was Thiers, returned from exile and now a determined foe of Napoleon. On January 11, 1864, he delivered a well-publicized address in which he called for further reforms. He insisted on freedom of the press, except for slander, free elections, and personal freedom from violence and arbitrary arrest. He also wanted majority public opinion to direct the government; this all meant ministerial responsibility and an end to the government sponsorship of particular candidates. He suggested further that if these changes were not soon made, the day would come when the country would demand them. Thiers seemed to be offering cooperation if the Emperor would accept his suggestions. Napoleon refused and Thiers became progressively more of an obstructionist. Because the Empire did fall, it has been interesting to speculate on whether Napoleon in fact missed an opportunity to establish a truly effective regime with one of France's ablest statesmen as an ally instead of a critic. At any rate, Thiers' offer was seen by the Emperor as blackmail; the old Orléanist had overrated his nuisance value. By 1870 Napoleon did accept most of Thiers recommendations. What he missed was a chance to speed up liberalization. Had he done this in 1864 after the elections of 1863, it would have been publicized as an admission of weakness; but we may observe with the easy wisdom of hindsight that the parliamentary regime would have had several years of functioning before facing its supreme test in 1870. On the other hand, although the still moderately Orléanist Thiers might cooperate, the question remained of what dedicated republicans like Gambetta would do.

The 1860s were generally a period of foreign policy embarrassments for the Second Empire; the Mexican fiasco was the most damaging before 1866. Mexico, however, was far away; but Prussia's defeat of Austria at Sadowa (July 3, 1866) was a comparable diplomatic defeat for Napoleon, and he liberalized further as his critics poured forth a torrent of abuse. The Senate was now allowed a truly legislative function, which gave France two working houses. Further, ministers could be interrogated from the floor of the Legislative Body and press restrictions were relaxed. Rather than gratitude, more criticisms were heard as Thiers declared that the real test of the Emperor's good intentions would be seen by the new men to be appointed as ministers. When most of the old faces reappeared with no republican in the cabinet, Thiers called it all a hoax and continued his opposition. The Emperor was disturbed but was not about to be stampeded into hasty action. He still had a considerable following and did enjoy some successes in the 1860s although they were modest in retrospect and in contrast to his failures. He was popular in Algeria, where the work of colonization proceeded rapidly. In Senegal the foundations were being laid for what became French West Africa. Another success was the construction and opening of the Suez Canal in 1869. A cooperative venture with Britain resulted in French control of most of Indo-China. From August of 1860, to June of 1861, French troops, in diplomatic cooperation with Britain, helped end the Syrian massacres of Christians. Despite the trade treaty, the aid to Britain in the Far East and support of her cause in Syria, Napoleon never enjoyed much confidence among statesmen in London, aside from Palmerston. Mexico and Sadowa overshadowed all his successes in the 1860s and were crucial for the Emperor's career. To the number of problems facing Napoleon late in his reign must be added his failing health. By 1870 he was in almost continuous pain from kidney stones.

The low point of the Empire came in 1869. The criticism now amounted to slander, as exemplified in the writing of Henri Rochefort in *La Lanterne* and Victor Hugo in *Le Rappel*. Opposition objectives had broadened to include separation of church and state, free secular education, and elimination of a standing army. Gambetta was eloquent on these points, while campaigning for the election of more republicans. Interestingly enough, most of the critics were not against the dynasty. In the voting for candidates for the Legislative Body, the opposition attracted 3.5 million votes or about 45 per cent. The official candidates managed to win a majority of less than a million votes, a shameful rebuke. The Emperor, sick and aging, wondered what to do. Many of his friends had died, including Morny and Niel, and it seemed clear that somehow power had to be turned over to younger men. He saw in Ollivier a republican to whom power could perhaps be entrusted. He had no confidence whatever in Thiers.

On New Years Day of 1870, Napoleon decreed ministerial responsibility. A ministry could now be dismissed by adverse votes in the Legislative Body. Again, the reform looked forced, but it was so significant that the Emperor finally received a portion of the praise he deserved. He had brought the French to a system of real parliamentary government where the prestige of a dynasty enhanced a popular democracy. It was to be the nation's most practical approach to such a government, and for Napoleon III to have allowed and fashioned it was a major achievement. He had "crowned the edifice with liberty" as he promised, and in May, a plebescite was held asking approval or disapproval of the constitutional changes made since 1860. The vote of 1869 was in everyone's mind and republicans worked to create a larger opposition. The Emperor was apprehensive, but to his pleasure and the amazement of many, over 3 million more people supported the regime than had the previous year. The election was one of the Emperor's greatest public triumphs, but it was a short-lived one because the Empire was soon swept aside in the defeat of the Franco-Prussian War.

The Second Empire was a period of enormous economic and social progress in France. Though there were temporary setbacks, essentially the nation enjoyed a prosperity for which the regime could claim much of the credit. Before proclaiming the Empire, Louis Napoleon had publicly declared that an empire at this stage in French history would mean a determined program of social improvements. He also declared that because it was old-fashioned for states to wage war over mere boundary problems, any empire of his would mean peace. As it worked out, he was grossly in error about prognosticating peace, but he was accurate in his expectation of extensive social improvement. Probably any government in power for very long after 1848 would have presided over an economy which was expanding and bringing general prosperity. Many aspects of the remarkable growth occurring under the Empire were continuations of programs begun during the July Monarchy, as, for example, in the case of railway construction. This naturally raises the question of just how important Napoleon's role was in the developing prosperity. Although the Emperor never went so far as to insist that government had an obligation to assure employment, he believed that its role encompassed much more than providing law and order; it had for example, a special responsibility to encourage improved living standards. His officials worked closely with businessmen, who were the obvious producers of "progress" and economic well-being. His policies proved more of a boon to the middle class than to the truly poor but this does not negate his efforts to support change. He always claimed that he owed his position to the nation's masses, some 29 million in number. He insisted that where earlier governments were concerned for the welfare of the million educated citizens who supported them, he was reaching over their heads and basing his support on the other 29 million. A spokesman for "the people," he would institute programs which would benefit them. If businessmen enjoyed more advantages than the peasants, it was not from a lack of good intentions at the top. His attempts to work through the business community reflects his Saint-Simonian faith in the key importance of the entrepreneur to society. Thus, although programs were not directly aimed at the peasantry, the conditions were created for economic improvement and change in one's lot, no mean achievement in a nation like France at mid-century.

It is well to remember that Louis Napoleon was at heart an earnest ideologue who would have been happy as a member of the Frankfurt Parliament debating the pros and cons of an ideal constitution. He was as interested in social questions as Louis Blanc, who had visited him at Ham. Essentially humanitarian and romantic at heart, as a Bonaparte there were the added ingredients of militarism and republicanism in his make-up. Thus one can see the plotter, the authoritarian Caesar, and at the same time the Saint-Simonian. The dominant economic system was capitalism rather than feudalism and the new leaders were the businessmen who became honored technicians in a Bonapartist society where the lower classes were to be protected and employed rather than exploited.

Napoleon had no difficulty in attracting to government service men like Michel Chevalier, Achille Fould, Prosper Enfantin, and the Péreire brothers, all Saint-Simonian believers whose main interests were in business rather than politics. A corresponding group also appeared in the Legislative Body. They were not Bonapartists and they had no sense of party affiliation. They had similarly served Louis Philippe without being Orléanists. As minister of the interior, Morny was an invaluable liaison with this group and shared many of their perspectives at the same time that he was close to the Emperor. Napoleon thus believed in very close cooperation with the business community; at the same time, he retained the perspective of an outsider. That he never fully assumed its more limited values is clear from his support of free trade, which in the Cobden-Chevalier Treaty was strongly opposed by French business leaders.

Up to this time the government in France had done relatively little to promote business. The most support had unquestionably come under Louis Philippe, where an officialdom friendly to business had enabled the aggressive entrepreneur to find greater opportunities. Under Louis Napoleon, however, the government itself created vast reservoirs of credit which offered unparalleled business opportunities. A host of newly formed joint-stock investment companies and land banks extended large amounts of credit to support new industrial enterprises. Many of the small investment companies were shortly merged into two large units, the *Crédit Foncier* to promote agricultural experimentation and the *Crédit Mobilier* for other types of large-scale business ventures. Ironically, the funds supporting the initial companies came from treasury reserves which were accumulated under Louis Philippe and had somehow not been expended in 1848. With loans readily available, local governments and aggressive businessmen alike embarked on interesting construction and manufacturing programs. As the economy reacted favorably, the old *Haute Banque* and the Rothschilds began to extend more credit. These institutions had been reluctant to support the schemes of Louis Napoleon and their excessive caution, coupled with the Bank of France's inadequate funding at the time, forced him to encourage more daring experimentation in banking. During the Second Empire much of the dramatically expanding economy stemmed from the founding of the *Crédit Mobilier* and the *Crédit Foncier* in 1852. They were in accord with Saint-Simonian ideology and their adoption may be clearly credited to Louis Napoleon and his advisors. This initiative in economic affairs gave rise to one of the most appropriate references to this Bonapartist Emperor who believed in free trade among nations but active government support for business development at home—"Saint-Simon on horseback."

The new instruments of credit, coupled with overt encouragement on the part of officialdom, led to an era of public and private construction. In communications the most spectacular development occurred in the expanded program of railroad building. The plans for a number of the lines had been finished in 1842 but actual work had lagged, so that when Louis Philippe fell, less than 2,000 kilometers had been completed. By 1870, rail trackage in France amounted to almost 16,000 kilometers. Rail lines were built radially out from Paris, connecting the capital with major ports, provincial centers, and boundary points of entry. New lines also connected the various provincial cities with one another. The economic consequence of the rail program was a vast increase in trade and wealth, and the bounds of the domestic market were expanded for virtually all manufacturers. The telegraph was a new communication device which, introduced and expanded greatly under the Second Empire, also emphasized the dominant position of the leading cities. The extensive employment created in the construction of the lines proved to be among the more modest of the economic advantages flowing from the railroads.

A fundamental change took place in rural France. In addition to the stimulation of trade and commerce, a vital development was that many small communities were for the first time really put in close contact with Paris and other large cities. Complacently agrarian and unconcerned with the outer world, these cultural islands were awakened and introduced to the advantages made by progress during the previous century. This result of improved transportation was clear within two or three decades as these communities began to send talent to the cities and became more sophisticated users and producers of goods themselves. Besides the major role played by the railroad, the government had also supervised extensive road building and completed many highways as well as an intricate network of secondary roads.

Improved communications were also furthered by a program of canal construction. This had lagged earlier because of the idea that possibly canals would not be needed in the face of the quicker service provided by the railroad. The economy was expanding so rapidly, however, that it became clear that both systems would be fully utilized. At the same time overseas transportation was being promoted by the creation of new maritime companies, which provided transatlantic service and contributed to the particular growth of the ports of Le Havre, Bordeaux, and Saint-Nazaire. In the technology of water transportation this was an era of change from sail to steam, with steam tonnage increasing eightfold between 1848 and 1858. Witness to the great expansion of trade is the statistic that in the same period technologically obsolescent sail tonnage increased by 50 per cent. The world of communication in France was markedly different in 1870 than it had been in 1850, and much of the change may be attributed to imperial policies.

Accompanying the rapid changes in communication was an enormous increase in vital industrial products. Steel and cast iron production more than doubled and the manufacture of machinery spurted 70 per cent, naturally triggering production and consumption in allied areas as the credit structure encouraged men with entrepreneurial instincts. Coke and coal production also surged but could not keep up with the demand. All of this led to a proliferation of lighter consumer industries because the middle class was growing rapidly and was eager to spend its new and rapidly growing income for up-to-date goods. This they were able to do in recently founded department stores such as the Bon Marché, established in 1853, which were flourishing marvels of efficiency and merchandising.

With so many new firms enjoying such rapid success, rampant speculation was probably inevitable. The Bourse found its activities increased manyfold as the numbers of businessmen working to assure careful and proper funding of the multiple new enterprises grew. Because many government officials had advance information on new projects, temptations for quick wealth were present and many indulged themselves, either directly investing or simply "selling" information. So many important imperial officials yielded to the opportunity that the idea spread that the Empire was an exercise in shady plotting and immorality. Morny and Saint-Arnaud were prime suspects in this regard. Napoleon worried about the charges of corruption that republican spokesmen leveled at the regime, and although he proposed stringent steps against speculation, it continued.

In the midst of all the economic prosperity, the expanded urban labor force experienced little change in its living conditions. The workers were carefully watched by the police because they had a reputation for radicalism and their savage fighting during the June Days was still a vivid memory. Part of the liberalization program in the 1860s included the legalization of unions (1868) and strikes (1864). Beginnings were also made in sickness insurance and old-age pensions, welcome measures for workers who may have been radical at heart but never opposed the Empire and were satisfied to be fully employed.

Naturally the bourgeoisie was the class which enjoyed the most change in terms of growth, new wealth, and prestige. The example of Louis Philippe's reign as a businessman's regime pales by comparison. Indeed the cascading opportunities for new business success effectively challenged many minds which in other circumstances would have been more interested in politics. As a group, businessmen were long impervious to republican efforts to create dissatisfaction with imperial policy. They believed in material progress, and the challenge of finding new techniques absorbed their enormous skills.

In 1855 and 1867, expositions in Paris displayed to the world the products of the new technologies. Millions of visitors, including many sovereigns, came to see the new wonders of machinery and steel. In the 1867 exposition, besides the official exhibits there were numerous booths emphasizing sheer amusement. This contributed markedly to the reputation of Paris as a great tourist city where light and risqué entertainment overlooked the stricter conventions of morality.

In addition to being attracted by advances in technology and pure pleasure, tourists were also impressed by physical changes in the city of Paris itself. A massive rebuilding program had transformed Paris from a tangle of miserable alleyways to a city with broad thoroughfares. Many old buildings with intrinsic beauty had earlier been obscured by the crowding of dwellings near them and the whole city had reeked with a thousand stenches. In rebuilding the capital, Napoleon III made one of his most enduring and praiseworthy domestic contributions. He entrusted the task to a prefect with a reputation for strict efficiency, Baron Haussmann (1809–1891) who wielded his authority ruthlessly. This was necessary, for such a major attack against such a large concentration of property owners could not have been carried out in the nineteenth century by anything less than an autocratic regime. When the work was finished, the city was hardly recognizable as the Paris of 1848. Broad boulevards, carefully placed, brought light and a sense of spaciousness into the heart of the city. Republicans declared that Napoleon did this so that barricades would be impossible. The Emperor was enough of a schemer not to be ignorant of the advantages deriving from an opportunity to use artillery and cavalry against urban mobs, but to attribute his rebuilding program to this reason is surely ungracious. Squares were created near buildings which either attracted traffic because of their function or were architecturally significant. Of course, the tearing down of old buildings involved widescale condemnations. Speculation and corruption were at every hand, prices rose drastically, and the government paid the inflated costs. New buildings generally followed a preconceived plan, which resulted in a considerable amount of conformity. Guilty perhaps of this criticism, nonetheless the project produced buildings which blended well with the boulevards and squares in a fashion still dignified and impressive.

One by-product of the rebuilding was to have long-term social consequences. It was decided to allocate large areas in the center of the city to professional, tourist, and bureaucratic types of business; factories were placed on the periphery. As a result, the core of the city became almost exclusively bourgeois and workers settled nearer the factories. Previously, workers had merely occupied the upper floors of buildings which housed business and professional men in the lower, more comfortable, floors. Housing in the center of the renovated city was now too expensive for workers. Massive working-class districts developed outside the old confines of the city; it was to these areas that peasants came when leaving the countryside. These outer suburbs, despite their newness, were grimy. The workers and middle class became physically separated and seemed remote from one another. They no longer met regularly in the course of daily life and they could more easily suspect one another's aims and loyalties. Further, the workers could be more militantly organized and now developed a firmer sense of solidarity; these factors are crucial to understanding French social and political history since 1880.

While noting the changes in Paris, we should also observe that similar, though smaller, renovations occurred in other French cities. Most industrial centers increased in population, some by as much as 300 per cent—and construction seemed to be going on everywhere. Enormous fortunes were made and impressive seaside resorts were built as the middle class now joined the aristocracy in its taste for luxury and expensive vacations. Even the workers, who could not afford such vacations, ended up with public parks to enjoy and regular incomes over long periods. Though the gains were inequitable, the alterations in patterns of living were so extensive that few lives remained untouched.

Thus, Napoleon III left France a more prosperous and a pleasanter place in which to live. Opportunities for advancement were much more broadly available, more economic freedom existed, and the nation possessed the most advanced political structure then existing in a major state on the Continent. While accomplishing this, he was plagued by diplomatic failures of enormous proportions (we shall touch on these elsewhere), he was badgered by relatives and an intractable wife, and his health was failing. Consistently criticized in the 1860s by the republicans, he was regarded by many simply as an autocratic old *roué*. The man has proved difficult for historians to categorize with confidence; but there can be no doubt that the Second Empire was an age of dramatic peaceful domestic progress, inspired and supported by an imperial regime and headed by an emperor whose inclinations bordered on the socialistic.

CHAPTER 25

Reform by Tsarist Decree

Reform in nineteenth-century Russia came by Tsarist initiatives rather than from explicit demands articulated from below, as in the case of France and even England. Few leaders in history have been personally responsible for more fundamental reform than that accomplished by the Tsar-Liberator, Alexander II (1818–1881). At the time of his accession in March of 1855, the winds of change released by the French Revolution had not yet penetrated the Russian social system. Personal relationships were less enlightened and considerably more barbaric than conditions in the Austrian Empire prior to 1848.

The redoubtable Nicholas, Europe's strongest supporter of aristocratic conservatism, had not only crushed the independence movement in Hungary but also kept Russia free of the contagious ideas

Alexander II. (Courtesy of Historical
Pictures Service, Chicago.)

circulating in that chaotic year. His armies, which were very capable
in countering liberalism, were inadequate to expel the French and
British forces which invaded the Crimea. A vaunted offensive to
drive the Western armies into the sea was unequal to the task. Widespread indignation and amazement at the incompetence of British
officers and supply services during the struggle obscured the vastly
greater failures on the Russian side. The militaristic Nicholas, the
"gendarme of Europe," died as both his army and bureaucracy were
being proved grossly incompetent.

Alexander II, thirty-seven years old in 1855, showed little of his
father's interest in militarism and was not as emotionally committed
to the issues leading to the war. He was, therefore, in a position to
negotiate peace as soon as possible. Both sides, however, had made
such a point of possessing Sebastopol that either it had to fall or
the siege had to be successfully lifted before any negotiations could
succeed. The city held on for another six months before falling.
Although the allies could be elated over their success, the Russian
defenses had been so heroic that the conditions existed for a mu-
tually honorable settlement. An interesting and slowly developing

Franco-Russian entente gave assurances that although the settlement would make clear who had won the war and who had lost, the Russians would not come off badly. Alexander was thus able to obtain peace with honor despite the loss of the war.

The compelling social problem in Russia at mid-century was serfdom and the issue of emancipation. Military defeat exposed the inefficiency of the system; the bureaucracy especially was unmasked as incredibly corrupt and incompetent. Before his accession Alexander had given little indication that he would rule any differently than his father, who had allowed him some administrative training and had trusted him to be regent in his absence. Nicholas had been concerned about serfdom, but after the mid-1840s, he despaired of finding a practical solution which would not alienate the nobility. With Alexander, however, circumstances were quite different. Defeat had aroused national pride and there was widespread sentiment for reform. Alexander was much freer to embark on programs of reform than the autocratic Nicholas had been. While never abandoning his autocracy, Alexander faced most of Russia's domestic problems squarely and inaugurated epochal humanitarian programs, which he saw as essential to Russian strength. There was no ultimate scheme for limited monarchy even remotely in the back of his mind. Probably too many historians have attributed generous motives to Alexander, seeing him as the reform-minded ruler gradually disillusioned. Accused of vacillation and indecision, he nevertheless emancipated the serfs and accomplished it in the face of widespread opposition among the aristocracy. Despite shortcomings and some half measures, this was a gigantic social undertaking and could easily have occasioned extensive bloodshed and unrest. Accompanying other important but less dramatic reforms, the over-all impact was to alter Russian society so much that the nation's domestic history was set on a new course.

Alexander openly declared himself against serfdom barely a year after his father's death. In an often quoted address to the nobility in Moscow on March 30, 1856, he exhorted them to take the initiative in ridding the nation of serfdom before such change began from below without any chance of their controlling it. This suggestion generally went unheeded, although in 1857 some of the nobles in Lithuania accepted the idea of serf emancipation, but without any grants of land. It was probably unrealistic to expect the nobility to initiate proposals even as enlightened as these from Lithuania. The vested interests of the most powerful class, after all, made extremely difficult an issue which was far more complex than, for example,

Britain's Irish problem. Alexander worked consistently for the end of serfdom despite the prestige of those defending the system. German influence in the Russian court life proved significant. The Tsar's mother, Charlotte, was Prussian; his wife, Marie, came from Hesse-Darmstadt; and his sister married the King of Württemberg— all areas where serfdom had been abolished and was regarded as an uncivilized and antequated institution. Alexander had received a humanistic education and was well aware of the eloquence with which serf freedom was being advocated by such Russian authors as Turgenev. Adherents to the idea of emancipation were scarce among high officials, but they did include the minister of the interior, Sergei Lanskoe; his assistant, Nicholas Milyutin; and the foreign minister, A. M. Gorchakov.

Beginning in 1857, major committees were formed to study emancipation. Ideas submitted by local committees were evaluated and in February of 1861, a policy was framed for the entire country. The committees were generally composed of aristocrats who emphatically opposed emancipation. They willingly accepted the idea that perhaps some reforms could be adopted to improve serf living conditions, but that was about the extent of their initiative. Without the Tsar's insistence that a formula to end serfdom be found, the old system would have drifted on. In Russia the Crown provided the driving force for reform; unlike France under Louis XVI, it was willing to coerce its own aristocracy to bring improvements to the lower classes. The Tsar provided the example in 1859 when he issued the first of a series of decrees freeing Crown serfs by 1866.

Aside from the reluctance of the nobility (some 250,000 nobles held serfs) to free their serfs, the committees faced difficult problems in devising a practical formula for emancipation. For one thing, the pattern of serf-noble relationships had never been as explicit as in Central and Western Europe. Serf living conditions were wretched, and although legally they were not slaves, nobles could and did sell them. There was no question that the serf was to render labor without pay, but noble obligations were less clearly understood. Also the whole matter of land ownership was obscure. Indeed, it seemed more obvious that the nobles owned the serfs than that they owned the land, and many serfs sincerely believed that although they belonged to the noble, the land was theirs. Contributing to the confusion was the considerable variety in Russia, which reflected the country's growth and the unique history of many of its regions. In the heart of historic Russia the practice had developed, stemming from Mongol invasion days, of redistributing land among the village families as the size of the families varied. Thus, every two decades or so, a re-assessment was made in terms of the practical working of the land. The attitude prevailed that a man worked land which really belonged to the village but was his temporarily. This was especially suggestive to members of the committees, who had to consider not only this practice but also the problem that areas of Estonia and Livonia had been strongly influenced by the Napoleonic code, which had been in force in Poland since 1807. During the discussions, the nobles gradually retreated before those few spokesmen for reform who had the prestige of the Tsar supporting them. It became easier for them to acquiesce when it was explained that serf owners would be indemnified. It was presumed that the serf, soon to be a free peasant, would continue to work the same land and that all that remained was to find a device for accomplishing this. The nobles were skeptically compliant, and the serfs heard rumors of their impending freedom with mounting anticipation.

The solution approved by Alexander disappointed many peasants but was probably as enlightened as conditions permitted. Except in the West, where individual ownership was common, the land was assigned to the *mir* (the village commune), which was then responsible for seing that it was tilled by the peasants. The nobles were given forty-nine-year bonds as compensation and these were to be retired through payments from the *mir*. Over half of Russia's arable land was thus given indirectly to the peasants, who were expected to work it for forty-nine years until the payments were completed. These "redemption" payments came as a harsh surprise to the peasants who had not expected that freedom would entail further work. Indeed, the *mir* drove the peasants harshly in order to meet the payments and often proved a more exacting master than had many of the nobles. The *mir* supervised peasant labor and coerced those who were slackers, even punishing some by sending them to Siberia. At first the peasants believed that somehow the nobles had subverted the wishes of the Tsar. Disillusioned and forced to work as hard as ever, a great change had, nonetheless, occurred. Both the peasant and the noble now depended on a money economy while earlier practices of communal property ownership received strong sanction, establishing the idea that such arrangements were sound and natural. The nobles, of course, retained a great deal of property, especially forests and grazing land. The peasant found that besides working his own land for the *mir,* he had to make money payments for grazing rights. He needed money regularly, and in this regard his life had become more complicated. In the division of land a considerable inequity existed. Peasants who had been serfs on crown or state lands were favored with much larger lots (in some cases double the size) than their compatriots received, and their redemption payments were also lighter. Some rioting occurred, but essentially the new system was implemented peacefully. Adjudication of disputes was a responsibility met by the nobility, whose appointees showed great tact and administrative ability. The smoothness of the transition was due to the peasants' belief that these men fairly considered their best interests.

Many interesting ramifications of emancipation took place. Among the peasants themselves a class structure began to develop as the brightest and most aggressive found ways to exploit their own kind and the system. The most successful group came to be known as the kulaks. One result of serf freedom made a negative impact on Russia's small but growing industrial plant. The serf laborer took his new freedom to mean that he could return to agriculture; consequently, thousands simply left the factories. Emancipation had not created or expanded a mobile work force; instead it reduced the number of men available for industrial labor. This temporarily retarded industrial growth, but newer and better machinery soon caught up. At the same time, despite an overall rising death rate in nineteenth-century Russia, there was a striking increase in population. In the nine years following emancipation an increase of about 14 per cent occurred—from 73.6 to 84.5 million.

In Poland the settlement with the peasants was an aspect of the over-all Polish problem. The crucial event of the 1860s for Poland was an uprising in January of 1863. Alexander had made a few moderate concessions to Polish pride but refused any major gestures such as restoring the Polish Diet or allowing a separate Polish army. The revolt was an exercise in futility which further engendered intense hatred. Led by nobles and students with help from townsmen and clergy, it lacked support from the peasants. It never had an effective functioning government or even a real army. At best it was a spirited guerilla-type uprising which never menaced Russian control. Its leaders desperately hoped for foreign intervention, but unfortunately, Polish nationalism's most distinguished friend, Napoleon III, was embarrassingly committed in Mexico at the time and reduced to nothing more than instigating a combination of Franco-British-Austrian protests to the Tsar. When Bismarck gave his approval to the Tsar's crushing of the insurgents, possibilities of outside aid for them became virtually nil. In dealing with the revolt Alexander was every bit as rigorous as his father. Congress

Poland came to an end and the area now became merely the Vistula region of Russia. Polish nationalism had received a crushing blow but the peasants were rewarded for their apathetic refusal to aid in the revolt. They received larger grants of land than the Russian peasants and were still allowed use of noble pastures and forest lands. The Polish nobility was indemnified for the loss of direct services through a land tax which everyone paid, including the owners of large estates. Thus the nobles helped to pay for their own losses and a system had been created which assured a deepening gulf between peasants and nobles. The prospect of the peasants aiding the nobles in any future revolt had been made especially remote. Polish peasants had gained handsomely through the failure of Polish nationalism, though Western reformers hardly applauded this by-product of autocracy.

Significant results of the emancipation in Russia was the new importance of the *mir* as an administrative center and the lending of state support to the idea of the collective organization of land and its usage. The latter idea attracted socialist theoreticians and made Russia a land of special promise for them.

As free men, the peasants suddenly became involved in a whole host of legal questions relating to money obligations and contracts. The pressing need for clarification led to a series of legal and judicial reforms. Previously the legal apparatus resembled a corrupt and inefficient court-martial system, with summary justice meted out to virtually defenseless victims by judges who themselves felt no security. A number of judgeships now became elective, well paid, and secure, thereby assuring more independent judgments. The judiciary was separated from the regular government; the jury system was introduced; and equality before the law was proclaimed. Trials were opened to the public and cases were to be tried orally. Also provisions were made for appeal courts, so that, as far as possible, a fair and open system based on equality was introduced. Corruption diminished rapidly and the new court structure readily acquired a reputation for impartiality and justice. The new structure (authorized in 1864 but implemented throughout the 1860s) was a deliberate copy of French and British practice and, unlike the collective arrangement of land, could not be regarded as a natural outgrowth of earlier Russian history. The main defect was an acute shortage of trained personnel. The previous system had failed to prepare either enough lawyers or judges to handle the large amount of new legal work. Considering this shortage, the new system was a striking success. At the same time there were areas where the reforms came slowly. For example, corporal punishment was abandoned by official decree in 1863, yet there were 5,452 examples of it between 1866 and 1868, 10,884 between 1872 and 1874. In the 1870s the Third Section virtually ignored the new reforms.

Judicial reforms were accompanied by the formation (in 1864) of district and provincial assemblies called *zemstvos*. Seats were held by representatives from peasant assemblies in the *mirs,* towns people and nobles. The *zemstvo* provided administrative leadership in a number of local problem areas, such as maintenance of roads and bridges, charitable institutions, elementary education, sanitation, and agriculture. It kept track especially of crop maturation and took appropriate relief measures if famine threatened. The *zemstvo* met a few days every year to appoint men to an executive committee. These officials were conscientious but were handicapped in that their authority was subordinated to that of the provincial governor and they were expressly ordered not to communicate with the representatives of other *zemstvos*. Expenses were paid by direct local real estate taxes. The *zemstvos* were remarkably free of corruption and there was little indication of class tension or hatred. Peasants and nobles sat and worked peacefully together in mutual concern for solving common problems. Many people were thus trained in the complexities of local government and their horizons were broadened. Outsiders have seen in the *zemstvo* the germ of representative government, and enthusiastic reformers then hoped that Alexander would complete the system of representative assemblies with a national *zemstvo*, but this proved a vain expectation. The emancipation had created an acute need for a new bureaucratic structure at the bottom but not especially at the top.

There were, meanwhile, other reforms. The failure in the Crimean War had focused the Tsar's attention on the need for a massive and immediate reform of the army. The hated system of military colonies was ended, along with corporal punishment. Training procedures were carefully reviewed and greater care was given to the selection and instruction of officers. The whole military establishment was decentralized and the obligation of male conscription was instituted on a basis of class equality. Although a system of exemptions modified this, it was a popular and constructive step ahead. Among less significant changes, moderate press reform was introduced in 1865, but because decisions on censorship were placed in the hands of imperial authorities, real guarantees of press freedom were lacking. Alexander II had voluntarily relaxed censorship when he came to the throne, but no guarantees existed against a return to harsher standards.

Alexander's role was the same in all the reforms. He would initiate the various changes by imperial decree, after an appropriate committee or committees had investigated (also on his initiative) and discovered the need for specific improvements. The reforms, however, inevitably led to greater expectations. This was probably in the nature of things, because the programs he instigated were profound and, occurring contemporaneously, they created an atmosphere of dynamism and hope. A point often ignored regarding the Tsar was that he reformed not because he was a liberal, but because the particular reforms he allowed seemed to be essential for the creation of a strong Russia. He was an honest conservative who agreed with many of his father's ideas, but he did not see social reform as meaning political reform. When liberal enthusiasts wanted more change, he halted and appeared to vacillate. By the mid-1870s he seemed to be sponsoring a number of half measures; as a result, he was accused of abandoning true reform.

Alexander's reign began with a flurry of new journalistic endeavor encouraged by the relaxed censorship. In the wake of defeat in the Crimea, papers were critical of the bureaucracy and called loudly for emancipation. Although many new papers were founded, Russia's distances between major population centers made the less frequent magazines more practical conveyors of news and opinion. These publications were important symptoms of the widespread unrest and ferment building up among the intelligentsia at large and in the universities. During Nicholas' reign the old opposition between the Westerners and the Slavophiles had gradually been altered. Disillusioned Westerners perceived not only that Western Europe was unable to solve its poverty problems but that the advent of machinery seemed to intensify them. Alexander Herzen was a leading example of this change in outlook. He saw 1848 as a grandiose failure for liberal principles and came to have more sympathy for the *mir* and its development. The socialistic aspects of Russian life now attracted the Westerners, who became the core of a liberal movement demanding further reform. Chernyshevsky called for Fourier-type phalansters in a new system where the emphasis was to be clearly on democracy in an agrarian setting. Part of the new ferment was a revival of nationalistic feeling in response to the Polish revolt; and the emancipation, with its addition of administrative functions in the *mir,* gave added impulse to the continuing

Slavophile movement. All these intellectuals were similar in many respects to the liberals of Western Europe, especially in their clamoring for more representative institutions. They thought they saw movement in the direction of their goals in the emancipation, in the *zemstvos,* and in jury trials. They were, however, utterly alienated by the regime when the reforms seemed to stop short of a national constitution and a national *zemstvo.*

At this point a new intellectual movement appeared, nihilism. This drew its inspiration from the disappointments that imperial reforms were not more comprehensive, combined with a youthful enthusiasm for further change per se. It acquired a large following among the educated elite, especially in the generation attending the universities since the accession of Alexander II. The nihilists systematically turned their backs on the historic foundations of their educational system, rejecting alike the classics and the teachings of the Slavophiles. They claimed to be supporting no ideology other than that which proclaimed the unacceptability of the present system. The government showed its alarm by trying to censor their publications and by more carefully controlling admission to the universities. The nihilists read widely in Western European philosophers and social critics and debated their ideas with little appreciation for the context in which these insights were initially presented. Many nihilists were young nobles emotionally concerned for the harsh lot of the peasantry. They blamed the whole range of social institutions for what they denounced as the grossest miscarriage of justice. Science attracted their interest, for here was truth unvarnished by social institutions. Although scientific study enjoyed a new popularity, to the government it became associated with nihilism and was clearly subversive. Many nihilists were sent to Siberia; others fled to Western Europe, where they could write and propagandize relatively unhindered. The nihilist movement lacked roots, but as an intellectual current its indirect influence was profound.

Out of the tumult of ideas came three clear paths which could be followed, and Russia tried all three. Michael Bakunin (1814–1876), acclaimed for an escape from Siberia in 1862, called for the end of all institutions, including the family. He prescribed open violence as the manner of achieving this. The economist Nicholas Chernyshevsky saw the possibilities for evolution toward some sort of socialism. Peter Lavrov believed that improvement in the peasant's life would come slowly through education and that those who were educated should go among the peasantry and educate them. Many students vacillated between one or another of these courses.

An attempt to implement Lavrov's ideas occurred in the so-called Narodnik movement, 1872–1875. Intellectuals wearing peasant dress appeared in the villages and tried to get the peasants to agitate for more reform and more rights. Between 2,000 and 3,000, many of them young people and women, enthusiastically joined in this campaign. Their approach, however, was too radical for the stolid peasantry, who distrusted them and frequently turned them in to the Tsar's police. The episode was an exercise in utter futility, despite its elevated objectives. Unfortunately, this failure turned many reformers toward the blatantly violent program of Bakunin. The peasants had appeared to be a useless instrument in the cause of their own betterment. Only the question of land moved them; on politics and socialism they were essentially inert.

The reform movement now adopted terrorism as a tactical device; in 1876 in St. Petersburg, an insurrectionist society called Land and Liberty was formed. Branches were organized in the main cities and towns and assassinations of public officials soon resulted from this organized wave of anarchistic feeling. Most of the murders were carried out by zealous young people who were impatient with a government which by the late 1870s, they saw as essentially reactionary and inactive on the question of further reform. One of the most dramatic assassinations occurred in 1878, when the chief of police in St. Petersburg, General Feodor Trepov, was shot by Vera Zasulich, a young girl of noble birth. Brought to trial, the evidence against her was compelling, but the jurors acquitted her. Sympathizers among the spectators prevented her rearrest by the police and smuggled her out of the country. Such actions turned jury trials into a farce and encouraged firmer administrative policies. The government was goaded thus to more reactionary administrative action, whereas the terrorists, who had no constructive policies themselves, stepped up the pace of their activities. The actual assassins numbered only a few hundred, but they received help in the form of secure hiding places from a public which, on the surface, appeared stoically uncommitted.

In 1879 the radical ranks generally divided into two groups; a moderate wing named The Blank Partition (of Property) led by George Plekhanov (1857–1918), which continued to emphasize propaganda, and a smaller extremist wing called The Will of the People. The majority was dominated by intellectuals more than activists and formed the core of the later Social Democrats. The more aggressive group comprised Jacobin types, known subsequently as the Socialist Revolutionaries; late in 1879, they sentenced the Tsar to death. The publicity which they gave this decision, coupled with bold attempts on Alexander's life, alarmed the Tsar and he appointed a Supreme Regulating Commission for the Maintenance of the Governmental System and Social Tranquility. This was headed by General Loris-Melikov (1825?–1888), who was given dictatorial powers to combat the forces of revolution.

Melikov tried at once to restore public confidence in the imperial government. He had no intention of working for a national assembly yielding directly to threat or force. He received innumerable suggestions regarding liberal goals which he could bring to Russia but most involved some sort of popular representation at the highest levels of decision making. He moderated press censorship and Slavophile views quickly circulated to a wide reading public. The "Third Section" lost its identity as a separate unit, being merged with other police forces; and within the ministries a number of reactionaries were replaced by men of liberal leanings. This was a clear move to attract responsible liberal support against the terrorists and initial reactions were most promising. After six months, Melikov advised disbanding the special commission and he was named minister of the interior, though his functions more resembled those of a prime minister. Melikov had shown great ability in meeting a very difficult situation and, as was the case with Turgot over a century before in France, in retrospect we may speculate about what might have been if this man could have had a decade of power.

In February of 1881, Melikov presented a report to Alexander which recommended a culminating reform that would satisfy those who were calling for some sort of national assembly. He was perhaps a bit optimistic about how it would be accepted, because his proposition stopped well short of national representation. Still, the germ of such an idea was present. Special committees would be appointed to consider further reforms and their reports would be considered by a General Committee composed of Tsarist appointees and delegates elected by the *zemstvos* and the towns. This body would merely make recommendations; the power of decision would remain with the Tsar in consultation with his Council of State. This was far from a national legislative body, but it did provide for local interests to have a voice in the highest councils while opening the door for further reforms. Alexander received the report on February 9, 1881, and on March 13th he gave it his approval. Unfortunately, while he was debating his decision, a small terrorist group completed its plans for his murder, and on the very day he gave his approval to Melikov's proposal, they succeeded in their aim. Alexander was

The labels on the illustration read:

Tcherkess of the Emperor's Guard

Tcherkess sitting on coachman's side, mortally wounded.

The Emperor.

Colonel of the Police Dvorchetski.

Colonel Dvorchetski's sledge in which the Emperor was brought to the Winter Palace.

Tcherkess of the suite of the Emperor killed.

An officer mortally wounded.

Butcher boy killed.

The assassination of Alexander II. (Courtesy of Historical Pictures Service, Chicago.)

mutilated from a bomb explosion at close range and died in less than two hours.

The assassins had killed the Tsar but their brutal act turned public opinion against terroism far more emphatically than any new proposals of Melikov could have. The death of Alexander II ended any immediate prospects for further reform in Russia. For all of his vacillation and despite his questionable motives and reluctance to grant political concessions, Alexander had introduced enormous changes in Russia. The fervor with which more was demanded was a measure of how overdue such reforms were. Although his reign saw some unrest and sporadic violence, millions of persons had been freed.

IX

Nineteenth-Century Intellectual Vitality

CHAPTER 26

Nineteenth-Century Science

Science in Europe during the nineteenth century showed enormous vitality, both in the theoretical and applied areas. In the latter case, new standards of comfort and health were broadly present in urban areas, giving obvious verification to the idea of progress. Expositions displayed and publicized bewildering arrays of new inventions and stimulated further alterations in traditional patterns of living.

In theoretical or pure science, the period represents a vital and orderly progression from issues and problems indicated in the eighteenth century. That era had constituted in many ways an adjustment to a new world view, and the generations immediately following Newton busily explored the implications of his insights. In the nineteenth century the pursuit of new knowledge accelerated sharply. Newton's system became entrenched with better calculations on the planets, comets, and moon; laboratory techniques became much more sophisticated; and profound advances were made in every field. No scientist appeared whose impact was comparable to Newton's but it was a far more productive century for scientific activity than any to that time.

Periods of scientific, intellectual, or artistic development rarely fit the dates which the political-diplomatic historian selects as his guideposts, and this generalization is especially true for the nineteenth century. The French Revolution, as a traumatic watershed, had its equivalent in intellectual life in the work of Newton. The French Revolution and the subsequent upheaval in much of Europe did not seriously impede scientific activity; the advance in knowledge was steady and attracted the finest minds. The splintering of knowledge into rigidly defined fields, a professionalization of the disciplines, greatly accelerated during the century; but at the century's beginning, intellectuals can be found moving with ease from one type of scientific pursuit to another. A distinguished example of this was the literary giant Johann Wolfgang von Goethe (1749–1832). A study of his work reveals not only the artistic writer but also a creative scientist whose work had enduring merit. A 1940 bibliography of Goethe's impact on science carried no less than 4,500 titles.

Goethe's scientific interests were broad. In mineralogy, geology, and mining he was an avid collector but authored no major contributions. He did, however, discover and describe, in 1823, a former volcano, not previously identified as such, in Bohemia near Marienbad. He also was among the first to recognize that many erratic materials in Europe must be accounted for by a vast ice sheet. More important was his research on skulls, where he demonstrated that humans had the intermaxillary bone. This bone in the upper jaw carries the incisors, but previously it had only been identified in mammals other than man. Goethe accomplished this independently, but at the same time as a Parisian anatomist, Felix Vicq d'Azyr. Goethe's report was the more profound and is regarded as basic to the foundation of scientific morphology and comparative anatomy. In botany he made a fundamental contribution in his insistence on the existence of, and search for, the *Urpflanze,* or archetype, the plant form so elemental that all others could be traced to it. This led to the development of comparative morphology in botany. He also worked with the theory of color, but his findings here lacked broad acceptance, although they did lead to advances in physiological optics and sensory physiology. In much of his work he came close to implications of evolution but never dealt directly with this issue. In his insistence on archetypes, for inanimate as well as animate life, he was dealing with an idea important to evolutionary theory, but he made no effort to view his work in this context. Goethe was an interesting example of a modern "renaissance man" whose contributions spread across broad spectrums of knowledge. Nineteenth-century developments were to make the reappearance of such a person especially unlikely, for the rapid accumulation of knowledge and the growing identification of fields resulted in channeling one's interest more narrowly and then requiring greater study before work at the frontier of a discipline could begin.

The century saw an enormous acquisition of information concerning the physical features of the world itself. The most important geographer was Alexander von Humbolt (1769–1859), an indefatigable traveler and an encyclopedic recorder of nature. His descriptions of Central America were of special value and brought him celebrity status. His minute presentations of flora and fauna opened a new world to a Europe with a developing romantic interest in far away places. His final magnum opus was the multivolume *Cosmos,* the first volume of which appeared in 1845, when he was seventy-six years of age. Completed thirteen years later, this work was an attempt to present the fruit of scientific achievement since 1700 in a way which would show that in the vast disparity and diversity of data, there was an over-all unity. Crammed with scientific detail, it purported to present nature as it was, with no particular reference to any religious power operating within or outside that nature. By inference this sort of science was independent of nondata and the unity in the universe was to be seen from and through consideration of the mass of sheer data. The facts spoke for themselves. Alexander's brother, Wilhelm, was an active figure in education and in diplomacy, and between them the name of von Humbolt became one of the most distinguished in Germany. Alexander's work proved to be a prelude to a feverish rush to discover more about the earth's surface, and a flowering of exploratory missions occurred.

The interest in acquiring descriptive information about the world was matched by considerable activity in the field of geology, where the most important figure was Charles Lyell (1797–1875). Before Lyell there were two opposing views regarding the way in which change occurred in the earth. There was a "catastrophist" theory, which allowed for miraculous and sudden occurrences, and there was a "uniformitarian" explanation, which saw change taking place slowly by processes going on everywhere in the same fashion. The two views vied after 1780, with the uniformitarians gradually gain-

ing, despite the catastrophists' closeness to Biblical presentations of
the world's origin and their opponents' great demands on the credi-
bility of their audience when they posited fantastically long periods
of time for change to occur. Paleontology was an especial aid to the
uniformitarians, but the work of Lyell made their victory virtually
complete.

Lyell's *Principles of Geology* appeared in three volumes between
1830 and 1833. Here he explained clearly the details of uniformitarianism, postulating that the processes now readily observed in
progress (volcanic action; earthquakes creating faults; river action;
erosion from cold, heat, and rain; decaying vegetation; and so on)
had been going on in the same fashion for eons and could account
for the current configuration of continents and land masses. The
Bible was not to be taken seriously as a scientific work. Catastro-
phism was simply out of vogue in most intellectual circles after Lyell,
who found a wide audience. People came to accept the idea that
the earth was far more ancient than had been thought earlier. New
editions of the *Principles* came out in rapid succession, each with
additional data as other investigators were adding to the expanding
body of knowledge. It is an interesting curiosity that this work,
trumpeting truth through the impartial study of the facts of a nature
operating in an even and mechanical fashion, carried a frontispiece
which was a romantic sketch of a classical Greek setting.

If the uniformitarians were correct about the earth being much
older, it was natural to ask if the same were true about man on the
earth. Lyell turned readily to this problem and in 1863 published
The Geological Evidences of the Antiquity of Man. Here he presented a composite picture of early man which was in accord with the
uniformitarian view of the earth's antiquity. Of special importance
was evidence of primitive farming tools and weapons, such as arrow-
heads, found in strata long buried. This indicated man's appearance
on earth as coming many thousands of years ahead of earlier specula-
tions and contrasted markedly with literal accounts in the Old Testament. At the same time Lyell had provided a great deal of solid
material for those in the 1860s who were arguing for evolution. Lyell
was not a major developer of any aspect of evolutionary theory;
rather, he regarded himself as won over to the idea that all life forms
were evolving. He did not see how fossils really proved that changes
had occurred directly from one form to another. Darwin, however,
was to give Lyell credit for contributing to his own insights and most
geologists were to see their field as providing basic evidence for evolution. Geology had been a recognized area for scientific study since

1780, but Lyell's work, especially the *Principles,* gave it the formal organization and substance which has since characterized the field. Charles Lyell was the founder of modern geology.

Advances in understanding change in the earth as a whole were matched by new insights in physics and in chemistry. As steam engines became more common, the exact relationship between energy, work, and heat attracted many sophisticated minds, especially in Germany (Herman von Helmholtz, 1821–1894), France (Sadi Carnot, 1796–1832), and England (William Thompson, Lord Kelvin, 1824–1907). The high point of these investigations came at midcentury. In 1847 von Helmholtz announced the law of the conservation of energy, known as the first law of thermodynamics. This stated simply that the amount of energy existing was constant. This energy, as heat, could be changed into work, but whatever amounts were transferred, there was neither loss nor gain. On the heels of this came another insight, this one with frightening implications. In 1852 Lord Kelvin announced a second law of thermodynamics, a statement on the dissipation of energy. Although agreeing that the total energy would be constant, it held that in the conversion process some heat becomes dissipated, so that the resulting available total does not constitute an equal amount of useful energy. Since, therefore, heat is being lost, a gradual cooling of the planet is in progress and we may postulate an eventual lifeless, workless, and cold environment. These two laws caught the imagination of researchers, and late in the century extensive experimentation in thermodynamics yielded enormous quantities of data.

Modern atomic theory was largely formulated in the nineteenth century, though, of course, enormous refinements were made after 1900. In 1804 John Dalton (1766–1844) suggested that the weights of atoms of two elements could be computed by measuring the ratios of the simplest compounds of those elements. This led to a series of experiments with gases, resulting in 1811 in the molecular concept put forth by the Italian physicist Count Avograde (1776–1856). Molecular studies then flourished, with intricate chemical experimentation further yielding more sophisticated statements. Lord Kelvin remained in the forefront of these studies and in 1881 suggested that the diameter of an atom was between one ten-millionth and one hundred-millionth of a centimeter. Many of these new researches shared a concern with the phenomena of heat, energy, and patterns of movement; an important by-product of this research was the new field of organic chemistry. It was an age of exhilarating new discoveries; every decade made clearly defined advances.

A field of special progress was the study of electricity and magnetism. Many men contributed new information but probably Alessandro Volta (1745–1827), Hans Oersted (1777–1851), and André Ampère (1775–1836) were best known early in the century. Electricity and magnetism had previously not been thought of as belonging to a common area of study. Michael Faraday (1791–1867), however, brought this work to its fruition, and thereby gained a solid reputation as an ingenious experimenter. He produced the first electric dynamo, which opened the way to electric motors and a host of other inventions. Lord Kelvin was also active in these researches, as was James Maxwell (1831–1879), who put the new knowledge into its precise mathematical language. His 1881 *Treatise on Electricity and Magnetism* defined in fundamental equations the final development of electrical theory.

As the century wore on, chemistry became an increasingly productive field of research, with atomic studies making particular progress. John Dalton was largely responsible for the essential statement of the unchangeable nature of the atom as it was to be understood for over a century. Two undramatic but important advances must be noted. Early in the century J. J. Berzelius (1779–1848) devised a system of symbols to represent the various chemical elements. Simple as this appears, it facilitated research by giving chemistry an exact and concise language of its own. Later, in 1869, Dmitri Mendeleyev (1834–1907) brought together the fruit of many researchers' labors by drawing up the periodic table. This was an arrangement of the elements in the order of their atomic weights. When presented in this fashion it became possible to predict the discovery of other elements and to note particular characteristics in the sequence; for example, every eighth was similar, and certain "families" of elements became apparent. It was a very mechanical procedure but focused new research productively.

The nineteenth century saw remarkable discoveries in the field of bacteriology. The relationship between disease and bacteria was demonstrated through painstaking laboratory work, especially that of Louis Pasteur (1822–1895) and Robert Koch (1843–1910). Pasteur carried on experiments in fermentation, which cast serious doubt on the widely held notion that life arose spontaneously ("heterogenesis") and at the same time suggested the existence of bacteria in the air. By altering the temperature he was able to stop the progress of fermentation in wines. He concluded that if such bacterial reproduction could be limited in wines, a similar control could be developed for disease in animals. He moved readily to the germ theory of dis-

Louis Pasteur. (Courtesy of Historical Pictures Service, Chicago.)

ease and thence to the development of a number of vaccines for a frontal attack on the whole spectrum of disease. Most dramatic perhaps was his vaccine for rabies. Robert Koch was among the first, following implications of Pasteur's work, to describe the bacteria responsible for anthrax, and Pasteur developed an appropriate vaccine. Koch also identified the germ responsible for tuberculosis and went on to other, less dramatic, contributions. The result of his and Pasteur's work was to pinpoint the enormous potential for human betterment to flow from bacteriology, with its strong reliance on exact studies in the laboratory.

In biology the most prominent figure was Charles Darwin, who received most of the distinction for giving a more solid foundation to the theory of evolution. His work and its impact will be discussed later, but here we should note his immediate forebears in evolutionary theory. In the eighteenth century, Georges Louis Buffon (1707–1788) came very close to a statement of evolution. He commented on how species might change their form and noted especially the role played by environmental change. His observations on evolution were couched in highly conditional language so that he would escape censure, but from a distance his message was clear. His ideas were largely intuitive and lacked systematic proof. Nonetheless, he was the director of Europe's largest zoological garden and had published an impressive *Natural History* which was filled with detail and noted significant cases of changes in species.

Following Buffon was Jean Baptiste de Lamarck (1744–1829), an accomplished botanist and geologist who stated explicitly much of what Buffon had implied. He produced a specific account of evolution based on what he regarded as adequate evidence. He accepted the uniformitarian notion of massive time spans as the context in which the changes in species occurred. He published a *Natural History of Invertebrates* (1815–1822) in seven volumes and a careful work on the *Fossil Shells of the Paris Region* (1825), where he demonstrated command of the scientific and naturalistic data required by his theory. Lamarck's main idea was that the environment pressing on an animal could promote its development in specific ways. His most famous example was of the giraffe forced to stretch his neck in order to feed on high leaves. Accustomed to this over a lifetime, the acquired habit or characteristic was handed on to the next generation by heredity. Species thus are not changed, but their appearance is altered. Lamarck was the object of strong criticism because he seemed to imply that a creature could change some of its attributes merely by willing it and by changing his habits. His theory was more open to question, however, on the matter of the inheritance of acquired characteristics.

While Lamarck was formulating his ideas, Erasmus Darwin (1731–1802), grandfather of Charles, was also speculating about evolution as suggested to him from his study of botany. Many of the major ideas developed by Charles may be found simply presented by Erasmus but lacking in the enormity of detail Charles was to bring to his expositions. For example, Erasmus wrote of the desire for survival, of sexual selection, and of protective coloration. Indeed, he was bolder than Lamarck in that he decided that species themselves evolved. Thus Charles Darwin had prepared and ready for his use a number of ideas which, though imperfectly explored, still were part of his cultural inheritance. His task to some extent was to decide whether the data he had acquired should be fit into the older framework and whether or not that framework should be itself altered. It was interesting that Charles Darwin recoiled from Lamarck's theory but was never specific himself on how the variations occurred on which he constructed his own theory. He readily adopted the uniformitarians' contribution of vast reaches of time but was disturbed by the second law of thermodynamics, which implied that the time available had not been nearly as long. Consequently, he modified later editions of his *Origin of the Species* to take this into account but never was at ease on the damage the second law suggested.

Other work in biology was equally fundamental, especially the research on plant and animal cells (cytology). In the 1830s the cell theory, wherein each cell comes from an earlier cell, was developed from work by a German botanist, Matthias Schleiden (1804–1881), and a German zoologist, Theodor Schwann (1810–1882). In 1844 protoplasm within the cell was identified as an area deserving of far more research. August Weismann (1834–1914), another German zoologist, made an especially important contribution by proving that the sort of acquired characteristic basic to Lamarck (and important also to Darwin) simply could not be transmitted from one generation to another. The work on the cell coincided with the work chemists were doing with the atom; the biologists and chemists both felt they had found a basic natural unit.

At the end of the century, publicity was suddenly attracted to the work of Gregor Mendel (1822–1884), who in the 1860s conducted a series of experiments cross-breeding peas. It was the most productive study of heredity to date and for the first time variations in a species could be explained. It was a major supplement to evolutionary theory and spurred many researchers to test Mendel's finding with other life forms.

While new knowledge about the world, its composition, and the intricacies of its make-up was pouring in, there was similar attention turned to the role of man's activities as a creature (once evolved) on the earth's surface. As in the pure sciences, new standards of accuracy were developed for the study and writing of history, or "scientific" history, as it came to be called. One man, Leopold von Ranke (1795–1886), at the University of Berlin, introduced the new values which constituted the beginning of modern historical scholarship. Its hallmark was the standard of rigorous and detached objectivity. The historian's task was to present the story of the past "exactly as it happened" (*wie es eigentlich gewesen*), without reference to the events and issues of the writer's own day. Religious and national apologetics and polemics were categorically to be dismissed as serious history, an enormous stride forward, and memoirs were to be seen for what they were, highly egocentric documents, to be used by the historian with great care.

More than any other historian Ranke was responsible for the emphasis on original documents which came to characterize historical

Leopold von Ranke. (Courtesy of Historical Pictures Service, Chicago.)

writing. Documents were of course to be carefully scrutinized and the techniques for this Ranke developed in the seminar, a teaching device which he was the first to employ for historical instruction. He traveled broadly in order to study documents in various archives and was the first scholar to use archival materials well. His was a pioneering venture in this regard and his study of Venetian ambassadorial reports was of special significance. The result of such attention to documents was an overemphasis on political and diplomatic history, simply because such records were most likely to be preserved in archives holding the documentary remnants of past official regimes. These records were not then well catalogued and were not freely open to the public. Merely to get historians to start systematic study of these materials was to put the writing of history on a more solid foundation.

As a writer, Ranke was prolific. In his long life he authored fifty-two volumes, all of a high quality. At the age of eighty-five in 1880, his health was still good and he started a *Universal History*. Of all his writing, this project attracted the most valid criticism, because the volumes relating to antiquity revealed that he had not kept up with advances in the area since his youth, and much work had been done in the interim. Ranke did not regard his first work as being of solid merit because it was based on printed works and not on documents. This was his study on *The History of the Romance and Teutonic Peoples 1494–1514,* a remarkable book revealing highly sophisticated organizational ability. His other works are all fine examples of the values he propounded in his seminar, where he trained a host of young scholars who themselves spread his methods to other universities in Germany and abroad. A history of the papacy and a host of national histories flowed from his pen, solidly establishing the new scientific history. Ranke's work was pleasant reading and his books found a wide market. His followers, however, were often lesser men, and the dry-as-dust historical monograph, freighted with abstruse documentary citations, came to stand in many minds for the scientific history of Ranke, an unfortunate perversion.

As a practicing historian at the University of Berlin, Ranke was exposed to its bewildering swirl of intellectual ferment. He found special interest in the educational reforms of Wilhelm von Humbolt and in Hegel's ideas on liberty. Trained in philosophy and well read in Thucydides, Livy, and Herodotus, he also was influenced by the work of Edmund Burke. Keenly aware of historic and philosophic traditions, he probably did not understand the potential for profound change which science and technology were generating in his own day. Mass popular movements and economic forces play a small part in his studies, for he closely followed his documents, which were heavily political and diplomatic. These materials failed to suggest intense passions. Lord Acton criticized him for allowing such slavish reliance on documents to blind him to deep emotional drives. Men were both better and worse than Ranke's documents allowed him to present them. Prussian patriots and nationalists generally rebelled at Ranke's objective cosmopolitanism; other critics insisted that objectivity was simply impossible.

Despite the validity of some of these criticisms, especially of his vaunted attempt at objectivity, Ranke certainly came as close as any of his critics to meeting such an exalted standard. Further, he formed some clear conclusions from his historical study. He was emphatic on the role of ideas in history. These ideas, or intellectual forms which were generalizations from observed reality, clearly existed and moved men. Examples of this were nationalism, Protestantism, and liberalism. The historian could be expected to describe these ideas and their working but not to judge them. Some ideas, he believed, were dangerous and the historian should point out that a concept— for instance, popular sovereignty—could threaten the stability of virtually all of Europe's governments. He believed that there was a moral force acting in human affairs. His work had a vaguely religious nature; he could not prove a divine will directing things but he did see many imperfectly understood forces at work. States for him were intellectual entities and creations of the human spirit. National character is developed by people in contact with other peoples, and although no people should attempt to live by and for itself alone, each should safeguard its own individuality. People have their personality from their association with their particular group and the wise statesman will know the history of his state. To Ranke, the great man was one able to give substance to existing tendencies. These were surely interesting insights and were restrained at a time when intemperate action was being advised on every hand.

Ranke's impact was enormous. The German historical seminar became famous and was widely copied in Europe and the United States. Although perversions of his methodology quickly developed, he had marked the procedures by which more rationally accepted accounts of the past could be obtained. A major tribute to his achievement is the observation that his career spelled the death knell to the widely ranging type of philosophic writing which could trace human history in a few bold strokes, as Hegel did in noting the progress of liberty or Marx did in noting history as the story of class struggle. After Ranke, speculators had to be more limited and pay far more attention to what was now a more solid knowledge of the past.

CHAPTER 27

Portents
of Another Age

It was virtually inevitable that a towering intellectual figure like Hegel would evoke some opposition and reaction. Although in his own day he had far more disciples than critics, the very spurring of the formulation of alternatives was yet another Hegelian contribution, albeit indirect. A case in point would be Schopenhauer's stubborn insistence on his own variety of idealism.

Another major philosophic position formulated partially in deliberate revulsion against Hegel is the work of Sören Kierkegaard (1813–1855), a profound Danish thinker. Kierkegaard was not a professional philosopher and presented his ideas in essays written in Danish. Consequently, much of the corpus of his thought went unnoticed for decades. Ludwig Feuerbach (1804–1872) studied portions of his attack on Hegel; but, by and large, his ideas had little direct impact until the twentieth century, when his writing became the seminal statement of modern existentialism. This perspective on life, which has proved most attractive since 1900, was formulated as an attempt to explain the author's reaction against many of the forces and conventions of his own time. Widely acclaimed Hegelian idealism was merely one element against which he was in rebellion.

To an unusually large degree Kierkegaard's philosophy was rooted psychologically in his own alienation from society; it speaks volumes about the changes in Europe that his lonely perspective should attract such an enthusiastic following a half century later. The son of a businessman, he grew up in the stern and somber environment of Danish Lutheranism. In a moment of illness and great emotion his father explained how he had once cursed God. This confession implanted in the youth the sense that Christianity was a great moral testing ground where one sought salvation from a wrathful God. In 1841 he incurred social disgrace when he broke off an engagement to a vivacious girl some twelve years his junior. Essentially introverted, this humiliating experience made him melancholy and even more inner-directed. He believed he had made the proper decision but obviously society disapproved. He turned to writing, especially essays, in which he examined the role of personal decision in human affairs, making this central to the development of his philosophy. By giving emphasis and special value to decision, he at once became an opponent of any writers supporting determinism, the most recent and well known being, of course, Hegel. The loneliness of social censure, combined with a personality already overwhelmed by awe of God's wrath for those who erred, led Kierkegaard to try to demonstrate that his actions were proper; he was an introvert trying to explain his condition. Life was a hard and emotionally trying experience and he desperately wanted to make the proper decisions so that he would avoid hell and arrive in heaven. The mood of much of his writing may be seen from the following titles: *The Stages on Life's Way, Either Or, Fear and Trembling, Sickness unto Death,* and *Died Young and Miserable.* To these should be added *Philosophic Fragments* and *Concluding Unscientific Postscripts* for a brief listing of works containing the outlines of his basic philosophy.

For Kierkegaard, as for many philosophers, attention to a few definitions is crucial. *Truth,* for example, does not mean simply "that which is in accord with the facts" or "what is objectively real"; instead, it is what is *subjectively* grasped. *This subjectivity is activity on the part of the subject* and is especially grasped when one makes a decision. *Reality, or existence, is, then, subjective activity;* this is all a person can *know* to exist. The more passionate existence comprises intense subjective activity, engaged in when a difficult choice or decision is to be made. We know and grasp this kind of subjectivity; all else is mere phenomena that are outside our area of subjective knowledge and that exist as uncertain symbols which we experience as sense data. Only in decision do we grasp and experience certainty. Here is reality and we live it; in making a decision we choose between alternatives, neither factually overwhelming. We choose on faith because there is objective uncertainty and in this decision our very being is being torn in opposite directions; we experience intense passion and pain. The moment of decision is one of intense existence—we exist and we know we exist.

There can be no such thing as an existential system, because existence means decision and is forever changing and incomplete. Kierkegaard maintained that a logical system might be possible; but only for God alone, and such a system would be beyond human apprehension. Hegel's system he found especially illogical. In trying to understand Christianity, Kierkegaard oriented it toward his insistence on the reality of subjectivity. Christianity offers an individual eternal happiness and assumes the possibility of choosing to accept or reject it, but acceptance is not easy. He rejected traditional proofs of God's existence. To accept, he argued, requires intense and passionate subjectivity. "Christianity is spirit—spirit is inwardness. Inwardness is subjectivity. Subjectivity is essentially passion, and in its maximum an infinite passionate personal interest in one's own happiness."

In his discussion of the moral qualities of human life, Kierkegaard was penetrating and his ideas impressed a number of twentieth-century theologians and novelists. A world where problems of loyalty to one's church and nation became ever more pronounced, where belief in ideologies conflicted with national requirements, or where patriotism required acts of formal illegality, seized on existentialism, with its praise for acts of passion which found their justification within one's own self rather than in a pronouncement of society. German socialists supporting their nation's war effort in World War I were in this position, as were members of various undergrounds fighting Germans in World War II. Similarly, the Christian whose nation asks that a man take the life of another may face such a choice. Although Kierkegaard wrote to explain himself, many since his day have seen their problem in his.

Another nineteenth-century writer whose work was enormously important for the twentieth century was Auguste Comte (1798–

1857). He enjoyed considerable prestige in his own day, but his analytic powers were less substantial than those of Kierkegaard. Comte was much impressed by advances being made in the sciences, and like intellectuals a century before, he believed in the extension of scientific methods into all phases of human life.

Auguste Comte. (Courtesy of Historical Pictures Service, Chicago.)

Comte was basically a social reformer, a liberal who believed in science, education, and enlightenment. He published his ideas in pamphlets, but especially in the *Positive Philosophy* (six volumes, 1830) and the *Positive Polity* (four volumes, 1851–1854). He saw vast changes taking place and he speculated about how society might be altered to take advantage of the new knowledge being produced so rapidly. From his study came the definition of the positive position in philosophy, the foundations of sociology, and a humanistic but nontheistic religion.

As a philosopher Comte returned to Hume, generally disregarding Kant's effort to solve the problems raised by Hume. He accepted

Hume's critique of causation and used it to attack traditional theology and metaphysics. His comment on Hume was that Hume simply pointed out that we lack certainty about the world. Nonetheless, the positive content of science remains. One should merely recognize the limitations of what science really is and that it does not give us knowledge of the world beyond our senses. However, science does justify the prediction of the future course of sensory objects with a high degree of probability. This is the only knowledge possible, but it is positive and it is adequate for our purposes. Carefully extended, this knowledge will solve most of our problems; we need merely to remember that this knowledge is description and not explanation. Science is an empirical statement, telling what rather than why. Data can be collected about humans and societies as well as falling bodies or chemicals and so the behavior of people and societies can be scientifically pursued. Statements of uniformities can be made; humans are merely more complex subjects. Essentially there is no difference in the type of study; consequently, broad, general laws of society and history may be devised. Indeed, a science of society and history is possible.

As Comte looked at human history, he detected three major stages. The first stage was theological; the world was explained in terms of anthropomorphic spirits, social organization tended to be militaristic, and leadership was often personal or by class. The second stage was metaphysical. This began in the Middle Ages and amounted to a depersonalizing of the first stage. Here forces like nature and natural law came into being; politically, bourgeoise society is organized about such abstractions as the rights of man. In the third stage, the positive stage ushered in by Comte, science unencumbered by useless and deceptive beliefs records regularities and offers predictions but does not speculate on ultimate questions. Society would be based on the findings of the science of sociology which would produce the laws of social behavior, a fitting climax for this new field which Comte saw as the cream of the sciences. Man's freedom is that, with these insights, he has to a large extent the possibility to control himself and his environment.

Comte then proceeded to outline what the general social pattern would be in the new society. Progress to him was the increase of large-scale organization, because this demonstrated intelligent cooperation over a wide area. In such organization, an equilibrium exists, because opposing social forces (conservatism—liberalism, egotism —altruism) have been balanced, with a resulting maximum of peace and productivity. Education will make people realize the value of large-scale organization. In his society he describes three general categories of people. Besides the commoners there are the new patricians, an aristocracy of leadership comprised generally of bankers and businessmen, whose virtue is that they are experts in large-scale organization. His highest class is that of the new priests. These are the experts, intellectuals, scientists, educators, ministers of the positive church, and above all, sociologists. They are the real shapers of public opinion and policy and they have great prestige but low incomes. All will follow their advice, because all are properly educated.

This was an optimistic vision but Comte believed it was practical. He argued that to implement it would require an interim period of dictatorship when positivist intellectuals would introduce the details of the new system. Such a dictatorship would respect civil rights and be a period of peace, rather than violently revolutionary, because changes would be genuinely willed by the people and would be in their interest. Comte thought such a time had come when he heard of Louis Napoleon's *coup d'état*, but he was quickly disillusioned.

The Comtean humanistic religion of humanity was replete with symbolism and rituals and was designed mainly as an educational device to promote attitudes supporting the new society. From this evolved a number of ethical-culture societies and a twentieth-century humanist movement. Hardly a profound thinker, Comte embraced progress and the scientific developments of his age; he by-passed the whole area of fundamental truths. His was a practical and optimistic message, or as he would say, a positive program.

The last half of the century produced another philosopher whose major impact, like Kierkegaard's, came well after his own life span. Friedrich Nietzsche (1844–1900) also resembled the father of existentialism in that the germ of much of his later attitudes may be seen in the circumstances of his youth. He came from a religious family and was sent to Pforta, the Eton of Prussia. Here the supreme values centered on military drill and athletics. The young Nietzsche, however, was physically weak and a poor athlete; consequently, he developed a marked inferiority complex. He was, however, a brilliant student and excelled in Greek, Latin, and grammar. He recognized his own intellectual superiority and developed a hostility for the brand of Christian instruction he was offered, a rigid, gloomy, and dogmatic Lutheranism. He came out of Pforta with a hatred for Christianity and an admiration for sheer power, for Greece, and for early Greek tragedies.

Two specific incidents in his early life also contributed to his respect for power. His own inabilities were emphasized when he was thrown from a horse. In 1870, the most his military aptitudes justified was service in the medical corps. From this vantage point, however, he was able to see a charge of Prussian hussars. He found it a thrilling and inspiring sight, an expression of the will to power, a phrase he was to make famous. His writing was inspired and emphasized feeling, as Kierkegaard did passion, in an interesting change in philosophy after the lofty and often ponderous logic of Kant and Hegel.

Nietzsche was a brilliant writer and his credentials as a man of letters were imposing. His philosophy was presented unsystematically in a series of works. Like many philosophers he admired the Greeks, but unlike the others, the Greeks he esteemed were those of the early fifth century, men of instinct and passion, examples of the Dionysiate principle. He criticized those usually revered, especially Socrates, who wrought what Nietzsche regarded as a great disservice to humanity by his insistence that it was better to submit to injustice than to commit injustice. Nietzsche was persuasively dogmatic and more poetic than logical, as may be seen in *Human All Too Human, Thus Spake Zarathustra, Beyond Good and Evil,* and *The Will to Power.* In these works he argued against the values of Christianity and democracy, the twin evils, he believed, that were promoting the decay of civilization. He saw aristocratic values in danger of being destroyed because they were being leveled to the plane of the common man. He issued a warning to Europe's aristocracies and gave them an emotional argument for their own existence. In Nietzsche the declining aristocracies found a satisfying justification to resist reform and to retain their power. After 1900 he was the fashionable topic of conversation in German high society, an intriguing reassertion of *ancien régime* values and an argument against democracy, socialism, communism, trade unionism, bourgeoise liberalism, and other threats to Europe's then crumbling social order. His language also proved suggestively potent after World War I, when fascism arose. His was an interesting reaction against many forces of his day, but in seeking to understand the implications of evolutionary theory, he was as advanced as any in his generation. In 1889, his creative powers were cut short and for the last decade of his life he was insane.

Nietzsche's major contribution was his insight that life is not merely a struggle for existence. The will is really a will to power. The basic characteristic of the life force is to extend its control over its environment and other living things. A living thing continuously discharges its strength; persons freely take risks as the will exerts itself. Life, properly understood, is a striving to control, a will to power. This will to power was as important a contribution to thought as Schopenhauer's world as will and idea; but even more significant was Nietzsche's presentation of its implications in history, where he coupled it with evolutionary theory and his hostility to Christianity.

As Nietzsche presented the human record, the Jews and Christians were responsible for a transvaluation of values. They had condemned and substituted for the true values of a master or ruling class the attitudes of a slave class. Some early Romans, early Greeks, and early Jews possessed the energy and conquering vitality of a master race, but their values became distorted as their prophets performed a grotesque miracle by successfully propagating the idea that the superior values were those of humility, meekness, mercifulness, and long-suffering. These are slave attitudes. The most extreme case of this perversion Nietzsche claimed could be found in the teachings of Christ. Christianity, with its slave morality, thrived because most persons in antiquity really were slaves, or virtually so. When their overlords were also taken in, then the slave morality was imposed on all Europe. A measure of the extent of the disease may be seen when rulers speak of representing the people and of "serving" the people. Man had been brutalized. Instead of being aggressively proud, he was reduced to the position of a pigmy with rights, spouting praises for democracy, freedom, security, diligence, and happiness. In the nineteenth century such development was progressing at an appalling pace and unless something was done by those believing in the nobler values, democracy and socialism would continue the pell-mell perversion of human possibilities. What was needed, he claimed, was for Europe's aristocracies to reassert themselves. They were the carriers of the truly high virtues and had for centuries been responsible for whatever real progress man had made. Another transvaluation of values was now needed, to redress the damage done by the Jews and Christians. All this inflated the egos of the aristocrats, who had earlier been justifying their privileged status because of service, an essentially slave idea. The Nazis later were attracted by some of Nietzsche's vocabulary, but they did not like his failure to laud service to the state, and they were also disturbed by his praise of individualism.

Nietzsche's metaphysic was a blending of the ideas of progress, evolution, and a garbled understanding of the science of his day. His doctrine of eternal recurrence provides the general background for his discussions of leadership and ethics. According to this doctrine, the whole course of the universe must repeat itself in cyclical fashion. He postulates that the world is eternal becoming; for him, the idea of creation is meaningless. He also limited space and force (or energy) and stated that because time is limitless, the dispositions of force must repeat themselves. To the weak and the unhappy, to life's failures or slaves, this is a shattering idea; but to the strong and successful, it is encouraging. He has reduced hope for the poor and boosted the morale of the rich and powerful.

In this cyclical view of life and experience, the striving for power continuously goes on and mankind is gradually moving upward (despite the transvaluation!). At every stage there are always free spirits who are preparing the way for the superman (*Übermensch*), or man of the next stage. These are prophets and forerunners who keep mankind from degenerating. The free spirit expresses to a high degree the will to power and values things accordingly. The free spirit has a different sort of moral code; indeed, traditional morality began with the herd and the herding animal and reflects a slave mentality. The free spirit operates according to a higher morality for a select few. This is not to be judged by intent or consequences, but by the extent of it as an expression of the will to power. Self-sacrifice is folly and should be set aside, as should be deep prejudices regarding the truth. Also to be abandoned is a feeling of dependence and loyalty to others. All of this added up to a master-race ethic which could be ruthlessly imposed on others. The master group would have special privileges, which it both needed and deserved. Christianity worked against the conditions leading to the superman and, if left unchallenged, would turn men into brutes, a complete violation of human destiny suggested by the cycles of evolution.

Many details of Nietzsche's scheme were open to question but his language was highly suggestive. In the will to power, a solid contribution to philosophic thought, and in his master race, his *übermensch,* and the special moral code for free spirits, he gave history some slogans and expressions which the Nazis turned to their own purposes. The introverted boy who admired the physical prowess that he himself lacked became the man who gloried in the will to power so evident in a cavalry charge. It was the age of blood and iron and unifications by force, of advanced races meeting clearly inferior races in far corners of the world. In Nietzsche, an evolutionary view of the world presented a picture of life where power, nobility, and independent action were enshrined.

While Nietzsche was glorifying the use of force and Bismarck was employing it, the world of music produced Richard Wagner, whose work personified German nationalism so effectively that his chords found their way into Nazi programs and propaganda films half a century later. As a technician Wagner's accomplishment was much like that of Karl Marx, whom we will subsequently discuss. He took forms that his predecessors and contemporaries had developed and produced his own eclectic product. Although the contributions of others were only vaguely disguised, his work had a distinct and impressive quality. His was a martial and ponderously effective nationalism, and perhaps the finest example of how music could be put to the service of a militant romantic nationalism.

Wagner owed an enormous intellectual debt to two major composers, Berlioz and Meyerbeer. From Berlioz he absorbed the capacity to produce vast orchestral productions, and he readily borrowed extensively from his model's work. From Meyerbeer, a talented German composer who made impressive contributions to French grand opera, Wagner learned the techniques of staging, the coordination of music and lyrics, the musical setting of a scene, and the meticulous concern for the entire impact of the production.

Wagner emphasized the integration of music, poetry, and action to create a total program. Even more than Meyerbeer he did most of the work himself. He experimented with orchestra, often dividing it so that the soloist could create a different effect. He felt free to improvise, all in the name of the integration of several forms of artistic expression. The fact that the various arts he was dealing with (music, literature, theater) had unique characteristics which often made their blending awkward did not deter him. He proved to have unequal talent in these areas and he would have regarded it as a sign of failure that in the twentieth century, his productions are usually presented in truncated form. One of his favorite central themes was that a wicked soul can only be saved by the love of a pure woman. Ironically, extra information was often required in the program to get his intellectual message across to the audience. This was a problem which Berlioz never had, because he was working only with music and the moods it could create. As Wagner produced his multiple arts, he assumed the heights of a creative genius and a Wagnerian cult shortly developed. Appropriate to a romantic view of genius, he was a difficult associate and managed to criticize and to quarrel with many who had been initially impressed with his work, including Berlioz, Meyerbeer, and Nietzsche. His relationship with each of these three was a fascinating encounter between men of talent and insight. His break with Nietzsche was particularly symbolic, because the philosopher had been especially attracted by the musician's loneliness in trying to weld together disparate art forms. The figure of the genius at work, driven by his art, had an epic quality which Nietzsche appreciated. Ultimately, however, he decided that Wagner's art was mostly ersatz and that a great talent was really catering to popular impulses of the moment. Despite his difficult personality, Wagner did a great deal to popularize the opera, and the orchestra especially received a new importance in operatic productions. His was a fresh and vitalizing influence and his opening of the Festival Opera House in Beyreuth in 1876 was a major event in the history of music.

Johannes Brahms. (Courtesy of Historical Pictures Service, Chicago.)

Another German composer of the same period was Johannes Brahms (1833–1897). By the mid and late 1800s many flamboyant artists were exploring new types of scales and new theories of chord connections. In this environment Brahms was a symbol of tradition and conservatism. Conscious of romantic tendencies and at heart warm and sensitive, he found, nonetheless, that he could express these attitudes within the strict classical forms already established for symphonies, concertos, piano pieces, or songs. He was a prolific composer of music of a high quality, his greatest work perhaps being his German Requiem of 1868. Though he enjoyed wide recognition in his own lifetime, he was singled out for criticism by followers of Wagner, who decried his lack of experimentation.

The result of the careers of Wagner and Brahms was that there appeared to be a special vitality and quality to German music. This was, of course, a pre-eminence which could be associated with Central Europe for over a century, but late in the nineteenth century it served to stimulate an interest in the musical abilities of other nationalities. Nationalism in music was hardly new, but now it received unprecedented attention, with many clearly recognizable national schools appearing, another legacy of the nineteenth century.

CHAPTER 28

Additional Dimensions to the Century's Intellectual Life

The intellectual vitality of nineteenth-century Europe can hardly be understood by only considering the growing sophistication in philosophy, music, social and political theory, and the sciences. At a lower level a dynamo of ideas was in ferment. Practical and non-philosophic criticisms of institutions abounded, and rising literacy and educational levels stimulated even greater traffic in ideas. Many episodes occurred which, lacking continentwide or even national impact in themselves, cumulatively were symptomatic of altered conditions and contributed a new tone to European life.

Two interesting developments in religion typify the diversity of new developments. The Oxford Movement in England, had it occurred two decades earlier, would have been branded as sheer ro-

365

manticism. This was, however, more of an intellectual than an emotional phenomenon and its romanticism consisted mainly in its sense of appreciation for an aged and historic institution, the Catholic Church. The most prominent figure in the Oxford Movement was John Henry Newman (1801–1890), but scarcely less important were John Keble (1792–1866) and Edward Pusey (1800–1882). These were the most active of a group of Anglican clergymen who believed that their church needed a revitalization. Centered at Oxford, they wrote and preached learned praises of medieval Christianity. Keble helped to initiate the movement with his *Christian Year*, published in 1827. Six years later he gave a memorable sermon entitled "National Apostasy" which outlined the specific objects of the new reformers. An interesting intellectual movement, it caused the Anglican clergy, as individuals and as a body, to reconsider its faith and practices. A storm of sermons and pamphlets supported and attacked the new critics, often called Puseyites or Tractarians (from their writing in *Tracts for the Times*).

In harking back to the Middle Ages, they took the position that essentially the Anglican church was a development from the Catholic Church of that era. Indeed, it was not a Protestant church. Accordingly, they argued, Anglican ceremonies and doctrines should be as much in accord as possible with those of Roman Catholicism and Greek Orthodoxy. This in effect was a denial of much of the character of the Reformation in England and naturally drew the ire of many clergymen. Their critics regarded this as an obvious scheme to "Romanize" the Anglican church, which to them was properly Protestant and anti-Papal. A traumatic moment came in 1845, when Newman and a number of his followers left the Anglicans to join the Roman Catholic Church. Newman had decided that to remain Anglican was heretical and really meant furthering religious schism. It was an obvious implication of the whole Oxford Movement, though a majority failed to follow Newman's example. Employing brilliant prose, Newman argued that Christ's Church was an infallible guide. In Catholic circles he rose rapidly, becoming a cardinal in 1879, and his beliefs about the importance of ceremony and the medieval Church led to a strengthening of Catholic forces.

Among the Anglicans, Newman's ideas continued to be aggressively promoted by Pusey. The Anglicans experienced a sort of religious revival but in its renewed vigor, this church took on three distinct characters. Those following the Oxford spokesmen supported a church very similar to the Catholic in its ritual and sacramental structure, even with a version of transubstantiation. Rooted in a pre-Reformation view of their faith, these became known as "high church." Those who rejected the Oxford leaders and insisted on the less ritualistic and the distinctly reformatory and evangelical character of their faith as a Protestant movement were known as "low church." There also developed a "broad" church made up of believers concerned mainly with reaching an accommodation between religion and science, hoping that the emotional and comforting context of religion might be retained and at the same time accepting science, with its appearance of obvious truth. The over-all result for the Anglicans was a new vitality at a time when materialism increasingly posed a threat to all faiths.

In France the Catholic Church was also the scene of a reforming and renovating effort, the foundation of Liberal Catholicism. This became a movement espousing social democracy through a program to protect workers by factory legislation and the founding of labor unions under church auspices. Anticipating some of the ideas of Leo XIII, the movement was one of ferment and frustration in France between 1825 and 1860. We have already noted how the agitation and romantic writings of Lamennais eventually attracted papal censure. His most distinguished follower was Charles de Montalembert, who became uncomfortable when his ideas progressively found a smaller audience. Somewhat like the utopian socialists, they were perhaps in advance of their times, stubbornly unrealistic, irritated that their recommendations were not more avidly accepted by those in authority.

Lamennais accepted the ultramontanism of de Maistre but assigned to the Papacy a new mission. He insisted that the Pope should assume a special sort of jurisdiction over all men, granting such rights as freedom of the press and education. He would in effect put monarchs in the service of the Papacy, hardly a practical idea in the 1820s, especially when conservative monarchs apprehensively regarded freedom of the press as reflecting the republicanism of the French Revolution. In a trip to Rome in 1824 Lamennais tried to persuade Leo XII to assume greater leadership in promoting democratic principles but received little encouragement. The regime of Charles X also refused to cooperate in such a program and Lamennais found himself opposed by the leaders of the Gallican clergy.

Believing that ultimately the Papacy would have to adopt the cause of peoples against governments, Lamennais enthusiastically supported the idea of political revolution in France, Poland, Italy, and anywhere that democratic principles appeared to be served by the defiance of authority. He founded *L'Avenir* to promote his ideas of Catholic democracy and its articles made explicit his opposition to the Gallicans. Both he and they appealed to Rome for support. In 1831 Lamennais and Montalembert traveled to Rome to present their case to the supreme pontiff, now Gregory XVI. Lamennais could hardly believe that the Papacy would refuse to accept the sweeping authority he suggested, but the Pope supported the Gallicans. In *Mirari vos* he condemned the values of Lamennais. It was a severe blow and Liberal Catholicism as a movement was stopped abruptly in its growth.

Among workers the effect of Lamennais' failure was to plant a sense of futility and skepticism regarding religion. The Church appeared unconcerned with their plight, because the Gallicans were so oriented toward upper-class interests. Lamennais, however, had had an unrealistic view of the Papacy's position in Europe. The Pope was largely beholden to the reactionary secular governments whose denial of freedom of the press, conscience, and education Lamennais was criticizing; consequently, the Pope was hardly in a position to promote his program. A clergy close to the workers was an intriguing idea to many in the lower priesthood; and in their ranks Lamennais' impact was substantial. While Newman was asking religion to harken back to the Middle Ages, Lamennais would have it come to grips with nineteenth-century problems of social democracy.

Few intellectuals promoting equality and freedom were more emphatic than the philosophic radical we have mentioned earlier, John Stuart Mill. His doctrines were yet another reaction to the ferment of change and, coinciding with a massive growth of liberal strength in England, were impressive for their flexibility. Liberty for him was a matter of sheer utility rather than an inference from natural law. His *On Liberty* (1859) was a calm and logical explanation of why and how governments should promote individual liberty. Indeed, personal liberty should be so rigorously protected by government that it could only be interfered with in cases of self-protection or threatened harm to others. There was no playing on emotions or appeal to historic institutions in his writing; rather, his were sober, commonsense arguments.

In his considerations of economic life, Mill combined a laissez-faire approach with some sympathy for collectivism and government control. He argued that because wealth was produced by natural laws over which man had no control, in this area there should be *laissez faire,* though he did question the idea of the sanctity of private property. However, the distribution of that wealth was different. Distribution took place through institutions devised by man, and these were capable of changing their goals and of being subverted. Therefore, regulations were appropriate and even necessary to assure fair working of the distributive process. Collectives or cooperatives might be instituted in the interest of fair distribution and a maximum of social utility. He believed further that workers might form unions. The Reform Bill of 1832 was not broad enough for Mill, who wanted all men to have the vote. The role of women and children in industry disturbed him and he urged that they be protected by legislation. While he accepted the basic position of the classical economists, he favored pragmatic adjustments to assure the most utility. A gospel of progress rooted in classical economics, it was thus a flexible utilitarianism and attracted support among intellectuals of the middle and upper classes, despite his emphasis on democracy, which was offensive to many.

The rapidly changing scene to which Newman, Lamennais, Mill, and others were responding was characterized by an almost bewildering display of inventions. These were often the practical result of scientific advances, and in this form the general public frequently became aware of the creative work being done in the laboratory. The expositions, the first held in 1851 at London's Crystal Palace, were effective devices introducing new gadgetry to an interested and curious public. Technology flourished as never before and, in industrial development, helped to create the social issues disturbing thoughtful intellectuals.

In the nineteenth century the whole process of inventions became the object of intensive study, especially in German universities and technical schools. The organization and application of new knowledge received high priority with the result that inventions became a product, the volume and nature of which could be predicted and controlled. Knowledge became professionalized and categorized systematically, with rigorous well-defined programs of study to assure the careful training of new workers in the disciplines. The amateurism and romantic coincidence of talent and inspiration characterizing invention before the industrial revolution gave way to the orderly pursuit of rational procedures which produced new gadgets and inventions in great numbers. This tapping of nature's secrets buttressed a materialistic view of the world and contributed to the steady erosion or disintegration of romanticism as an acceptable and coherent outlook on life. As the century progressed, romanticism became fragmented and more divorced from the work-a-day world. Living conditions clearly underwent rapid alteration, especially in urban areas, as the flood of inventions continued. Science and technology were achieving a liberation of man comparable to the freedoms promised in the French Revolution. The idea of progress appeared justified, especially in the second half of the century, and the mood in scientific circles was one of heady optimism.

In medicine the discoveries of Pasteur and advances in cellular theory found immediate application. Especially important was Joseph Lister (1827–1912), who brought modern standards of cleanliness to surgery. Lister was particularly concerned about the infections which seemed to develop after each case of surgery. When he learned, in 1860, of Pasteur's ideas about bacteria being in the air and of the germ theory of disease, he concluded that the infections probably came from outside rather than from within the affected area. Carbolic acid was used to control sewerage odors, and Lister guessed that this chemical might also kill the bacteria causing the infection. He sprayed the wound with the acid, as well as the operating room, and treated bandages in a carbolic mixture. The result was a near elimination of surgical infection. This, combined with the development (in the United States) of anaesthesia, led to a drastic reduction in deaths from surgery. With the patient quiet and protected from the full force of the shock to his system, the surgeon could work with more care and deliberation. The operations were thus more efficient, and with postoperative infections avoided, recovery was speeded.

Based less on an understanding of science than on administrative study and an incisive common sense was the work of Florence Nightingale (1820–1910). Forever to be associated with the suffering of the English army in the Crimean War, she instituted modern nursing practices and made nursing an honorable calling. It speaks volumes for the neglect of the sick before her time that she could renovate nursing by insisting that a nurse's main responsibility consisted of "the proper use of fresh air, light, warmth, cleanliness, quiet and . . . diet." She noted that ventilation was not necessarily the same as cold air and also that the night air should not be dreaded. Indeed "pure night air from without" was to be preferred to "foul night air from within," a choice people seldom made correctly. She combatted the lack of cleanliness and sanitation while insisting that nurses be considerate, efficient, and selfless in their ministering to patients.

It was appropriate to the age that Florence Nightingale received her chance to demonstrate her methods from the public concern over the casualties from illness and neglect publicized in the press. Armies had been suffering appalling losses from disease from time immemorial but now a public press duly informed the people of these losses—10,053 Englishmen died from disease alone in one seven-month period, an appalling indictment.

As the century wore on, and the wonders of medicine and technology appeared to fulfill the wildest expectations of believers in progress, a disturbing aspect of the early decades of the century continued and became even more pronounced. The grimy circumstances of life near the factory grew worse and far more extensive with the general growth both of population and of industry. While the marvels of the age were evident, it was only to be expected that those not sharing in them were to be objects of pity, evoking strong humanitarian sentiments condemning the circumstances responsible for their lot. Socialists, of course, flourished in this environment, but also there appeared some impressive critiques authored by writers comprising a naturalistic and realistic school.

An interesting critic was John Ruskin (1819–1900). Much of his career was given over to art criticism, where his work established new standards. He argued that art presented the attitudes of the artist and reflected the spirit of his age. He also helped to popularize Gothic tastes. Gradually he came to consider social and economic problems and to criticize strongly the society about him. Ruskin especially indicted the factory system for creating sheer ugliness. It had made the world a horrible place, fit for animals but not for men. His prescription was unrealistic for the enormity of the problem but still had some results. He concluded that men should return to medieval concepts of craftsmanship which put a premium on a man's creativity. His indictment was deserved but his answer reflected an idealistic view of the Middle Ages. He reasoned that man must work, for to live without work was inherently wrong; however, work without taste or art was merely brutality. A sharp critic of the barren aesthetic nature of worker existence, his efforts led to support for an arts and crafts movement which, ironically, flourished outside the world of the deprived and impoverished.

William Morris (1834–1896) echoed some of Ruskin's ideas. He too found a grim sordidness in a society where the factory system could warp men's souls. He wondered if the concept of beauty had been lost, and if it had been, whether it could be restored to a world which had forgotten it. His answer also emphasized individual performance in arts and crafts. An amazingly talented man, he dabbled with radical socialism, promoting a sort of anarchism without violence. He wrote poetry and was a passably good painter. He was also a printer, a bookbinder, and an importer of tapestries, stained glass, and furniture. He did a great deal to popularize an interest in crafts, though like Ruskin, those he reached were mostly not living in the factory slums.

In nineteenth-century literature there was a particular interest in revealing life as it was, which resulted in an outpouring of "realistic" and "naturalistic" writing that also encompassed the appearance of the psychological novel. Throughout, the seamier side of human nature was laid bare as well as the corrosive effects of money and poverty. These literary developments by no means replaced romanticism, which continued, perhaps its most powerful proponent being Victor Hugo. Hugo's pen, however, ranged vigorously over a variety of subjects; he was an eloquent iconoclast and waxed lyrically and powerfully against literary tradition. A sheer romantic with a powerful command of language, he was neither an analytical thinker nor a careful social critic, although he embarked on all sorts of emotional tirades and some of his writing was very close to crude propaganda. Hugo took sides in the topical issues of his day, but his emotional involvement (as in *Napoléon le Petit*) often blunted the force of his position. The realist, on the other hand, tended to pay so much attention to the accuracy of the situation he was drawing that his own personal feeling, though often clear, was considerably muted.

In Charles Dickens (1812–1870) Britain produced a skillful author who centered his attention on the lower middle class and the workers. He tended to make his characters either cruelly inhuman or morally pure, villains or heroes, and he was guilty of maudlin sentimentality. His comedy lacked urbanity or subtlety, but he was a potent critic of corruption, stupidity, and a range of social abuses. In *David Copperfield* and *Hard Times* he was at his best.

Victorian realism at its most potent appears in the novels of Thomas Hardy (1840–1928), who, despite living well into the twentieth century, completed his career in fiction in 1895. His was a powerful indictment of society and the way in which persons appeared to be trapped by their environment. His workers and peasants were starkly realistic and the somber crudeness that his prose evoked cast a pall over the buoyant optimism which the idea of progress had created and new scientific and technological developments seemed to promise. Hardy's message seemed a negation of this hope which was planted by the publicity of expositions and newspapers. He was a sobering reminder that the lower classes were living quite different lives from those of the prosperous.

Across the English Channel, French literature also came to portray vividly the grimy side of factory life. While Hugo continued his thunderous perorations, Honoré de Balzac (1799–1850), Gustave Flaubert (1821–1880), and Emile Zola (1840–1902) were distinguished authors establishing different traditions in French letters.

Balzac's major work, the *Comédie Humaine,* was a whole series of separate works which provided different views of French society. Most concerned with portraying members of the bourgeoisie, his view of them was most unflattering. With elaborate detail he described the life of the middle class, finding its members greedy, self-centered, ignorant, and obnoxious. He carefully placed his characters in a complex environment which tempted and molded them. His accounts were peopled with many villains but there were few heroes, and he was unable to describe generosity or love with the verve and effectiveness so apparent when he was portraying greed and hatred.

Gustave Flaubert was a different sort of realist. Like Balzac he found the bourgeoisie and their values revolting; but unlike Balzac, he believed an author should labor to keep his own prejudices out of his writing. *Madame Bovary* was his finest work. A careful stylist, he excelled at presenting the hopes and passions motivating ordinary people. He had a romantic streak which broke forth from time to time and was pronounced in *Salammbo,* which was filled with pictorial richness. Even Madame Bovary, whom he drew with detailed care, was a woman driven by romantic notions. In short, his realism was contrived in its stylistic excellence and modified by romanticism. Emile Zola was a realist who rigorously examined his subjects in order, like the scientist studying his data, to discover basic laws in human experience. More a naturalist then a realist, he saw man buffeted and brutalized by forces of nature which knew no favorites. Man had become little more than a slow-witted brute; again the indictment of the evils of industrial development are explicit. Zola had clear sympathies for the working classes. He regarded the rank exploitation of labor as a practice ignoring an enormous potential for good which underlined the human price being paid for progress. *Germinal* was one of his major works and its realism evokes compassion for the lot of the miners whose grimy labor was essential for modern society.

Elsewhere in Europe writers were producing similarly realistic works. The German dramatist Gerhart Hauptmann (1862–1946), portrayed in *The Weavers* the wretched living conditions of weavers in Silesia, as he understood them from tales of his grandfather told to him by his father. His was a masterful portrayal in that the picture of economic exploitation is presented so vividly that the audience is drawn into a mood of both sympathy and irritation at their circumstance. The indictment of this brand of capitalism is clear. His heroes are unheroic victims of an inhumane system which turned stolid, good citizens into a roaring mob. Skillfully written to produce an atmosphere of horror and fear, its final pathetic note is one of despair, because there are no prospects of improved conditions. This play was a devastatingly effective piece of social criticism.

Feodor Dostoyevsky (1821–1881), perhaps the most perceptive of Russian writers, created the psychological novel. His work, of which the finest probably was *Crime and Punishment,* was profoundly moving. A victim of four years in Siberian exile among criminals, he described human degradation and the requirements to overcome one's evil. Bestial and cruel instincts and the Russian character generally are laid bare; he finds relief possible through intense suffering, the degree of suffering matching the intensity of the evil. It was a new type of realism.

Another variety of realism was apparent in the dramas of Henrik Ibsen (1828–1906). Ibsen was a blunt critic of hypocrisy. His plays centered about individuals becoming caught in society's web and their attempts to work out their destiny, in the process keeping or losing their right to respect. Business success resulting from deceit in dealings with others he carefully probed in *Pillars of Society.* A believer in personal freedom, Ibsen was concerned about the strictures placed on women in society. Attacking the temptation to follow public opinion, his incisive critiques exposed the moral price often exacted of people trying to live in modern society.

The story of cultural achievement in Europe must include the progress of literacy and education among the middle and lower classes. During the century the world of ideas and taste rapidly expanded beyond the comfortable confines of the aristocracy and was indirectly promoted by the growth of industry and the expanding middle class. The Church and its priesthood had earlier been a device for presenting knowledge to the public, but now other possibilities opened up. Serious music could be heard by the general public at concerts, and various festivals and performances were priced low enough that vast numbers became exposed to nonreligious compositions of the finest quality.

The development of railroads was of major importance in introducing urban ideas to residents of small towns and villages. The impact of the expositions on the thinking of the lower classes is impossible to gauge completely, but it can hardly be overrated.

Special trains to London (1851) and Paris (1855, 1867) carried millions of ordinary people to see the marvels which education could produce. Six million people, for example, attended the Exposition in 1851.

Public education markedly expanded in nineteenth-century Europe and was highlighted by the growing republicanism in France and the 1867 Reform Bill in England, which led to the Forster Education Act of 1870. A basic element both reflecting and promoting the popular educational level was the newspaper press. In Britain it has often been presumed that newspapers made their impact on the lower classes during the 1880s and 1890s as a direct result of the Education Act. In these decades a number of inexpensive papers appeared and flourished, but newspapers for the masses in England were much older than this. The newspaper, in the first place, was an eighteenth-century development, a device by which businessmen engaged in commerce could keep informed. Along with magazines and periodicals, the newspaper came to be a thoroughly middle-class institution. Of all the newspapers in England, *The Times* was the most prestigious. From 1816 well into the 1830s a number of efforts were made to create a working-class press. These failed but the idea of a Sunday paper did catch on. It had a wide lower-class circulation, which reflected its radical politics and the popularity of its special features, such as novels, almanacs, gory reporting, and ballads. After 1840 special Sunday editions managed to outsell even *The Times*.

A newspaper was a normal part of a reform movement. The Chartists had their journalists writing for a working-class readership. In Paris there were in 1848 a plethora of short-lived and underfinanced journals directed for the most part at the lower classes. Technological developments in printing and rail circulation made it possible to print larger editions and to sell them cheaper. Major urban centers thus were able to communicate their values over a broad area; at the same time, a healthy provincial press developed. From all this it was clear that literacy among the lower classes, especially in cities, did not uniformly await a comprehensive educational program. A popular press, of course, was an earmark of democracy, especially when accompanied by legislation supporting press freedom. It also pandered to unsophisticated tastes; but for all that it was a great cultural medium and brought a modicum of real education to many people.

During the entire century there was a continuous European cultural impact on other areas of the world. Areas owing an allegiance to a European state naturally shared access to the mother country's cultural, social, and political development. Canada would be an example of this. The United States was also closely attuned to literary developments in Britain, mainly because of common language. The British, of course, exported their culture wherever they claimed new lands during the race for colonies late in the century. In this regard they differed little from other imperial powers. The French cultural impact in Algeria and later in Equatorial Africa provides another example. Even the Belgians planted much of their culture in the Congo. The missionaries were of special significance as transmitters of European civilization to non-Europeans.

There were other interesting examples of the exportation of European civilization which were not accompanied by colonization or political control. In the eastern Mediterranean a substantial French cultural impact stemmed from the business ties of France with Egypt and the Levant. These ties dated from 1799 and were stimulated by the French Syrian expedition in 1860–1861. In Palestine there developed a small island of Germanic culture as a result of the short-lived Anglo-Prussian Jerusalem bishopric.

In South America there was an interesting admiration for France and some of her leaders. The figures of Simón Bolívar and Napoleon Bonaparte were epic examples of heroic leadership to the military in many South American countries. Despite a heritage of Spanish rule and despite growing trade connections with Britain and the United States, it was to Paris and French culture that the South American aristocracy frequently turned. The resurgence of Bonapartism under Louis Napoleon especially impressed them, and news of his fall at Sedan was received with a sense of shock by both the aristocracy and military.

The United States was fed throughout the century by a stream of immigrants from Western and Central Europe. The influx from England merely enhanced cultural attitudes already established, but the Irish brought with them their firm allegiance to Catholicism, allowing that faith to develop swiftly in hitherto largely Protestant cities along the Atlantic seaboard. Most other nationalities were less pronounced in their impact, but of major importance were two distinct waves of German immigrants. In the wake of the 1848 revolution, many German liberals fled Central Europe and found a sanctuary in the United States. They tended to settle in an area bounded roughly by Cincinnati, Milwaukee, and Kansas City. Most distinguished of this group was Karl Schurz. As a people they were hardworking, liberal, and avid supporters of excellence in education. They brought with them the tendency to form literary societies and

Kant groups and generally brought a high cultural tone to many communities in the Midwest. Their numbers were enhanced by another Germanic influx following the foundation of the German Empire, when Prussian regulations on conscription were extended to lands in South Germany and to new areas along the Rhine. This group was not the educated elite the earlier group had been, but its average age was younger and it was equally energetic. Between the two groups the German cultural contribution to American letters and values was substantial. They stood in marked contrast to many of the other immigrants, who were often unlettered masses of Europe's poor. Talented Jews from Eastern Europe were part of a later movement, along with large numbers of Armenians and Italians.

European civilization in the nineteenth century was vigorous at virtually every level. Striking advances in basic research were accompanied by an amazing technological vitality. Applications of knowledge wrought basic changes in the level of popular culture, much of it closely associated with the increasing size and power of the middle class. Growing literacy and rising living standards all promoted the vitality of European culture in general. At the same time, basic features of this culture were being exported, carrying European standards of morality, progress, and cultural excellence over the globe.

X

Change Through Violence

CHAPTER 29

Karl Marx and Charles Darwin

In Part VIII we noted that some liberal reform accompanied by a considerable amount of material progress occurred under the leadership of well-established governments. This orderly change barely covered an undercurrent of violence which boiled to the surface in 1848 and was afterward etched vividly in the recollections of many people. In this context it was natural that European society produced two brilliant men, both of whom accepted violence and sought to explain its proper function.

In Karl Marx, socialism became "scientific" and was set on a new course. Earlier socialists had felt humanitarian twinges when thinking of the grinding poverty which machines and the concept of private property seemed to bring. With Karl Marx the reaction was more a sense of moral outrage. His response was not to devise a

The Karl Marx family with Friedrich Engels. (Courtesy of Historical Pictures Service, Chicago.)

scheme to modify the suffering, but rather, almost to glory in deteriorating conditions, because these indicated the rapid approach of a more vicious and fundamental struggle. No sentimental believer in altruism as a means of alleviating suffering, he insisted that, from his study of history and philosophy and his basically realistic point of view, he had been able to discern the laws of historical change. The "Newton of the social sciences" had at last appeared.

Pre-Marxism socialists were well known for their carefully worked-out plans which were to bring better conditions for the laboring masses. Marx, however, had no such explicitly drawn vision of the good society. He had, rather, a "scientific" blueprint for historical development which assured the workers a better day. The label of "utopian" (rather than "scientific") does less than justice to the careful attention to facts which many early socialists exhibited. Indeed, the label could be applied to Marx himself regarding his unrealistic final historic stage. In his almost complete reluctance to admit logical errors, he was a sheer dogmatist. An energetic and abusive prophet with a closed mind, a far less attractive personality than any of the earlier socialists, his name and his doctrines came eventually to touch the lives of millions. His ideas as presented, developed, and misrepresented have become such a force in modern history that no astute citizen or statesman can afford to ignore them. It needs, however, to be fully recognized that in his name there have been many travesties of his ideas. This has been especially the case in the twentieth century.

Although Marx stands as a great watershed in the history of social and economic thought, the corpus of his philosophy was based heavily on the ideas around him in the 1830s and 1840s. Major elements came from the classical economists, supplemented by Hegelian insights which he had acquired as a student in Berlin. Marx may be regarded as perhaps the greatest of the "classical" economists. His was an eclecticism which borrowed heavily from English writers on economic theory, but he so arranged the constituent parts that the result was new and distinctly radical.

Intellectually, his debt to England was enormous. The English experience provided him with the most advanced example of an expanding capitalism. Its political decisions after the Reform Bill also resulted in a fund of detailed information about the system's most glaring failures. The very openness of English politics made available to any potential critic a mass of data, collected and published by Parliament. A major aspect of Marx's critique of capitalism, as distinct from previous critics, was that he could be so specific about the system's callous inhumanity. Previous theorizers—the utopians generally—lacked such precise information and could be more readily answered by defenders of the status quo. His more explicit drawing of the indictment against the bourgeoisie and their system goes far to explain the anger and frustration with which they reacted to Marx. He compounded their cause for anger when he argued that the forces at work in history were moving against them and then suggested the pattern by which they would be overthrown. Little wonder that Marx is a major figure in capitalism's gallery of rogues.

Besides using the data provided by the government to support his indictment of the system, he was also frustrating to the business aristocracy because of his open reliance on theories which they had accepted as virtually sacred. In the world of ideas, few (if any) Englishmen are more respected than John Locke. This seventeenth-century theorist found that the infusion of labor into land made the latter an extension of one's person, thus deserving of special rights of protection from unjust acts of a sovereign. The main thrust of Locke's remarks was concerned with limiting a sovereign, but this subsidiary point—the "labor theory of value"—continued as a generally accepted axiom. Debates among economic theorists questioned how to measure the value and the doctrine underwent a number of refinements. It was Ricardo's particular version which Marx borrowed, the concept that the labor required to produce an item was the true measure of its exchange value and that things had value only in exchange rather than in use. Arguing from Ricardo, Marx presented the worker as the basic creator of value.

As if this reliance on two English writers were not enough, he also accepted the bulk of Adam Smith's ideas. Supply and demand were real forces which were forever present and could be studied and predicted. He further added emphasis to another aspect of Ricardo, the iron law of wages. When he combined these in a package, buttressed with factual examples, the result was unique and especially tempting to persons who were hostile to the system. Applying the labor theory of value to manufactured items as well as land, he developed his theory of surplus value. The worker, who creates value in goods, is paid, because of supply and demand in the labor marketplace, for only part of the value he has created. The difference is retained by the manager and is as much an act of robbery as the unjust tax against property collected without the owner's consent. An overabundance of labor in this period of developing capitalism, of course, kept the price of labor low, thus assuring bare subsistence wages and the highest maximum "robbery" by the managers. Thus, with basic theories accepted by owners and managers themselves, Marx devised an explanation of economic history which painted them as the blackest of recent villains. He did concede that they had supplanted earlier exploitative classes which were worse. The bourgeoisie were the current class in control of the means of production; and Karl Marx explained to his own satisfaction how they were becoming ever more wealthy, thus separating themselves from the true creators of wealth by an increasing margin. The tendency was toward monopoly; eventually there would result a situation where the working class would achieve such a sense of identity and alienation from the rest of society that it would rise in revolution. This proletarian revolution would resemble the French Revolution in its violence and vitality. The dreaded connotation of mob violence which the French Revolution conjured up to most cultivated people served to make the figure of Marx anathema to those who were comfortable in the system. Marx was calling for revolution and the dispossession of the managerial classes to assure economic justice. In the name of morality he seemed to be espousing the rankest sort of social upheaval and murder. From the viewpoint of nineteenth-century liberalism, this was especially reprehensible because the men to be dispossessed (murdered?) were to be displaced simply because they had succeeded in their competitive situation. They were to be punished for success, which was shockingly immoral from a bourgeois perspective.

Karl Marx made an enormous contribution to the study of history. Most obvious was his insistence on the primacy of economic motivation in human affairs. Prior to Marx, there had been some concern for economic motivation, although it was usually not as central as other considerations. Thucydides remains a model of balanced historical writing in terms of the careful treatment of a number of different types of motives which account for human action. By his singleminded emphasis on the drive for gain, Marx forced a complete reconsideration of the known human record; in many instances, the result was a more careful and realistic explanation for the past. Social classes had been recognized before, but in economic terms Marx provided a useful and instructive method for understanding their emergence and continuing activity. After Marx any scholarly study of history which neglected economic considerations could not be regarded as adequate. This alone was a towering achievement.

Marx was a brilliant example of the person who expects to discover lessons from history which can be immediately applied. His theory of history presumed uniformity in human nature and motivation which, once understood, could be a guiding factor in one's immediate plans. Being an activist as well as an intellectual, he explicitly traced what the human record meant for the furtherance of social justice in his own day. His bold and almost ruthless prescription for the present and future particularly disturbed the holders of economic and political power. Had he not added a call and program of action to his ideas on history and economics, he would not have disturbed nearly so many people. Another aspect of his program which was regarded as dangerous was his insistence that the process of change would come from the working class itself. Previous reformers appealed to the upper classes to aid the less fortunate. The Marxist critique of this approach was that it was unrealistic because it depended on altruism; at best the result would be the degrading dole. Marx called his socialistic system communistic to avoid any possibility of being confused with previous and current socialists, who were distinctly "utopian" and not "scientific." His was a call of action to the lower portions of the social scale, an insistence that they dispossess forcibly those responsible for their wage slavery. Because he also wrote that workers in all nations had more in common with each other than with persons in classes directly above them, the Marxist position appeared distinctly unpatriotic in its insistence on international class solidarity. In this regard it should be noted that Marx was promoting at the workers' level the sort of international identity which was especially evident among Europe's aristocracies in the eighteenth century. Nationalism was the pervading force which countered both of these "internationals."

We have noted that the corpus of Marx's system was a vast eclecticism owing much to English antecedents. His synthesis was at the same time a particular intellectual triumph in that it brought together a number of currents which, to his day, had been moving in opposite directions. The rationalism of the Enlightenment had ignored the strivings of the human will to which the romantic period paid so much attention. The equality of the French Revolution only fleetingly escaped the strictures of a class orientation. The view of a universe rent with contradictory concepts was intriguing but under Hegel remained largely a metaphysical consideration. With a philosophical insistence on unity, Marx brought together these opposing concepts in a unified scheme, perhaps best described as "historical materialism." This eclectic synthesis was as unique a contribution as Immanuel Kant's earlier attempt to account for both ideas and objects but was far more laden with prospects for direct action. Marx created an action-oriented version of truth which carried a promise of economic justice for the first time in history.

The importance of Hegel in Marx's intellectual development can hardly be overrated. At Berlin Marx had been one of the "Young Hegelians," and in the dialectic he found a basic key to social action and organization. Hegel had also explicitly emphasized the importance of history as a key to the unfolding of the present, but he had not been especially rigorous in applying the dialectic to history. It was Marx who brought together the dialectical relationship of basic ideas as taught by Hegel with the historical facts of class-structured societies where the pursuit of economic gain put classes and individuals against one another. To the Hegelian vision of a world of clashing dialectical relationships, Marx added an emphasis on materialism, resulting in a world of "stuff" in conflict. Thus, the Marxian synthesis was based on a more rigorous view of history, on the most creative thinking in philosophic idealism, and on a vast array of specific data concerning capitalism in its most advanced stage. These made his socialism "scientific" and gave to his prescriptions for change a force which other alternatives lacked. His intellectual achievement was an awesome triumph and created a vast watershed in the development of socialistic thinking.

The name of Marx is most closely associated with the "Communist Manifesto" which, hastily written and propagandistic, contained the gist of much of his ideas. He also applied his new perspective to the revolution of 1848 in France, to Louis Napoleon's *coup d'état* in 1851, and to other current events. His analyses of contemporary issues and problems were particularly acute considering that he had no special or confidential sources of information regarding policy making. Possessing the temperament of an activist as well as a theorist, his early work was interrupted frequently by participation in various plots. He was especially active in the unsuccessful Rhenish disturbances in 1848. He was also delayed in his work by extreme poverty. Though he thundered against bourgeois values, he was a dutiful and responsible family man; while working on *Das Kapital,* he and his family lived under excruciatingly poignant circumstances. Undernourished and ever cold from the dankness of London's climate, he was saddened by the death of three of his children, including his only son Edgar. A lesser spirit would have been broken, and even Marx began to despair of completing his project. His emphatic dogmatism was also a handicap which complicated his study when changes occurred in English capitalism that did not fit his basic pattern. He was psychologically incapable of compromise and once his overall plan was worked out, he proved unwilling to moderate his ideas in the face of either logical arguments or sheer data. He finally completed the first volume of *Das Kapital,* but Friedrich Engels (1820–1895) was responsible for the publication of the last two volumes, which he compiled from scattered notes left by Marx at his death in 1883. Ironically, by the time his classic work appeared, it was somewhat superfluous. The world did not need *Das Kapital* to know the ideas of Karl Marx. Further, the work lacked the cohesiveness and unity which his overall position contained, characteristics which were obvious in the "Manifesto." Reflecting the influence of Victor Considerant, the "Manifesto" was sweeping and an improper vehicle for a detailed and scholarly presentation. In *Das Kapital,* however, there was no constraining influence and Marx appeared as a relatively undisciplined writer, allowing himself to digress and to be painfully repetitive. He presented a vast compendium of economic data which he had only partially digested and was most effective when indicating the evils that machine production seemed to encourage. Though he wrote of classes, his eye was on people; and the pain of one who has suffered comes into his pages as a burning moral indignation against the managerial elite and their spokesmen controlling governments. He portrayed a vitally productive system, controlled by essentially evil men whose immorality can be measured in the lives of squalor evident among the workers. He found no men of integrity in government service (a high sense of duty such as the Prussian bureaucracy was noted for was not a topic which he cared to write much about). Rather, he saw corruption and bribery on a broad scale. These he attacked, and was nearly incapable of criticizing another man's ideas without at the same time impugning his integrity.

For decades Marx lived and wrote in England; and, while he found there most of his data, he never became active in current labor movements. It was a significant period of developing trade unionism but Marx lived and labored in the company of other continental exiles and radicals. His great collaborator in England, Friedrich Engels, was similarly of German origin. Engels, at critical periods, gave money to Marx. He also helped to provide much of the "feel" for the actual conditions in the factories of England which Marx combined with statistical data and a historical perspective conditioned by Hegelian presuppositions.

After 1848 the most important organizational role played directly by Marx concerned the First International, as the International Workingmen's Association was commonly called. This organization tried to develop international solidarity among various socialist and labor organizations and was consistent with Marx's ideas. In practice it attracted English trade union leaders and a fair spectrum of radicals from the Continent. After extensive correspondence, the first meeting was held in London in September of 1864. Here, as in subsequent meetings, Marx was a forceful and intolerant debater who dominated the proceedings. His credentials for leadership at this point were questionable for the first volume of *Das Kapital* was still three years from publication. In this association he came face to face with other renowned social critics whose ideas were often as logically rigorous as his own and equally oriented toward goals emphasizing social justice. Marx had earlier penned a critique of Proudhon's ideas and now was publicly challenged by defenders of the famed anarchist. There were also contending principles put forth by men as disparate as Bakunin and Mazzini, besides spokesmen for other varieties of socialism. The legendary Bakunin was frankly anarchistic, whereas Mazzini thought in terms of an international society to further political revolutions. Such challenges served to bring out the most negative and combative elements in Karl Marx, and he ruthlessly bludgeoned all opposition to his own ideas. Marx was able to dominate the sessions and successfully opposed efforts by Mazzini to give the organization a strong and centralized structure. In arguing for a looser format, Marx alienated Mazzini, who dropped out of the International. The result was that social reform movements were encouraged to develop a national cohesiveness but not an international permanent bureaucracy. Bakunin, of course, was at the other extreme from Mazzini, and Marx equally combated him, formally driving him from the International during the Lyon meeting in 1872. Mazzini wanted republican states, Bakunin wanted states destroyed, and Marx wanted the states taken over by socialists. In this group of continental radicals and republicans, the English trade unionists were, to say the least, ill at ease.

The International met annually and considered a number of specific problems. The congress held in Geneva (1866), Lausanne (1867), Brussels (1868), and Basel (1869) voted on questions ranging from the issue of Polish freedom to communal ownership of major communications, such as telegraph, canal, and rail systems. The organization moved from the defense of labor on specific issues such as wage levels to an outright attack on the whole system of wages. Gradually it came to support the complete Marxian position on the class struggle.

The movement was too weak to have any direct impact on current affairs. The International approved of the Commune, but the fate of the Communards was as doomed as those of the earlier insurgents in Poland. To have favored the Commune, in fact, proved a mistake because it was far too bloody an example of defiance to be so lavishly praised; and many potential supporters were repelled. The main importance of the First International was its impact on the course of later socialism in Europe. Socialist parties grew rapidly, and in 1889 a Second International was organized. By the 1890s it was clear that Karl Marx's particular brand of socialist thought was regarded as representative, the German Social Democrats' Erfurt Program of 1891 constituting a model for socialist parties over the world, and debate raged over whether it should be accepted with or without modifications. Spokesmen for his position in later generations proved to be just as hard and intolerant of dissent, arguing just as vigorously for the inevitability of the class struggle and the social and political injustices stemming from private property. Marx had put his stamp on a whole ideological movement, ultimately affecting millions of people.

While Karl Marx was busily documenting and arguing for his version of social change through violence, England was also the setting for the propagation of another intellectual account for change which frankly accepted violence as a fact of life. The same society that tolerated the fiery socialist produced Charles Darwin (1809–1882), the scholarly writer who gave the theory of evolution new currency and support. Like Marx he was an affectionate family man but there ends the similarity in personality. Darwin could never have brought himself to match Marx in pouring invective on those with whom he might have an intellectual disagreement. His conclusions, however, were equally significant and, like those of Marx, appeared to be solidly buttressed with an impressive array of data. With Darwin as its Newton, biology became yet another science with explosive implications for modern man.

Darwin's work—and the development of his ideas—constitutes an interesting example of the interplay of concepts taking place in mid-nineteenth-century England. As a youth Darwin gave little promise of a career of much significance, to the despair of his father. He appeared unmotivated by his classical education or his subsequent study of medicine and religion at Edinburgh and Cambridge, respectively. He had shown some interest in science, and this led his professor of botany to arrange for his appointment in 1831 as a naturalist on the *Beagle*. A momentous episode in the history of ideas, at the time there was little to suggest the special importance of this combination.

The *Beagle* was a naval vessel, sent from England to collect information about the coast of South America. All sorts of information was to be gathered and accurate coastal maps were to be drawn, charting currents and depths. Then only twenty-two years of age, Darwin supervised the collection of thousands of specimens of marine life. During the five-year voyage his personal commitment to the study of various forms of life became fixed. When he was not seasick, his enthusiasm for his work was intense; and he gradually became curious about the relationships between various species. It was the continuation of this questioning which proved so fruitful after his return to England.

An interesting by-product of Darwin's work has been the special attention which historians have called to this voyage of the *Beagle*. The results of the expedition were enormous, but often overlooked is the point that this was but one of many such trips undertaken in the 1830s and 1840s. As records of the French Academy make clear, during the reign of Louis-Philippe, France was especially active in sending out exploratory missions. They ranged over much of the globe and had objectives nearly identical to that of the *Beagle*. There was great activity and concern with knowing more about distant places. Typical was a Belgian expedition in 1841–1842 into the interior of Abyssinia. Led by Blondeel van Cuelenbroeck, a diplomat who managed to turn up in a number of crisis situations (Constantinople prior to the Crimean War, Mexico during Maximilian, the Congo), this was a fact-gathering expedition, producing data on the flora and fauna of the region. What separated the *Beagle* from these other ventures was the later impact of Darwin's writing. The others had able collectors but only the *Beagle* had Darwin.

Back in England the young Darwin pored over his specimens, putting them in order. Unlike most other naturalists of the day, he tried to see the larger pattern in which his data had significance. As he pondered the variety of life represented before him, he decided that his evidence allowed him to question a time-honored doctrine called the fixity of the species. It seemed obvious that the species were in the course of great change and that this change was in the direction of progressively more specialized or differentiated characteristics. The pattern of change was from the more simple to the more complex, and if this was true for all his examples, might it not be true for all life at all times? This was a speculative conclusion he arrived at by meditating on his data and it is a fine example of how a great idea may arise. For Darwin the gnawing problem was to explain *why* and *how* the change occurred, after he had decided that it did occur. What was the *mechanism* of the change? To put the question in this language indicates an interesting perspective on the development of life in its many forms.

Darwin found part of his answer in reading Malthus' *Essay on Population*. Malthus was concerned with the problem of human overpopulation in terms of food supply. Darwin took up this general idea and applied it more widely to plant and animal life. Overpopulation clearly created a situation where a struggle for survival ensued. Those survived to procreate who were the *fittest*—thus through *natural selection* the *survival of the fittest* occurred. In this fashion characteristics not conducive to survival or having no special survival value tended to disappear. The fertility of both plants and animals assured a continuing struggle; thus the concept of fixed species was misleading, providing at best a temporary guide for a serious student. Progressive and constant change was apparent everywhere and the only real fixity was change itself. The struggle for survival made not only for progressive adaptation but also for great casualties. The struggle occurred between members of a species, between species, and also between forces of nature itself and the forms of life. The result was a situation of vicious struggle and the rule of the claw. It was the law of the jungle with violence on every hand—another version of progress through violence.

Like Marx, Darwin's achievement was largely to take current ideas and to put them together, with more raw data, into a distinctive new package. In Darwin's case, more of the ingredients were close at hand; thus, intellectually, his achievement shows less sheer brilliance than was the case with Marx. Evolution as a theory was old. It enjoyed a resurgence as part of the general acceptance of the idea of progress. Its most distinguished recent supporter had been Lamarck, whose explanations were based on the inheritance of acquired characters. Lyell's work had vastly extended the time during which change could occur, and serious thinkers had come to the point where evolution as a concept could be elevated in status if the notion of the fixity of the species could be shown to be false and a convincing explanation for continuing change could be put forth. Darwin had nothing to do with posing the general problem or with isolating its central issue. Darwin's formulation of natural selection occurred simultaneously with a similar explanation by Alfred Wallace, another naturalist. The classical economists had made commonplace the idea of a world in which humans competed, with the less able being driven to the wall. And Herbert Spencer (1820–1903) had developed a thoroughgoing theory of evolution by April, 1857, over a year before the ideas of Darwin and Wallace were first presented in a formal paper. Indeed, Spencer's theory, being more philosophical, was more inclusive, dealing, as he put it, "with the universe as a whole from gas to genius," whereas Darwin dealt only with organic evolution, which he claimed to treat "simply as a naturalist." Spencer had also given currency to the expression *survival of the fittest*. It was Darwin's particular formulation which the intellectual world was prepared to accept at the time; and, in contrast with Spencer, its very specificity seemed to provide the kind of certainty required when dealing with so serious a problem as undermining the concept of the fixity of the species. In a very real sense, Darwin was the man of the hour—his exact formulation seemed to be what his age wanted and was groping toward.

When his data and explanation seemed to sweep away the last

barrier to open acceptance of evolution, then a torrent of analyses of the theory's implications appeared. Many clerics were appalled at the simplistic notion that man had evolved from the ape and attacked the doctrine of evolution as being ungodly and contrary to Genesis. The debate took the form of a dichotomy between science and religion; heated disputes raged at the popular level while intellectuals generally regarded the issue as relegated to past history. On the strictly scientific level, it was not clear that Darwin's data really supported his conclusions; but the public seized on the social ramifications of the theory. Often labeled Social Darwinism, this became a profound new justification for the transgressions of men against their fellows which had been going on for centuries. Individually and in groups, the competition for survival was a continuing law of life with the "fittest" surviving to procreate. The weakest and poorest perpetually fell in a never-ending struggle. It was a blunt and direct recognition of the violence evident in international relations and in social and economic affairs. At the same time that violence was explained, an inference of confidence and superiority was also clear. Current survivors were clearly at the top of the evolutionary scale. The change forever going on was always to the more specialized and sophisticated—there was little hint of extensive retrogression—thus nineteenth-century society could look back to earlier ages with a sense of smug satisfaction. Progress, great expectations, and violence were all of a package.

Lest there be any doubt about the broader social meaning of evolution, many writers promptly alerted the public. Herbert Spencer promoted acceptance of evolution and placed it in a more cosmic context. Thomas Huxley eagerly publicized the theory and especially attacked the clerical opposition to the idea. In *Physics and Politics* (1869) Walter Bagehot explained how natural selection operated in the development of human history and in philosophy; and Friedrich Nietzsche placed evolution close to the center of his thought. The doctrine which appeared to be proved in the field of biology seemed readily adaptable to social development and was as important in the formation of attitudes late in the century as Newton's work was to the Enlightenment.

In Darwinian terms the ruthless and competitive exploitation occurring in the business world was perfectly understandable and indeed natural. In the relations between states, war was also normal and the Machiavellian policies of Bismarck were to be similarly understood as in accord with the basic law of life. Great decisions and advances occurred through "blood and iron," and statecraft was no profession for the timid or weak. Especially glaring were the implications of the theory for imperialism. Political and economic servitude was a "natural" consequence of a different level on the evolutionary scale because the most advanced cultures were those which had developed more sophisticated and superior weapons. There was little attention to Christian principles, which in contrast to evolution appeared both weak and impractical. Expressions like the "white man's burden" became mere covers for the rankest sort of imperialistic exploitation.

Romanticism continued through the nineteenth century and enjoyed a particular vitality late in the century. The role of the Great Man in history was an engaging theme, especially when seen in terms of evolutionary theory. Figures like Luther and Napoleon acquired an even more cosmic reputation than they had earlier enjoyed. Their great contribution was that by breaking up an established order—"breaking the cake of custom," as Bagehot put it —they made it possible for the race to make a forward step. Laws tended to fix people in place, so a fomenter was needed for the ongoing progress of civilization. Thus Napoleon was important for ending the Holy Roman Empire, which made possible the later formation of both Italy and Germany. And the upheaval of the French Revolution had made it possible for him to give France a whole series of enlightened domestic improvements. The nineteenth century remembered Napoleon Bonaparte clearly, and it had another such heroic type in Bismarck. Carlyle and others were publicizing such extraordinary men whose appearance could be neatly explained by evolutionary theory.

Darwin was obviously working with a cluster of ideas which had broader import than those of Karl Marx. Both brought significant insights and new data to bear on issues many other men had studied. Both were apostles of progress and both found a central role for violence. It was perhaps more fundamental in Darwin's work than in Marx's, though Marx was more directly attuned to the present and a segment of its immediate problems. It is interesting that these men expressed their ideas in a Victorian society which was accumulating vast wealth and where those in polite society lived more and more immune from the life of the jungle that Marx and Darwin described. After the passing of these two, the world of men could never be the same; their impact was as significant as the French Revolution.

CHAPTER 30

The Crimean War and Italian Unification

While socialism was suggesting alternate patterns of social organization and many of its proponents were advocating violence, the diplomatic structure devised at Vienna underwent a major alteration. The Crimean War opened the door to forceful changes in Central Europe and allowed the forces of nationalism, so long in fetters, to burst forth in a successful realignment of the international power structure.

The diplomatic precedents to the Crimean War comprised an intriguing and confused interaction of religious, economic, political, and personal ambitions—a situation well documented, well studied but still requiring caution and humility in trying to judge correctly the relative importance of the various factors leading to hostilities. A headlong confrontation of many sets of interests encouraged both boldness and caution in leaders, and the complexity of the issues almost assured that honest mistakes would be made and that honest intentions would be misunderstood and vilified. None of the leading statesmen wanted the war which, tragically, they all eventually felt compelled to fight in the unfolding of yet another phase of the Eastern Question.

The war grew out of a dispute between Catholic and Orthodox Christians over rights of maintenance and precedence in worship at common shrines in the Holy Land. The Sultan had a record of ambivalence in granting concessions to both groups, and over the years each had found an outside power to champion its interests. France had long been the spokesman for Catholic Europe, whereas the Tsar of Russia supported the Orthodox position. In 1850, Louis Napoleon authorized representations at Constantinople in behalf of the Catholic Christians of Europe; it was in direct response to this particular phase of the dispute that negotiations became entangled and eventually broke down. Louis then was continuing a French policy which heads of state in Paris had pursued spasmodically since 1740 and directly since 1819. Catholic treaty concessions dated from the Middle Ages, as did Orthodox rights. The Tsar's position was explicit in the Treaty of Kuchuk Kainarji of 1774 and was reaffirmed several times later. Thus both France and Russia had treaties designating them as spokesmen for the respective Christians and both put pressure on the Sultan for decisions in their favor. The Sultan, of course, could not have cared less about who worshipped when in Jerusalem, but he did not want to alienate either France or Russia. In espousing the Catholic cause Louis Napoleon was consciously performing yet another favor for Catholic interests within France while filling a traditional role of French leadership. His actions were not primarily intended to be anti-Russian, though in this context they could not be otherwise. It should especially be noted that he was supporting the Catholics of Europe in their position well before the Tsar gave his condescending recognition to Louis as his friend (rather than brother) Napoleon III. Also of note is the absence of Great Britain in the early talks regarding the Holy Places.

The British became a party to the negotiations because of long-standing interest in the power structure of the Eastern Mediterranean and because of extensive trade patterns and opportunities in the Ottoman Empire and in Russia. They were understandably unmoved by arguments between Catholics and Orthodox Christians. When the issue became, as it shortly did, the right of the Tsar to claim protective sovereignty over Turkish Orthodox subjects and especially when he occupied the significant wheat-producing provinces of Moldavia and Wallachia, then Britain's voice became among the most vocal in Constantinople. Finally, both France and Great Britain claimed they were fighting in behalf of Ottoman sovereignty, an interesting posture for two states who had aided the Greeks to break away from Ottoman rule.

The patterns of trade had encouraged a growing Anglo-Russian rift. Britain had declined as a buyer of Russian grain and shifted her purchases more to the Ottoman provinces of Moldavia and Wallachia. At the same time, a small but growing industry in Russia made that nation less reliant on British finished goods, and both states recognized a lucrative market in the backward Ottoman Empire. The business community in Britain divided between a policy which would come to an accommodation with Russia and share the Ottoman market, and an alternative which would pressure the Turk to keep Russian goods out and give Britain a virtual monopoly. Proponents of the first course urged a policy of cooperation and friendship with Russia; they supported Lord Aberdeen. The latter course had its spokesman in Lord Palmerston and his blunt anti-Russian policies. Although parliamentary and public opinion were behind Palmerston, Victoria's personal hostility to this minister kept Aberdeen in office and created a situation where it was difficult for outsiders, like Nicholas, to anticipate British policy. This ambiguous situation in London was compounded in Constantinople where Britain's spokesman was Stratford Canning, a sworn enemy of Nicholas (who years before had refused to accept him as ambassador at St. Petersburg) and vigorously independent of policy made in London.

Nicholas had often referred to the Ottoman Empire as the "Sick Man." Though the Russian Tsar had helped the Greeks to break away, he had taken measures supporting the Sultan against rebellious subordinates and had assumed a role much like a protector. Like most statesmen, Nicholas recognized the risks of war if the Sultan were unable to maintain domestic order; therefore in 1844, he talked with British leaders in London and came to what he regarded as an understanding: neither Russia nor Britain would act without consulting the other if a future Ottoman crisis were to arise. Ironically, in the disputes over the Holy Places, the Sultan temporized and appeared to yield, now before one, now before another, and finally followed Canning, who spoke with the most authority. It was a perfect illustration of the point which Nicholas had been stressing. The Turk really was not his own master. Indeed, in February of 1853, the Sultan had acquiesced to the demands of a special Austrian mission regarding troop locations and religious problems in Bosnia. Nicholas sent Prince Menschikoff to Constantinople on a special mission (March–May, 1853) which he saw as merely another version of the same procedure. In the past, blunt demands and threats yielded results from the Turk. Nicholas had just brought peace in a Danish dispute by a threat and a naval demonstration. Threats and force, after all, had just saved Europe from revolution and he regarded Anglo-French demands at Constantinople as nothing less than the forces of revolution at work. Napoleon wrote a personal letter to Nicholas hoping to dissuade him from rash action and received a reply commenting that if need be, Russia in 1854 would prove herself as worthy as she was in 1812. A proud man feeling a great sense of responsibility for the order of 1815, the Tsar was incapable of much compromise.

The Russian occupation of the provinces of Moldavia and Wallachia (July 2, 1853) was on a pretext which was provided for by treaty; but Britain, France, and Turkey claimed this was a violation of Ottoman sovereignty. Had she had designs on these provinces, Russia could, of course, have taken them outright in 1849, instead of occupying them for a time after crushing the 1848 revolution in Wallachia. Nicholas claimed that he now reoccupied them as a show of force to counter the dispatch of the French and English fleets to waters outside the Dardanelles, a device to strengthen Anglo-French diplomats trying to pressure the Sultan. In response to the Russian occupation, the British and French fleets entered the Black Sea in defiance of the Straits Convention of 1841. Hasty attempts in Vienna to mediate the dispute failed. Tempers flared when, on November 30, 1853, a decrepit Turkish fleet was sunk at Sinope by modern Russian ships; the British public was now ready to go to war. The friendly Tsar of 1844 had become the destroyer of freedom in Hungary and Palmerston's anti-Russian sentiments carried the day. Led by a prime minister who favored friendship with Russia, Britain went to war against Russia to support a Moslem power in a dispute with Orthodox Christians. She did this in alliance with Napoleon III, who proved to be in the most authoritarian phase of his reign. He was equally a destroyer of popular liberties; but he had at least a plebiscite to support his position, something which Nicholas, of course, would never have considered.

In light of the foregoing considerations war was probably unavoidable. Terrible errors of judgment were made during the drift toward hostilities which no major leader really wanted. The poor state of preparation of the major armies belie arguments that any leader plotted war. Neither the British, French, nor Russian army had been alerted for war. Both of the Turk's allies viewed her with contempt and distrust. It was a fateful and tragic course of events.

France and Great Britain became formal allies of the Ottoman Empire on March 12, 1854. Committed now to war to defend Ottoman sovereignty, the two historic enemies signed a military alliance on April 10, looked to their armies, and began joint planning. They assumed that the Russians would quickly cross the Danube and soon be outside Constantinople. This presumption of easy mobility against the Turks underlaid all early Anglo-French planning, which centered on how to save the Ottoman capital. The Russians proved unable to take Turkish fortified towns south of the Danube and thereby threw off the estimates made in London and Paris. The Turkish army was far better than the allies had estimated for they gave too much priority to precision on the drill field. French and British errors about the Russians and the Turks were matched by equally erroneous estimates of their own forces which were shortly to embark to "save" Constantinople. Britain had not fought a serious war since 1815 and her military engagements were managed in the colonial office. The army Britain now fielded was woefully outdated; in effect, it was Wellington's army without Wellington. Many of the men and even the cannon had been at Waterloo. Its officer corps was aged; its generals were veterans of the war against Napoleon I; and the chief engineering officer, Sir John Burgoyne, had been in uniform since 1789. The British commander-in-chief was Lord Raglan, a nephew of Wellington's who had lost an arm at Waterloo and thereafter had held a desk job. The whole force was antiquated and poorly organized.

The French army was that of Louis Napoleon's *coup d'état* of December 1851, and its commander was Marshal de Saint-Arnaud, who had been war minister at the time of the coup. His supporting officers had survived the personal loyalty requirement and all bore the stamp of the Algerian campaigns. Far younger than their British counterparts, they looked on themselves as hardened soldiers and on their allies as amateurs. The British officers regarded them as rabble because they were not of the titled aristocracy. It was difficult to evaluate the French experience in Algeria, because they had not really encountered a fully armed foe. Many observers were skeptical about the outcome when two such questionable armies met Russian forces. Russia's army seemed impressive. She enjoyed a reputation for being a vast artillery power. Under Nicholas, however, the army had progressively atrophied, and although it had been equal to the task of subduing Hungary, it now proved to be inadequate against a determined foe.

When the allied armies arrived to defend Constantinople, the Russians were still barely south of the Danube, a circumstance the allies had completely unforeseen. The French, who had landed at Gallipoli, now marched to Varna and were joined there by the British. At this point interminable discussions produced little action and many petty disagreements. Meanwhile, the Russians recrossed the Danube and abandoned the principalities. This action had followed an Austrian threat which left Nicholas feeling betrayed and deserted. Indeed both Austria and Prussia formally assumed neutral positions, but in this context Austrian neutrality was an anti-Russian act, and when seen in light of Russia's recent service for Austria in Hungary, it was truly close to betrayal. Had Austria been an active Russian ally, a limited war probably would not have resulted.

With the Russians neither facing the allied force nor endangering the Ottoman Empire, the need for the war was gone, but the armies were in the field and there were clamors for "victory." Saint-Arnaud was in poor health, but when he had insisted on having the command, Napoleon had not the heart to refuse him. The Marshal wanted a great victory and so he supported the idea of an invasion of the Crimea, where the enemy, as he put it, would not be able to flee but would be forced to stand and fight. The allied armies invaded the Crimea on September 14, 1854, with the expectation that after one engagement they would enter the great naval fortress of Sebastopol and the war would be over. There were, all the while, unbelievably confused supply arrangements for both the British and French armies, an aspect of the war which grew progressively worse. Saint-Arnaud was partially correct in that the Russians did elect to fight, and on September 20, the battle of Alma occurred. It was the victory Saint-Arnaud had craved, but shortly afterward he gave up the command and died at sea en route home. The Russians retreated and began feverishly to erect fortifications outside Sebastopol, at the same time sinking ships in the harbor entrance to prevent allied naval shelling at close range. The British and French now gathered around the perimeter of the city and on Burgoyne's advice began an enormous buildup of ammunition to sustain a protracted period of shelling. On October 17, they began the artillery bombardment, intended as a preliminary to assault. To their amazement they discovered that Sebastopol's defenders were more than able to match their firepower. The Russian commander in the city was Todleben, the only soldier to earn a solid military reputation in the war. The assault was canceled; for the first time, the sober reality was faced that they had to spend a winter in the Crimea. Further, they were on the barren heights and the enemy had civilized shelter.

The hardships of winter turned the British and Russian supply services into a shambles. The French were somewhat more fortunate because of their Algerian experience, but it was a difficult period for ordinary soldiers in all the armies. Military activity was limited to spasmodic cannon fire while everyone worried more about the day-to-day problems of keeping warm and getting enough food. The Charge of the Light Brigade on October 25 was an appropriate testimonial to the level of much of the leadership. The poor supply situation led to scandals in London and the fall of Aberdeen's ministry. Palmerston finally became prime minister and began an avid search for mercenaries. Sardinia entered the war on the allied side with her expenses paid by Britain, who had great difficulty in attracting enough men to the colors. Recruitment of special forces went on in Switzerland and various German states. The British were very conscious of numbers because the French provided many more troops, manned a substantial share of the British trenches for them, and on occasion even gave them rations. This made it embarrassing to insist, as the British did, on an equal voice in decisions. Popular feeling in England was turning against the war; more and more Englishmen felt that Britain had been hoodwinked by Napoleon. Ironically, in Paris there was grumbling that the British tricked the French into fighting their war and that it was getting too expensive.

When the war settled into a stalemate, Napoleon III grew impatient and suggested going to the Crimea to take personal control. This appalled everyone, especially his aides, who saw their personal positions jeopardized if he were killed. The British reacted instinctively against the idea of a Bonaparte at the head of an army. He was dissuaded but insisted that his tactical suggestions be tried; after all, he fancied himself a military authority from his studies at Ham. He resorted to explicit telegraphic instructions which sorely tried tempers and loyalties in the Crimea.

While the struggle continued, sporadic diplomatic talks were going on in Vienna. At the death of Tsar Nicholas, the prospects for a peace settlement became more encouraging. It lacked only a dramatic victory to save everyone's face, and if Sebastopol would fall, that would be adequate. The Russian defense had been sufficiently heroic that the Tsar could negotiate with honor, and the allies could discuss terms now that they had achieved their objective of taking the fortress. Statesmen all recognized the opportunity for peace, but to their frustration the fortress continued to resist attack. Finally, on September 8, 1855, the allies mounted a furious attack which succeeded. The city fell and the psychological conditions for peace were complete. The Malakoff, a key bastion, fell to the French and made the rest of the city indefensible, but the British had been repulsed in their sectors of the attack. They resented the glory claimed by the French but had not the heart to argue strongly for continued war. After some desultory expeditions against minor points along the Black Sea coast, the war came to an end and a peace conference was held in Paris in 1856.

This war, which was so lacking in military brilliance, had enormous diplomatic repercussions, barely hinted at in the terms of the peace. The neutralization of the Black Sea was agreed upon, and a decision on the status of Moldavia and Wallachia was deferred. Neutral rights during wartime were clarified in a series of regulations. This was a real contribution to international law, because Prussia, Belgium, and Sweden especially had encountered some perplexing conflicts of interest during the struggle; and regulations specifying just what was, and was not, an effective blockade, for example, were sorely needed. The question of safe navigation on the Danube was turned over to an international commission. Russia relinquished territory at the river's mouth and in Bessarabia. A more crucial point at Paris was the formal admittance of the Ottoman Empire to the concert of European powers, thus correcting a major oversight of the Congress of Vienna. Nothing was stipulated about Catholic and Orthodox rights regarding Holy Places, although Russia did give up her claim of protecting Christians within Turk lands. Meanwhile French, British, and Austrian diplomats had drawn up a program of liberalization for Christians who were Turkish subjects and pressured the Turks to accept it. This made clear the citizenship duties and privileges of the Christians but did not reflect decisions regarding Catholic or Orthodox priorities in the Holy Land. Many of these specific points at issue had ironically been settled during the Menschikoff mission before hostilities had begun.

Important as these considerations were, they pale in significance compared with other aspects of the situation. European international stability had been maintained for forty years through the cooperation of the major conservative powers, Russia, Austria, and Prussia. These "Holy Alliance Powers" had managed to keep the structure designed at Vienna fairly intact despite minor alterations. The crucial relationship between Austria and Russia was severed during the Crimean War. Despite Russia's aid in crushing Hungary, Austrian interests in the Balkans had increased and she viewed Russian activity in this area with suspicion. Adopting an understandable but shortsighted view during the war, Austria desperately tried to stay neutral, partly to save money and partly because she was apprehensive about Russian claims regarding Christian subjects within the Ottoman Empire. Despite the brilliance of her generals, she had not been able to control Hungary without outside assistance and now she had forfeited the expectation of ever receiving that assistance again. In remaining neutral, Austria had given the signal for her own potential disintegration, an obvious point to statesmen at Paris and to her restive subject populations. The Sardinian spokesman at Paris, Cavour, was disappointed in not gaining the duchy of Parma as a reward for helping the allies, but he did persuade Britain's Lord Clarendon to make a blunt and scathing indictment of Austrian influence in Italy. As A. J. P. Taylor has observed, the stake in the Crimean War was Central Europe. Austria's diplomatic isolation was an open invitation for renewed nationalistic movements in that area.

Besides this, France could claim to have broken the system of Vienna. A Napoleon in alliance with Britain had defeated Russia; France had become the dominant power on the Continent. The reforming Tsar needed his army at home, creating a situation where for nearly two decades Russian troops were not to be a factor in dispositions in Central Europe. A moderate Franco-Russian rapprochement took place toward the end of the war and extended until the Polish Revolt, a further encouragement for France to be more active in Central Europe. Napoleon III was at the apex of his prestige; and, but for the pressure of circumstances, seemed prepared merely to enjoy what he had achieved. In the immediate wake of the war, he embarked on no new international schemes and did nothing to correct deficiencies which combat had revealed in his army. As a leader of France, he had succeeded beyond his dreams; and his empress, Eugénie, had provided him with a son, so that the dynasty seemed assured. Unfortunately for his peace of mind, Austria's isolation was too inviting to Italian nationalists and Napoleon had made too many statements about some day doing "something" for Italy. Men and events now plunged him on a downhill course.

Count Camillo Cavour (1810–1861), Sardinia's premier, had concluded from talking with Napoleon that under the proper conditions the French Emperor would aid Sardinia in a war against Austria. He also concluded that although the British would not openly give help, neither would they allow Austria to crush Sardinia completely. Thus, Cavour felt safe to prepare for yet another Sardinian effort to expel Austria from Italy. The Countess Castiglione (Cavour's cousin) was sent to France to have an affair with Napoleon so that she could keep reminding him that Italy needed help. Cavour pursued a policy of studied insolence regarding Austria, deliberately goading them to war while building up his army. All this attracted volunteers from the rest of Italy and gained the cooperation of other leading Italian nationalists such as Garibaldi and Daniele Manin. Mazzini refused to help and continued in his own fashion to plot sporadic and unsuccessful insurrections. Napoleon remained sympathetic but some catalytic event was needed to rouse him to more active participation.

Such an event occurred on January 14, 1858, when Felice Orsini almost succeeded in assassinating Napoleon and the Empress. His bombs killed or wounded nearly 200 persons and the imperial couple were shaken by their brush with death. At his trial and in letters to the Emperor, Orsini so eloquently stated the case for Italian freedom that Eugénie was moved to admiration. She now began to involve herself in diplomatic questions and slowly came to realize that Italian independence and papal secular power were nearly incompatible. Eugénie argued passionately for Orsini's life to be spared, but the counterthreat of resignation by the Emperor's ministers if he were not executed made Napoleon carry through the death sentence. Ironically, at heart Napoleon approved Orsini's cause and allowed wide publicity for the conspirator's pleas for Italy. French protests were delivered to Turin and also to London, where the assassins had completed their plot. Although Victor Emmanuel brusquely refused the French protests, his bluntness created a favorable impression on Napoleon. Napoleon now began to consider concrete ways of helping "Italy" and he arranged a private conference with Cavour in July at Plombières. Many historians have presented Napoleon as duped by Cavour into a committment to liberate Italy. In fact, Cavour's role was very nearly passive. The French Emperor clearly laid out his intention to aid in expelling Austria from Italy, and he stipulated his price. He discussed how he thought Italy would be organized after Austria was driven out. He had no intention whatever of unifying Italy. Cavour was thinking more in terms of a greater Sardinia than of a united Italy. Unification came as a consequence of subsequent events, but it was not a stated intention at Plombières.

While Cavour listened, Napoleon was explicit in his proposition. He judged that it would take 300,000 men to expel Austria from the peninsula and he was ready to provide 200,000. For this he expected the province of Savoy, and possibly Nice, and that his cousin, Prince Napoleon, would marry Victor Emmanuel's fifteen-year-old daughter, Clotilde. Besides an extension of French influence in Italy, Napoleon envisioned a loose Italian confederation of four states—the Papal States and the Kingdoms of Naples, Central Italy, and Upper Italy. He desired that Cavour arrange somehow for Austria to declare war and appear as the guilty party. Some of these ideas had been suggested in May, so Cavour was hardly taken by surprise. That he never accepted the strictures involved in the scheme for a four-state confederation and that events turned out differently is hardly evidence that at Plombières the Emperor was tricked into agreeing to aid Sardinia. Cavour's reaction was to do what was expected of him. He arranged the marriage, increased the size of Sardinia's army, and continued the deliberate provocation of Austria.

A widespread latent distrust of Napoleon was clear and many statesmen correctly assumed that he was engaged in a plot to combat Austria in Italy. On New Year's Day, 1859, Napoleon pointedly observed to Austria's ambassador in Paris, Baron Hübner, that he regreted relations between France and Austria were not as good as he would like. The diplomats of Europe now debated how war might be averted. Shortly, Napoleon began to have second thoughts and characteristically vacillated, hoping that perhaps a congress on Italy could be arranged or that Austria's hold might be moderated or eliminated without the cost and risks of war. In Paris he found few important supporters for a war in Italy, and Prussia's attitude caused particular apprehension. Although Britain opposed Austrian control of Italy, she was equally against a French army there and also was concerned about losing markets in Northern Italy during any hostilities. Meanwhile Austria reacted firmly to the petty provocations of Savoy and enlarged her garrisons. Following several vague and ineffectual suggestions for a congress to discuss Italy, Britain's Lord Malmesbury proposed that Austria, France, and Sardinia all demobilize at once and then meet for a congress. Napoleon agreed, and Cavour, feeling betrayed, also reluctantly agreed. Austria, however, refused (April 23) and unilaterally demanded Sardinian demobilization within three days. Cavour was elated. He refused the ultimatum and Austrian troops invaded Sardinia. Cavour had succeeded in fostering a situation where Austria appeared the aggressor. The Austrian decision was a major diplomatic blunder which saved Cavour, for he had lost control of the situation. To the diplomats of Europe, all watching Italy, there was little question of Austria's culpability and France was able to go to the assistance of a small state "unjustly" attacked, with a minimum of international misgivings.

Cavour was delighted and never doubted that the French aid would be more than enough to defeat the Austrians. Napoleon was as good as his word and quickly sent his army into Italy, half by sea, landing at Genoa, and half through the Alps. This time he would not be denied a role with the army. Leaving the Empress as regent, he departed for Genoa, arriving there on May 12. The allied armies cooperated fairly well and their officers showed a higher caliber of judgment than the Austrians. French and Sardinian arms won the battle of Magenta on June 4, a victory resulting largely from better troop dispositions and harder fighting. Though Austrian troops fought well, in most engagements they faced greater numbers and were continually in retreat. After a joyous ride through the streets of Milan, Napoleon and Victor Emmanuel moved further east, where Austrian forces had concentrated. The Emperor Franz Joseph had joined his army and substantial reinforcements had also arrived. Now the Austrians numbered more than the Franco-Sardinian force (190,000 men to 174,000; 22,600 horses to 14,500; and 752 guns to 522), but they proved unable to gain any practical advantage from this. The armies met at Solferino on June 24, where three nearly separate actions occurred. Napoleon was in command of the allied force and gave the orders which led to victory, the only personal military victory in his career. French troops fought furiously and the Austrians finally retreated. Austrian losses were 22,000 compared with 17,000 for the French. The Austrians now moved into strong defensive positions. Siege equipment was then en route from France and nearly everyone expected a long, vigorous struggle. Instead, Napoleon contacted Franz Joseph and at Villafranca the two emperors arranged an armistice, followed on July 12 by terms of peace.

The settlement of Villafranca caught all observers by surprise. Cavour was furious and resigned from office. He felt betrayed because the campaign had liberated only Lombardy; the Austrians were still in Venetia and the peace terms allowed her to remain there, still an Italian power. Cavour's anger about Napoleon's independent action had been balanced by a wave of revolutionary outbreaks in the peninsula during May. The Emperor suspected that Cavour had perhaps instigated them and had more extensive designs than he intended to sanction. It was clear that movements were under way which Napoleon could not control, so after two important victories, he was satisfied to see Austria remain in Italy, though in a reduced role.

SWITZERLAND

AUSTRIAN EMPIRE

TYROL

• Trent

VENETIA

LOMBARDY

Verona • Venice • • Trieste

Novara • Magenta Custoza

Milan • Solferino • Villafranca

ISTRIA

PIEDMONT

SAVOY

to France 1860

Turin •

Po R.

KINGDOM

• Ferrara

PARMA

Genoa •

MODENA

• Bologna

ROMAGNA

FRANCE

NICE

Nice •

Leghorn • Arno R.

Florence •

TUSCANY

THE MARCHES

• Castelfidardo

PAPAL

STATES

UMBRIA

ELBA

ABRUZZI

Tiber R.

THE PATRIMONY

• Rome

OTTOMAN EMPIRE

DALMATIA

ADRIATIC SEA

CORSICA (FR.)

OF

SARDINIA

SARDINIA

Cagliari •

TYRRHENIAN SEA

Gaeta •

• Bari

CAMPANIA

• Naples

APULIA

• Taranto

KINGDOM OF THE TWO SICILIES

CALABRIA

Palermo •

Messina •

• Reggio

SICILY

MEDITERRANEAN SEA

UNIFICATION OF ITALY, 1859-1870

AFRICA

Kingdom of Sardinia before 1859

To Kingdom of Sardinia: 1859 ▮ 1860

To Kingdom of Italy: 1866 1870

Italia Irredenta

A number of other considerations motivated the French Emperor, but their relative weight is difficult to ascertain. He had been appalled at the sight of the mass physical suffering and death which littered the battlefields. With the Austrians in stronger positions, the prospects were for more casualties and perhaps a war of attrition. Meanwhile Prussia had mobilized some 400,000 men along the Rhine and France had only bare cadres in the garrisons facing them. This threat to French security was being criticized by nationalists at home, who, ironically, would have liked a war on the Rhine more than one in Italy. The Prussian mobilization had also been an ominous gesture to the Austrians, who would have preferred direct help in Italy, although this might have seriously alienated Britain. Meanwhile the Catholics apprehensively viewed the revolts in Italy as a threat to the Pope's secular holdings. The general unpopularity of the war at home surprised Napoleon; consequently, for all these and perhaps other considerations, he negotiated peace and left Italy.

The Sardinians were dismayed, but Napoleon had assured vast changes. While France received Nice and Savoy, extensive annexations to Piedmont occurred in Central Italy; and Garibaldi conquered Sicily, Naples, and much of the papal territories, all of which he delivered to Sardinia. On March 17, 1861, the Kingdom of Italy was proclaimed. It was really a greater Sardinia which included the whole peninsula except Venetia, which remained Austrian, and Rome, where French troops still protected the Pope. Instead of gratitude to France, the new state was irritated that Austria had not been driven entirely out of Italy and its subsequent policy in Paris put continual emphasis on this point. The new state acquired Venetia in 1866 and unification was completed in 1870, when the French left Rome. Napoleon had, indeed, done "something for Italy." Not many people truly appreciated his efforts and even historians have been loath to give him much credit. For all of Cavour's intriguing, he needed Napoleon's sword to cut the Gordion knot of Austrian force.

CHAPTER 31

German Unification

{the Danish War;
the Austro-Prussian War;
and the Franco-Prussian War}

Of all the forceful alterations in the diplomatic power structure of the nineteenth century, few were more central to Europe's later history than the unification of Germany. Through a frank use of "blood and iron" in a policy of *realpolitik,* Otto von Bismarck (1815–1898) boasted in his memoirs of how he had created the new German state which both logic and history demanded. This Iron Chancellor's recollections after the fact presented historians with a neat and well-organized explanation of his motives and triumphs. Although his version was easier to accept than to modify, serious studies have since made clear that he pursued a chancy, devious path beset with doubt and uncertainty. The creation of the modern German Empire was the supreme achievement of Bismarck. To note that others created opportunities for him or that he made other important contributions in no way detracts from the enormity of this particular triumph of statesmanship.

Born in 1815, Bismarck grew to manhood watching contemptuously as liberal efforts to govern were sporadic failures, the most notable being the Frankfurt Assembly. A bona fide Junker aristocrat and a shrewd judge of men, he came to have a wider vision than his class. A realist in politics, he recognized how men's actions could be swayed by ideologies. His loyalty to a Prussia ruled by the Hohenzollerns was remarkably inflexible; he looked askance at the growing middle and lower classes while he worked to assure a greater and stronger Prussia. A servant of the state, he unswervingly served its interests as he saw them; and until 1870, his role was much like Cavour's in Italy. He shared no romantic view of a united Germany, but rather thought in terms of a greater Prussia. The greater Prussia proved large enough to include most of Europe's Germans, except the Catholic Germans in Austria, who were left outside of the new Empire but who were not regarded by Bismarck as a serious loss. In his view, in the Rhine valley and in Bavaria he already had too many of these religious sources of potential disloyalty. Nationalism in Germany, under Bismarckian control, led to a new nation-state which at first was Prussian directed. This involved a rejection of the old idea of a massive universal empire of Germans, a concept the Hapsburgs had been nursing for centuries. A Hapsburg-Hohenzollern opposition on this larger issue had been in the making since at least 1740, and it was Bismarck's triumph to settle this question in favor of the Prussian dynasty. In effect, he created *a new division of Germans,* a point often overlooked, in such a way that two large states emerged, one Germanic and one multinational, in the heart of Europe.

Bismarck's leadership in the expansion of Prussia began in September of 1862, when he was recalled from the Paris embassy to find the despondent King William (1797–1888) on the point of abdication. The monarch's frustration stemmed from liberal opposition to additional funds for military reforms which both William and von Roon, the war minister, were convinced were essential to correct inadequacies revealed in the 1859 mobilization. Bismarck proposed to continue the reforms, collecting and spending the additional monies despite the attitudes or votes of members of the lower house. Liberals were fearful that the military buildup could result in their own repression. They argued that for the government to act in defiance of the lower house was unconstitutional, a consideration which failed to move Bismarck, who regarded them as men of limited vision and little practical experience in government. For four years he collected and spent funds without proper sanction, though it was later given ex post facto.

Bismarck became minister-president of Prussia at a critical time. The 1848 concessions to liberal reform promised by Frederick William IV had been nominally implemented in a spirit of increased reluctance, and blatant pressure kept many liberal spokesmen out of the lower house. The government was openly authoritarian and blithely ignored such constitutional guarantees as freedom of the press. When William replaced his brother (declared insane in 1858), he quickly rescinded the most reactionary features of the system. Although more liberals now appeared in the lower house, the struggle to free Italy of Austrian control stimulated a rash of liberal and nationalistic propaganda in Prussia and the other non-Austrian German states.

During Austria's agony in Italy, Prussia mobilized her army along the Rhine, a gesture which worried both France and Austria. Bismarck had spent most of the 1850s as an openly anti-Austrian delegate to the reconstituted Diet in Frankfurt, and while relations were deteriorating between France and Austria, he was sent to St. Petersburg as Prussian ambassador. He spent three years in Russia making important contacts and acquiring a feel for Russian attitudes toward European problems. In 1859 he believed that Prussia should absorb North Germany while Austria was helplessly mired in Italy. There is little evidence to indicate that he considered a practical extension of Prussian authority to include South Germany until years after he was in power. Austria was his main opponent until he added the southern states to Prussian objectives; then France became the enemy. Bismarck saw the simple mobilization of 1859 as a lost opportunity when such large areas were available merely for the taking. His political analysis was correct except that the mobilization had not gone nearly as smoothly as it looked to outsiders. Extensive and expensive military reforms were needed and appropriate plans were drawn up as euphoric sentiments for change in the Germanies were mushrooming. In 1862 Bismarck was assigned to the Paris embassy, where for a short three months he closely observed Napoleon III. He thus came to power with a significant background in diplomacy and a proved record of authoritarian and anti-Austrian sentiments. Bismarck's appointment was a disappointment to liberals who had hoped to win their struggle against increased funds for militarism. In the north and central German states there was strong sentiment for a new German state led by a liberalized Prussia. William's early decisions had seemed to encourage this hope which carried also the prospect of a significant reduction of Austrian authority in central Germany. The south German states were hoping that such a move would result in a liberalization of Austria, in whose orbit they expected to remain. The appointment of a man with such authoritarian sentiments as those of Bismarck, sent a shudder through liberal ranks, where there was little sentiment for a revitalized, reactionary leadership.

While defying the liberals on the budget question, Bismarck took two moves designed to gain liberal and national support against Austria. He recognized the new Kingdom of Italy and completed Zollverein negotiations with France for a German version of the Cobden-Chevalier Treaty of 1860. Austria was strongly opposed to this extension of free trade practice in the Germanies and publicized her objections. The Prussian initiatives indicated a new, independent, and anti-Austrian orientation and contained the hint of the kind of alliance which could be erected against Austria.

By the end of 1862 Austria had been humbled in Italy by France, was still the object of Italian bitterness over Venetia, had a clear Prussian rival in Germany, and was still remembered by Russia for "betrayal" in the Crimean War. To make things worse, a Franco-Russian entente had a distinctly anti-Austrian flavor. In the midst of these realities Bismarck was working to take advantage of the Franco-Russian feeling against Austria when the Polish revolt broke out. This anti-Russian violence ruined the Franco-Russian entente when Napoleon III openly lauded this latest example of nationalism and tried to support the Poles by organizing a conference which would lead to joint protestations to Alexander II. The French Emperor was unprepared to give practical help to the Poles and for him the result of the whole episode was that he had sacrificed his close relationship with Russia but gained nothing in return. Within France, Napoleon had hoped to win the gratitude of both the Catholics and friends of Polish nationalism but alienated both by what they regarded as his halfway measures.

Bismarck quickly decided that the Poles had no chance for success, so he assured Alexander (the Alvensleben Convention) that Poles attempting to escape by crossing the Prussian frontier would be arrested and turned back to tsarist forces. This was unpopular among German liberals, but many historians have praised Bismarck for having a clearer sense of basic realities than Napoleon III. He had taken an inexpensive step, alienating only liberal sentiment, which already opposed him, and for this gesture, he won the gratitude of Alexander II. To this facile analysis, however, should be added the idea that the Polish upheaval was a great misfortune to Bismarck, for it placed in opposition his two potential allies against Austria. He had to lose one of them. Characteristically, he described his actions as successful and deliberate; but, in fact, Prussia was diplomatically weaker as a result of the Polish episode. Further, the price of Russian friendship was more expensive than it appeared on the surface. Like many republicans in 1848, Napoleon III saw Prussia as a sort of "Northern Piedmont," and so Bismarck had alienated early in his tenure in office the one great power which genuinely believed Prussia should unify northern Germany (the limit of Bismarck's ambitions at the time). The thought that Bismarck had cheaply purchased Russian gratitude has been grossly overstated. Instead of gratitude, the reaction of Russian statesmen was that he meddled in a situation in which he was unwanted. There was never a real danger that Russia could not control the revolt and they resented Prussia's offer to help crush the Poles, as well as the suggestion that Prussia might have to occupy part of Poland. From Russia's view, the convention kept Prussia out of Poland and exposed Bismarck as an opportunist willing to take advantage of a neighbor's adversity. The diplomacy of the Polish revolt was no success for Bismarck. Rather, it was perhaps the nadir of his experience as a leader in the period prior to 1871.

More to Bismarck's credit as a statesman was the 1864 Danish War over Schleswig-Holstein. Here his conduct and control of events showed the astute finesse which has often been attributed to all his initiatives. Writers of historical narratives tend to present one issue or episode at a time, but the bewildering swirl of issues requiring Bismarck's attention in 1863 can hardly be imagined. While dealing with Poland and trying to lead a reluctant William, who frankly suspected his coarse minister, he still had to parry the invectives of liberals at home. Meanwhile there was a rising clamor for liberal reform in Germany at large, which led to a call by Franz Joseph, in 1863, for a meeting of princes in Frankfurt to discuss practical ways in which the Confederation might be altered. Bismarck cajoled William into refusing to attend, despite the fact that this Austrian initiative by the foreign minister, Rechberg, looked to a strengthing of Austria in Germany by liberalizing and *coming to terms with Prussia as an equal.* To Rechberg this would strengthen the Confederation vis-à-vis France, an obvious need for Austria after the defeat in Italy. Bismarck completely refused to cooperate and Rechberg was also opposed at home by conservatives who believed Austria should continue as the dominant power in the Confederation. At the

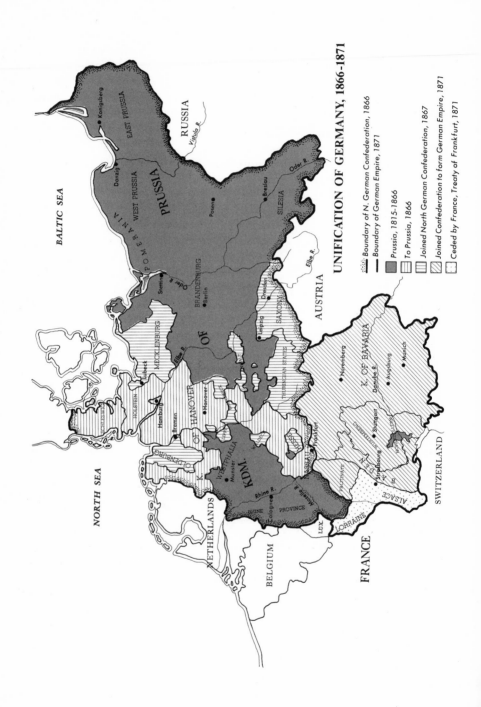

UNIFICATION OF GERMANY, 1866-1871

Boundary of N. German Confederation, 1866
Boundary of German Empire, 1871

Prussia, 1815-1866
To Prussia, 1866
Joined North German Confederation, 1867
Joined Confederation to form German Empire, 1871
Ceded by France, Treaty of Frankfurt, 1871

BALTIC SEA

RUSSIA

Königsberg

EAST PRUSSIA

Vistula R.

Danzig

WEST PRUSSIA

P O M E R A N I A

PRUSSIA

Oder R.

Breslau

Posen

SILESIA

Stettin

Oder R.

BRANDENBURG

Berlin

OF

Elbe R.

AUSTRIA

MECKLENBURG

Lübeck

Elbe R.

Leipzig

Dresden

SAXONY

NORTH SEA

SCHLESWIG

HOLSTEIN

Hamburg

Bremen

K. OF HANOVER

Hanover

THURINGIAN STATES

Nürnberg

K. OF BAVARIA

Munich

Augsburg

Danube R.

OLDENBURG

K.

WESTPHALIA

Münster

KDM.

NASSAU

Frankfurt

WÜRTTEMBERG

Stuttgart

HOHENZOLLERN

NETHERLANDS

RHINE PROVINCE

Cologne

Rhine R.

Moselle R.

RHINE

PALATINATE

Strasbourg

ALSACE

SWITZERLAND

BELGIUM

LUX.

LORRAINE

FRANCE

414

same time the aged problem of the duchies of Schleswig and Holstein simmered toward a new outburst which Bismarck skillfully exploited.

As a topic in European diplomacy, the Schleswig-Holstein dispute rivals the most complex. In comparison with the multitude of interwoven subissues, Bismarck's solution was simplicity itself, unencumbered as it was with any respect for the past, for the legal positions of parties to the problem, or for the feelings of the particular populations involved. For us to come abruptly to this problem as it existed in the mid-nineteenth century, ignoring its involved roots, has the virtue of putting us much in the position of Bismarck, who looked back mainly to the London Protocol of May 1852, a document which had ended the previous tangled chapter regarding the duchies. This agreement had been negotiated by outsiders (England, Austria, France, Prussia, Russia, Sweden, Denmark) and regulated the status of the duchies. They were to be jointly *administered* through the person of the King of Denmark. This solution ignored the overwhelmingly Germanic population of the duchies but was accepted as an expedient in the midst of other issues disturbing Europe. By 1863 German national feeling in the duchies was aroused when, in response to intense Danish nationalistic pressures, Denmark's Frederick VII moved formally to incorporate Schleswig into his kingdom, a violation of the Protocol which aroused the Germans. Then the Danish monarch died, succeeded (November 18, 1863) by Christian IX (1818–1906), who came to the throne through the female line. Meanwhile, Frederick, the Duke of Augustenburg, had laid claims to both provinces, attempting to create a new German state despite the fact that his father had earlier relinquished his claims in return for a sizable cash payment. The German Confederation recognized the Salic Law and consequently branded Christian's hold on the provinces illegal. Authorizing the use of force to detach the provinces from Denmark, it supported Augustenburg, despite his father's agreement. Bismarck sensed in this situation an opportunity both to test the newly reformed Prussian army and to extend Prussia's influence in North Germany. Accordingly, he sent Prussian troops into the duchies, independent of the Saxon and Hanoverian forces sent by the Confederation. He represented Prussia as acting in defense of the London Protocol, opposing both the recent pretensions of the Danish crown and the Duke of Augustenburg. Austria also adopted a policy independent of the Confederation and joined Bismarck in war against Denmark. Otherwise Prussia would have acted alone, because the other non-Danish signatories to the Protocol left the issue to be decided by the principals in the field. Napoleon III had issued another unsuccessful call for an international congress, which only encouraged Austria to cooperate with Prussia. It is worth observing that nationalism in the affected area meant nothing to Bismarck. He was engaged in a program of Prussian aggrandizement, with German nationalism incidental to his thinking, merely one of many factors to be weighed and acted upon or counteracted.

The military phase of the struggle is of scant significance in military history other than as a demonstration that the Prussian reforms were progressing effectively. The Austrians did little more than accompany the Prussians, who broke Danish defensive efforts by taking the stronghold of Duppel on April 18. The Danes had abandoned the wholly German Holstein without a struggle, but they made a vigorous attempt to keep Schleswig and hoped for English and Swedish assistance. These powers, however, had been irritated by the Danish violations of the Protocol and remained neutral. When a new London conference of the major powers failed to solve the problem (partly through Bismark's machinations), it was left to the Danes, Prussians, and Austrians to find a solution. In effect, the Danes had been abandoned and they lost the disputed provinces. Bismarck had not anticipated the situation which now developed and a most unsatisfactory arrangement regarding occupation of the two provinces resulted. On one point he was adamant; there should be no recognition of Augustenburg's claims, even though he was now being supported by Austria. In Prussia Bismarck was virtually alone on this issue. German nationalists, conservatives, liberals, the war minister von Roon, the Crown Prince, and even King William, all had a sentimental feeling that Augustenburg deserved help. Bismarck managed, however, to convince them that such an arrangement would merely create an anti-Prussian Austrian ally in an area where Prussia might logically expect to expand.

The Austrian cooperation with Prussia was fleetingly unnatural, generated by her suspicion of Prussian designs and the reluctance to agree to a Napoleonic conference. The Confederation was weakened through the bilateral Austro-Prussian decisions; and after the peace, signed in Vienna in October, the two powers were openly rivals. With the hour for an open assault on Austria near at hand, Bismarck began to make appropriate diplomatic arrangements. The two major German powers held the provinces of Schleswig and Holstein (also Lauenburg), but what disposition was to be made of them? In the Convention of Gastein (August, 1865) their joint occupation and administration was arranged in a fashion that almost assured petty disturbances. Here Bismarck had a source of friction which could be fanned into a cause for war almost at will. Having arranged this, he then worked to make sure that when war came, Austria would have no ally.

At this point, the key to Austrian isolation in Europe was Napoleon III. Russia was still estranged from Vienna and the new Italian kingdom regarded Austria as its greatest enemy. France had sown bitterness in Vienna during 1859, but the continuance of this could not be taken for granted. Napoleon had, after all, gone to Villafranca and Austria had been grateful to emerge from that war still in possession of Venetia. Sensing, perhaps, the future need for allies, the French Emperor had moved to restore good feeling with the power he had just defeated. In offering the Mexican crown to the brother of Franz Joseph he was, in effect, trying to repeat the sort of rapprochement which he had earlier been able to develop with Russia after her defeat in the Crimea. This pathetic effort to gain friendship in Vienna was hopelessly counterbalanced by his calls for congresses on Poland and Schleswig-Holstein, because the Austrians had no desire for open discussions of boundaries and the question of nationalities. A truly close rapprochement with Vienna was also hampered by Napoleon's feeling that somehow he must get Austria to relinquish Venetia. Bismarck had also declined Napoleon's suggestions for congresses and now he needed to be sure of French attitudes. Therefore, in October of 1865, he traveled to Biarritz, south of Bordeaux, to confer with Napoleon, a trip which was impressive testimony to the importance of France under Napoleon III this late in the Empire.

In these discussions Bismarck added to his earlier impressions of the Emperor and carried away the feeling that in a situation of crisis elsewhere, the Emperor would probably not act. From this interestingly prophetic observation has come the view that at Biarritz (like Plombières) the Emperor was somehow tricked by a shrewder mind. Biarritz resembled Plombières only in that both meetings discussed a future clash of arms and that in each case the situation afterward did not benefit French prestige in Europe. The meeting is usually not seen in the context of Napoleon's rebuffs at trying to bring the Great Powers to a conference to discuss the problems of nationalism in Europe. Also he was sensitive to criticisms that after he had said a great deal about nationalism, he had "abandoned" the Poles and the Danes. Simultaneously, he was engaged in an attempt to please Italy by recalling French troops from Rome, but his success here proved only temporary and the attempt led to further ill will.

Often overlooked is the fact that Napoleon still believed in a new Germany with Prussian leadership. This did not rule out other German states in his thinking, especially the prospect of a French satellite state in the Rhine area. At Biarritz Bismarck was asking Napoleon merely to remain neutral while Prussia made the modifications which Napoleon happened to believe nationalism required in Central Europe. The Emperor was not convinced that Prussia was strong enough to accomplish this, but in case she were, he listened to hints from Bismarck of compensations for France in the revised power structure. At the same time, Napoleon saw in Prussia's plot against Austria an opportunity to make amends with the Italians by arranging for the eventual transfer of Venetia.

At Biarritz as at Plombières, two genuine Machiavellians faced each other and no wool was pulled over anyone's eyes. Napoleon's objects were somewhat more altruistic than those of his rival statesmen. He seems truly to have believed in the principle of nationalism and that Europe would find peace in a structure of "completed nationalities." Further, he believed in the congress system as a device for settling disputes and problems. He was, of course, the leader of France, and he expected to enhance French prestige, but his vision was also broad and humane, which is more than can be said of either Cavour or Bismarck.

After Biarritz, Napoleon used his influence to bring Prussia and Italy together. These powers agreed (April, 1866) that should a war break out within ninety days between Prussia and Austria, Italy would support Prussia and be rewarded with Venetia. Bismarck had assured not only French neutrality but also a two-front war for his enemy. As hostilities were stealthily being plotted by Bismarck, the Austrians sensed that a showdown in Germany was near at hand. To complete the situation, from Napoleon's viewpoint, the Austrians approached the French leader and bought his promise of neutrality by agreeing to give up Venetia. They also mentioned a French client state along the Rhine emerging from future readjustments after the struggle with Prussia. Diplomatically, Napoleon's position was particularly strong. He needed, however, to have an army near the frontier ready to march to enforce the various agreements, written, verbal, and hinted. Failure to take this precaution led to disaster for France.

After the Convention of Gastein, a concerted Austro-Prussian rivalry developed in Frankfurt over how the Confederation should be reformed. Both powers were aggressive in seeking a new constitutional situation reflecting their own advantage; the minor states, though leaning toward Austria, opposed both. Austria raised the question of the future disposition of the duchies and called a meeting of Holsteiners to discuss the issue. Bismarck declared this to be a violation of Gastein and occupied Holstein. Austria responded by persuading the Federal Diet in Frankfurt to condemn Prussia's action; and Bismarck then went to war, technically against the Confederation but actually against Austria.

The Seven Weeks' War between Prussia and Austria had profound ramifications for later decades of European history. Italy was militarily no more a match for Austria than she was before Napoleon had aided her in 1859. Her defeat in 1866 on both land and sea was humiliating. Her ally was successful, however, and so she gained Venetia. Prussia's army now showed impressive results of the reforms. This included not only more sophisticated weaponry (their "needle gun" fired much faster than the muzzle loaders and could be reloaded while lying down instead of standing), but also careful planning of troop movements by rail. Prussia had a considerable advantage in that much of non-Austrian Germany had a well-developed rail network, whereas Austria had only one major line extending north from Vienna. Consequently, this line was overworked while Prussian troops efficiently moved against Austria's allies in North Germany (Hanover, Nassau, Frankfurt, Hesse-Cassel) and penetrated Bohemia by three routes. Efficiency in the inherently expensive process of mobilization and troop movement proved to be a great asset for Prussia. By incorrect timing in both 1859 and 1866, Austria absorbed a considerable financial burden which hampered her war effort. The main battle, Königgrätz (Sadowa) on July 3, 1866, was a masterpiece of planning; Austria's defeat was very nearly complete. Austrian pretensions to a dominant role in German affairs were at an end. As Napoleon had driven her out of Italy, now Bismarck expelled her from Germany. A major reconstitution of the power structure in Central Europe had occurred. Any who doubt whether it matters who wins or loses in war should contemplate the consequences, immediate and long range, of this brief struggle. The birth of the new Germany by blood and iron was almost complete. There was a human cost in the loss of lives in Bismarck's wars, but this was surely minor when put beside the enormity of the change suddenly made possible.

Königgrätz came as a great surprise to Napoleon III. It is still a question why the Prussian army reforms had not been better understood in Paris. In discussions on the wisdom of a military demonstration toward the Rhine frontier, Napoleon overruled his ministers and decided against it. Meanwhile hasty and pretentious messages were sent to Bismarck, who, after a brief period of apprehension that the French might use force, became progressively more terse and blunt. Napoleon approved of massive reorganization in North Germany but insisted (and Bismarck agreed) that the South German states retain their independence. The value of this was modified, however, when Bismarck negotiated offensive and defensive alliances with the southern states and when they re-entered the Zollverein. Napoleon had expected that they might form a southern confederation, but they failed to move in this direction. For the French Emperor the most humiliating aspect came when Bismarck flatly refused any "compensations" for France to balance the vast accretion of Prussian power. Napoleon quickly realized that failure to make a military gesture had been a mistake. His reaction was merely to keep suggesting various alternate forms of compensation, mentioning Belgium and Luxembourg and the Rhine as a frontier. Bismarck merely received these in writing and bided his time.

For Napoleon everything seemed to have failed. French authority in both Italy and Germany was compromised and the Mexican expedition became an ever-increasing failure. Opponents of the government in the Legislative Body consistently criticized this venture, which seemed costly without any practical gain for France. In another major miscalculation, Napoleon had thought the South would win the Civil War in the United States. After the North won, diplomatic pressure was exerted to get the French army out of Mexico. Napoleon's commitment to Maximilian had been to keep 25,000 men there, but only until Maximilian was in control himself. The French Emperor had carefully explained to Maximilian that in order to succeed he must identify with the people's cause. A Hapsburg could probably not understand such a lesson born of the French Revolution. At any rate, Maximilian identified quickly with the upper clergy and aristocracy and even managed to alienate segments of these. Juarez had the loyalty of the native population to himself; when Napoleon began the orderly withdrawal of his troops, Maximilian's days in power were numbered. He refused Napoleon's advice to abdicate and was executed on June 19, 1867. News of his death came to Paris during the Exposition and cast a pall of failure over the dazzling display of technical progress. To the royalty of Europe it appeared that Maximilian's life was the price exacted to pay for a Napoleonic attempt at overseas imperialism.

The number of French troops in Mexico had never been very large, and the presence of French troops there was not the reason

Napoleon failed to make a threatening gesture in the wake of Königgrätz. Mexico was a great propaganda failure because Napoleon was never able to answer his critics convincingly. His bids for compensation, entered when it was too late to force them, were simply pathetic. Nonetheless, we would not write this sort of judgment now had France won the war in 1870. However, she lost, and that defeat attracted forever criticism of her diplomacy during 1866–1870. The onus of failure settled on the Emperor after Sadowa, yet, ironically, an aggressive military display to secure compensations would have stirred further opposition in France. The public wanted prestige but did not want to pay additional taxes or to see conscription enforced on a broader scale. At the same time, the most avid critics in the Legislative Body were orating on the virtues of eliminating the standing army. Napoleon was alarmed at the proved effectiveness of Prussia's army and recognized that the French army had not been kept abreast of new developments. With little support among his entourage and in the face of a torrent of political opposition, he tried to push modernization of the army. The task could have been accomplished in the three remaining years that history allotted him if he had been more authoritarian and had ignored both the sensibilities of the lower house and public sentiment. In 1870 the army was not ready and the Emperor paid the price for this short-coming while those who had eagerly worked to cut military expenditures faulted him for not being energetic and forceful enough in foreign affairs.

Following the war with Austria, Bismarck gained a retroactive sanction for the monies he had been collecting since 1862 in defiance of liberal sentiment. His successes had proved the correctness of the policies they had questioned; in a spirit of admiration, many of his former protagonists now moved to erase from the record the proof of their shortsightedness. The Prussian statesman had deliberately fomented the war with Austria, a struggle which was an obvious culmination of Hohenzollern-Hapsburg rivalry since the days of Frederick II and Maria Theresa. There is little reliable evidence to suggest that Bismarck looked beyond the acquisition of North Germany for Prussia before the outcome of the struggle with Austria. Once he had founded the North German Confederation (with a constitutional structure somewhat anticipating that of the Empire), he sensed an opportunity to make a similar extension of Prussia into South Germany and began to work just as deliberately for a war with France. Humiliated by failure to gain anything for France after Sadowa and publicly rebuked over a clumsy, unsuccessful attempt to obtain Luxembourg, Napoleon III could not possibly allow Prussian expansion to include South Germany. Sensing this, Bismarck directly prepared for war with France.

Spain had played a major role in the fall of Napoleon Bonaparte and it was appropriate that this unfortunate land be involved in the demise of the Second Empire. This time it provided the occasion for the event rather than the basic motivation. Queen Isabella's rule had come to an end in September of 1868. On the 29th she arrived in France as a royal exile, to the embarrassment of Napoleon III. Though a person of easy morality himself, he was as appalled as others by the flagrant immorality and scandal associated with Isabella. Furthermore, she represented reactionary government at a time when Napoleon III was liberalizing as rapidly as he could. Bitterly criticized for foreign policy failures, this pitiful example of rejected royalty was yet another political liability.

The expulsion of Isabella opened the way to six years of Spanish instability while the nation experimented with provisional government, monarchy, and republicanism. Throughout this time there were Carlist intrigues or uprisings in the background. In the early phase of this fluid situation, a search for a successor to Isabella centered on a number of young princes. France was interested in preventing the Duke of Montpensier, a son of Louis Philippe, from wearing the crown. When it appeared that the choice would be Leopold of Hohenzollern-Sigmaringen, French critics observed that France was being encircled by states ruled by a single dynasty, as in the days before the War of Spanish Succession. Napoleon at first saw no serious problem regarding this particular candidacy, because he had been a leading influence in assuring to Leopold's brother, Charles, the throne of Rumania. William of Prussia, as head of the family, acted to prevent Leopold's acceptance when he realized that popular excitement began to build up in Paris against the prince. In this situation, however, Bismarck sensed the diplomatic means for a war with France. Sentiment in the south German states in the winter of 1869–1870 was distinctly anti-Prussian, and Bismarck realized that it would take war to bring them into his new German state as well as to make France accept the change. Thus he seized on the Hohenzollern candidacy and helped to turn the episode into a prelude to war.

Jingoistic sentiment ran high in both Berlin and Paris, with Bismarck doing all he could in the Prussian capital to promote irresponsible journalism. This was equalled by the Parisian press while Napoleon's new government assumed a pro-Austrian stance and in

a park at Ems, a resort, Count Vincent Benedetti, the French ambassador to Berlin, insisted on impossible guarantees from William.
The Prussian monarch refused the demands (July 13) and sent a
telegram to Berlin describing the encounter. It is interesting to note
that if the issue had been truly the Spanish crown, then the French
should have delivered their remonstrances to the provisional government in Madrid. The real issue, however, was the massive extension of Prussian power in Central Europe. The candidacy
conveniently focused the sentiments for revenge for Sadowa and the
nationalists and other critics of Napoleon's policies were aroused
against Prussia. As the situation was deteriorating, Bismarck publicized the so-called Ems dispatch after editing it to make the French
demands sound more insulting than they were, thus feeding the
journalistic fires for war. He also released the text of earlier demands
by Napoleon for compensation at the expense of lands bounding
France to the east and north, thus assuring revulsion in Britain
against the French Emperor. Napoleon had just been overwhelmingly supported at the polls and was about to face the supreme crisis
of his political life. Wracked with pain, he resigned himself to the
test, feeling himself largely a victim of events. Removed from his
direct control were the ministries, foreign policy, the press, the Empress, and the dispositions and condition of the army. Efforts to
devise a league of neutrals to save peace failed because in both Berlin
and Paris there were men and crowds determined on war. It came on
July 19, 1870.

History has applauded the genius of Bismarck for arranging the
diplomatic isolation of France. The perspective, however, needs to
be expanded. The issue was settled not so much by the fact of French
isolation as it was by the inability of the French army to defeat that
of Prussia. In none of the struggles of Napoleon III had France faced
more than one opponent, a military luxury the first Napoleon rarely
enjoyed. While Bismarck associated the South German states with
him in the venture, the major forces were Prussian. An additional
aspect of the situation was that, had the French enjoyed some initial
successes, there was a likelihood of both Austria and Italy coming
into the struggle against Prussia. Despite Bismarck's moderation after
Königgrätz, Austria was still resentful of the cavalier way she had
been pushed out of much of Germany and was a factor to be watched
in 1870. Thus, the diplomatic and military situation was not nearly
as bleak for France as it has often been described. The Emperor's
basic war plan was for a rapid thrust into the South German states,
which assured the entry of both Italy and Austria into the war.

The failure of France in 1870 was the failure of her military leadership. The reforms of the previous few years had only partially modernized the army. The *chassepot* (a form of machine gun) was a devastating weapon and most of the units had them. They had not been equipped with new breech-loading rifles because of adverse votes on the military budget in the Legislative Body. The ordnance and logistics services were a shambles, with men and equipment poorly coordinated. The Emperor left Paris by rail, hoping to join an army fit for a quick descent into South Germany. He found confusion and units in disarray, barely ready to give battle to the invading Prussians, who made an even more dramatic use of the railroad for troop movements than in 1866. The emphasis was on mobility, and when the French assumed a defensive posture in a strong position, as Bazaine did at Metz, the Prussians merely left a besieging force and swept on. The French officers were hopelessly outclassed. In the military as in other areas of government Napoleon's administrative structure had failed to bring to the fore men of real genius. The army's rank and file fought well but were overcome by Prussian speed and ingenuity. The issue was settled at the battle of Sedan, where, on September 2, 1870, Napoleon and an entire army were captured. The Emperor had roamed from one force to another, his authority diminished when Bazaine became commander-in-chief. In vain, he purposely exposed himself to enemy fire so that his demise might be honorable and fitting a Bonaparte. At Paris the news of Sedan triggered the fall of the Empire; the Empress left for England and radicals and republicans tried to organize further resistance. Paris withstood a siege until January 28, 1871, but the issue could not remain long in doubt as the major question seemed to be who could properly negotiate for France. Meanwhile Bismarck's most ambitious objectives had been more than achieved. His success was symbolically validated at Versailles on January 18, 1871, when William was proclaimed Emperor of Germany. Prussian arms had diminished the power of Austria's emperor and they were responsible for the end of the Second Empire. Blood and iron had created a new Emperor and a "unified" Germany which was to retain essentially the same boundaries for over seventy years.

CHAPTER 32

Disturbing Portents

In 1871, an era of national unifications seemed successfully closed: the new Hohenzollern German Empire had been proclaimed and the Italians had moved at last into their natural historic capital, Rome. These triumphs of calculated aggression promised a relaxing of tensions to persons who had believed that a divided Italy and Germany had been responsible for centuries of Great Power rivalry to control these areas. The creation of these two nations, however, led to other problems which, in their own way, were disquieting portents for the future.

A by-product of the fall of the Second Empire at the hands of the Prussian army was the Paris Commune, which lasted from March 26 until May 28, 1871. This brief episode in French history, together

425

with the memory of the 1848 June Days, was to emphasize and exaggerate social divisions for many decades. The whole experience demonstrated the special position of Paris within France and also the growing cohesiveness of the more radical urban elements.

It should be recalled that despite the Emperor's modernization of the city, he had never been truly accepted in the French capital. He had taken in this a measure of pride that he was one ruler forced on the city by the rest of the nation, rather than the reverse, which was the usual case. For all his power and good intentions, he had done little to aid the worker directly; consequently, at the outset of the war, the attitude of radical and republican urban elements was that they had been ignored and suppressed for over twenty years. They also remembered that the propertied classes had turned the army on them in 1848. When the Empire fell, they enthusiastically endorsed republicanism and manned the city's defenses in a four-month siege which brought them to the verge of starvation while they waited for a rescue which never came. Bismarck needed somebody who would have authority to negotiate, so he allowed an armistice during which elections could be held. Most of France, wearied of the war, voted largely for the monarchists, who promised peace. The new assembly, led by Thiers, began negotiations with the Germans and, after moving to Versailles, attempted to disarm the National Guard in Paris. It also reduced payments to guardsmen and authorized the renewal of debt collections, such as rent, which had been in abeyance during the emergency. These measures infuriated urban republicans, who felt that agrarian spokesmen were selling out the cities and monarchists were betraying the national honor. In an emotional rejection of the Assembly, they rose in revolt, established a Guard-oriented communal government, and called on other cities in France to follow their example. Thiers found himself unable to move in force against the city until troops captured earlier by the Germans could be released to him. Morale soared in the city and radical agitators preached defiance of the monarchist assembly. There were all sorts of demagogues, but no special brand of militant socialism or communism dominated affairs. German troops watched in amusement as Thiers, on April 2, 1871, finally launched an all-out attack. The communards fought a vigorous house-to-house defense, killing all whose loyalty to their cause was suspect. The attacking army similarly gave no quarter in one of the bloodiest weeks (May 21–28, 1871) in the history of revolutionary activity. From a worker's viewpoint, the forces of property and reaction had again ordered the army to kill fellow Frenchmen who happened to be of a lower and largely propertyless class. The toll in lives was duplicated in property destruction (including Thiers' residence) which encompassed the looting and burning of government records. This latter circumstance has especially handicapped researchers on Second Empire topics; an example of this was the sacking of Marshal Canrobert's quarters, during which the bulk of his personal papers were burned. Thousands were killed and deported to penal colonies as the mood for revenge was allowed full rein. Because many of the most radical leaders were killed, subsequent French republicanism entered a moderate phase. The Commune was not an experiment in communism, despite its attempt to coordinate the city's energies for defense. Karl Marx saw it as an interesting example of a workers' uprising which lacked leadership. His followers, however, have been more enthusiastic in assigning it an important place in the history of communism. Some members of the International belonged on the ninety-member council, but the main thrust of the whole movement had been a wounded patriotism and a rejection of rural monarchist and clerical leadership. The suggestion has been made that Bismarck gave Thiers the troops to crush the revolt because the two leaders were partners in a bourgeoise move against the lower classes but this is to give to the Prussian statesman a dimension which hardly fits. The bitter upheaval created within France such deep social divisions and hatreds that when the monarchists then quarreled over the kind of new government to emerge, France was no longer a power to stir the apprehensions of the rest of Europe.

Another by-product of the Italian and German unifications was a major constitutional readjustment in Austria. In 1860 and 1861, both decentralized and centralized schemes for modifying the Empire were attempted but neither enjoyed much success. More local autonomy meant surrender of power to the landed aristocrats, whereas increased control from Vienna meant more Germanization. All voices seemed agreed that some concessions to the various nationalities were needed, but in what fashion and to what extent were matters of debate and indecision. From the experimentation Austria acquired a *Reichsrat,* a two-house legislative body modeled somewhat on Britain's Parliament. The biggest single problem for the government was to decide what should be done about the Hungarians. There had been no Magyar contribution to the war effort in 1859 and the Hungarians made no secret of their delight at the embarrassment of the dynasty and the army. The subsequent defeat by Prussia was the main catalyst in this domestic issue and dictated a pro-Hungarian solution. Francis Deak had been demanding restitution of the Hungarian constitutional rights of 1848; and after König-grätz, Vienna had little choice but to accede. At this point Franz Joseph was more interested in restoring Austrian prestige in Germany than he was in domestic reform. Bismarck's lenient Treaty of Prague and the restraint of his generals, who wanted a victory parade in Vienna, had not won much favor from the Austrian Emperor. The experience merely made Franz Joseph more willing to come to a quick and practical solution of his internal problems. He remained more interested in the Germany he was expelled from than in the Balkan vistas that Bismarck had hinted were now open to him.

In 1867 Vienna finally gave the Hungarians all they wanted. In a compromise called the *Ausgleich,* the Empire was essentially divided into two equal parts. Austria remained an empire and Hungary became a kingdom. In this "Dual Monarchy" there was personal union as Franz Joseph was both emperor and king and the two states shared common ministries of foreign affairs, finance, and war. Each were parliamentary states functioning under a constitution and delegates from both parliaments were to consult annually on common problems. On the surface a concession to Hungarian nationalism, it was, in fact, much more. Austria was openly still an empire with Germans controlling subject Poles, Czechs, Ruthenians, and Slovenes. The Hungarians similarly embraced Serbs, Croats, Slovaks, and Rumanians residing in Transylvania. In effect, two dominant ethnic groups were controlling subject peoples for whose nationalistic aspirations they had little sympathy. They openly regarded their charges as uncivilized and barbarian races fit to be ruled and exploited. Serfdom had formally disappeared in 1848 but this had not led to startling changes in living conditions among the lower classes. Landless peasants were pawns in the hands of landed aristocrats who possessed vast wealth and political power. The *Ausgleich* was simply a decision by the Germans to share the leadership with the Magyars, a judgment stemming directly from their humiliation in 1859 and 1866. Bismarck's unification in Central Europe was a triumph for one form of nationalism, but for Austria it opened the door to more multinationalism. The problem of sovereignty in most of Germany was solved, but the resulting truncated Austrian Empire was being urged to follow essentially an imperialistic program against less civilized peoples in the Balkans. Having surrendered her control of Hungary she was hardly well equipped to carry on a vigorous program of compensation. It was perhaps natural that she turned only slowly to the southeast. Königgrätz and Sedan dictated a nation-state solution to the German problem but condemned Austria to a continuation of a multinational structure which had been shorn of its earlier prestige as a historic universal empire. Lacking a powerful army, she was encouraged to re-create in the Balkans with even more disparate peoples, a system which had just failed in Germany. To many observers it seemed a futile path and predictions were rife that the Dual Monarchy would not last. With such skeptical initial apprehensions, its half century of existence was one of the surprises bequeathed by the nineteenth century. Prussian aggression and German nationalism had spelled defeat and multinationalistic imperialism for Austria. Constitutionalism in Bismarck's new Germany was a device to prevent democracy, and in the Dual Monarchy it was similarly nondemocratic. Only slowly was the suffrage broadened. The Magyars had strenuously resented being controlled by the Germans in Vienna, but when they achieved self-control, they proved harsher than the Germans with their subject peoples. In Austria adult male suffrage came in 1907, whereas in Hungary, by 1914 barely a quarter of adult males were able to vote.

While Austria was being forced to alter her historic role in Central Europe, the Ottoman Empire was also set on a new course. Internationally, the Congress of Paris had declared the Turkish Empire to be a full member of the European concert or family of nations; and the Powers pledged themselves to guarantee its sovereignty. Because the British, French, and Sardinians had ostensibly fought the Crimean War to protect Ottoman integrity, this was a natural point to be insisted on by these victors. In February of 1856, however, the Sultan had been pressured to accept a document, the Hatt-i Humayum, which embodied a wide range of reforms dealing with Christian civil rights. The Hatt-i Humayun had been drawn up by the Austrians, British, and French; at Paris, its position as a key statement of new Ottoman domestic policy was emphasized. This outside meddling in the Sultan's affairs was similar to that attributed to Nicholas of Russia before the war and indicates that, as the Tsar had often suggested, the Sultan was not master in his own house.

The Congress assumed a similar role regarding the principalities of Wallachia and Moldavia. After the war which was to support the Sultan against Russian invasion of these areas, the Ottoman ruler's authority there was only nominal. The Russian occupation was followed by an Austrian occupation and when both had withdrawn by March of 1857, elections were held to determine whether the two principalities should be united. A wave of nationalistic feeling had swept through the region and widespread consternation attended the results of the blatantly corrupt balloting which had helped to give victory to those opposing union. This was essentially a vote for the Sultan and for divided but parallel institutions of government. The frustrated unionists found their views echoed on the international plane by Russia, France, Prussia, and Sardinia, who blamed the Sultan for the chicanery at the ballot boxes and severed diplomatic relations with Constantinople. The British at first supported the Sultan, but Napoleon III persuaded them to reverse their stand. In new elections (September, 1859) the unionists were successful and the two principalities established identical political structures. This was as far as outsiders had expected union to go but now the native Rumanians seized the initiative and in both Moldavia and Wallachia selected Alexander Cuza (1820–1873) as the governing prince (*hospodar*). Unification was thus very nearly completed and a new country virtually founded, to the irritation of the Great Powers. However, in the wake of the Franco-Austrian war in Italy there was little sentiment to do more than grumble, and by 1862 the Sultan accepted the union. Formal independence came only in 1878; but, in effect, the Rumanians were functioning as a separate state after 1866, when Cuza was overthrown and replaced by Prince Charles (1839–1914) of Hohenzollern-Sigmaringen. This prince, who became King Charles I in 1881, had Beauharnais connections and was supported by Napoleon III. The peaceful founding of Rumania was the product of the Franco-Russian entente which operated between 1856 and 1863 and was a further evidence of the continual erosion of the Sultan's authority, which went on through most of the century. Another result of this Franco-Russian cooperation was a strengthening of local autonomy in both Serbia and Montenegro, again at the expense of the Sultan. From the mid-1860s, looking back over a decade, the government in Constantinople must have wondered whether it had gained anything at all from the support of Western Europe in the struggle with Russia.

Nationalism was spreading rapidly in the Balkans, bringing added complications to the so-called Eastern Question. Unfulfilled nationalism was a gnawing issue outside the Ottoman Empire and no equally strong major economic or social forces were at work to blunt or counter its impact. Poland was restive; subject peoples in Austria-Hungary were potential sources for agitation; and by 1870 a major segment of Europe, extending from Greece to the Baltic, was an attractive breeding ground for nationalistic outbreaks representing a number of cultural and ethnic groups. Nationalism by 1871 became a movement closely associated with force, thanks largely to Bismarck. Liberalism and cosmopolitanism tended to be discarded, especially by Polish nationalists, who believed they had been betrayed in 1863 by liberals in the West. The new nationalism seemed hardly humanitarian at all, as in France the sentiment fed on a feeling of revenge for the loss of Alsace and Lorraine. Indeed many European liberals frankly admired the authoritarian militarism of Bismarck, so obviously great and historic were the changes he had accomplished. They were spared the foreknowledge that German unification was of far more profound significance than even they realized. In the meantime, a Bismarck legend, somewhat like the Napoleonic Legend, appeared as liberals turned their backs on many of their own principles to applaud success. The same success inspired many Germans overseas, who also looked to the Iron Chancellor with pride and gratitude. He had made them stand taller in the world and they were delighted. Within Germany patriotism became equated with Prussian militarism and the new Empire was set on a course which eventually proved to be both dangerous and disastrous for millions of people.

The contagion of nationalism which was swiftly spreading in Europe had its effect directly in the writing of history itself. Among smaller ethnic groups there was a feverish search for uniqueness in background or origins, a concern with documenting the idea that their culture had a long and truly separate character. The best-known illustration of the interrelationship of nationalism and the writing of history is the Prussian school of historians. Its composite product was both a recommendation and a justification for German unification under Prussia. The educators of an age, they pointed out what tradition had marked as Germany's destiny and in effect helped to make Prussian aggression both palatable and proper. These recorders of the past thus played an important role in their own present and unwittingly but dramatically proved the value of history as a socially and politically useful tool. Writing in German, their works were widely read as they appeared in the context of public prestige for history which Leopold von Ranke had helped to create. Documented and seeming to meet the highest canons of scientific history, the message was clear that what had happened politically in Central Europe was "right." A flowering of studies on medieval Germany, the Lutheran revolt, and the Thirty Years' War set the context for von Sybel (1817–1895), Droysen (1808–1884), and finally Treitschke (1834–1896). The cumulative impact of these three men was a glorification of Hohenzollern and Prussian leadership. Von Sybel was a student of Ranke's and his early work on the First Crusade, combined with his founding and editing of the *Historische*

Zeitschrift, gave his name the aura of authority. He became active in politics; as a result, his study on the founding of the German Empire was an important but flawed work. Droysen was also involved in politics as a member of the Frankfurt Parliament and came to his politically laden studies after early work of high quality on antiquity. He helped to focus German thinking on the leadership qualities of the house of Hohenzollern, especially in his descriptions of Prussian foreign policy before Frederick the Great and during the War of Liberation. Like von Sybel, he had a scrupulous regard for documents and meticulously included them in his narratives. Heinrich von Treitschke made von Sybel and Droysen appear as completely objective historians. His study of nineteenth-century Germany has valuable documentary material, but despite the trappings of scholarship it is one of the most biased works ever written by a serious scholar. The Hohenzollerns are, of course, on a pedestal whereas opponents of Prussia and its dynasty are condemned with all the feeling that nationalism can inspire. He thus censures democrats, internationalists, Jews, pacifists, socialists, Catholics, Austrians, Englishmen, Russians, Frenchmen, non-Prussian Germans of the smaller states, and other broad categories of nonpatriotic Prussians. In Treitschke's hands, historical writing lost its sense of objectivity. It became emotional propaganda and its potential in promoting divisive national hatreds and rivalries was clear. Treitschke glorified armed conquest and declared any hope of abolishing war to be not only preposterous but immoral, as in Nietzschean flourishes, he found war to be glorious and sublime, a law of life, veritably the will of God.

XI

A New Politics
of the Status Quo,
1870–1890

CHAPTER 33

An Era of
Bismarckian Diplomacy,
1871–1890

Following the proclamation of the German Empire at Versailles in 1871, European diplomacy entered a distinctly new phase. Until 1890, Otto von Bismarck, now chancellor to an Emperor, dominated the scene. It was perhaps fitting that the man instrumental in creating the Europe of 1871 should have the task of initially providing its diplomatic leadership. Despite many uncertainties and some failures, Bismarck so successfully manipulated the ambitions abounding in Europe that the story of international relations for two more decades appears neatly structured as though fitting a basic plan. From his retirement Bismarck later explained how he had followed such a design. Most historians have been prone to accept his analysis because it seemed to be in accord with known facts. From our present perspective the German leader remains an intriguing and extraor-

435

Bismarck addressing the Reichstag. (Courtesy of Historical Pictures Service, Chicago.)

dinary diplomat but hardly as prescient and in control of events as he would have liked us to believe.

European diplomacy between 1870 and 1890 was reminiscent of the years from 1815 to 1848, when another German statesman dominated diplomatic discussions. The similarities were interesting but the differences revealed how much Europe had been changed. Like Metternich in 1815, Bismarck had helped create the world of 1871 and his future efforts were devoted to maintaining it with as little change as possible. It was to be a new era of status quo politics between states, so far as Bismarck could manage it. The key to the new status quo was to be a cooperative foreign policy between the three eastern powers, Germany, Austria-Hungary, and Russia. Such a cooperation would, in effect, be a sort of resurrection of the old Holy Alliance. The sight of these three conservative powers acting together to provide stability among European states would have pleased Metternich.

Bismarck, however, was not Metternich and the new Germany was not the old Austria. Temperamentally, Metternich was of the eighteenth century but by 1871, there was little left of the gracious cosmopolitanism permeating higher society in the previous century. Bismarck was a conservative, to be sure, but he was first and foremost a Prussian nationalist. His new Germany was really a triumphant and conquering Prussia with little sympathy for the humane values of the Enlightenment. With his sense of hard realism, problems of national unrest and friction could be seen for exactly what they were. There would be no equating of an urge for national independence with an attack on the social order, and there was no new equivalent for the sense of dread and terror felt by Metternich's generation for The Revolution. The new leadership was pragmatic. It thought in terms of security through balanced tensions rather than assuming a moralistic view of protecting the values of civilized society. One of the prices paid for the new realism was that it was unconvincing for Bismarck to pose as a moral leader when an occasion such as the *Kulturkampf* suggested such a role.

After 1871 Bismarck saw his task as ensuring the security of Germany. Through successive resorts to "blood and iron" he had created the new situation in Europe and now wanted no further territorial changes. The poacher had turned game warden. Having just flouted and altered the political pattern of the Continent, he now became an ardent spokesman for the sanctity of treaties and the new arrangement of political power. From his point of view, Prussia was now a "completed state." There would be no problem if the other major powers were satisfied with their boundaries as of 1871, but this was not the case. Nationalists and liberals had long expected that with a united Germany and a united Italy, many of Europe's political problems would be solved. Unfortunately, the two new powers had been created at the expense of other states; consequently, an era opened with anxieties and frustrations as deep and dangerous as those of the age just ended. Bismarck recognized the sources of new instability and, with a remarkable candor, set about their control.

As the German chancellor surveyed the European scene in 1871, he saw one major threat to peace, France. He had privately opposed the transfer of Alsace and Lorraine on the grounds that such a use of victory would assure permanent French hostility. He noted that a proud people would never acquiesce for long in such a settlement, but the military arguments for taking these territories were compelling. Over the centuries most French invasions of South Germany had passed through these provinces. The geography of this part of Europe made their control essential if South Germany were to be defended—a new obligation about to fall to the Prussian leaders. History has proved both Bismarck and his generals to be largely correct. For years French politicians representing all levels of the political spectrum called for a restoration of Alsace and Lorraine, and many explicitly demanded a war of revenge. It proved also to be true that by holding the key routes into South Germany, the German army could protect that area from French invasion. When he bowed to the military arguments, Bismarck then presumed the continuous enmity of France. This hostility, however, could be tolerated because it had been just proved that France was no match for the new Germany. A French war of revenge was not a practical danger to Germany *unless* France found an ally. This general rationale governed much of Bismarck's diplomacy for the next nineteen years. German security rested on French diplomatic isolation. Continuation of the same isolation which had helped defeat Napoleon III became the basic objective for German diplomacy.

While French hostility was seen as an underlying threat to peace, another danger was the sense of shock at the enormous military power demonstrated by the Germans. It was one thing to see Germany united; but that French influence should be so reduced and that the new power in Central Europe should be such an armed colossus was disturbing to many capitals. Even British leaders, who had so distrusted Napoleon III, were now apprehensive. Bismarck had expected that Britain would continue to follow a policy of "splendid" isolation, but her renewed interest in Empire now made her more apprehensive of any state in a position to hamper her "life-lines." In London there was also a renewed anxiety about the security of the Low Countries. What guarantee was there that the new Germany really had no further territorial ambitions? Bismarck quickly recognized these new attitudes and took special care that no overt German actions could be regarded as aimed at England.

On the Continent Bismarck moved quickly to promote close understanding with those states which could be potential French allies for a successful war of revenge, Austrian-Hungary and Russia. His task was eased because these countries, like Britain, were impressed by the show of raw power just demonstrated against France. In Vienna especially there was concern for good relations with the new Germany. After Sadowa, *despite Bismarck's restraint* of Prussian generals who wanted a victory march in Vienna, Austrian statesmen began thinking in terms of a war of revenge. They had not fully accepted the idea that Sadowa meant their near exclusion from German affairs. Of course, the logic of this position should have made them allies of Napoleon III in 1870. When they failed to help France and the Second Empire fell, their hopes for a major comeback as a

German power were shattered. Bismarck's hints that Austria might find compensation elsewhere (the Balkans) became acceptable after 1871, once the finality of her expulsion from Germany was clear. In the historic rivalry between Hapsburg and Hohenzollern for influence in Germany, the Prussian dynasty had won. Once this was accepted in Vienna, they could give more systematic attention to opportunities presented by the still-decaying Ottoman Empire.

Centuries of conflict with the Turk also supported the logic of Hapsburg expansion to the southeast, but for this now to be vigorously pushed, it was essential that the Hungarians cooperate and peacefully accept their place in the Dual Monarchy. The idea of hostility between Vienna and Berlin would have to be replaced by as close a relationship as possible in order to assure German diplomatic support for advances in the Balkans. This was an historic change, and with the Hungarian Andrassy (1823–1890) in the foreign ministry, it was ably carried out. Initial steps in the program for closer relations with Germany began at Ischl, Gastein, and Salzburg during August and September, 1871, when Emperor Franz Joseph met for comprehensive talks with Germany's new emperor, William. Both leaders were accompanied by their respective foreign ministers and all recognized the importance of Austria's altered role in Europe. A year later (September, 1872) the emperors again met, this time in Berlin, and were joined by Russia's Tsar Alexander II, who was apprehensive about the growing Austro-German friendship. The talks were amicable but portents of the future abounded in discussions of the Ottoman Empire held by Andrassy and Russia's chancellor, Gorchakov (1798–1883). Bismarck's encouragement of Austria to move into the Balkans disregarded completely the equally historic Russian interest in Ottoman lands. That Austria and Russia would view each other's designs in the Balkans with great suspicion was merely a continuation of a former posture, though Austria's interest in the area had become far more vital. So long as Germany gave diplomatic support to this new Austrian course, it was assured that France would find no encouragement in Vienna for a struggle to recover Alsace and Lorraine.

Russia's position proved difficult, in the long run, for Bismarck to control; and after he left office, the event he had dreaded and worked against for years came to pass—France found an ally in Russia. Such a development, however, had not occurred while Bismarck was directing German policy. On the surface there was little to draw France and Russia together. The rapprochement between the two powers after the Crimean War had not lasted beyond the Polish revolt in 1863, when Napoleon criticized Russian repression. Bismarck had adopted a pro-Russian stance at that time and had agreed to the substantial modification of the Black Sea neutralization clause in the settlement at the Congress of Paris. These acts had helped to keep Russia neutral in 1870, and after Napoleon had fallen, France adopted a republican regime which appeared to make any approaches to imperial Russia quite unlikely. Bismarck, however, was apprehensive of a Franco-Russian agreement and diligently worked against it. He presumed too much French interest in such an arrangement during the 1870s but was accurate in his reading of French policy from the mid-1880s on.

Out of this complex of interests grew the *Dreikaiserbund,* a very loose alliance which had for Germany the object of assuring the continuance of French isolation. However, the central figure, strictly speaking, so far as formal documents were concerned, was Russia, and the central issue was the problem of Austro-Russian competition in the Balkans. In May of 1873, Russia negotiated with Germany a military agreement which provided that each would provide 200,000 troops to the other if either were attacked by another power. This meant little to Germany but gave Russia reassurances should Balkan problems lead to hostilities with Austria. The following month in Vienna, a less explicit but equally important understanding was reached between Austria and Russia. The respective emperors agreed to consult with one another in case difficulties were to arise between them, an apparent possibility then in the Balkans. In October, Germany declared its support of this latter agreement; consequently, a loose interlocking structure had evolved. The powers were all conservative, dedicated to monarchical government, and anxious to avoid outright hostilities. Dangers arising from conflicting ambitions in the Balkans seemed to have been anticipated and at the same time Bismarck had his security from France. The whole arrangement was fragile and rested to a large extent on the good judgment of the emperors themselves. A new, conservative, Holy Alliance type of structure had been created. Like Prussia, Russia, and Austria between 1815 and 1848, peace was to be maintained by efforts to keep the status quo and the three major states pledged to pursue common foreign policies. Peace proved almost as elusive as it had in the earlier Metternich era, but at least the structure seemed to prevent major wars.

Italy was the only other power Bismarck had to consider, but it came into the post-1871 period with interesting frustrations. Unification of the peninsula was complete but a number of avid nationalists still called attention to Italians not yet included in the new state. They wanted still more land to assure the return of their "brothers," specifically Trieste and the southern Trentino, territories controlled by Austria. A cry that Italians living in these lands should be freed from the foreign yoke created ill will in Austria, who was already irritated over her earlier losses in Italy. While statesmen in Rome in the early 1870s managed to keep this movement subdued, Victor Emmanuel II negotiated Italian adhesion to the *Dreikaiserbund*. This was a very loose and vague arrangement, less binding even than those between the three major powers. Italy's incentive for this agreement was that she feared that the monarchist-oriented government in France might intervene in behalf of the Pope, who had refused to come to terms with the new secular state in Rome. Later Italian ambitions in North Africa were to drive her even further from harmonious relations with France.

In Bismarck's thinking the new treaty structure which Balkan appetites had helped to create was still oriented toward the danger of a revanchist France. Almost as if to confirm his apprehensions, a "war scare" occurred in 1875. Characteristically, the Prussian statesman's role in the developing situation is obscure and he remains suspect to this day.

Many elements contributed to the "scare," but prominent among them was the phenomenal French recovery after 1871. The peace treaty had included a 5-billion-franc indemnity, a provision designed to drain off French surpluses and to provide an excuse for a German occupation of French territory for an extended period. The enormous sum to be delivered by March, 1874, was intended to be virtually an impossible goal; but, to the amazement of Europe, France delivered the required funds early. Consequently, German troops left France in September of 1873, and the massive flow of funds into Germany was an inflationary factor in the economy east of the Rhine. At the same time, the French openly embarked on a program of military reform. France appeared to be economically strong and to be girding for war. In addition, there was widespread consternation in France regarding Bismarck's coercive measures against the Catholic Church in Germany. In this context many important Germans, especially officers in the upper echelons of the army, began to discuss the merits of a preventive war. This idea finally appeared in the German press, most notably an article published in Berlin entitled "Is War in Sight?" Bismarck is suspected of having been responsible for publication of the article as a warning to the French. In Paris the royalist foreign minister, the Duke Decazes, seized the situation as an opportunity to portray Germany as in effect threatening France. The result was that both Britain and Russia, through their ambassadors in Berlin, expressed consternation at such talk, to the irritation of Bismarck. Because they refrained from trying to get the French to discontinue their military reforms, the German chancellor saw the situation as revealing the fragility of the new alliance and he became even more determined that France should not find a Continental ally. The French regarded the episode as a diplomatic triumph, but it could not be further exploited because the position of the monarchist government of MacMahon was steadily eroding. With the anticlerical republican upsurge, France appeared less an immediate danger and the attention of diplomats was diverted to a new Eastern crisis.

Another chapter in the Eastern Question began with a revolt in Bosnia and Herzogovina in mid-summer of 1875. It ended with the Congress of Berlin in 1878. Causes of the upheaval were the familiar grievances of non-Turk Christians associated with Turkish rule. Because Ottoman rule was laced with corruption and incompetence over a broad area, as well as being antinational and anti-Christian, the revolt, once started, met with considerable sympathy among other subject groups and quickly spread through the Balkan peninsula. By the following summer both Serbia and Montenegro had formally declared war on the Ottoman Empire and Bulgaria was in full insurrection. Left alone by outsiders, the Turks could probably have maintained their sovereignty in all areas of unrest; indeed, their army was remarkably successful against the Serbs, and the Bulgarians were put down with especial severity. The Great Powers, however, became involved.

Britain had been tempted to do nothing so long as the Turks maintained control and were not coerced by another major power. This comfortable stance became untenable after the repression in Bulgaria, when Gladstone piously condemned the "Horrors," scoring points against his political opponent then in office, Benjamin Disraeli. While the British were becoming less neutral, the Austrians and Russians could not resist the temptation to fish in troubled waters. A complex negotiation centered on the so-called Andrassy Note, which detailed a program of reform for the Turks. Austria's motives, however, were suspect, for Andrassy coveted Bosnia and Herzogovina. At the same time, the Russians were also drawn into events and, like the British, were divided at home about what their policy should be. The Pan-Slavs wanted a militantly pro-Serb, anti-Turk policy; others favored using Russian influence to prevent any basic changes. The Pan-Slavs proved more successful; finally, in April of 1877, Russia went to war against Turkey, an act which helped to place Britain emphatically in an anti-Russian, pro-Turkish posture, a considerable change considering the public outcry against the Bulgarian horrors.

Through the preliminaries to war Bismarck was little more than an observer participating in diplomacy but doing nothing to alter the paths being followed by other powers. He had, in fact, little control in the situation. He regretted the idea that Austria and Russia might come to blows over a Balkan dispute but seemed to lack the ingenuity to come up with a solution. On this occasion he was lucky, for Austrian and Russian troops did not meet, despite their opposing objectives. Bismarck, like most others caught up in the situation, reacted to events as well as he could but showed no special brilliance.

The Russian objective in the war was to move quickly on Constantinople; but, as in the early phase of the Crimean War, they found it easier to cross the Danube than to continue to the Ottoman capital. Instead of Silistria, this time it was Plevna where the Turks made a brave stand. For five months, from July to December, 1877, Plevna resisted attack. When it finally fell, its heroic defense had stirred public emotion in Britain to sympathize with the Turk and to forget the horrors. Ironically, the siege had brought forth as much heroism on the part of the beseiging Russians, but somehow this did not create as favorable an impact on the popular imagination. Instead, when Plevna fell and the Russians could resume their push to Constantinople, they were again seen as avaricious aggressors against a weak, victimized Turkey (instead of defenders of Christians being massacred) and a cool attitude toward Russian aims was clear in the chancellories of Europe.

The siege had depleted Russian strength and when the Turks could no longer resist, the Treaty of San Stefano was quickly negotiated on March 3, 1878. The terms of this settlement sent shock waves through Central and Western Europe, though from a dispassionate point of view, they merely validated Russian aims in the Balkans and the fact that Russia had won the war. As in the Franco-Prussian War the loser, the Turks in this case, was to pay a large indemnity and lose some territory as well. Reforms favoring Christians in Bosnia and Herzogovina were to be expected and the insistence on independence for Serbia and Montenegro was a reasonable stipulation for a victorious power motivated strongly by sentiments of Pan-Slavism. There was a rationale as well for Russian expansion, at Ottoman expense, in Asia. Consequently, the transfer of Batum, Bayazed, Kars, and Ardahan caused no great objection. The most important feature of the treaty, however, was the portion dealing with Bulgaria. A new Bulgarian state was to be formed which clearly would be little more than a Russian satellite. Especially disturbing was the provision for its new boundaries. Because the Dobrudja was to be considered a compensation to Rumania for the transfer of Bessarabia to Russia, the Bulgarian southern boundary was extended to the Aegean, thus appearing to provide Russia with an outlet to the Mediterranean which by-passed Constantinople. If implemented, San Stefano would constitute a major upset of the power structure in southeastern Europe. The nations who had been content to watch the Russo-Turk struggle without getting too involved now became alarmed.

Austria-Hungary and Great Britain found the new settlement especially unacceptable. Of the outside powers these had been the most involved and Andrassy took the diplomatic initiative while Britain actually sent her fleet to Constantinople in response to a sentiment close to war fever at home. British diplomacy also became active and coalesced with Austrian frustration at the settlement which allowed for no compensatory gains for herself in the Balkans. (Earlier Russia had led her to believe she would get Bosnia if there were Russian gains.) Bismarck realized that San Stefano simply was unacceptable as it stood. Not exactly sure what was in the offing, he agreed to a call by Andrassy for the major states to meet in a congress at Berlin to review the Eastern Question thoroughly. Accordingly, between June 13 and July 13 in 1878, the German capital hosted the most impressive array of diplomats to assemble between 1856 and 1919. Bismarck, Gorchakov, Andrassy, and Disraeli were merely the brightest stars in a body containing the best diplomatic minds of Europe.

Between March and June notes and missions frantically laid the groundwork for the discussions regarding the viability of San Stefano. In this period the Russians failed to win Austrian acquiescence to their gains while the British scored a striking success in coming to agreements with Russia, Turkey, and Austria. In view of the British agreements, which involved a much smaller Bulgaria, Bismarck seemed to have an opportunity to remain out of the issue. This was to be the posture which he affected but failed to maintain. When the Congress actually met, Russia arrived having already accepted the idea of retreating on San Stefano but willing to see what face-to-face re-examination of the issues might produce.

Russian spokesmen were especially anxious to see what Bismarck's position in the crisis would be. Their agreement with Britain was secret so that to many of the diplomats arriving in the German capital, there was an appearance of more flexibility than was actually the case. The particular issue showed clearly the inadequacy of the loose *Dreikaiserbund* as a device to preserve peace and Bismarck was in a quandary about how to handle the situation. He wanted, of course, to see a settlement which both Austria and Russia would accept in good faith, but this appeared virtually impossible. The English agreements dictated the type of peace to emerge unless Germany were to object. Bismarck adopted the pose of a genial host, an "honest broker," and declared himself really uninterested in Balkan affairs and pained that his friends were so upset over the area. He had, of course, helped direct Austrian interests in that direction. During the conference he played on Continental apprehensions regarding the British, who were forever interfering in the affairs of others and slyly gave advice to "watch out for the Jew," Disraeli. Nonetheless, his pretended neutrality was seen by the Russians for exactly what it was, a reluctant support for the Austrian position—in effect, an insistence on a basic revision of the Treaty of San Stefano. With others opposed to Russia, to be neutral was to leave Russia isolated, and they believed that Bismarck had deserted them. And he had, though with reluctance.

The hero of the meeting, despite Bismarck's omnipresence, was Disraeli. It was probably the high point in his career. The settlement denied the Russians the enlarged Bulgaria and handed Austria administrative rights in Bosnia and Herzogovina, thus granting "compensation" to Austria for the Russian increase in prestige in the Balkans. Russia retained Batum, Kars, Ardaham, and southern Bessarabia, a modest return for the expensive and successful war she had fought. Britain was delighted that the revised Bulgaria did not border on the Aegean. As her reward from the Turks for promising earlier to defend them against further Russian aggression, she occupied Cyprus. Rumania, Montenegro, and Serbia were declared independent states. Many reforms were stipulated for various parts of the Ottoman Empire, which in this phase of the Eastern Question was completely powerless to decide its future. In the gradual breakup of the Sultan's domains, the Greeks had hoped for major gains but were brushed aside at Berlin. Thus the Greeks, as well as the Bulgarians and Russians, were irritated by the outcome of the conference. The Serbs were apprehensive about the Austrian intrusion into Bosnia and Herzogovina and disappointed at their loss of some lands that San Stefano had given them. The Congress had revised

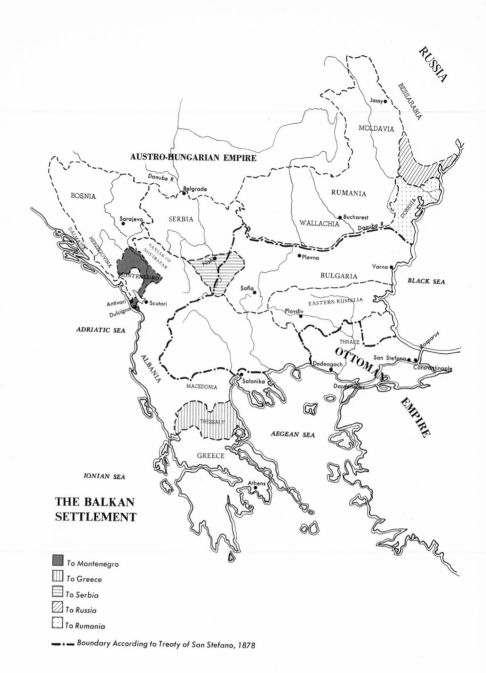

RUSSIA

BESSARABIA

Jassy

MOLDAVIA

AUSTRO-HUNGARIAN EMPIRE

Danube R.

Belgrade

RUMANIA

BOSNIA

Sarajevo

SERBIA

WALLACHIA

Bucharest

DOBRUJA

HERZEGOVINA

SANJAK OF NOVIBAZAR

Danube R.

DALMATIA

MONTENEGRO

Niš

Plevna

Varna

BLACK SEA

Antivari

Scutari

BULGARIA

Sofia

Dulcigno

EASTERN RUMELIA

ADRIATIC SEA

Plovdiv

THRACE

Bosporus

ALBANIA

San Stefano

OTTOMAN

Constantinople

Dedeagach

MACEDONIA

Salonika

Dardanelles

EMPIRE

THESSALY

AEGEAN SEA

GREECE

IONIAN SEA

Athens

THE BALKAN
SETTLEMENT

To Montenegro

To Greece

To Serbia

To Russia

To Rumania

—·— Boundary According to Treaty of San Stefano, 1878

446

San Stefano so that Britain and Austria could live with a newly diminished Ottoman Empire, but it created its own share of bitterness and frustration.

An undramatic but interesting feature of the Congress was the role of the French spokesman, W. H. Waddington. Unobtrusively he managed to contribute a French voice in the decisions; considering the humiliation of 1870, his role at Berlin was remarkable. France had significant economic interests in many of the Balkan areas. She was especially involved as the major creditor of the Ottoman Empire and was concerned over territorial adjustments which were to deprive that Empire of half its "European" holdings. Waddington's voice was also given attention because of the apprehensions of the other powers. French friendship was still worth cultivating and Waddington left the Congress with its approval for a French penetration of Tunis. Italy, the other new "Great Power" besides Germany, played an insignificant role at Berlin. Because Austria was on the side the major decisions supported, it was obviously no time for Italians to hope for success in claiming more of Austrian territory. She was irritated over the green light given France in Tunis; and Bismarck delighted in the idea that in rewarding France for some of the economic losses she would suffer in the Balkans, he had helped assure friction between France and Italy. The hero was Disraeli, but the stamp of Bismarck was also clear.

If German policy had not really been in control before the Congress of Berlin, it followed a remarkably aggressive and successful path afterward. In 1878 Bismarck had been forced to choose between Austria and Russia. He tried to disguise the choice, but his situation was clear to diplomats. When he could avoid decision no longer, he had supported Austria. His reasoning for preferring Vienna over St. Petersburg was that in any alliance, Berlin would always be able to decide policy and to dictate to Vienna; however, Russia, in a similar arrangement, would always insist on an equal voice. This rationale is intriguing when one considers 1914, the "blank check," and the basic decisions then made in Vienna. Germany lacked a Bismarck in 1914. In choosing Austria in 1878, Bismarck also felt that if he abandoned her in her Balkan ambitions, she would be far more likely than Russia to turn to France. After the Congress, therefore, the German statesman approached the Austrians and negotiated an Austro-German alliance (October, 1879). This Dual Alliance was an obvious implication of the Congress and was to prove the basic feature of future German policy. The five-year renewable treaty provided that if Russia attacked either party, the other would aid in the defense. If either were attacked by some other power, such as France, then the other would be neutral unless France had Russia as an ally. In the latter contingency both Germany and Austria would fight together. Bismarck regarded this treaty as helping Germany's defensive posture against the French danger. He thought Russia would hesitate to attack Austria in the Balkans if she knew an attack on Austria would bring Germany to her aid. It was clear that for the treaty to be operable, one had to be "attacked." Thus, Austria could not attack Russia in the Balkans and expect help, so the alliance might be a damper on Austrian aggressiveness in Southeastern Europe.

Compelling as his logic was for the Austrian alliance in 1879, Bismarck was disturbed by the rupture in Russo-German relations caused by the Balkan crisis. The split had occurred because of secondary considerations and not because of any basic dispute between Russia and Germany. He retained the notion that the French were eager for any opportunity for a war to recover Alsace and Lorraine and it bothered him that Russia was free of any treaty obligations to Germany and was just "drifting" and available for a French alliance. Russia, however, had her eye more on Austria and the Balkans than on France, and to Bismarck's delight she approached Germany with suggestions for renewal agreements. The result of this was a resurrection in June, 1881, of the old *Dreikaiserbund,* in effect a broadening of the Dual Alliance with Austria. Discussions would take place regarding future Balkan crises and if any of the three powers were attacked by a fourth (France), then the other two were to remain neutral. In this arrangement the Russians felt they were more likely to receive German sympathy for their Balkan ambitions, which at the same time would act as a brake on Austria. Again the Balkans had brought Bismarck his alliances, and although the Austrians now participated with some hesitation, he still had his security from France. Indeed, everything seemed to be favoring German policy and Italy asked to be part of the new alliance structure. This came as a direct consequence of the Berlin encouragement to the French to move into Tunis.

In May of 1882, after negotiating with Austria at Bismarck's insistence, Italy joined Austria and Germany, forming the historic Triple Alliance. She now had a promise of help if she were engaged in a war with France. For this she had agreed to aid Germany or Austria if they were attacked by France or to aid either if they were attacked by any two or more powers. For Bismarck this guarantee of aid was regarded as of little importance, because the core of his policy remained the Dual Alliance. He had, however, managed to keep the other major powers, besides England, outside the grasp of French diplomacy. In another bonus for Germany, the British invaded Egypt, a direct blow to French economic interests. The French were truly isolated.

In 1884 the *Dreikaiserbund* was easily renegotiated to extend another three years. In that time Balkan intrigues again brought Austrian and Russian objectives face to face. Russia had become embroiled in Bulgarian politics, where she saw her dominant position threatened by Austria. Austria had already negotiated treaties with Serbia (1881) and Rumania (1883). When Germany associated herself with the Rumanian treaty, Russia realized that her earlier advantages in the Balkans were gradually being eroded. Rail construction in Bulgaria constituted Austrian economic penetration and spurred active Russian intrigues and countermeasures. To Bismarck's dismay, Austro-Russian suspicion and mutual antipathy regarding the Balkans became so pronounced that it was impossible for him to obtain a further extension of the *Dreikaiserbund* after 1887. The provision calling for consultations and discussions regarding Balkan interests had always been a dead letter. Although Bismarck could do little more than watch as Austria and Russia became more hostile over the Balkans, he felt no real danger so long as neither was available for a French alliance. He worried about Russia "drifting free," but the Russians gave him a way out of this central concern. They proposed that a Russo-German treaty be negotiated to replace the *Dreikaiserbund* when it expired. This would be somewhat along the lines of the Dual Alliance.

At this juncture Bismarck felt that he had little choice but to accede to the Russian suggestions. The result was the so-called Reinsurance Treaty signed on June 18, 1887. Both parties would be neutral if either were at war with another power unless Russia were an aggressor against Austria or Germany an aggressor against France. Bismarck felt that he had "reinsured" German security by again joining with Russia in a treaty arrangement. It was less satisfactory than a renewal of the *Dreikaiserbund,* but it was the best choice available. It was especially important because in the 1880s French capital had been seeking investments in Russia, which the Prussian statesman saw as dangerous.

This Reinsurance Treaty has been criticized as being essentially immoral so far as Bismarck was concerned. Technically, it was not inconsistent with other German treaties; but in actuality, Germany's position would have been embarrassing indeed had Austria and

Russia gone to war during the life of the treaty. As it was, Bismarck gave an impression of sober honesty in the negotiations, even reading to the Russian ambassador, Shuvalov, the text of the Dual Alliance. In his defense it should be noted that statecraft followed intricate formal procedures which essentially covered the fact that the law among nations was really the law of the jungle. Further, Bismarck did have an obligation to provide German security as well as he could; by binding Russia to an alliance with Germany, he was effectively removing her from any immediate French blandishments. The wisdom of this rationale became clear after Bismarck's dismissal when the Russo-German treaty was not renewed and a rapid Franco-Russian accommodation (1892) took place. When the very thing Bismarck had dreaded for twenty years occurred, the prospects of war were significantly enhanced.

Russian objectives in the treaty were fairly obvious, though perhaps excessively optimistic. They expected the pact to moderate Austrian opposition to her designs in the Balkans. It called for supporting the status quo in that troubled region; as the Russians saw it, this meant German diplomatic recognition of a Russian preponderance in Bulgaria. At the time, Bulgaria was in turmoil over a struggle between Russian agents and sympathizers and Bulgarian nationalists under Prince Alexander of Battenberg, who had worked to root out Russian influences. Alexander was forced to abdicate and during an interregnum from September 4, 1886, to July 4, 1887, the Russians debated open military occupation of the country. There appeared to be some German support for Russia in this crisis, and Austria was restrained, which lessened the danger of overt Russian military action.

Bismarck's role in this situation was typical of how he viewed his obligations of support for Russian objectives agreed in the treaty. In effect, Bismarck received the comfort of having Russia a part of his alliance structure without really giving much for it. The requirement to support Russian interest in the status quo was deftly avoided when the situation attracted other powers, especially Austria and England. Aiding in this were the Mediterranean Agreements of February and December of 1887. Germany acceded to the first but not the second, though her closest ally, Austria, was a party to both. Britain and Italy were central to both agreements, which insisted on the maintenance of the status quo if at all possible in the Mediterranean, the Aegean, the Adriatic, and the Black Sea. They had a distinct anti-French orientation and, in the context of Russo-Balkan interests, were also anti-Russian. Thus any serious Russian aggression in the Balkans would surely bring England as well as Austria into the situation and Russia would be blocked despite German "support." As Bismarck saw the problem, the Reinsurance Treaty combined with the Mediterranean Agreements maintained German security. Despite what looked like an accommodation with Russia (and all of this was secret), the whole weight of German diplomacy was distinctly pro-Austrian as well as anti-French. In effect, Russian objectives were really on the fringe of German policy and never central to it.

On March 18, 1890, Bismarck was dismissed from office by William II (1859–1941). As widely noted at the time, it was the end of an era. For three decades the wily Junker aristocrat had played a brilliant role in Europe's diplomacy. After ten years of successfully promoting war, he had worked just as effectively for twenty years in behalf of peace. His triumphs were so striking that as brilliant a diplomatic coup as Disraeli's 1875 acquisition of the controlling shares in the Suez Canal seemed almost to deserve second place. Similarly, the hero of the 1878 Congress was really Disraeli, yet "the honest broker" managed to be the center of attention. He dominated diplomatic circles after the triumph of Prussian arms at Sadowa and at Sedan. There can be no questioning his sincerity for peace following 1870 and, given the circumstances outside his direct control in south-eastern Europe, he must receive substantial credit for the diplomacy which, though allowing a Russo-Turk war, still prevented war between two major powers. His object was continuance of the status quo of 1871 and he saw the best guarantee of this to be through cooperation between the three conservative empires, Germany, Russia, and Austria-Hungary. This line-up was somewhat reminiscent of the old Holy Alliance except that Russia's role was reduced and the new Germany played a more commanding role than Prussia ever had.

In the conduct of German policy, Bismarck showed himself uncompromising. After the dramatic success of the army prior to 1871, an intrusion of some of its spokesmen into the area of decision making might have been expected. Bismarck, however, treated them as technicians whose advice could be sought on occasion. In 1887, he thwarted an effort of the military men to encourage Austrian leaders to believe Germany would support them if war with Russia came over Bulgaria. Bismarck clearly indicated that he intended to make policy himself and was able to keep army men in a subordinate role. The episode indicated, however, the influence that the army in Germany could have if not opposed by an unusually strong man. In

November, 1887, another interesting situation revealed Bismarck's awareness of the power of economic considerations. In a move to hinder Russian policy in the Balkans, he made it impossible for the Russians to use their securities as collateral for loans from the Reichsbank. This had its calculated effect in the short run, but in the long run it helped to turn Russian bankers to Paris for capital and to make Bismarck himself partly responsible for the developing Franco-Russian alliance.

In a broader context, the period from 1870 to 1890 is usually seen as a first phase in the complicated background of World War I. Historians relating these two decades to the hostilities between Great Powers erupting in 1914 have generally had harsh words for Bismarck. In his striving for German security and peace, he managed to erect an alliance structure which required statesmen with talent and resourcefulness. When he was followed by lesser men, he was an obvious target for criticism for creating the system. Further, as a result of his policies the idea spread that security required allies and the French anxiously tried to promote a situation where the Triple Alliance could not dominate European relations. In his defense, of course, it may again be pointed out that the French were able to start erecting the Triple Entente only after Bismarck left office. His object for Germany after 1871 was peace in his time, and he succeeded in this. Perhaps he should not be judged by the problems of another age.

Another criticism of the diplomacy of the 1870s and 1880s was that so much of it was secret. This secrecy enhanced the chances of mistakes and became an acute problem in 1914, when many statesmen were unclear about specific obligations of other powers. Bismarck, however, hardly created secret diplomacy; he merely excelled in the game as he found it. He made no attempt to raise the moral level of diplomacy or the world he lived in. As a confirmed practitioner of *Realpolitik,* he recognized hatreds as part of life. Thus he presumed and accepted the idea of continual French animosity. He never made serious attempts to mollify the French but assumed that they were continuously plotting to gain revenge. Considering the history of French domestic and foreign policy between 1871 and 1914, it appears that Bismarck may have been on solid ground in this evaluation. The moralist, however, would insist that the Prussian statesman was in error when he did not work harder for French friendship. He had, after all, been able to appease Austria and her expulsion from German affairs was as much an affront, and as damaging historically, as the defeat and loss of territory suffered by

France. Considering the talents of the man, perhaps possibilities other than simply devising a structure of balanced tensions existed for assuring German security. After his time, eventually most of Europe had its place in an enormous diplomatic Leviathan which assured a massive conflagration when it went out of control. By 1914, however, twenty-four years had passed since Bismarck left office and he had been dead for sixteen years. The history of European diplomacy after 1890, when it was guided by lesser men, properly belongs to the story of the twentieth century.

CHAPTER 34

Domestic and Economic Adjustments in Germany, France, Britain, Russia, and Italy, 1870–1890

In the decades following 1870 Europe underwent enormous economic change. Such progress had already been a distinguishing feature of the century but now it vastly accelerated. The German and Italian unifications contributed to this, as well as the general trend toward free trade which occurred by the 1860s. Further, banking facilities had markedly increased, so that larger enterprises could be launched. A rapidly growing middle class now avidly pursued business, and in its quest for higher profits, it began to expect government aid. Indeed, the business community began to see the promotion of business as a major function of government. Their laissez-faire attitudes moderated considerably when they discovered the enormous advantages possible from cooperating with officialdom. A general weakening of liberal parties resulted as an alliance developed between businessmen and the conservative parties in power. At the same time, the expanding industrial plant was utilizing an expanded work force, much of which appeared from the massive influx of people from the countryside to the cities. Between the remarkable population growth under way and the exodus from the country, there was a phenomenal increase in the size of existing cities and in the number of cities. These aspects of rapid economic and social growth were pronounced in England and Germany between 1870 and 1890, and much of the rest of Europe also experienced rapid change. It is a truism that French population and industrial growth lagged, but life in France nonetheless underwent considerable change. Italy, Austria, and Russia were not as vitally affected, yet the impulses of progress were also clear in these areas. Sweden joined the ranks of important economic powers in this period.

All governments had to confront a number of new developments resulting from these patterns of growth. The vast laboring force in the new cities dwarfed those of the industrial plants existing only a few decades earlier. There was a problem of defining the proper role of government in the new environment. Altered political alignments were in the offing as the conservatives who formerly represented largely agrarian noble interests now found themselves courted by the business elite. The new industrial society was enormously profitable and the incentives were strong to invest in other lands. This resulted in increased pressure on governments to pursue colonial programs and to assume a responsibility to protect these investments. Such, in much abbreviated form, was the general context in which many statesmen and politicians tried to play out their lives, with a modicum of awareness of the new forces and a substantial reliance on old formulas.

In Germany especially the accommodation to new circumstances was perhaps the most obvious and most successful. Characteristically, Bismarck addressed himself to the solution of German domestic problems with as much dedication, authoritarianism, and ingenuity as he showed in foreign affairs. His immediate domestic problem resulting from his successful struggle with France was to formulate a constitutional structure for the new state that his policies and the Prussian army had created. Modeled largely on the constitution of the North German Confederation, his constitution for the German Empire was designed as much to hide the sources of power as to pay lip-service to such popular notions as the secret ballot and universal suffrage for males over twenty-five. Essentially, Prussia dominated the new government, which was based on a combination of a number of unequal states. The relative strengths of the states were carefully stipulated, but the attention to such detail meant little when seen beside the preponderance of Prussian control. The new Germany was an enlarged Prussia and was frankly considered in this light by most statesmen, including Bismarck.

Authoritarian as the system was, an active political life developed in the lower house, the Reichstag. Here 397 elected members debated legislation but lacked the basic power of the purse. Though not allowed to play a major role in making policy, they could obstruct legislation and were such valid indicators of popular sentiment that the government watched their proceedings carefully.

Six political parties were represented in the Reichstag—the Conservatives, Free Conservatives, National Liberals, Progressives, Catholics (or Center), and the Social Democrats. The first four existed before unification and Bismarck was experienced in dealing with them. The Conservatives were a Prussian party, mostly Junkers, who supported the idea of divine-right (Lutheran) monarchy and had little respect for lower-class participation in government. Their basic loyalty was to Prussia and they regarded the creation of the Empire with some apprehension. The Free Conservatives resembled the Conservatives in many ways but they were neither so numerous nor so narrowly Prussian, and they supported the Empire. These two parties were the original supporters of Bismarck. The National Liberals were a more truly imperial or national party in that they existed in all the states of the Empire. These were the wealthier businessmen, who were liberal in the traditional nineteenth-century meaning of the word. Offshoots from the Progressives, with whom Bismarck had earlier contested regarding the military budget, by 1871 the National Liberals were willing to forgive and forget as they applauded both the unification and the inclusion of a popular lower house in the new constitutional system. This was the largest party with growth potential and became Bismarck's main source of support in the Reichstag in the 1870s. The Progressives comprised an intelligentsia, a middle-class party which supported parliamentary government according to the English model and opposed militarism. They became victims of Bismarck's dramatic successes and never rivalled the other parties.

After the unification two new parties became a special concern to Bismarck. The Catholic, or Center, party was based mainly in new areas added to Prussia, that is, Bavaria and lands along the Rhine. Because of their confessional obligations, Bismarck never regarded them as Germans whose loyalty could be relied on implicitly. A party of peasants and workers, its ranks were militant and grew swiftly when attacked by Bismarck. The other new party, the socialist Social Democrats, also increased rapidly and was strongly based in industrial areas. Like the National Liberals, it naturally grew with industrial expansion and, like the Catholics, became more militant when attacked by Bismarck, who saw it as resembling the Catholics in that it was guided by an international ideology and appeared not to be an integral part of German nationalism. Bismarck worried as much about the Catholics and the Social Democrats as he did about France finding an ally. Consequently, his policies regarding these two parties became the center of German political life from 1871 to 1890.

Shortly after unification Bismarck became embroiled in a bitter struggle against the Catholic Center party. The origins of this encounter were diverse and extremely complex. The Papacy's *Syllabus of Errors* and doctrine of Papal Infallibility combined to condemn liberalism generally and secularism in particular. The result was a sharpening of Church–state opposition in many areas, including Germany. Bismarck was disturbed by the appeal of the Center party to the electorate and also by the idea that their loyalty to the Empire was probably not as strong as their loyalty to Rome. At the same time he recognized the Papacy's close relationship to France, whom he believed was encouraging all opposition to the new German Empire. When the Papacy's attitudes criticizing modern liberalism alienated the National Liberals, Bismarck sensed an opportunity to gain their support by attacking Catholicism in Germany. Such a move would also please the Protestant Conservatives and aid in developing a sense of unity in the Empire. There was the further possibility that in the guise of attacking Catholicism, Bismarck could introduce restrictive legislation which would have the effect of equally curtailing the power of the Lutheran Church. Interestingly enough, the Conservatives opposed Bismarck's religious legislation almost as much as the Catholics did.

The attack against the Catholics, known as the *Kulturkampf*, was embodied in legislation called the May Laws (enacted piecemeal in May of 1873, 1874, and 1875). These bills reduced the role of the Church in education and in the appointment of priests. Bishops' prerogatives were restricted, the Jesuits were expelled and other orders suppressed, and marriage was made a civil function in all the Empire. The Church was hurt but fought back vigorously; its discipline and organizational structure so proved its strength that in 1877 the Catholics were stronger at the polls than they had been in 1872, before the struggle. The National Liberals had supported Bismarck but began to insist on a series of special considerations as the price of their support. He sensed that his attack on the Church was unsuccessful and also began to doubt whether the Catholics were as much of a menace to authoritarian government as the socialists or even the National Liberals and Progressives. Further, he was not a man to be pressured, so he decided to seek another parliamentary base in the Reichstag. His opportunity came in 1878, when Pius IX was succeeded by Leo XIII (1810–1903), who initiated improved relations with Germany. The repressive legislation was gradually dropped and Bismarck welcomed the aid of the Church (which he had called the Black International) in a new struggle. His enemy was now the Red International, socialism. He made this transition in his power base in the popular house as successfully as he had earlier moved from reliance on Conservatives to backing from the National Liberals. He had really failed in his struggle with the Catholics, but this had been well masked.

In his attack on socialism Bismarck followed the familiar policy of legislative repression, a series of "exceptional laws" giving special police authorization to coerce and suppress socialists. These laws were in force from 1878 to 1890 and drove the socialists underground. Like the Catholics, after the shock of the early attack, the repression brought out the socialists' latent organizational ability and determination to survive. The result was an increase in the number of socialist deputies to the Reichstag. In 1877 there were nine Social Democrats in the Reichstag; in 1890 there were twelve. Again Bismarck had failed.

The Chancellor's struggles with both the Catholics and the socialists are full of meaning for modern society, for they brilliantly illustrate the futility of authoritarianism when turned against ideas and beliefs which have been long implanted, as in the case of the Catholics, or are wedded to powerful economic issues, as were those of the socialists. Two groups which were political irritants to the body politique in Germany became major forces when attacked by the state, a sobering lesson that history has only partially absorbed.

The record of Bismarck's failures in two great domestic struggles should not blind us to a number of his striking successes on the home front. An immediate problem after the proclamation of the Empire and its constitutional structure had been decided was to create a sense of unity strong enough that the new state would have a life of its own. A long-standing handicap to German unity had been "particularism," an exaggerated sense of regional and local pride and loyalty, present in many parts of the new Empire. Further, the new state was composed of a number of diverse elements, despite a common heritage in literature. Unification brought many disparate areas together. The resulting divisive influences might well have proved too great for the new system. Catholics and Protestants (mostly Lutherans) shared a common citizenship when the agrarian and industrial areas were united. Opposing views on tariffs highlighted the Empire's diversity. The prospects for real unity must at times have seemed remote, even to Bismarck.

The imperial chancellor moved quickly, however, to bind the whole region closer together. In general, there was an extension of Prussian bureaucratic institutions into many of the newly acquired lands, a good example being the 1875 transformation of the Prussian bank into a bank for all Germany. Currency became uniform in all the states and the entire fiscal structure was consolidated. At the same time a similar centralization and coordination occurred in the railroad system. There was also consolidation of legal systems. Gradually Germany became a genuinely centralized economic unit which went far to promote a new sense of identity.

An interesting domestic development was Bismarck's support of protectionism. An era of prosperity created excessive speculation which was further encouraged by the flow of French funds in payment of the indemnity. When the economic euphoria turned into depression, industrialists and agrarian interests alike called for protective tariffs. Bismarck saw an interesting opportunity; he would obtain money for the treasury (consistently in the red) through the tariffs; he would receive credit for restoring prosperity which would come through German control of their own market; and he would gain the support of the protectionists. As a by-product of this policy he could help heal the wounds resulting from the *Kulturkampf*, because the Center party, having a large agrarian constituency, favored protection. They would replace those National Liberals opposing protection and he would emerge with a new power base. He achieved this but the more important result was that protection proved a great boon to German industrial development. It was an interesting repudiation of the general *laissez-faire* position.

Perhaps Bismarck's most important domestic achievement lay in the field of social welfare. As a by-product of his struggle with the Social Democrats, he sponsored a series of measures designed to improve the lot of workers. These reforms clearly came from above and smacked of paternalism and have been labeled an example of state socialism. The most important feature of the program involved workers' insurance for accidents, illness, and old age. These were to aid the workers without doing violence to the capitalistic system, which was particularly energetic in the 1880s. Bismarck hoped to create in the worker such a feeling of gratitude to the state that he would be much less responsive to socialist blandishments. Naturally, the socialists called these reforms bribes and proponents of *laissez faire* were appalled at such government interference. He had given a massive social insurance program to the laborers of a major state, much ahead of other states; despite his motives, he deserves high praise for this achievement. Ironically, the workers continued to support socialism in greater numbers.

Bismarck's long public career came to an end in 1890, when he was ordered to resign. It was a bitter pill for the old statesman. He had been able to persuade and cajole William I to listen to his advice most of the time. William had been followed by Frederick III, who was dying of cancer at the time of his accession and ruled only from March 9 to June 15, 1888. His successor, William II, was twenty-nine and approached his office with youthful enthusiasm and a totally different point of view from that held by his father, grandfather, or Bismarck. He and his revered chancellor soon were at odds over several issues—labor policy, private audiences with his ministers, and Russian policy. Finally he forced Bismarck out of office. It was the end of an era and probably William was correct when he observed that for all his major contributions to German history, Bismarck belonged to an earlier time. Bismarck still referred to 1848 and to his attempts to outwit Napoleon III. William clearly brought a freshness and new vitality to affairs; his wider outlook on the world and more sympathetic perspective on labor issues promised a new course for Germany. Energy, youth, and aggressiveness were to mark a new German policy which lacked the shrewdness of the old *realpolitiker*. For Germany the twentieth century began in 1890.

French domestic history in the two decades after 1871 is the story of the nation's recovery from the twin disasters of the Franco-Prussian War and the Commune. The fall of Bonapartism left a power vacuum which the republicans eventually filled, but in the special circumstances attending the defeat, a royalist majority controlled the National Assembly, which had been elected to negotiate a peace. This was accomplished when the Treaty of Frankfurt was ratified in mid-May of 1871, before the collapse of the Commune. Having made peace, the Assembly decided to continue as a governing body and to prepare for some sort of royalist regime. The first decade of the Third Republic is largely the story of how the royalist majority was gradually eroded in the Assembly by a swelling tide of republican sentiment which was widespread and clearly evident once political issues were seen in contexts other than peace or war. The royalists missed a superb opportunity mainly through their internal divisions. The supporters of the Count of Chambord and the Count of Paris, the Legitimists and Orléanists, respectively, were unable to cooperate. Slowly their support in the Assembly grew weaker as by-elections kept returning republicans. The Assembly had given executive authority to Thiers, who earned widespread gratitude by crushing the Commune and also by paying ahead of schedule the massive indemnity due the Germans, thus removing the German garrisons. Looking to a strengthened army, the French adopted a system of compulsory military service and began refortifying the eastern frontier. All the while, intrigues among royalists continued until Thiers, whose whole career had really been oriented toward Orléanism, endorsed a real republic. Consequently, he was soon forced out of office (May 24, 1873) by the combined royalists and was replaced by Marshal MacMahon (1808–1893). The plotting went on, complicated by the presence of Bonapartists and by a split in republican ranks. In 1875 a series of laws finally established the basis of government and the National Assembly was dissolved. In new elections for the recently authorized Senate and Chamber of Deputies, republicans were successful in the lower house and almost won the Senate. With MacMahon still president, the royalists dominated the bureaucracy as well as the Senate, but republican gains continued. By January, 1879, the republicans controlled the Senate as well as the Chamber and MacMahon resigned. Jules Grévy (1807–1891) became president and finally the Third Republic was solidly established, though it had been proclaimed only two days after Sedan. Its constitution had come into existence in a piecemeal fashion and comprised a collection of different statutes. In the new structure the control of the budget resided in the lower house and the president was elected to a seven-year term by the combined vote of the Senate and Chamber sitting together. Ministerial responsibility to the lower house was emphatic, as the premium was on representation and rights rather than efficient administration. It was a ramshackle type of system but managed to last longer than any other since 1789. Ministries came and went as coalition governments promoted instability at the top, but an efficient bureaucracy assured continuity to government programs.

After MacMahon left office, political life was controlled by the republicans. They were, however, divided. The Moderate Republicans were the dominant group for at least a decade. This was the party of the propertied, middle class. Led by Jules Ferry (1832–1893), their most important achievement in the 1880s was the introduction of significant educational reform. Openly attacking the Church, they established a whole system of secular schools which paralleled those of the clergy. The government looked askance at the clerical schools and ordered them to extol patriotism. Naturally, the secular schools were rigorously republican. At the same time a vigorous colonial program created opportunity for extensive overseas investments, which attracted support from the business classes. Substantial imperial gains occurred in Southeast Asia and in Africa. Tunisia and Madagascar were also important additions as France played a prominent role in the new wave of imperialism prevalent in the last third of the century.

The Moderate Republicans were strongly opposed by the royalists and clerical forces, but they also faced formidable protagonists in the Radical Republicans, led by Georges Clemenceau (1841–1929). The Radicals would cooperate with the Moderates when the issue was the republic itself, and they were also vigorously anticlerical. Their membership came from the lower class, where property was more suspect and where there were few incentives to colonial expansion. They opposed the imperialism of the Moderates largely on the grounds that it was a distractive frittering of resources at a time when the nation should be girding itself for a war of revenge to recover Alsace and Lorraine.

Though the republicans were clearly in control in the 1880s, Gambetta's death in 1882 and that of Ferry in 1885 were severe blows to French political life. At this time France began to experience what became a frustrating characteristic of government under the Third Republic, a series of ministries where portfolios were continuously being juggled, with no strong men giving direction to affairs. By now the idea of revenge was becoming chronic in local politics and was virtually synonymous with patriotism. In this atmosphere a "man on horseback" suddenly appeared who appealed to all the prejudices of those unhappy with the Republic. The minister of war, General Boulanger (1837–1891), adopted an aggressive, decisive pose which seemed to stand for a positive program. His dynamism attracted a broad following. His program, however, was vague and consisted only of a war of revenge and the idea that the president should be elected by the people, a procedure reminiscent of the Second Republic. From 1886 to 1889 he was the center of attention and appeared progressively more popular. He finally reached a point where he had either to engineer some sort of coup or to stand trial on charges of conspiracy, which his opponents in the Senate brought against him. He backed away from the situation and fled to Belgium, but his supporters—avid nationalists, royalists, and clerics—were left exposed. The republicans joined ranks and drove many of these from government office. A major challenge to the system had thus been passed.

Another test was to come in the Dreyfus Case, which lasted from 1894 until 1906. This situation also raised questions of the role of the military, the clergy, the royalists, and the chauvinistic nationalists. The forces which had supported Boulanger again ranged against the republicans, and again the republicans won. This episode, though, belongs as much to the story of France on the eve of World War I as it does to that of nineteenth-century France. Similarly, a whole wave of anticlerical legislation resulting in the 1905 separation of church and state is a climax to long-standing republican opposition to the clergy but occurs in a context well removed from the circumstances of the 1880s. By 1890 the republic was beyond Sedan by two decades and had significantly defeated royalism, clericalism, and unreasoning militarism. These would all appear later, but successively the forces of republicanism were becoming stronger, a trend which was clear by 1890.

Economically, the decades between 1871 and 1891 were particularly transitional. French industry was expanding but, in a relative sense, lagged behind other major states. France suffered from a stationary birth rate as well as inadequate coal supplies to power a major economic expansion. Ironically, she had plenty of capital seeking investment, and this proved a strong stimulus to imperialism; considerable sums were used speculatively in other European states, especially in Russia. The working class had a reputation for radicalism since the black days in its history—June of 1848 and the Commune of 1871—when the propertied class had turned the army on the workers. Because the Commune had taken a heavy toll among labor spokesmen, a relative lull in labor agitation occurred. Hoping to gain labor support, the Radical Republicans promoted legislation which, in 1884, made both strikes and unions legal. The unions soon became organized on a wide scale, but this story too belongs mostly to the twentieth century. Socialism was not as effective in France as in Germany, but its spokesmen nevertheless appeared in the Chamber of Deputies in the 1880s. They represented several varieties of socialism but cooperated with the Radical Republicans on most issues. During the Dreyfus Case they were supporters of the regime.

During this era, Britain enjoyed a remarkably expanding economy as the consequences of free trade brought riches and prosperity. Except for a grim year in 1870 when crops failed and depression conditions encouraged a wave of strikes among the ever increasing labor force, the chief continuing irritant for political leaders was the perennial Irish question. Against this backdrop of dynamic growth two extraordinary men vied for power, each with his own prescription for national strength, William Gladstone and Benjamin Disraeli. Protagonists of classic proportions, between 1868 and 1880, both governed for six years and both left their own personal stamp on the nation's history.

The Second Reform Bill of 1867 set the stage for the high point in their rivalry, a confrontation which had been gradually developing for years. As young men, both had been conservatives under Peel but gradually had taken different paths in reaction to Peel's leadership. Gladstone, temperamentally conservative and against basic social reform, came to embrace middle-class liberalism. For him Peel's acquiescence to pressures for reform had not been adequate. He promoted a flood of domestic reform legislation but was not truly interested in seeing middle-class privileges extended to the workers. Considering this basic orientation, his ministry of 1868–1874 was especially remarkable. Disraeli was a genuine conservative but had a much broader perspective than many in his class. He too had reacted against Peel but his position was that Peel's decision to support the repeal of the Corn Laws was, in effect, a betrayal of principle. He became Peel's successor as the Conservative leader and spokesman. Though more interested in imperialism, he worked diligently to encourage his party to become more responsive to the needs of labor and give to Toryism a sense of social consciousness. Both were able debaters. Gladstone's speeches reflected a puritanical conviction of right as well as a command of intricate detail. Disraeli was the witty irritant who poked fun and ridicule at the sobriety of his opponent. Each was a perfect foil of the other.

Gladstone's first ministry began December 9, 1868, as a result of the November elections, the first in which those receiving the suffrage in 1867 were able to vote. These voters had turned in large numbers against Disraeli who, despite giving them the vote, still represented the Tory aristocracy. With a substantial mandate, Gladstone set upon a twofold course. He tried to face the Irish problem squarely while embarking upon an ambitious program of domestic reform. Though he was frustrated at not being able to accomplish more, he made remarkable progress regarding Ireland and was phenomenally successful in his domestic legislative objectives.

Many Irish frustrations had been centered on the established church, the Church of England, which had been long supported by lands taken during the Reformation. Anglican ideals had remained foreign to the Irish population and resentments smouldered at the wealth being accumulated by a church unsupported by a population which had remained stoically Catholic. Gladstone's Disestablishment Act (1869) removed the formal monopoly enjoyed by the Anglicans in Ireland and freed the Irish from forced contributions to the Anglican church. This was a bold decision but Gladstone had made it part of his 1866 campaign. It naturally drew the wrath of Anglican clergy and the Conservatives, but it passed nonetheless.

The religious problem was solved, but Gladstone was not so fortunate in his attempt to do something about the land issue. Here the worst features of an absentee ownership system prevailed and Gladstone introduced a Land Act in 1870 which sought to eliminate the obvious economic exploitation. The measure passed but proved to be inadequate. In theory it hampered the landowner's ability to evict rent-paying peasants, but in practice rents were uncontrolled and the owner was as free as ever to hand out evictions for nonpayment of rent. More thorough legislation was required to follow this halting early step in solving the problem.

In domestic reform, Gladstone pushed through a phenomenal amount of important legislation. Perhaps the most significant was the Forster Education Act, which allowed for a major extension of public education. The general object was to provide education for children in the large class of new voters. Gladstone had, in fact, inherited this problem from Disraeli. When political power was granted to the lower classes, the need for their education was obvious. The Act provided for government inspection of all schools, the creation of new schools, and the better financing of existing schools, many being administered by the Church of England. Problems of religious instruction were compromised, to the general satisfaction of all groups. Another educational reform, important but less sweeping, eliminated the religious qualification for admission to Oxford and Cambridge.

Other reforms included the adoption of the secret ballot, a measure sorely needed in local elections. There was also legislation which streamlined the judiciary and speeded up the hearing of cases. Gladstone's impact was pronounced in the army, where he eliminated the system of purchasing commissions and introduced competitive examinations. He also reduced the term of active service from twelve to six years. However, the soldier remained for six more years in the reserves and thus provided for a large trained reserve force, an element lacking in Britain heretofore.

All these measures had an important impact on British life but they served to irritate many people. Further, they were reforms which, however fundamental, lacked glamor. Gladstone's popular support began to dwindle. He was under constant attack by Disraeli, who cavalierly dismissed Gladstone's achievements as "harassing legislation." The prime minister was especially vulnerable to criticism in the area of foreign policy. His only success here had been the settlement of the Alabama claims, and the recognition of the validity of the claims appeared humiliating to many Englishmen. Disraeli was sharp in his indictment of foreign policy. While Gladstone had been concerned with the width of school desks, Germany had been unified, Napoleon III had fallen, and the treaty of Paris had been partially repudiated by Alexander II. What, asked Disraeli, had been Britain's role in these events? Recognizing the growing opposition, Gladstone gave way; in the general election of February, 1874, Disraeli's Conservatives returned to power.

The new ministry had no intention whatever of tackling the problems of Ireland or of doing much in the field of domestic legislation. Its meager record here included a few bills regarding public health, protection for women and children employed in textile factories, and slum housing, all of which were little more than noncontroversial housekeeping chores.

Disraeli had roundly criticized Gladstone for inattention to foreign policy and here he centered his own attention. He shortly announced two bold measures which occasioned wide publicity. Late in 1875 he procured for Britain a large portion (44 per cent) of the shares in the Suez Canal. He had taken advantage of the bankrupt Egyptian Khedive to purchase what amounted to a controlling interest in the Canal. Coming only six years after its opening, the negotiation had the drama and importance of a coup. It appealed to the public imagination and it set the nation on an imperialistic course in Egypt. Disraeli followed this success with a scheme for Victoria to assume the title of Empress of India, a title which then happened to be vacant. The Queen was highly flattered and Disraeli shortly became the Earl of Beaconsfield.

The climax of Disraeli's career was the Congress of Berlin, where despite Bismarck's presence, the powers came to the solution of the

Benjamin Disraeli as seen by *Punch*. (Courtesy of Historical Pictures Service, Chicago.)

Bulgarian crisis which British diplomacy had arranged in earlier agreements. Russian ambitions were blunted; Turkey had been shored up through another crisis; and Britain gained control of Cyprus. Britain's influence in European affairs could hardly have been more prominent.

Along with the successes, an aggressive foreign policy also brought its problems. For Disraeli two unpopular wars, the Afghan War and the Zulu War, proved the start of a swing of public support away from the Conservatives. Increasing his vulnerability was the 1879 depression. Gladstone sensed an opportunity to dislodge Disraeli and, in November of 1879, he embarked on a major effort to crystal-

William Gladstone on campaign. (Courtesy of Historical
Pictures Service, Chicago.)

lize opinion against the ministry; this was the Midlothian campaign,
one of the most intense in British history. With telling invective and
moral condescension, he charged the Tories with fiscal mismanage-
ment which prolonged the depression. In addition, he faulted them
for pursuing a disastrous foreign policy; and he made Disraeli appear
responsible for all sorts of barbarities occurring abroad, especially
massacres in Afghanistan. He described the Conservatives as placing
Britain staunchly against freedom, justice, and liberty. Britain should
be supporting freedom, especially in the Balkans, which should be
free. Above all, the Turk should not be supported when he was
guilty of such things as the Bulgarian "horrors." The attack was
effective and in March, 1880, Disraeli's party was defeated.

Shortly after Gladstone returned to power, Disraeli died (April

19, 1881). His successor as leader of the Conservatives was the Marquis of Salisbury (1830–1903), who shared Disraeli's preoccupation with foreign affairs. Gladstone returned to office with every intention of concentrating on the Irish problem and domestic legislation but, as in 1868, he was forced to deal with the legacy left him by Disraeli. He could not escape substantial involvement in foreign problems. He was at once caught up in the details of Balkan boundary problems stemming from the Congress of Berlin. He showed himself opposed to unilateral actions by Great Powers and revealed a faith in international cooperation and European concert, ideas contrasting with Bismarck's reliance on balanced tensions. Imperial involvements were constant and culminated for him in the death of General Gordon at Khartum in January, 1885. The government was vigorously denounced for not sending aid sooner and in June Gladstone resigned.

Despite these diversions, he did carry through a new Reform Bill in 1884 which added 2 million people to the voting public, double the number added in 1867. He also introduced a bill redistributing seats in the House of Commons, bringing the representation more in line with existing population concentrations. All the while he wrestled with the problem of Ireland. It seemed increasingly clear that home rule was the answer, but before he came to this decision he was replaced in office by Salisbury, who began cooperating with Parnell on a program of land ownership. When Gladstone again returned to office the issue of home rule was introduced in April, 1886. An emotional, bitter debate finally resulted in the bill's defeat and Salisbury formed another ministry, this one to last from 1886 to 1892. Gladstone brooded about home rule and waited for another chance to come to power. When it came, he was eighty-three. Salisbury's ministry proved to be relatively lackluster, with imperial questions receiving his interest, but Ireland remained unsettled and domestic labor disputes became more prominent. Trade unionism expanded significantly but the major headlines went to Britain's part in the partitioning of Africa.

The 1870s and 1880s in Britain had seen great industrial progress reflected in Liberal attempts to pass appropriate legislation to serve the needs of a swelling electorate. Overseas Britain returned to an active role in world diplomacy after a measure of withdrawal under Gladstone's first ministry. All the while the Irish problem defied solution but finally occupied a place of first priority on Gladstone's agenda in 1890.

In Russia, the assassination of Alexander II in 1881 ushered in a period of reaction and repression. Under the new monarch, thirty-six-year-old Alexander III (1845–1894), a deliberate and systematic attempt was made to return to the standards of Nicholas I. Reform was presented as having been a dreadful mistake, proved so when it led to the murder of the highest of public officials, and the Tsar lost little time in discarding the recommendations of Loris Melikov. A measure of the determination of the Tsar was that he embarked upon this autocratic and illiberal course despite a clear warning from the revolutionary agitators. They declared openly in a manifesto that autocracy as a form of government was evil and that they would persevere in creating a representative government in Russia, despite the peril of death or exile. They pointed to two possible routes to achieve the new system. Either the Tsar would voluntarily call for a representative assembly or else one would be summoned after a violent revolution. The warning was to the point and Alexander's response was equally blunt, "God orders us to stand firm. . . ." This response, incidentally, coincided with advice he received from Germany's William I to make no concessions to the radicals. He was, in effect, his own first minister and was a more direct and singleminded person than his father. Under his leadership autocracy stood for a known point of view, rigorously and efficiently applied. He regarded the murder of his father as proof of liberalism's failure, a view which happened to coincide with his basic orientation on life. His thinking had long been colored by the ideas of Constantine Pobedonostsev (1827–1907), his former tutor but now Procurator of the Holy Synod, the Tsar's special censor in all religious questions. Pobedonostsev was against virtually all aspects of Western liberalism. Juries merely freed the guilty, press freedom meant slander, elections invited corruption, democratic government merely allowed the rich to govern, and religious freedom meant schism. All these had occurred in the West, where societies were decadent. Such ideas, of course, closely coincided with the point of view of the Slavophiles, who greeted with joy Alexander III's emphatic turn against liberalism.

The instrument of much of the repression was V. C. Plehve, who controlled the police. He apprehended those responsible for Alexander II's death and applied relentless pressure to all suspected revolutionary groups. At the same time a rigorous censorship made the dissemination of radical views very difficult and the number of successful revolutionary agitators dwindled. Though sporadic instances of public violence occurred, by and large, the reign of Alexander III became one of relative calm.

Repression was applied systematically on a number of fronts. In

The Hanging of the assassins of Alexander II. (Courtesy of Historical Pictures Service, Chicago.)

education its impact was comprehensive and stifling at the higher levels. Universities were made a responsibility of the ministry of the interior, which carefully scrutinized the curriculum. Students and professors alike were carefully watched, and those showing liberal tendencies were forced out of the system. Censorship was applied to the possession of forbidden books as well as to the writing of inflammatory tracts. Similar pressures existed at the secondary level. A scheme approved by Alexander called for making the primary school system the responsibility of the church rather than of the *zemstvos*. Only prohibitive expense prevented this change from being carried out. In an age when France was trying to free herself from clerical shackles, the Russian government desired a closer connection with its established church.

In religion Alexander's reign saw a pronounced emphasis on orthodoxy. Virtually all dissenters were discriminated against; pressure was strong to support the established church. This was a portion of the deliberate program of "Russification" which the Tsar had decided upon. It involved an emphasis on the uniqueness and rightness of Russia's institutions and the Great Russian language. The police were kept busy trying to force minorities into the Russian mold. The more ambitious attempts to coerce minorities involved the outlawing of Polish in Poland and German in the Baltic provinces. There were accompanying restrictions on the rights to hold public office. This sort of pressure was especially severe as applied to Jews. Under Alexander I they had been forced to live in fifteen of the western provinces (especially Lithuania and Poland) and this area became known as the Jewish Pale of Settlement. Some notable exceptions to the regulations were made in cases of certain professions. This enforced segregation remained on the statute books but little attempt at enforcement was made during Alexander II's reign, when many Jews had resettled outside the Pale. Alexander III ordered the law to be strictly enforced and many Jews who had long lived undisturbed outside the Pale were now uprooted. There were many other discriminations against Jews and they were the victims of outright looting and massacres. One result of this pressure was a large exodus of Russian and Polish Jews to the United States.

Another consequence of the repression was the forcible transfer of hosts of political prisoners to Siberia. These unfortunates became part of the labor force in a number of projects accompanying a major Russian push to the east. Such a move had won Bismarck's approval. He commented that as an European power Russia really could play no constructive role. She merely absorbed "Nihilism and other diseases" from the West. In Asia, however, was her real mission, because "there she stands for civilization." The push east was largely powered by the Russification program which required self-sufficiency. It was also possible because while Alexander III had been ruthlessly crushing all liberal tendencies, a vast flow of foreign capital came into Russia and major industrial expansion was beginning. These were well advanced by the death of Alexander in 1894, and were to continue under the guidance of Sergius Witte, the minister of finance, who came to office in 1892. As occurred earlier in the West, the new industrialization was fed by a steady stream of labor from the countryside and a large oversupply of workers soon developed. The urban laborer lived in abject misery and was particularly hurt during the famine of 1891–1892. He also was vulnerable to radical propaganda when Alexander II's regime was followed by one less efficient. In the countryside the famine resulted in sporadic disorders, which the government met by modifying both the redemption obligations and the poll tax requirement. There had developed in Russia more of a sense of class consciousness; especially pronounced was the appearance of an urban middle class with values much like those in Western Europe. Alexander III's rule had been short but it proved to be just as distinctive a period for Russia as the reigns of Alexander I, Nicholas I, or Alexander II.

A special disappointment in the decades following 1870 was the new Kingdom of Italy. Nationalists and liberals had expected much from the unification but conditions in Italy sharply contrasted to the remarkable vitality of the new German Empire to the north. Italy, however, faced a number of problems which had no counterpart in Germany and the similarity of the two unification movements had tended to obscure the dissimilarities. There had been in Italy nothing like the Zollverein, which had done so much to create a sense of a German economic community. When Prussia absorbed other German states, she gained highly literate, sophisticated, and economically advanced populations. In Italy there was no such common level of wealth or cultural attainment. Widespread illiteracy was the rule in much of southern Italy and, in effect, Sardinia had absorbed areas which were economically and culturally deprived. It was almost as though an imperialistic relationship had developed between the north and the south. Unification had been supported in northern Italy by a large middle class but no such class existed in the southern portion of the peninsula. In a very real sense, a civilizing and pioneering effort was required on the part of the new government.

A particularly disruptive, special problem associated with the new Italy was the antipathy between the government and the Papacy. The unification had been opposed by the Pope, who regarded the whole movement as a secular attack on papal lands and prerogatives. Until 1929 neither Pius IX nor his successors recognized the secular Italian state and they assumed the posture of being prisoners in the Vatican. Because Catholicism was so much a part of Italian life, it created a crisis of conscience for many able men who would normally have been attracted to government service. Thus the regime was to be denied the services of some of the nation's best minds, this in a society with acute bureaucratic and social problems. Corruption and incompetence were to be continuing plagues in Italy.

In politics, party leaders resorted to obstructionism for its own sake, electoral manipulation through bribery and, when necessary, beatings by thugs and hoodlums. The public welfare seemed openly subordinated to staying in power as a prime object of politics. Elections were heatedly contested as the rotativism common in the Iberian peninsula was about the only perversion of political practices not engaged in. The spoils system became a device to buy off opponents and a major objective of a rising politician was to gather enough of a following that he needed to be bought off. With such ethics in practice, it is no wonder that constitutional government in Italy lacked public admiration. The right (Giovanni Lanza and Marco Minghetti) enjoyed power until 1876, when they lost out to a leftist (Agostino Depretis) coalition. The overwhelming consideration of both groups, however, had been merely to stay in office. Socialism was not an issue until 1891, when a formal Italian socialist party was organized in Milan. The premier at the time, Francesco Crispi, attacked it with the methods of Bismarck, with the same lack of success. Socialism was to grow with industrialization, which proceeded rapidly in the north but very slowly in the south.

Despite the self-centered objectives of most politicians, the new kingdom vigorously attacked the problem of the great diversity between north and south. Its policies were often hampered by incompetence, but nonetheless great strides were made. An enormous spurt in rail construction gave a priority to lines connecting important centers in the south. At the same time the army and navy swelled to enormous proportions for peacetime, because Italian leaders believed that large military forces were appropriate for Italy's new role as a major power. Besides, she still wanted more land, especially Trieste and the Trentino. These ideas were a bit too ambitious and resulted in a particularly heavy tax burden. The poorest in the population were unmercifully exploited (by taxes on sugar, bread, tobacco, salt) to pay for these symbols of national prestige; but for a time after 1876, the budget was balanced. Probably the most constructive by-product of the military program was that many of the poor, and especially many southerners, were recruited and given the rudiments of an elementary education. Further, they were deliberately assigned to units in other parts of the peninsula so that their horizons were significantly broadened. The same sort of educational function was served by the bureaucracy which particularly attracted southerners, who soon filled a majority of government jobs. Despite all this, however, material and economic progress in Italy was not significant when compared with the giant strides being taken elsewhere in Europe and despite her military build-up (third in naval power by 1885), she never quite achieved the status of a Great Power.

CHAPTER 35

Christianity Under Attack

Early in the nineteenth century, most of the varieties of Christianity had undergone a pietistic renaissance, with evangelicalism becoming a common feature of organized religion. Thus the churches had reflected, absorbed, and harmonized with the dominant cultural mood. As the century wore on, however, a number of social and cultural developments resulted in a basic challenge to organized Christianity. The general problem was acute for both Protestants and Catholics, although particular threats varied in intensity for these two major wings of Christianity.

The material progress of the century, so evident to any observer, gave a sense of dynamism to society and the human condition. The demand was widespread for institutions that would be sufficiently flexible to direct or at least adjust to the rapidly occurring changes.

Nineteenth-century political history is focused largely on this topic. In this context the religions of Europe, with their traditional emphases on answers to problems generated by agrarian societies, came to appear irrelevant, when they were not openly obstructionist. While this was occurring, advances of knowledge in two main areas led to serious crises for Europe's clergymen. The issue was joined between 1860 and 1890 as both Protestants and Catholics responded vigorously to attacks.

A particular challenge was the doctrine of evolution as presented by Darwin. Evolution was not a new idea but advances in biology and geology provided an impressive array of solid new evidence. From geology came the concept of uniformitarianism and the problem of accounting for fossils. The world now appeared to be far older than had previously been thought and changes seemed to have occurred very gradually, instead of, as a rival view had held, through catastrophes. From studying biology Darwin had abandoned the idea of fixity of the species and he suggested that natural selection was the mechanism explaining the change in life forms.

From the point of view of religion, evolution raised questions about creation as explained in Genesis. It also implied that man was subject to the natural laws governing other forms of life; no divine origin had set him aside from other living beings. A storm of clerical protest, much of it Protestant and centered in England and Germany, at once attacked Darwin's version of evolution. Clergymen defined and discussed the theory as it appeared to them in a very unsophisticated version: Was man descended from the monkey? They thundered emotionally from their pulpits, convincing much of their semieducated public but failing when debating intellectuals. In T. H. Huxley, Darwinism produced a defender who excelled in discussions at a popular level and so the clergy were challenged here also. Virtually all intellectuals came to accept the doctrine; and by the end of the century, most theologians had stopped their open opposition. Their initial response had made the clerics appear hostile to new learning, a great tactical error, for they quickly lost the support of important members of the intellectual community.

A second shock for nineteenth-century organized Christianity stemmed from the development of a segment of historical research called Biblical criticism. When the scientific standards of Leopold von Ranke were applied to the study of the Bible, many people found the results profoundly unsettling. With so much historical and philological research being pursued, it was natural that the most fundamental document of Christianity would be studied, using the new standards being applied to other texts from antiquity. A "lower criticism" developed, concerning itself with identifying the basic Biblical text, and "higher criticism" explored questions of accuracy, motivation and authorship. The attempt to require documentary proof of the Bible's validity as a source implied a weak faith and resulted in substantial doubt when the composition of the Bible proved to be far more complex than had been remotely anticipated.

These studies had been conducted primarily by German scholars, with Tübingen being a particularly important center. The cumulative effect of the research of Julius Wellhausen, F. C. Bauer, D. F. Strauss, and others showed that the Bible comprised a vast collection of songs, mythical beliefs, and early literature. Contradictory accounts of the same events, along with varieties of style, led to major revisions of thought regarding the authorship of many portions of the Bible. Genesis was especially suspect, and the idea that Moses authored the first five books in the Old Testament simply became untenable. As a literal presentation of events, the Bible was no longer to be trusted from the viewpoint of scientific history. However, there proved to be a moral and inspirational consistency to the work which gave it high ethical value. Christianity's Hebraic roots received sympathetic study and at the same time the "historical Jesus" was presented in human terms as an understandable moral prophet.

This scholarship on the Continent came to England largely in the second half of the century. Here it appeared in the context of another example of new knowledge resulting in an attack on the foundations of religion. By initially opposing it with fervor, the clergy again appeared to be taking a position opposed to the findings of free inquiry; they seemed afraid of truth.

The new criticism created the greatest problem for Protestants who had concentrated much of their religious point of view on the idea that the Scriptures constituted literal truth, an embarrassing remnant from the Reformation but still central to most fundamentalist sects. The Catholics were less severely damaged for they had never taken such a narrow position on the Bible. Indeed they had urged its validity as a spiritual document, insisting that it must be properly seen in combination with the writings of the Church Fathers and the course of Church history. Because all these were the foundations of the Catholic faith, the new findings of scholars did not constitute a fundamental attack.

At the same time evolution and Biblical criticism were disturbing clergymen, anthropological studies were similarly raising questions about the ethical practices and standards preached by Christianity. The very secularity of the pursuit for new knowledge seemed to lend special credence to a relativistic view of moral behavior; a religious justification for behavior seemed antiquated.

While organized religion was facing these attacks based on new knowledge, its foundations were also being eroded by the social consequences of industrial progress. As workers gathered in grimy dwellings around the factories, there was an inadequate adjustment of the various faiths to the new situation. Not enough new churches were built in the expanding cities and the clergy were far too slow in recognizing the developing problem. The worker came to be as poverty-stricken spiritually as he was materially. Industrialization appeared to have a particularly brutalizing effect on the worker. The spiritual result was a wave of "de-Christianization" (or outright paganism) which swept through urban industrial populations in mid- and late century. It was particularly evident in Belgium, becoming a source of concern to that small nation's leaders. Liberals generally saw this problem as a major challenge. They believed almost devoutly in machine production as a vehicle of progress and assumed that such a good for mankind *per se* need not necessarily result in such appalling urban slums. Socialists seized on the obviously exploitive character of the situation to launch attacks on the institutions which fostered or allowed such conditions to develop. Organized religion was prominent among their targets and the success of their attacks had the effect of stimulating further "de-Christianization." Socialism itself took on much of the crusading and moral qualities provided by earlier Christianity and provided an emotional support for the new urban class which had been neglected by the church. Christianity was in grave danger of being found socially and intellectually inadequate to the new society which the French and the industrial revolutions had spawned.

A major Protestant reaction to the attack of both the evolutionists and the upholders of Biblical criticism was to turn inward to its own resources. This self-examination resulted in a renewed emphasis on fundamentalism and the spirit of piety. Essentially an emotional response, it utterly ignored the substance of the intellectual questions being asked. Personal salvation and the reading of God's word became more important than disputations on points of historical or philological accuracy.

Because good works were also important characteristics of the person who was close to God, a number of movements began which were explicitly oriented toward helping others, especially the poor.

Debates on dogma were replaced with a strong sense of social mission, both at home and in the world at large. In England Charles Kingsley, Frederick Maurice, and John Ludlow worked to produce a type of Christian socialism. They moved into the vacuum created by the failure of Chartism and tried to form a Christian Cooperative Commonwealth. They appealed to producers to treat workers as Christians and spoke out against the class hatreds and ruthlessness associated with competitive industrial society. They saw a better world resulting from workers and producers combining with the church and embracing Christian love as a rule of life. But the cooperatives they sponsored were underfinanced and failed. The movement resembled the earlier utopians in their appeal to the altruistic impulses of those in power. This experiment typified many Protestant activities designed to stimulate the loyalty of workers to the system by alleviating their most desperate problems. In this respect the movement was conservative and distinctly nonrevolutionary.

In Germany the Christian Social Labor Party was organized in 1878 mainly to provide a patriotic and Christian version of social improvement as an alternative to the Marxist programs being offered the workers. This was a shortlived experiment but much of its practical program was directly taken over by Bismarck when he introduced his own industrial legislation.

In the nonpolitical sphere another example of the new thrust of Protestantism may be seen in the founding of the Salvation Army in 1878. Here a major commitment was made to reach the slum dwellers spiritually. Showmanship, piety, and determination combined in a remarkably successful venture. The clergy turned enthusiastically to programs of social work as dozens of "missions" appeared in the slums. An evangelical revivalism resulted from this turn from theological study to practical action and the churches embarked on a social mission. Such work earlier had been largely confined to charitable functions, which paled in comparison with this new movement. A more intellectual version was the Christian Social Union organized in 1889. Here religious study was promoted and an attempt made to combine the traditional Anglican position with the new criticism and a doctrine of social welfare. It lacked the vitality and effectiveness of the more activist Salvation Army. A less ambitious program was the Y.M.C.A., which was to minister to young urban males. Thus the Protestants turned to an emphasis on direct action and a personalized Christianity which offered salvation through living a better life.

The Catholics were in a position much different from that of the

Protestants. They had, after all, lived for a long time with the problem of literal meaning of the Bible and also the pedantic criticisms of linguists who questioned its textual accuracy (a renowned critic had been Erasmus). Evolution and de-Christianization were problems, but more pressing was the fact that the Church, including the Papacy itself, was under direct attack by the secular state. This was a crucial immediate problem and appeared on two fronts, in Italy and in Germany.

The Pope who had to face these issues was Pius IX, the man who had been hailed in liberal circles at the time of his selection in 1846. The upheavals of 1848 made him turn from liberal causes to become a supporter of conservatism. Although he accepted the protection of French troops and was in fact unable to follow an independent policy, his instincts were hardly frustrated by his protectors. Italian unification was a crucial blow to Pius IX's ego, for in the process he lost virtually all his secular holdings, all but Rome in 1859–1860 and Rome itself in 1870. Thus the creation of modern Italy was seen by the Papacy as a direct blow to the Church. The Papacy had built an extensive temporal power just so the Pope would not be at the mercy of secular princes. Now this protection was gone and Pius moodily refused to cooperate with the new state.

Unlike Italy, Germany had been unified with little need for diplomatic consideration of the Papacy or papal territories. After unification, however, Bismarck quickly showed himself to be militantly opposed to Catholicism in his new Germany. Branding the Roman church as the "Black International," he struck out at what he regarded as the Church's intrusion into nonreligious areas of life. He believed that his actions would be popular because he sensed a public reaction against Pius IX's pretensions of superiority, especially as they appeared in the dogma of Papal Infallibility. An obvious lashing out against the losses in territory, Pius had sought to compensate somewhat for this by enhancing the spiritual and moral power of the Church. Bismarck at the time was trying to crush particularist sentiment and to develop widespread acquiescence to Prussian institutions. Thus he saw the Catholics along the Rhine and in Bavaria as potentially unreliable, and he prepared a series of coercive bills calculated to make it difficult for the Catholic Center Party to promote itself and its candidates. He also reduced the Church role in education and welfare. As if to verify Bismarck's analysis, Pius reacted to the measure providing that marriage was a civil matter by simply stating that any laws restricting or ending the religious authority of the Church were null and void. This, of course, resulted in more curtailing of Church functions as the secular state's relations with the Vatican steadily deteriorated. At the same time, in France the obvious clerical ties of the monarchists during the early years of the Third Republic resulted in their influence being explicitly opposed and curtailed by the republicans once they were firmly in power. For Pius IX the developments in Europe between 1848 and his death in 1878 were one long nightmare. Although buffeted by political forces largely beyond his control, still he fought back with obstinacy.

After the attack on papal authority in 1848, a wave of support for the Pope had swept through the Catholic populations of Europe, resulting in new popularity for ultramontanism and a consequent weakening of liberal Catholicism. Pius seized on this sentiment to negotiate a number of concordats in the early 1850s and also expanded the functions of the Church in several areas, including Holland and England. At the same time he moved to enhance his authority further by proclaiming, on December 8, 1854, the doctrine of the Immaculate Conception of the Virgin Mary to be an article of faith. This idea had been accepted for centuries at the popular level but had never received papal sanction. During the Middle Ages scholars such as Saint Anselm had studied the matter but stopped short of affirming that solid bases existed for the belief. Pius took this step on his own authority and won broad support among the masses. It was his first major impact on the development of doctrine and foreshadowed a massive contribution in this area, his pontificate being the most productive since the sixteenth century.

Ten years later to the day, Pius showed the extent of his alienation from the dominant trends of his age. He had from time to time criticized various aspects of modern society and he now presented these criticisms in a composite form. Known commonly as the *Syllabus of Errors,* this document placed the Church in a reactionary position on almost every major issue. As could be expected, it appalled the dwindling ranks of liberals in the Church and delighted the ultramontanes, who applauded this initiative at a time when papal holdings were a bare shred of what they had been before the French army entered northern Italy in 1859.

The *Syllabus* was a carefully constructed, scholarly work, couched in technical language and intended for the guidance of bishops. Like Darwin's work, its content was seen in somewhat altered form when it was discussed at the popular level. Its message seemed more dogmatic and uncompromising than was the actual case when the document was considered in its entirety. In France Bishop Felix

Dupanloup wrote a defense of the *Syllabus* which pointed out that it was dealing with ideas in the abstract but that in their application the Church was flexible enough to allow consideration for special circumstances; he insisted that the last thing that should be believed was that these condemnations represented an uncompromising stand. This attempt to soften the impact of the *Syllabus* was widely applauded in Catholic circles but was not as convincing as if Pius IX himself had offered this explanation. Indeed, the ideas in the *Syllabus,* expressed starkly in truncated form, may very well have been a true picture of Pius IX's intentions, and no amount of qualifying considerations could change the fact that the errors condemned did constitute much of the fabric of liberal and progressive ideas then current in Europe. The eightieth error explicitly condemned was the idea that the Pope "can and should reconcile and align himself with progress, liberalism, and modern civilization."

The entire *Syllabus* merits careful study but its breadth may be indicated here by noting a few of the propositions explicitly condemned. Rationalism in religion stemming from the Enlightenment was rejected; miracles and prophecies are not poetic or mythical inventions; Christ was no mythical fiction and faith in Christ is not unreasonable; reason is neither the main path to knowledge nor the judge of good and evil or the true and the false. A pietistic sort of pantheism had also survived and it too drew papal fire. The growing sense of freedom in Europe since the French Revolution had encouraged the idea that any person should be "free to embrace and profess that religion which . . . he shall believe true." Pius condemned this and the idea that men might find salvation through any religion, explicitly denying that Protestantism made it "equally possible to please God as in the Catholic Church." He especially reaffirmed the right of the Church to "exercise its authority without the permission and assent" of the secular civil power, including the "care and dominion over temporal things." He further condemned the growing attack on clerical education which many secular governments were encouraging. He disallowed government interference in the selection of bishops, the suppression of religious orders, and the superiority of civil law when it might be in conflict with canon law or Church policy. After a series of propositions implying Church authority and independence from secular control, he bluntly put the issue in another form; persons were in error who maintained that church and state should be separated. His reassertion of Church prerogatives against secular attack in Italy was clear but his target was broader. He condemned as well democratic procedures when he denied that authority was "the result of numerical superiority." The right of rebellion so enshrined in English history was similarly condemned when he insisted that legitimate princes should be obeyed. At the same time he reasserted the propriety of having the Catholic Church as a sole religion in a state and disagreed that non-Catholic immigrants should be legally allowed to practice their own religions. He explicitly condemned the idea that marriage was not a proper sacrament and opposed defining matrimony as merely a civil contract. Divorce was also condemned.

In sum, the *Syllabus* appeared as a series of condemnations of the liberalism apparent in the upheavals of 1830 and 1848 as well as the increase in domestic functions being assumed by the secular state. Republicanism was also a special target, along with the intrusion of governments into fields like education. Although the specific points had been earlier condemned, their issuance all in a package at this particular time, when the Papacy had lost much of its lands, drew special attention to the document as being more in tune with the reactionary sentiments of Charles X than the progressive ideas of constitutional monarchy. It is little wonder that the *Syllabus* attracted wide attention. It also served to make a number of immediate developments appear in a context of special defiance of the Church. This was the case, for instance, in the broad educational reform undertaken in England under the Forster Act and also in the final unification of Italy, which appeared as the supreme act of secular aggression against the Church.

While the *Syllabus* was still the object of broad discussion, Pius issued a call for a Vatican Council, which convened in December, 1869. The Council dealt with a number of problems, including the issue of the supremacy of Pope or Church council, a problem unresolved since the Middle Ages. The Pope was judged superior and the Church itself a divine-right monarchy, although bishops through whom the Pope was to rule were also divinely sanctioned. The most dramatic conclusion of the Council was the doctrine of Papal Infallibility when the Pope spoke *ex cathedra* on faith or morals. Some liberals (Johann J. I. von Döllinger and Lord John E. E. Acton) had tried to prevent such a decision but their efforts were ineffectual. The few bishops who had held reservations about the wisdom of the doctrine readily accepted it when it became official. It was a resounding triumph for Pius IX and undoubtedly the high point of his pontificate. Like other doctrines it was broadly misunderstood at the popular level.

Papal superiority had hardly been established within the Church when the last vestiges of the papal temporal holdings were lost in the final stage of Italian unification. The new government offered to respect the Pope's spiritual position and to pay him an amount equal to his former income from his lands. Pius rejected the money and posed as a prisoner, but accepted other aspects of his situation as defined in the law of guarantees.

The Pope's problems with the government of Italy were shortly matched by intense friction with the new German Empire. Here the initiative in the struggle rested largely with Bismarck, but Pius' role was characteristic, stubborn resistance. Bismarck's main motive was political; he wanted a united realm and he saw religious variety as a distintegrating influence, especially when the Catholics organized politically, forming the Center Party. It was not a doctrinal matter to him, although the National Liberals he was cooperating with were strongly anticlerical. The struggle involved intense persecution of Catholicism. The state made the open conduct of Church business almost impossible but could not prevent the growth of political support for the Center Party. A stalemate developed and in the midst of it Pius IX died in 1878.

The next pontificate, that of Leo XIII, 1878–1903, appeared to contrast markedly to the rule of Pius IX. The new Pope was a talented diplomat with an acute awareness of the complexities of modern society. His formal positions and public statements buttressed an impression of a Papacy coming to grips with social problems associated with progress. His posture and attitudes conveyed a sense of a modernized Papacy—so emphatic was this that observers were often amazed at the news from the Vatican. That such an impression could be made spoke highly for the talents of Leo XIII. Although almost anyone following Pius IX would have appeared liberal, essentially Leo agreed with his predecessor on basic issues. Indeed, he remarked shortly after Pius' death "that modern society should end by reconciling itself . . . to the *Syllabus*." He believed in the right of the Church to regulate its own affairs, the temporal power of the Papacy, close church-state cooperation, and vigorous ultramontanism. The main difference really was that he turned a sympathetic and cooperative face toward the world and toward the avowed enemies of the Church. Merely to assume this posture made a number of things possible.

The first major success of the new pontificate was the ending of the *Kulturkampf*. The nature of Pius IX's personality had made conciliation impossible even though Bismarck recognized that his attempt to coerce the Catholic Church in Germany had been a mistake. On the day he became Pope, Leo initiated new discussions of the problem and Bismarck seized the opportunity. Both put on a bold front, Leo demanding that the coercive May Laws be rescinded and Bismarck refusing such an open response to papal wishes. In June of 1879 the minister of public worship, Dr. Falk, resigned. Falk had introduced the May Laws and was associated with their implementation. Enforcement lapsed and the German government, in effect, ended the open warfare on the Church, as a result gaining Center Party help in its program of protectionist tariff legislation and support in the struggle against socialism, the "Red" international. A measure of the value Bismarck came to attach to good relations with the Papacy may be seen from an 1885 colonial dispute between Germany and Spain over the Caroline Islands. Arbitration was finally agreed on and Bismarck suggested Leo XIII as arbitrator. This pleased and flattered the Pope but irritated anticlerical sentiment in Germany. Leo decided in favor of Spain but Bismarck accepted the Pope's tactful and almost obsequious explanation, replying in diplomatic terminology (with the word *Sire*) which implied that the Pope was really a temporal monarch, despite the losses of Papal territories. Leo's relationship with Germany illustrates well how he could seem responsible for a new course without doing more than appearing cooperative. The conditions for change had been present in Germany and not of his making, but he received much of the credit for the improved situation for Catholics.

Leo came to the Papacy at a difficult time, to say the least. Anticlericalism was strong in many areas besides Germany, a particularly disturbing problem existing in France. Here the Church was closely associated with monarchism and shared its fate. Indeed, many of republicanism's sharpest barbs were aimed at the Church, which Gambetta dramatically had singled out as the real enemy. A systematic, legislative attack on clerical education came in the early 1880s when the Third Republic appeared solidly beyond the threat of any monarchist restoration. The Catholic reaction was to support the ambitions of General Boulanger and when he failed, they were again in the position of appearing to be against republican institutions. Leo decided that open defiance of the republic was an unproductive course and instructed Catholics in France to accept the republic as a legitimate form of government, to cooperate with it, and to work within its structure to improve relations with the Church. The formal name for this move was the *ralliement,* a curious development which was opposed by many Catholics although some did follow the guidance of the Papacy. Ironically, Leo counseled Catholics in France to cooperate with the secular state while he continued Pius IX's refusal to come to terms with the Italian government. His efforts at reconciliation in France were badly hampered by the Catholic role in the Dreyfus case, which further discredited the Church and contributed markedly to the final separation of church and state in 1905, two years after Leo's death. The Napoleonic contributions to French Catholicism, the Concordat and the Falloux Law, had been reversed.

Leo XIII is best known for his support of social Catholicism, the key document being *Rerum novarum,* an encyclical issued in 1891. He placed the Church officially and emphatically in the position of supporting economic justice for the urban worker. In the details of this new initiative, Leo borrowed heavily from the earlier experience of Germany's Bishop Ketteler. This prelate had been instrumental in combating socialism among the workers through a Catholic union movement. He had also been a force in the Center Party.

Social Catholicism involved state regulation of industrial leaders to ensure that workers would be treated justly. Labor itself was encouraged to form Catholic unions, which Leo thought of as modern guilds. Attitudes dating from before 1789 were evident in his program. Leo saw a class-structured society where Christian goodwill and harmony existed in contrast to the Marxian outlook of warring classes. Laissez-faire attitudes were never strong in agrarian Catholic areas, so that state interference or regulation did not seem as obnoxious as it did in many parts of Western Europe. Leo defended private property and believed that a proper Christian spirit among the classes would make socialistic appeals fall on deaf ears. All of this led to Catholic varieties of socialism, although socialism itself, despite some laudable goals, was regarded as being too materialistic and irreligious. The various labor unions founded under Catholic auspices were relatively unsuccessful and Catholic attempts to form political parties were also of limited significance. Despite this, the idea that the Church was formally committed to justice for the industrial worker brought it a remarkable amount of new support and prestige. Leo saw the workers as merely urban peasants and his chief purpose was to retain the support for the Church of this lowest and more numerous social class. His efforts represented an attempt to develop a base other than in the aristocracy, a tie which in France was proving well-nigh fatal. There was also the danger of becoming entirely too responsive to the interests of capitalists.

Leo XIII was important in the movement known as modernism. He encouraged scientific and humanistic study, believing that there would be no conflict between them if both were seeking truth. This involved an acceptance and encouragement of much of the new criticism and attracted attention to the religious experience itself, rather than the formulation of doctrines. Leo explicitly promoted the study of Thomas Aquinas, whose ideas were tolerant to such a position. The modernists went well beyond a position congenial to Leo but were more of a problem for his successor, Pius X, who condemned modernism in 1907. Leo XIII's policies, however, had encouraged this growth.

By 1890 the Catholics and Protestants alike had entered the field of social welfare, greatly concerned with the conditions attendant upon the development of industrial society. Here they met the socialist face to face and neither cleric nor socialist received much help from the capitalist or from most politicians. As utopian in some respects as pre-Marxian socialists, still the churches faced the problems of the urban poor and manfully struggled with de-Christianization, which was continually on the increase. Doctrinal debates became muted in favor of programs of direct assistance and social welfare. Christianity was haltingly moving to meet the problems of industrial society.

CHAPTER 36

The Resurgence of European Imperialism, 1870–1890

Between 1870 and 1890 a resurgence of imperialism occurred which was to continue well into the twentieth century. While Bismarck was astutely trying to maintain the status quo of 1871 within Europe, an enormous extension of European overseas power was beginning. By 1900 almost 150 million people living in areas covering more than 10 million square miles became subjects of one or another of the European states. This increase in sovereignty added new diplomatic problems to an already tense situation and provided new testing areas for comparisons of will and power. The new colonial movement was so swift and virulent that it amazed even its participants and contrasted markedly with the nearly quiescent period in imperial history preceding 1870.

488

After 1815 the states of Europe were mainly concerned with domestic problems or issues relating to Continental stability. Britain was an exception in that her efforts to maintain control of Latin American markets represented a type of economic imperialism. She also added to her holdings, gaining New Zealand, parts of Canada and Australia, and the Punjab. These, however, were undramatic gains and were largely instances of an extension of a sovereignty already established. Russian penetration east of the Urals and the United States' push westward were illustrations of similar expansion. France was a better example of imperialism in the accepted sense. Her conquest of Algeria, along with the footholds gained in Senegal and Cochin China, was Europe's most conspicuous overseas movement during this period.

While statesmen in the decades immediately following 1815 were not absorbed by imperial questions, nonetheless progressive economic transformations at home were directing the attention of businessmen to opportunities overseas. Further, the appearance of masses of partially employed workers living in privation in the cities, as well as the conditions of depression which swept much of Western Europe in the 1840s, prompted political leaders to consider colonization as an outlet for what they regarded as an excess in population. Belgium under Leopold I was the most prominent example of this, the King almost continuously exploring chances to create an overseas colony. Many of that young nation's political leaders agreed with their sovereign that a colony would guarantee prosperity. They and the burgeoning business community saw imperialism in largely mercantilistic terms. No major colony resulted from these early impulses but the probing was indicative of trends which after 1870 were not to be denied.

Ironically, across the Channel the power with the largest empire was moving toward free trade and the national acceptance of laissez-faire economics. Her statesmen were taking the position that colonies were really not worth the trouble. This was, however, a temporary stance, as later in the scramble for more land Britain emerged with larger gains than any other nation. The business conditions giving rise to acceptance of laissez-faire economics had been altered by the very rapidity and volume of industrial growth; so that when new opportunities for imperial expansion occurred, Britain, too, played a major role. Talk of colonies not being worth the trouble or of mercantilism being old-fashioned became rare. At first Britain reacted to opportunities and situations when they developed, as in the imperial ventures of Disraeli and Gladstone, but by the later part of the century Britain was as avidly seeking additional overseas territory as the other powers.

There were a number of specific factors responsible for the renewed surge of imperialism after 1870. These may be categorized as political, economic, or religious but there was a considerable variety of colonial situations and all involved intricate combinations of motives. The topic is so complex that we may be on safe grounds only when we insist that any simple analysis is wrong. Such remarks as "capitalism is by nature anti-imperialist" or "the economic quintessence of imperialism is monopoly capitalism" just will not do. Doubtless the changed domestic scene in Europe played a large part; statesmen were no longer apprehensive about the spector of the French Revolution, because many of its values had been accepted with the admission of much of the middle class to a voice in policy-making. When this same growing class pointed to riches and prestige to be gained abroad, the holders of power proved interested and willing to support imperialistic schemes.

Fundamental to the movement was the acquisition of new geographic knowledge, especially about Africa. In 1800 virtually nothing was known of Central Africa. The same ignorance existed regarding vast reaches of Asia as well as much of North America and Antarctica—in all, nearly half the earth's land mass. Africa was literally the Dark Continent, known vaguely through trading settlements at points along her coast and a few centers of civilization along the Mediterranean and at the Cape of Good Hope. Sporadic explorations continued through the first half of the century but the "opening" of the continent flowed largely from the explorations of David Livingston and Henry Stanley. Livingston's travels in Africa spanned twenty-two years (1849–1871) and ended as Stanley's began. The result of these explorations, along with the opening of China and Japan, brought to Europe the realization that the world's land expanse was much more varied than earlier thought. An avalanche of information about new cultures appeared. At the same time the Suez Canal made the Mediterranean more important as an avenue to the East, steam transportation bringing these strange and vast lands closer to hand. The railroad contributed to this through the construction of major trunk lines which enabled raw materials and finished goods to be moved rapidly. Steamships and railroads were partners in the new imperialism; their effect on commerce was enormous.

Meanwhile in Europe sophisticated entrepreneurial techniques had pushed through another major industrial revolution. This resulted in production increased beyond anyone's imagination and a strong insistence by businessmen that new markets be found and that governments aid in the search. As competition increased, they welcomed news of backward areas with teeming millions and no established industry. Most of Asia and Africa were potential customers and textile manufacturers were agog at the thought of providing clothing for these population masses. At the same time it was clear that vast sources of raw materials had been discovered in close proximity to abundant supplies of native labor. In such a situation it is little wonder that mercantilist ideas revived and flourished.

Simultaneously, Europe's burgeoning industrial system was creating large sums of capital for which business leaders were seeking investments. The home industry absorbed large amounts, but domestic profits were modest when compared with the return from imperialistic ventures. Some of the surplus found its way into financing trunk railroads. French capital helped support Russia's move east; and in backward areas European engineers and entrepreneurs feverishly set to work building docks, roads, and warehouses. Emphasis was placed on communications and transportation as well as on creating local sources of power besides native labor. The laying of telegraph lines starkly symbolized the intrusion of a more technologically advanced culture in many areas, and the construction of massive dams gave notice of the intention to remain. The wealth and influence of the men engaged in these projects almost assured that their respective governments would play an active role in protecting their investments if ever they were threatened. So strong was the growing entrepreneurial elite by the 1880s that few governments openly defied it; and Bismarck appeared out of step with the trends of his age by ignoring their cries for an aggressive imperial program.

Another incentive for nations to embark on a frankly imperialistic course was political. To be a colonial power carried a special status which became an aspect of late nineteenth-century nationalism, especially among the Great Powers. To acquire colonies was an evidence of dynamism and growth, a proof that one's state and nationality were politically and culturally prominent. Rampant patriotism and national pride encouraged political leaders to extend their country's holdings, to provide their people with a larger "place in the sun."

France was a prominent example of national pride supporting imperialism. Her vision of her own importance had been badly shaken by the humiliation of the Franco-Prussian War and, above all, by the loss of Alsace-Lorraine. Republican leaders during the 1880s had no difficulty in finding support for a vigorous compensatory increase in colonial holdings overseas and extended French sovereignty in Africa and Southeast Asia. Alsace-Lorraine, however, was so close to home that despite enormous colonial gains, the desire for the return of these lost provinces was never blunted. French colonial initiatives under the Third Republic accompanied a humiliating inferiority complex.

Great Britain's new imperial expansion seemed almost effortless and was particularly marked by a sense of national pride. This dated from Disraeli's achievements and was his special legacy to his countrymen. A smug confidence and optimism marked Great Britain's colonial program, which seemed a striking example of how success breeds success. The public outcry over General Gordon's murder at Khartoum shows how little the nation was prepared for setbacks abroad. Gladstone's delay in supporting Gordon was seen not as a tactical error, but as a betrayal of the nation's destiny and world image.

In 1878 Russia's ambitions in Europe had been blocked at Berlin. Her intrigues in Bulgaria continued, but essentially her progress in the Balkans had been halted and she turned the bulk of her expansionist energies toward the East. Impressive gains east of the Urals, however, never quite compensated for the prestige of increases in the Balkans; and so, like France and Alsace-Lorraine, her renewal of energies in this area was easily predicted and only a matter of time.

Newly united Italy and Germany were in different positions in the fresh imperialistic struggle. Neither had an immediate colonial past to build on. Some business leaders were clamoring for an aggressive colonial program to compensate for the headstart of other powers. Colonies would also be proof of status. Italy readily succumbed to these temptations, embarking on an extensive program in North Africa. Both Italy and Germany saw colonies as a solution to population pressure, but both were also concerned that a population movement out to colonies seemed to involve a loss of valuable talent. In this light it is interesting to ponder the observation of Cecil Rhodes, Britain's great imperialist, who saw imperialism as the answer to the urban unemployment caused by industrialization. The unemployed must be sent out to forestall civil war at home. In Germany a strong business community waged a vigorous campaign to urge the government to enter the colonial race, but Bismarck refused until the mid-1880s. He was convinced that colonies did not add significantly to a nation's strength and, more important, that an aggressive colonial program by any nation merely assured that country's eventual collision of interests with Great Britain. As an element in his over-all foreign policy, imperialism was to be avoided for Germany but to be encouraged for others, especially France. To a large extent the series of colonial incidents after 1890 bore out his basic viewpoint. Such a perspective, however, did not placate the businessmen who saw opportunities for vast profits going to others nor did it satisfy patriots like William II, who desired the appearance of importance more than the substance of power.

A characteristic feature of much colonial activity was the presence of the Christian missionary, both Catholic and Protestant. The new awareness that there were millions of other people in the world became a challenge to Christendom; because there were souls needing salvation, the churches of Europe developed large overseas mission programs at the same time that they were addressing themselves to the de-Christianization problems of their own cities. In many areas the missionary appeared well in advance of any other European, and his primitive schools and chapels became outposts of European civilization. To many Europeans, the "white man's burden" was a serious and conscientious obligation; to others it became an excuse to acquire advantage. Religious leaders helped to frame public attitudes supporting imperialism; but more often than not, political leaders saw them as means to a national end. The murder of a missionary by savages in a distant land became one of the most potent excuses to assume political control over alien populations.

Imperialism in the late nineteenth century played a significant role in the spread of European values and standards. Added to the earlier colonial experience, the result was a virtual Europeanizing of the world. This extension of Western civilization was even more thoroughgoing and remarkable than that of Greek and Roman culture centuries before. Europe was the smallest continent, yet she managed to impose her culture and basic ideas on the rest.

Europeans were able to achieve such success because their way of life provided them with several advantages when opposing the peoples of Asia or Africa. An enormous asset was their bureaucratic-national state, this political device which had grown over the centuries. With all its red tape, corruption, overlapping jurisdictions and entrenched special interests which hampered flexibility and made radical departures in policy difficult, still the European state proved to be a vastly superior device for providing specialists (whether soldiers or technicians) than any of the native political units encountered in Africa or Asia. It was a striking testimonial to the uniqueness of Western institutions.

The testing of institutional strength occurred most obviously in scattered military confrontations, which often determined the fate of millions of natives. European armies were more carefully organized, more professionally led and better armed than the hordes which often faced them. Their enemies were rarely better than a poorly disciplined irregular cavalry. Sophisticated European artillery and machine guns found no equivalent in the weapons used to oppose them. An example of the advantage enjoyed by the Europeans in combat may be seen from an engagement at Palikao when on September 21, 1880, a force of 40,000 Chinese cavalry intercepted 800 Frenchmen. Far from stopping the French, the Chinese were themselves dispersed. Another military advantage flowed from European naval standards. They never struggled with any native fleets of any consequence and never encountered fortifications which could stand up to their shell fire. Thus Europeans sailed into native harbors and rivers at will, shelling villages point blank and rapidly transporting armies deep into hostile territory with little resistance.

Once the land fell under the control of Europeans, they implanted their own economic system, which also proved much more advanced than any devised by the natives. Handicraft economies, wherever they were that advanced, were no match for the machine-produced goods of Europe, and the native systems quickly succumbed. The Europeans integrated their colonies into their own economies with appalling results for the natives. The new means of production and distribution were controlled by Europeans and the natives sank into a state of utter economic servitude. The populations of much of Asia and Africa paid a horrendous price for the advanced civilization to which they had become exposed. As in earlier centuries, the European showed himself at times to be completely ruthless.

In some instances the penetration of an area was through the existing elite. Native leaders needing funds, weapons, or protection often became clients of outsiders. Where these rulers were already exploiting their people, in many cases the change in sovereignty took place without the populations concerned even being aware that they had new masters. Usually the Europeans were content with economic exploitation and did little to interfere with the local social customs. Missionaries attempted to proselytize, of course, but aside from this, local religions were respected so long as native practices did not interfere with the exploitation.

Primitive communications and tribal jealousies prevented the native populations from joining against the outsiders. Further, they were attacked piecemeal and lacked a sense of the over-all attack being made on their territories. Eventually, in the twentieth century, a number of native nationalisms began to appear. Interestingly, because they were direct responses to European rule, their nationalism followed the territorial divisions that their colonial masters had established rather than more fundamental tribal or ethnic groupings. Japan came to serve as a prime example of a developing nationalism that adopted European techniques in order to become strong enough to combat those attempting to exploit her. Indeed, Japan herself became an imperialistic power. The whole age was one of imperialism and Europeans were only the most spectacular of the peoples engaged in the movement.

The new wave of imperialism may be regarded as beginning in 1876 when Leopold II (1835–1909) of Belgium called together in Brussels an international meeting of explorers and geographers to consider further systematic study of Africa. This conference led to the start of a colonial empire in the Congo, and the speed and publicity surrounding the move tempted other statesmen also to embark on colonial schemes in Africa. The result was the so-called scramble for Africa in which European states rushed pell mell to discover and acquire the choicest regions.

Leopold's meeting in 1876 was avowedly to promote exploration and, above all, to work toward elimination of the slave trade. Livingston, whose explorations were motivated by personal curiosity, and a desire to spread Christianity and to end the slave trade, would have been pleased by the many statements of high moral purpose. The International Association for the Exploration and Civilization of Central Africa was founded to carry on the noble objectives expressed in Brussels. A number of national subcommittees were also established but most languished. The Belgian committee, however, was aggressively active. It negotiated treaties with Congolese chieftains, founded trading posts, and hired Henry Stanley (1841–1904) to pursue these activities vigorously in Central Africa. By 1882 this committee took the name of the International Association of the Congo and declared that its major concern was trade. Leopold was the guiding spirit in this association. It was a private company with neither diplomatic standing nor any formal tie with the Belgian state. Despite the King's pious moral statements, the object was profit and this led to unmerciful exploitation. Stanley proved to have similar interests and, with the two men working together, the bases were laid through a series of protectorates for Leopold to acquire the Congo. In 1885 the International Association won formal recognition by the Great Powers as the Congo Free State, with Leopold as sovereign. He literally possessed the whole area and had won the sanction of diplomats for his new state by making the most emphatic and righteous statements about the philanthropic work he wished to carry out at his own expense in Central Africa.

The Congo Free State became a mockery of altruistic or humanitarian pursuits. A personal belonging of Leopold II, the Belgian state's first direct connection came in 1889 when Belgium was named Leopold's heir in the Congo. In 1890 the government was given the right to acquire the colony in ten years in return for a loan and subsidy. Essentially, the monarch controlled the Congo Free State. Vast tracts were set aside as state lands; others were crown lands; and in addition the King had large interests in companies whose major work was the exploitation of concessions he had granted them.

Early to acquire new sovereignty in Africa, Leopold was also among the first to see the enormous exploitive potential in the Dark Continent. The word *Free* in the state's title was without meaning so far as the Congolese population was concerned. Expressions like *freedom of trade* bore no relation to the ruthless regime settled on the natives. The main freedom was that of native exploitation. Beckoning the eager Belgian entrepreneurs were prospects for enormous profits rivaling the riches acquired by overseas companies in trade in the East Indies centuries earlier. One Belgian company with a capital of 10,000 pounds sterling yielded a net profit in six years of 370,000 pounds. A similarly impressive investment was a return of over 730,000 pounds in four years from costs amounting to 40,-200 pounds. In this latter case the stock rose from a value of 250 Belgian francs to 16,000 francs in 1906. How much Leopold made personally is a matter of speculation but it was surely an enormous sum.

The source of this wealth was largely rubber and ivory, which the natives were forced to collect. These products, as well as land, were stipulated by decree as belonging to the state. Therefore, the natives could not sell ivory or rubber to any Europeans. They were merely to collect them for specified state or company officials. The various native tribes were given quotas which were rigorously enforced. Failure to meet the quotas resulted at first in the sequestering of native women as hostages. If quotas still were not met, officials turned native troops into the villages to pillage and kill. Many of these were cannibals and a reign of terror resulted. These natives who had been turned against their fellows were carefully rationed in the number of cartridges they were allowed. For every shell expended they were to present a right hand. The result of this grisly requirement was that when they shot at game or missed when firing at people, they brutally turned on living people, cutting off their hands. Such tactics contributed to both a massive drop in the population and vast profits.

This monstrous exploitation continued for many years. Aside from the parties involved, little was known of Congolese conditions. There were no charges brought by victims of the system in courts of law. Some missionaries were concerned, but these regarded Leopold as a great philanthropist and patron. Some Protestant missionaries objected privately to the maltreatment of natives, but even they believed that the King was unaware of what was being done in his name. This charitable position was eventually exposed; and finally, in 1908, a storm of unfavorable world opinion resulted in Leopold's relinquishing his sovereignty and turning the Congo over to the Belgian government. His had been a sordid stewardship. For us, it stands as a prime example of the new imperialistic movement, with all its questionable motives, and it illustrates well the advantages gained for Europeans through the sharp differentiation of technological development between European and native cultures.

Leopold's activities in the Congo had just started when the statesmen of Europe awakened to the new situation. The publicity attending the new explorations had also alerted people. The French moved to duplicate Leopold's techniques in the territory north of the Congo River. Building on explorations of this region by Savorgnan de Brazza (1852–1905) between 1875–1878, they founded Brazzaville and assumed an extensive protectorate which came to comprise much of French Equatorial Africa. Recognizing that vast new regions had been opened to outside appropriation, Bismarck and Jules Ferry jointly decided on a conference of the major powers in order to establish some ground rules for the coming "scramble for Africa." The conference itself was a consequence of exactly the sort of misunderstanding between major powers that the meeting would try to prevent in the future. The Portuguese had a flimsy claim to the mouth of the Congo River and in 1884 the British announced their support for Portugal's claim. If the claim were sustained, Leopold's activities in Central Africa would be hampered. The Belgian monarch at once turned to France and to Germany for help. Bismarck had recently begun to relent in his stolid opposition to colonies and saw Britain's interference here as an omen of what might befall German efforts in Africa. Jules Ferry, in Paris, absolutely refused to accept the idea of Portugal controlling the mouth of the Congo, also a French access route, and so he agreed to support Leopold, providing France would be given the first chance to acquire Congolese territory if the Belgian monarch ever sold it. Thus both the French and German governments supported Leopold and called the conference which met in Berlin from November 16, 1884, to February 28, 1885. When the British came to the meeting, the basic decision regarding Portugal's claim had already been decided. They accepted the decision, insisting only on some agreements to assure equality of opportunity in future competition for territory. A kind of open door was agreed on so far as the "scramble" was concerned. Leopold received full recognition for his claims. Freedom of navigation and trade was to prevail and slavery and the slave trade were to be eliminated. In the Congo these provisions were close to a mockery of what happened. The powers all agreed that new sovereignty was to come after the notification of the other powers of the effective occupation of an area not already occupied by Europeans. It was a simple rule and was an invitation for imperialists to move as quickly as possible to occupy the blank areas on their maps. It obviously allowed Italy and Germany to be partners in the new colonial race, despite their recent unification and lack of a colonial heritage. The conference was a triumph for Leopold, who successfully continued his pose as a great patron and philanthropist. As in 1878 Bismarck was the genial host with no direct involvement in the specific issue but an interest in the over-all situation.

Another conference was held in Brussels in 1889 to reconsider how to stamp out the slave trade, which had proved difficult to eradicate. It also considered ways to improve native living standards and debated how his access to firearms and alcohol might be controlled. There was no way, however, to enforce any decisions of the conference, and Leopold and other exploiters continued to ignore the native as a human being. Technically, slavery was abolished wherever possible but the systems of forced labor introduced by the Europeans were just as harsh and inhumane.

France under the Third Republic made extensive gains in Africa, beginning with Tunis in 1881. In French Equatorial Africa and French West Africa she created an enormous colonial empire. At the same time she gained Djibouti (1888), and imperial planners in Paris began to think in terms of an east-west link across the continent.

In German colonial history 1884 was an important year. Before the convening of the Berlin Conference, Bismarck relented in his opposition to colonies and announced a protectorate over Southwest Africa. The British were irritated but had no valid complaint because Bismarck had inquired of their intentions in the area but had received no clear response. This act of encouragement to the imperialists in Germany led them to increase their clamor. They soon added the Cameroons and Togoland to their holdings and in 1890 they acquired German East Africa (Tanganyika). German gains had been substantial in Africa for a state whose main leader was skeptical about colonialism.

Italy was disappointed about the French acquisition of Tunisia, but in the late 1880s she established the colony of Eritrea along the Red Sea. She was singularly unsuccessful in the division of Africa, suffering a humiliating defeat in 1896 at the hands of the Ethiopians.

Prominent in the colonial race in Africa were the British, who were for a time interested in the idea of a Cape to Cairo railroad. This fell through in 1890, when the Germans moved into Tanganyika, but nonetheless Britain's gains were enormous. Much of the story of British policy in Africa centers on Cecil Rhodes (1853–1902), whose Kimberley diamond mines financed an extensive imperialistic program for over ten years after 1888. Diamonds and gold, rather than rubber and ivory, were the particular magnets of greed pursued by the British.

Western imperialism between 1870 and 1890 also was an important feature of Asian history, although the movement lacked the coordination obvious in the partitioning of Africa. There was more emphasis on trade concessions, especially in coastal ports, from which spheres of influence were staked out by the Europeans. Closer to the African pattern was the French move in 1883 to extend their Southeast Asian holdings. Ignoring protests from China, they absorbed Annam and French Indo-China took its basic form. Germany, France, and Britain also made gains in Oceania.

The two decades after 1890 saw increased imperial activity. The Great Powers weathered a series of diplomatic crises involving colonies. Statesmen sensed the growing danger of war and were appalled when in 1904 Russia was resoundingly defeated by a non-European power, Japan.

The new imperialism after 1870 did have its positive side. In places where the exploitation was not too extreme, the Europeans did bring a more sophisticated civilization to backward areas. Slavery did end and educational systems were founded. Road and rail connections between new cities helped to open up the interior of the continent to outside influences. The missionaries served a humane role and were responsible for much of the groundwork in introducing natives to European customs. The new bureaucracies provided for legal systems which brought to the native populations a sense of personal rights, although there was a great chasm between theory and practice in much of Africa.

Considering the advantages Europeans expected to gain when they embarked on imperialism, there were some horrendous miscalculations and disappointments. The colonies never did become a great settling ground for the surplus populations of Europe. The urban poor simply did not lend themselves well to the role of colonial adventurers. Very few emigrated to Africa or Asia.

On the financial level, there proved to be a number of speculators or profiteers who amassed vast treasures but no national economies were enhanced. Thus, while Leopold II was reaping an enormous personal fortune from the Congo, military and bureaucratic expenses forced the Congo Free State to borrow money. The wealth flowed to individuals and not to state treasuries. From a national point of view the colonies simply did not pay their way. Another disappointment was that the new areas never filled their proper role in a mercantilistic sense. The colonies were a source of raw materials but never provided an adequate market for the finished goods of the parent European nation. The African natives did not copy the attitudes, habits, and dress of the Europeans. Even had they desired to, they were unable to acquire the necessary purchasing power as a consequence of the exploitive or forced systems of labor.

Despite these drawbacks, the competition for colonies enhanced the prestige of the nations involved. National pride was both served and flattered and, like many appetites, tended to grow with the feeding. As the race for ever more colonies continued, an exaggerated sense of national honor ran greater risks of being offended over some modest encounter between minor forces in some far away tropical jungle. Such an incident occurred at Fashoda in 1898 and diplomats shuddered, fearing that one of the nineteenth century's basic forces, nationalism, was about to yield some bitter fruit.

XII

Conclusion

CHAPTER 37

A Century's Finale

When Bismarck ended his public career in 1890, Europe was at peace; France had no major ally and Russia was committed to Germany. After unifying Germany, the Iron Chancellor had kept his new nation out of war and secure for twenty years. Four years after he left office, the French and Russians negotiated a military convention and the struggle Bismarck had plotted to avoid was in sight. In twenty years it came, and in retrospect, it seemed almost inevitable. The states of Europe had stumbled from one crisis to another. The danger of a vast conflagration was recognized by most statesmen and became progressively more acute until in 1914 the diplomatic machinery for peace and security broke down. World War I was a leadership failure of appalling proportions.

The nineteenth century had been a remarkable age of diplomacy.

503

Metternich, Nicholas I, Napoleon III, Palmerston, Cavour, Disraeli, and Bismarck were leaders who, whatever their other failings, managed to prevent more than localized wars in Europe. These towering figures allowed the forces of nationalism a measure of success but prevented them from disrupting the continent. After 1890 and before 1914, the most prominent leader was William II, but he hardly belongs in such a distinguished list. He fancied himself as a sort of Disraeli who would instill in his nation a sense of pride in empire and increase his country's role in the world at large. An energetic and flamboyant headline hunter, he was no match for the standard set by Europe's earlier leaders; and instead of contributing to the working of the system, he contributed, at least as much as any other man, to its downfall. There was no great statesman following Bismarck and the structure devised at Vienna and adjusted in 1856 and 1878 was unable to survive. The ideologies unleashed during the Revolution were to grow during the century and similarly the nationalism of the Revolution could only be partially blunted by Vienna. A new structure was probably needed which would take account of nationalism; but, after 1890, the major countries were all pursuing selfish objectives with little regard for placing priority on peace. Bismarck's perspective on the world was largely restricted to the boundaries of Europe; but at least he tried to understand, as well as take advantage of, the basic interests of all the major states of the continent. No European ruler in the quarter century following 1890 did as much.

William's attitude concerning colonies was a major new element in the diplomatic world. In this regard he is perhaps merely representative of his age. Most leaders were enthusiastically promoting unrestrained imperialism and Bismarck's reluctant acquiescence merely made William's strong support for the cause the more pronounced. In this wider view he regarded himself as being a modern man rather than a particularistic German like Metternich and Bismarck, who saw only Europe from the Atlantic to the Urals. Intent on enhancing German status in the world at large, he tended to downgrade dangers lurking within Europe. He discounted the peril of Russia and even of the Franco-Russian Alliance. At the same time the German foreign office felt that a proper alliance structure for Germany would be one in which Britain would join the Triple Alliance. Efforts to encourage this were too ambitious though not without some justification. In London, Joseph Chamberlain was working for a bilateral Anglo-German alliance. He was never able to get much popular support for this and was handicapped by the strong

German preference that Britain join the Triple Alliance as well as by the Kaiser's stand in the Boer War (Kruger Telegram), which especially irritated the English. These negotiations fell through by 1901; thus, Germany had lost Russia and had approached but alienated Great Britain. Both, of course, were to develop a close relationship with France. To add to the contradiction in German policy, her imperial program placed her in a competitive position with Britain—as Bismarck had predicted—and especially militated against a British alliance. At the same time, to buttress colonial ambitions, the Germans, following the advice of Admiral Alfred von Tirpitz, in 1898 embarked on a major program of naval construction. The decision was to build a fleet so powerful that no country could challenge it, thus providing protection for German colonies and commerce as well as enhancing German diplomatic prestige. This naval program was the object of special apprehension among Britain's leaders, and contributed as much as anything else to their acceptance of a policy of alliances to replace the isolation they had practiced for so long.

This change of attitude on Britain's part was, like Germany's emphasis on overseas expansion, a new element in the international chessboard. The Boer War had brought a storm of protest and Britain felt alone in the world. Despite her industrial strength and naval power, she now decided that she needed allies and in 1902 negotiated a five-year alliance with Japan. From this time on, she became actively engaged in seeking security arrangements with other powers. Having rebuffed German efforts to join the Triple Alliance, the logic of the situation seemed to dictate what came to pass, that she should move closer to Germany's potential enemies, the members of the Franco-Russia military convention. In 1904 an *entente cordiale* with France was negotiated, followed in 1907 by another with Russia. Now the Triple Alliance was matched by a Triple Entente and the stage was set for the struggle to come.

The Triple Entente had been formed in the shadows of the Triple Alliance. While a number of diplomatic crises were aggravating relations, Russia's defeat by Japan in 1904–1905 made the French question the value of Russia as an ally and realize the advantages of an arrangement with Britain. The ententes followed a series of compromises, especially involving conflicting claims in Egypt, Morocco, and Persia. That such rivalries could be settled was a hopeful sign, but in later incidents, where the opposing parties were members of the rival treaty systems, the mood to compromise was less and the danger to peace correspondingly higher. In effect, Europe stood at the brink of war after 1907 and the fact that she avoided it for another seven years was due more to chance than design. The situation was more acute than any Bismarck had even postulated and was unmatched by any crisis since 1815.

By 1900 the economic condition of Europe was one of great promise. Germany was undergoing industrial expansion at a bewildering rate. She had, in fact, gone from a very early phase of industrial development, characterized by small plants, directly to the massive corporation. By this course, she managed to pass over the long period in England where laissez-faire principles were admired and extended with the growth of business. In Germany there was no similar predictable growth in liberal ranks matching industrial expansion. The cartel system developed, welcomed by most Germans as a natural growth. To limit competition and to work to achieve a monopoly seemed good sense, especially when it was clearly more efficient. Thus there was no German equivalent to efforts in the United States to break up giant trusts, and large-scale corporate development was unhampered. Cartels were loose structures and individual companies retained their management. They did, however, work out agreements on prices, production schedules and techniques, and distribution arrangements. Cartels were especially common in the electrical, chemical, mining, and steel industries. *Horizontal* cartels were those formed by companies producing like products who would otherwise be competitors. *Vertical* cartels were comprised of firms contributing to the entire production of an item, from acquisition of raw materials to sale in the marketplace. The cartel system forced German industrialists to develop a broad view of their situation and they became apprehensive about the possibility of being cut off from raw materials and markets, both largely based overseas. This led them to support William's ambitions for Germany to become a great colonial power possessing a strong navy. The new capitalist was a skilled financier promoting a diffused ownership of corporations while control and management remained in the hands of a few. Through imaginative stock financing he amassed vast sums for the development of enormous plants producing a torrent of products, making the accessibility of raw materials and markets even more crucial.

The growth of cartels in Germany was the most dramatic development in large-scale industrial expansion. Outside Germany much of Europe was also rapidly industrializing; the most impressive growth occurred within an area that could be bounded by lines drawn roughly between Glasgow, Stockholm, Trieste, Florence, and

Barcelona. Outside this "inner" area of industrial progress, conditions remained largely agrarian, although some cities contained modest industrial beginnings. Investment capital flowed across national lines with few restrictions and much of the agrarian "outer" Europe stood in a colonial economic relationship to the major financial centers. The growing Russian industrial plant, however, was able to rival Central European penetration of the Balkans.

All this economic progress had been accompanied by a growth of labor organizations. Workers were not only more numerous but better educated, and they possessed a sense of solidarity. The result was a continuous flow of members into labor unions and increasing support for socialism. Labor unions had flourished in Britain alongside other sporadic efforts to help the lot of the workers, such as Chartism and varieties of Christian Socialism. The ideals of the latter were taken up in the 1880s by the Fabian Society, a group of intellectuals who managed to convince the traditional parties that programs of social reform should replace unrestrained *laissez faire*. The unions were led by socialist intellectuals but were not themselves socialist. Unions had been legal and growing in number since 1875 but they became politically active after the anti-union Taff Vale decision of 1901. Combining with some socialist groups, the Labor Party was formed and first showed its potential in 1905 when it won twenty-nine seats in the House of Commons. Both Liberals and Conservatives were amazed but warmly welcomed the new members, passing the Trades Disputes Act in 1906 which voided the Taff Vale decision and put labor unions in a privileged position.

In France trade unionism flourished during the Third Republic but the overriding concept was syndicalism. The spirit of revolution permeated the movement, and emphasis was placed on keeping it alive. Militantly promoting direct action, the unions opposed bourgeois institutions, including the state and its bodies, such as the Chamber of Deputies. The strike was their major weapon and the general strike the supreme weapon. To the extent that this aspect of unionism had an ideologue, it was Georges Sorel (1847–1922). He saw the industrial proletariat as potentially a modern crusading force whose will and strength would overthrow bourgeois capitalism and establish a proletarian socialism. His philosophy was a heavy blend of Marx and Nietzsche. The development of broad union organization on industrial bases resulted in great power for labor. The strike was used frequently and Sorel encouraged union members to carry on sabotage when working, the slogan being "poor work for poor pay." Although syndicalist methods were concrete, objectives remained ill defined. After 1900, strikes became more common and, with virtually all French labor represented in the comprehensive General Confederation of Labor, the massive general strike became possible. When it occurred on May Day of 1906, labor history in France entered a new phase.

Socialism on the continent appeared after 1900 in a number of varieties; and we have already noted Leo XIII's Catholic socialism. There was a substantial copying of Bismarck's brand of state socialism, especially in Scandinavia, where labor relations never were characterized by the bitterness found elsewhere. The most important socialist organization was the German Social Democratic Party, which owed much of its early vigor to the leadership of Ferdinand Lassalle (1825–1864). In 1875 it had resulted from a fusion of the German Workingmen's Association with the Social Democratic Labor Party. In 1891, after the retirement of Bismarck, the party formulated a program of minimum and maximum demands during a memorable congress at Erfurt. This Erfurt Program became the model for socialist parties over the world. The maximum demands involved the abolition of private property and the establishment of a cooperative commonwealth. The less dramatic minimum demands offered a practical set of objectives which were also attractive to nonsocialist reformers. They called for universal suffrage, proportional representation, freedom of speech and assembly, separation of church and state, free secular education, a public militia instead of a standing army, civil equality of men and women, the eight-hour day, heavy income and inheritance taxes, and general factory reforms. These were popular issues in Germany and Social Democrats were elected to the Reichstag in ever greater numbers. In 1912, 110 Social Democrats took seats as a result of 4.25 million votes.

Within the party—and most socialist parties suffered the same internal dilemma—the issue of revisionism posed a difficult problem. Essentially, the point was made by Eduard Bernstein (1850–1933) and others that Marx's ideas and tactics should be revised in light of the continuing history of capitalism. Specifically, the middle class did not seem to be disappearing, peasant proprietorships were increasing, and consolidation of industries did not mean a complete consolidation of wealth because more stockholders appeared. On these and other points Marx had erred in his prediction and although the goal was still to be socialism, the strategy and program of Marx needed revision. Another major alteration was the idea that a violent revolution might not be necessary and that one should cooperate with other progressives and work within, instead of outside, the governmental structure.

Whether to revise or not was an issue in all socialist parties; in Germany, Bernstein was opposed by August Bebel (1840–1913) and Karl Kautsky (1854–1938), who argued that any current reforms were only bribes. A famous debate on this subject occurred in 1904 at the International Socialist Congress at Amsterdam. Here Bebel defended a rigid Marxist position with systematic logic and was opposed by Jean Jaurès (1859–1914), who spoke eloquently for revision. Jaurès was especially against militarism and the open resort to unprovoked force. The congress supported Bebel but in most parties the revisionists were the more successful. The most fateful example of this same dichotomy was in Russia. There the Bolsheviks under Lenin supported the orthodox Marxist line and opposed the Mensheviks, whose most effective spokesman, Georgi Plekhanov (1857–1918), argued for revision and for the peaceful, slow, and natural development of socialism under a protective shell of capitalism. Socialism thus was fragmented as it came into the twentieth century, but it was nonetheless to be a major force attracting a wide following and able leaders.

During the century a particularly disturbing type of social critic had been the anarchist. Patron saints of anarchism were William Godwin and Pierre-Joseph Proudhon. Emphasizing reason and justice, respectively, they authored the ideology of anarchism. Although also a writer, Michael Bakunin (1814–1876) was primarily an activist, plotting the overthrow of existing regimes wherever there seemed an opportunity. His exploits became legendary and four years of Siberian exile along with eight years in various prisons made him a genuine revolutionary martyr. He preached, among other things, that the urge to destroy was creative. He had a passion for forming revolutionary societies but most of his plots failed. Anarchism was also praised in *The Ego and Its Own* by Max Stirner (Johann Schmidt, 1806–1856). He placed more emphasis on personal liberation and egotism, but the message was the same, the end of all social and moral bonds imposed on people. Toward the end of the century the anarchists were closely associated with the nihilists and their program of action became oriented toward the deed of violence. A wave of assassinations (President Carnot of France, Italy's King Humbert, Empress Elizabeth of Austria) led people to view anarchists with shock and horror. In Russia, especially, anarchism came to be irrational terrorism, plundering, or simply robbery. The movement had assumed a level close to sheer vandalism and lacked the ideological commitment apparent earlier in Bakunin or Proudhon. These people destroyed for destruction's sake and were no part of the organized reform movement stirring in Russia and about to come to the surface in 1905.

At the same time two interesting Russian intellectuals put a new face on anarchism. Near the end of his life Count Leo Tolstoy (1828–1910), the great author of *War and Peace* and *Anna Karenina,* became so critical of the government as an institution that he personally rejected the state and denied the validity of property. He emphasized Christian love and a general return to nature. Life to him seemed more real and closer to Christian truth if lived humbly and close to nature. He rejected the formal church as a structural device which, like the state, impeded love and the simple life and was, on occasion, an agent of oppression and even violence. His answer was not revolution but rather a refusal to obey the state. Among those influenced by his doctrine of passive defiance was Mohandas Gandhi (1869–1948). While Tolstoy was espousing love and the simple life, Prince Peter Kropotkin (1842–1921) was arguing for an anarchism based on the general idea of mutual assistance. A prince and a distinguished geographer, he enjoyed an entrée into polite society. He was an able debater and writer and his prestige as a scientist, like Tolstoy's reputation as an author, enhanced the credentials of his particular brand of anarchism. Indeed, the reputations of Tolstoy and Kropotkin made many serious people reconsider anarchism, and Kropotkin himself was a popular speaker to bourgeois audiences. A count and a prince who were promoting anarchy were intriguing sources of amused speculation. Kropotkin saw revolution as an evolutionary gradual development which was perfectly natural and certainly not frightening. This was a sophisticated and perhaps unrealistic view of revolution and clearly not what Bakunin had worked for. Kropotkin emphasized mutual aid as a basis for true society, the best example being the Middle Ages, where the whole social structure rested on mutual contracts. Such an association creates a collective sense of justice, which is the real essence of society. Because such a development (society) is a natural phenomenon and really antedates man himself, there is no need whatever for artificial restraints such as the state. His was a benevolent anarchism, based on education and the recognition that mutual assistance is in line with the enlightened self-interest. Thus anarchism, like socialism, was coming into the twentieth century fragmented, split between the intellectual critics of society and the blind attacks of hoodlums.

By 1900 Britain was experiencing economic anxiety as the nation faced stiff competition in the world's markets. Her two major competitors were the United States and Germany and both of these nations were producing goods of equal or better quality frequently at lower prices. More imaginative salesmanship and greater attention to the customer's particular needs, especially by the Germans, also accounted for Britain's losses in the marketplace. Britain's period of ascendancy was over; and she faced the future with a belated recognition that she desperately needed to establish technical schools and to reassess her policy of free trade. German industry had flourished in large measure because her producers were assured of the home market by tariffs and consequently could compete at cost or slightly less than cost in the world's markets. They captured large segments of the British colonial market and much of her home market as well. The colonial secretary, Joseph Chamberlain, published in 1897 a report that detailed the products with dwindling sales and the reasons each was failing in competition with foreign rivals. It was a sobering recital and the business community became concerned about its faltering position in the world economy. Modernization, imaginative sales approaches, and tariffs were obvious remedies but were not implemented in time to stem the competition.

The turn of the century was also witness to an accelerating armaments race. Following the Franco-Prussian War the Prussian system of conscription was copied across the continent in the name of defense and security. The cost, however, was high and resulted in staggering taxes. Italy, which we have noted previously in this regard, was only one case in point. In 1899 the Hague Peace Conference met at the suggestion of Nicholas II (1868–1918) of Russia to explore ways of controlling or limiting armaments, in the interest of both peace and economy. Twenty-six countries were represented but there was little sincere support for the idea. Germany emphatically opposed reductions of land forces and Britain as adamantly refused to give up her position of dominance at sea. Another Hague meeting in 1907 proved no more successful and bilateral talks between the Germans and British also failed. So the arms race continued. Armies grew larger and weapons and ships became more expensive; and Germany and Great Britain became more and more accustomed to seeing each other in rival positions.

In France the Dreyfus case served to continue and inflame hatred for the Germans. The defeat of 1870 had engendered deep feeling and this was kept alive, as Bismarck had predicted, by the territorial arrangement giving Germany control of the strategic areas of Alsace and Lorraine. That these provinces became important in the developing steel industry added one more reason for the French to deplore their loss. The charge that Dreyfus had conveyed secret information to the Germans added a great deal to the tension of the case which had great implications for the Third Republic. It was clear that the Germans were *the* enemy and that threats to the nation's security which involved Germany touched an acutely sensitive nerve. When added to anti-Semitism and the issue of clerical influence in the French army, a domestic crisis of major proportions was virtually inevitable.

Insistent voices for social change in Russia could not be delayed after the nation lost the war with Japan. Industrial development had quickened significantly after 1890. Rail construction and iron production showed great increases as did coal mining, where Russia's output during the 1890s increased by 131 per cent compared with a German increase of 52 per cent. In the same decade the value of her industrial production doubled. This economic vitality lent sinews to the demands for reform but the peasantry was not sharing in the new wealth. Agrarian riots and industrial strikes were particularly clear evidences that the system was broadly disliked. Open pleasure was apparent as news spread of the assassination of V. C. Plehve (1846–1904), the minister of internal affairs, who had used force to maintain order. Appropriate to the increasing gravity of the situation was the circumstance that Plehve had come to office after the murder of his predecessor. The crescendo of unrest was clear and as the news from the Orient continued to be unfavorable, the Tsar's government issued a series of decrees, finally calling for a Duma, meant initially to be a "legislative deliberative" body. Leaders for reform planned to assume broad functions and a wave of enthusiasm over the changes produced other developments. No political parties, for example, were legal before 1905. New regulations did not specify their legality, but by 1906 they were generally accepted by all, including public officials, as a regular feature of the system. Thus in the most conservative and reactionary of states the leadership was acceding to demands for change. An outlet was provided for the churning cauldron of discontent stemming from the greater wealth and the expectations associated earlier with formal freedom. Enormous changes in Russia could have been predicted.

By 1900 in most of Europe the gap between rich and poor existed as it always had but now there was a greater awareness among the poor that their lot could be improved. Agitators were, of course, diligently informing them of how they were not sharing enough in the total productivity of the state. Besides the rich and poor, there was a rapidly growing middle class, fed largely by a stream of talent from below. Its increasing size and wealth had forced most governments formerly staffed by aristocrats to share power, and although poverty still existed among the peasantry, especially in much of Eastern and Southern Europe, the prospects for improvement were not nearly as bleak as heretofore. As cities grew so did the problems of the urban poor, many of whom were skilled workers. Socialists diligently tried to organize their discontent, but met with difficulty. Part of their problem was that the poor could also realize the gradations of wealth and status above them, and consequently it was more difficult to focus rebellion—other than against the system. It may be argued that the poor did not take a "have" and "have not" view of life, and thus could not be effectively organized on this basis.

Meanwhile, for many in the upper classes life had a confident and lighthearted air to it. But in a decade and a half the holocaust of World War I was to overwhelm the Continent. A complete shattering of governments and society occurred; belief in "progress" was replaced by pessimism and despair. Optimism and confidence were to disappear as major features of the European scene. An age truly died between 1914 and 1918.

On the intellectual level a persuasive case may be made (and has been by H. Stuart Hughes in *Consciousness and Society*) for the idea that after 1890 a new generation of thinkers consciously dealt with the problems of a society already in deep trouble. A number of German, French, Austrian, and Italian intellectuals shared the feeling that European institutions and values had outlived much of their usefulness and were inadequate to the new circumstances of life. For these men World War I was the supreme statement that the structures of the nineteenth century were unacceptable. There is a unity to the period extending from 1890 to 1930 where the recognition of the problem is validated by the war which underlined the need for basic attempts at an intellectual reconstruction. Thus, intellectually, the nineteenth century ends in 1890; names like Georges Sorel, Max Weber, Henri Bergson, Vilfredo Pareto, Benedetto Croce, and Sigmund Freud properly belong in analyses of the twentieth century. These men all had deep roots, of course, in the previous age. The generation of the 1890s, which was actively productive for about forty years was, for the most part, born in the third quadrant of the nineteenth century and educated in its institutions. Georges Sorel and Vilfredo Pareto obviously built on the past as they studied, criticized, and modified many of the tenets of Marxism. On the other hand, the insights of Schopenhauer and Nietzsche on the will played virtually no part in the development of Sigmund Freud's ideas.

An exception to this group, yet very much a part of it in terms of his importance for the twentieth century, was Wilhelm Dilthey (1833–1911). In his make-up were the major cultural trends of the century and before—he embodied respect for the Enlightenment, the romantic movement as represented by Schleiermacher, the philosophy of Kant and Hegel, and the rigor of Ranke's standards in history. It was a rich inheritance. As a philosopher or theoretician of history, Dilthey is of primary importance, his main ideas appearing in his *Einleitung in die Geisteswissen-schaften* and in drafts for a work on a critique of historical reason which he never finished. This latter work was to be modeled on Kant's epic studies of pure and practical reason. His major achievement was to indicate clearly the ways in which natural science and cultural science (or history and the social sciences) differed. He sought to show that although these areas of inquiry were data oriented, their practitioners used and ascribed meaning to the data differently. He rebelled against positivism and sociology and found economics and psychology to be more helpful in his particular approach to understanding the special province of history. Separating the historian from the social scientist was the fact that the former's work required more than drawing abstractions from data. History demands imagination and involves the attempt of the historian to relive the past. His capturing a historical experience and presenting it on paper is a matter of art more than of science, although, of course, the attempt to be analytical is a recourse to scientific standards. Thus the artistic, humanistic, and literary dimensions of history are made clear and provide the complement which Ranke's values needed to present a comprehensive view of history's nature and function. New knowledge in the field of psychology was of crucial importance, for history was arid and superficial when seen and practiced as a mere positivistic collection and analysis of data—that is, when history was treated as a social science. In Dilthey history received a clearer definition, a clearer status, and new assignments.

An interesting contrast to Dilthey may be seen in the major life work of his contemporary Herbert Spencer (1820–1903). This self-appointed philosopher of evolution published a mass of material, much of which has failed to influence later generations. By the end of his life he appeared to be more of an anachronism than a vital contributor to the intellectual life of his time. Still actively writing, his recommendations for society were politely set aside. Despite poor health, after thirty-six years he had completed (in 1896) his magnum opus, *The System of Synthetic Philosophy*, while writing several other works, including an eight-volume study of *Descriptive Sociology*. He was renowned but saddened that socialism was growing rapidly and that both militarism and materialism were so much on the ascent. The measure of his failure is that despite his enormous productivity, he failed to provide an imaginative interpretation of the idea of evolution for the next generation; the vitality and import of this notion is to be read in others. Spencer failed to speak to later ages and his reputation has declined rapidly in this century. A major handicap was that he knew little philosophy and, despite the philosophical implications of his writing, he made no effort to acquaint himself with the positions suggested by previous thinkers. He read to obtain illustrative material for the books he was writing rather than to learn of previous work in a field. He had read about a dozen pages of Emerson and less than fifty of Carlyle, yet the ideas of both these men impressed him deeply. He admitted familiarity with Rousseau "at second hand." When in 1883 it was pointed out to him that Kant had an ethical doctrine similar to his own in some respects, he acknowledged that it might be "helpful to ascertain definitely what were Kant's views." He was then sixty-three years old. He thought for some time that he could substitute the theory of evolution for the idea of progress but his most important contribution was his emphasis on the idea of a philosophic synthesis, that all knowledge existed in a coordinated relationship and made possible a philosophic synthesis. Knowledge is a coherent whole with a place for all facts and experience. After Kant and Hegel, the philosophy of Spencer was rather a tired note on which to end the century.

Between 1800 and 1900 European society and civilization had undergone remarkable change. In almost every measurable respect, 1900 represented an enormous advance and the period truly was an Age of Progress. As the twentieth century may some day be regarded as a time of adjustment to the implications of Freud and of $E = mc^2$, so the nineteenth was characterized by an extension and adaptation, in the face of strong opposition, of the principles of the French Revolution entwined with Enlightened and Romantic attitudes toward life. The forces of liberalism and nationalism struggled against entrenched autocracy but helped to power an imperialism which was often as reprehensible as any nineteenth-century conservative or reactionary regime in Europe.

Political power was no longer the exclusive province of the aristocracy. In varying degrees the middle and lower classes were sharing in the governmental process, and the rapid growth of socialism promised even wider participation. Political parties had proliferated over the continent during the century. Public opinion was extremely important by 1900, and the rapidly increasing literacy, combined with a growing newspaper press, led to increased interest in national and world events.

The century was not without its lost causes. Monarchy and the conservative position in politics generally were in retreat. In France the Legitimists, Orléanists, and Bonapartists had their turn in power but by 1900 could hardly be regarded as practical alternatives to the Third Republic. To be regretted was the lack of acceptance of Napoleon III's propagandistic remark that to go to war over mere boundary issues or provinces was old-fashioned. The Congress System also had greater potential than it was allowed to show. Throughout the century the Eastern Question managed to reappear continually in such a form that traditional diplomacy was never adequate and left this dilemma as a grim legacy for the future. Europe's vitality overseas similarly left a number of unsolved issues. These were, however, to be posed and resolved in European terms, an impressive tribute to the extent of the transplanting of European values and social attitudes.

An enormous increase in man's understanding of nature had occurred. Indeed, so many new laws appeared to have been learned that many believed that all which remained for experimenters was to carry numerical relationships out a few more places. All the basic laws were known and the world's greatest era of science was over. It was a confident but erroneous appraisal. The ramifications of scientific progress in terms of industrial production and higher living standards for wide segments of Europe's population defy description. The impact of railroads alone made an incalculable change in social conditions. The economic and social advantages of urban life had led to a rapid growth of cities. Old defensive city walls were torn down and suburbs were incorporated into the local political structure. Generals bemoaned the fact that capitals now were indefensible but advances in military technology had virtually assured this anyway. The rebuilding of Paris demonstrated the potential for urban grandeur, while the expositions and new department stores advertised the bewildering array of conveniences which technology was producing. Economic and social progress were dramatic and obvious to nearly all, though it needs to be observed that these remarks apply more to Central and Western Europe than to Eastern and Southeastern Europe.

As the century ended, a heady sense of optimism lingered, though many intellectuals were ill at ease in a society which they discerned was seriously deficient. The rapid acceleration of German economic power was easily recognizable and accompanied by growing international tension. German diplomatic aggressiveness added to a growing apprehension of Germany. It was a dangerous situation calling for skilled leadership. Improved military technology had enhanced each state's destructive power, and nationalism now was far more dangerous than the variety which Metternich tried to combat. The need for leadership, unfortunately, was unrelated to the supply. Instead of being able to avert war, Europe's leaders after 1900 helped to assure it. The structure devised in 1815 at Vienna was to be swept away between 1914 and 1918.

BIBLIOGRAPHICAL
SUGGESTIONS

The intriguing developments occurring between the French Revolution and the coming of World War I may be studied in great detail from a host of careful studies written by competent historians. For this era the literature in the English language alone is massive and so rapidly increasing that any attempt to provide a comprehensive guide to it necessarily will be frustrating, as the flood of new works make bibliographies simply measures of the literature at the date of compilation. Nonetheless, a number of bibliographies provide superb guidelines for the student wishing to begin reading more deeply. Of course, the entries in the subject index of the card catalogue of any library provide a listing of works immediately available. For a wealth of helpful information see *The Guide to Historical Literature* (1931), which is dated but was much more successful in its task than its less rigorous successor, *The American Historical Association's Guide to Historical Literature* (1961). The bibliographies

518

in the separate volumes of *The Rise of Modern Europe* (1934 seq.) series edited by W. L. Langer are superb and have been continuously updated in later printings. Most textbooks contain bibliographies, many of a high order. Particularly outstanding examples of text guides to English language materials may be found in R. R. Palmer and J. Colton, *A History of the Modern World* (3rd ed., 1965); D. Thomson, *Europe Since Napoleon* (2nd ed., 1962); and in the third edition of R. Ergang, *Europe since Waterloo* (1967). Authoritative commentary on many works is available also in the many problems books widely available. Most notable are the bibliographic essays in the *Problems in European Civilization* series published by D. C. Heath & Co. and in the *European Problems Studies* published by Holt, Rinehart & Winston. Each of the titles in these two series contains excerpts from the spectrum of interpretations extant on a topic, providing a student with a ready introduction to historical study at a sophisticated level. Many titles in these series pertain to nineteenth-century subjects. Bibliographical and historiographical articles are published regularly in the scholarly journals and the serious student should especially examine past issues of *The Journal of Modern History* and *The American Historical Review*. Most specialized studies contain bibliographies, two impressive examples of which are A. J. P. Taylor's *The Struggle for Mastery in Europe 1848–1918* (1954) and L. Gershoy's "New Annotated Bibliography" in his 1964 edition of *The French Revolution and Napoleon*. In G. Wright's *France in Modern Times* (1960), the literature on periods of French history is discussed in a series of chapters, each entitled "The Varieties of History." These chapters illuminate the text directly as well, in their total, as providing a comprehensive survey of the most important works on French history since 1760. From the titles already mentioned, the volume of material available is obvious. Following is a brief indication of some particular books one could use to begin further study, presented in the order of the organizational pattern of this volume (12 parts). There are many superb monographs omitted and it would require the wisdom of Job to justify one's selection of any particular short list of titles. Suffice it to say that this author has found some of the books which follow especially helpful.

PART I
A Century and Its Birth

Few works provide satisfactory single volume treatment of the whole nineteenth century above the textbook level, but H. Hearder's *Europe in the Nineteenth Century* (1966) attempts this with considerable success. On the same order is R. F. Leslie, *The Age of Transformation, 1789–1871* (1964) and I. Collins, *The Age of Progress* (1964). These are superb but give minimal attention to intellectual developments. A particularly suggestive work is L. C. B. Seaman, *From Vienna to Versailles* (1955). Six volumes of the *Cambridge Modern History—The Eighteenth Century* (1909), *The French Revolution* (1904), *Napoleon* (1906), *The Restoration* (1907), *The Growth of Nationalities* (1909), and *The Latest Age* (1910)—contain much sound material, although the series as a whole needs updating, a process being attempted with only moderate success in the *New Cambridge Modern History—The American and French Revolutions 1763–93* (1965), *War and Peace in an Age of Upheaval 1793–1830* (1965), *The Zenith of European Power 1830–70* (1960), and *Material Progress and World-wide Problems 1870–98* (1962). A reliable guide to much of the period may be found in the *Rise of Modern Europe* series, the particular volumes being: L. Gershoy, *From Despotism to Revolution* (1949); C. Brinton, *A Decade of Revolution* (1934); G. Brunn, *Europe and the French Imperium* (1938); F. B. Artz, *Reaction and Revolution* (1934); W. L. Langer, *Political and Social Upheaval, 1832–52* (1969); R. C. Binkley, *Realism and Nationalism* (1935); and C. J. H. Hayes, *A Generation of Materialism* (1941). The general period of the French Revolution and Napoleon has inspired an enormous literature. Distinguished French scholars some of whose works have been translated into English include H. Sée, A. Aulard, A. Mathiez, and G. Lefebvre. Representative fine studies written in English are: F. Ford, *Robe and Sword* (1953); C. Becker, *Heavenly City of the Eighteenth Century Philosophers* (1932); G. R. Havens, *The Age of Ideas* (1955); D. Dakin, *Turgot and the Ancien Regime in France* (1939); C. V. Easum, *Prince Henry of Prussia, Brother of Frederick the Great* (1942); P. Farmer, *France Reviews her Revolutionary Origins* (1944); R. R. Palmer, *Twelve Who Ruled* (1941); D. Greer, *The Incidence of the Terror* (1935); C. Brinton, *The Jacobins* (1930); P. Geyl, *Napoleon: For and Against* (1949); J. B. Morton, *Brumaire, the Rise of Bonaparte* (1948); W. C. Langsam, *The Napoleonic Wars and German Nationalism in Austria* (1930); R. B. Holtman, *Napoleonic Propaganda* (1950); R. W. Phipps, *The Armies of the First French Republic and the Rise of the Marshals of Napoleon I* (5 vols., 1926–39); G. P. Gooch, *Germany and the French Revolution* (1920); P. R. Sweet, *Friedrich von Gentz, Defender of the Old Order* (1941); and G. Lacour-Gayet, *Talleyrand, 1754–1838* (3 vols., 1928–31).

PART II

The Conditions of Peace

The Congress of Vienna and its implementation, in both the foreign and domestic policies of the nations involved, centers on Metternich and the fact of Napoleonic defeat. Our account owes much to H. A. Kissinger's *A World Restored* (1957) which acutely sets forth the perspectives of the various powers. Also of value are H. Nicolson, *The Congress of Vienna* (1946); E. V. Gulick, *Europe's Classical Balance of Power* (1955); and G. Ferrero, *The Reconstruction of Europe* (1941). C. K. Webster has authored many brilliant studies, of special importance here are *The Congress of Vienna 1814–1815* (1934) and *The European Alliance 1815–1825* (1929). Metternich's memoirs are available in English (5 vols., 1880–82) and while H. von Srbik wrote the finest biography (3 vols. in German in 1925) of Metternich, the student will find P. Shroeder's *Metternich's Diplomacy at its Zenith* (1962) a careful and thorough work. Of equal importance are E. J. Knapton, *The Lady of the Holy Alliance: the Life of Julie de*

Krüdener (1939); and L. I. Strakhovsky, *Alexander I of Russia, The Man Who Defeated Napoleon* (1947). Broader presentations of nineteenth century diplomacy may be read in B. Jelavich, *A Century of Russian Foreign Policy 1814–1914* (1964); R. W. Seton-Watson, *Britain in Europe 1789–1914* (1937); and R. Albrecht-Carrié, *A Diplomatic History of Europe Since the Congress of Vienna* (1958). Domestic conservatism is covered in works portraying various national histories. More detailed would be F. B. Artz, *France Under the Bourbon Restoration 1814–1830* (1931); R. J. White, *From Waterloo to Peterloo 1815–1819* (1957); and W. M. Simon, *Failure of the Prussian Reform Movement, 1807–19* (1955).

PART III

Changing Conditions of Life

Much of this portion is based on the early chapters of P. N. Stearns, *European Society in Upheaval: Social History Since 1800* (1967), a very fine study. Important also are P. A. M. Taylor, *The Industrial Revolution in Britain* (1958); T. S. Ashton, *The Industrial Revolution 1760–1830* (1948); J. T. Ward, *The Factory Movement, 1830–1855* (1962); M. C. Buer, *Health, Wealth and Population in the Early Days of the Industrial Revolution* (1926); A. L. Dunham, *The Industrial Revolution in France, 1815–1848* (1955); A. F. Weber, *The Growth of Cities in the Nineteenth Century* (1899); and J. H. Clapham, *The Economic Development of France and Germany, 1815–1914* (1936). Patterns of trade may be studied in R. E. Cameron, *France and the Economic Development of Europe, 1800–1914* (1961) and W. O. Henderson, *The Zollverein* (1939). Among works exploring the emergence of early liberalism and socialism are: G. de Ruggiero, *The History of European Liberalism* (1927); H. J. Laski, *The Rise of European Liberalism* (1936); E. Halévy, *The Growth of Philosophic Radicalism* (1949); G. C. Iggers, *The Cult of Authority: The Political Philosophy of the Saint-Simonians* (1958); and F. E. Manuel, *The New World of Henri Saint-Simon* (1956).

PART IV

The Romantic Movement

Nineteenth-century intellectual history may be found presented in a broader context in G. L. Mosse, *The Culture of Western Europe* (1961); J. H. Randall, Jr., *The Making of the Modern Mind* (1926); C. Brinton, *Ideas and Men* (1950); R. N. Stromberg, *An Intellectual History of Modern Europe* (1966); and in volume three of the third revised edition of *An Intellectual and Cultural History of the Western World* (1965) by H. E. Barnes. Also of value is J. Bronowski and B. Mazlish, *The Western Intellectual Tradition: Leonardo to Hegel* (1960). More specific studies would include: N. E. Hudson, *Ultra-royalism and the French Restoration* (1936); R. H. Soltau, *French Political Thought in the Nineteenth Century* (1931); B. Croce, *European Literature in the Nineteenth*

Century (1924); J. H. Bruford, *Culture and Society in Classical Weimar, 1775–1806* (1962); A. Guerard, *Reflections on the Napoleonic Legend* (1924); J. L. Talmon, *Political Messianisms: The Romantic Phase* (1960); M. Elwin, *The First Romantics* (1948); A. Einstein, *Music in the Romantic Era* (1947); G. Grove, *Beethoven, Schubert, Mendelssohn* (1952); J. Barzun, *Berlioz and the Romantic Century* (2 vols., 1950) and *Romanticism and the Modern Ego* (1943); G. P. Gooch, *History and Historians in the Nineteenth Century* (1949); K. W. Swart, *The Sense of Decadence in Nineteenth Century France* (1964); F. C. Gill, *Romantic Movement and Methodism* (1937); R. B. Brandt, *The Philosophy of Schleiermacher* (1945); V. Grønbech, *Religious Currents in the Nineteenth Century* (1964); K. S. Latourette, *Christianity in a Revolutionary Age*, Vols. I and II: *The Nineteenth Century in Europe; Background and the Roman Catholic Phase* (1958) and *The Protestant and Eastern Churches* (1959); and S. Hook, *From Hegel to Marx* (1936). A desire for more fundamental and exhaustive but rewarding study would lead to examination of particular titles by Kant, Fichte, Hegel, and others mentioned in our narrative.

PART V

Liberal and Nationalistic Adjustments, 1820–1832

British policy and difficulties in the working of the Vienna settlement may be examined in two fine works by C. K. Webster, *The Foreign Policy of Castlereagh, 1815–1822* (1925) and *Britain and the Independence of Latin America, 1812–1830* (1944). Also to be commended are H. Temperley, *The Foreign Policy of Canning, 1822–1827* (1925); C. W. Crawley, *The Question of Greek Independence* (1930); C. M. Woodhouse, *The Greek War of Independence* (1952); and A. J. Whyte, *The Evolution of Modern Italy* (1959). In general the upheavals between 1825 and 1832 are covered in separate studies each dealing with a single case, such as A. Mazour, *The First Russian Revolution, 1825: The Decembrist Movement, Its Origins, Development, and Significance* (1937). The Belgian Revolt is discussed in Ch. XVI of Vol X (*The Restoration*) of the *Cambridge Modern History*. The best accounts of this revolution are to be found in French language works, such as H. Pirenne's classic history of Belgium. Of special interest, however, is J. A. Betley, *Belgium and Poland in International Relations, 1830–1831* (1960). For Poland see R. F. Leslie, *Polish Politics and the Revolution of November 1830* (1956). The 1830 Revolution in France is well treated in many national histories. The account in this volume owes much to the work of V. W. Beach, especially his "The Polignac Ministry: A Re-evaluation," *University of Colorado Studies,* Series in History, No. 3, January, 1964; and his "The Fall of Charles X of France: A Case Study of Revolution," *ibid.,* No. 2, November, 1961. Recently G. F. Rudé has called our attention again to the role of the crowd in history—*The Crowd in the French Revolution* (1959) and *The Crowd in History: A Study of Popular Disturbances in France and England, 1730–1848* (1964). For Paris in 1830 see especially D. Pinkney's

"The Crowd in the French Revolution of 1830," *American Historical Review* (October, 1964).

PART VI
Another Attempt at Stability and Order:
The Limited Recognition of New Forces

Reforms in Britain prior to and following the Great Reform Bill of 1832 are well presented in E. L. Woodward, *The Age of Reform, 1815–1870* (1941). Among less comprehensive, more specific studies are: J. A. Reynolds, *Catholic Emancipation in Ireland, 1823–9* (1956); R. G. Cowherd, *The Politics of English Dissent, 1815–48* (1956); A. Brady, *Huskisson and Liberal Reform* (1928); G. M. Trevelyan, *Lord Grey of the Reform Bill* (1920); H. W. C. Davis, *The Age of Grey and Peel, 1832–41* (1929); and W. R. Brock, *Lord Liverpool and Liberal Toryism, 1820–1827* (1941). For Louis Philippe's reign, see T. E. B. Howarth, *The Citizen-king* (1961); J. Lucas-Dubreton, *The Restoration and the July Monarchy* (1929); J. M. S. Allison, *Thiers and the French Monarchy, 1797–1848* (1926); D. O. Evans, *Social Romanticism in France, 1830–1848* (1951); D. Johnson, *Guizot; Aspects of French History, 1787–1874* (1963); and S. Mellon, *The Political Uses of History* (1958). For Russia, see N. V. Riasanovsky, *Nicholas I and Official Nationality in Russia, 1825–1855* (1959); G. T. Robinson, *Rural Russia Under the Old Regime* (1949); J. Blum, *Lord and Peasant from the Ninth to the Nineteenth Century* (1961). Nicholas has attracted few Western historians except for diplomacy where research may be profitably pursued in non-Russian archives. However, most surveys of Russian history give adequate presentations of his reign. For Prussia and Austria in this period, see relevant portions of T. S. Hamerow, *Restoration, Revolution, Reaction* (1958); H. Treitschke, *History of Germany in the Nineteenth Century* (7 vols., 1915–19); A. J. P. Taylor, *The Hapsburg Monarchy, 1809–1918* (1948); and R. A. Kann, *A Study in Austrian Intellectual History* (1960). Among many studies of the diplomacy of this period are: C. K. Webster, *The Foreign Policy of Palmerston, 1830–41* (2 vols., 1951); H. C. F. Bell, *Lord Palmerston* (2 vols., 1936); P. E. Moseley, *Russian Diplomacy and the Opening of the Eastern Question in 1838 and 1839* (1934); V. J. Puryear, *International Economics and Diplomacy in the Near East 1834–53* (1935); J. A. R. Marriott, *The Eastern Question* (1940); and E. J. Parry, *The Spanish Marriages* (1936).

PART VII
1848—Western and Central Europe in Turmoil

There is an extensive literature on 1848 and perhaps the best comprehensive account is P. Robertson, *The Revolutions of 1848: A Social History* (1952). A sampling of more limited works might include: L. B. Namier, *1848: The Revolution of the Intellectuals* (1946); V. Valentin, *1848: Chapters of German History* (1940); G. M. Trevelyan, *Manin and the Venetian Revolution of 1848* (1923);

A. J. P. Taylor, *The Italian Problem in European Diplomacy, 1847–1849* (1934); R. J. Rath, *The Viennese Revolution of 1848* (1957); D. C. McKay, *The National Workshops* (1933); L. Loubere, *Louis Blanc* (1961); K. Marx, *The Class Struggle in France, 1848 to 1850* (1850) and *The Eighteenth Brumaire of Louis Bonaparte* (1914); B. D. Gooch, *Belgium and the February Revolution* (1963); A. Schwarzenberg, *Prince Felix zu Schwarzenberg, Prime Minister of Austria, 1848–1852* (1926); and J. A. R. Marriott, *The French Revolution of 1848 in its Economic Aspects* (2 vols., 1913). The French Second Republic has been the separate topic of only a few studies. P. de la Gorce has authored a work in French which has not yet been translated into English. Most accounts treat this regime as a chapter in the coming to power of Louis Napoleon. See, for example, R. Arnaud, *The Second Republic and Napoleon III* (1930); E. Bourgeois, "The French Republic (1848–52)" (Ch. V in vol. XI of the *Cambridge Modern History*); and F. A. Simpson's *The Rise of Louis Napoleon* (1909) and *Louis Napoleon and the Recovery of France* (1923).

PART VIII

Peaceful Domestic Progress

An extensive literature details Britain's domestic history during the reign of Victoria. For the earlier years of her rule, see G. M. Young, *Early Victorian England, 1830–1865* (2 vols., 1935); W. L. Burn, *The Age of Equipoise* (1964); J. L. and B. Hammond, *The Age of the Chartists, 1832–54* (1930); D. G. Barnes, *A History of the English Corn Laws from 1660 to 1846* (1930); F. E. Gillespie, *Labour and Politics in England, 1850–1867* (1927); A. Briggs, *Victorian People* (1955); and W. E. Williams, *The Rise of Gladstone to the Leadership of the Liberal Party, 1859–1868* (1934). The Second Empire has been magisterially treated in French by T. Delord, E. Ollivier, and P. de la Goroe. Among English language studies, the following are important and representative: T. Zeldin's *The Political System of Napoleon III* (1958) and *Emile Ollivier and the Liberal Empire of Napoleon III* (1963); D. H. Pinkney, *Napoleon III and the Rebuilding of Paris* (1958); L. M. Case, *French Opinion on War and Diplomacy during the Second Empire* (1954); R. L. Williams, *Gaslight and Shadow: The World of Napoleon III* (1957); T. A. B. Corley, *The Democratic Despot* (1961); J. M. Thompson, *Louis Napoleon and the Second Empire* (1955); and A. L. Dunham, *The Anglo-French Treaty of 1860* (1930). A particularly unflattering but important view may be found in J. S. Schapiro, *Liberalism and the Challenge of Fascism: Social Forces in England and France, 1815–1870* (1949). Russia during the reign of Alexander II may be studied in national histories as well as in: W. E. Mosse, *Alexander II and the Modernization of Russia* (1959); S. Graham, *Tsar of Freedom: The Life and Reign of Alexander II* (1935); M. B. Petrovich, *The Emergence of Russian Pan-Slavism, 1856–1870* (1956); H. Seton-Watson, *The Decline of Imperial Russia, 1855–1914* (1952); D. Footman, *Red Prelude* (1945); and in much of S. R. Tompkins, *The Russian Intelligentsia: Makers of the Revolutionary State* (1957).

PART IX

Nineteenth-Century Intellectual Vitality

Intellectual giants are best studied from their own works but these often need to be seen in the context of the state of knowledge at the time of their composition. Thus selected chapters in histories of science, literature, philosophy or religion may be most helpful in approaching a man's ideas. Representative special studies are: R. Magnus, *Goethe as a Scientist* (1949); H. Butterfield, *Man on His Past* (1955); I. W. Mueller, *John Stuart Mill and French Thought* (1956); D. G. Charlton, *Positivist Thought in France, 1852–1870* (1959); W. M. Simon, *European Positivism in the Nineteenth Century* (1963); B. Glass, ed., *Forerunners of Darwin* (1959); T. von Laue, *Leopold Ranke: The Formative Years* (1950); F. C. Lea, *The Tragic Philosopher* (1957); O. Chadwick, *The Mind of the Oxford Movement* (1960); B. Mazlish, *The Riddle of History* (1966); J. D. Rosenberg, *The Darkening Glass: A Portrait of Ruskin's Genius* (1961); E. Johnson, *Charles Dickens: His Tragedy and Triumph* (2 vols., 1953); E. M. Grant, *The Career of Victor Hugo* (1945); G. Lukacs, *Studies in European Realism* (1950); S. Zweig, *Balzac* (1946); F. R. Love, *Young Nietzsche and the Wagnerian Experience* (1963); L. Stein, *The Racial Thinking of Richard Wagner* (1950); R. J. Dubos, *Louis Pasteur, Free Lance of Science* (1951); C. Woodham-Smith, *Florence Nightingale* (1951); W. W. Cheyne, *Lister and His Achievement* (1925); H. Leichentritt, *Music, History and Ideas* (1938); M. Slonim, *The Epic of Russian Literature: From Its Origin Through Tolstoy* (1950); A. N. Whitehead, *Science and the Modern World* (1926); B. W. Downs, *Ibsen: The Intellectual Background* (1946); H. de Terra, *The Life and Times of Alexander von Humbolt, 1769–1859* (1955).

PART X

Change Through Violence

There is a large and ever-increasing literature on both Marx and Darwin, of which the following are but samples: J. Barzun, *Darwin, Marx, Wagner* (1941); L. Schwarzschild, *The Red Prussian: The Life and Legend of Karl Marx* (1947); E. H. Carr, *Karl Marx: A Study in Fanaticism* (1934); G. Lichtheim, *Marxism, an Historical and Critical Study* (1961); G. Himmelfarb, *Darwin and the Darwinian Revolution* (1959); W. Irvine, *Apes, Angels and Victorians* (1955); L. Eiseley, *Darwin's Century* (1958); and A. Ellegard, *Darwin and the General Reader* (1958). Among many studies of the wars and diplomacy between 1852 and 1871, see: H. W. V. Temperley, *England and the Near East: The Crimea* (1936); G. B. Henderson, *Crimean War Diplomacy and Other Essays* (1947); W. E. Mosse. *The Rise and Fall of the Crimean System, 1855–1871* (1963); B. D. Gooch, *The New Bonapartist Generals in the Crimean War* (1959); L. D. Steefel, *The Schleswig-Holstein Question* (1932); N. N. Barker, *Distaff Diplomacy: The Empress Eugenie and the Foreign Policy of the Second Empire* (1967); F.

Darmstaedter, *Bismarck and the Creation of the Second Reich* (1948); C. W. Hallberg, *Franz Joseph and Napoleon III, 1852–1864* (1955); W. R. Thayer, *Life and Times of Cavour* (2 vols., 1911); D. M. Smith, *Cavour and Garibaldi, 1860* (1954); O. Pflanze, *Bismarck and the Development of Germany* (1963); H. von Sybel, *The Founding of the German Empire by William I* (7 vols., 1890–1898); C. W. Clark, *Franz Joseph and Bismarck: The Diplomacy of Austria before the War of 1866* (1934); M. Howard, *The Franco-Prussian War* (1961); and T. W. Riker, *The Making of Rumania: A Study of an International Problem, 1856–1866* (1931). For the Commune and its immediate background, see M. Kranzberg, *The Siege of Paris, 1870–1871* (1950); F. Jellinek, *The Paris Commune of 1871* (1937); and R. L. Williams, *The French Revolution of 1870–1871* (1969) which has a particularly fine bibliographical essay. Nationalism in German historians may be studied in G. C. Iggers, *The German Conception of History* (1968) and A. Dorpalen's *Heinrich von Treitschke* (1957) is an incisive presentation.

PART XI

A New Politics of the Status Quo, 1870–1890

The diplomacy of the 1871–1890 period is often regarded as a phase in the background of World War I and many studies of the coming of that struggle include careful attention to events in the two decades prior to the retirement of Bismarck. Such a perspective is helpful in understanding the causes of the war but often overlooks the issues as seen by the generation of leaders who failed to live much beyond 1900. For studies centering in the earlier period, see: B. H. Sumner, *Russia and the Balkans, 1870–1880* (1937); R. W. Seton-Watson, *Gladstone, Disraeli and the Eastern Question* (1936); W. N. Medlicott, *The Congress of Berlin and After* (1938) and *Bismarck, Gladstone, and the Concert of Europe* (1956); E. Eyck, *Bismarck and the German Empire* (1955); P. Knaplund, *The Foreign Policy of Mr. Gladstone* (1935); W. L. Langer, *The Franco-Russian Alliance* (1930) and *European Alliances and Alignments, 1871–1890* (1951). Domestic affairs may be studied in national histories and biographies, as well as works such as: L. Levine, *Syndicalism in France* (1914); F. H. Brabant, *The Beginning of the Third Republic in France* (1940); E. M. Acomb, *French Laic Laws, 1879–1889* (1941); J. Rothney, *Bonapartism After Sedan* (1969); J. T. Joughin, *The Paris Commune in French Politics, 1871–1880* (1955); W. H. Dawson, *The German Empire, 1867–1914* (2 vols., 1919); R. H. Bowen, *German Theories of the Corporative State, with special reference to the period 1870–1919* (1949); H. M. Lynd, *England in the 1880's* (1945); L. P. Curtis, *Coercion and Conciliation in Ireland, 1880–1892* (1963); J. L. Hammond, *Gladstone and the Irish Nation* (1938); J. Walkin, *The Rise of Democracy in Prerevolutionary Russia* (1962); and R. Hostetter, *The Italian Socialist Movement, 1860–1882* (1958). For the fate of organized Christianity amidst nineteenth-century movements, see: J. L. Altholz, *The Churches in the Nineteenth Century* (1967); S. W. Halperin, *Italy and the Vatican at War* (1939); L. P. Wallace, *The Papacy and European Diplomacy, 1869–1878* (1948); H. de Dorlodot, *Darwinism and Catholic Thought* (1914); A. M. P. Fogarty, *Christian Democracy in Western Europe, 1820–1953* (1957); and D. O. Wagner, *The Church of England and Social Reform Since 1854* (1930). Among many works on phases of the resurgence of European imperialism, see R. I. Lovell, *The Struggle for South Africa, 1875–1899* (1934); R. Slade, *King Leopold's Congo* (1962); T. F. Power, *Jules Ferry and the Renaissance of French Imperialism* (1944); M. E. Townsend, *Origins of German Colonialism, 1871–1885* (1921); A. J. P. Taylor, *Germany's First Bid for Colonies, 1884–1885* (1938); W. L. Langer, *The Diplomacy of Imperialism, 1890–1902* (1951); and H. Feis, *Europe: The World's Banker, 1870–1914* (1930).

PART **XII**
The End of the Nineteenth Century

Studies covering aspects of the 1890–1914 period are virtually all laden with the perspective of seeing a society headed for war. A brilliant work with a broader and more suggestive point of view is H. S. Hughes, *Consciousness and Society* (1958). Representative titles of turn-of-the-century topics not oriented toward prewar diplomacy are G. Chapman, *The Dreyfus Case: A Reassessment* (1955); J. A. Nichols, *Germany After Bismarck: The Caprivi Era, 1890–1894* (1958); C. W. Schorske, *German Social Democracy, 1905–1907* (1955); G. Woodcock, *Anarchism* (1962); A. Noland, *The Founding of the French Socialist Party, 1893–1905* (1956); and D. W. Treadgold, *Lenin and His Rivals, 1889–1906* (1955).

INDEX

540 *Index*

EUROPE IN 1900

SCOTLAND

Edinburgh

Belfast

UNITED KINGDOM

IRELAND

Newcastle

Dublin

ENGLAND

WALES

London

Amsterdam

NETHERLANDS

NORTH SEA

Rhine R.

GER

KDM. O.

KDM

BELGIUM

Brussels

Cologne

Frankfurt

LUX.

Mainz

ATLANTIC OCEAN

Brest

Seine R.

Paris

Versailles

FRENCH

Loire R.

Orleans

REPUBLIC

LORRAINE

ALSACE

Bern

SWITZ.

Bordeaux

Rhone R.

Milan

KINGDOM

Duero R.

KDM. OF PORTUGAL

Ebro R.

Madrid

OF

Barcelona

Marseille

CORSIC

Lisbon

Tagus R.

Valencia

BALEARIC IS.

SARDINI

SPAIN

Cadiz

Tangier

Gibraltar (Br.)

MEDITERRANEAN